Learning in Graphical Models

Jianmei Zhang
Depart ment of CS

Adaptive Computation and Machine Learning

Learning in Graphical Models

edited by
Michael I. Jordan

The MIT Press
Cambridge, Massachusetts
London, England

First MIT Press edition, 1999.

Originally published by Kluwer Academic Publishers, Dordecht, The Netherlands

©1998 Kluwer Academic Publishers

Printed and bound in the United States of America.

Library of Congress Cataloging-in-Publication Data

Learning in graphical models / edited by Michael I. Jordan.
    p. cm. — (Adaptive computation and machine learning)
    Originally published: Boston : Kluwer Academic Publishers, 1998.
    Includes bibliographical references and index.
    ISBN 0-262-60032-3 (pbk. : alk. paper)
    1. Graphical modeling (Statistics) I. Jordan, Michael Irwin
1956– . II. Series.
QA279.L375 1998b
519.6—dc21
                                                         98-38260
                                                            CIP

Contents

Series Foreword

The goal of building systems that can adapt to their environments and learn from their experience has attracted researchers from many fields, including computer science, engineering, mathematics, physics, neuroscience, and cognitive science. Out of this research has come a wide variety of learning techniques that have the potential to transform many industrial and scientific fields. Recently, several research communities have begun to converge on a common set of issues surrounding supervised, unsupervised, and reinforcement learning problems. The MIT Press Series on Adaptive Computation and Machine Learning seeks to unify the many diverse strands of machine learning research and to foster high-quality research and innovative applications.

This book collects recent research on representing, reasoning, and learning with belief networks. Belief networks (also known as graphical models and Bayesian networks) are a widely applicable formalism for compactly representing the joint probability distribution over a set of random variables. Belief networks have revolutionized the development of intelligent systems in many areas. They are now poised to revolutionize the development of learning systems. The papers in this volume reveal the many ways in which ideas from belief networks can be applied to understand and analyze existing learning algorithms (especially for neural networks). They also show how methods from machine learning can be extended to learn the structure and parameters of belief networks. This book is an exciting illustration of the convergence of many disciplines in the study of learning and adaptive computation.

Preface

Graphical models are a marriage between probability theory and graph theory. They provide a natural tool for dealing with two problems that occur throughout applied mathematics and engineering—uncertainty and complexity—and in particular they are playing an increasingly important role in the design and analysis of machine learning algorithms. Fundamental to the idea of a graphical model is the notion of modularity—a complex system is built by combining simpler parts. Probability theory provides the glue whereby the parts are combined, insuring that the system as a whole is consistent, and providing ways to interface models to data. The graph theoretic side of graphical models provides both an intuitively appealing interface by which humans can model highly-interacting sets of variables as well as a data structure that lends itself naturally to the design of efficient general-purpose algorithms.

Many of the classical multivariate probabilistic systems studied in fields such as statistics, systems engineering, information theory, pattern recognition and statistical mechanics are special cases of the general graphical model formalism—examples include mixture models, factor analysis, hidden Markov models, Kalman filters and Ising models. The graphical model framework provides a way to view all of these systems as instances of a common underlying formalism. This has many advantages—in particular, specialized techniques that have been developed in one field can be transferred between research communities and exploited more widely. Moreover, the graphical model formalism provides a natural framework for the design of new systems.

This book presents an in-depth exploration of issues related to learning within the graphical model formalism. Four of the chapters are tutorial articles (those by *Cowell, MacKay, Jordan, et al.*, and *Heckerman*). The remaining articles cover a wide spectrum of topics of current research interest.

The book is divided into four main sections: **Inference, Independence, Foundations for Learning**, and **Learning from Data**. While the sections can be read independently of each other and the articles are to a large extent self-contained, there also is a logical flow to the material. A full appreciation of the material in later sections requires an understanding of the material in the earlier sections.

The book begins with the topic of probabilistic inference. **Inference** refers to the problem of calculating the conditional probability distribution of a subset of the nodes in a graph given another subset of the nodes. Much effort has gone into the design of efficient and accurate inference algorithms. The book covers three categories of inference algorithms—exact algorithms, variational algorithms and Monte Carlo algorithms. The first chapter, by *Cowell*, is a tutorial chapter that covers the basics of exact inference, with particular focus on the popular junction tree algorithm. This material should be viewed as basic for the understanding of graphical models. A second chapter by *Cowell* picks up where the former leaves off and covers advanced issues arising in exact inference. *Kjærulff* presents a method for increasing the efficiency of the junction tree algorithm. The basic idea is to take advantage of additional independencies which arise due to the particular messages arriving at a clique; this leads to a data structure known as a "nested junction tree." *Dechter* presents an alternative perspective on exact inference, based on the notion of "bucket elimination." This is a unifying perspective that provides insight into the relationship between junction tree and conditioning algorithms, and insight into space/time tradeoffs.

Variational methods provide a framework for the design of approximate inference algorithms. Variational algorithms are deterministic algorithms that provide bounds on probabilities of interest. The chapter by *Jordan*, *Ghahramani*, *Jaakkola*, and *Saul* is a tutorial chapter that provides a general overview of the variational approach, emphasizing the important role of convexity. The ensuing article by *Jaakkola* and *Jordan* proposes a new method for improving the mean field approximation (a particular form of variational approximation). In particular, the authors propose to use mixture distributions as approximating distributions within the mean field formalism.

The inference section closes with two chapters on Monte Carlo methods. Monte Carlo provides a general approach to the design of approximate algorithms based on stochastic sampling. *MacKay*'s chapter is a tutorial presentation of Monte Carlo algorithms, covering simple methods such as rejection sampling and importance sampling, as well as more sophisticated methods based on Markov chain sampling. A key problem that arises with the Markov chain Monte Carlo approach is the tendency of the algorithms to exhibit random-walk behavior; this slows the convergence of the algorithms. *Neal* presents a new approach to this problem, showing how a sophisticated form of overrelaxation can cause the chain to move more systematically along surfaces of high probability.

The second section of the book addresses the issue of **Independence**. Much of the aesthetic appeal of the graphical model formalism comes from the "Markov properties" that graphical models embody. A Markov property is a relationship between the separation properties of nodes in a graph (e.g., the notion that a subset of nodes is separated from another subset of nodes, given a third subset of nodes) and conditional independencies in the family of probability distributions associated with the graph (e.g., A is independent of B given C, where A, B and C are subsets of random variables). In the case of directed graphs and undirected graphs the relationships are well understood (cf. Lauritzen, 1997). Chain graphs, however, which are mixed graphs containing both directed and undirected edges, are less well understood. The chapter by *Richardson* explores two of the Markov properties that have been proposed for chain graphs and identifies natural "spatial" conditions on Markov properties that distinguish between these Markov properties and those for both directed and undirected graphs. Chain graphs appear to have a richer conditional independence semantics than directed and undirected graphs

The chapter by *Studeny* and *Vejnarova* addresses the problem of characterizing stochastic *dependence*. Studeny and Vejnarova discuss the properties of the multiinformation function, a general information-theoretic function from which many useful quantities can be computed, including the conditional mutual information for all disjoint subsets of nodes in a graph.

The book then turns to the topic of learning. The section on **Foundations for Learning** contains two articles that cover fundamental concepts that are used in many of the following articles. The chapter by *Heckerman* is a tutorial article that covers many of the basic ideas associated with learning in graphical models. The focus is on Bayesian methods, both for parameter learning and for structure learning. *Neal* and *Hinton* discuss the expectation-maximization (EM) algorithm. EM plays an important role in the graphical model literature, tying together inference and learning problems. In particular, EM is a method for finding maximum likelihood (or maximum a posteriori) parameter values, by making explicit use of a probabilistic inference (the "E step"). Thus EM-based approaches to learning generally make use of inference algorithms as subroutines. Neal and Hinton describe the EM algorithm as coordinate ascent in an appropriately-defined cost function. This point of view allows them to consider algorithms that take partial E steps, and provides an important justification for the use of approximate inference algorithms in learning.

The section on **Learning from Data** contains a variety of papers concerned with the learning of parameters and structure in graphical models. *Bishop* provides an overview of latent variable models, focusing on probabilistic principal component analysis, mixture models, topographic maps and time series analysis. EM algorithms are developed for each case. The article by *Buhmann* complements the Bishop article, describing methods for dimensionality reduction, clustering, and data visualization, again with the EM algorithm providing the conceptual framework for the design of the algorithms. Buhmann also presents learning algorithms based on approximate inference and deterministic annealing.

Friedman and *Goldszmidt* focus on the problem of representing and learning the local conditional probabilities for graphical models. In particular, they are concerned with representations for these probabilities that make explicit the notion of "context-specific independence," where, for example, A is independent of B for some values of C but not for others. This representation can lead to significantly more parsimonious models than standard techniques. *Geiger, Heckerman*, and *Meek* are concerned with the problem of model selection for graphical models with hidden (unobserved) nodes. They develop asymptotic methods for approximating the marginal likelihood and demonstrate how to carry out the calculations for several cases of practical interest.

The paper by *Hinton, Sallans*, and *Ghahramani* describes a graphical model called the "hierarchical community of experts" in which a collection of local linear models are used to fit data. As opposed to mixture models, in which each data point is assumed to be generated from a single local model, their model allows a data point to be generated from an arbitrary subset of the available local models. *Kearns, Mansour*, and *Ng* provide a careful analysis of the relationships between EM and the K-means algorithm. They discuss an "information-modeling tradeoff," which characterizes the ability of an algorithm to both find balanced assignments of data to model components, and to find a good overall fit to the data.

Monti and *Cooper* discuss the problem of structural learning in networks with both discrete and continuous nodes. They are particularly concerned with the issue of the discretization of continous data, and how this impacts the performance of a learning algorithm. *Saul* and *Jordan* present a method for unsupervised learning in layered neural networks based on mean field theory. They discuss a mean field approximation that is tailored to the case of large networks in which each node has a large number of parents.

Smith and *Whittaker* discuss tests for conditional independence tests in graphical Gaussian models. They show that several of the appropriate statistics turn out to be functions of the sample partial correlation coefficient. They also develop asymptotic expansions for the distributions of the test statistics and compare their accuracy as a function of the dimensionality of the model. *Spiegelhalter, Best, Gilks*, and *Inskip* describe an application of graphical models to the real-life problem of assessing the effectiveness of an immunization program. They demonstrate the use of the graphical model formalism to represent statistical hypotheses of interest and show how Monte Carlo methods can be used for inference. Finally,

Williams provides an overview of Gaussian processes, deriving the Gaussian process approach from a Bayesian point of view, and showing how it can be applied to problems in nonlinear regression, classification, and hierarchical modeling.

This volume arose from the proceedings of the International School on Neural Nets "E.R. Caianiello," held at the Ettore Maiorana Centre for Scientific Culture in Erice, Italy, in September 1996. Lecturers from the school contributed chapters to the volume, and additional authors were asked to contribute chapters to provide a more complete and authoritative coverage of the field. All of the chapters have been carefully edited, following a review process in which each chapter was scrutinized by two anonymous reviewers and returned to authors for improvement.

There are a number of people to thank for their role in organizing the Erice meeting. First I would like to thank Maria Marinaro, who initiated the ongoing series of Schools to honor the memory of E.R. Caianiello, and who co-organized the first meeting. David Heckerman was also a co-organizer of the school, providing helpful advice and encouragement throughout. Anna Esposito at the University of Salerno also deserves sincere thanks for her help in organizing the meeting. The staff at the Ettore Maiorana Centre were exceedingly professional and helpful, initiating the attendees of the school into the wonders of Erice. Funding for the School was provided by the NATO Advanced Study Institute program; this program provided generous support that allowed nearly 80 students to attend the meeting.

I would also like to thank Jon Heiner, Thomas Hofmann, Nuria Oliver, Barbara Rosario, and Jon Yi for their help with preparing the final document.

Finally, I would like to thank Barbara Rosario, whose fortuitous attendance as a participant at the Erice meeting rendered the future conditionally independent of the past.

Michael I. Jordan

PART I : INFERENCE

INTRODUCTION TO INFERENCE FOR BAYESIAN NETWORKS

ROBERT COWELL
City University, London.
The School of Mathematics, Actuarial Science and Statistics,
City University, Northampton Square, London EC1E 0HT

1. Introduction

The field of Bayesian networks, and graphical models in general, has grown enormously over the last few years, with theoretical and computational developments in many areas. As a consequence there is now a fairly large set of theoretical concepts and results for newcomers to the field to learn. This tutorial aims to give an overview of some of these topics, which hopefully will provide such newcomers a conceptual framework for following the more detailed and advanced work. It begins with revision of some of the basic axioms of probability theory.

2. Basic axioms of probability

Probability theory, also known as inductive logic, is a system of reasoning under uncertainty, that is under the absence of certainty. Within the Bayesian framework, probability is interpreted as a numerical measure of the degree of consistent belief in a proposition, consistency being with the data at hand.

Early expert systems used deductive, or Boolean, logic, encapsulated by sets of production rules. Attempts were made to cope with uncertainty using probability theory, but the calculations became prohibitive, and the use of probability theory for inference in expert systems was abandoned. It is with the recent development of efficient computational algorithms that probability theory has had a revival within the AI community.

Let us begin with some basic axioms of probability theory. The probability of an event A, denoted by $P(A)$, is a number in the interval [0,1], which obeys the following axioms:

1 $P(A) = 1$ if and only if A is certain.

2 If A and B are mutually exclusive, then $P(A \text{ or } B) = P(A) + P(B)$.

We will be dealing exclusively with discrete random variables and their probability distributions. Capital letters will denote a variable, or perhaps a set of variables, lower case letter will denote values of variables. Thus suppose A is a random variable having a finite number of *mutually exclusive states* $(a_1, \ldots, a_n)$. Then $P(A)$ will be represented by a vector of non-negative real numbers $P(A) = (x_1, \ldots, x_n)$ where $P(A = a_i) = x_i$ is a scalar, and $\sum_i x_i = 1$.

A basic concept is that of conditional probability, a statement of which takes the form: *Given the event $B = b$ the probability of the event $A = a$ is x, written $P(A = a \mid B = b) = x$*. It is important to understand that this is not saying: "If $B = b$ is true then the probability of $A = a$ is x". Instead it says: "If $B = b$ is true, and any other information to hand is irrelevant to A, then $P(A = a) = x$". (To see this, consider what the probabilities would be if the state of A was part of the extra information).

Conditional probabilities are important for building Bayesian networks, as we shall see. But Bayesian networks are also built to facilitate the calculation of conditional probabilities, namely the conditional probabilities for variables of interest given the data (also called evidence) at hand.

The fundamental rule for probability calculus is the product rule[1]

$$P(A \text{ and } B) = P(A \mid B)P(B). \tag{1}$$

This equation tells us how to combine conditional probabilities for individual variables to define joint probabilities for sets of variables.

3. Bayes' theorem

The simplest form of Bayes' theorem relates the joint probability $P(A \text{ and } B)$ – written as $P(A, B)$ – of two events or hypotheses A and B in terms of marginal and conditional probabilities:

$$P(A, B) = P(A \mid B)P(B) = P(B \mid A)P(A). \tag{2}$$

By rearrangement we easily obtain

$$P(A \mid B) = \frac{P(B \mid A)P(A)}{P(B)}, \tag{3}$$

which is Bayes' theorem.

This can be interpreted as follows. We are interested in A, and we begin with a *prior* probability $P(A)$ for our belief about A, and then we observe

---

[1]Or more generally $P(A \text{ and } B \mid C) \equiv P(A \mid B, C)P(B \mid C)$.

B. Then Bayes' theorem, (3), tells us that our revised belief for A, the *posterior* probability $P(A \mid B)$ is obtained by multiplying the prior $P(A)$ by the ratio $P(B \mid A)/P(B)$. The quantity $P(B \mid A)$, as a function of varying A for fixed B, is called the *likelihood* of A. We can express this relationship in the form:

$$\textbf{posterior} \quad \propto \quad \textbf{prior} \times \textbf{likelihood}$$
$$P(A \mid B) \quad \propto \quad P(A)P(B \mid A).$$

Figure 1 illustrates this prior-to-posterior inference process. Each diagram

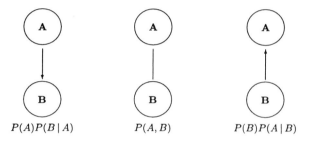

$$P(A)P(B \mid A) \qquad P(A, B) \qquad P(B)P(A \mid B)$$

Figure 1. Bayesian inference as reversing the arrows

represents in different ways the joint distribution $P(A, B)$, the first represents the prior beliefs while the third represents the posterior beliefs. Often, we will think of A as a possible "cause" of the "effect" B, the downward arrow represents such a causal interpretation. The "inferential" upwards arrow then represents an "argument against the causal flow", from the observed effect to the inferred cause. (We will not go into a definition of "causality" here.)

Bayesian networks are generally more complicated than the ones in Figure 1, but the general principles are the same in the following sense. A Bayesian network provides a model representation for the joint distribution of a set of variables in terms of conditional and prior probabilities, in which the orientations of the arrows represent influence, usually though not always of a causal nature, such that these conditional probabilities for these particular orientations are relatively straightforward to specify (from data or eliciting from an expert). When data are observed, then typically an inference procedure is required. This involves calculating marginal probabilities conditional on the observed data using Bayes' theorem, which is diagrammatically equivalent to reversing one or more of the Bayesian network arrows. The algorithms which have been developed in recent years allows these calculations to be performed in an efficient and straightforward manner.

4. Simple inference problems

Let us now consider some simple examples of inference. The first is simply Bayes' theorem with evidence included on a simple two node network; the remaining examples treat a simple three node problem.

4.1. PROBLEM I

Suppose we have the simple model $X \to Y$, and are given: $P(X)$, $P(Y \mid X)$ and $Y = y$. The problem is to calculate $P(X \mid Y = y)$.

Now from $P(X)$, $P(Y \mid X)$ we can calculate the marginal distribution $P(Y)$ and hence $P(Y = y)$. Applying Bayes' theorem we obtain

$$P(X \mid Y = y) = \frac{P(Y = y \mid X)P(X)}{P(Y = y)}. \tag{4}$$

4.2. PROBLEM II

Suppose now we have a more complicated model in which X is a parent of both Y and Z: $Z \leftarrow X \to Y$ with specified probabilities $P(X)$, $P(Y \mid X)$ and $P(Z \mid X)$, and we observe $Y = y$. The problem is to calculate $P(Z \mid Y = y)$. Note that the joint distribution is given by $P(X, Y, Z) = P(Y \mid X)P(Z \mid X)P(X)$. A 'brute force' method is to calculate:

1. The joint distribution $P(X, Y, Z)$.
2. The marginal distribution $P(Y)$ and thence $P(Y = y)$.
3. The marginal distribution $P(Z, Y)$ and thence $P(Z, Y = y)$.
4. $P(Z \mid Y = y) = P(Z, Y = y)/P(Y = y)$.

An alternative method is to exploit the given factorization:

1. Calculate $P(X \mid Y = y) = P(Y = y \mid X)P(X)/P(Y = y)$ using Bayes' theorem, where $P(Y = y) = \sum_X P(Y = y \mid X)P(X)$.
2. Find $P(Z \mid Y = y) = \sum_X P(Z \mid X)P(X \mid Y = y)$.

Note that the first step essentially reverses the arrow between X and Y. Although the two methods give the same answer, the second is generally more efficient. For example, suppose that all three variables have 10 states. Then the first method in explicitly calculating $P(X, Y, Z)$ requires a table of 1000 states. In contrast the largest table required for the second method has size 100. This gain in computational efficiency by exploiting the given factorizations is the basis of the arc-reversal method for solving influence diagrams, and of the junction-tree propagation algorithms. The following example shows the same calculation using propagation on a junction tree.

4.3. PROBLEM III

Suppose now that we are given the *undirected* structure $ZX - X - XY$, and probabilities $P(Z, X)$, $P(X)$ and $P(Y, X)$. Again the problem is to calculate $P(Z \mid Y = y)$. Note that:

$$
\begin{aligned}
P(Z, X) &= P(Z \mid X)P(X) \\
P(Y, X) &= P(Y \mid X)P(X) \\
P(X, Y, Z) &= P(Z, X)P(Y, X)/P(X).
\end{aligned}
$$

The calculational steps now proceeds using a 'message' in step 1 which is 'sent' in step 2:

1. Calculate $\bar{P}(X) \equiv \sum_Y P(X, Y = y)$.
2. Find $\bar{P}(Z, X) \equiv P(Z, X)\bar{P}(X)/P(X)$.
3. Find $P(Z, Y = y) = \sum_X \bar{P}(Z, X)$.
4. Find $P(Z \mid Y = y) = P(Z, Y = y)/\sum_Z P(Z, Y = y)$

5. Conditional independence

In the last example we had that

$$
P(X, Y, Z) = P(Y \mid X)P(Z \mid X)P(X),
$$

from which we get

$$
\begin{aligned}
P(Y \mid Z, X) &= \frac{P(X, Y, Z)}{P(Z, X)} \\
&= \frac{P(Y \mid X)P(Z \mid X)P(X)}{P(Z, X)} \\
&= P(Y \mid X)
\end{aligned}
$$

and likewise for $P(Z \mid Y, X) = P(Z \mid X)$. Hence given $X = x$ say, we obtain $P(Y \mid Z, X = x) = P(Y \mid X = x)$ and $P(Z \mid Y, X = x) = P(Z \mid X = x)$. This is an example of conditional independence (Dawid(1979)). We associated the graph $Z \leftarrow X \rightarrow Y$ with this distribution, though this is not unique. In fact the joint probability can be factorized according to three distinct directed graphs:

$$
\begin{aligned}
Z \leftarrow X \rightarrow Y &: P(X, Y, Z) = P(X)P(Y \mid X)P(Z \mid X). \\
Z \rightarrow X \rightarrow Y &: P(X, Y, Z) = P(Y \mid X)P(X \mid Z)P(Z). \\
Z \leftarrow X \leftarrow Y &: P(X, Y, Z) = P(X \mid Y)P(Z \mid X)P(Y).
\end{aligned}
$$

Each of these factorizations follows from the conditional independence properties which each graph expresses, viz $Z \perp\!\!\!\perp Y \,|\, X$, (which is to be read as "Z is conditionally independent of Y given X") and by using the general factorization property:

$$
\begin{aligned}
P(X_1, \ldots X_n) &= P(X_1 \,|\, X_2, \ldots, X_n) P(X_2, \ldots, X_n) \\
&= P(X_1 \,|\, X_2, \ldots, X_n) P(X_2 \,|\, X_3, \ldots, X_n) P(X_3, \ldots, X_n) \\
&= \vdots \\
&= P(X_1 \,|\, X_2, \ldots, X_n) \ldots P(X_{n-1} \,|\, X_n) P(X_n).
\end{aligned}
$$

Thus for the third example

$$
P(X, Y, Z) = P(Z \,|\, X, Y) P(X \,|\, Y) P(Y) = P(Z \,|\, X) P(X \,|\, Y) P(Y).
$$

Note that the graph $Z \to X \leftarrow Y$ does not obey the conditional independence property $Z \perp\!\!\!\perp Y \,|\, X$ and is thus excluded from the list; it factorizes as $P(X, Y, Z) = P(X \,|\, Y, Z) P(Z) P(Y)$.

This example shows several features of general Bayesian networks. Firstly, the use of the conditional independence properties can be used to simplify the general factorization formula for the joint probability. Secondly, that the result is a factorization that can be expressed by the use of directed acyclic graphs (DAGs).

6. General specification in DAGs

It is these features which work together nicely for the general specification of Bayesian networks. Thus a Bayesian network is a directed acyclic graph, whose structure defines a set of conditional independence properties. These properties can be found using graphical manipulations, eg *d-separation* (see eg Pearl(1988)). To each node is associated a conditional probability distribution, conditioning being on the parents of the node: $P(X \,|\, \mathrm{pa}(X))$. The joint density over the set of all variables U is then given by the product of such terms over all nodes:

$$
P(U) = \prod_X P(X \,|\, \mathrm{pa}(X)).
$$

This is called a *recursive factorization* according to the DAG; we also talk of the distribution being graphical over the DAG. This factorization is equivalent to the general factorization but takes into account the conditional independence properties of the DAG in simplifying individual terms in the product of the general factorization. Only if the DAG is complete will this formula and the general factorization coincide, (but even then only for one ordering of the random variables in the factorization).

6.1. EXAMPLE

Consider the graph of Figure 2.

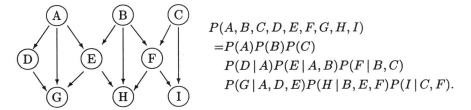

$$P(A, B, C, D, E, F, G, H, I)$$
$$= P(A)P(B)P(C)$$
$$P(D \mid A)P(E \mid A, B)P(F \mid B, C)$$
$$P(G \mid A, D, E)P(H \mid B, E, F)P(I \mid C, F).$$

Figure 2.   Nine node example.

It is useful to note that marginalising over a childless node is equivalent to simply removing it and any edges to it from its parents. Thus for example, marginalising over the variable H in the above gives:

$$P(A, B, C, D, E, F, G, I) = \sum_H P(A, B, C, D, E, F, G, H, I)$$

$$= \sum_H P(A)P(B)P(C)P(D \mid A)P(E \mid A, B)P(F \mid B, C)$$
$$P(G \mid A, D, E)P(H \mid B, E, F)P(I \mid C, F)$$
$$= P(A)P(B)P(C)P(D \mid A)P(E \mid A, B)P(F \mid B, C)$$
$$P(G \mid A, D, E)P(I \mid C, F) \sum_H P(H \mid B, E, F)$$
$$= P(A)P(B)P(C)P(D \mid A)P(E \mid A, B)P(F \mid B, C)$$
$$P(G \mid A, D, E)P(I \mid C, F),$$

which can be represented by Figure 2 with H and its incident edges removed.

Directed acyclic graphs can always have their nodes linearly ordered so that for each node X all of its parents pa(X) precedes it in the ordering. Such and ordering is called a *topological ordering* of the nodes. Thus for example $(A, B, C, D, E, F, G, H, I)$ and $(B, A, E, D, G, C, F, I, H)$ are two of the many topological orderings of the nodes of Figure 2.

A simple algorithm to find a topological ordering is as follows: Start with the graph and an empty list. Then successively delete from the graph any node which does not have any parents, and add it to the end of the list. Note that if the graph is not acyclic, then at some stage a graph will be obtained in which no node has no parent nodes, hence this algorithm can be used as an efficient way of checking that the graph is acyclic.

Another equivalent way is to start with the graph and an empty list, and successively delete nodes which have no children and add them to the beginning of the list (cf. marginalisation of childless nodes.)

6.2. DIRECTED MARKOV PROPERTY

An important property is the *directed Markov property*. This is a conditional independence property which states that a variable is conditionally independent of its non-descendents given it parents:

$$X \perp\!\!\!\perp \mathrm{nd}(X) \,|\, \mathrm{pa}(X).$$

Now recall that the conditional probability $P(X \,|\, \mathrm{pa}(X))$ did not necessarily mean that if $\mathrm{pa}(X) = \pi^*$ say, then $P(X = x) = P(x \,|\, \pi^*)$, but included the caveat that any other information is irrelevant to X for this to hold. For the DAGs this 'other information' means, from the directed Markov property, knowledge about the node itself or any of its descendents. For if all of the parents of X are observed, but additionally observed are one or more descendents D_X of X, then because X influences D_X, knowing D_X and $\mathrm{pa}(X)$ is more informative than simply knowing about $\mathrm{pa}(X)$ alone. However having information about a non-descendent does not tell us anything more about X, because either it cannot influence or be influenced by X either directly or indirectly, or if it can influence X indirectly, then only through influencing the parents which are all known anyway.

For example, consider again Figure 2. Using the previous second topological ordering we may write the general factorization as:

$$
\begin{aligned}
P(A, B, C, D, E, F, G, I, H) =& P(B) \\
& * P(A \,|\, B) \\
& * P(E \,|\, B, A) \\
& * P(D \,|\, B, A, E) \\
& * P(G \,|\, B, A, E, D) \\
& * P(C \,|\, B, A, E, D, G) \\
& * P(F \,|\, B, A, E, D, G, C) \\
& * P(I \,|\, B, A, E, D, G, C, F) \\
& * P(H \,|\, B, A, E, D, G, C, F, I)
\end{aligned}
\tag{5}
$$

but now we can use $A \perp\!\!\!\perp B$ from the directed Markov property to simplify $P(A \,|\, B) \to P(A)$, and similarly for the other factors in (5) etc, to obtain the factorization in Figure 2. We can write the general pseudo-algorithm of what we have just done for this example as

> Topological ordering +
> General factorization +
> Directed Markov property
> $\implies$ Recursive factorization.

7. Making the inference engine

We shall now move on to building the so called "inference engine" to introduce new concepts and to show how they relate to the conditional independence/recursive factorization ideas that have already been touched upon. Detailed justification of the results will be omitted, the aim here is to give an overview, using the use the fictional ASIA example of Lauritzen and Spiegelhalter.

7.1. ASIA: SPECIFICATION

Lauritzen and Spiegelhalter describe their fictional problem domain as follows:

> Shortness-of-breath (**D**yspnoea) may be due to **T**uberculosis, **L**ung cancer or **B**ronchitis, or none of them, or more than one of them. A recent visit to **A**sia increases the chances of **T**uberculosis, while **S**moking is known to be a risk factor for both **L**ung cancer and **B**ronchitis. The results of a single **X**-ray do not discriminate between **L**ung cancer and **T**uberculosis, as neither does the presence or absence of **D**yspnoea.

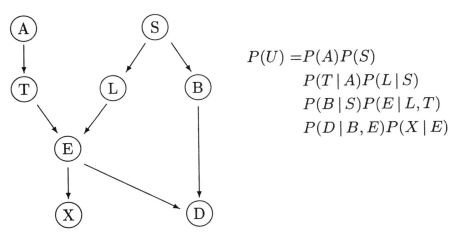

$$P(U) = P(A)P(S)$$
$$P(T \mid A)P(L \mid S)$$
$$P(B \mid S)P(E \mid L, T)$$
$$P(D \mid B, E)P(X \mid E)$$

Figure 3. ASIA

The network for this fictional example is shown in Figure 3. Each variable is a binary with the states ("yes", "no"). The **E** node is a logical node taking value "yes" if either of its parents take a "yes" value, and "no" otherwise; its introduction facilitates modelling the relationship of **X**-ray to **L**ung cancer and **T**uberculosis.

Having specified the relevant variables, and defined their dependence with the graph, we must now assign (conditional) probabilities to the nodes. In real life examples such probabilities may be elicited either from some large database (if one is available) as frequency ratios, or subjectively from the expert from whom the structure has been elicited (eg using a fictitious gambling scenario or probability wheel), or a combination of both. However as this is a fictional example we can follow the third route and use made-up values. (Specific values will be omitted here.)

7.2. CONSTRUCTING THE INFERENCE ENGINE

With our specified graphical model we have a representation of the joint density in terms of a factorization:

$$P(U) = \prod_V P(V \mid \mathrm{pa}(V)) \qquad (6)$$

$$= P(A)\ldots P(X \mid E). \qquad (7)$$

Recall that our motivation is to use the model specified by the joint distribution to calculate marginal distributions conditional on some observation of one or more variables. In general the full distribution will be computationally difficult to use directly to calculate these marginals directly. We will now proceed to outline the various stages that are performed to find a representation of $P(U)$ which makes the calculations more tractable. (The process of constructing the inference engine from the model specification is sometimes called *compiling* the model.)

The manipulations required are almost all graphical. There are five stages in the graphical manipulations. Let us first list them, and then go back and define new terms which are introduced.

1. Add undirected edges to all co-parents which are not currently joined (a process called *marrying parents*).
2. Drop all directions in the graph obtained from Stage 1. The result is the so-called *moral graph*.
3. *Triangulate the moral graph*, that is, add sufficient additional undirected links between nodes such that there are no cycles (ie. closed paths) of length 4 or more distinct nodes without a short-cut.
4. Identify the *cliques* of this triangulated graph.
5. Join the cliques together to form the *junction tree*.

Now let us go through these steps, supplying some justification and defining the new terms just introduced as we go along. Consider first the joint density again. By a change of notation this can be written in the form

$$P(U) \;=\; \prod_V a(V, \mathrm{pa}(V)) \tag{8}$$

$$\;=\; a(A)\ldots a(X, E). \tag{9}$$

where $a(X, \mathrm{pa}(X)) \equiv P(V \,|\, \mathrm{pa}(V))$. That is, the conditional probability factors for V can be considered as a function of V and its parents. We call such functions *potentials*. Now after steps 1 and 2 we have an undirected graph, in which for each node both it and its set of parents in the original graph form a complete subgraph in the moral graph. (A complete graph is one in which every pair of nodes is joined together by an edge.) Hence, the original factorization of $P(U)$ on the DAG G goes over to an equivalent factorization on these complete subsets in the moral graph G^m. Technically we say that the distribution is graphical on the undirected graph G^m. Figure 4 illustrates the moralisation process for the Asia network. Now let us de-

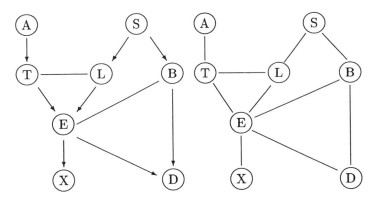

Figure 4. Moralising Asia: Two extra links are required, $A - S$ and $L - B$. Directionality is dropped after all moral edges have been added.

note the set of cliques of the moral graph by C^m. (A clique is a complete subgraph which is not itself a proper subgraph of a complete subgraph, so it is a maximal complete subgraph.) Then each of the complete subgraphs formed from $\{V\} \cup \mathrm{pa}(V)$ is contained within at least one clique. Hence we can form functions a_C such that

$$P(U) = \prod_{c \in C^m} a_C(V_C)$$

where $a_C(V_C)$ is a function of the variables in the clique C. Such a factorization can be constructed as follows: Initially define each factor as unity, i.e.,

$a_C(V_C) = 1$ for all cliques in C^m. Then for each factor $P(V \mid \mathrm{pa}(V))$ find one
and only one clique which contains the complete subgraph of $\{V\} \cup \mathrm{pa}(V)$
and multiply this conditional distribution into the function of that clique
to obtain a new function. When this is done the result is a potential representation of the joint distributions in terms of functions on the cliques of
the moral G^m.

Note that by adding the extra edges in the moralisation process it is
not possible to read of all of the conditional independences of the original
DAG, though they are still there "buried" in the numerical specification.
Those which remain "visible" in the moral graph are used to exploit the
efficient local computations which will be described later.

8. Aside: Markov properties on ancestral sets

In fact the moral graph is a powerful construction for elicudating conditional independence. First we require some more definitions. A node A is
an ancestor of a node B if either (i) A is a parent of B or (ii) A is an
ancestor of (at least) one of the parents of B. The ancestral set of a node
is the node itself and the set of its ancestors. The ancestral set of a set
of nodes Y is the union of the ancestral sets of the nodes in Y. A set S
separates the sets A and B if every path between a node $a \in A$ and $b \in B$
passes through some node of S. With these definitions we have:

Lemma 1

    Let P factorize recursively according to $\mathcal{G}$. Then

$$A \perp\!\!\!\perp B \mid S$$

whenever A and B are separated by S in $(\mathcal{G}_{\mathrm{An}(A \cup B \cup S)})^m$, the moral graph
of the smallest ancestral set containing $A \cup B \cup S$.

Lemma 2

    Let A, B and S be disjoint subsets of a directed, acyclic graph $\mathcal{G}$. Then S
d-separates A from B if and only if S separates A from B in $(\mathcal{G}_{\mathrm{An}(A \cup B \cup S)})^m$.

What these lemmas tell us is that if we want to check conditional independences we can either look at d-separation properties or the smallest
ancestral sets of the moral graphs – they are alternative ways of calculation.

To understand why ancestral set come into the picture, let us consider
the following simple algorithm for finding them. Suppose that we have the
graph G and that we wish to find the ancestral set of a set of nodes $Y \subseteq U$.
Then successively delete nodes from G which have no children, provided
they are not in the set Y. When it is not possible any longer delete any
nodes, the subgraph left is the minimal ancestral set.

Now recall that deleting a childless node is equivalent to marginalising over that node. Hence the marginal distribution of the minimal ancestral set containing $A \perp\!\!\!\perp B \,|\, S$ factorizes according to the sub-factors of the original joint distribution. So these lemmas are saying that rather than go through the numerical exercise of actually calculating such marginals we can read it off from the graphical structure instead, and use that to test conditional independences. (Note also that the directed Markov property is also lurking behind the scenes here.) The "moral" is that when ancestral sets appear in theorems like this it is likely that such marginals are being considered.

9. Making the junction tree

The remaining three steps of the inference-engine construction algorithm seem more mysterious, but are required to ensure we can formulate a consistent and efficient message passing scheme. Consider first step 3 – adding edges to the moral graph G^m to form a triangulated graph G^t. Note that adding edges to the graph does not stop a clique of the moral graph formed from being a complete subgraph in G^t. Thus for each clique in C^m of the moral graph there is at least one clique in the triangulated graph which contains it. Hence we can form a potential representation of the joint probability in terms of products of functions of the cliques in the triangulated graph:

$$P(U) = \prod_{c \in C^t} a_C(X_C)$$

by analogy with the previous method outline for the moral graph. The point is that after moralisation and triangulation there exists for each a node-parent set at least one clique which contains it, and thus a potential representation can be formed on the cliques of the triangulated graph.

While the moralisation of a graph is unique, there are in general many alternative triangulations of a moral graph. In the extreme, we can always add edges to make the moral graph complete. There is then one large clique. The key to the success of the computational algorithms is to form triangulated graphs which have small cliques, in terms of their state space size.

Thus after finding the cliques of the triangulated graph – stage 4 – we are left with joining them up to form a junction tree. The important property of the junction tree is the *running intersection property* which means that if variable V is contained in two cliques, then it is contained in every clique along the path connecting those two cliques. The edge joining two cliques is called a separator. This joining up property can always be done, not necessarily uniquely for each triangulated graph. However the choice of tree is immaterial except for computational efficiency considerations. The junction tree captures many, but not necessarily all, of the conditional independence properties of the distribution on the original DAG. It loses some of the conditional independences by the process of adding extra edges to the moral graph. However it does retain conditional independence between (not necessarily neighbouring) cliques given separators between them. It is because of this fact that local computation with message passing becomes possible. The running intersection property ensures *consistence* in the message passing between cliques, and the cliques become the basic unit of the local computation, ie., they define the granularity of the computational algorithms. If the cliques are of manageable size then local computation is possible. Figure 5 shows a triangulated version of Asia and a possible junction tree.

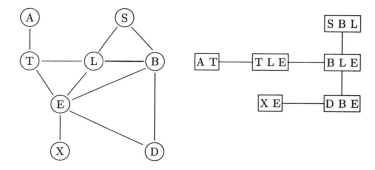

Figure 5. Junction tree for Asia

10. Inference on the junction tree

We will summarise some of the basic results of message passing on the junction tree. We have seen that we can form a potential representation of the joint probability using functions defined on the cliques:

$$P(U) = \prod_{C \in C^t} a_C(X_C).$$

This can be generalized to include functions on the separators (the intersections of neighbouring cliques) to form the following so called *generalized potential representation*:

$$P(U) = \frac{\prod_{C \in C^t} a_C(X_C)}{\prod_{S \in S^t} b_S(X_S)}.$$

(for instance by making the separator functions the identity). Now, by sending messages between neighbouring cliques consisting of functions of the separator variables only, which modify the intervening separator and the clique receiving the message, but in such a way that the overall ratio of products remains invariant, we can arrive at the following *marginal representation*:

$$p(U) = \frac{\prod_{C \in \mathcal{C}} p(C)}{\prod_{S \in \mathcal{S}} p(S)}. \tag{10}$$

Marginals for individual variables can be obtained from these clique (or separator) marginals by further marginalisation.

Suppose that we observe "evidence" $\mathcal{E} : X_A = x_A^*$. Define a new function P^* by

$$P^*(x) = \begin{cases} P(x) & \text{if } X_A = x_A^* \\ 0 & \text{otherwise.} \end{cases} \tag{11}$$

Then $P^*(U) = P(U, \mathcal{E}) = P(\mathcal{E})P(U \mid \mathcal{E})$. We can rewrite (11) as

$$P^*(U) = P(U) \prod_{v \in A} l(v), \tag{12}$$

where $l(v)$ is 1 if $x_v = x_v^*$, 0 otherwise. Thus $l(v)$ is the *likelihood function* based on the partial evidence $X_v = x_v^*$. Clearly this also factorizes on the junction tree, and by message passing we may obtain the following *clique-marginal representation*

$$p(V \mid \mathcal{E}) = \frac{\prod_{C \in \mathcal{C}} p(C \mid \mathcal{E})}{\prod_{S \in \mathcal{S}} p(S \mid \mathcal{E})}. \tag{13}$$

or by omitting the normalization stage,

$$p(V, \mathcal{E}) = \frac{\prod_{C \in \mathcal{C}} p(C, \mathcal{E})}{\prod_{S \in \mathcal{S}} p(S, \mathcal{E})}. \tag{14}$$

Again marginal distributions for individual variables, conditional upon the evidence, can be obtained by further marginalisation of individual clique tables, as can the probability (according to the model) of the evidence, $P(\mathcal{E})$.

11. Why the junction tree?

Given that the moral graph has nice properties, why is it necessary to go on to form the junction tree? This is best illustrated by an example, Figure 6:

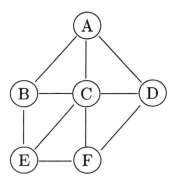

Figure 6.   A non-triangulated graph

The cliques are (A, B, C), (A, C, D), (C, D, F), (C, E, F) and (B, C, E) with successive intersections (A, C), (C, D), (C, F), (C, E) and (B, C). Suppose we have clique marginals $P(A, B, C)$ *etc.*. We cannot express $P(A, B, C, D)$ in terms of $P(A, B, C)$ and $P(A, C, D)$ – the graphical structure does *not* imply $B \perp\!\!\!\perp D|(A, C)$. In general there is no closed for expression for the joint distribution of all six variables in terms of its cliques marginals.

12.   Those extra edges again

Having explained why the cliques of the moral graph are generally not up to being used for local message passing, we will now close by indicating where the extra edges to form a triangulated graph come from.

Our basic message passing algorithm will be one in which marginals of the potentials in the cliques will form the messages on the junction tree. So let us begin with our moral graph with a potential representation in terms of functions on the cliques, and suppose we marginalise a variable Y say,which belongs to more than one clique of the graph, say two cliques, C_1 and C_2, with variables $Y \cup Z_1$ and $Y \cup Z_2$ respectively. They are cliques, but the combined set of variables do not form a single clique, hence there must be at least one pair of variables, one in each clique, which are not joined to each other, u_1 and u_2 say.

Now consider the effect of marginalisation of the variable Y. We will have

$$\sum_Y a_{C_1}(Y \cup Z_1)a_{C_2}(Y \cup Z_2) \equiv f(Z_1 \cup Z_2),$$

a function of the combined variables of the two cliques minus Y. Now this function cannot be accommodated by a clique in the moral graph because the variables u_1 and u_2 are not joined (and there may be others).

Hence we cannot form a potential representation of the joint distribution of $P(U - Y)$ on the moral graph with node Y removed. However, if we fill in the missing edges between the pairs of variables of the two cliques, then this marginal can be accommodated, and we can find a potential representation for $P(U - Y)$ on the reduced moral graph having these extra edges. This is why one adds edges to the moral graph, to be able to accommodate such intermediate marginal expressions. It turns out that one must fill-in sufficiently to form a triangulated graph, and doing so results in being able to set up a consistent message passing scheme.

13. Suggested further reading

Pearl is one of the pioneers who helped Bayesian methods for uncertain reasoning become popular in the artificial intelligence community. His textbook (Pearl, 1988) contains a wealth of material, from introducing probability theory and arguments for its use; axiomatics for graphical models; Markov properties; etc, to propagation in singly connected DAGs (ie prior to the development of making junction trees and propagating with them.) A good collection of papers on uncertain reasoning is Shafer and Pearl(1990), which covers not only probabilistic reasoning but also other formalisms for handling uncertainty. This also contains good overviews by the editors explaining the historical significance of the selected papers. An introductory review for probabilistic expert systems is (Spiegelhalter *et al.*, 1993). Each of these three references contain a large number of references for further reading.

Dawid(1979) introduced the axiomatic basis for treating conditional independence. More recent accounts of conditional independence with emphasis on graphical models and their Markov properties are given by Whittaker(1990) and Lauritzen(1996). (The latter also contains proofs of the lemmas stated in section 8.)

The Asia example was given by Lauritzen and Spiegelhalter(1988), who showed how to do consistent probability calculations in multiply connected DAG's using propagation, (it is also reprinted in (Shafer and Pearl, 1990)). Junction trees arise in other areas and are known by different names (eg join trees in relational databases); see (Lauritzen and Spiegelhalter, 1988) for more on this and also the discussion section of that paper. A recent and general formulation of propagation in junction trees is given by Dawid(1992). A recent introductory textbook on Bayesian networks is (Jensen, 1996).

References

Dawid, A. P. (1979). Conditional independence in statistical theory (with discussion). *Journal of the Royal Statistical Society, Series B*, **41**, pp. 1–31.

Dawid, A. P. (1992). Applications of a general propagation algorithm for probabilistic expert systems. *Statistics and Computing*, **2**, pp. 25–36.

Jensen, F. V. (1996). *An introduction to Bayesian networks*. UCL Press, London.

Lauritzen, S. L. (1996). *Graphical models*. OUP.

Lauritzen, S. L. and Spiegelhalter, D. J. (1988). Local computations with probabilities on graphical structures and their application to expert systems (with discussion). *Journal of the Royal Statistical Society, Series B*, **50**, pp. 157–224.

Pearl, J. (1988). *Probabilistic inference in intelligent systems*. Morgan Kaufmann, San Mateo.

Shafer, G. R. and Pearl, J. (ed.) (1990). *Readings in uncertain reasoning*. Morgan Kaufmann, San Mateo, California.

Spiegelhalter, D. J., Dawid, A. P., Lauritzen, S. L., and Cowell, R. G. (1993). Bayesian analysis in expert systems. *Statistical Science*, **8**, pp. 219–47.

Whittaker, J. (1990). *Graphical models in applied multivariate statistics*. John Wiley and Sons, Chichester.

ADVANCED INFERENCE IN BAYESIAN NETWORKS

ROBERT COWELL
City University, London.
The School of Mathematics, Actuarial Science and Statistics,
City University, Northampton Square, London EC1E 0HT

1. Introduction

The previous chapter introduced inference in discrete variable Bayesian networks. This used evidence propagation on the junction tree to find marginal distributions of interest. This chapter presents a tutorial introduction to some of the various types of calculations which can also be performed with the junction tree, specifically:

- Sampling.
- Most likely configurations.
- Fast retraction.
- Gaussian and conditional Gaussian models.

A common theme of these methods is that of a localized message-passing algorithm, but with different 'marginalisation' methods and potentials taking part in the message passing operations.

2. Sampling

Let us begin with the simple simulation problem. Given some evidence $\mathcal{E}$ on a (possibly empty) set of variable X_E, we might wish to simulate one or more values for the unobserved variables.

2.1. SAMPLING IN DAGS

Henrion proposed an algorithm called *probabilistic logic sampling* for DAGs, which works as follows. One first finds a topological ordering of the nodes of the DAG $\mathcal{G}$. Let us denote the ordering by $(X_1, X_2, \ldots, X_n)$ say after relabeling the nodes, so that all parents of a node precede it in the ordering, hence any parent of X_j will have an index $i < j$.

Assume at first that there is no evidence. Then one can sample X_1 from $P(X_1)$ to obtain x_1^* say. Then one samples a state for node X_2. Now if X_2 has no parents, then we can sample from $P(X_2)$ to obtain x_2^* say. Otherwise it has X_1 as a parent (by the topological ordering there are no other possibilities); hence we can sample from $P(X_2 \,|\, X_1 = x_1^*)$. In general in the jth stage we can sample from $P(X_j \,|\, \mathrm{pa}(X_j) = \pi^*)$ because all the parents will have already been sampled themselves and be in some definite state π^*. When we have sampled each of the nodes, we will obtain the case $u^* = (x_1^*, x_2^*, \dots, x_n^*)$ with probability $P(U = u^*)$, ie sampled correctly from the full distribution $P(U)$. If we wish to generate a set of such cases, we begin over again with X_1. Each such case will be sampled independently.

Now suppose that we have evidence on one or more nodes. The previous scheme can still be applied, but one now introduces rejection steps to ensure samples are drawn from the correct distribution $P(U \,|\, \mathcal{E})$. Thus suppose we are at stage j, but that the state of X_j is known from the evidence to be $x_j^\dagger$ say. We cannot simply set $x_j^* = x_j^\dagger$ and then continue, because the resulting case will not have been drawn at random from the correct distribution. Instead, one samples X_j to obtain x_j^* say. Then, if it is the case that $x_j^* = x_j^\dagger$, we proceed to sample the next node, otherwise we start again at X_1, discarding all of the values generated for the current case. This rejection step ensures the correct balancing of probabilities so that when a complete case is successfully generated it is drawn from the distribution of interest. This rejection sampling is Henrion's probabilistic logic sampling.

However a problem is that with even quite small networks, let alone large ones, rejection increases exponentially with the number of nodes bearing evidence. We shall now see how the junction tree can be used to sample efficiently even with evidence.

2.2. SAMPLING USING THE JUNCTION TREE

Let us assume that we have propagated evidence and have a marginal representation of the joint probability on the junction tree:

$$P(U \,|\, \mathcal{E}) = \prod_C P(C \,|\, \mathcal{E}) / \prod_S P(S \,|\, \mathcal{E}).$$

To draw an analogy to the direct sampling from the DAG, let us now suppose that a clique is fixed as root, and that the edges of the junction tree are made directed as follows: the edges are directed between cliques and separators such that they all point away from the root. The result is a directed graph which because it is also a tree is also acyclic. Let us label the cliques and separators $(C_0, S_1, C_1, \dots, S_m, C_m)$ such that C_0 is the root clique, that this ordering is a topological ordering of the nodes in the directed tree, and with S_i the parent of C_i; see Figure 1. (Note that this notation

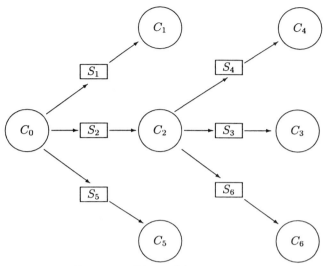

Figure 1. Directed junction tree.

has a subtlety that the tree is connected, but the disconnected case is easily dealt with.) Then we may divide the contents of the parent separator S_i into the clique table in C_i to obtain the following representation:

$$P(U \mid \mathcal{E}) = P(X_{C_0} \mid \mathcal{E}) \prod_{i=1}^{m} P(X_{C_i \setminus S_i} \mid X_{S_i}, \mathcal{E}).$$

This is called the *set-chain* representation, and is now in a form similar to the recursive factorization on the DAG discussed earlier, and can be sampled from in a similar manner. The difference is that instead of sampling individual variables at a time, one samples groups of variables in the cliques.

Thus one begins by sampling a configuration in the root clique, drawing from $P(X_{C_0} \mid \mathcal{E})$ to obtain $x^*_{C_0}$ say. Next one samples from $P(X_{C_1 \setminus S_1} \mid x^*_{S_1}, \mathcal{E})$ where the states of the variables for X_{S_1} are fixed by $x^*_{C_0}$ because $X_{S_1} \subset X_{C_0}$. One continues in this way, so that when sampling in clique C_i the variables X_{S_i} will already have been fixed by earlier sampling, as in direct sampling from the DAG. Thus one can sample directly from the correct distribution and avoid the inefficiencies of the rejection method.

3. Most likely configurations

One contributing reason why local propagation on the junction tree to find marginals "works" is that there is a "commutation behaviour" between the operation of summation and the product form of the joint density on the tree, which allows one to move summation operations through the terms in the product, for example:

$$\sum_{A,B,C} f(A,B)f(B,C) = \sum_{A,B} \left(f(A,B) \sum_C f(B,C) \right).$$

However summation is not the only operation which has this property; another very useful operation is maximization, for example:

$$\max_{A,B,C} f(A,B)f(B,C) = \max_{A,B} \left(f(A,B) \max_C f(B,C) \right),$$

provided the factors are non-negative, a condition which will hold for clique and separator potentials representing probability distributions.

3.1. MAX-PROPAGATION

So suppose we have a junction tree representation of a probability distribution

$$P(U,\mathcal{E}) = \prod_C a(C) / \prod_S b(S)$$

and we pass messages of the form

$$b^*(S) = \max_{C\backslash S} a(C),$$

(which can be performed locally through the commutation property above) what do we get? The answer is the *max-marginal* representation of the joint density:

$$P(U,\mathcal{E}) = \frac{\prod_C P^{\max}(C,\mathcal{E})}{\prod_S P^{\max}(S,\mathcal{E})} \equiv \frac{\prod_C \max_{U\backslash C} P(U,\mathcal{E})}{\prod_S \max_{U\backslash S} P(S,\mathcal{E})}.$$

The interpretation is that for each configuration c^* of the variables in the clique C, the value $P_C^{\max}(c^*)$ is the highest probability value that any configuration of all the variables can take subject to the constraint that the variables of the clique have states c^*. (One simple consequence is that this most likely value appears at least once in every clique and separator.)

To see how this can come about, consider a simple tree with two sets of variables in each clique:

$$P(A,B,C,\mathcal{E}) = a(A,B)\frac{1}{b(B)}a(B,C).$$

Now recall that the message passing leaves invariant the overall distribution. So take $\boxed{AB}$ to be the root clique, and send then the first message, a maximization over C:

$$b^*(B) = \max_C a(B, C).$$

after "collecting" this message we have the representation:

$$P(A, B, C, \mathcal{E}) = \left(a(A, B) \frac{b^*(B)}{b(B)} \right) \frac{1}{b^*(B)} a(B, C).$$

The root clique now holds the table obtained by maximizing $P(A, B, C, \mathcal{E})$ over C, because

$$
\begin{aligned}
P^{\max}(A, B, \mathcal{E}) &\equiv \max_C P(A, B, C, \mathcal{E}) \\
&= \max_C \left(a(A, B) \frac{b^*(B)}{b(B)} \right) \frac{1}{b^*(B)} a(B, C) \\
&= \left(a(A, B) \frac{b^*(B)}{b(B)} \right) \max_C \frac{1}{b^*(B)} a(B, C) \\
&= \left(a(A, B) \frac{b^*(B)}{b(B)} \right).
\end{aligned}
$$

By symmetry the distribute message results in the second clique table holding the max-marginal value $\max_A P(A, B, C, \mathcal{E})$ and the intervening separator holding $\max_{A,C} P(A, B, C, \mathcal{E})$. The more general result can be obtained by induction on the numbers of cliques in the junction tree. (Note that one can pass back to the sum-marginal representation from the max-marginal representation by a sum-propagation.)

A separate but related task is to find the configuration of the variables which takes this highest probability. The procedure is as follows: first from a general potential representation with some clique C_0 chosen as root, perform a collect operation using maximization instead of summation. Then, search the root clique for the configuration of its variables, c_0^* say, which has the highest probability. Distribute this as extra "evidence", fixing successively the remaining variables in the cliques further from the root by finding a maximal configuration consistent with the neighbouring clique which has also been fixed, and including the states of the newly fixed variables as evidence, until all cliques have been so processed. The union of the "evidence" yields the most likely configuration. If there is "real" evidence then this is incorporated in the usual way in the collect operation. The interpretation is that the resulting configuration acts as a most likely explanation for the data.

Note the similarity to simulation, where one first does a collect to the root using ordinary marginalisation, then does a distribute by first randomly selecting a configuration from the root, and then randomly selecting configurations from cliques successively further out.

3.2. DEGENERACY OF MAXIMUM

It is possible to find the degeneracy of the most likely configuration, that is the total number of distinct configurations which have the same maximum probability $P^{\max}(U \,|\, \mathcal{E}) = p^*$ by a simple trick. (For most realistic applications there is unlikely to be any degeneracy, although this might not be true for eg. genetic-pedigree problems.) First one performs a max-propagation to obtain the max-marginal representation. Then one sets each value in each clique and separator to either 0 or 1, depending on whether or not it has attained the maximum probability value, thus:

$$I_C(x_C \,|\, \mathcal{E}) = \begin{cases} 1 & \text{if } P_C^{\max}(x_C \,|\, \mathcal{E}) = p^* \\ 0 & \text{otherwise,} \end{cases}$$

and

$$I_S(x_S \,|\, \mathcal{E}) = \begin{cases} 1 & \text{if } P_S^{\max}(x_S \,|\, \mathcal{E}) = p^* \\ 0 & \text{otherwise.} \end{cases}$$

Then

$$I(U \,|\, \mathcal{E}) = \prod_C I_C(x_C \,|\, \mathcal{E}) \Big/ \prod_S I_S(X_S \,|\, \mathcal{E})$$

is a potential representation of the indicator function of most likely configurations, a simple sum-propagation on this will yield the degeneracy as the normalization.

3.3. TOP N CONFIGURATIONS

In finding the degeneracy of the most likely configuration in the previous section, we performed a max-propagation and then set clique elements to zero which did not have the value of the highest probability. One might be tempted to think that if instead we set to zero all those elements which are below a certain threshold $p < 1$ then we will obtain the number of configurations having probability $\geq p$. It turns out that one can indeed find these configurations after one max-propagation, but unfortunately not by such a simple method. We will discuss a simplified version of an algorithm by Dennis Nilsson which allows one to calculate the top N configurations by a sequence of propagations. (Nilsson(1997) has recently shown how they can be found after a single max-propagation.)

To begin with assume that we have no evidence. The first step is to have an ordering of the nodes, any ordering will do. Let us write this as $(X_1, X_2, \ldots, X_n)$, and let the j-th node have k_j states $(x_j^1, \ldots x_j^{k_j})$. We now do a max-propagation, and find the most likely configuration, denoted by $M^1 = (x_1^{m_1^1}, \ldots x_n^{m_n^1})$. Necessarily the second-most likely configuration, $M^2 = (x_1^{m_1^2}, \ldots x_n^{m_n^2})$, must differ from the most likely configuration in the state of at least one variable. So now we perform a further n max-propagations with "pseudo-evidence" $\mathcal{E}_j$ as follows.

$$
\begin{aligned}
\mathcal{E}_1 &= X_1 \neq x_1^{m_1^1} \\
\mathcal{E}_2 &= X_1 = x_1^{m_1^1} \text{ and } X_2 \neq x_2^{m_2^1} \\
\mathcal{E}_3 &= X_1 = x_1^{m_1^1} \text{ and } X_2 = x_2^{m_2^1} \text{ and } X_3 \neq x_3^{m_3^1} \\
&\vdots \\
\mathcal{E}_n &= X_1 = x_1^{m_1^1} \text{ and } \ldots X_{n-1} = x_{n-1}^{m_{n-1}^1} \text{ and } X_n \neq x_n^{m_n^1}
\end{aligned}
$$

By this procedure we partition the remaining set of configurations, excluding the most likely one M^1 we have already found. Hence one, and only one, of them has the second most likely configuration M^2, which can be found by looking at the (max-)normalizations of each.

Suppose the second most likely configuration was found in the jth set, ie by propagating $\mathcal{E}_j = X_1 = x_1^{m_1^1}$ and $\ldots X_{j-1} = x_{j-1}^{m_{j-1}^1}$ and $X_j \neq x_j^{m_j^1}$. Now the third most likely configuration M^3 is to be found either in the other set of propagations, or it disagrees with the M^1 and M^2 configuration in at least one place. To find out which we need to perform a further $n - j + 1$ propagations using "evidence" for each as follows:

$$
\begin{aligned}
\mathcal{E}_j^1 &= \mathcal{E}_j \text{ and } X_j \neq x_j^{m_j^2} \\
\mathcal{E}_j^2 &= \mathcal{E}_j \text{ and } X_j = x_j^{m_j^2} \text{ and } X_{j+1} \neq x_{j+1}^{m_{j+1}^2}, \\
&\vdots \\
\mathcal{E}_j^{n-j+1} &= \mathcal{E}_j \text{ and } \ldots X_{n-1} = x_{n-1}^{m_{n-1}^2} \text{ and } X_n \neq x_n^{m_n^2}.
\end{aligned}
$$

This further partitions the allowed states. After propagating these we can find the third most likely configuration. We can then find the fourth most likely configuration by essentially performing a similar partition on the third most likely configuration etc. The idea is quite simple, the main problem to develop a suitable notation to keep track of which partition one is up to.

If we have prior evidence, then we simply take this into account at the beginning, and ensure that the partitions do not violate the evidence. Thus for example if we have evidence about m nodes being in definite states, then instead of n propagations being required to find M^2 after having found M^1, we require instead only $n - m$ further propagations.

One application of finding a set of such most likely explanations is to explanation, ie, answering what the states of the unobserved variables are likely to be for a particular case. We have already seen that the most likely configuration offers such an explanation. If instead we have the top 10 or 20 configurations, then in most applications most of these will have most variables in the same state. This can confirm the diagnosis for most variables, but also shows up where diagnosis is not so certain (in those variables which differ between these top configurations). This means that if one is looking for a more accurate explanation one could pay attention to those variables which differ between the top configurations, hence serve to guide one to what could be the most informative test to do (cf. value of information).

The use of partitioned "dummy evidence" is a neat and quite general idea, and will probably find other applications.[1]

4. A unification

One simple comment to make is that minimization can be performed in a similar way to maximization. (In applications with logical dependencies the minimal configuration will have zero probability and there will be many such configurations. For example in the ASIA example half of the 256 configurations have zero probability.)

Another less obvious observation is that sum, max and min-propagation are all special cases of a more general propagation based upon L^p norms, used in functional analysis. Recall that the L^p norm of a non-negative real-valued function is defined to be

$$L^p(f) = \left(\int_{x \in X} f^p(x) dx \right)^{\frac{1}{p}}$$

For $p = 1$ this gives the usual integral, for $p \to \infty$ this give the maximum of the function over the region of integration, and for $p \to -\infty$ we obtain the minimum of f.

We can use this in our message propagation in our junction tree: the marginal message we pass from clique to separator is the L^p marginal,

---

[1]See for example (Cowell, 1997) for sampling without replacement from the junction tree.

defined by:

$$b_S^*(X_S) = \left(\sum_{X_C \setminus X_S} a_C^p(X_C) \right)^{\frac{1}{p}}$$

So that we can obtain the L^p marginal representation:

$$P(U \mid \mathcal{E}) = \frac{\prod_{C \in \mathcal{C}} P_C^{L^p}(X_C \mid \mathcal{E})}{\prod_{S \in \mathcal{S}} P_S^{L^p}(X_S \mid \mathcal{E})}$$

which is an *infinite-family* of representations. Apart from the L^2 norm, which may have an application to quadratic scoring of models, it is not clear if this general result is of much practical applicability, though it may have theoretical uses.

5. Fast retraction

Suppose that for a network of variables X we have evidence on a subset of k variables U: $\mathcal{E} = \{\mathcal{E}_u : u \in U^*\}$, with $\mathcal{E}_u$ of the form "$X_u = x_u^*$" Then it can be useful to compare each item of evidence with the probabilistic prediction given by the system for X_u on the basis of the remaining evidence $\mathcal{E}_{\setminus\{u\}}$: "$X_v = x_v^*$ for $v \in U \setminus \{u\}$", as expressed in the conditional density of X_u given $\mathcal{E}_{\setminus\{u\}}$. If we find that abnormally low probabilities are being predicted by the model this can highlight deficiencies of the model which could need attention or may indicate a rare case is being observed.

Now one "brute force" method to calculate such probabilities is to perform k separate propagations, in which one takes out in turn the evidence on each variable in question and propagates the evidence for all of the remaining variables.

However it turns out that yet another variation of the propagation algorithm allows one to calculate all of these predictive probabilities in one propagation, at least for the case in which the joint probability is strictly positive, which is the case we shall restrict ourselves to here. (For probabilities with zeros it may still be possible to apply the following algorithm; the matter depends upon the network and junction tree. For the Shafer-Shenoy message passing scheme the problem does not arise because divisions are not necessary.) Because of the computational savings implied, the method is called *fast-retraction*.

5.1. OUT-MARGINALISATION

The basic idea is to work with a potential representation of the prior joint probability even when there is evidence. This means that, unlike the earlier sections, we do not modify the clique potentials by multiplying them by the evidence likelihoods. Instead we incorporate the evidence only into forming the messages, by a new marginalisation method called *out-marginalisation*, which will be illustrated for a simple two-clique example:

$$\boxed{\text{A B}}\!\!-\!\!-\!\!\boxed{\text{B C}}$$

Here A, B and C are disjoint sets of variables, and the clique and separator potentials are all positive. Suppose we have evidence on variables $\alpha \in A$, $\beta \in B$ and $\gamma \in C$. Let us denote the evidence functions by h_α, h_β and h_γ, where h_α is the product of the evidence likelihoods for the variables $\alpha \in A$ etc. Then we have

$$
\begin{aligned}
P(ABC) &= g(AB) \otimes \frac{1}{g(B)} \otimes g(BC) \\
P(ABC, \mathcal{E}_\alpha) &= P(ABC)h_\alpha \\
P(ABC, \mathcal{E}_\gamma) &= P(ABC)h_\gamma \\
P(ABC, \mathcal{E}_\alpha, \mathcal{E}_\gamma) &= P(ABC)h_\alpha h_\gamma.
\end{aligned}
$$

where the g's are the clique and separator potentials.

We take the clique $\boxed{AB}$ as root. Our first step is to send an *out-marginal message* from $\boxed{BC}$ to $\boxed{AB}$ defined as:

$$g^*(B) = \sum_C g(BC)h_\gamma.$$

That is we only incorporate into the message that subset of evidence about the variables in C, thus excluding any evidence that may be relevant to the separator variables B. Note that because we are using the restriction that the joint probability is non zero for every configuration, this implies that the potentials and messages are also non zero. Sending this message leaves the overall product of junction tree potentials invariant as usual:

$$P(ABC) = \frac{g(AB)g^*(B)}{g(B)} \otimes \frac{1}{g^*(B)} \otimes g(BC).$$

Now let us use this representation to calculate

$$P^{out}(AB, \mathcal{E}_{\backslash A \cup B}) \equiv \sum_C P(ABC, \mathcal{E}_\gamma)$$

$$= \sum_C P(ABC) h_\gamma$$

$$= \sum_C \frac{g(AB)g^*(B)}{g(B)} \otimes \frac{1}{g^*(B)} \otimes g(BC) h_\gamma$$

$$= \frac{g(AB)g^*(B)}{g(B)} \otimes \frac{1}{g^*(B)} \left(\sum_C g(BC) h_\gamma = g^*(B) \right)$$

$$= \frac{g(AB)g^*(B)}{g(B)}.$$

This shows that the content of the clique $\boxed{AB}$ is simply the out-margin of the joint probability. We can now send and out-margin message back, and by symmetry the content of the clique $\boxed{BC}$ will also be the out-margin of the joint probability, with marginalisation taken over A. The separator potential $g(B)$ is also an out-marginalisation: $\sum_A P^{out}(AB, \mathcal{E}_{\backslash A \cup B}) h_\alpha \equiv P^{out}(B, \mathcal{E}_{\backslash B})$. We thus arrive at the following out-marginal representation of the joint probability:

$$P(ABC) = P^{out}(AB, \mathcal{E}_{\backslash A \cup B}) \frac{1}{P^{out}(B, \mathcal{E}_{\backslash B})} P^{out}(BC, \mathcal{E}_{\backslash B \cup C}).$$

Further out-marginalisation of these clique potentials will then yield the desired predictive probabilities for the individual variables having evidence.

In general we have the following out-marginal representation:

$$P(U) = \frac{\prod_C P^{out}(C, \mathcal{E}_{\backslash C})}{\prod_S P^{out}(S, \mathcal{E}_{\backslash S})},$$

which follows, from the simple two-clique case previously described, by induction on the number of cliques in the tree.

Fast retraction, where applicable, has another use besides comparing predictive probabilities against evidence. Consider the previous way of dealing with evidence, in which the clique potentials are multiplied by the evidence likelihoods. After propagating evidence about one case, one might wish to alter the evidence to look at another case. To do this would require a re-initialisation of the junction tree. However, by propagating evidence with fast-retraction, then because the tree always retains a potential representation of the joint probability, there is no need to re-initialise the junction tree between cases.

6. Modelling with continuous variables

All examples and discussion has have been restricted to the special case of discrete random variables. In principle, however, there is no reason why we should not build models having continuous random variables as well as, or instead of, discrete random variables, with more general conditional probability densities to represent the joint density, and use local message passing to simplify the calculations. In practice the barrier to such general applicability is the inability of performing the required integrations in closed form representable by a computer. (Such general models can be analyzed by simulation, for example Gibbs sampling.)

However there is a case for which such message passing is tractable, and that is when the random variables are such that the overall distribution is multivariate-Gaussian. This further extends to the situation where both discrete and continuous random variables coexist within a model having a so called *conditional-gaussian* joint distribution.

We will first discuss Gaussian models, and then discuss the necessary adjustments to the theory enabling analysis of mixed models with local computation.

7. Gaussian models

Structurally, the directed Gaussian model looks very much like the discrete models we have already seen. The novel aspect is in their numerical specification. Essentially, the conditional distribution of a node given its parents is given by a Gaussian distribution with expectation linear in the values of the parent nodes, and variance independent of the parent nodes. Let us take a familiar example:

$$\boxed{Y} \to \boxed{X} \to \boxed{Z}.$$

Node Y, which has no parents, has a normal distribution given by

$$N_Y(\mu_Y; \sigma_Y^2) \propto \exp\left(\frac{-(y - \mu_Y)^2}{2\sigma_Y^2}\right),$$

where μ_Y and σ_Y are constants. Node X has node Y as a parent, and has the conditional density:

$$N_X(\mu_X + \beta_{X,Y}y; \sigma_X^2) \propto \exp\left(\frac{-(x - \mu_X - \beta_{X,Y}y)^2}{2\sigma_X^2}\right),$$

where μ_X, $\beta_{X,Y}$ and σ_X are constants. Finally, node Z has only X as a parent; its conditional density is given by

$$N_Z(\mu_Z + \beta_{Z,X}x; \sigma_Z^2) \propto \exp\left(\frac{-(z - \mu_Z - \beta_{Z,X}x)^2}{2\sigma_Z^2}\right).$$

In general, if a node X had parents $\{Y_1, \ldots, Y_n\}$ it would have a conditional density:

$$N_X(\mu_X + \sum_i \beta_{X,Y_i}y_i; \sigma_X^2) \propto \exp\left(\frac{-(x - \mu_X - \sum_i \beta_{X,Y_i}y_i)^2}{2\sigma_X^2}\right).$$

Now the joint density is obtained by multiplying together the separate component Gaussian distributions:

$$
\begin{aligned}
P(X, Y, Z) &= N_Y(\mu_Y; \sigma_Y^2)N_X(\mu_X + \beta_{X,Y}y; \sigma_X^2)N_Z(\mu_Z + \beta_{Z,X}x; \sigma_Z^2) \\
&\propto \exp\left(-\frac{1}{2}(x - \mu_X, y - \mu_Y, z - \mu_Z)K(x - \mu_X, y - \mu_Y, z - \mu_Z)^T\right),
\end{aligned}
$$

where K is a symmetric (positive definite) 3×3 matrix, and T denotes transpose. In a more general model with n nodes, one obtains a similar expression with an $n \times n$ symmetric (positive definite) matrix.

Expanding the exponential, the joint density can be written as:

$$\exp\left((x \quad y \quad z)\begin{pmatrix}h_X \\ h_Y \\ h_Z\end{pmatrix} - \frac{1}{2}(x \quad y \quad z)\begin{pmatrix}K_{XX} & K_{XY} & K_{XZ} \\ K_{YX} & K_{YY} & K_{YZ} \\ K_{ZX} & K_{ZY} & K_{ZZ}\end{pmatrix}\begin{pmatrix}x \\ y \\ z\end{pmatrix}\right)$$

where $h_X = \mu_X/\sigma_X^2 + \mu_Z\beta_{Z,X}/\sigma_Z^2$ etc. This form of the joint density is the most useful for constructing local messages, and indeed local messages will consist of functions of this type. Let us now define them and list the properties we shall be using.

7.1. GAUSSIAN POTENTIALS

Suppose we have n continuous random variables $X_1, \ldots, X_n$. A Gaussian potential in a subset $\{Y_1, \ldots, Y_k\}$ of variables is a function of the form:

$$\exp\left(g + (y_1 \quad \cdots \quad y_k)\begin{pmatrix}h_1 \\ \vdots \\ h_k\end{pmatrix} - \frac{1}{2}(y_1 \quad \cdots \quad y_k)\begin{pmatrix}K_{1,1} & \cdots & K_{1,k} \\ \vdots & \ddots & \vdots \\ K_{k,1} & \cdots & K_{k,k}\end{pmatrix}\begin{pmatrix}y_1 \\ \vdots \\ y_k\end{pmatrix}\right)$$

where K is a constant positive definite $k \times k$ matrix, h is a k dimensional constant vector and g is a number. For shorthand we write this as a triple, $\phi = (g, h, K)$. Gaussian potentials can be multiplied by adding their respective triples together:

$$\phi_1 * \phi_2 = (g_1 + g_2, h_1 + h_2, K_1 + K_2).$$

Similarly division is easily handled:

$$\phi_1/\phi_2 = (g_1 - g_2, h_1 - h_2, K_1 - K_2).$$

These operations will be used in passing the "update factor" from separator to clique.

To initialize cliques we shall require the extension operation combined with multiplication. Thus a Gaussian potential defined on a set of variables Y is extended to a larger set of variables by enlarging the vector h and matrix K to the appropriate size and setting the new slots to zero. Thus for example: $\phi(x) = \exp(g + x^T h - \frac{1}{2} x^T K x)$ extends to

$$\phi(x, y) = \phi(x) = \exp\left(g + (x \quad y) \begin{pmatrix} h \\ 0 \end{pmatrix} - \frac{1}{2} (x \quad y) \begin{pmatrix} K & 0 \\ 0 & 0 \end{pmatrix} \begin{pmatrix} x \\ y \end{pmatrix} \right).$$

Finally, to form the messages we must define marginalisation, which is now an integration. Let us take Y_1 and Y_2 to be two sets of distinct variables, and

$$\phi(y_1, y_2) = \exp\left(g + (y_1 \quad y_2) \begin{pmatrix} h_1 \\ h_2 \end{pmatrix} - \frac{1}{2} (y_1 \quad y_2) \begin{pmatrix} K_{1,1} & K_{1,2} \\ K_{2,1} & K_{2,2} \end{pmatrix} \begin{pmatrix} y_1 \\ y_2 \end{pmatrix} \right)$$

so that the h and K are in blocks. Then integrating over Y_1 yields a new vector h and matrix K as follows:

$$h = h_2 - K_{2,1} K_{1,1}^{-1} h_1$$

$$K = K_{2,2} - K_{2,1} K_{1,1}^{-1} K_{1,2}.$$

(Discussion of the normalization will be omitted, because it is not required except for calculating probability densities of evidence.) Thus integration has a simple algebraic structure.

7.2. JUNCTION TREES FOR GAUSSIAN NETWORKS

Having defined the directed Gaussian model, the construction of the junction tree proceeds exactly as for the discrete case, as far as the structure is concerned. The difference is with the initialization.

A Gaussian potential of correct size is allocated to each clique and separator. They are initialized with all elements equal to zero.

Next for each conditional density for the DAG model, a Gaussian potential is constructed to represent it and multiplied into any one clique which contains the node and its parents, using extension if required.

The result is a junction tree representation of the joint density. Assuming no evidence, then sending the clique marginals as messages results in the clique marginal representation, as for the discrete case:

$$P(U) = \prod_C P(X_C) / \prod_S P(X_S).$$

Care must be taken to propagate evidence. By evidence $\mathcal{E}$ on a set of nodes Y we mean that each node in Y is observed to take a definite value. (This is unlike the discrete case in which some states of a variable could be excluded but more than one could still be entertained.) Evidence about a variable must be entered into every clique and separator in which it occurs. This is because when evidence is entered on a variable it reduces the dimensions of every h vector and K matrix in the cliques and separators in which it occurs.

Thus for example, let us again take Y_1 and Y_2 to be two sets of distinct variables, and

$$\phi(y_1, y_2) \propto \exp\left(\begin{pmatrix} y_1 & y_k \end{pmatrix} \begin{pmatrix} h_1 \\ h_k \end{pmatrix} - \frac{1}{2} \begin{pmatrix} y_1 & y_k \end{pmatrix} \begin{pmatrix} K_{1,1} & K_{1,2} \\ K_{2,1} & K_{2,2} \end{pmatrix} \begin{pmatrix} y_1 \\ y_2 \end{pmatrix} \right)$$

so that the h and K are again in blocks. Suppose we now observe the variables of Y_2 to take values y_2^*. Then the potentials become modified to $h = h_1 - y_2^* K_{2,1}$ and $K = K_{1,1}$.

After such evidence has been entered in every clique and separator, then the standard propagation will yield the clique-marginal density representation with evidence included. Further within clique marginals then gives the (Gaussian) distributions on individual nodes.

7.3. EXAMPLE

Let us take out three node example again, with initial conditional distributions as follows:

$$\boxed{Y} \longrightarrow \boxed{X} \longrightarrow \boxed{Z}$$

$$
\begin{aligned}
N(Y) &= N(0, 1) \\
N(X \mid Y) &= N(y, 1) \\
N(Z \mid X) &= N(x, 1)
\end{aligned}
$$

The cliques for this tree are $\boxed{\text{X Y}}$ and $\boxed{\text{X Z}}$. After initializing and propagating, the clique potentials are

$$\phi(x,y) \;\propto\; \exp\left(-\frac{1}{2}\,(x\ \ y)\begin{pmatrix} 1 & -1 \\ -1 & 2 \end{pmatrix}\begin{pmatrix} x \\ y \end{pmatrix}\right)$$

$$\phi(x,z) \;\propto\; \exp\left(-\frac{1}{2}\,(x\ \ z)\begin{pmatrix} 1.5 & -1 \\ -1 & 1 \end{pmatrix}\begin{pmatrix} x \\ z \end{pmatrix}\right)$$

with separator $\phi(x) \propto \exp(-x^2/4)$; Now if we enter evidence $X = 1.5$, say, then the potentials reduce to:

$$\phi(X = 1.5, y) \propto \exp(1.5y - y^2)$$

and

$$\phi(X = 1.5, z) \propto \exp(1.5z - \frac{1}{2}z^2),$$

because in this example X makes up the separator between the two cliques. The marginal densities are then:

$$P(Y) = N(0.75, 0.5) \text{ and } P(Z) = N(1.5, 1).$$

Alternatively, suppose we take $\boxed{\text{X Y}}$ as the root clique, and enter evidence that $Z = 1.5$. Then the message from $\boxed{\text{X Z}}$ to $\boxed{\text{X Y}}$ is given by $\phi(X) \propto \exp(1.5x - 0.75x^2)$ so that after propagation the clique potential on $\boxed{\text{X Y}}$ is of the form:

$$\phi(x,y) \propto \exp\left((x\ \ y)\begin{pmatrix} 1.5 \\ 0 \end{pmatrix} - \frac{1}{2}(x\ \ y)\begin{pmatrix} 2 & -1 \\ -1 & 2 \end{pmatrix}\begin{pmatrix} x \\ y \end{pmatrix}\right)$$

with marginal densities

$$P(X) = N(1, 2/3) \text{ and } P(Y) = N(1/2, 2/3).$$

8. Conditional Gaussian models

As we have seen, the treatment of Gaussian networks is much the same as for discrete models. The minor differences are in (1) the nature of the potentials employed, and (2) evidence has to be entered into every clique and separator.

The passage to mixed models proceeds with some more important differences. The first is a restriction in the modeling stage: *continuous variables are not allowed to have discrete children*, ie. discrete nodes can only have discrete parents. The conditional probabilities specified for discrete nodes differ in character to those of continuous nodes. The former are again simple tables, as for discrete models, the latter are Gaussian potentials, but with the constants g, vectors h and matrices K indexed by the parent configurations of the discrete parents. Also, because certain sub configurations of discrete variables might not be allowed, we need to include indicator functions on the Gaussian potentials and we have to more careful with the normalization constants g.

The following is a brief guide to the theory, for more details see the original paper by Lauritzen, whose notation we follow closely here.

8.1. CG-POTENTIALS

The set of variables V is partitioned into the *discrete* variables (Δ) and continuous variables (Γ), thus $V = \Delta \cup \Gamma$. Let $x = (i, y)$ denote a typical element of the joint state space with i denoting the values of the discrete variables and y the values of the continuous variables. The joint density is assumed to be a *CG distribution*, which means that it has the form f with

$$f(x) = f(i, y) = \chi(i) \exp \left\{ g(i) + y^T h(i) - y^T K(i) y / 2 \right\},$$

where $\chi(i) \in \{0, 1\}$ indicates whether f is positive at i. The triple (g, h, K) is called the *canonical characteristics* of the distribution; it is only defined for $\chi(i) > 0$ but when that is the case one can define the *moment characteristics*, denoted by the triple $\{p, \xi, \Sigma\}$ and given by

$$\xi(i) = K(i)^{-1} h(i), \quad \Sigma(i) = K(i)^{-1}.$$

Inverting, we have the canonical characteristics are $K(i) = \Sigma(i)^{-1}$, $h(i) = K(i)\xi(i)$, and

$$g(i) = \log p(i) + \left\{ \log \det K(i) - |\Gamma| \log(2\pi) - \xi(i)^T K(i) \xi(i) \right\} / 2.$$

As for the Gaussian networks, we generalize CG distributions to *CG potentials* which are any functions ϕ of the form

$$\phi(x) = \phi(i, y) = \chi(i) \exp\{g(i) + y^T h(i) - y^T K(i) y / 2\}.$$

$K(i)$ is restricted to be symmetric, though not necessarily invertible. However we still call the triple (g, h, K) the canonical characteristics, and if for all i, $\chi(i) > 0$ and $K(i)$ is positive definite then the moment characteristics are given as before.

Multiplication, division and extension proceed as for the Gaussian potentials have already been discussed. Marginalisation is however different, because adding two CG potentials in general will result in a mixture of CG potentials – a function of a different algebraic structure. Thus we need to distinguish two types of marginalisation – *strong* and *weak*.

8.2. MARGINALISATION

Marginalising continuous variables corresponds to integration. Let

$$y = \begin{pmatrix} y_1 \\ y_2 \end{pmatrix}, \quad h = \begin{pmatrix} h_1 \\ h_2 \end{pmatrix}, \quad K = \begin{pmatrix} K_{11} & K_{12} \\ K_{21} & K_{22} \end{pmatrix}$$

with y_1 having dimension p and y_2 dimension q with K_{11} is positive definite. Then the integral $\int \phi(i, y_1, y_2) \, dy_1$ is finite and equal to a CG potential $\tilde{\phi}$ with canonical characteristics given as

$$\begin{aligned} \tilde{g}(i) &= g(i) + \left\{ p \log(2\pi) - \log \det K_{11}(i) + h_1(i)^T K_{11}(i)^{-1} h_1(i) \right\} / 2 \\ \tilde{h}(i) &= h_2(i) - K_{21}(i) K_{11}(i)^{-1} h_1(i) \\ \tilde{K}(i) &= K_{22}(i) - K_{21}(i) K_{11}(i)^{-1} K_{12}(i). \end{aligned}$$

Marginalising discrete variables corresponds to summation. Since in general addition of CG potentials results is a mixture of CG potentials, an alternative definition based upon the moment characteristics $\{p, \xi, \Sigma\}$ is used which does result in a CG potential; however it is only well defined for $K(i, j)$ positive definite. Specifically, the marginal over the discrete states of ϕ is *defined* as the CG potential with moment characteristics $\{\tilde{p}, \tilde{\xi}, \tilde{\Sigma}\}$ where

$$\tilde{p}(i) = \sum_j p(i, j), \quad \tilde{\xi}(i) = \sum_j \xi(i, j) p(i, j) / \tilde{p}(i), \quad \text{and}$$

$$\tilde{\Sigma}(i) = \sum_j \Sigma(i, j) p(i, j) / \tilde{p}(i) + \sum_j \left(\xi(i, j) - \tilde{\xi}(i) \right)^T \left(\xi(i, j) - \tilde{\xi}(i) \right) p(i, j) / \tilde{p}(i).$$

Note that the latter can be written as

$$\tilde{p}(i) \left(\tilde{\Sigma}(i) + \tilde{\xi}(i)^T \tilde{\xi}(i) \right) = \sum_j p(i, j) \left(\Sigma(i, j) + \xi(i, j)^T \xi(i, j) \right).$$

so that if $\Sigma(i, j)$ and $\xi(i, j)$ are independent of j then they can be taken through the summations as constants. This observation is used to define a marginalisation over both continuous and discrete variables: First marginalise over the the continuous variables and then over the discrete variables. If, after marginalising over the continuous variables the resulting pair (h, K) is independent of the discrete variables to be marginalised over, (summation over these discrete variables then leaves the pair (h, K)

unmodified), we say that we have a *strong marginalisation*. Otherwise one sums over the discrete variables using the moment characteristics, and the overall marginalisation is called a *weak marginalisation*.

Weak and strong marginalisation satisfy composition:

$$\sum_A \left(\sum_B \phi_{A \cup B \cup C} \right) = \sum_{A \cup B} \phi_{A \cup B \cup C},$$

but in general only the strong marginalisation satisfies

$$\sum_A (\phi_{A \cup B} \psi_B) = \psi_B \left(\sum_A \phi_{A \cup B} \right).$$

Under both type of marginalisation, a 'marginalised' density will then have the correct moments to order 2, i.e.

$$P(I = i) = \tilde{p}(i), \quad \mathbf{E}(Y \mid I = i) = \tilde{\xi}(i), \quad \mathbf{V}(Y \mid I = i) = \tilde{\Sigma}(i),$$

where the correct CG distribution is used to take expectations.

8.3. MAKING THE JUNCTION TREE

The non-closure of cg-potentials under marginalisation of discrete variables means that we have to adjust to how we construct the junction tree and pass messages in it. The first step is to construct the junction tree. First we moralize the DAG in the usual way. Then we triangulate by a restricted elimination ordering.[2] Specifically, we first eliminate all of the continuous variables, and then we eliminate the discrete variables. Then from the resulting cliques we can construct a junction tree. Now we must select a root. Unlike the previous pure cases, we cannot freely choose any clique of the junction tree. Instead we choose a so called *strong root* defined as follows:

Any clique R which for any pair A, B of cliques themselves neighbours on the tree with A closer to R than B satisfies

$$(B \setminus A) \subseteq \Gamma \text{ or } (B \cap A) \subseteq \Delta.$$

Thus, when a separator between two neighbouring cliques is not purely discrete, the clique furthest away from the root has only continuous vertices extra beyond the separator.

---

[2]One way to triangulate a graph is to take an ordering of the nodes and give all of the nodes the status 'unmarked'. One then works through each node in turn, marking it and joining all pairs of its unmarked neighbours. The ordering is called an *elimination ordering*. Finding good triangulations is then equivalent to finding good elimination orderings.

8.4. PROPAGATION ON THE JUNCTION TREE

The point of this restriction is that on the collect operation, only strong marginalisations are required to be performed. This is because our restricted elimination ordering - getting rid of the continuous variables first, is equivalent to doing the integrations over the continuous variables before marginalising any of the discrete variables.

Thus our message passing algorithm takes the form:

1. Initialization: Set all clique and separator potentials to zero with unit indicators, and multiply in the model specifying potentials using the extension operation where appropriate.
2. Enter evidence into all clique and separator potentials, reducing vector and matrix sizes as necessary.
3. Perform a collect operation to the strong root, where the messages are formed by strong marginalisation by first integrating out the redundant continuous variables, and then summing over discrete variables.
4. Perform a distribute operation, using weak marginalisation where appropriate when mixtures might be formed on marginalising over the discrete variables.

The result is a representation of the joint CG-distribution including evidence, because of the invariant nature of the message passing algorithm. Furthermore, because of the use of weak marginalisation for the distribute operation, the marginals on the cliques will themselves be CG-distributions whose first two moments match that of the full distribution. The following is an outline sketch of why this could be.

First by the construction of the junction tree, all collect operations are strong marginals, so that after a collect-to-root operation the root clique contains a strong marginal. Now suppose, for simplicity, that before the distribute operation we move to a set-chain representation (cf. section 2.2). Then apart from the strong root, each clique will have the correct joint density $P(X_{C_i \setminus S_i} \mid X_{S_i})$ where S_i is the separator adjacent to the clique C_i on the path between it and the strong root. Now on the distribute operation the clique C_i will be multiplied by a CG-potential which will either be a strong marginal or a weak marginal. If the former then the clique potential will be the correct marginal joint density. If the latter then we may write the clique potential as the product $P(X_{C_i \setminus S_i}) * Q(X_{S_i})$ where Q is the correct weak marginal for the variables X_{S_i}. Now consider taking an expectation of any linear or quadratic function of the X_{C_i} with respect to this "density". We are free to integrate by parts. However, choosing to integrate wrt. $X_{C_i \setminus S_i}$ first means that we form the expectation wrt the correct CG-density $P(X_{C_i \setminus S_i} \mid X_{S_i})$, and will thus end up with a correct expectation (which will be a linear or quadratic function in the X_{S_i}) multiplied by the correct weak marginal $Q(X_{S_i})$. Hence performing these integrations we will obtain the correct expectation of the original function wrt the true joint density.

For brevity some details have been skipped over here, such as showing that the separator messages sent are correct weak marginals. Detailed justifications and proofs use induction combined with a careful analysis of the messages sent from the strong root on the distribute operation. See the original paper for more details.

9. Summary

This tutorial has shown the variety of useful applications to which the junction-tree propagation algorithm can be used. It has not given the most general or efficient versions of the algorithms, but has attempted to present the main points of each so that the more detailed descriptions in the original articles will be easier to follow. There are other problems, to which the junction-tree propagation algorithm can be applied or adapted to, not discussed here, such as:

- Influence diagrams: Discrete models, with random variables, decisions and utilities. Potentials are now doublets representing probabilities and utilities. Junction tree is generated with a restricted elimination generalising that for cg-problems to emulate solving the decision tree.
- Learning probabilities. Nodes presenting parametrisations of probabilities can be attached to networks, and Bayesian updating performed using the same framework.
- Time series. A network can represent some state at a given time, and they can be chained together to form a time-window for dynamic modelling. The junction tree can be expanded and contracted to allow forward-prediction or backward smoothing.

Doubtless new examples will appear in the future.

10. Suggested further reading

Probabilistic logic sampling for Bayesian networks is described by Henrion(1988). A variation of the method – *likelihood-weighting sampling* – in which rejection steps are replaced by a weighting scheme is given by Shachter and Peot(1989). Drawing samples directly from the junction tree is described by Dawid(1992), which also shows how the most likely configuration can be found from the junction tree. The algorithm for finding the N- most likely configurations is due to Nilsson(1994), who has also developed a more efficient algorithm requiring only one max-propagation on the junction tree. L^p-propagation is not described anywhere but here.

Fast retraction is introduced in (Dawid, 1992) and developed in more detail in (Cowell and Dawid, 1992).

Gaussian networks are described by Shachter and Kenley(1989), who use arc-reversal and barren-node reduction algorithms for their evaluation. (The equivalence of various evaluation schemes is given in (Shachter *et al.*, 1994).) The treatment of Gaussian and conditional-gaussian networks is based on the original paper by Lauritzen(1992). For pedagogical reasons this chapter specialized the conditional-gaussian presentation of (Lauritzen, 1992) to the pure gaussian case, to show that the latter is not so different from the pure discrete case. Evaluating influence diagrams by junction-trees is treated in (Jensen *et al.*, 1994). For an extensive review on updating probabilities (Buntine, 1994). Dynamic junction trees for handling time series is described by Kjærulff(1993). See also (Smith *et al.*, 1995) for an application using dynamic junction trees not derived from a DAG model.

References

Buntine, W. L. (1994). Operations for learning with graphical models. *Journal of Artificial Intelligence Research*, **2**, pp. 159–225.

Cowell, R. G. (1997). Sampling without replacement in junction trees, Research Report 15, Department of Actuarial Science and Statistics, City University, London.

Cowell, R. G. and Dawid, A. P. (1992). Fast retraction of evidence in a probabilistic expert system. *Statistics and Computing*, **2**, pp. 37–40.

Dawid, A. P. (1992). Applications of a general propagation algorithm for probabilistic expert systems. *Statistics and Computing*, **2**, pp. 25–36.

Henrion, M. (1988). Propagation of uncertainty by probabilistic logic sampling in Bayes' networks. In *Uncertainty in Artificial Intelligence*, (ed. J. Lemmer and L. N. Kanal), pp. 149–64. North-Holland, Amsterdam.

Jensen, F., Jensen, F. V., and Dittmer, S. L. (March 1994). From influence diagrams to junction trees. Technical Report R-94-2013, Department of Mathematics and Computer Science Aalborg University, Denmark.

Kjærulff, U. (1993). A computational scheme for reasoning in dynamic probabilistic networks. Research Report R-93-2018, Department of Mathematics and Computer Science, Aalborg University, Denmark.

Lauritzen, S. L. (1992). Propagation of probabilities, means and variances in mixed graphical association models. *Journal of the American Statistical Association*, **87**, pp. 1098–108.

Nilsson, D. (1994). An algorithm for finding the most probable configurations of discrete variables that are specified in probabilistic expert systems. M.Sc. Thesis, Department of Mathematical Statistics, University of Copenhagen.

Nilsson, D. (1997). An efficient algorithm for finding the M most probable configurations in a probabilistic expert system. Submitted to *Statistics and Computing*.

Shachter, R. D., Andersen, S. K., and Szolovits, P. (1994). Global conditioning for probabilistic inference in belief networks. In *Proceedings of the Tenth Conference on Uncertainty in Artifical Intelligence*, pp 514–522.

Shachter, R. and Kenley, C. (1989). Gaussian influence diagrams. *Management Science*, **35**, pp. 527–50.

Shachter, R. and Peot, M. (1989). Simulation approaches to general probabilistic inference on belief networks. In *Uncertainty in Artificial Intelligence 5*, (ed. M. Henrion, R. D. Shachter, L. Kanal, and J. Lemmer), pp. 221–31. North-Holland, North-

Holland.

Smith, J. Q., French, S., and Raynard, D. (1995). An efficient graphical algorithm for updating the estimates of the dispersal of gaseous waste after an accidental release. In *Probabilistic reasoning and Bayesian belief networks*, (ed. A. Gammerman), pp. 125–44. Alfred Waller, Henley-on-Thames.

INFERENCE IN BAYESIAN NETWORKS USING NESTED JUNCTION TREES

UFFE KJÆRULFF

Department of Computer Science, Aalborg University
Fredrik Bajers Vej 7E, DK-9220 Aalborg Ø, Denmark

Abstract. The efficiency of inference in both the Hugin and the Shafer-Shenoy architectures can be improved by exploiting the independence relations induced by the incoming messages of a clique. That is, the message to be sent from a clique can be computed via a factorization of the clique potential in the form of a junction tree. In this paper we show that by exploiting such nested junction trees in the computation of messages both space *and* time costs of the conventional propagation methods may be reduced. The paper presents a structured way of exploiting the nested junction trees technique to achieve such reductions. The usefulness of the method is emphasized through a thorough empirical evaluation involving ten large real-world Bayesian networks and both the Hugin and the Shafer-Shenoy inference algorithms.

1. Introduction

Kim and Pearl (1983) first formulated inference in a Bayesian network through message passing, but for singly connected networks only. Later this was extended to multiply connected networks, where the messages are passed in a junction tree (or join tree) corresponding to the network (Lauritzen and Spiegelhalter, 1988; Jensen *et al.*, 1990; Shafer and Shenoy, 1990). More precisely, a posterior probability distribution for a particular variable can be computed by sending messages inward from the leaf nodes of the tree toward the root node containing the variable of interest. If a subsequent outward propagation of messages from the root toward the leaves is performed, all nodes (or cliques) will then contain the correct posterior distributions (at least up to a normalizing constant).

51

The Hugin and the Shafer-Shenoy propagation methods will be reviewed briefly in the following; for more in-depth presentations, consult above references. We shall assume that all variables of a Bayesian network are discrete.

2. Bayesian Networks and Junction Trees

A Bayesian network can be defined as a pair $(\mathcal{G}, p)$, where $\mathcal{G} = (V, E)$ is an acyclic, directed graph or, more generally, a chain graph (Frydenberg, 1989) with vertex set V and edge set E, and p is a discrete probability function with index set V. To each vertex $v \in V$ corresponds a (discrete) random variable X_v with domain $\mathcal{X}_v$. Similarly, a subset $A \subseteq V$ corresponds to a set of variables X_A with domain $\mathcal{X}_A = \times_{v \in A} \mathcal{X}_v$. Elements of $\mathcal{X}_A$ are denoted $x_A = (x_v)$, $v \in A$.

A probability function $\kappa_v(x_v, x_{\mathrm{pa}(v)})$ is specified for each variable X_v, where $\mathrm{pa}(v)$ denotes the parents of v (i.e., the set of vertices of $\mathcal{G}$ from which there are directed links to v). If $\mathrm{pa}(v)$ is non-empty, κ_v is a conditional probability distribution for X_v given $X_{\mathrm{pa}(v)}$; otherwise, κ_v is a marginal probability distribution for X_v.

The joint probability function $p_V = p$ for X_V is Markov with respect to the acyclic, directed graph $\mathcal{G}$. That is, $\mathcal{G}$ is a map of the independence relations represented by p: each pair of vertices not connected by a directed edge represents an independence relation. Thus, $\mathcal{G}$ is often referred to as the independence graph of p. The probability function p being Markov with respect to $\mathcal{G}$ implies that p factorizes according to $\mathcal{G}$:

$$p = \prod_{v \in V} \kappa_v.$$

For a more detailed account of Markov fields over directed graphs, consult e.g. the work of Lauritzen *et al.* (1990.

Exact inference in Bayesian networks involves the computation of marginal probabilities for subsets $C \subseteq V$, where each C induces a fully connected (i.e., complete) subgraph of an undirected graph derived from $\mathcal{G}$. (Formally, a set $A \subseteq V$ is said to *induce* a subgraph $\mathcal{G}_A = (A, E \cap A \times A)$ of $\mathcal{G} = (V, E)$.) A fixed set $\mathcal{C}$ of such complete subsets can be used no matter which variables have been observed and no matter for which variables we want posterior marginals. This is the idea behind the junction tree approach to inference.

The derived undirected graph is created through the processes of moralization and triangulation. In moralization an undirected edge is added between each pair of disconnected vertices with common children and, when this has been completed, all directed edges are replaced by undirected ones. In the triangulation process we keep adding undirected edges (*fill-ins*) to the moral graph until there are no cycles of length greater than three without a chord (i.e., an edge connecting two non-consecutive vertices of the cycle).

The maximal complete subsets of the triangulated graph are called *cliques*. It can easily be proved that an undirected graph is triangulated if and only if the cliques can be arranged in a tree structure such that the intersection between any pair of cliques is contained in each of the cliques on the path between the two. A tree of cliques with this property is referred to as a *junction tree*. Now, inference can be performed by passing messages between neighbouring cliques in the junction tree.

3. Inference in Junction Trees

In the following we will briefly review the junction tree approach to inference. For a more in-depth treatment of the subject consult e.g. the book of Jensen (1996).

In the Hugin architecture, a potential table ϕ_C is associated with each clique, C. The link between any pair of neighbouring cliques, say C and D, shall be denoted a *separator*, and it is labelled by $S = C \cap D$. Further, with each separator, S, is associated one or two potential tables ('mailboxes'). The Hugin algorithm uses one mailbox per separator, referred to as ϕ_S, and the Shafer-Shenoy algorithm uses two mailboxes, referred to as ϕ_S^{in} and ϕ_S^{out}.

In addition, we assign each function κ_v, $v \in V$, to a clique, C, such that $\{v\} \cup \text{pa}(V) \in C$. That is, for each clique, C, is associated a subset of the conditional probabilities specified for the Bayesian network. Let $\mathcal{K}_C$ denote this subset, and define

$$\psi_C = \prod_{\kappa \in \mathcal{K}_C} \kappa.$$

As mentioned above, inference in a junction tree is based on message passing. The scheduling of message passes is controlled by the following rule: a clique, C, is allowed to send a message to a neighbour, D, if C has received messages from all of its neighbours, except possibly from D, and C has not previously sent a message to D. Thus propagation of messages is initiated in leaf cliques and proceeds inwards until a 'root' clique, R, has received messages from all of its neighbours. (Note that any clique may be root.) The root clique is now fully informed in the sense that it has got information (via its neighbours) from all cliques of the junction tree, and thus $p_R \propto \phi_R$, with the proportionality constant being the probability of the evidence (i.e., observations), if any. An outward propagation of messages from R will result in $p_C \propto \phi_C$ for all $C \in \mathcal{C}$, where $\mathcal{C}$ denotes the set of cliques.

A message is passed from clique C to clique D via separator $S = C \cap D$, as follows:

1. C generates the message $\phi_S^* = \sum_{C \setminus S} \phi_C$ and sends it to D.
2. D absorbs the message such that $\sum_{D \setminus S} \phi_D = \phi_S^*$, where ϕ_D is the clique potential for D after the absorption.

Now, assume that we are performing the inward pass, and that clique C is absorbing messages $\phi_{S_1}^*, \ldots, \phi_{S_n}^*$ from neighbouring cliques $C_1, \ldots, C_n$ and sending a message $\phi_{S_0}^*$ to clique C_0. This is done as follows.

1. Absorb messages $\phi_{S_1}^*, \ldots, \phi_{S_n}^*$: $\phi_C^* = \psi_C \prod_{i=1}^{n} \phi_{S_i}^*$

2. Generate message $\phi_{S_0}^*$: $\phi_{S_0}^* = \sum_{C \setminus S} \phi_C^*$

3. Store received messages:
   if algorithm = Hugin then
       $\phi_{S_i} \leftarrow \phi_{S_i}^*, i = 1, \ldots, n$
   else
       $\phi_{S_i}^{\text{in}} \leftarrow \phi_{S_i}^*, i = 1, \ldots, n$

4. If algorithm = Hugin, then store clique potential: $\phi_C \leftarrow \phi_C^*$

5. Discard $\phi_C^*, \phi_{S_1}^*, \ldots, \phi_{S_n}^*$

6. Send $\phi_{S_0}^*$ to C_0

(Note that if C is the root clique, we skip steps 2 and 6.) Thus, considering the inward pass, the only difference between the Hugin and the Shafer-Shenoy algorithms is that the Hugin algorithm stores the clique potential. Storing the clique potential increases the space cost, but (most often) reduces the time cost of the outward pass, as we shall see shortly.

Next, assume that we are performing the outward pass, and that clique C receives a message, $\phi_{S_0}^*$, from its 'parent clique' C_0 (i.e., the neighbouring clique on the path between C and the root clique), and sends messages $\phi_{S_1}^*, \ldots, \phi_{S_n}^*$ to its remaining neighbours, $C_1, \ldots, C_n$. (The ϕ^*'s should not be confused by the similar potentials of the inward pass.) This is done as follows.

1. Absorb message $\phi_{S_0}^*$:
   if algorithm = Hugin then
   $$\phi_C^* = \phi_C \frac{\phi_{S_0}^*}{\phi_{S_0}}$$
   for $i = 1$ to n do

$$\phi^*_{S_i} = \sum_{C \backslash S_i} \phi^*_C$$

 else

  for $i = 1$ to n do

$$\phi^*_C = \psi_C \phi^*_{S_0} \prod_{j=1,\ldots,i-1,i+1,\ldots,n} \phi^{in}_{S_j}$$

$$\phi^*_{S_i} = \sum_{C \backslash S_i} \phi^*_C$$

2. Store $\phi^*_{S_0}$:

 if algorithm = Hugin then

  $\phi_{S_0} \leftarrow \phi^*_{S_0}$

 else

  $\phi^{out}_{S_0} \leftarrow \phi^*_{S_0}$

3. If algorithm = Hugin, then store clique potential: $\phi_C \leftarrow \phi^*_C$

4. Discard ϕ^*_C and $\phi^*_{S_0}$

5. Send $\phi^*_{S_1}, \ldots, \phi^*_{S_n}$

Inference in junction trees may be very expensive due to the generation of clique potentials, ϕ^*_C. Thus, if the generation of these can be relaxed, both space and time savings can be obtained. This is what is exploited in the nested junction trees approach.

4. Nested Junction Trees

In a Bayesian network $(\mathcal{G} = (V, E), p)$ each potential κ_v, $v \in V$, induces a complete subgraph $(\mathrm{fam}(v), \mathrm{fam}(v) \times \mathrm{fam}(v))$ of the moral graph of $\mathcal{G}$, where $\mathrm{fam}(v) = \{v\} \cup \mathrm{pa}(v)$. In general, a set of potentials, $\xi_{U_1}, \ldots, \xi_{U_m}$, with index sets $U_1, \ldots, U_m \subseteq V$ induce an undirected graph, $\mathcal{H} = (U, \bigcup_i U_i \times U_i)$ $(U = \bigcup_i U_i)$, where each ξ_{U_i} induces a complete subgraph $(U_i, U_i \times U_i)$ of $\mathcal{H}$ and the potential

$$\xi_U = \prod_i \xi_{U_i}$$

is Markov with respect to $\mathcal{H}$ (i.e., $\mathcal{H}$ is an independence graph of ξ_U). Thus, if triangulating $\mathcal{H}$ does not result in a complete graph, we can build a junction tree corresponding to the triangulated graph, and then exploit the message passing principle for computing marginals of ξ_U. Assume that $\xi_{U_1}, \ldots, \xi_{U_m}$ are the potentials involved in computing a message (i.e., a marginal), say $\phi^*_{S_0}$, in a clique C. That is, $\xi_{U_1}, \ldots, \xi_{U_m}$ are the incoming messages and the κ_v's associated with C. Then, instead of computing the clique potential

$$\phi_C^* = \prod_i \xi_{U_i}$$

(cf. Step 1 of the above inward algorithm), inducing a complete graph, and marginalizing from ϕ_C^* to compute $\phi_{S_0}^*$ (cf. Step 2 of the above inward algorithm), we might be able to exploit conditional independence relationships between variables of S_0 given the remaining variables of C in computing $\phi_{S_0}^*$ through message passing in a junction tree residing inside C (which, remember, is a clique of another, larger junction tree). This, in essence, is the idea pursued in the present paper. In principle, this nesting of junction trees can extend to arbitrary depth. In practice, however, we seldomly encounter instances with depth greater than three to four.

As a little sidetrack, note the following property of triangulations. Let C be a clique of a junction tree corresponding to a triangulation of a moral graph $\mathcal{G}$, let $\mathcal{K}_C = \{\phi_{V_1}, \ldots, \phi_{V_m}\}$, and let $C_1, \ldots, C_n$ be the cliques connected to C via separators $S_1, \ldots, S_n$. Triangulating the graph induced by $V_1 \cup \cdots \cup V_m \cup S_1 \cup \cdots \cup S_n$ results in a complete graph, unless the triangulation of $\mathcal{G}$ contains a superfluous fill-in: a fill-in between vertices u and v is superfluous if $\{u, v\} \not\subseteq S_i$ for each $i = 1, \ldots, n$, because then C can be split into two smaller neighbouring cliques $C' = C \setminus \{u\}$ and $C'' = C \setminus \{v\}$ with C_i, $i = 1, \ldots, n$, connected to C' if $v \in C_i$, to C'' if $u \in C_i$, or, otherwise, to either C' or C''.

Therefore, assuming the triangulation to be minimal in the sense of not containing any superfluous fill-ins, the nested junction tree principle cannot be applied when a clique, C, receives messages from all of its neighbours, or when a clique potential ϕ_C is involved in the computation (cf. the outward pass of the Hugin algorithm). However, in the inward pass and in the outward pass of the Shafer-Shenoy algorithm, any non-root clique receives messages from all but one, say C_0, of its neighbours, making it possible to exploit the junction tree algorithm for generating the message to C_0.

To illustrate the process of constructing nested junction trees, we shall consider the situation where clique C_{16} is going to send a message to clique C_{13} in the junction tree of a subnet, here called Munin1, of the Munin network (Andreassen *et al.*, 1989). Clique C_{16} and its neighbours are shown in Figure 1. The variables of $C_{16} = \{22, 26, 83, 84, 94, 95, 97, 164, 168\}$ (named corresponding to their node identifiers in the network) have 4, 5, 5, 5, 5, 5, 5, 7, and 6 possible states, respectively.

The undirected graph induced by the potentials $\phi_{S_1}^*$, $\phi_{S_2}^*$, $\phi_{S_3}^*$, and ϕ_{V_1} may be depicted as in Figure 2. At first sight this graph looks quite messy, and it might be hard to believe that its triangulated graph will be anything but complete. However, a closer examination reveals that the graph

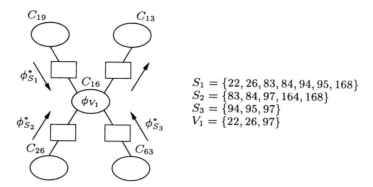

Figure 1. Clique C_{16} receives messages $\phi_{S_1}^*$, $\phi_{S_2}^*$, and $\phi_{S_3}^*$ from cliques C_{19}, C_{26}, and C_{63}, respectively. Based on these messages and the probability potential, $\phi_{V_1} = P(97 \mid 22, 26)$, a message must be generated and sent to clique C_{13}.

is already triangulated and that its cliques are $\{83, 84, 97, 164, 168\}$ and $\{22, 26, 83, 84, 94, 95, 97, 168\}$.

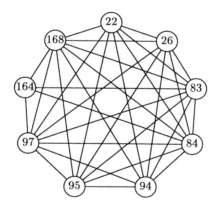

Figure 2. The undirected graph induced by potentials $\phi_{S_1}^*$, $\phi_{S_2}^*$, $\phi_{S_3}^*$, and ϕ_{V_1}.

So, the original 9-clique (i.e., clique containing nine variables) with a table of size $2,625,000$ has been reduced to a junction tree with a 5-clique and an 8-clique with tables of total size $381,000$ (including a separator table of size 750).

Thus encouraged we shall try to continue our clique break-down. In the two-clique junction tree, the 5-clique has associated with it only potential $\phi_{S_2}^*$, so it cannot be further broken down. The 8-clique, on the other hand, has got the remaining three potentials associated with it. These potentials (i.e., $\phi_{S_1}^*$, $\phi_{S_3}^*$, and ϕ_{V_1}) induce the graph shown in Figure 3.

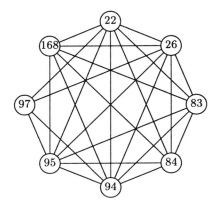

Figure 3. The undirected graph induced by potentials $\phi_{S_1}^*$, $\phi_{S_3}^*$, and ϕ_{V_1}.

This graph also appears to be triangulated and contains the 5-clique $\{22, 26, 94, 95, 97\}$ and the 7-clique $\{22, 26, 83, 84, 94, 95, 168\}$ with tables of total size $78,000$ (including a separator table of size 500). Thus, the space cost is reduced by a factor of $375,000/78,000 \approx 5$.

In this junction tree, the 7-clique cannot be further broken down since it contains only one potential. The 5-clique, however, contains two potentials, $\phi_{S_3}^*$ and ϕ_{V_1}, and can therefore possibly be further broken down. The two potentials induce the graph shown in Figure 4, hence a further break-down is possible as the graph is triangulated and contains two cliques.

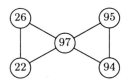

Figure 4. The undirected graph induced by potentials $\phi_{S_3}^*$ and ϕ_{V_1}.

Now, no further break-down is possible. The resulting nested junction tree, shown in Figure 5, has a total space cost of $81,730$, which is significantly less than the original $2,625,000$. Carrying out the nesting to this depth, however, has a big time cost. To see this, let us describe how the computation of $\phi_{S_0}^*$ (the message to C_{13}) proceeds. To compute $\phi_{S_0}^*$ we need to perform an inward propagation of messages in the (C_a, C_b) junction tree. However, since neither C_a nor C_b contain all variables of S_0, we need to perform multiple message passes from C_b to C_a (or vice versa). For example, letting C_a be the root clique of the inward pass, we need to send a message from C_b for each instantiation of the variables in

$(C_b \cap S_0) \setminus C_a = \{22, 26, 94, 95\}$; that is, $4 \times 5 \times 5 \times 5 = 500$ messages must be sent via separator $\{83, 84, 97, 168\}$ in order to generate $\phi^*_{S_0}$. Sending a message from C_b to C_a involves inward propagation of messages in the (C_c, C_d) junction tree, but, again, since neither C_c nor C_d contain all variables of the (C_a, C_b) separator, we need to send multiple message from C_d to C_c (or vice versa). For example, letting C_c be the root clique of the inward pass at this level, we need to send 5 messages from C_d (i.e., one for each instantiation of the variables in $(C_d \cap \{83, 84, 97, 168\}) \setminus C_c = \{97\}$) for each of the 500 messages to be sent from C_b (actually from C_c) to C_a. Similarly, for each message sent from C_d to C_c, 20 messages must be sent from C_e to C_f (or 25 messages from C_f to C_e). Clearly, it becomes a very time consuming job to generate $\phi^*_{S_0}$, exploiting nesting to this extent.

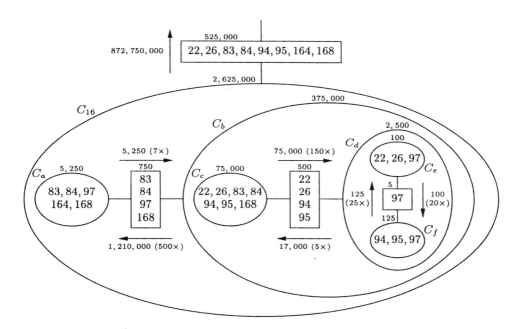

Figure 5. The nested junction tree for clique C_{16} in Munin1. Only the connection to neighbour C_{13} is shown. The small figures on top of the cliques and separators indicate table sizes, assuming no nesting. The labels attached to the arrows indicate (1) the time cost of sending a single message, and (2) the number of messages required to compute the separator marginal one nesting level up.

A proper balance between space and time costs will most often be of interest. We shall address that issue in the next section.

Finally, however, let us briefly analyze the case where C_b is chosen as root instead of C_a (see Figure 6). First, note that, since C_b contains the three potentials $\phi^*_{S_1}$, $\phi^*_{S_3}$ and ϕ_{V_1}, and receives message potentials, $\phi^1_S, \ldots, \phi^7_S$, from C_a via $S = \{83, 84, 97, 168\}$, C_b collapses to a complete subgraph. The time cost of computing the first clique potential, $\phi^*_{C_b} =$

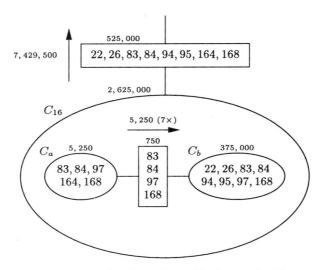

Figure 6. The nested junction tree for clique C_{16} in Munin1, with C_b being the root clique (i.e., the message to be generated by C_{16} is computed via inward message propagation with C_b as root). The labels attached to the arrows indicate (1) the time cost of sending a single message, and (2) the number of messages required to compute the separator marginal one nesting level up.

$\phi^*_{S_1} * \phi^*_{S_3} * \phi_{V_1} * \phi^1_S$, has a time cost of $4 \times 375,000$. Using the Hugin algorithm, the time cost of computing the remaining six clique potentials is $6 \times (750 + 375,000)$. Each marginalization of the clique potentials has a time cost of $525,000$ (this is a conservative measure based on the larger of the $\phi^*_{C_b}$ and the $\phi^*_{S_0}$ tables). Thus, the total time cost of generating $\phi^*_{S_0}$, using C_b as root, is

$$4 \times 375,000 + 6 \times (750 + 375,000) + 7 \times 525,000 = 7,427,500.$$

The space and time costs of conventional (i.e., non-nested) message generation is $2,625,000$ and $5 \times 2,625,000 = 13,125,000$, respectively. Thus, in this case, using the nested junction trees approach provides savings of 85% and 43%, respectively, of space and time costs.

5. Space and Time Costs

In order to evaluate the applicability of the nested junction tree approach, we must compare its space and time costs with those of the conventional junction tree approaches.

5.1. CONVENTIONAL APPROACH

The space and time costs (denoted c_s and c_t, respectively) of conventional Hugin and Shafer-Shenoy message passing for a single clique are shown in Figures 7 and 8 for, respectively, inward and outward message passing. In Figure 7, clique C receives messages from outward neighbours $C_1, \ldots, C_n$ via separators $S_1, \ldots, S_n$, and, if it is not the root clique, sends a message to the inward neighbour C_0 via S_0. In Figure 8, having received a message from the inward neighbour C_0, unless it is the root clique, clique C sends messages to the outward neighbours.

5.1.1. *Inward*

The cost of message processing in clique C during the inward pass in shown in Figure 7. Note that, using the Shafer-Shenoy algorithm with $|\mathcal{K}_C| > 1$

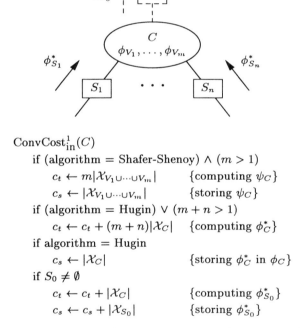

$\mathrm{ConvCost}^1_{\mathrm{in}}(C)$
  if (algorithm = Shafer-Shenoy) $\wedge$ $(m > 1)$
    $c_t \leftarrow m|\mathcal{X}_{V_1 \cup \cdots \cup V_m}|$ {computing ψ_C}
    $c_s \leftarrow |\mathcal{X}_{V_1 \cup \cdots \cup V_m}|$ {storing ψ_C}
  if (algorithm = Hugin) $\vee$ $(m + n > 1)$
    $c_t \leftarrow c_t + (m + n)|\mathcal{X}_C|$ {computing ϕ_C^*}
  if algorithm = Hugin
    $c_s \leftarrow |\mathcal{X}_C|$ {storing ϕ_C^* in ϕ_C}
  if $S_0 \neq \emptyset$
    $c_t \leftarrow c_t + |\mathcal{X}_C|$ {computing $\phi_{S_0}^*$}
    $c_s \leftarrow c_s + |\mathcal{X}_{S_0}|$ {storing $\phi_{S_0}^*$}

Figure 7. Space and time costs of receiving messages from outward neighbours and sending to the inward neighbour.

(or, equivalently, $m > 1$), computing and storing $\psi_C = \prod_i \phi_{V_i}$ will save time during the outward pass, since ψ_C is then going to be reused. However, since m is typically small (less than three to four), we might want to save the space required, $|\mathcal{X}_{V_1 \cup \cdots \cup V_m}|$, and use a little extra time during the outward pass, recomputing ψ_C. Anyway, we shall assume that ψ_C is stored in the inward pass.

In general, with $m + n$ tables contributing to the clique potential, ϕ_C^*, the time cost of computing ϕ_C^* is $(m + n)|\mathcal{X}_C|$. Note that if information on the domain of the contributing potentials are utilized, this cost may be reduced (Shenoy, 1996). For simplicity, we shall, however, refrain from using such refined methods of combination.

The Hugin algorithm will always compute ϕ_C^* and store it in ϕ_C, whereas the Shafer-Shenoy algorithm will only compute ϕ_C^* when more than one table contribute to it. If C is not the root clique (i.e., $S_0 \neq \emptyset$), the message, $\phi_{S_0}^*$, to clique C_0 is generated.

5.1.2. *Outward*

The cost of message processing in clique C during the outward pass is shown in Figure 8. Note that using the Hugin algorithm, there will be a clique table, ϕ_C, if message processing in C in the inward pass was based on the conventional method; otherwise, ϕ_C $(= \phi_C^*)$ must be generated. Note that we shall always assume an outward pass to be preceded by an inward pass.

Using the Shafer-Shenoy algorithm with C being a leaf clique, we do not have to do anything, since $\phi_C^* = \phi_{S_0}^*$, unless $\mathcal{K}_C \neq \emptyset$ in which case $\phi_C^* = \psi_C \phi_{S_0}^*$. Note the difference between the two algorithms: the Hugin algorithm computes ϕ_C^* only once, whereas the Shafer-Shenoy algorithm does it n times, unless only one table contributes to ϕ_C^* in which case we marginalize directly from that table. The number of tables contributing to ϕ_C^* when generating the message, $\phi_{S_i}^*$, to C_i equals $n + 1$ (i.e., tables $\psi_C, \phi_{S_0}^*, \phi_{S_1}^{in}, \ldots, \phi_{S_{i-1}}^{in}, \phi_{S_{i+1}}^{in}, \ldots, \phi_{S_n}^{in}$) if $S_0 \neq \emptyset$ and $\mathcal{K}_C \neq \emptyset$, n if either $S_0 = \emptyset$ or $\mathcal{K}_C = \emptyset$ (but not both), and $n - 1$ if both $S_0 = \emptyset$ and $\mathcal{K}_C = \emptyset$.

5.2. NESTED APPROACH

In describing the costs associated with the nested junction tree approach, we shall distinguish between message processing at level 1 (i.e., the outermost level) and at deeper levels.

5.2.1. *Level 1*

The processing of messages in a non-root clique C (i.e., receiving messages from neighbours $C_1, \ldots, C_n$ via separators $S_1, \ldots, S_n$, and sending to clique C_0) may involve inference in a junction tree induced by $V_1 \cup \cdots \cup V_m \cup S_1 \cup \cdots \cup S_n$ (see Figure 9). Note that, in this setup, C may either be involved in inward message passing using either algorithm, or it may be involved in outward Shafer-Shenoy message passing. In the inward case, $C_1, \ldots, C_n$ are

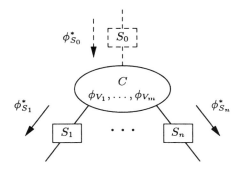

$\mathrm{ConvCost}_{\mathrm{out}}^1(C)$

   if algorithm = Hugin

     if $S_0 \neq \emptyset$

       if ϕ_C exists   {conventional inward message processing in C}

$$c_t \leftarrow |\mathcal{X}_{S_0}| + |\mathcal{X}_C| \quad \{\text{computing } \phi_C^* = \phi_C \frac{\phi_{S_0}^*}{\phi_{S_0}}\}$$

       else

$$c_t \leftarrow (m + n + 1)|\mathcal{X}_C|\{\text{computing } \phi_C^* = \phi_{S_0}^* \prod_{i=1}^n \phi_{S_i} \prod_{j=1}^m \phi_{V_j}\}$$

       for $i = 1$ to n

$$c_t \leftarrow c_t + |\mathcal{X}_C| \quad \{\text{computing } \phi_{S_i}^* = \sum_{C \setminus S_i} \phi_C^*\}$$

     else

       if $(S_0 \neq \emptyset) \wedge (n = 0) \wedge (m > 0)$ {C is a leaf clique with $\mathcal{K}_C \neq \emptyset$}

         $c_t \leftarrow c_t + 2|\mathcal{X}_C|$ {computing $\phi_C^* = \psi_C \phi_{S_0}^*$}

       for $i = 1$ to n

         if $r > 1$ {r is the number of tables contributing to ϕ_C^*}

$$c_t \leftarrow c_t + r|\mathcal{X}_C| \quad \{\text{computing } \phi_C^* = \psi_C \phi_{S_0}^* \prod_{j=1,\ldots,i-1,i+1,\ldots,n} \phi_{S_j}^{\mathrm{in}}\}$$

$$c_t \leftarrow c_t + |\mathcal{X}_C| \quad \{\text{computing } \phi_{S_i}^* = \sum_{C \setminus S_i} \phi_C^*\}$$

$$c_s \leftarrow c_s + |\mathcal{X}_{S_i}| \quad \{\text{storing } \phi_{S_i}^* \text{ in } \phi_{S_i}\}$$

Figure 8. Space and time costs of receiving a message from the inward neighbour and sending to the outward neighbours. Note that $r = n + 1$ if $m > 0 \wedge S_0 \neq \emptyset$, $r = n$ if $m > 0 \vee S_0 \neq \emptyset$, and $r = n - 1$ if $m = 0 \wedge S_0 = \emptyset$.

the outward neighbours and C_0 the inward. In the outward case, C_0 is the outward neighbour to which C is going to send, and $C_1, \ldots, C_n$ includes the inward neighbour plus the remaining outward neighbours. (Recall that, assuming a minimal triangulation, computing a marginal in a root clique cannot be done through inference in an induced junction tree.)

The message $\phi_{S_0}^*$ is generated through inference in the level 2 junction tree. Thus, the cost of message processing in clique C equals the cost of performing inward propagation towards a root clique in the level 2 junction

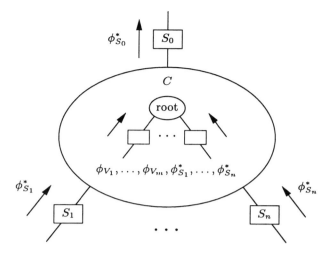

$\text{NestedCost}^1_{\text{in/out}}(C)$

$c_s \leftarrow c_s^{\text{root}}$ {space cost of inward propagation towards clique 'root'}

$c_t \leftarrow c_t^{\text{root}}$ {time cost of inward propagation towards clique 'root'}

$c_s \leftarrow c_s + |\mathcal{X}_{S_0}|$ {storing $\phi_{S_0}^*$}

Figure 9. Space and time costs of receiving n messages and sending 0 or 1, where the relevant marginal is computed in a junction tree induced by $V_1 \cup \cdots \cup V_m \cup S_1 \cup \cdots \cup S_n$.

tree (see below) plus the space cost of storing $\phi_{S_0}^*$. In Section 6, we shall describe how the cost of performing inward propagation towards a root clique is calculated.

5.2.2. *Level 2 or deeper — conventional*

We shall now analyze the space and time costs of conventional message passing in junction trees at level 2 or deeper. Since the purpose of performing inference in a junction tree at level $l > 1$ is to generate a message from the clique at level $l - 1$ containing the junction tree, we should only perform inward message passing towards a root clique to compute a marginal or (more typically) a set of marginals.

Consider the situation in Figure 10 where clique C receives messages from its outward neighbours in a junction tree at level $l > 1$ which is contained in a clique, say C^*, at level $l - 1$, wanting to send a message to a neighbour via separator S^*. Note that C^* can be engaged in either inward or outward message processing, and that the potentials involved in that operation are those defining the junction tree containing clique C.

Now, since an S^*-marginal is going to be generated and C might share

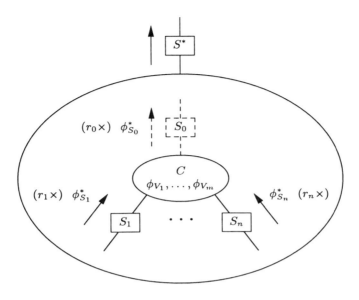

$\mathrm{ConvCost}_{\mathrm{in}}^{>1}(C)$
    if algorithm $=$ Hugin
        if $m + n > 1$

$c_t \leftarrow (m+n)\lvert\mathcal{X}_C\rvert$	{computing the first ϕ_C^*}
$c_s \leftarrow \lvert\mathcal{X}_C\rvert$	{storing ϕ_C^*}
$c_t \leftarrow c_t + \sum_{i=1}^{n} r^i(\lvert\mathcal{X}_{S_i}\rvert + \lvert\mathcal{X}_C\rvert)$	{comp. rem. $\sum_{i=1}^{n}(r_i - 1)\prod_{j=1}^{i-1} r_j\ \phi_C^*$'s}

        else
            if $(a > 1) \wedge (m > 1)$ {$a =$ number of absorptions}

$c_t \leftarrow m\lvert\mathcal{X}_{V_1 \cup \cdots \cup V_m}\rvert$	{computing $\psi_C = \prod_i \phi_{V_i}$}
$c_s \leftarrow \lvert\mathcal{X}_{V_1 \cup \cdots \cup V_m}\rvert$	{storing ψ_C}
$c_t \leftarrow c_t + (n+1)\prod_i r_i\lvert\mathcal{X}_C\rvert$	{computing $\prod_i r_i\ \phi_C^*$'s}

            else
                if $(a > 0) \vee (m > 1)$

$c_t \leftarrow c_t + (m+n)\prod_i r_i\lvert\mathcal{X}_C\rvert$	{computing $\prod_i r_i\ \phi_C^*$'s}

    $c_s \leftarrow c_s + \sum_{i=2}^{n}(r_i - 1)\lvert\mathcal{X}_{S_i}\rvert$ {storing multiple messages for each $i > 1$}
    if $S_0 \neq \emptyset$

$c_s \leftarrow c_s + \lvert\mathcal{X}_{S_0}\rvert$	{storing $\phi_{S_0}^*$'s}
$c_t \leftarrow c_t + r_0\lvert\mathcal{X}_C\rvert$	{comp. $r_0 = \lvert\mathcal{X}_{(C \cap S^*) \setminus C_0}\rvert \prod_{i=1}^{n} r_i\ \phi_{S_0}^*$'s}

    else

$c_t \leftarrow c_t + \prod_i r_i \max\{\lvert\mathcal{X}_{S^*}\rvert, \lvert\mathcal{X}_C\rvert\}$	{computing $\prod_i r_i$ marginals}

Figure 10. Space and time costs of receiving messages from outward neighbours and sending to the inward neighbour in a junction tree at nesting level greater than 1.

variables with S^* which it does not share with clique C_0 to which it is going to send (assuming $S_0 \neq \emptyset$), C will have to send $|\mathcal{X}_{(C \cap S^*) \setminus C_0}|$ messages to C_0. That is, a message must be sent for each configuration $x_{(C \cap S^*) \setminus C_0}$ for C_0 to be able to generate appropriate messages to its inward neighbour, or to generate the S^*-marginal if C_0 is the root clique. Furthermore, if, for the same reason, C's outward neighbours are sending multiple messages to C, the number of messages needed to be sent from C will be multiplied by the product of the number of messages received from the outward neighbours. This way of computing arbitrary marginals in a junction tree is referred to as *variable firing* by Jensen (1996); an alternative called *variable propagation* (Xu, 1994) might be worth considering, but will shall refrain from that in the present paper.

Denote by r_i the number of messages that outward neighbour C_i have to send to C, $i = 1, \ldots, n$. Assuming that the messages are scheduled such that $C_2, \ldots, C_n$ send all of their messages in one batch, and that C_1 synchronizes its activity with C such that, for each message received from C_1, C processes all combinations of messages from $C_2, \ldots, C_n$, we need extra storage of size $(r_i - 1)|\mathcal{X}_{S_i}|$ for each $i > 1$. Thus, for each combination of messages from the outward neighbours, C either sends $|\mathcal{X}_{(C \cap S^*) \setminus C_0}|$ messages to C_0, or, if $S_0 = \emptyset$, generates the part of the S^*-marginal corresponding to the actual combination of messages. (Note that, typically, $|C| < |S^*|$.)

Using the Hugin algorithm, the first step taken by C is to compute (the first) $\phi_C^* = \prod_{i=1}^m \phi_{V_i} \prod_{j=1}^n \phi_{S_j}^*$, which have time cost $(m+n)|\mathcal{X}_C|$. The remaining $\prod_i r_i - 1 = \sum_i r^i$ combinations of messages are processed by replacing one message at a time such that r^i replacements are performed for messages originating from C_i, where $r^i = (r_i - 1) \prod_{j=1}^{i-1} r_j$. Note that replacing a message from C_i involves $|\mathcal{X}_{S_i}|$ divisions and $|\mathcal{X}_C|$ multiplications.

Using the Shafer-Shenoy algorithm, we distinguish two cases: (i) the number of combinations of messages (i.e., the number of absorptions, a) is greater than 1 *and $m > 1$*, and (ii) $a > 0$ *or $m > 1$*. In case (i), it pays (wrt. time) to compute $\psi_C = \prod_i \phi_{V_i}$ before computing the multiple ϕ_C^*'s, the time cost of which therefore is $(n + 1) \prod_i r_i |\mathcal{X}_C|$. Case (ii) is similar except that ψ_C is not computed, since $\prod_i \phi_{V_i}$ is only going to be computed once.

If C is the root clique, the S^*-marginal is going to be composed. For each of the $\prod_i r_i$ ϕ_C^*'s computed we must compute the corresponding S^*-marginal. The time cost of generating an S^*-marginal equals the larger of $|\mathcal{X}_{S_0}|$ and $|\mathcal{X}_C|$.

5.2.3. *Level 2 or deeper — nested*

The processing of messages in a non-root clique C at level $l > 1$, where the message, $\phi_{S_0}^*$, to be sent is generated through inference in an induced junction tree at level $l + 1$, is shown in Figure 11. This situation resembles

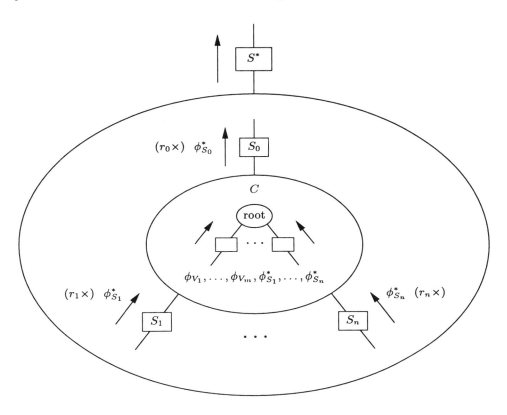

$$\text{NestedCost}_{\text{in}}^{>1}(C)$$

$c_s \leftarrow c_s^{\text{root}}$	{space cost of inward prop. towards 'root'}
$c_t \leftarrow c_t^{\text{root}}$	{time cost of inward prop. towards 'root'}
$c_s \leftarrow c_s + |\mathcal{X}_{S_0}|$	{storing $\phi_{S_0}^*$}
$c_t \leftarrow c_t |\mathcal{X}_{(C \cap S^*) \setminus C_0}| \prod_i r_i$	{inward prop. $|\mathcal{X}_{(C \cap S^*) \setminus C_0}| \prod_i r_i$ times}
$c_s \leftarrow c_s + \sum_{i=2}^{n} (r_i - 1)|\mathcal{X}_{S_i}|$	{storing multiple messages for each $i > 1$}

Figure 11. Space and time costs of receiving messages from outward neighbours and sending to the inward neighbour in a junction tree at nesting level greater than 1.

the situation shown in Figure 9, the only difference being that C may receive multiple messages from each outward neighbour, and that it may have to send multiple messages to clique C_0. Since C needs to perform $\prod_i r_i$ absorptions, with each absorption corresponding to an inward pass in the junction tree at level $l + 1$, and $|\mathcal{X}_{(C \cap S^*) \setminus C_0}|$ marginalizations for each combination of messages, a total of $|\mathcal{X}_{(C \cap S^*) \setminus C_0}| \prod_i r_i$ inward passes must be performed in the level $l + 1$ tree.

5.3. SELECTING COST FUNCTION

Now, depending on the level, directionality of propagation, and algorithm used, we should be able to select which of the five cost functions given in Figures 7–11 to use. In addition, we need a function for comparing two pairs of associated space and time costs to select the smaller of the two. To determine which of two costs, say $c = (c_s, c_t)$ and $c' = (c'_s, c'_t)$, is the smaller, we compare the linear combinations $c_s + \gamma c_t$ and $c'_s + \gamma c'_t$, where the time factor γ is chosen according to the importance of time cost. The algorithm Cost(C) for selecting the minimum cost is shown in Figure 12, where '$\prec$' refers to the cost comparison mentioned above.

$\text{Cost}(C)$
    if level $= 1$
        if (direction $=$ inward) $\vee$ (algorithm $=$ Shafer-Shenoy)
            if $\text{ConvCost}^1_{\text{in}}(C) \prec \text{NestedCost}^1_{\text{in/out}}(C)$
                $c = \text{ConvCost}^1_{\text{in}}(C)$
            else
                $c = \text{NestedCost}^1_{\text{in/out}}(C)$
        else
            $c = \text{ConvCost}^1_{\text{out}}(C)$
    else
        if $\text{ConvCost}^{>1}_{\text{in}}(C) \prec \text{NestedCost}^{>1}_{\text{in}}(C)$
            $c = \text{ConvCost}^{>1}_{\text{in}}(C)$
        else
            $c = \text{NestedCost}^{>1}_{\text{in}}(C)$

Figure 12. Selecting cost functions and the minimum cost associated with message processing in clique C.

5.4. SUM OF COSTS

Under a given time factor, γ, the overall minimum space and time costs of inward or outward propagation of messages towards/from a given root clique, R, can now be computed as

$$c^R = \sum_{C \in \mathcal{C}} \text{Cost}(C) + c_s^{\text{temp}}, \qquad (1)$$

where

$$c_s^{\text{temp}} = \begin{cases} \max_{S \in \mathcal{S}} |\mathcal{X}_S| + \max_{\{C \mid \phi_C \text{ not stored}\}} |\mathcal{X}_C| & \text{if outward Hugin prop.} \\ \max_{C \in \mathcal{C}} |\mathcal{X}_C| & \text{if Shafer-Shenoy prop.} \\ 0 & \text{otherwise.} \end{cases}$$

During outward Hugin propagation we need auxiliary space when generating messages; thus, a space of size $\max_{S \in \mathcal{S}} |\mathcal{X}_S|$ suffices. Further, for each clique, C, for which ϕ_C was not stored during the inward pass (since a nested junction tree was applied to generate the message), we need temporary storage for the clique potential ϕ_C^*. Thus we add the maximal table size for such cliques.

Using the Shafer-Shenoy algorithm, we need auxiliary space for temporary clique potentials both for the inward and the outward pass. (In computing the sum of the c^R's for inward and outward propagation, c_s^{temp} should only be added once.)

Note that $c_s^{\text{temp}} = \max_{C \in \mathcal{C}} |\mathcal{X}_C|$ may be an approximation when one or more $\text{Cost}(C)$'s originate from $\text{NestedCost}_{\text{in/out}}^1(C)$; thus, $\max_{C \in \mathcal{C}} |\mathcal{X}_C|$ is an upper limit.

6. Propagating Costs

All of the cost functions mentioned above are relative to a given root clique, R, and we are therefore only able to compute the cost of probability propagation (inward or outward) with R as root. However, we want to select the root clique such that the associated cost is minimal, and, therefore, we must be able to compute the 'root cost' c^C for each clique $C \in \mathcal{C}$.

Assuming that root clique R has neighbours $C_1, \ldots, C_n$, Equation 1 can be re-expressed as

$$c^R = \text{Cost}(R) + \sum_{i=1}^{n} c^{C_i \setminus R} + c_s^{\text{temp}}, \qquad (2)$$

where $c^{C_i \setminus R}$ denotes the root cost in the subtree rooted at C_i and with the R-branch cut off. Note that, since

$$c^{C_i \setminus R} = \text{Cost}(C_i) + \sum_{C \in \text{neighbours}(C_i) \setminus \{R\}} c^{C \setminus C_i},$$

the root costs can be computed through inward propagation of costs. This is illustrated in Figure 13, where each clique C sends the cost message $\mathrm{Cost}(C) + \sum_{i=1}^{n} c^{C_i \backslash C}$ to its inward neighbour C_0.

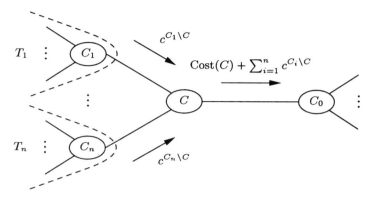

Figure 13.   Propagating costs of probability propagation.

Thus, what lacks to compute the root cost for C_i, $i = 1, \ldots, n$, is $c^{R \backslash C_i}$ (i.e., the root cost for the subtree rooted at R and with the C_i-branch cut off). However, this is nothing but the cost message sent from R to C_i if we perform outward propagation of costs from R. That is, after a full propagation of costs (i.e., inward and outward) we can easily compute the root cost of any clique.

Note that $\mathrm{Cost}()$ depends on the directionality (i.e., inward or outward). So, to compute the root costs for both inward and outward probability propagation we need to perform two full cost propagations.

7. Experiments

To investigate the practical relevance of nested junction trees, the cost propagation scheme described above has been implemented and run on a variety of large real-world networks.

The following networks were selected. The KK network (50 variables) is an early prototype model for growing barley. The Link network (724 variables) is a version of the LQT pedigree by Professor Brian Suarez extended for linkage analysis (Jensen and Kong, 1996). The Pathfinder network (109 variables) is a tool for diagnosing lymph node diseases (Heckerman *et al.*, 1992). The Pignet network (441 variables) is a small subnet of a pedigree of breeding pigs. The Diabetes network (413 variables) is a time-sliced network for determining optimal insulin dose adjustments (Andreassen *et al.*, 1991). The Munin1–4 networks (189, 1003, 1044, and 1041 variables, respectively) are different subnets of the Munin system (Andreassen *et al.*, 1989).

The Water network (32 variables) is a time-sliced model of the biological processes of a water treatment plant (Jensen *et al.*, 1989).

The average space and time costs of performing a probability propagation is measured for each of these ten networks. Tables 1–4 summarize the results obtained for inward Hugin propagation, inward Shafer-Shenoy propagation, full Hugin propagation (i.e., inward and outward), and full Shafer-Shenoy propagation, respectively. All space/time figures should be read as millions of floating point numbers/arithmetic operations. The first pair of space/time columns lists the costs associated with conventional junction tree propagation. The remaining three pairs of space/time columns show, respectively, the least possible space cost with its associated time cost, the costs corresponding to the highest average relative saving, and the least possible time cost with its associated space cost. The largest average relative savings were found by running the algorithm with various γ-values for each network. The optimal values, γ^*, are shown in the rightmost columns.

TABLE 1. Space and time costs for inward Hugin propagation using (i) the conventional approach, and the nested junction trees approach with (ii) maximum nesting (minimum space cost), (iii) maximum average relative saving of space and time costs, and (iv) minimum time cost.

| Network | Conventional | | Nested | | | | | | |
| | | | $\gamma = 0$ | | $\gamma = \gamma^*$ | | $\gamma = 100$ | | |
	Space	Time	Space	Time	Space	Time	Space	Time	γ^*
KK	15.1	50.3	0.7	1119.1	6.7	40.9	8.3	37.5	0.30
Link	28.1	83.3	0.3	29692.3	11.5	62.5	12.3	61.7	0.30
Pathfinder	0.2	0.7	0.1	1.1	0.2	0.6	0.2	0.6	0.25
Pignet	0.8	2.2	0.04	61.8	0.3	2.0	0.6	1.8	0.25
Diabetes	11.0	33.1	0.5	90.0	0.9	34.6	5.3	29.1	0.15
Munin1	207.7	728.7	19.9	95818.2	68.4	315.9	68.8	315.3	0.30
Munin2	3.2	9.7	0.5	203.7	1.5	9.5	2.4	8.4	0.30
Munin3	3.7	12.1	0.5	85.8	1.5	9.9	2.4	9.4	0.25
Munin4	18.3	64.2	4.9	1128.1	6.3	63.0	12.9	50.0	0.30
Water	8.6	28.3	0.6	3532.7	2.7	26.1	3.9	22.3	0.15

As anticipated, for all networks but Pathfinder, the time costs associated with minimum space costs ($\gamma = 0$) are much larger than the time costs of conventional propagation. Thus, although maximum nesting yields minimum space cost, it is not recommended in general, since the associated time cost may be unacceptably large. The Pathfinder network behaves differently because that nesting is only possible to a very limited degree.

TABLE 2. Space and time costs for inward Shafer-Shenoy propagation using (i) the conventional approach, and the nested junction trees approach with (ii) maximum nesting (minimum space cost), (iii) maximum average relative saving of space and time costs, and (iv) minimum time cost.

| | Conventional | | Nested | | | | | | |
| | | | $\gamma = 0$ | | $\gamma = \gamma^*$ | | $\gamma = 100$ | | |
Network	Space	Time	Space	Time	Space	Time	Space	Time	γ^*
KK	7.9	52.2	6.0	787.9	6.8	42.7	7.0	42.4	0.15
Link	4.5	83.3	2.1	587.4	3.6	76.1	4.0	73.8	0.05
Pathfinder	0.1	0.7	0.1	1.3	0.1	0.7	0.1	0.7	0.10
Pignet	0.3	2.2	0.2	4.0	0.2	2.4	0.3	2.1	0.15
Diabetes	1.2	33.9	0.5	51.0	0.7	36.2	1.2	33.3	0.05
Munin1	97.7	728.8	79.2	31260.7	85.3	379.3	88.0	368.6	0.10
Munin2	0.7	9.9	0.2	50.7	0.4	11.1	0.7	9.1	0.05
Munin3	0.7	12.2	0.2	324.0	0.5	12.0	0.7	10.5	0.05
Munin4	3.0	64.3	1.1	235.7	2.1	52.6	2.4	51.4	0.05
Water	6.1	29.2	5.3	115.8	5.9	27.1	6.1	26.9	0.15

However, as the $\gamma = \gamma^*$ columns show, a moderate increase in the space costs tremendously reduces the time costs. (The example in Figure 5 demonstrates the dramatic effect on the time cost as the degree of nesting is varied.) In fact, for $\gamma = \gamma^*$, the time costs of nested computation are either roughly identical or smaller than those of conventional computation, while space costs are still significantly reduced for most of the networks.

Interestingly, for all networks the minimum time costs ($\gamma = 100$) are less than the time costs of conventional propagation, and, of course, the associated space costs are also less than in the conventional case, since the saving on the time side is due to nesting which inevitably reduces the space cost.

Comparing Tables 3 and 4 with $\gamma = \gamma^*$, we note, somewhat surprisingly, that the time costs of a full Hugin propagation are consistently smaller than those obtained using the Shafer-Shenoy algorithm, while the space costs are either comparable or smaller for the Hugin algorithm. Note, however, that the γ^*'s are significantly smaller in the Shafer-Shenoy case, indicating an attempt to keep the space costs under control.

ACKNOWLEDGEMENTS

I wish to thank Steffen L. Lauritzen for suggesting the cost propagation scheme, Claus S. Jensen for providing the Link and Pignet networks, David

TABLE 3. Space and time costs for a full Hugin propagation using (i) the conventional approach, and the nested junction trees approach with (ii) maximum nesting (minimum space cost), (iii) maximum average relative saving of space and time costs, and (iv) minimum time cost.

| Network | Conventional | | Nested | | | | | | |
| | | | $\gamma = 0$ | | $\gamma = \gamma^*$ | | $\gamma = 100$ | | |
	Space	Time	Space	Time	Space	Time	Space	Time	γ^*
KK	15.8	93.3	1.4	1162.2	2.7	104.1	9.0	80.5	0.20
Link	28.4	164.1	0.5	29773.2	7.2	164.6	12.6	142.6	0.20
Pathfinder	0.2	1.2	0.1	1.6	0.2	1.1	0.2	1.1	0.15
Pignet	0.9	4.5	0.1	64.1	0.4	4.3	0.6	4.1	0.20
Diabetes	11.0	59.5	0.6	116.5	1.0	61.0	5.3	55.5	0.15
Munin1	213.3	1362.3	25.5	96451.8	74.0	949.6	74.4	948.8	0.15
Munin2	3.2	18.7	0.6	212.6	1.4	19.0	2.4	17.3	0.20
Munin3	3.8	23.6	0.5	97.3	1.4	21.6	2.5	20.8	0.15
Munin4	18.4	119.4	5.0	1183.2	5.5	122.1	13.0	105.2	0.20
Water	9.0	46.3	1.0	3550.7	3.2	44.0	4.4	40.3	0.15

TABLE 4. Space and time costs for a full Shafer-Shenoy propagation using (i) the conventional approach, and the nested junction trees approach with (ii) maximum nesting (minimum space cost), (iii) maximum average relative saving of space and time costs, and (iv) minimum time cost.

| Network | Conventional | | Nested | | | | | | |
| | | | $\gamma = 0$ | | $\gamma = \gamma^*$ | | $\gamma = 100$ | | |
	Space	Time	Space	Time	Space	Time	Space	Time	γ^*
KK	9.0	153.6	7.1	889.3	7.9	114.9	8.1	114.4	0.05
Link	6.8	263.1	4.5	767.1	6.0	222.5	6.4	220.8	0.05
Pathfinder	0.1	2.1	0.1	2.6	0.1	2.1	0.2	2.0	0.05
Pignet	0.5	7.0	0.3	8.9	0.4	7.1	0.5	6.8	0.05
Diabetes	1.8	80.9	1.1	97.9	1.3	82.0	1.8	79.0	0.05
Munin1	117.0	2411.9	98.4	32943.8	105.8	1309.1	110.9	1263.4	0.05
Munin2	1.1	31.6	0.6	72.4	0.8	31.2	1.1	29.2	0.05
Munin3	1.2	44.8	0.7	356.6	1.0	44.1	1.2	42.5	0.05
Munin4	4.9	209.9	3.0	381.3	3.1	199.4	5.7	154.9	0.01
Water	6.7	60.6	5.9	147.3	6.5	55.5	6.6	55.3	0.15

Heckerman for providing the Pathfinder network, Kristian G. Olesen for providing the Munin networks, and Steen Andreassen for providing the Diabetes network.

References

Andreassen, S., Hovorka, R., Benn, J., Olesen, K. G. and Carson, E. R. (1991) A model-based approach to insulin adjustment, *in* M. Stefanelli, A. Hasman, M. Fieschi and J. Talmon (eds), *Proceedings of the Third Conference on Artificial Intelligence in Medicine*, Springer-Verlag, pp. 239–248.

Andreassen, S., Jensen, F. V., Andersen, S. K., Falck, B., Kjærulff, U., Woldbye, M., Sørensen, A. R., Rosenfalck, A. and Jensen, F. (1989) MUNIN — an expert EMG assistant, *in* J. E. Desmedt (ed.), *Computer-Aided Electromyography and Expert Systems*, Elsevier Science Publishers B. V. (North-Holland), Amsterdam, Chapter 21.

Frydenberg, M. (1989) The chain graph Markov property, *Scandinavian Journal of Statistics*, **17**, pp. 333–353.

Jensen, F. V. (1996) *An Introduction to Bayesian Networks*. UCL Press, London.

Jensen, F. V., Kjærulff, U., Olesen, K. G. and Pedersen, J. (1989) Et forprojekt til et ekspertsystem for drift af spildevandsrensning (an expert system for control of waste water treatment — a pilot project), *Technical report*, Judex Datasystemer A/S, Aalborg, Denmark. In Danish.

Jensen, C. S. and Kong, A. (1996) Blocking Gibbs sampling for linkage analysis in large pedigrees with many loops, *Research Report R-96-2048*, Department of Computer Science, Aalborg University, Denmark, Fredrik Bajers Vej 7, DK-9220 Aalborg Ø.

Jensen, F. V., Lauritzen, S. L. and Olesen, K. G. (1990) Bayesian updating in causal probabilistic networks by local computations, *Computational Statistics Quarterly*, **4**, pp. 269–282.

Heckerman, D., Horvitz, E. and Nathwani, B. (1992) Toward normative expert systems: Part I. The Pathfinder project, *Methods of Information in Medicine*, **31**, pp. 90–105.

Kim, J. H. and Pearl, J. (1983) A computational model for causal and diagnostic reasoning in inference systems. In *Proceedings of the Eighth International Joint Conference on Artificial Intelligence*, pp. 190–193.

Lauritzen, S. L., Dawid, A. P., Larsen, B. N. and Leimer, H.-G. (1990) Independence properties of directed Markov fields, *Networks*, **20**, pp. 491–505.

Lauritzen, S. L. and Spiegelhalter, D. J. (1988) Local computations with probabilities on graphical structures and their application to expert systems. *Journal of the Royal Statistical Society, Series B*, **50**, pp. 157–224.

Shafer, G. and Shenoy, P. P. (1990) Probability propagation, *Annals of Mathematics and Artificial Intelligence*, **2**, pp. 327–352.

Shenoy, P. P. (1996) Binary Join Trees, *in* D. Geiger and P. Shenoy (eds.), *Proceedings of the Twelfth Conference on Uncertainty in Artificial Intelligence*, Morgan Kaufmann Publishers, San Francisco, California, pp. 492–499.

Xu, H. (1994) Computing marginals from the marginal representation in Markov trees, *in Proceedings of the Fifth International Conference on Information Processing and Management of Uncertainty in Knowledge-Based Systems (IPMU)*, Cite Internationale Universitaire, Paris, France, pp. 275–280.

BUCKET ELIMINATION: A UNIFYING FRAMEWORK FOR PROBABILISTIC INFERENCE

R. DECHTER
Department of Information and Computer Science
University of California, Irvine
dechter@ics.uci.edu

Abstract.
Probabilistic inference algorithms for belief updating, finding the most probable explanation, the maximum a posteriori hypothesis, and the maximum expected utility are reformulated within the *bucket elimination* framework. This emphasizes the principles common to many of the algorithms appearing in the probabilistic inference literature and clarifies the relationship of such algorithms to nonserial dynamic programming algorithms. A general method for combining conditioning and bucket elimination is also presented. For all the algorithms, bounds on complexity are given as a function of the problem's structure.

1. Overview

Bucket elimination is a unifying algorithmic framework that generalizes dynamic programming to accommodate algorithms for many complex problem-solving and reasoning activities, including directional resolution for propositional satisfiability (Davis and Putnam, 1960), adaptive consistency for constraint satisfaction (Dechter and Pearl, 1987), Fourier and Gaussian elimination for linear equalities and inequalities, and dynamic programming for combinatorial optimization (Bertele and Brioschi, 1972). Here, after presenting the framework, we demonstrate that a number of algorithms for probabilistic inference can also be expressed as bucket-elimination algorithms.

The main virtues of the bucket-elimination framework are *simplicity* and *generality*. By simplicity, we mean that a complete specification of bucket-elimination algorithms is feasible without introducing extensive terminology (e.g., graph concepts such as triangulation and arc-reversal), thus making the algorithms accessible to researchers in diverse areas. More important, the uniformity of the algorithms facilitates understanding, which encourages cross-fertilization and technology transfer between disciplines. Indeed, all bucket-elimination algorithms are similar enough for any improvement to a single algorithm to be applicable to all others expressed in this framework. For example, expressing probabilistic inference algorithms as bucket-elimination methods clarifies the former's relationship to dynamic programming and to constraint satisfaction such that the knowledge accumulated in those areas may be utilized in the probabilistic framework.

The generality of bucket elimination can be illustrated with an algorithm in the area of deterministic reasoning. Consider the following algorithm for deciding satisfiability. Given a set of clauses (a clause is a disjunction of propositional variables or their negations) and an ordering of the propositional variables, $d = Q_1, ..., Q_n$, algorithm *directional resolution* (DR) (Dechter and Rish, 1994), is the core of the well-known Davis-Putnam algorithm for satisfiability (Davis and Putnam, 1960). The algorithm is described using *buckets* partitioning the given set of clauses such that all the clauses containing Q_i that do not contain any symbol higher in the ordering are placed in the bucket of Q_i, denoted $bucket_i$.

The algorithm (see Figure 1) processes the buckets in the reverse order of d. When processing $bucket_i$, it resolves over Q_i all possible pairs of clauses in the bucket and inserts the resolvents into the appropriate lower buckets. It was shown that if the empty clause is not generated in this process then the theory is satisfiable and a satisfying truth assignment can be generated in time linear in the size of the resulting theory. The complexity of the algorithm is exponentially bounded (time and space) in a graph parameter called *induced width* (also called *tree-width*) of the *interaction graph* of the theory, where a node is associated with a proposition and an arc connects any two nodes appearing in the same clause (Dechter and Rish, 1994).

The belief-network algorithms we present in this paper have much in common with the resolution procedure above. They all possess the property of compiling a theory into one from which answers can be extracted easily and their complexity is dependent on the same induced width graph parameter. The algorithms are variations on known algorithms and, for the most part, are not new, in the sense that the basic ideas have existed for some time (Cannings *et al.*, 1978; Pearl, 1988; Lauritzen and Spiegelhalter, 1988; Tatman and Shachter, 1990; Jensen *et al.*, 1990; R.D. Shachter and Favro, 1990; Bacchus and van Run, 1995; Shachter, 1986; Shachter, 1988; Shimony and Charniack, 1991; Shenoy, 1992). What we are presenting here is a syntactic and uniform exposition emphasizing these algorithms' form

---

Algorithm directional resolution
Input: A set of clauses φ, an ordering $d = Q_1, ..., Q_n$.
Output: A decision of whether φ is satisfiable. If it is, an equivalent output theory; else, an empty output theory.
1. **Initialize:** Generate an ordered partition of the clauses, $bucket_1, ..., bucket_n$, where $bucket_i$ contains all the clauses whose highest literal is Q_i.
2. For $p = n$ to 1, do
• **if** $bucket_p$ contains a unit clause, perform only unit resolution. Put each resolvent in the appropriate bucket.
• **else,** resolve each pair $\{(\alpha \vee Q_p), (\beta \vee \neg Q_p)\} \subseteq bucket_p$. If $\gamma = \alpha \vee \beta$ is empty, φ is not satisfiable, else, add γ to the appropriate bucket.
3. **Return:** $\bigcup_i bucket_i$.

Figure 1. Algorithm *directional resolution*

as a straightforward elimination algorithm. The main virtue of this presentation, beyond uniformity, is that it allows ideas and techniques to flow across the boundaries between areas of research. In particular, having noted that elimination algorithms and clustering algorithms are very similar in the context of constraint processing (Dechter and Pearl, 1989), we find that this similarity carries over to all other tasks. We also show that the idea of *conditioning*, which is as universal as that of elimination, can be incorporated and exploited naturally and uniformly within the elimination framework.

Conditioning is a generic name for algorithms that search the space of partial value assignments, or partial conditionings. Conditioning means splitting a problem into subproblems based on a certain condition. Algorithms such as *backtracking* and *branch and bound* may be viewed as conditioning algorithms. The complexity of conditioning algorithms is exponential in the conditioning set, however, their space complexity is only linear. Our resulting hybrid of conditioning with elimination which trade off time for space (see also (Dechter, 1996b; R. D. Shachter and Solovitz, 1991)), are applicable to all algorithms expressed within this framework.

The work we present here also fits into the framework developed by Arnborg and Proskourowski (Arnborg, 1985; Arnborg and Proskourowski, 1989). They present table-based reductions for various NP-hard graph problems such as the independent-set problem, network reliability, vertex cover, graph k-colorability, and Hamilton circuits. Here and elsewhere (Dechter and van Beek, 1995; Dechter, 1997) we extend the approach to a different set of problems.

Following preliminaries (section 2), we present the bucket-elimination algorithm for belief updating and analyze its performance (section 3). Then, we extend the algorithm to the tasks of finding the most probable explanation (section 4), and extend it to the tasks of finding the maximum a posteriori hypothesis (section 5) and for finding the maximum expected utility (section 6). Section 7 relates the algorithms to Pearl's poly-tree algorithms and to join-tree clustering. We then describe schemes for combining the conditioning method with elimination (section 8). Conclusions are given in section 9.

2. Preliminaries

Belief networks provide a formalism for reasoning about partial beliefs under conditions of uncertainty. It is defined by a directed acyclic graph over nodes representing random variables that takes value from given domains. The arcs signify the existance of direct causal influences between the linked variables, and the strength of these influences are quantified by conditional probabilities. A belief network relies on the notion of a directed graph.

A *directed graph* is a pair, $G = \{V, E\}$, where $V = \{X_1, ..., X_n\}$ is a set of elements and $E = \{(X_i, X_j)|X_i, X_j \in V, i \neq j\}$ is the set of edges. If $(X_i, X_j) \in E$, we say that X_i points to X_j. For each variable X_i, the set of parent nodes of X_i, denoted $pa(X_i)$, comprises the variables pointing to X_i in G, while the set of child nodes of X_i, denoted $ch(X_i)$, comprises the variables that X_i points to. Whenever no confusion can arise, we abbreviate $pa(X_i)$ by pa_i and $ch(X_i)$ by ch_i. The family of X_i, F_i, includes X_i and its child variables. A directed graph is *acyclic* if it has no directed cycles. In an *undirected graph*, the directions of the arcs are ignored: (X_i, X_j) and (X_j, X_i) are identical.

Let $X = \{X_1, ..., X_n\}$ be a set of random variables over multivalued domains, $D_1, ..., D_n$. A *belief network* is a pair (G, P) where G is a directed acyclic graph and $P = \{P_i\}$, where P_i denotes probabilistic relationships between X_i and its parents, namely conditional probability matrices $P_i = \{P(X_i|pa_i)\}$. The belief network represents a probability distribution over X having the product form

$$P(x_1, ..., x_n) = \Pi_{i=1}^n P(x_i|x_{pa_i})$$

where an assignment $(X_1 = x_1, ..., X_n = x_n)$ is abbreviated to $x = (x_1, ..., x_n)$ and where x_S denotes the projection of a tuple x over a subset of variables S. An evidence set e is an instantiated subset of variables. $A = a$ denotes a partial assignment to a subset of variables A from their respective domains. We use upper case letter for variables and nodes in a graph and lower case letters for values in variable's domains.

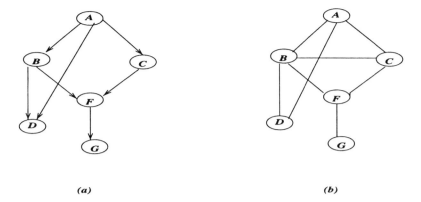

Figure 2.   belief network $P(g, f, d, c, b, a) = P(g|f)P(f|c, b)P(d|b, a)P(b|a)P(c|a)$

Example 2.1 *Consider the belief network defined by*

$$P(g, f, d, c, b, a) = P(g|f)P(f|c, b)P(d|b, a)P(b|a)P(c|a).$$

Its acyclic graph is given in Figure 2a. In this case, $pa(F) = \{B, C\}$.

The following queries are defined over belief networks: 1. *belief updating* namely, given a set observations, computing the posterior probability of each proposition, 2. *Finding the most probable explanation (mpe)*, or, given some observed variables, finding a maximum probability assignment to the rest of the variables 3. *Finding the maximum aposteriori hypothesis (map)*, or, given some evidence, finding an assignment to a subset of hypothesis variables that maximizes their probability, and finally, 4. given also a utility function, finding an assignment to a subset of decision variables that *maximizes the expected utility of the problem (meu)*.

It is known that these tasks are NP-hard. Nevertheless, they all permit a polynomial propagation algorithm for singly-connected networks (Pearl, 1988). The two main approaches to extending this propagation algorithm to multiply-connected networks are the *cycle-cutset* approach, also called *conditioning*, and *tree-clustering* (Pearl, 1988; Lauritzen and Spiegelhalter, 1988; Shachter, 1986). These methods work well for sparse networks with small cycle-cutsets or small clusters. In subsequent sections bucket-elimination algorithms for each of the above tasks will be presented and relationship with existing methods will be discussed.

We conclude this section with some notational conventions. Let u be a partial tuple, S a subset of variables, and X_p a variable not in S. We use (u_S, x_p) to denote the tuple u_S appended by a value x_p of X_p.

Definition 2.2 (elimination functions) *Given a function h defined over subset of variables S, where $X \in S$, the functions $(min_X h)$, $(max_X h)$,*

$(mean_X h)$, and $(\sum_X h)$ are defined over $U = S - \{X\}$ as follows. For every $U = u$, $(min_X h)(u) = \min_x h(u, x)$, $(max_X h)(u) = \max_x h(u, x)$, $(\sum_X h)(u) = \sum_x h(u, x)$, and $(mean_X h)(u) = \sum_x \frac{h(u,x)}{|X|}$, where $|X|$ is the cardinality of X's domain. Given a set of functions $h_1, ..., h_j$ defined over the subsets $S_1, ..., S_j$, the product function $(\Pi_j h_j)$ and $\sum_J h_j$ are defined over $U = \cup_j S_j$. For every $U = u$, $(\Pi_j h_j)(u) = \Pi_j h_j(u_{S_j})$, and $(\sum_j h_j)(u) = \sum_j h_j(u_{S_j})$.

3. An Elimination Algorithm for Belief Assessment

Belief updating is the primary inference task over belief networks. The task is to maintain the probability of singleton propositions once new evidence arrives. Following Pearl's propagation algorithm for singly-connected networks (Pearl, 1988), researchers have investigated various approaches to belief updating. We will now present a step by step derivation of a general variable-elimination algorithm for belief updating. This process is typical for any derivation of elimination algorithms.

Let $X_1 = x_1$ be an atomic proposition. The problem is to assess and update the belief in x_1 given some evidence e. Namely, we wish to compute $P(X_1 = x_1|e) = \alpha \cdot P(X_1 = x_1, e)$, where α is a normalization constant. We will develop the algorithm using example 2.1 (Figure 2). Assume we have the evidence $g = 1$. Consider the variables in the order $d_1 = A, C, B, F, D, G$. By definition we need to compute

$$P(a, g = 1) = \sum_{c,b,f,d,g=1} P(g|f)P(f|b,c)P(d|a,b)P(c|a)P(b|a)P(a)$$

We can now apply some simple symbolic manipulation, migrating each conditional probability table to the left of summation variables which it does not reference, we get

$$= P(a) \sum_c P(c|a) \sum_b P(b|a) \sum_f P(f|b,c) \sum_d P(d|b,a) \sum_{g=1} P(g|f) \qquad (1)$$

Carrying the computation from right to left (from G to A), we first compute the rightmost summation which generates a function over f, $\lambda_G(f)$ defined by: $\lambda_G(f) = \sum_{g=1} P(g|f)$ and place it as far to the left as possible, yielding

$$P(a) \sum_c P(c|a) \sum_b P(b|a) \sum_f P(f|b,c)\lambda_G(f) \sum_d P(d|b,a) \qquad (2)$$

$$bucket_G = \quad P(g|f), g = 1$$
$$bucket_D = \quad P(d|b, a)$$
$$bucket_F = \quad P(f|b, c)$$
$$bucket_B = \quad P(b|a)$$
$$bucket_C = \quad P(c|a)$$
$$bucket_A = \quad P(a)$$

Figure 3.   Initial partitioning into buckets using $d_1 = A, C, B, F, D, G$

Summing next over d (generating a function denoted $\lambda_D(a, b)$, defined by $\lambda_D(a, b) = \sum_d P(d|a, b)$), we get

$$P(a) \sum_c P(c|a) \sum_b P(b|a)\lambda_D(a, b) \sum_f P(f|b, c)\lambda_G(f) \qquad (3)$$

Next, summing over f (generating $\lambda_F(b, c) = \sum_f P(f|b, c)\lambda_G(f)$), we get,

$$P(a) \sum_c P(c|a) \sum_b P(b|a)\lambda_D(a, b)\lambda_F(b, c) \qquad (4)$$

Summing over b (generating $\lambda_B(a, c)$), we get

$$P(a) \sum_c P(c|a)\lambda_B(a, c) \qquad (5)$$

Finally, summing over c (generating $\lambda_C(a)$), we get

$$P(a)\lambda_C(a) \qquad (6)$$

The answer to the query $P(a|g = 1)$ can be computed by evaluating the last product and then normalizing.

The bucket-elimination algorithm mimics the above algebraic manipulation using a simple organizational devise we call *buckets*, as follows. First, the conditional probability tables (*CPTs*, for short) are partitioned into buckets, relative to the order used $d_1 = A, C, B, F, D, G$, as follows (going from last variable to first varaible): in the bucket of G we place all functions mentioning G. From the remaining CPTs we place all those mentioning D in the bucket of D, and so on. The partitioning rule can be alternatively stated as follows. In the bucket of variable X_i we put all functions that mention X_i but do not mention any variable having a higher index. The resulting initial partitioning for our example is given in Figure 3. Note that observed variables are also placed in their corresponding bucket.

This initialization step corresponds to deriving the expression in Eq. (1). Now we process the buckets from top to bottom, implementing the

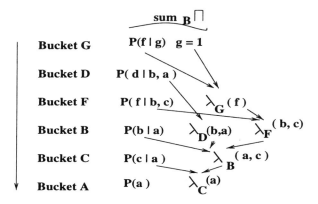

Figure 4.   Bucket elimination along ordering $d_1 = A, C, B, F, D, G$.

right to left computation of Eq. (1). $Bucket_G$ is processed first. Processing a bucket amounts to eliminating the variable in the bucket from subsequent computation. To eliminate G, we sum over all values of g. Since, in this case we have an observed value $g = 1$ the summation is over a singleton value. Namely, $\lambda_G(f) = \sum_{g=1} P(g|f)$, is computed and placed in $bucket_F$ (this corresponds to deriving Eq. (2) from Eq. (1)). New functions are placed in lower buckets using the same placement rule.

$Bucket_D$ is processed next. We sum-out D getting $\lambda_D(b, a) = \sum_d P(d|b, a)$, that is computed and placed in $bucket_B$, (which corresponds to deriving Eq. (3) from Eq. (2)). The next variable is F. $Bucket_F$ contains two functions $P(f|b, c)$ and $\lambda_G(f)$, and thus, following Eq. (4) we generate the function $\lambda_F(b, c) = \sum_f P(f|b, c) \cdot \lambda_G(f)$ which is placed in $bucket_B$ (this corresponds to deriving Eq. (4) from Eq. (3)). In processing the next $bucket_B$, the function $\lambda_B(a, c) = \sum_b (P(b|a) \cdot \lambda_D(b, a) \cdot \lambda_F(b, c))$ is computed and placed in $bucket_C$ (deriving Eq. (5) from Eq. (4)). In processing the next $bucket_C$, $\lambda_C(a) = \sum_{c \in C} P(c|a) \cdot \lambda_B(a, c)$ is computed (which corresponds to deriving Eq. (6) from Eq. (5)). Finally, the belief in a can be computed in $bucket_A$, $P(a|g = 1) = P(a) \cdot \lambda_C(a)$. Figure 4 summarizes the flow of computation of the bucket elimination algorithm for our example. Note that since throughout this process we recorded two-dimensional functions at the most, the complexity the algorithm using ordering d_1 is (roughly) time and space quadratic in the domain sizes.

What will occur if we use a different variable ordering? For example, lets apply the algorithm using $d_2 = A, F, D, C, B, G$. Applying algebraic manipulation from right to left along d_2 yields the following sequence of derivations:

$$P(a, g = 1) = P(a) \sum_f \sum_d \sum_c P(c|a) \sum_b P(b|a) \, P(d|a, b) P(f|b, c) \sum_{g=1} P(g|f) =$$

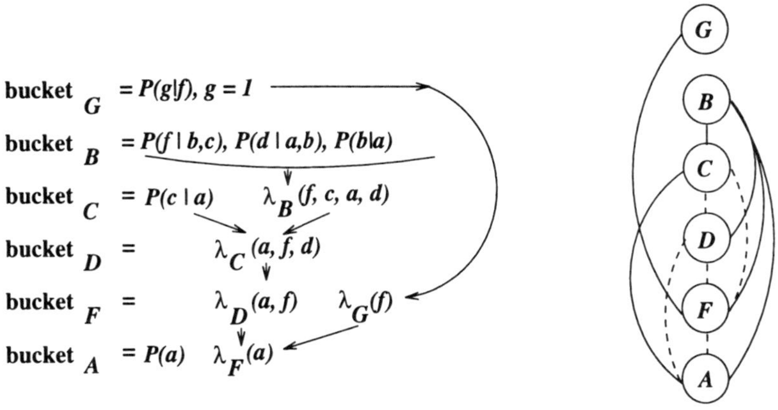

bucket $_G$ $= P(g|f), g = 1$

bucket $_B$ $= P(f \mid b,c), P(d \mid a,b), P(b|a)$

bucket $_C$ $= P(c \mid a)$ $\lambda_B (f, c, a, d)$

bucket $_D$ $=$ $\lambda_C (a, f, d)$

bucket $_F$ $=$ $\lambda_D (a, f)$ $\lambda_G (f)$

bucket $_A$ $= P(a)$ $\lambda_F (a)$

(a)   (b)

Figure 5. The buckets output when processing along $d_2 = A, F, D, C, B, G$

$P(a) \sum_f \lambda_G(f) \sum_d \sum_c P(c|a) \sum_b P(b|a) \; P(d|a,b) P(f|b,c) =$
$P(a) \sum_f \lambda_G(f) \sum_d \sum_c P(c|a) \lambda_B(a, d, c, f) =$
$P(a) \sum_f \lambda_g(f) \sum_d \lambda_C(a, d, f) =$
$P(a) \sum_f \lambda_G(f) \lambda_D(a, f) =$
$P(a) \lambda_F(a)$

The bucket elimination process for ordering d_2 is summarized in Figure 5a. Each bucket contains the initial $CPTs$ denoted by P's, and the functions generated throughout the process, denoted by λs.

We summarize with a general derivation of the bucket elimination algorithm, called *elim-bel*. Consider an ordering of the variables $X = (X_1, ..., X_n)$. Using the notation $\bar{x}_i = (x_1, ..., x_i)$ and $\bar{x}_i^j = (x_i, x_{i+1}, ..., x_j)$, where F_i is the family of variable X_i, we want to compute:

$$P(x_1, e) = \sum_{x = \bar{x}_2^n} P(\bar{x}_n, e) = \sum_{\bar{x}_2^{(n-1)}} \sum_{x_n} \Pi_i P(x_i, e|x_{pa_i}) =$$

Seperating X_n from the rest of the variables we get:

$$\sum_{x = \bar{x}_2^{(n-1)}} \Pi_{X_i \in X - F_n} P(x_i, e|x_{pa_i}) \cdot \sum_{x_n} P(x_n, e|x_{pa_n}) \Pi_{X_i \in ch_n} P(x_i, e|x_{pa_i}) =$$

$$\sum_{x = \bar{x}_2^{(n-1)}} \Pi_{X_i \in X - F_n} P(x_i, e|x_{pa_i}) \cdot \lambda_n(x_{U_n})$$

where

$$\lambda_n(x_{U_n}) = \sum_{x_n} P(x_n, e|x_{pa_n}) \Pi_{X_i \in ch_n} P(x_i, e|x_{pa_i}) \qquad (7)$$

Algorithm elim-bel
Input: A belief network $BN = \{P_1, ..., P_n\}$; an ordering of the variables, $d = X_1, ..., X_n$; evidence e.
Output: The belief in $X_1 = x_1$.
1. **Initialize:** Generate an ordered partition of the conditional probability matrices, $bucket_1, ..., bucket_n$, where $bucket_i$ contains all matrices whose highest variable is X_i. Put each observed variable in its bucket. Let $S_1, ..., S_j$ be the subset of variables in the processed bucket on which matrices (new or old) are defined.
2. **Backward:** For $p \leftarrow n$ downto 1, do
for all the matrices $\lambda_1, \lambda_2, ..., \lambda_j$ in $bucket_p$, do
• (bucket with observed variable) if $X_p = x_p$ appears in $bucket_p$, assign $X_p = x_p$ to each λ_i and then put each resulting function in appropriate bucket.
• **else,** $U_p \leftarrow \bigcup_{i=1}^{j} S_i - \{X_p\}$. Generate $\lambda_p = \sum_{X_p} \Pi_{i=1}^{j} \lambda_i$ and add λ_p to the largest-index variable in U_p.
3. **Return:** $Bel(x_1) = \alpha P(x_1) \cdot \Pi_i \lambda_i(x_1)$ (where the λ_i are in $bucket_1$, α is a normalizing constant).

Figure 6. Algorithm *elim-bel*

Where U_n denoted the variables appearing with X_n in a probability component, excluding X_n. The process continues recursively with X_{n-1}.

Thus, the computation performed in the bucket of X_n is captured by Eq. (7). Given ordering $X_1, ..., X_n$, where the queried variable appears first, the *CPT*s are partitioned using the rule described earlier. To process each bucket, all the bucket's functions, denoted $\lambda_1, ..., \lambda_j$ and defined over subsets $S_1, ..., S_j$ are multiplied, and then the bucket's variable is eliminated by summation. The computed function is $\lambda_p : U_p \to R$, $\lambda_p = \sum_{X_p} \Pi_{i=1}^{j} \lambda_i$, where $U_p = \cup_i S_i - X_p$. This function is placed in the bucket of its largest-index variable in U_p. The procedure continues recursively with the bucket of the next variable going from last variable to first variable. Once all the buckets are processed, the answer is available in the first bucket. Algorithm elim-bel is described in Figure 6.

Theorem 3.1 *Algorithm elim-bel compute the posterior belief $P(x_1|e)$ for any given ordering of the variables.* □

Both the peeling algorithm for genetic trees (Cannings *et al.*, 1978), and Zhang and Poole's recent algorithm (Zhang and Poole, 1996) are variations of elim-bel.

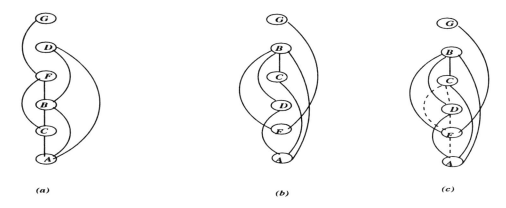

Figure 7. Two ordering of the moral graph of our example problem

3.1. COMPLEXITY

We see that although elim-bel can be applied using any ordering, its complexity varies considerably. Using ordering d_1 we recorded functions on pairs of variables only, while using d_2 we had to record functions on four variables (see $Bucket_C$ in Figure 5a). The arity of the function recorded in a bucket equals the number of variables appearing in that processed bucket, excluding the bucket's variable. Since recording a function of arity r is time and space exponential in r we conclude that the complexity of the algorithm is exponential in the size of the largest bucket which depends on the order of processing.

Fortunately, for any variable ordering bucket sizes can be easily read in advance from an ordered associated with the elimination process. Consider the *moral graph* of a given belief network. This graph has a node for each propositional variable, and any two variables appearing in the same CPT are connected in the graph. The moral graph of the network in Figure 2a is given in Figure 2b. Let us take this moral graph and impose an ordering on its nodes. Figures 7a and 7b depict the ordered moral graph using the two orderings $d_1 = A, C, B, F, D, G$ and $d_2 = A, F, D, C, B, G$. The ordering is pictured from bottom up.

The *width* of each variable in the ordered graph is the number of its *earlier* neighbors in the ordering. Thus the width of G in the ordered graph along d_1 is 1 and the width of F is 2. Notice now that using ordering d_1, the number of variables in the initial buckets of G and F, are also 1, and 2 respectively. Indeed, in the initial partitioning the number of variables mentioned in a bucket (excluding the bucket's variable) is always identical to the width of that node in the corresponding ordered moral graph.

During processing we wish to maintain the correspondance that any two nodes in the graph are connected if there is function (new or old) deefined on both. Since, during processing, a function is recorded on all the variables apearing in a bucket, we should connect the corresponding nodes in the graph, namely we should connect all the earlier neighbors of a processed variable. If we perform this graph operation recursively from last node to first, (for each node connecting its earliest neighbors) we get the *the induced graph*. The width of each node in this induced graph is identical to the bucket's sizes generated during the elimination process (see Figure 5b).

Example 3.2 *The induced moral graph of Figure 2b, relative to ordering $d_1 = A, C, B, F, D, G$ is depicted in Figure 7a. In this case the ordered graph and its induced ordered graph are identical since all earlier neighbors of each node are already connected. The maximum induced width is 2. Indeed, in this case, the maximum arity of functions recorded by the elimination algorithms is 2. For $d_2 = A, F, D, C, B, G$ the induced graph is depicted in Figure 7c. The width of C is initially 1 (see Figure 7b) while its induced width is 3. The maximum induced width over all variables for d_2 is 4, and so is the recorded function's dimensionality.*

A formal definition of all the above graph concepts is given next.

Definition 3.3 *An ordered graph is a pair (G, d) where G is an undirected graph and $d = X_1, ..., X_n$ is an ordering of the nodes. The width of a node in an ordered graph is the number of the node's neighbors that precede it in the ordering. The width of an ordering d, denoted $w(d)$, is the maximum width over all nodes. The induced width of an ordered graph, $w^*(d)$, is the width of the induced ordered graph obtained as follows: nodes are processed from last to first; when node X is processed, all its preceding neighbors are connected. The induced width of a graph, $w*$, is the minimal induced width over all its orderings. The tree-width of a graph is the minimal induced width plus one (Arnborg, 1985).*

The established connection between buckets' sizes and induced width motivates finding an ordering with a smallest induced width. While it is known that finding an ordering with the smallest induced width is hard (Arnborg, 1985), usefull greedy heuristics as well as approximation algorithms are available (Dechter, 1992; Becker and Geiger, 1996).

In summary, the complexity of algorithm elim-bel is dominated by the time and space needed to process a bucket. Recording a function on all the bucket's variables is time and space exponential in the number of variables mentioned in the bucket. As we have seen the induced width bounds the arity of the functions recorded; variables appearing in a bucket coincide with the earlier neighbors of the corresponding node in the ordered induced moral graph. In conclusion:

Theorem 3.4 *Given an ordering d the complexity of elim-bel is (time and space) exponential in the induced width $w^*(d)$ of the network's ordered moral graph.* □

3.2. HANDLING OBSERVATIONS

Evidence should be handled in a special way during the processing of buckets. Continuing with our example using elimination on order d_1, suppose we wish to compute the belief in $A = a$ having observed $b = 1$. This observation is relevant only when processing $bucket_B$. When the algorithm arrives at that bucket, the bucket contains the three functions $P(b|a)$, $\lambda_D(b, a)$, and $\lambda_F(b, c)$, as well as the observation $b = 1$ (see Figure 4).

The processing rule dictates computing $\lambda_B(a, c) = P(b = 1|a)\lambda_D(b = 1, a)\lambda_F(b = 1, c)$. Namely, we will generate and record a two-dimensioned function. It would be more effective however, to apply the assignment $b = 1$ to each function in a bucket separately and then put the resulting functions into lower buckets. In other words, we can generate $P(b = 1|a)$ and $\lambda_D(b = 1, a)$, each of which will be placed in the bucket of A, and $\lambda_F(b = 1, c)$, which will be placed in the bucket of C. By so doing, we avoid increasing the dimensionality of the recorded functions. Processing buckets containing observations in this manner automatically exploits the cutset conditioning effect (Pearl, 1988). Therefore, the algorithm has a special rule for processing buckets with observations: the observed value is assigned to each function in the bucket, and each resulting function is moved individually to a lower bucket.

Note that, if the bucket of B had been at the top of our ordering, as in d_2, the virtue of conditioning on B could have been exploited earlier. When processing $bucket_B$ it contains $P(b|a), P(d|b, a), P(f|c, b)$, and $b = 1$ (see Figure 5a). The special rule for processing buckets holding observations will place $P(b = 1|a)$ in $bucket_A$, $P(d|b = 1, a)$ in $bucket_D$, and $P(f|c, b = 1)$ in $bucket_F$. In subsequent processing, only one-dimensional functions will be recorded.

We see that the presence of observations reduces complexity. Since the buckets of observed variables are processed in linear time, and the recorded functions do not create functions on new subsets of variables, the corresponding new arcs should not be added when computing the induced graph. Namely, earlier neighbors of observed variables should *not* be connected.

To capture this refinement we use the notion of *adjusted induced graph* which is defined recursively as follows. Given an ordering and given a set of observed nodes, the adjusted induced graph is generated by processing from top to bottom, connecting the earlier neighbors of unobserved nodes only. The *adjusted induced width* is the width of the adjusted induced graph.

Theorem 3.5 *Given a belief network having n variables, algorithm elim-bel when using ordering d and evidence e, is (time and space) exponential in the adjusted induced width $w^*(d, e)$ of the network's ordered moral graph.* □

3.3. FOCUSING ON RELEVANT SUBNETWORKS

We will now present an improvement to elim-bel whose essence is restricting the computation to relevant portions of the belief network. Such restrictions are already available in the literature in the context of existing algorithms (Geiger *et al.*, 1990; Shachter, 1990).

Since summation over all values of a probability function is 1, the recorded functions of some buckets will degenerate to the constant 1. If we could recognize such cases in advance, we could avoid needless computation by skipping some buckets. If we use a topological ordering of the belief network's acyclic graph (where parents precede their child nodes), and assuming that the queried variable starts the ordering[1], we can recognize skipable buckets dynamically, during the elimination process.

Proposition 3.6 *Given a belief network and a topological ordering $X_1, ..., X_n$, algorithm elim-bel can skip a bucket if at the time of processing, the bucket contains no evidence variable, no query variable and no newly computed function.* □

Proof: If topological ordering is used, each bucket (that does not contain the queried variable) contains initially at most one function describing its probability conditioned on all its parents. Clearly if there is no evidence, summation will yield the constant 1. □

Example 3.7 *Consider again the belief network whose acyclic graph is given in Figure 2a and the ordering $d_1 = A, C, B, F, D, G$, and assume we want to update the belief in variable A given evidence on F. Clearly the buckets of G and D can be skipped and processing should start with $bucket_F$. Once the bucket of F is processed, all the rest of the buckets are not skipable.*

Alternatively, the relevant portion of the network can be precomputed by using a recursive marking procedure applied to the ordered moral graph. (see also (Zhang and Poole, 1996)).

Definition 3.8 *Given an acyclic graph and a topological ordering that starts with the queried variable, and given evidence e, the marking process works as follows. An evidence node is marked, a neighbor of the query variable is marked, and then any earlier neighbor of a marked node is marked.*

---

[1]otherwise, the queried variable can be moved to the top of the ordering

---

Algorithm elim-bel

. . .

2. **Backward:** For $p \leftarrow n$ downto 1, do
for all the matrices $\lambda_1, \lambda_2, ..., \lambda_j$ in $bucket_p$, do
• (bucket with observed variable) **if** $X_p = x_p$ appears in $bucket_p$, then
substitute $X_p = x_p$ in each matrix λ_i and put each in appropriate bucket.
• **else**, *if $bucket_p$ is NOT skipable*, then
$U_p \leftarrow \bigcup_{i=1}^{j} S_i - \{X_p\}$ $\lambda_p = \sum_{X_p} \Pi_{i=1}^{j} \lambda_i$. Add λ_p to the largest-index
variable in U_p.

. . .

Figure 8.   Improved algorithm elim-bel

The marked belief subnetwork, obtained by deleting all *unmarked* nodes, can be processed now by elim-bel to answer the belief-updating query. It is easy to see that

Theorem 3.9 *The complexity of algorithm elim-bel given evidence e is exponential in the adjusted induced width of the marked ordered moral subgraph.*

Proof: Deleting the unmarked nodes from the belief network results in a belief subnetwork whose distribution is identical to the marginal distribution over the marked variables. $\square$

4. An Elimination Algorithm for mpe

In this section we focus on the task of finding the most probable explanation. This task appears in applications such as diagnosis and abduction. For example, it can suggest the disease from which a patient suffers given data on clinical findings. Researchers have investigated various approaches to finding the *mpe* in a belief network. (See, e.g., (Pearl, 1988; Cooper, 1984; Peng and Reggia, 1986; Peng and Reggia, 1989)). Recent proposals include best first-search algorithms (Shimony and Charniack, 1991) and algorithms based on linear programming (Santos, 1991).

The problem is to find x^0 such that $P(x^0) = \max_x \Pi_i P(x_i, e|x_{pa_i})$ where $x = (x_1, ..., x_n)$ and e is a set of observations. Namely, computing for a given ordering $X_1, ..., X_n$,

$$M = \max_{\bar{x}_n} P(x) = \max_{\bar{x}_{n-1}} \max_{x_n} \Pi_{i=1}^{n} P(x_i, e|x_{pa_i}) \qquad (8)$$

This can be accomplished as before by performing the mximization operation along the ordering from right to left, while migrating to the left, at each step, all components that do not mention the maximizing variable. We get,

$$M = \max_{x = \bar{x}_n} P(\bar{x}_n, e) = \max_{\bar{x}_{(n-1)}} \max_{x_n} \Pi_i P(x_i, e | x_{pa_i}) =$$

$$\max_{x = \bar{x}_{n-1}} \Pi_{X_i \in X - F_n} P(x_i, e | x_{pa_i}) \cdot \max_{x_n} P(x_n, e | x_{pa_n}) \Pi_{X_i \in ch_n} P(x_i, e | x_{pa_i}) =$$

$$\max_{x = \bar{x}_{n-1}} \Pi_{X_i \in X - F_n} P(x_i, e | x_{pa_i}) \cdot h_n(x_{U_n})$$

where

$$h_n(x_{U_n}) = \max_{x_n} P(x_n, e | x_{pa_n}) \Pi_{X_i \in ch_n} P(x_i, e | x_{pa_i})$$

Where U_n are the variables appearing in components defined over X_n. Clearly, the algebraic manipulation of the above expressions is the same as the algebraic manipulation for belief assessment where summation is replaced by maximization. Consequently, the bucket-elimination procedure *elim-mpe* is identical to elim-bel except for this change. Given ordering $X_1, ..., X_n$, the conditional probability tables are partitioned as before. To process each bucket, we multiply all the bucket's matrices, which in this case are denoted $h_1, ..., h_j$ and defined over subsets $S_1, ..., S_j$, and then eliminate the bucket's variable by maximization. The computed function in this case is $h_p : U_p \rightarrow R$, $h_p = \max_{X_p} \Pi_{i=1}^{j} h_i$, where $U_p = \cup_i S_i - X_p$. The function obtained by processing a bucket is placed in the bucket of its largest-index variable in U_p. In addition, a function $x_p^o(u) = argmax_{X_p} h_p(u)$, which relates an optimizing value of X_p with each tuple of U_p, is recorded and placed in the bucket of X_p.

The procedure continues recursively, processing the bucket of the next variable while going from last variable to first variable. Once all buckets are processed, the *mpe* value can be extracted in the first bucket. When this *backwards* phase terminates the algorithm initiates a *forwards* phase to compute an *mpe* tuple.

Forward phase: Once all the variables are processed, an *mpe* tuple is computed by assigning values along the ordering from X_1 to X_n, consulting the information recorded in each bucket. Specifically, once the partial assignment $x = (x_1, ..., x_{i-1})$ is selected, the value of X_i appended to this tuple is $x_i^o(x)$, where x^o is the function recorded in the backward phase. The algorithm is presented in Figure 9. Observed variables are handled as in elim-bel.

Example 4.1 *Consider again the belief network of Figure 2. Given the ordering $d = A, C, B, F, D, G$ and the evidence $g = 1$, process variables from last to the first after partitioning the conditional probability matrices into buckets, such that $bucket_G = \{P(g|f), g = 1\}$, $bucket_D = \{P(d|b, a)\}$,*

Algorithm elim-mpe
Input: A belief network $BN = \{P_1, ..., P_n\}$; an ordering of the variables, d; observations e.
Output: The most probable assignment.
1. **Initialize:** Generate an ordered partition of the conditional probability matrices, $bucket_1, ..., bucket_n$, where $bucket_i$ contains all matrices whose highest variable is X_i. Put each observed variable in its bucket. Let $S_1, ..., S_j$ be the subset of variables in the processed bucket on which matrices (new or old) are defined.
2. **Backward:** For $p \leftarrow n$ downto 1, do
for all the matrices $h_1, h_2, ..., h_j$ in $bucket_p$, do
• (bucket with observed variable) **if** $bucket_p$ contains $X_p = x_p$, assign $X_p = x_p$ to each h_i and put each in appropriate bucket.
• **else**, $U_p \leftarrow \bigcup_{i=1}^{j} S_i - \{X_p\}$. Generate functions $h_p = \max_{X_p} \Pi_{i=1}^{j} h_i$ and $x_p^o = argmax_{X_p} h_p$. Add h_p to bucket of largest-index variable in U_p.
3. **Forward:** Assign values in the ordering d using the recorded functions x^o in each bucket.

Figure 9. Algorithm *elim-mpe*

$bucket_F = \{P(f|b, c)\}$, $bucket_B = \{P(b|a)\}$, $bucket_C = \{P(c|a)\}$, *and* $bucket_A = \{P(a)\}$. *To process* G, *assign* $g = 1$, *get* $h_G(f) = P(g = 1|f)$, *and place the result in* $bucket_F$. *The function* $G^o(f) = argmax h_G(f)$ *is placed in* $bucket_G$ *as well. Process* $bucket_D$ *by computing* $h_D(b, a) = \max_d P(d|b, a)$ *and putting the result in* $bucket_B$. *Record also* $D^o(b, a) = argmax_D P(d|b, a)$. *The bucket of* F, *to be processed next, now contains two matrices:* $P(f|b, c)$ *and* $h_G(f)$. *Compute* $h_F(b, c) = \max_f p(f|b, c) \cdot h_G(f)$, *and place the resulting function in* $bucket_B$. *To eliminate* B, *we record the function* $h_B(a, c) = \max_b P(b|a) \cdot h_D(b, a) \cdot h_F(b, c)$ *and place it in* $bucket_C$. *To eliminate* C, *we compute* $h_C(a) = \max_c P(c|a) \cdot h_B(a, c)$ *and place it in* $bucket_A$. *Finally, the mpe value is given in* $bucket_A$, $M = \max_a P(a) \cdot h_C(a)$, *is determined, along with the mpe tuple, by going forward through the buckets.*

The backward process can be viewed as a compilation (or learning) phase, in which we compile information regarding the most probable extension of partial tuples to variables higher in the ordering (see also section 7.2).

Similarly to the case of belief updating, the complexity of elim-mpe is bounded exponentially in the dimension of the recorded matrices, and those are bounded by the induced width $w^*(d, e)$ of the ordered moral graph. In summary:

Theorem 4.2 *Algorithm elim-mpe is complete for the mpe task. Its complexity (time and space) is $O(n \cdot exp(w^*(d, e)))$, where n is the number of variables and $w^*(d, e)$ is the e-adjusted induced width of the ordered moral graph.* $\Box$

5. An Elimination Algorithm for MAP

We next present an elimination algorithm for the map task. By its definition, the task is a mixture of the previous two, and thus in the algorithm some of the variables are eliminated by summation, others by maximization.

Given a belief network, a subset of hypothesized variables $A = \{A_1, ..., A_k\}$, and some evidence e, the problem is to find an assignment to the hypothesized variables that maximizes their probability given the evidence. Formally, we wish to compute $\max_{\bar{a}_k} P(x, e) = \max_{\bar{a}_k} \sum_{\bar{x}_{k+1}^n} \Pi_{i=1}^n P(x_i, e|x_{pa_i})$ where $x = (a_1, ..., a_k, x_{k+1}, ..., x_n)$. In the algebraic manipulation of this expression, we push the maximization to the left of the summation. This means that in the elimination algorithm, the maximized variables should initiate the ordering (and therefore will be processed last). Algorithm *elim-map* in Figure 10 considers only orderings in which the hypothesized variables start the ordering. The algorithm has a backward phase and a forward phase, but the forward phase is relative to the hypothesized variables only. Maximization and summation may be somewhat interleaved to allow more effective orderings; however, we do not incorporate this option here. Note that the relevant graph for this task can be restricted by marking in a very similar manner to belief updating case. In this case the initial marking includes all the hypothesized variables, while otherwise, the marking procedure is applied recursively to the summation variables only.

Theorem 5.1 *Algorithm elim-map is complete for the map task. Its complexity is $O(n \cdot exp(w^*(d, e)))$, where n is the number of variables in the relevant marked graph and $w^*(d, e)$ is the e-adjusted induced width of its marked moral graph.* $\Box$

6. An Elimination Algorithm for MEU

The last and somewhat more complicated task we address is that of finding the maximum expected utility. Given a belief network, evidence e, a real-valued utility function $u(x)$ additively decomposable relative to functions $f_1, ..., f_j$ defined over $Q = \{Q_1, ..., Q_j\}$, $Q_i \subseteq X$, such that $u(x) = \sum_{Q_j \in Q} f_j(x_{Q_j})$, and a subset of decision variables $D = \{D_1, ...D_k\}$ that are assumed to be root nodes, the meu task is to find a set of decisions

---

Algorithm elim-map

Input: A belief network $BN = \{P_1, ..., P_n\}$; a subset of variables $A = \{A_1, ..., A_k\}$; an ordering of the variables, d, in which the A's are first in the ordering; observations e.

Output: A most probable assignment $A = a$.

1. **Initialize:** Generate an ordered partition of the conditional probability matrices, $bucket_1, ..., bucket_n$, where $bucket_i$ contains all matrices whose highest variable is X_i.

2. **Backwards** For $p \leftarrow n$ downto 1, do

for all the matrices $\beta_1, \beta_2, ..., \beta_j$ in $bucket_p$, do

• (bucket with observed variable) **if** $bucket_p$ contains the observation $X_p = x_p$, assign $X_p = x_p$ to each β_i and put each in appropriate bucket.

• **else,** $U_p \leftarrow \bigcup_{i=1}^{j} S_i - \{X_p\}$. If X_p not in A and if $bucket_p$ contains new functions, then $\beta_p = \sum_{X_p} \Pi_{i=1}^{j} \beta_i$; else, $X_p \in A$, and $\beta_p = \max_{X_p} \Pi_{i=1}^{j} \beta_i$ and $a^0 = argmax_{X_p}\beta_p$. Add β_p to the bucket of the largest-index variable in U_p.

3. **Forward:** Assign values, in the ordering $d = A_1, ..., A_k$, using the information recorded in each bucket.

Figure 10. Algorithm *elim-map*

$d^o = (d^o_1, ..., d^o_k)$ that maximizes the expected utility. We assume that the variables *not* appearing in D are indexed $X_{k+1}, ..., X_n$. Formally, we want to compute

$$E = \max_{d_1, ..., d_k} \sum_{x_{k+1}, ... x_n} \Pi_{i=1}^{n} P(x_i, e|x_{pa_i}, d_1, ..., d_k)u(x),$$

and

$$d^0 = argmax_D E$$

As in the previous tasks, we will begin by identifying the computation associated with X_n from which we will extract the computation in each bucket. We denote an assignment to the decision variables by $d = (d_1, ..., d_k)$ and $\bar{x}_k^j = (x_k, ..., x_j)$. Algebraic manipulation yields

$$E = \max_d \sum_{\bar{x}_{k+1}^{n-1}} \sum_{x_n} \Pi_{i=1}^{n} P(x_i, e|x_{pa_i}, d) \sum_{Q_j \in Q} f_j(x_{Q_j})$$

We can now separate the components in the utility functions into those mentioning X_n, denoted by the index set t_n, and those not mentioning X_n, labeled with indexes $l_n = \{1, ..., n\} - t_n$. Accordingly we get

$$E = \max_d \sum_{\bar{x}_{k+1}^{(n-1)}} \sum_{x_n} \Pi_{i=1}^{n} P(x_i, e|x_{pa_i}, d) \cdot (\sum_{j \in l_n} f_j(x_{Q_j}) + \sum_{j \in t_n} f_j(x_{Q_j}))$$

$$E = \max_d [\sum_{\bar{x}_{k+1}^{(n-1)}} \sum_{x_n} \Pi_{i=1}^n P(x_i, e | x_{pa_i}, d) \sum_{j \in l_n} f_j(x_{Q_j})$$

$$+ \sum_{\bar{x}_{k+1}^{(n-1)}} \sum_{x_n} \Pi_{i=1}^n P(x_i, e | x_{pa_i}, d) \sum_{j \in t_n} f_j(x_{Q_j})]$$

By migrating to the left of X_n all of the elements that are not a function of X_n, we get

$$\max_d [\sum_{\bar{x}_{k+1}^{n-1}} \Pi_{X_i \in X - F_n} P(x_i, e | x_{pa_i}, d) \cdot (\sum_{j \in l_n} f_j(x_{Q_j})) \sum_{x_n} \Pi_{X_i \in F_n} P(x_i, e | x_{pa_i}, d)$$

$$\tag{9}$$

$$+ \sum_{\bar{x}_{k+1}^{n-1}} \Pi_{X_i \in X - F_n} P(x_i, e | x_{pa_i}, d) \cdot \sum_{x_n} \Pi_{X_i \in F_n} P(x_i, e | x_{pa_i}, d) \sum_{j \in t_n} f_j(x_{Q_j})]$$

We denote by U_n the subset of variables that appear with X_n in a probabilistic component, excluding X_n itself, and by W_n the union of variables that appear in probabilistic and utility components with X_n, excluding X_n itself. We define λ_n over U_n as (x is a tuple over $U_n \cup X_n$)

$$\lambda_n(x_{U_n} | d) = \sum_{x_n} \Pi_{X_i \in F_i} P(x_i, e | x_{pa_i}, d) \tag{10}$$

We define θ_n over W_n as

$$\theta_n(x_{W_n} | d) = \sum_{x_n} \Pi_{X_i \in F_n} P(x_i, e | x_{pa_i}, d) \sum_{j \in t_n} f_j(x_{Q_j})) \tag{11}$$

After substituting Eqs. (10) and (11) into Eq. (9), we get

$$E = \max_d \sum_{\bar{x}_{k+1}^{n-1}} \Pi_{X_i \in X - F_n} P(x_i, e | x_{pa_i}, d) \cdot \lambda_n(x_{U_n} | d) [\sum_{j \in l_n} f_j(x_{Q_j}) + \frac{\theta_n(x_{W_n} | d)}{\lambda_n(x_{U_n} | d)}]$$

$$\tag{12}$$

The functions θ_n and λ_n compute the effect of eliminating X_n. The result (Eq. (12)) is an expression, which does not include X_n, where the product has one more matrix λ_n and the utility components have one more element $\gamma_n = \frac{\theta_n}{\lambda_n}$. Applying such algebraic manipulation to the rest of the variables in order yields the elimination algorithm *elim-meu* in Figure 11. We assume here that decision variables are processed last by elim-meu. Each bucket contains utility components θ_i and probability components, λ_i. When there is no evidence, λ_n is a constant and we can incorporate the marking modification we presented for elim-bel. Otherwise, during processing, the algorithm generates the λ_i of a bucket by multiplying all its

---

Algorithm elim-meu

Input: A belief network $BN = \{P_1, ..., P_n\}$; a subset of variables $D_1, ..., D_k$ that are decision variables which are root nodes; a utility function over X, $u(x) = \sum_j f_j(x_{Q_j})$; an ordering of the variables, o, in which the D's appear first; observations e.

Output: An assignment $d_1, ..., d_k$ that maximizes the expected utility.

1. Initialize: Partition components into buckets, where $bucket_i$ contains all matrices whose highest variable is X_i. Call probability matrices $\lambda_1, ..., \lambda_j$ and utility matrices $\theta_1, ..., \theta_l$. Let $S_1, ..., S_j$ be the probability variable subsets and $Q_1, ..., Q_l$ be the utility variable subsets.

2. Backward: For $p \leftarrow n$ downto $k+1$, do
for all matrices $\lambda_1, ..., \lambda_j, \theta_1, ..., \theta_l$ in $bucket_p$, do
- (bucket with observed variable) **if** $bucket_p$ contains the observation $X_p = x_p$, then assign $X_p = x_p$ to each λ_i, θ_i and put each resulting matrix in appropriate bucket.
- **else,** $U_p \leftarrow \bigcup_{i=1}^j S_i - \{X_p\}$ and $W_p \leftarrow U_p \cup (\bigcup_{i=1}^l Q_i - \{X_p\})$. If bucket contains an observation or new λ's, then $\lambda_p = \sum_{X_p} \Pi_i \lambda_i$ and $\theta_p = \frac{1}{\lambda_p} \sum_{X_p} \Pi_{i=1}^j \lambda_i \sum_{j=1}^l \theta_j$; else, $\theta_p = \sum_{X_p} \Pi_{i=1}^j \lambda_i \sum_{j=1}^l \theta_j$. Add θ_p and λ_p to the bucket of the largest-index variable in W_p and U_p, respectively.

3. Forward: Assign values in the ordering $o = D_1, ..., D_k$ using the information recorded in each bucket of the decision variable.

Figure 11. Algorithm *elim-meu*

probability components and summing over X_i. The θ of bucket X_i is computed as the average utility of the bucket; if the bucket is marked, the average utility of the bucket is normalized by its λ. The resulting θ and λ are placed into the appropriate buckets.

The maximization over the decision variables can now be accomplished using maximization as the elimination operator. We do not include this step explicitly, since, given our simplifying assumption that all decisions are root nodes, this step is straightforward. Clearly, maximization and summation can be interleaved to some degree, thus allowing more efficient orderings.

As before, the algorithm's performance can be bounded as a function of the structure of its *augmented graph*. The augmented graph is the moral graph augmented with arcs connecting any two variables appearing in the same utility component f_i, for some i.

Theorem 6.1 *Algorithm elim-meu computes the meu of a belief network augmented with utility components (i.e., an influence diagram) in $O(n \cdot$*

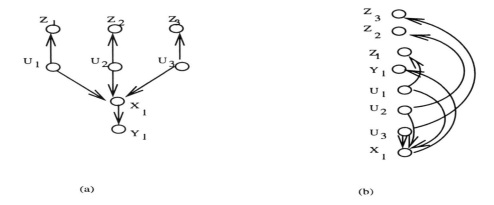

Figure 12.   (a) A poly-tree and (b) a legal processing ordering

$exp(w^*(d, e))$, where $w^*(d, e)$ is the induced width along d of the augmented moral graph. $\square$

Tatman and Schachter (Tatman and Shachter, 1990) have published an algorithm that is a variation of elim-meu, and Kjaerulff's algorithm (Kjæaerulff, 1993) can be viewed as a variation of elim-meu tailored to dynamic probabilistic networks.

7.   Relation of Bucket Elimination to Other Methods

7.1. POLY-TREE ALGORITHM

When the belief network is a poly-tree, both belief assessment, the mpe task and map task can be accomplished efficiently using Pearl's poly-tree algorithm (Pearl, 1988). As well, when the augmented graph is a tree, the *meu* can be computed efficiently. A poly-tree is a directed acyclic graph whose underlying undirected graph has no cycles.

We claim that if a bucket elimination algorithm process variables in a topological ordering (parents precede their child nodes), then the algorithm coincides (with some minor modifications) with the poly-tree algorithm. We will demonstrate the main idea using bucket elimination for the mpe task. The arguments are applicable for the rest of the tasks.

Example 7.1 *Consider the ordering $X_1, U_3, U_2, U_1, Y_1, Z_1, Z_2, Z_3$ of the poly-tree in Figure 12a, and assume that the last four variables are observed (here we denote an observed value by using primed lowercase letter and leave other variables in lowercase). Processing the buckets from last to first, after the first four buckets have been processed as observation buckets, we get*
$bucket(U_3) = P(u_3), P(x_1|u_1, u_2, u_3), P(z\prime_3|u_3)$
$bucket(U_2) = P(u_2), P(z\prime_2|u_2)$

$bucket(U_1) = P(u_1), P(z\prime_1|u_1)$
$bucket(X_1) = P(y\prime_1|x_1)$
When processing bucket(U_3) by elim-mpe, we get $h_{U_3}(u_1, u_2, u_3)$, which is placed in bucket(U_2). The final resulting buckets are
$bucket(U_3) = P(u_3), P(x_1|u_1, u_2, u_3), P(z\prime_3|u_3)$
$bucket(U_2) = P(u_2), P(z\prime_2|u_2), h_{U_3}(x_1, u_2, u_1)$
$bucket(U_1) = P(u_1), P(z\prime_1|u_1), h_{U_2}(x_1, u_1)$
$bucket(X_1) = P(y\prime_1|x_1), h_{U_1}(x_1)$
We can now choose a value x_1 that maximizes the product in X_1's bucket, then choose a value u_1 that maximizes the product in U_1's bucket given the selected value of X_1, and so on.

It is easy to see that if elim-mpe uses a topological ordering of the poly-tree, it is time and space $O(exp(|F|))$, where $|F|$ is the cardinality of the maximum family size. For instance, in Example 7.1, elim-mpe records the intermediate function $h_{U_3}(X_1, U_2, U_1)$ requiring $O(k^3)$ space, where k bounds the domain size for each variable. Note, however, that Pearl's algorithm (which is also time exponential in the family size) is better, as it records functions on single variables only.

In order to restrict space needs, we modify elim-mpe in two ways. First, we restrict processing to a subset of the topological orderings in which sibling nodes and their parent appear consecutively *as much as possible.* Second, whenever the algorithm reaches a set of consecutive buckets from the same family, all such buckets are combined and processed as one *super-bucket.* With this change, elim-mpe is similar to Pearl's propagation algorithm on poly-trees.[2] Processing a super-bucket amounts to eliminating all the super-bucket's variables without recording intermediate results.

Example 7.2 *Consider Example 7.1. Here, instead of processing each bucket of U_i separately, we compute by a brute-force algorithm the function $h_{U_1, U_2, U_3}(x_1)$ in the super-bucket of U_1, U_2, U_3 and place the function in the bucket of X_1. We get the unary function*
$$h_{U_1, U_2, U_3}(x_1) = \max_{u_1, u_2, u_3} P(u_3)P(x_1|u_1, u_2, u_3)P(z\prime_3|u_3)P(u_2)P(z\prime_2|u_2)P(u_1)P(z\prime_1|u_1).$$

The details for obtaining an ordering such that all families in a poly-tree can be processed as super-buckets can be worked out, but are beyond the scope of this paper. In summary,

Proposition 7.3 *There exist an ordering of a poly-tree, such that bucket-elimination algorithms (elim-bel, elim-mpe, etc.) with the super-bucket modification have the same time and space complexity as Pearl's poly-tree algorithm for the corresponding tasks. The modified algorithm's time complexity is exponential in the family size, and it requires only linear space.* □

---

[2] Actually, Pearl's algorithm should be restricted to message passing relative to one rooted tree in order to be identical with ours.

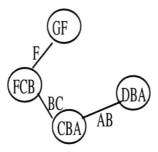

Figure 13.   Clique-tree associated with the induced graph of Figure 7a

7.2. JOIN-TREE CLUSTERING

Join-tree clustering (Lauritzen and Spiegelhalter, 1988) and bucket elimination are closely related and their worst-case complexity (time and space) is essentially the same. The sizes of the cliques in tree-clustering is identical to the induced-width plus one of the corresponding ordered graph. In fact, elimination may be viewed as a directional (i.e., goal- or query-oriented) version of join-tree clustering. The close relationship between join-tree clustering and bucket elimination can be used to attribute meaning to the intermediate functions computed by elimination.

Given an elimination ordering, we can generate the ordered moral induced graph whose maximal cliques (namely, a maximal fully-connected subgraph) can be enumerated as follows. Each variable and its earlier neighbors are a clique, and each clique is connected to a parent clique with whom it shares the largest subset of variables (Dechter and Pearl, 1989). For example, the induced graph in Figure 7a yields the clique-tree in Figure 13, If this ordering is used by tree-clustering,the same tree may be generated.

The functions recorded by bucket elimination can be given the following meaning (details and proofs of these claims are beyond the scope of this paper). The function $h_p(u)$ recorded in $bucket_p$ by elim-mpe and defined over $\cup_i S_i - \{X_p\}$, is the maximum probability extension of u, to variables appearing later in the ordering and which are also mentioned in the clique-subtree rooted at a clique containing U_p. For instance, $h_F(b,c)$ recorded by elim-mpe using d_1 (see Example 3.1) equals $\max_{f,g} P(b,c,f,g)$, since F and G appear in the clique-tree rooted at (FCB). For belief assessment, the function $\lambda_p = \sum_{X_p} \Pi_{i=1}^{j} \lambda_i$, defined over $U_p = \cup_i S_i - X_p$, denotes the probability of all the evidence e^{+p} observed in the clique subtree rooted at a clique containing U_p, conjoined with u. Namely, $\lambda_p(u) = P(e^{+p}, u)$.

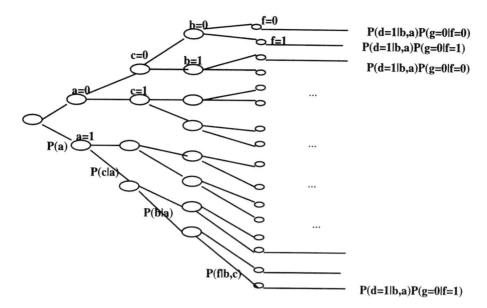

Figure 14. probability tree

8. Combining Elimination and Conditioning

A serious drawback of elimination algorithms is that they require considerable memory for recording the intermediate functions. Conditioning, on
the other hand, requires only linear space. By combining conditioning and
elimination, we may be able to reduce the amount of memory needed yet
still have performance guarantee.

Conditioning can be viewed as an algorithm for processing the algebraic
expressions defined for the task, from left to right. In this case, partial
results cannot be assembled; rather, partial value assignments (conditioning
on subset of variables) unfold a tree of subproblems, each associated with
an assignment to some variables. Say, for example, that we want to compute
the expression for mpe in the network of Figure 2:

$$M = \max_{a,c,b,f,d,g} P(g|f)P(f|b,c)P(d|a,b)P(c|a)P(b|a)P(a)$$

$$= \max_a P(a) \max_c P(c|a) \max_b P(b|a) \max_f P(f|b,c) \max_d P(d|b,a) \max_g P(g|f).$$

$$(13)$$

We can compute the expression by traversing the tree in Figure 14, going
along the ordering from first variable to last variable. The tree can be
traversed either breadth-first or depth-first and will result in known search
algorithms such as best-first search and branch and bound.

Algorithm elim-cond-mpe
Input: A belief network $BN = \{P_1, ..., P_n\}$; an ordering of the variables, d; a subset C of conditioned variables; observations e.
Output: The most probable assignment.
Initialize: $p = 0$.

1. For every assignment $C = c$, do
   - $p_1 \leftarrow$ The output of elim-mpe with $c \cup e$ as observations.
   - $p \leftarrow \max\{p, p_1\}$ (update the maximum probability).
2. **Return** p and a maximizing tuple.

Figure 15. Algorithm *elim-cond-mpe*

We will demonstrate the idea of combining conditioning with elimination on the mpe task. Let C be a subset of conditioned variables, $C \subseteq X$, and $V = X - C$. We denote by v an assignment to V and by c an assignment to C. Clearly,

$$\max_x P(x, e) = \max_c \max_v P(c, v, e) = max_{c,v} \Pi_i P(x_i, c, v, e | x_{pa_i})$$

Therefore, for every partial tuple c, we compute $\max_v P(v, c, e)$ and a corresponding maximizing tuple

$$(x_V^o)(c) = argmax_V \Pi_{i=1}^n P(x_i, e, c | x_{pa_i})$$

by using the elimination algorithm while treating the conditioned variables as observed variables. This basic computation will be enumerated for all value combinations of the conditioned variables, and the tuple retaining the maximum probability will be kept. The algorithm is presented in Figure 15.

Given a particular value assignment c, the time and space complexity of computing the maximum probability over the rest of the variables is bounded exponentially by the induced width $w^*(d, e \cup c)$ of the ordered moral graph adjusted for both observed and conditioned nodes. In this case the induced graph is generated without connecting earlier neighbors of both evidence and conditioned variables.

Theorem 8.1 *Given a set of conditioning variables, C, the space complexity of algorithm elim-cond-mpe is $O(n \cdot exp(w^*(d, c \cup e)))$, while its time complexity is $O(n \cdot exp(w^*(d, e \cup c) + |C|))$, where the induced width $w^*(d, c \cup e)$, is computed on the ordered moral graph that was adjusted relative to e and c.* $\square$

When the variables in $e \cup c$ constitute a cycle-cutset of the graph, the graph can be ordered such that its adjusted induced width equals 1. In this case elim-cond-mpe reduces to the known loop-cutset algorithms (Pearl, 1988; Dechter, 1990).

Clearly, algorithm elim-cond-mpe can be implemented more effectively if we take advantage of shared partial assignments to the conditioned variables. There is a variety of possible hybrids between conditioning and elimination that can refine the basic procedure in elim-cond-mpe. One method imposes an upper bound on the arity of functions recorded and decides dynamically, during processing, whether to process a bucket by elimination or by conditioning (see (Dechter and Rish, 1996)). Another method which uses the super-bucket approach, collects a set of consecutive buckets into one super-bucket that it processes by conditioning, thus avoiding recording some intermediate results (Dechter, 1996b; El-Fattah and Dechter, 1996).

9. Related work

We had mentioned throughout this paper many algorithms in probabilistic and deterministic reasoning that can be viewed as similar to bucket-elimination algorithms. In addition, unifying frameworks observing the common features between various algorithms had also appeared both in the past (Shenoy, 1992) and more recently in (Bistarelli *et al.*, 1997).

10. Summary and Conclusion

Using the bucket-elimination framework, which generalizes dynamic programming, we have presented a concise and uniform way of expressing algorithms for probabilistic reasoning. In this framework, algorithms exploit the topological properties of the network without conscience effort on the part of the designer. We have shown, for example, that if algorithms elim-mpe and elim-bel are given a singly-connected network then the algorithm reduces to Pearl's algorithms (Pearl, 1988) for some orderings (always possible on trees). The same applies to elim-map and elim-meu, for which tree-propagation algorithms were not explicitly derived.

The simplicity and elegance of the proposed framework highlights the features common to bucket-elimination and join-tree clustering, and allows for focusing belief-assessment procedures toward the relevant portions of the network. Such enhancements were accompanied by graph-based complexity bounds which are more refined than the standard induced-width bound.

The performance of bucket-elimination and tree-clustering algorithms is likely to suffer from the usual difficulty associated with dynamic programming: exponential space and exponential time in the worst case. Such performance deficiencies also plague resolution and constraint-satisfaction algorithms (Dechter and Rish, 1994; Dechter, 1997). Space complexity can be reduced using conditioning. We have shown that conditioning can be implemented naturally on top of elimination, thus reducing the space requirement while still exploiting topological features. Combining conditioning and elimination can be viewed as combining the virtues of forward and backward search.

Finally, no attempt was made in this paper to optimize the algorithms for distributed computation, nor to exploit compilation vs run-time resources. These issues can and should be addressed within the bucket-elimination framework. In particular, improvements exploiting the structure of the conditional probability matrices, as presented recently in (Santos *et al.*, in press; Boutilier, 1996; Poole, 1997) can be incorporated on top of bucket-elimination.

In summary, what we provide here is a uniform exposition across several tasks, applicable to both probabilistic and deterministic reasoning, which facilitates the transfer of ideas between several areas of research. More importantly, the organizational benefit associated with the use of buckets should allow all the bucket-elimination algorithms to be improved uniformly. This can be done either by combining conditioning with elimination, as we have shown, or via approximation algorithms as is shown in (Dechter, 1997).

11. Acknowledgment

A preliminary version of this paper appeared in (Dechter, 1996a). I would like to thank Irina Rish and Nir Freidman for their useful comments on different versions of this paper. This work was partially supported by NSF grant IRI-9157636, Air Force Office of Scientific Research grant AFOSR F49620-96-1-0224, Rockwell MICRO grants ACM-20775 and 95-043, Amada of America and Electrical Power Research Institute grant RP8014-06.

References

S. Arnborg and A. Proskourowski. Linear time algorithms for np-hard problems restricted to partial k-trees. *Discrete and Applied Mathematics*, 23:11–24, 1989.

S.A. Arnborg. Efficient algorithms for combinatorial problems on graphs with bounded decomposability - a survey. *BIT*, 25:2–23, 1985.

F. Bacchus and P. van Run. Dynamic variable ordering in csps. In *Principles and Practice of Constraints Programming (CP-95)*, Cassis, France, 1995.

A. Becker and D. Geiger. A sufficiently fast algorithm for finding close to optimal jnmction trees. In *Uncertainty in AI (UAI-96)*, pages 81–89, 1996.

U. Bertele and F. Brioschi. *Nonserial Dynamic Programming*. Academic Press, 1972.

S. Bistarelli, U. Montanari, and F Rossi. Semiring-based constraint satisfaction and optimization. *Journal of the Association of Computing Machinery (JACM)*, to appear, 1997.

C. Boutilier. Context-specific independence in bayesian networks. In *Uncertainty in Artificial Intelligence (UAI-96)*, pages 115–123, 1996.

C. Cannings, E.A. Thompson, and H.H. Skolnick. Probability functions on complex pedigrees. *Advances in Applied Probability*, 10:26–61, 1978.

G.F. Cooper. Nestor: A computer-based medical diagnosis aid that integrates causal and probabilistic knowledge. Technical report, Computer Science department, Stanford University, Palo-Alto, California, 1984.

M. Davis and H. Putnam. A computing procedure for quantification theory. *Journal of the Association of Computing Machinery*, 7(3), 1960.

R. Dechter and J. Pearl. Network-based heuristics for constraint satisfaction problems. *Artificial Intelligence*, 34:1–38, 1987.

R. Dechter and J. Pearl. Tree clustering for constraint networks. *Artificial Intelligence*, pages 353–366, 1989.

R. Dechter and I. Rish. Directional resolution: The davis-putnam procedure, revisited. In *Principles of Knowledge Representation and Reasoning (KR-94)*, pages 134–145, 1994.

R. Dechter and I. Rish. To guess or to think? hybrid algorithms for sat. In *Principles of Constraint Programming (CP-96)*, 1996.

R. Dechter and P. van Beek. Local and global relational consistency. In *Principles and Practice of Constraint programming (CP-95)*, pages 240–257, 1995.

R. Dechter. Enhancement schemes for constraint processing: Backjumping, learning and cutset decomposition. *Artificial Intelligence*, 41:273–312, 1990.

R. Dechter. Constraint networks. *Encyclopedia of Artificial Intelligence*, pages 276–285, 1992.

R. Dechter. Bucket elimination: A unifying framework for probabilistic inference algorithms. In *Uncertainty in Artificial Intelligence (UAI-96)*, pages 211–219, 1996.

R. Dechter. Topological parameters for time-space tradeoffs. In *Uncertainty in Artificial Intelligence (UAI-96)*, pages 220–227, 1996.

R. Dechter. Mini-buckets: A general scheme of generating approximations in automated reasoning. In *Ijcai-97: Proceedings of the Fifteenth International Joint Conference on Artificial Intelligence*, 1997.

Y. El-Fattah and R. Dechter. An evaluation of structural parameters for probabilistic reasoning: results on benchmark circuits. In *Uncertainty in Artificial Intelligence (UAI-96)*, pages 244–251, 1996.

D. Geiger, T. Verma, and J. Pearl. Identifying independence in bayesian networks. *Networks*, 20:507–534, 1990.

F.V. Jensen, S.L Lauritzen, and K.G. Olesen. Bayesian updating in causal probabilistic networks by local computation. *Computational Statistics Quarterly*, 4, 1990.

U. Kjæaerulff. A computational scheme for reasoning in dynamic probabilistic networks. In *Uncertainty in Artificial Intelligence (UAI-93)*, pages 121–149, 1993.

S.L. Lauritzen and D.J. Spiegelhalter. Local computation with probabilities on graphical structures and their application to expert systems. *Journal of the Royal Statistical Society, Series B*, 50(2):157–224, 1988.

J. Pearl. *Probabilistic Reasoning in Intelligent Systems*. Morgan Kaufmann, 1988.

Y. Peng and J.A. Reggia. Plausability of diagnostic hypothesis. In *National Conference on Artificial Intelligence (AAAI86)*, pages 140–145, 1986.

Y. Peng and J.A. Reggia. A connectionist model for diagnostic problem solving, 1989.

D. Poole. Probabilistic partial evaluation: Exploiting structure in probabilistic inference. In *Ijcai-97: Proceedings of the Fifteenth International Joint Conference on Artificial Intelligence*, 1997.

S.K. Anderson R. D. Shachter and P. Solovitz. Global conditioning for probabilistic inference in belief networks. In *Uncertainty in Artificial Intelligence (UAI-91)*, pages 514–522, 1991.

B. D'Ambrosio R.D. Shachter and B.A. Del Favro. Symbolic probabilistic inference in belief networks. *Automated Reasoning*, pages 126–131, 1990.

E. Santos, S.E. Shimony, and E. Williams. Hybrid algorithms for approximate belief updating in bayes nets. *International Journal of Approximate Reasoning*, in press.

E. Santos. On the generation of alternative explanations with implications for belief revision. In *Uncertainty in Artificial Intelligence (UAI-91)*, pages 339–347, 1991.

R.D. Shachter. Evaluating influence diagrams. *Operations Research*, 34, 1986.

R.D. Shachter. Probabilistic inference and influence diagrams. *Operations Research*, 36, 1988.

R. D. Shachter. An ordered examination of influence diagrams. *Networks*, 20:535–563, 1990.

P.P. Shenoy. Valuation-based systems for bayesian decision analysis. *Operations Research*, 40:463–484, 1992.

S.E. Shimony and E. Charniack. A new algorithm for finding map assignments to belief networks. In *P. Bonissone, M. Henrion, L. Kanal, and J. Lemmer ed., Uncertainty in Artificial Intelligence*, volume 6, pages 185–193, 1991.

J.A. Tatman and R.D. Shachter. Dynamic programming and influence diagrams. *IEEE Transactions on Systems, Man, and Cybernetics*, 1990.

N.L. Zhang and D. Poole. Exploiting causal independence in bayesian network inference. *Journal of Artificial Intelligence Research (JAIR)*, 1996.

AN INTRODUCTION TO VARIATIONAL METHODS FOR GRAPHICAL MODELS

MICHAEL I. JORDAN
Massachusetts Institute of Technology
Cambridge, MA

ZOUBIN GHAHRAMANI
University of Toronto
Toronto, Ontario

TOMMI S. JAAKKOLA
University of California
Santa Cruz, CA

AND

LAWRENCE K. SAUL
AT&T Labs – Research
Florham Park, NJ

Abstract. This paper presents a tutorial introduction to the use of variational methods for inference and learning in graphical models. We present a number of examples of graphical models, including the QMR-DT database, the sigmoid belief network, the Boltzmann machine, and several variants of hidden Markov models, in which it is infeasible to run exact inference algorithms. We then introduce variational methods, showing how upper and lower bounds can be found for local probabilities, and discussing methods for extending these bounds to bounds on global probabilities of interest. Finally we return to the examples and demonstrate how variational algorithms can be formulated in each case.

1. Introduction

The problem of probabilistic inference in graphical models is the problem of computing a conditional probability distribution over the values of some of the nodes (the "hidden" or "unobserved" nodes), given the values of other nodes (the "evidence" or "observed" nodes). Thus, letting H represent the set of hidden nodes and letting E represent the set of evidence nodes, we wish to calculate $P(H|E)$:

$$P(H|E) = \frac{P(H, E)}{P(E)}.$$ (1)

General exact inference algorithms have been developed to perform this calculation (Cowell, this volume; Jensen, 1996); these algorithms take systematic advantage of the conditional independencies present in the joint distribution as inferred from the pattern of missing edges in the graph.

We often also wish to calculate marginal probabilities in graphical models, in particular the probability of the observed evidence, $P(E)$. Viewed as a function of the parameters of the graphical model, for fixed E, $P(E)$ is an important quantity known as the *likelihood*. As is suggested by Eq. (1), the evaluation of the likelihood is closely related to the calculation of $P(H|E)$. Indeed, although inference algorithms do not simply compute the numerator and denominator of Eq. (1) and divide, they in fact generally produce the likelihood as a by-product of the calculation of $P(H|E)$. Moreover, algorithms that maximize likelihood (and related quantities) generally make use of the calculation of $P(H|E)$ as a subroutine.

Although there are many cases in which the exact algorithms provide a satisfactory solution to inference and learning problems, there are other cases, several of which we discuss in this paper, in which the time or space complexity of the exact calculation is unacceptable and it is necessary to have recourse to approximation procedures. Within the context of the junction tree construction, for example, the time complexity is exponential in the size of the maximal clique in the junction tree. As we will see, there are natural architectural assumptions that necessarily lead to large cliques.

Even in cases in which the complexity of the exact algorithms is manageable, there can be reason to consider approximation procedures. Note in particular that the exact algorithms make no use of the numerical representation of the joint probability distribution associated with a graphical model; put another way, the algorithms have the same complexity regardless of the particular probability distribution under consideration within the family of distributions that is consistent with the conditional independencies implied by the graph. There may be situations in which nodes or clusters of nodes are "nearly" conditionally independent, situations in which node probabilities are well determined by a subset of the neighbors of the node, or situations in which small subsets of configurations of variables contain most of the probability mass. In such cases the exactitude achieved by an exact algorithm may not be worth the computational cost. A variety of approximation procedures have been developed that attempt to identify and exploit such situations. Examples include the pruning algorithms of Kjærulff (1994), the "bounded conditioning" method of Horvitz, Suermondt, and Cooper (1989), search-based methods (e.g., Henrion, 1991), and the "localized partial evaluation" method of Draper and Hanks (1994). A virtue of all of these methods is that they are closely tied to the exact methods and thus are able to take full advantage of conditional independencies. This virtue can also be a vice, however, given the exponential growth in complexity of the exact algorithms.

A related approach to approximate inference has arisen in in applications of graphical model inference to error-control decoding (McEliece, MacKay, & Cheng, 1996). In particular, Kim and Pearl's algorithm for singly-connected graphical models (Pearl, 1988) has been used successfully as an iterative approximate method for inference in non-singly-connected graphs.

Another approach to the design of approximation algorithms involves making use of Monte Carlo methods. A variety of Monte Carlo algorithms have been developed (see MacKay, this volume, and Neal, 1993) and applied to the inference problem in graphical models (Dagum & Luby, 1993; Fung & Favero, 1994; Gilks, Thomas, & Spiegelhalter, 1994; Jensen, Kong, & Kjærulff, 1995; Pearl, 1988). Advantages of these algorithms include their simplicity of implementation and theoretical guarantees of convergence. The disadvantages of the Monte Carlo approach are that the algorithms can be slow to converge and it can be hard to diagnose their convergence.

In this chapter we discuss variational methods, which provide yet another approach to the design of approximate inference algorithms. Variational methodology yields deterministic approximation procedures that generally provide bounds on probabilities of interest. The basic intuition underlying variational methods is that complex graphs can be probabilistically simple; in particular, in graphs with dense connectivity there are averaging phenomena that can come into play, rendering nodes relatively insensitive to particular settings of values of their neighbors. Taking advantage of these averaging phenomena can lead to simple, accurate approximation procedures.

It is important to emphasize that the various approaches to inference that we have outlined are by no means mutually exclusive; indeed they exploit complementary features of the graphical model formalism. The best solution to any given problem may well involve an algorithm that combines aspects of the different methods. In this vein, we will present variational methods in a way that emphasizes their links to exact methods. Indeed, as we will see, exact methods often appear as subroutines within an overall variational approximation (cf. Jaakkola & Jordan, 1996; Saul & Jordan, 1996).

It should be acknowledged at the outset that there is as much "art" as there is "science" in our current understanding of how variational methods can be applied to probabilistic inference. Variational transformations form a large, open-ended class of approximations, and although there is a general mathematical picture of how these transformations can be exploited to yield bounds on probabilities in graphical models, there is not as yet a systematic algebra that allows particular variational transformations to be matched optimally to particular graphical models. We will provide illustrative examples of general families of graphical models to which variational methods have been applied successfully, and we will provide a general mathematical framework which encompasses all of these particular examples, but we are not as yet able to provide assurance that the framework will transfer easily to other examples.

We begin in Section 2 with a brief overview of exact inference in graphical models, basing the discussion on the junction tree algorithm. Section 3 presents several examples of graphical models, both to provide motivation for variational methodology and to provide examples that we return to and develop in detail as we proceed through the chapter. The core material on variational approximation is presented in Section 4. Sections 5 and 6 fill in some of the details, focusing on sequential methods and block methods, respectively. In these latter two sections, we also return to the examples and work out variational approximations in each case. Finally, Section 7 presents conclusions and directions for future research.

2. Exact inference

In this section we provide a brief overview of exact inference for graphical models, as represented by the junction tree algorithm (for relationships between the junction tree algorithm and other exact inference algorithms, see Shachter, Andersen, and Szolovits, 1994; see also Dechter, this volume, and Shenoy, 1992, for recent developments in exact inference). Our intention here is not to provide a complete description of the junction tree algorithm, but rather to introduce the "moralization" and "triangulation" steps of the algorithm. An understanding of these steps, which create data structures that determine the run time of the inference algorithm, will suffice for our

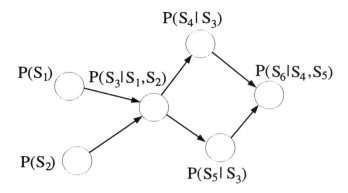

Figure 1. A directed graph is parameterized by associating a local conditional probability with each node. The joint probability is the product of the local probabilities.

purposes.[1] For a comprehensive introduction to the junction tree algorithm see Cowell (this volume) and Jensen (1996).

Graphical models come in two basic flavors—*directed* graphical models and *undirected* graphical models. A directed graphical model is specified numerically by associating local conditional probabilities with each of the nodes in an acyclic directed graph. These conditional probabilities specify the probability of node S_i given the values of its parents, i.e., $P(S_i|S_{\pi(i)})$, where $\pi(i)$ represents the set of indices of the parents of node S_i and $S_{\pi(i)}$ represents the corresponding set of parent nodes (see Fig. 1).[2] To obtain the joint probability distribution for all of the N nodes in the graph, i.e., $P(S) = P(S_1, S_2, \ldots, S_N)$, we take the product over the local node probabilities:

$$P(S) = \prod_{i=1}^{N} P(S_i|S_{\pi(i)}) \qquad (2)$$

Inference involves the calculation of conditional probabilities under this joint distribution.

An undirected graphical model (also known as a "Markov random field") is specified numerically by associating "potentials" with the cliques of the graph.[3] A potential is a function on the set of configurations of a clique

[1] Our presentation will take the point of view that moralization and triangulation, when combined with a local message-passing algorithm, are *sufficient* for exact inference. It is also possible to show that, under certain conditions, these steps are *necessary* for exact inference. See Jensen and Jensen (1994).

[2] Here and elsewhere we identify the ith node with the random variable S_i associated with the node.

[3] We define a clique to be a subset of nodes which are fully connected and maximal; i.e., no additional node can be added to the subset so that the subset remains fully connected.

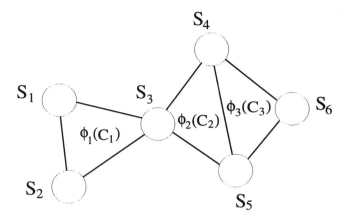

Figure 2.   An undirected graph is parameterized by associating a potential with each clique in the graph. The cliques in this example are $C_1 = \{S_1, S_2, S_3\}$, $C_2 = \{S_3, S_4, S_5\}$, and $C_3 = \{S_4, S_5, S_6\}$. A potential assigns a positive real number to each configuration of the corresponding clique. The joint probability is the normalized product of the clique potentials.

(that is, a setting of values for all of the nodes in the clique) that associates a positive real number with each configuration. Thus, for every subset of nodes C_i that forms a clique, we have an associated potential $\phi_i(C_i)$ (see Fig. 2). The joint probability distribution for all of the nodes in the graph is obtained by taking the product over the clique potentials:

$$P(S) = \frac{\prod_{i=1}^{M} \phi_i(C_i)}{Z}, \tag{3}$$

where M is the total number of cliques and where the normalization factor Z is obtained by summing the numerator over all configurations:

$$Z = \sum_{\{S\}} \left\{ \prod_{i=1}^{M} \phi_i(C_i) \right\}. \tag{4}$$

In keeping with statistical mechanical terminology we will refer to this sum as a "partition function."

The junction tree algorithm compiles directed graphical models into undirected graphical models; subsequent inferential calculation is carried out in the undirected formalism. The step that converts the directed graph into an undirected graph is called "moralization." (If the initial graph is already undirected, then we simply skip the moralization step). To understand moralization, we note that in both the directed and the undirected cases, the joint probability distribution is obtained as a product of local

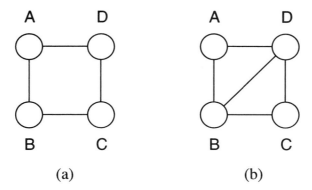

Figure 3.   (a) The simplest non-triangulated graph. The graph has a 4-cycle without a chord. (b) Adding a chord between nodes B and D renders the graph triangulated.

functions. In the directed case, these functions are the node conditional probabilities $P(S_i|S_{\pi(i)})$. In fact, this probability nearly qualifies as a potential function; it is certainly a real-valued function on the configurations of the set of variables $\{S_i, S_{\pi(i)}\}$. The problem is that these variables do not always appear together within a clique. That is, the parents of a common child are not necessarily linked. To be able to utilize node conditional probabilities as potential functions, we "marry" the parents of all of the nodes with undirected edges. Moreover we drop the arrows on the other edges in the graph. The result is a "moral graph," which can be used to represent the probability distribution on the original directed graph within the undirected formalism.[4]

The second phase of the junction tree algorithm is somewhat more complex. This phase, known as "triangulation," takes a moral graph as input and produces as output an undirected graph in which additional edges have (possibly) been added. This latter graph has a special property that allows recursive calculation of probabilities to take place. In particular, in a triangulated graph, it is possible to build up a joint distribution by proceeding sequentially through the graph, conditioning blocks of interconnected nodes only on predecessor blocks in the sequence. The simplest graph in which this is *not* possible is the "4-cycle," the cycle of four nodes shown in Fig. 3(a). If we try to write the joint probability sequentially as, for example, $P(A)P(B|A)P(C|B)P(D|C)$, we see that we have a problem. In particular, A depends on D, and we are unable to write the joint probability as a sequence of conditionals.

A graph is *not triangulated* if there are 4-cycles which do not have a *chord*, where a chord is an edge between non-neighboring nodes. Thus the

---

[4]Note in particular that Fig. 2 is the moralization of Fig. 1.

graph in Fig. 3(a) is not triangulated; it can be triangulated by adding a chord as in Fig. 3(b). In the latter graph we can write the joint probability sequentially as $P(A, B, C, D) = P(A)P(B, D|A)P(C|B, D)$.

More generally, once a graph has been triangulated it is possible to arrange the cliques of the graph into a data structure known as a *junction tree*. A junction tree has the *running intersection property*: If a node appears in any two cliques in the tree, it appears in all cliques that lie on the path between the two cliques. This property has the important consequence that a general algorithm for probabilistic inference can be based on achieving local consistency between cliques. (That is, the cliques assign the same marginal probability to the nodes that they have in common). In a junction tree, because of the running intersection property, local consistency implies global consistency.

The probabilistic calculations that are performed on the junction tree involve marginalizing and rescaling the clique potentials so as to achieve local consistency between neighboring cliques. The time complexity of performing this calculation depends on the size of the cliques; in particular for discrete data the number of values required to represent the potential is exponential in the number of nodes in the clique. For efficient inference, it is therefore critical to obtain small cliques.

In the remainder of this paper, we will investigate specific graphical models and consider the computational costs of exact inference for these models. In all of these cases we will either be able to display the "obvious" triangulation, or we will be able to lower bound the size of cliques in a triangulated graph by considering the cliques in the moral graph. Thus we will not need to consider specific algorithms for triangulation (for discussion of triangulation algorithms, see, e.g., Kjærulff, 1990).

3. Examples

In this section we present examples of graphical models in which exact inference is generally infeasible. Our first example involves a diagnostic system in which a fixed graphical model is used to answer queries. The remaining examples involve estimation problems in which a graphical model is fit to data and subsequently used for prediction or diagnosis.

3.1. THE QMR-DT DATABASE

The QMR-DT database is a large-scale probabilistic database that is intended to be used as a diagnostic aid in the domain of internal medicine.[5]

---

[5]The acronym "QMR-DT" refers to the "Decision Theoretic" version of the "Quick Medical Reference."

diseases

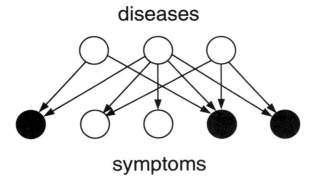

symptoms

Figure 4.   The structure of the QMR-DT graphical model. The shaded nodes represent evidence nodes and are referred to as "findings."

We provide a brief overview of the QMR-DT database here; for further details see Shwe, et al. (1991).

The QMR-DT database is a bipartite graphical model in which the upper layer of nodes represent diseases and the lower layer of nodes represent symptoms (see Fig. 4). There are approximately 600 disease nodes and 4000 symptom nodes in the database.

The evidence is a set of observed symptoms; henceforth we refer to observed symptoms as "findings" and represent the vector of findings with the symbol f. The symbol d denotes the vector of diseases. All nodes are binary, thus the components f_i and d_i are binary random variables. Making use of the conditional independencies implied by the bipartite form of the graph,[6] and marginalizing over the unobserved symptom nodes, we obtain the following joint probability over diseases and findings:

$$P(f, d) \;=\; P(f|d)P(d) \tag{5}$$

$$=\; \left[\prod_i P(f_i|d) \right] \left[\prod_j P(d_j) \right]. \tag{6}$$

The prior probabilities of the diseases, $P(d_j)$, were obtained by Shwe, et al. from archival data. The conditional probabilities of the findings given the diseases, $P(f_i|d)$, were obtained from expert assessments under a "noisy-OR" model. That is, the conditional probability that the ith symptom is

---

[6]In particular, the pattern of missing edges in the graph implies that (a) the diseases are marginally independent, and (b) given the diseases, the symptoms are conditionally independent.

absent, $P(f_i = 0|d)$, is expressed as follows:

$$P(f_i = 0|d) = (1 - q_{i0}) \prod_{j \in \pi(i)} (1 - q_{ij})^{d_j} \qquad (7)$$

where the q_{ij} are parameters obtained from the expert assessments. Considering cases in which only one disease is present, that is, $\{d_j = 1\}$ and $\{d_k = 0; k \neq j\}$, we see that q_{ij} can be interpreted as the probability that the ith finding is present if only the jth disease is present. Considering the case in which all diseases are absent, we see that the q_{i0} parameter can be interpreted as the probability that the ith finding is present even though no disease is present.

We will find it useful to rewrite the noisy-OR model in an exponential form:

$$P(f_i = 0|d) = e^{-\sum_{j \in \pi(i)} \theta_{ij} d_j - \theta_{i0}} \qquad (8)$$

where $\theta_{ij} \equiv -\ln(1 - q_{ij})$ are the transformed parameters. Note also that the probability of a positive finding is given as follows:

$$P(f_i = 1|d) = 1 - e^{-\sum_{j \in \pi(i)} \theta_{ij} d_j - \theta_{i0}} \qquad (9)$$

These forms express the noisy-OR model as a generalized linear model.

If we now form the joint probability distribution by taking products of the local probabilities $P(f_i|d)$ as in Eq. (6), we see that negative findings are benign with respect to the inference problem. In particular, a product of exponential factors that are linear in the diseases (cf. Eq. (8)) yields a joint probability that is also the exponential of an expression linear in the diseases. That is, each negative finding can be incorporated into the joint probability in a linear number of operations.

Products of the probabilities of positive findings, on the other hand, yield cross products terms that are problematic for exact inference. These cross product terms couple the diseases (they are responsible for the "explaining away" phenomena that arise for the noisy-OR model; see Pearl, 1988). Unfortunately, these coupling terms can lead to an exponential growth in inferential complexity. Considering a set of standard diagnostic cases (the "CPC cases"; see Shwe, et al. 1991), Jaakkola and Jordan (1997c) found that the median size of the maximal clique of the moralized QMR-DT graph is 151.5 nodes. Thus even without considering the triangulation step, we see that diagnostic calculation under the QMR-DT model is generally infeasible.[7]

---

[7]Jaakkola and Jordan (1997c) also calculated the median of the pairwise cutset size. This value was found to be 106.5, which also rules out exact cutset methods for inference for the QMR-DT.

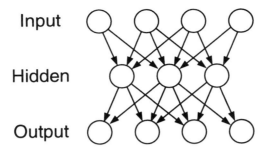

Input

Hidden

Output

Figure 5.   The layered graphical structure of a neural network. The input nodes and output nodes comprise the set of evidence nodes.

3.2. NEURAL NETWORKS AS GRAPHICAL MODELS

Neural networks are layered graphs endowed with a nonlinear "activation" function at each node (see Fig. 5). Let us consider activation functions that are bounded between zero and one, such as those obtained from the logistic function $f(z) = 1/(1 + e^{-z})$. We can treat such a neural network as a graphical model by associating a binary variable S_i with each node and interpreting the activation of the node as the probability that the associated binary variable takes one of its two values. For example, using the logistic function, we write:

$$P(S_i = 1 | S_{\pi(i)}) = \frac{1}{1 + e^{-\sum_{j \in \pi(i)} \theta_{ij} S_j - \theta_{i0}}} \tag{10}$$

where θ_{ij} are the parameters associated with edges between parent nodes j and node i, and θ_{i0} is the "bias" parameter associated with node i. This is the "sigmoid belief network" introduced by Neal (1992). The advantages of treating a neural network in this manner include the ability to perform diagnostic calculations, to handle missing data, and to treat unsupervised learning on the same footing as supervised learning. Realizing these benefits, however, requires that the inference problem be solved in an efficient way.

In fact, it is easy to see that exact inference is infeasible in general layered neural network models. A node in a neural network generally has as parents all of the nodes in the preceding layer. Thus the moralized neural network graph has links between all of the nodes in this layer (see Fig. 6). That these links are necessary for exact inference in general is clear—in particular, during training of a neural network the output nodes are evidence nodes, thus the hidden units in the penultimate layer become probabilistically dependent, as do their ancestors in the preceding hidden layers.

Thus if there are N hidden units in a particular hidden layer, the time complexity of inference is at least $O(2^N)$, ignoring the additional growth

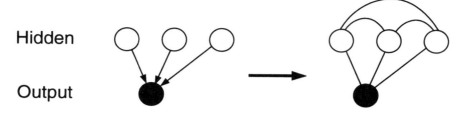

Hidden

Output

Figure 6. Moralization of a neural network. The output nodes are evidence nodes during training. This creates probabilistic dependencies between the hidden nodes which are captured by the edges added by the moralization.

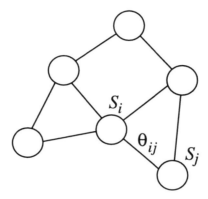

Figure 7. A Boltzmann machine. An edge between nodes S_i and S_j is associated with a factor $\exp(\theta_{ij} S_i S_j)$ that contributes multiplicatively to the potential of one of the cliques containing the edge. Each node also contributes a factor $\exp(\theta_{i0} S_i)$ to one and only one potential.

in clique size due to triangulation. Given that neural networks with dozens or even hundreds of hidden units are commonplace, we see that training a neural network using exact inference is not generally feasible.

3.3. BOLTZMANN MACHINES

A Boltzmann machine is an undirected graphical model with binary-valued nodes and a restricted set of potential functions (see Fig. 7). In particular, the clique potentials are formed by taking products of "Boltzmann factors"—exponentials of terms that are at most quadratic in the S_i (Hinton & Sejnowski, 1986). Thus each clique potential is a product of factors $\exp\{\theta_{ij} S_i S_j\}$ and factors $\exp\{\theta_{i0} S_i\}$, where $S_i \in \{0, 1\}$.[8]

---

[8]It is also possible to consider more general Boltzmann machines with multivalued nodes, and potentials that are exponentials of arbitrary functions on the cliques. Such models are essentially equivalent to the general undirected graphical model of Eq. (3)

A given pair of nodes S_i and S_j can appear in multiple, overlapping cliques. For each such pair we assume that the expression $\exp\{\theta_{ij}S_iS_j\}$ appears as a factor in one and only one clique potential. Similarly, the factors $\exp\{\theta_{i0}S_i\}$ are assumed to appear in one and only one clique potential. Taking the product over all such clique potentials (cf. Eq. (3)), we have:

$$P(S) = \frac{e^{\sum_{i<j} \theta_{ij}S_iS_j + \sum_i \theta_{i0}S_i}}{Z}, \tag{11}$$

where we have set $\theta_{ij} = 0$ for nodes S_i and S_j that are not neighbors in the graph—this convention allows us to sum indiscriminately over all pairs S_i and S_j and still respect the clique boundaries. We refer to the negative of the exponent in Eq. (11) as the *energy*. With this definition the joint probability in Eq. (11) has the general form of a *Boltzmann distribution*.

Saul and Jordan (1994) pointed out that exact inference for certain special cases of Boltzmann machine—such as trees, chains, and pairs of coupled chains—is tractable and they proposed a *decimation* algorithm for this purpose. For more general Boltzmann machines, however, decimation is not immune to the exponential time complexity that plagues other exact methods. Indeed, despite the fact that the Boltzmann machine is a special class of undirected graphical model, it is a special class only by virtue of its parameterization, not by virtue of its conditional independence structure. Thus, exact algorithms such as decimation and the junction tree algorithm, which are based solely on the graphical structure of the Boltzmann machine, are no more efficient for Boltzmann machines than they are for general graphical models. In particular, when we triangulate generic Boltzmann machines, including the layered Boltzmann machines and grid-like Boltzmann machines, we obtain intractably large cliques.

Sampling algorithms have traditionally been used to attempt to cope with the intractability of the Boltzmann machine (Hinton & Sejnowski, 1986). The sampling algorithms are overly slow, however, and more recent work has considered the faster "mean field" approximation (Peterson & Anderson, 1987). We will describe the mean field approximation for Boltzmann machines later in the paper—it is a special form of the variational approximation approach that provides lower bounds on marginal probabilities. We will also discuss a more general variational algorithm that provides upper and lower bounds on probabilities (marginals and conditionals) for Boltzmann machines (Jaakkola & Jordan, 1997a).

(although the latter can represent zero probabilities while the former cannot).

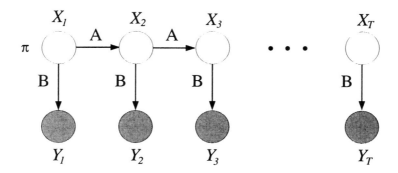

Figure 8. A HMM represented as a graphical model. The left-to-right spatial dimension represents time. The output nodes Y_i are evidence nodes during the training process and the state nodes X_i are hidden.

3.4. HIDDEN MARKOV MODELS

In this section, we briefly review hidden Markov models. The hidden Markov model (HMM) is an example of a graphical model in which exact inference is tractable; our purpose in discussing HMMs here is to lay the groundwork for the discussion of intractable variations on HMMs in the following sections. See Smyth, Heckerman, and Jordan (1997) for a fuller discussion of the HMM as a graphical model.

An HMM is a graphical model in the form of a chain (see Fig. 8). Consider a sequence of multinomial "state" nodes X_i and assume that the conditional probability of node X_i, given its immediate predecessor X_{i-1}, is independent of all other preceding variables. (The index i can be thought of as a time index). The chain is assumed to be homogeneous; that is, the matrix of transition probabilities, $A = P(X_i|X_{i-1})$, is invariant across time. We also require a probability distribution $\pi = P(X_1)$ for the initial state X_1.

The HMM model also involves a set of "output" nodes Y_i and an emission probability law $B = P(Y_i|X_i)$, again assumed time-invariant.

An HMM is trained by treating the output nodes as evidence nodes and the state nodes as hidden nodes. An expectation-maximization (EM) algorithm (Baum, et al., 1970; Dempster, Laird, & Rubin, 1977) is generally used to update the parameters A, B, π; this algorithm involves a simple iterative procedure having two alternating steps: (1) run an inference algorithm to calculate the conditional probabilities $P(X_i|\{Y_i\})$ and $P(X_i, X_{i-1}|\{Y_i\})$; (2) update the parameters via weighted maximum likelihood where the weights are given by the conditional probabilities calculated in step (1).

It is easy to see that exact inference is tractable for HMMs. The moralization and triangulation steps are vacuous for the HMM; thus the time

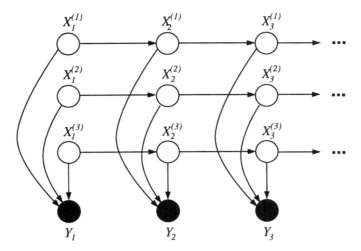

Figure 9. A factorial HMM with three chains. The transition matrices are $A^{(1)}$, $A^{(2)}$, and $A^{(3)}$ associated with the horizontal edges, and the output probabilities are determined by matrices $B^{(1)}$, $B^{(2)}$, and $B^{(3)}$ associated with the vertical edges.

complexity can be read off from Fig. 8 directly. We see that the maximal clique is of size N^2, where N is the dimensionality of a state node. Inference therefore scales as $O(N^2T)$, where T is the length of the time series.

3.5. FACTORIAL HIDDEN MARKOV MODELS

In many problem domains it is natural to make additional structural assumptions about the state space and the transition probabilities that are not available within the simple HMM framework. A number of structured variations on HMMs have been considered in recent years (see Smyth, et al., 1997); generically these variations can be viewed as "dynamic belief networks" (Dean & Kanazawa, 1989; Kanazawa, Koller, & Russell, 1995). Here we consider a particular simple variation on the HMM theme known as the "factorial hidden Markov model" (Ghahramani & Jordan, 1997; Williams & Hinton, 1991).

The graphical model for a factorial HMM (FHMM) is shown in Fig. 9. The system is composed of a set of M chains indexed by m. Let the state node for the mth chain at time i be represented by $X_i^{(m)}$ and let the transition matrix for the mth chain be represented by $A^{(m)}$. We can view the effective state space for the FHMM as the Cartesian product of the state spaces associated with the individual chains. The overall transition probability for the system by taking the product across the intra-chain transition

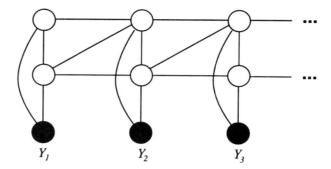

Figure 10. A triangulation of an FHMM with two component chains. The moralization step links states at a single time step. The triangulation step links states diagonally between neighboring time steps.

probabilities:

$$P(X_i|X_{i-1}) = \prod_{m=1}^{M} A^{(m)}(X_i^{(m)}|X_{i-1}^{(m)}), \qquad (12)$$

where the symbol X_i stands for the M-tuple $(X_i^{(1)}, X_i^{(2)}, \ldots, X_i^{(M)})$.

Ghahramani and Jordan utilized a linear-Gaussian distribution for the emission probabilities of the FHMM. In particular, they assumed:

$$P(Y_i|X_i) = \mathcal{N}(\sum_m B^{(m)} X_i^{(m)}, \Sigma), \qquad (13)$$

where the $B^{(m)}$ and Σ are matrices of parameters.

The FHMM is a natural model for systems in which the hidden state is realized via the joint configuration of an uncoupled set of dynamical systems. Moreover, an FHMM is able to represent a large effective state space with a much smaller number of parameters than a single unstructured Cartesian product HMM. For example, if we have 5 chains and in each chain the nodes have 10 states, the effective state space is of size 100,000, while the transition probabilities are represented compactly with only 500 parameters. A single unstructured HMM would require 10^{10} parameters for the transition matrix in this case.

The fact that the output is a function of the states of all of the chains implies that the states become stochastically coupled when the outputs are observed. Let us investigate the implications of this fact for the time complexity of exact inference in the FHMM. Fig. 10 shows a triangulation for the case of two chains (in fact this is an optimal triangulation). The cliques for the hidden states are of size N^3; thus the time complexity of

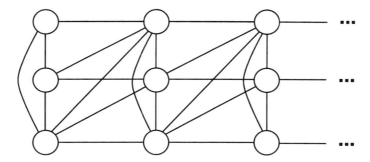

Figure 11.   A triangulation of the state nodes of a three-chain FHMM with three component chains. (The observation nodes have been omitted in the interest of simplicity).

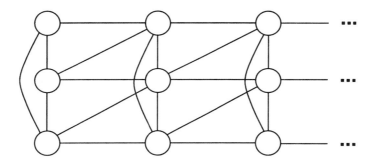

Figure 12.   This graph is not a triangulation of a three-chain FHMM.

exact inference is $O(N^3T)$, where N is the number of states in each chain (we assume that each chain has the same number of states for simplicity). Fig. 11 shows the case of a triangulation of three chains; here the triangulation (again optimal) creates cliques of size N^4. (Note in particular that the graph in Fig. 12, with cliques of size three, is *not* a triangulation; there are 4-cycles without a chord). In the general case, it is not difficult to see that cliques of size N^{M+1} are created, where M is the number of chains; thus the complexity of exact inference for the FHMM scales as $O(N^{M+1}T)$. For a single unstructured Cartesian product HMM having the same number of states as the FHMM—i.e., N^M states—the complexity scales as $O(N^{2M}T)$, thus exact inference for the FHMM is somewhat less costly, but the exponential growth in complexity in either case shows that exact inference is infeasible for general FHMMs.

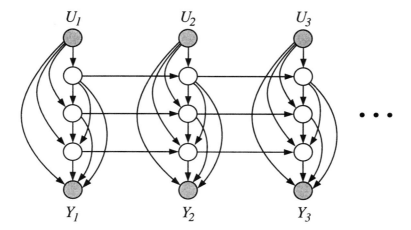

Figure 13. A hidden Markov decision tree. The shaded nodes $\{U_i\}$ and $\{Y_i\}$ represent a time series in which each element is an (input, output) pair. Linking the inputs and outputs are a sequence of decision nodes which correspond to branches in a decision tree. These decisions are linked horizontally to represent Markovian temporal dependence.

3.6. HIGHER–ORDER HIDDEN MARKOV MODELS

A related variation on HMMs considers a higher-order Markov model in which each state depends on the previous K states instead of the single previous state. In this case it is again readily shown that the time complexity is exponential in K. We will not discuss the higher–order HMM further in this chapter; for a variational algorithm for the higher–order HMM see Saul and Jordan (1996).

3.7. HIDDEN MARKOV DECISION TREES

Finally, we consider a model in which a decision tree is endowed with Markovian dynamics (Jordan, et al., 1997). A decision tree can be viewed as a graphical model by modeling the decisions in the tree as multinomial random variables, one for each level of the decision tree. Referring to Fig. 13, and focusing on a particular time slice, the shaded node at the top of the diagram represents the input vector. The unshaded nodes below the input nodes are the decision nodes. Each of the decision nodes are conditioned on the input and on the entire sequence of preceding decisions (the vertical arrows in the diagram). In terms of a traditional decision tree diagram, this dependence provides an indication of the path followed by the data point as it drops through the decision tree. The node at the bottom of the diagram is the output variable.

If we now make the decisions in the decision tree conditional not only on the current data point, but also on the decisions at the previous moment in time, we obtain a hidden Markov decision tree (HMDT). In Fig. 13, the horizontal edges represent this Markovian temporal dependence. Note in particular that the dependency is assumed to be level-specific—the probability of a decision depends only on the previous decision at the same level of the decision tree.

Given a sequence of input vectors U_i and a corresponding sequence of output vectors Y_i, the inference problem is to compute the conditional probability distribution over the hidden states. This problem is intractable for general HMDTs—as can be seen by noting that the HMDT includes the FHMM as a special case.

4. Basics of variational methodology

Variational methods are used as approximation methods in a wide variety of settings, include finite element analysis (Bathe, 1996), quantum mechanics (Sakurai, 1985), statistical mechanics (Parisi, 1988), and statistics (Rustagi, 1976). In each of these cases the application of variational methods converts a complex problem into a simpler problem, where the simpler problem is generally characterized by a decoupling of the degrees of freedom in the original problem. This decoupling is achieved via an expansion of the problem to include additional parameters, known as variational parameters, that must be fit to the problem at hand.

The terminology comes from the roots of the techniques in the calculus of variations. We will not start systematically from the calculus of variations; instead, we will jump off from an intermediate point that emphasizes the important role of convexity in variational approximation. This point of view turns out to be particularly well suited to the development of variational methods for graphical models.

4.1. EXAMPLES

Let us begin by considering a simple example. In particular, let us express the logarithm function variationally:

$$\ln(x) = \min_{\lambda} \{\lambda x - \ln \lambda - 1\}. \tag{14}$$

In this expression λ is the variational parameter, and we are required to perform the minimization for each value of x. The expression is readily verified by taking the derivative with respect to λ, solving and substituting. The situation is perhaps best appreciated geometrically, as we show in Fig. 14. Note that the expression in braces in Eq. (14) is linear in x with slope λ. Clearly, given the concavity of the logarithm, for each line having

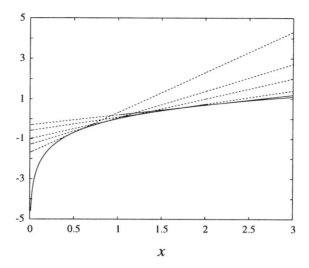

Figure 14. Variational transformation of the logarithm function. The linear functions $(\lambda x - \ln \lambda - 1)$ form a family of upper bounds for the logarithm, each of which is exact for a particular value of x.

slope λ there is a value of the intercept such that the line touches the logarithm at a single point. Indeed, $- \ln \lambda - 1$ in Eq. (14) is precisely this intercept. Moreover, if we range across λ, the family of such lines forms an upper envelope of the logarithm function. That is, for any given x, we have:

$$\ln(x) \leq \lambda x - \ln \lambda - 1, \tag{15}$$

for all λ. Thus the variational transformation provides a family of upper bounds on the logarithm. The minimum over these bounds is the exact value of the logarithm.

The pragmatic justification for such a transformation is that we have converted a nonlinear function into a linear function. The cost is that we have obtained a free parameter λ that must be set, once for each x. For any value of λ we obtain an upper bound on the logarithm; if we set λ well we can obtain a good bound. Indeed we can recover the exact value of logarithm for the optimal choice of λ.

Let us now consider a second example that is more directly relevant to graphical models. For binary-valued nodes it is common to represent the probability that the node takes one of its values via a monotonic nonlinearity that is a simple function—e.g., a linear function—of the values of the parents of the node. An example is the logistic regression model:

$$f(x) = \frac{1}{1 + e^{-x}}, \tag{16}$$

which we have seen previously in Eq. (10). Here x is the weighted sum of the values of the parents of a node.

The logistic function is neither convex nor concave, so a simple linear bound will not work. However, the logistic function is *log concave*. That is, the function

$$g(x) = -\ln(1 + e^{-x}) \tag{17}$$

is a concave function of x (as can readily be verified by calculating the second derivative). Thus we can bound the log logistic function with linear functions and thereby bound the logistic function by the exponential. In particular, we can write:

$$g(x) = \min_{\lambda}\{\lambda x - H(\lambda)\}, \tag{18}$$

where $H(\lambda)$ is the binary entropy function, $H(\lambda) = -\lambda \ln \lambda - (1-\lambda)\ln(1-\lambda)$. (We will explain how the binary entropy function arises below; for now it suffices to think of it simply as the appropriate intercept term for the log logistic function). We now take the exponential of both sides, noting that the minimum and the exponential function commute:

$$f(x) = \min_{\lambda}\left[e^{\lambda x - H(\lambda)}\right]. \tag{19}$$

This is a variational transformation for the logistic function; examples are plotted in Fig. 15. Finally, we note once again that for any value of λ we obtain an upper bound of the logistic function for all values of x:

$$f(x) \leq e^{\lambda x - H(\lambda)}. \tag{20}$$

Good choices for λ provide better bounds.

The advantages of the transformation in Eq. (20) are significant in the context of graphical models. In particular, to obtain the joint probability in a graphical model we are required to take a product over the local conditional probabilities (cf. Eq. (2)). For conditional probabilities represented with logistic regression, we obtain products of functions of the form $f(x) = 1/(1 + e^{-x})$. Such a product is not in a simple form. If instead we augment our network representation by including variational parameters— i.e. representing each logistic function variationally as in Eq. (20)—we see that a bound on the joint probability is obtained by taking products of exponentials. This is tractable computationally, particularly so given that the exponents are linear in x.

4.2. CONVEX DUALITY

Can we find variational transformations more systematically? Indeed, many of the variational transformations that have been utilized in the literature

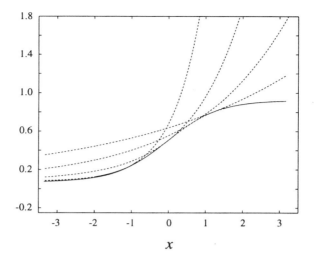

Figure 15. Variational transformation of the logistic function.

on graphical models are examples of the general principle of *convex duality*. It is a general fact of convex analysis (Rockafellar, 1972) that a concave function $f(x)$ can be represented via a *conjugate* or *dual* function as follows:

$$f(x) = \min_\lambda \{\lambda^T x - f^*(\lambda)\}, \tag{21}$$

where we now allow x and λ to be vectors. The conjugate function $f^*(\lambda)$ can be obtained from the following dual expression:

$$f^*(\lambda) = \min_x \{\lambda^T x - f(x)\}. \tag{22}$$

This relationship is easily understood geometrically, as shown in Fig. 16. Here we plot $f(x)$ and the linear function λx for a particular value of λ. The short vertical segments represent values $\lambda x - f(x)$. It is clear from the figure that we need to shift the linear function λx vertically by an amount which is the minimum of the values $\lambda x - f(x)$ in order to obtain an upper bounding line with slope λ that touches $f(x)$ at a single point. This observation both justifies the form of the conjugate function, as a minimum over differences $\lambda x - f(x)$, and explains why the conjugate function appears as the intercept in Eq. (21).

It is an easy exercise to verify that the conjugate function for the logarithm is $f^*(\lambda) = \ln \lambda + 1$, and the conjugate function for the log logistic function is the binary entropy $H(\lambda)$.

Although we have focused on upper bounds in this section, the framework of convex duality applies equally well to lower bounds; in particular

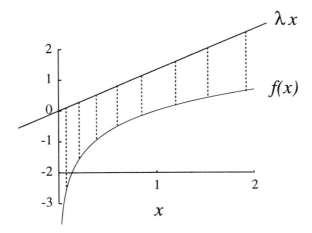

Figure 16. The conjugate function $f^*(\lambda)$ is obtained by minimizing across the deviations—represented as dashed lines—between λx and $f(x)$.

for *convex* $f(x)$ we have:

$$f(x) = \max_\lambda \{\lambda^T x - f^*(\lambda)\}, \tag{23}$$

where

$$f^*(\lambda) = \max_x \{\lambda^T x - f(x)\} \tag{24}$$

is the conjugate function.

We have focused on linear bounds in this section, but convex duality is not restricted to linear bounds. More general bounds can be obtained by transforming the argument of the function of interest rather than the value of the function (Jaakkola & Jordan, 1997a). For example, if $f(x)$ is concave in x^2 we can write:

$$f(x) = \min_\lambda \{\lambda x^2 - \bar{f}^*(\lambda)\}, \tag{25}$$

where $\bar{f}^*(\lambda)$ is the conjugate function of $\bar{f}(x) \equiv f(x^2)$. Thus the transformation yields a quadratic bound on $f(x)$. It is also worth noting that such transformations can be combined with the logarithmic transformation utilized earlier to obtain Gaussian representations for the upper bounds. This can be useful in obtaining variational approximations for posterior distributions (Jaakkola & Jordan, 1997b).

To summarize, the general methodology suggested by convex duality is the following. We wish to obtain upper or lower bounds on a function of interest. If the function is already convex or concave then we simply calculate the conjugate function. If the function is not convex or concave, then we look for an invertible transformation that renders the function convex or concave. We may also consider transformations of the argument of the function. We then calculate the conjugate function in the transformed space and transform back. For this approach to be useful we need to to find a transform, such as the logarithm, whose inverse has useful algebraic properties.

4.3. APPROXIMATIONS FOR JOINT PROBABILITIES AND CONDITIONAL PROBABILITIES

The discussion thus far has focused on approximations for the local probability distributions at the nodes of a graphical model. How do these approximations translate into approximations for the global probabilities of interest, in particular for the conditional distribution $P(H|E)$ that is our interest in the inference problem and the marginal probability $P(E)$ that is our interest in learning problems?

Let us focus on directed graphs for concreteness. Suppose that we have a lower bound and an upper bound for each of the local conditional probabilities $P(S_i|S_{\pi(i)})$. That is, assume that we have forms $P^U(S_i|S_{\pi(i)}, \lambda_i^U)$ and $P^L(S_i|S_{\pi(i)}, \lambda_i^L)$, providing upper and lower bounds, respectively, where λ_i^U and λ_i^L are (generally different) variational parameterizations appropriate for the upper and lower bounds. Consider first the upper bounds. Given that the product of upper bounds is an upper bound, we have:

$$
\begin{aligned}
P(S) &= \prod_i P(S_i|S_{\pi(i)}) \\
&\leq \prod_i P^U(S_i|S_{\pi(i)}, \lambda_i^U)
\end{aligned}
\tag{26}
$$

for any settings of values of the variational parameters λ_i^U. Moreover, Eq. (26) must hold for any subset of S whenever some other subset is held fixed, thus upper bounds on marginal probabilities can be obtained by taking sums over the variational form on the right-hand side of the equation. For example, letting E and H be a disjoint partition of S, we have:

$$
\begin{aligned}
P(E) &= \sum_{\{H\}} P(H, E) \\
&\leq \sum_{\{H\}} \prod_i P^U(S_i|S_{\pi(i)}, \lambda_i^U),
\end{aligned}
\tag{27}
$$

where, as we will see in the examples to discussed below, we choose the variational forms $P^U(S_i|S_{\pi(i)}, \lambda_i^U)$ so that the summation over H can be carried out efficiently (this is the key step in developing a variational method). In either Eq. (26) or Eq. (27), given that these upper bounds hold for any settings of values the variational parameters λ_i^U, they hold in particular for optimizing settings of the parameters. That is, we can treat the right-hand side of Eq. (26) or the right-hand side Eq. (27) as a function to be minimized with respect to λ_i^U. In the latter case, this optimization process will induce interdependencies between the parameters λ_i^U. These interdependencies are desirable; indeed they are critical for obtaining a good variational bound on the marginal probability of interest. In particular, the best global bounds are obtained when the probabilistic dependencies in the distribution are reflected in dependencies in the approximation.

To clarify the nature of variational bounds, note that there is an important distinction to be made between joint probabilities (Eq. (26)) and marginal probabilities (Eq. (27)). In Eq. (26), if we allow the variational parameters to be set optimally for each value of the argument S, then it is possible (in principle) to find optimizing settings of the variational parameters that recover the exact value of the joint probability. (Here we assume that the local probabilities $P(S_i|S_{\pi(i)})$ can be represented exactly via a variational transformation, as in the examples discussed in Section 4.1). In Eq. (27), on the other hand, we are *not* generally able to recover exact values of the marginal by optimizing over variational parameters that depend only on the argument E. Consider, for example, the case of a node $S_i \in E$ that has parents in H. As we range across $\{H\}$ there will be summands on the right-hand side of Eq. (27) that will involve evaluating the local probability $P(S_i|S_{\pi(i)})$ for different values of the parents $S_{\pi(i)}$. If the variational parameter λ_i^U depends only on E, we cannot in general expect to obtain an exact representation for $P(S_i|S_{\pi(i)})$ in each summand. Thus, some of the summands in Eq. (27) are necessarily bounds and not exact values.

This observation provides a bit of insight into reasons why a variational bound might be expected to be tight in some circumstances and loose in others. In particular, if $P(S_i|S_{\pi(i)})$ is nearly constant as we range across $S_{\pi(i)}$, or if we are operating at a point where the variational representation is fairly insensitive to the setting of λ_i^U (for example the right-hand side of the logarithm in Fig. 14), then the bounds may be expected to be tight. On the other hand, if these conditions are not present one might expect that the bound would be loose. However the situation is complicated by the interdependencies between the λ_i^U that are induced during the optimization process. We will return to these issues in the discussion.

Although we have discussed upper bounds, similar comments apply to lower bounds, and to marginal probabilities obtained from lower bounds on the joint distribution.

The conditional distribution $P(H|E)$, on the other hand, is the ratio of two marginal distributions; i.e., $P(H|E) = P(H, E)/P(E)$.[9] To obtain upper and lower bounds on the conditional distribution, we must have upper and lower bounds on both the numerator and the denominator. Generally speaking, however, if we can obtain upper and lower bounds on the denominator, then our labor is essentially finished, because the numerator involves fewer sums. Indeed, in the case in which $S = H \cup E$, the numerator involves no sums and is simply a function evaluation.

Finally, it is worth noting that variational methods can also be of interest simply as tractable approximations rather than as methods that provide strict bounds (much as sampling methods are used). One way to do this is to obtain a variational approximation that is a bound for a *marginal* probability, and to substitute the variational parameters thus obtained into the *conditional* probability distribution. Thus, for example, we might obtain a lower bound on the likelihood $P(E)$ by fitting variational parameters. We can substitute these parameters into the parameterized variational form for $P(H, E)$ and then utilize this variational form to calculate an approximation to $P(H|E)$.

In the following sections we will illustrate the general variational framework as it has been applied in a number of worked-out examples. All of these examples involve architectures of practical interest and provide concrete examples of variational methodology. To a certain degree the examples also serve as case histories that can be generalized to related architectures. It is important to emphasize, however, that it is not necessarily straightforward to develop a variational approximation for a new architecture. The ease and the utility of applying the methods outlined in this section depend on architectural details, including the choice of node probability functions, the graph topology and the particular parameter regime in which the model is operated. In particular, certain choices of node conditional probability functions lend themselves more readily than others to variational transformations that have useful algebraic properties. Also, certain architectures simplify more readily under variational transformation than others; in particular, the marginal bounds in Eq. (27) are simple functions in some cases and complex in others. These issues are currently not well understood and the development of effective variational approximations can in some cases require substantial creativity.

---

[9]Note that we treat $P(H, E)$ in general as a marginal probability; that is, we do not necessarily assume that H and E jointly exhaust the set of nodes S.

4.4. SEQUENTIAL AND BLOCK METHODS

Let us now consider in somewhat more detail how variational methods can be applied to probabilistic inference problems. The basic idea is that suggested above—we wish to simplify the joint probability distribution by transforming the local probability functions. By an appropriate choice of variational transformation, we can simplify the form of the joint probability distribution and thereby simplify the inference problem. We can transform some or all of the nodes. The cost of performing such transformations is that we obtain bounds or approximations to the probabilities rather than exact results.

The option of transforming only some of the nodes is important; it implies a role for the exact methods as subroutines within a variational approximation. In particular, partial transformations of the graph may leave some of the original graphical structure intact and/or introduce new graphical structure to which exact methods can be fruitfully applied. In general, we wish to use variational approximations in a limited way, transforming the graph into a simplified graph to which exact methods can be applied. This will in general yield tighter bounds than an algorithm that transforms the entire graph without regard for computationally tractable substructure.

The majority of variational algorithms proposed in the literature to date can be divided into two main classes: *sequential* and *block*. In the sequential approach, nodes are transformed in an order that is determined during the inference process. This approach has the advantage of flexibility and generality, allowing the particular pattern of evidence to determine the best choices of nodes to transform. In some cases, however, particularly when there are obvious substructures in a graph which are amenable to exact methods, it can be advantageous to designate in advance the nodes to be transformed. We will see that this block approach is particularly natural in the setting of parameter estimation.

5. The sequential approach

The sequential approach introduces variational transformations for the nodes in a particular order. The goal is to transform the network until the resulting transformed network is amenable to exact methods. As we will see in the examples below, certain variational transformations can be understood graphically as a sparsification in which edges are removed from the graph. A series of edge removals eventually renders the graph sufficiently sparse that an exact method becomes applicable. Alternatively, we can variationally transform all of the nodes of the graph and then reinstate the exact node probabilities sequentially while making sure that the resulting graph stays computationally tractable. The first example in the following section illustrates the latter approach and the second example illustrates the former approach.

Many of the exact methods provide tests that bound their run time. For example, one can run a greedy triangulation algorithm to upper bound the run time of the junction tree inference algorithm. If this estimated run time is sufficiently small, in terms of the overall time allotted to the inference procedure, the system can stop introducing variational transformations and run the exact procedure.

Ideally the choice of the order in which to transform nodes would be made optimally, that is, an ordering of the nodes would be chosen so that the resulting graph would be as simple as possible at each step (in particular, such that the maximal clique of the resulting triangulated graph would be as small as possible). Thus is a difficult problem, particularly given that a single ordering is unlikely to produce the simplest graph at each step; that is, different partial orders must be considered. In the literature to date heuristic procedures have been used to choose node orderings.

The sequential approach is perhaps best presented in the context of a specific example. In the following section we return to the QMR-DT network and show how a sequential variational approach can be used for inference in this network.

5.1. THE QMR-DT NETWORK

Jaakkola and Jordan (1997c) present an application of sequential variational methods to the QMR-DT network. As we have seen, the QMR-DT network is a bipartite graph in which the conditional probabilities for the findings are based on the noisy-OR model (Eq. (8) for the negative findings and Eq. (9) for the positive findings). Note that symptom nodes that are not findings—i.e., symptoms that are not observed—can simply be marginalized out of the joint distribution by omission and therefore they have no impact on inference. Moreover, as we have discussed, the negative findings present no difficulties for inference—given the exponential form of the probability in Eq. (8), the effects of negative findings on the disease probabilities can be handled in linear time. Let us therefore assume that the updates associated with the negative findings have already been made and focus on the problem of performing inference when there are positive findings.

Repeating Eq. (9) for convenience, we have the following representation for the probability of a positive finding:

$$P(f_i = 1|d) = 1 - e^{-\sum_{j \in \pi(i)} \theta_{ij} d_j - \theta_{i0}} \tag{28}$$

The function $1 - e^{-x}$ is log concave; thus, as in the case of the logistic function, we are able to express the variational upper bound in terms of

diseases

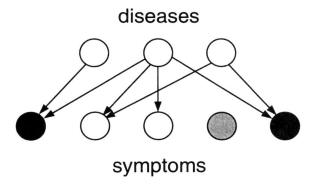

symptoms

Figure 17.   The QMR-DT graph after the lightly shaded finding has been subjected to a variational transformation. The effect is equivalent to delinking the node from the graph.

the exponential of a linear function. In particular:

$$1 - e^{-x} \le e^{\lambda x - f^*(\lambda)}, \tag{29}$$

where the conjugate function is as follows:

$$f^*(\lambda) = -\lambda \ln \lambda + (\lambda + 1) \ln(\lambda + 1). \tag{30}$$

Plugging the argument of Eq. (28) into Eq. (29), and noting that we need a different variational parameter λ_i for each transformed node, we obtain:

$$P(f_i = 1|d) \le e^{\lambda_i \left(\sum_{j \in \pi(i)} \theta_{ij} d_j + \theta_{i0} \right) - f^*(\lambda_i)} \tag{31}$$

$$= e^{\lambda_i \theta_{i0} - f^*(\lambda_i)} \prod_{j \in \pi(i)} \left[e^{\lambda_i \theta_{ij}} \right]^{d_j}. \tag{32}$$

The final equation displays the effect of the variational transformation. The exponential factor outside of the product is simply a constant. The product is taken over all nodes in the parent set for node i, but unlike the case in which the graph is moralized for exact computation, the contributions associated with the d_j nodes are uncoupled. That is, each factor $\exp(\lambda_i \theta_{ij})$ is simply a constant that is multiplied into the probability that was previously associated with node d_j (for $d_j = 1$). There is no coupling of d_j and d_k nodes as there would be if we had taken products of the untransformed noisy-OR. The graphical effect of the variational transformation is shown in Fig. 17; we see that the variational transformation essentially delinks the ith finding from the graph. In our particular example, the graph is now rendered singly connected and an exact inference algorithm can be invoked. (Recall that marginalizing over the *unobserved* symptoms simply removes them from the graph).

The sequential methodology utilized by Jaakkola and Jordan for inference in the QMR-DT network actually proceeds in the opposite direction. They first transform all of the nodes in the graph. They then make use of a simple heuristic to choose the ordering of nodes to reinstate, basing the choice on the effect of reinstating each node individually starting from the completely transformed state. (Despite the suboptimality of this heuristic, they found that it yielded an approximation that was orders of magnitude more accurate than that of an algorithm that used a random ordering). The algorithm then proceeds as follows: (1) Pick a node to reinstate, and consider the effect of reintroducing the links associated with the node into the current graph. (2) If the resulting graph is still amenable to exact methods, reinstate the node and iterate. Otherwise stop and run an exact method. Finally, (3) we must also choose the parameters λ_i so as to make the approximation as tight as possible. It is not difficult to verify that products of the expression in Eq. (32) yield an overall bound that is a convex function of the λ_i parameters (Jaakkola & Jordan, 1997c). Thus standard optimization algorithms can be used to find good choices for the λ_i.

Jaakkola and Jordan (1997c) presented results for approximate inference on the "CPC cases" that were mentioned earlier. These are difficult cases which have up to 100 positive findings. Their study was restricted to upper bounds because it was found that the simple lower bounds that they tried were not sufficiently tight. They used the upper bounds to determine variational parameters that were subsequently used to form an approximation to the conditional posterior probability. They found that the variational approach yielded reasonably accurate approximations to the conditional posterior probabilities for the CPC cases, and did so within less than a minute of computer time.

5.2. THE BOLTZMANN MACHINE

Let us now consider a rather different example. As we have discussed, the Boltzmann machine is a special subset of the class of undirected graphical models in which the potential functions are composed of products of quadratic and linear "Boltzmann factors." Jaakkola and Jordan (1997a) introduced a sequential variational algorithm for approximate inference in the Boltzmann machine. Their method, which we discuss in this section, yields both upper and lower bounds on marginal and conditional probabilities of interest.

Recall the form of the joint probability distribution for the Boltzmann machine:

$$P(S) = \frac{e^{\sum_{i<j} \theta_{ij} S_i S_j + \sum_i \theta_{i0} S_i}}{Z}. \tag{33}$$

To obtain marginal probabilities such as $P(E)$ under this joint distribution, we must calculate sums over exponentials of quadratic energy functions. Moreover, to obtain conditional probabilities such as $P(H|E) = P(H, E)/P(E)$, we take ratios of such sums, where the numerator requires fewer sums than the denominator. The most general such sum is the partition function itself, which is a sum over *all* configurations $\{S\}$. Let us therefore focus on upper and lower bounds for the partition function as the general case; this allows us to calculate bounds on any other marginals or conditionals of interest.

Our approach is to perform the sums one sum at a time, introducing variational transformations to ensure that the resulting expression stays computationally tractable. In fact, at every step of the process that we describe, the transformed potentials involve no more than quadratic Boltzmann factors. (Exact methods can be viewed as creating increasingly higher-order terms when the marginalizing sums are performed). Thus the transformed Boltzmann machine remains a Boltzmann machine.

Let us first consider lower bounds. We write the partition function as follows:

$$\sum_{\{S\}} e^{\sum_{j<k} \theta_{jk} S_j S_k + \sum_j \theta_{j0} S_j} = \sum_{\{S \setminus S_i\}} \sum_{S_i \in \{0,1\}} e^{\sum_{j<k} \theta_{jk} S_j S_k + \sum_j \theta_{j0} S_j}, \quad (34)$$

and attempt to find a tractable lower bound on the inner summand over S_i on the right-hand side. It is not difficult to show that this expression is log convex. Thus we bound its logarithm variationally:

$$\ln \left(\sum_{S_i \in \{0,1\}} e^{\sum_{j<k} \theta_{jk} S_j S_k + \sum_j \theta_{j0} S_j} \right)$$

$$= \sum_{\{j<k\} \neq i} \theta_{jk} S_j S_k + \sum_{j \neq i} \theta_{j0} S_j + \ln \left(\sum_{S_i \in \{0,1\}} e^{\sum_{j \neq i} \theta_{ij} S_i S_j + \theta_{i0} S_i} \right)$$

$$= \sum_{\{j<k\} \neq i} \theta_{jk} S_j S_k + \sum_{j \neq i} \theta_{j0} S_j + \ln \left(1 + e^{\sum_{j \neq i} \theta_{ij} S_j + \theta_{i0}} \right) \quad (35)$$

$$\geq \sum_{\{j<k\} \neq i} \theta_{jk} S_j S_k + \sum_{j \neq i} \theta_{j0} S_j + \lambda_i^L \left(\sum_{j \neq i} \theta_{ij} S_j + \theta_{i0} \right) + H(\lambda_i^L), \quad (36)$$

where the sum in the first term on the right-hand side is a sum over all pairs $j < k$ such that neither j nor k is equal to i, where $H(\cdot)$ is as before the binary entropy function, and where λ_i^L is the variational parameter associated with node S_i. In the first line we have simply pulled outside of the sum all of those terms not involving S_i, and in the second line we

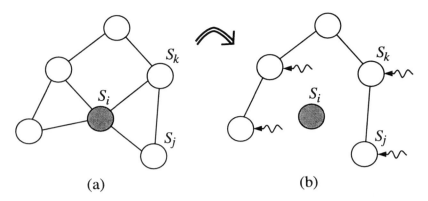

Figure 18.   The transformation of the Boltzmann machine under the approximate marginalization over node S_i for the case of lower bounds. (a) The Boltzmann machine before the transformation. (b) The Boltzmann machine after the transformation, where S_i has become delinked. All of the pairwise parameters, θ_{jk}, for j and k not equal to i, have remained unaltered. As suggested by the wavy lines, the linear coefficients have changed for those nodes that were neighbors of S_i.

have performed the sum over the two values of S_i. Finally, to lower bound the expression in Eq. (35) we need only lower bound the term $\ln(1 + e^x)$ on the right-hand side. But we have already found variational bounds for a related expression in treating the logistic function; recall Eq. (18). The upper bound in that case translates into the lower bound in the current case:

$$\ln(1 + e^{-x}) \geq \lambda x + H(\lambda). \tag{37}$$

This is the bound that we have utilized in Eq. (36).

Let us consider the graphical consequences of the bound in Eq. (36) (see Fig. 18). Note that for all nodes in the graph other than node S_i and its neighbors, the Boltzmann factors are unaltered (see the first two terms in the bound). Thus the graph is unaltered for such nodes. From the term in parentheses we see that the neighbors of node S_i have been endowed with new linear terms; importantly, however, these nodes have not become linked (as they would have become if we had done the exact marginalization). Neighbors that were linked previously remain linked with the same θ_{jk} parameter. Node S_i is absent from the transformed partition function and thus absent from the graph, but it has left its trace via the new linear Boltzmann factors associated with its neighbors. We can summarize the effects of the transformation by noting that the transformed graph is a new Boltzmann machine with one fewer node and the following parameters:

$$\tilde{\theta}_{jk} = \theta_{jk} \qquad\qquad j, k \neq i$$
$$\tilde{\theta}_{j0} = \theta_{j0} + \lambda_i^L \theta_{ij} \qquad\qquad j \neq i .$$

Note finally that we also have a constant term $\lambda_i^L \theta_{i0} + H(\lambda_i^L)$ to keep track of. This term will have an interesting interpretation when we return to the Boltzmann machine later in the context of block methods.

Upper bounds are obtained in a similar way. We again break the partition function into a sum over a particular node S_i and a sum over the configurations of the remaining nodes $S \backslash S_i$. Moreover, the first three lines of the ensuing derivation leading to Eq. (35) are identical. To complete the derivation we now find an upper bound on $\ln(1 + e^x)$. Jaakkola and Jordan (1997a) proposed using quadratic bounds for this purpose. In particular, they noted that:

$$\ln(1 + e^x) = \ln(e^{x/2} + e^{-x/2}) + x/2 \qquad (38)$$

and that $\ln(e^{x/2} + e^{-x/2})$ is a concave function of x^2 (as can be verified by taking the second derivative with respect to x^2). This implies that $\ln(1 + e^x)$ must have a quadratic upper bound of the following form:

$$\ln(1 + e^x) \leq \lambda x^2 + x/2 - \bar{g}^*(\lambda). \qquad (39)$$

where $\bar{g}^*(\lambda)$ is an appropriately defined conjugate function. Using these upper bounds in Eq. (35) we obtain:

$$\ln\left(\sum_{S_i \in \{0,1\}} e^{\sum_{j<k} \theta_{jk} S_j S_k + \sum_j \theta_{j0} S_j}\right) \leq \sum_{\{j<k\} \neq i} \theta_{jk} S_j S_k + \sum_{j \neq i} \theta_{j0} S_j$$
$$+ \lambda_i^U \left(\sum_{j \neq i} \theta_{ij} S_j + \theta_{i0}\right)^2 + \frac{1}{2}\left(\sum_{j \neq i} \theta_{ij} S_j + \theta_{i0}\right) - \bar{g}^*(\lambda_i^U), \qquad (40)$$

where λ_i^U is the variational parameter associated with node S_i.

The graphical consequences of this transformation are somewhat different than those of the lower bounds (see Fig. 19). Considering the first two terms in the bound, we see that it is still the case that the graph is unaltered for all nodes in the graph other than node S_i and its neighbors, and moreover neighbors of S_i that were previously linked remain linked. The quadratic term, however, gives rise to new links between the previously unlinked neighbors of node S_i and alters the parameters between previously linked neighbors. Each of these nodes also acquires a new linear term. Expanding Eq. (40) and collecting terms, we see that the approximate marginalization has yielded a Boltzmann machine with the following parameters:

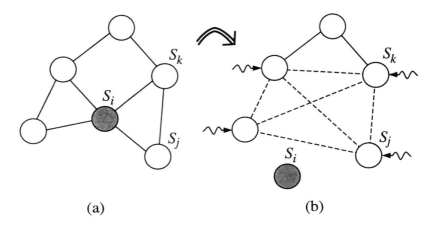

(a)   (b)

Figure 19.   The transformation of the Boltzmann machine under the approximate marginalization over node S_i for the case of upper bounds. (a) The Boltzmann machine before the transformation. (b) The Boltzmann machine after the transformation, where S_i has become delinked. As the dashed edges suggest, all of the neighbors of S_i have become linked and those that were formerly linked have new parameter values. As suggested by the wavy lines, the neighbors of S_i also have new linear coefficients. All other edges and parameters are unaltered.

$$\tilde{\theta}_{jk} = \theta_{jk} + 2\lambda_i^U \theta_{ji}\theta_{ik} \qquad\qquad j,k \neq i$$
$$\tilde{\theta}_{j0} = \theta_{j0} + \theta_{ij}/2 + 2\lambda_i^U \theta_{i0}\theta_{ij} + \lambda_i^U \theta_{ij}^2 \qquad j \neq i\ .$$

Finally, the constant term is given by $\theta_{i0}/2 + \lambda_i^U \theta_{i0}^2 - \bar{g}^*(\lambda_i^U)$.

The graphical consequences of the lower and upper bound transformations also have computational consequences. In particular, given that the lower bound transformation introduces no additional links when nodes are delinked, it is somewhat more natural to combine these transformations with exact methods. In particular, the algorithm simply delinks nodes until a tractable structure (such as a tree) is revealed; at this point an exact algorithm is called as a subroutine. The upper bound transformation, on the other hand, by introducing links between the neighbors of a delinked node, does not reveal tractable structure as readily. This seeming disadvantage is mitigated by the fact that the upper bound is a tighter bound (Jaakkola & Jordan, 1997a).

6. The block approach

An alternative approach to variational inference is to designate in advance a set of nodes that are to be transformed. We can in principle view this "block approach" as an off-line application of the sequential approach. In the case of lower bounds, however, there are advantages to be gained by developing a methodology that is specific to block transformation. In this section, we show that a natural global measure of approximation accuracy can be obtained for lower bounds via a block version of the variational formalism. The method meshes readily with exact methods in cases in which tractable substructure can be identified in the graph. This approach was first presented by Saul and Jordan (1996), as a refined version of mean field theory for Markov random fields, and has been developed further in a number of recent studies (e.g., Ghahramani & Jordan, 1997; Ghahramani & Hinton, 1996; Jordan, et al., 1997).

In the block approach, we begin by identifying a substructure in the graph of interest that we know is amenable to exact inference methods (or, more generally, to efficient approximate inference methods). For example, we might pick out a tree or a set of chains in the original graph. We wish to use this simplified structure to approximate the probability distribution on the original graph. To do so, we consider a family of probability distributions that are obtained from the simplified graph via the introduction of variational parameters. We choose a particular approximating distribution from the simplifying family by making a particular choice for the variational parameters. As in the sequential approach a new choice of variational parameters must be made each time new evidence is available.

More formally, let $P(S)$ represent the joint distribution on the graphical model of interest, where as before S represents all of the nodes of the graph and H and E are disjoint subsets of S representing the hidden nodes and the evidence nodes, respectively. We wish to approximate the conditional probability $P(H|E)$. We introduce an approximating family of conditional probability distributions, $Q(H|E, \lambda)$, where λ are variational parameters. The graph representing Q is not generally the same as the graph representing P; generally it is a sub-graph. From the family of approximating distributions Q, we choose a particular distribution by minimizing the Kullback-Leibler (KL) divergence, $D(Q\|P)$, with respect to the variational parameters:

$$\lambda^* = \mathrm{argmin}_\lambda \; D(Q(H|E, \lambda) \; \| \; P(H|E)), \tag{41}$$

where for any probability distributions $Q(S)$ and $P(S)$ the KL divergence is defined as follows:

$$D(Q\|P) = \sum_{\{S\}} Q(S) \ln \frac{Q(S)}{P(S)}. \tag{42}$$

The minimizing values of the variational parameters, λ^*, define a particular distribution, $Q(H|E, \lambda^*)$, that we treat as the best approximation of $P(H|E)$ in the family $Q(H|E, \lambda)$.

One simple justification for using the KL divergence as a measure of approximation accuracy is that it yields the best *lower bound* on the probability of the evidence $P(E)$ (i.e., the likelihood) in the family of approximations $Q(H|E, \lambda)$. Indeed, we bound the logarithm of $P(E)$ using Jensen's inequality as follows:

$$
\begin{aligned}
\ln P(E) &= \ln \sum_{\{H\}} P(H, E) \\
&= \ln \sum_{\{H\}} Q(H|E) \cdot \frac{P(H, E)}{Q(H|E)} \\
&\geq \sum_{\{H\}} Q(H|E) \ln \left[\frac{P(H, E)}{Q(H|E)} \right].
\end{aligned}
\tag{43}
$$

The difference between the left and right hand sides of this equation is easily seen to be the KL divergence $D(Q\|P)$. Thus, by the positivity of the KL divergence (Cover & Thomas, 1991), the right-hand side of Eq. (43) is a lower bound on $P(E)$. Moreover, by choosing λ according to Eq. (41), we obtain the tightest lower bound.

6.1. CONVEX DUALITY AND THE KL DIVERGENCE

We can also justify the choice of KL divergence by making an appeal to convex duality theory, thereby linking the block approach with the sequential approach (Jaakkola, 1997). Consider, for simplicity, the case of discrete-valued nodes H. The distribution $Q(H|E, \lambda)$ can be viewed as a vector of real numbers, one for each configuration of the variables H. Treat this vector as the vector-valued variational parameter "λ" in Eq. (23). Moreover, the log probability $\ln P(H, E)$ can also be viewed as a vector of real numbers, defined on the set of configurations of H. Treat this vector as the variable "x" in Eq. (23). Finally, define $f(x)$ to be $\ln P(E)$. It can be verified that the following expression for $\ln P(E)$:

$$
\ln P(E) = \ln \left(\sum_{\{H\}} e^{\ln P(H, E)} \right)
\tag{44}
$$

is indeed convex in the values $\ln P(H, E)$. Moreover, by direct substitution in Eq. (23):

$$
f^*(Q) = \min \left\{ \sum_{\{H\}} Q(H|E, \lambda) \ln P(H, E) - \ln P(E) \right\}
\tag{45}
$$

and minimizing with respect to $\ln P(H, E)$, the conjugate function $f^*(Q)$ is seen to be the negative entropy function $\sum_{\{H\}} Q(H|E) \ln Q(H|E)$. Thus, using Eq. (23), we can lower bound the log likelihood as follows:

$$\ln P(E) \geq \sum_{\{H\}} Q(H|E) \ln P(H, E) - Q(H|E) \ln Q(H|E) \qquad (46)$$

This is identical to Eq. (43). Moreover, we see that we could in principle recover the exact log likelihood if Q were allowed to range over all probability distributions $Q(H|E)$. By ranging over a parameterized family $Q(H|E, \lambda)$, we obtain the tightest lower bound that is available within the family.

6.2. PARAMETER ESTIMATION VIA VARIATIONAL METHODS

Neal and Hinton (this volume) have pointed out that the lower bound in Eq. (46) has a useful role to play in the context of maximum likelihood parameter estimation. In particular, they make a link between this lower bound and parameter estimation via the EM algorithm.

Let us augment our notation to include parameters θ in the specification of the joint probability distribution $P(S|\theta)$. As before, we designate a subset of the nodes E as the observed evidence. The marginal probability $P(E|\theta)$, thought of as a function of θ, is known as the *likelihood*. The EM algorithm is a method for maximum likelihood parameter estimation that hillclimbs in the log likelihood. It does so by making use of the convexity relationship between $\ln P(H, E|\theta)$ and $\ln P(E|\theta)$ described in the previous section.

In Section 6 we showed that the function

$$\mathcal{L}(Q, \theta) = \sum_{\{H\}} Q(H|E) \ln P(H, E|\theta) - Q(H|E) \ln Q(H|E) \qquad (47)$$

is a lower bound on the log likelihood for any probability distribution $Q(H|E)$. Moreover, we showed that the difference between $\ln P(E|\theta)$ and the bound $\mathcal{L}(Q, \theta)$ is the KL divergence between $Q(H|E)$ and $P(H|E)$. Suppose now that we allow $Q(H|E)$ to range over all possible probability distributions on H and minimize the KL divergence. It is a standard result (cf. Cover & Thomas, 1991) that the KL divergence is minimized by choosing $Q(H|E) = P(H|E, \theta)$, and that the minimal value is zero. This is verified by substituting $P(H|E, \theta)$ into the right-hand side of Eq. (47) and recovering $\ln P(E|\theta)$.

This suggests the following algorithm. Starting from an initial parameter vector $\theta^{(0)}$, we iterate the following two steps, known as the "E (expectation) step" and the "M (maximization) step." First, we maximize the bound $\mathcal{L}(Q, \theta)$ with respect to probability distributions Q. Second, we fix

Q and maximize the bound $\mathcal{L}(Q, \theta)$ with respect to the parameters θ. More formally, we have:

$$(\text{E step}): \quad Q^{(k+1)} = \text{argmax}_Q \; \mathcal{L}(Q, \theta^{(k)}) \qquad (48)$$

$$(\text{M step}): \quad \theta^{(k+1)} = \text{argmax}_\theta \; \mathcal{L}(Q^{(k+1)}, \theta) \qquad (49)$$

which is coordinate ascent in $\mathcal{L}(Q, \theta)$.

This can be related to the traditional presentation of the EM algorithm (Dempster, Laird, & Rubin, 1977) by noting that for fixed Q, the right-hand side of Eq. (47) is a function of θ only through the $\ln P(H, E|\theta)$ term. Thus maximizing $\mathcal{L}(Q, \theta)$ with respect to θ in the M step is equivalent to maximizing the following function:

$$\sum_{\{H\}} P(H|E, \theta^{(k)}) \ln P(H, E|\theta). \qquad (50)$$

Maximization of this function, known as the "complete log likelihood" in the EM literature, defines the M step in the traditional presentation of EM.

Let us now return to the situation in which we are unable to compute the full conditional distribution $P(H|E, \theta)$. In such cases variational methodology suggests that we consider a family of approximating distributions. Although we are no longer able to perform a true EM iteration given that we cannot avail ourselves of $P(H|E, \theta)$, we can still perform coordinate ascent in the lower bound $\mathcal{L}(Q, \theta)$. Indeed, the variational strategy of minimizing the KL divergence with respect to the variational parameters that define the approximating family is exactly a restricted form of coordinate ascent in the first argument of $\mathcal{L}(Q, \theta)$. We then follow this step by an "M step" that increases the lower bound with respect to the parameters θ.

This point of view, which can be viewed as a computationally tractable approximation to the EM algorithm, has been exploited in a number of recent architectures, including the sigmoid belief network, factorial hidden Markov model and hidden Markov decision tree architectures that we discuss in the following sections, as well as the "Helmholtz machine" of Dayan, et al. (1995) and Hinton, et al. (1995).

6.3. EXAMPLES

We now return to the problem of picking a tractable variational parameterization for a given graphical model. We wish to pick a simplified graph which is both rich enough to provide distributions that are close to the true distribution, and simple enough so that an exact algorithm can be utilized efficiently for calculations under the approximate distribution. Similar considerations hold for the variational parameterization: the variational parameterization must be representationally rich so that good approximations

are available and yet simple enough so that a procedure that minimizes the
KL divergence has some hope of finding good parameters and not getting
stuck in a local minimum. It is not necessarily possible to realize all of these
desiderata simultaneously; however, in a number of cases it has been found
that relatively simple variational approximations can yield reasonably accurate solutions. In this section we discuss several such examples.

6.3.1. *Mean field Boltzmann machine*

In Section 5.2 we discussed a sequential variational algorithm that yielded
upper and lower bounds for the Boltzmann machine. We now revisit the
Boltzmann machine within the context of the block approach and discuss
lower bounds. We also relate the two approaches.

Recall that the joint probability for the Boltzmann machine can be
written as follows:

$$P(S|\theta) = \frac{e^{\sum_{i<j} \theta_{ij} S_i S_j + \sum_i \theta_{i0} S_i}}{Z}, \tag{51}$$

where $\theta_{ij} = 0$ for nodes S_i and S_j that are not neighbors in the graph.
Consider now the representation of the conditional distribution $P(H|E,\theta)$
in a Boltzmann machine. For nodes $S_i \in E$ and $S_j \in E$, the contribution
$\theta_{ij} S_i S_j$ reduces to a constant, which vanishes when we normalize. If $S_i \in$
H and $S_j \in E$, the quadratic contribution becomes a linear contribution
that we associate with node S_i. Finally, linear terms associated with nodes
$S_i \in E$ also become constants and vanish. In summary, we can express the
conditional distribution $P(H|E,\theta)$ as follows:

$$P(H|E,\theta) = \frac{e^{\sum_{i<j} \theta_{ij} S_i S_j + \sum_i \theta_{i0}^c S_i}}{Z_c}, \tag{52}$$

where the sums are restricted to range over nodes in H and the updated
parameters θ_{i0}^c include contributions associated with the evidence nodes:

$$\theta_{i0}^c = \theta_{i0} + \sum_{j \in E} \theta_{ij} S_j. \tag{53}$$

The updated partition function Z_c is given as follows:

$$Z_c = \sum_{\{H\}} \left\{ e^{\sum_{i<j} \theta_{ij} S_i S_j + \sum_i \theta_{i0}^c S_i} \right\}. \tag{54}$$

In sum, we have a Boltzmann machine on the subset H.

The "mean field" approximation (Peterson & Anderson, 1987) for Boltzmann machines is a particular form of variational approximation in which a

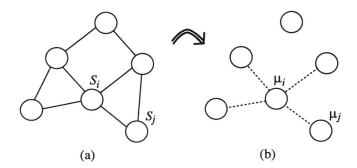

Figure 20.   (a) A node S_i in a Boltzmann machine with its Markov blanket. (b) The approximating mean field distribution Q is based on a graph with no edges. The mean field equations yield a deterministic relationship, represented in the figure with the dotted lines, between the variational parameters μ_i and μ_j for nodes j in the Markov blanket of node i.

completely factorized distribution is used to approximate $P(H|E,\theta)$. That is, we consider the simplest possible approximating distribution; one that is obtained by dropping *all* of the edges in the Boltzmann graph (see Fig. 20). For this choice of $Q(H|E,\mu)$, (where we now use μ to represent the variational parameters), we have little choice as to the variational parameterization—to represent as large an approximating family as possible we endow each degree of freedom S_i with its own variational parameter μ_i. Thus Q can be written as follows:

$$Q(H|E,\mu) = \prod_{i \in H} \mu_i^{S_i}(1 - \mu_i)^{1-S_i}, \tag{55}$$

where the product is taken over the hidden nodes H.

Forming the KL divergence between the fully factorized Q distribution and the P distribution in Eq. (52), we obtain:

$$D(Q\|P) = \sum_i [\mu_i \ln \mu_i + (1 - \mu_i)\ln(1 - \mu_i)]$$

$$- \sum_{i<j} \theta_{ij}\mu_i\mu_j - \sum_i \theta_{i0}^c \mu_i + \ln Z_c, \tag{56}$$

where the sums range across nodes in H. In deriving this result we have used the fact that, under the Q distribution, S_i and S_j are independent random variables with mean values μ_i and μ_j.

We now take derivatives of the KL divergence with respect to μ_i—noting that Z_c is independent of μ_i—and set the derivative to zero to obtain the following equations:

$$\mu_i = \sigma\left(\sum_j \theta_{ij}\mu_j + \theta_{i0}\right), \tag{57}$$

where $\sigma(z) = 1/(1 + e^{-z})$ is the logistic function and we define θ_{ij} equal to θ_{ji} for $j < i$. Eq. (57) defines a set of coupled equations known as the "mean field equations." These equations are solved iteratively for a fixed point solution. Note that each variational parameter μ_i updates its value based on a sum across the variational parameters in its Markov blanket (cf. Fig. 20b). This can be viewed as a variational form of a local message passing algorithm.

The mean field approximation for Boltzmann machines can provide a reasonably good approximation to conditional distributions in dense Boltzmann machines, and is the basis of a useful approach to combinatorial optimization known as "deterministic annealing." There are also cases, however, in which it is known to break down. These cases include sparse Boltzmann machines and Boltzmann machines with "frustrated" interactions; these are networks whose potential functions embody constraints between neighboring nodes that cannot be simultaneously satisfied (see also Galland, 1993). In the case of sparse networks, exact algorithms can provide help; indeed, this observation led to the use of exact algorithms as subroutines within the "structured mean field" approach pursued by Saul and Jordan (1996).

Let us now consider the parameter estimation problem for Boltzmann machines. Writing out the lower bound in Eq. (47) for this case, we have:

$$\ln P(E|\theta) \geq \sum_{i<j} \theta_{ij} \mu_i \mu_j + \sum_i \theta_{i0}^c \mu_i - \ln Z$$
$$- \sum_i [\mu_i \ln \mu_i + (1 - \mu_i) \ln(1 - \mu_i)] \tag{58}$$

Taking the derivative with respect to θ_{ij} yields a gradient which has a simple "Hebbian" term $\mu_i \mu_j$ as well as a contribution from the derivative of $\ln Z$ with respect to θ_{ij}. It is not hard to show that this derivative is $\langle S_i S_j \rangle$; where the brackets signify an average with respect to the unconditional distribution $P(S|\theta)$. Thus we have the following gradient algorithm for performing an approximate M step:

$$\Delta \theta_{ij} \propto (\mu_i \mu_j - \langle S_i S_j \rangle). \tag{59}$$

Unfortunately, however, given our assumption that calculations under the Boltzmann distribution are intractable for the graph under consideration, it is intractable to compute the unconditional average. We can once again appeal to mean field theory and compute an approximation to $\langle S_i S_j \rangle$, where we now use a factorized distribution on all of the nodes; however, the M step is now a difference of gradients of two different bounds and is therefore no longer guaranteed to increase $\mathcal{L}$. There is a more serious problem, moreover, which is particularly salient in unsupervised learning problems. If the data set of interest is a heterogeneous collection of sub-populations, such as in unsupervised classification problems, the unconditional distribution will generally be required to have multiple modes. Unfortunately the factorized mean field approximation is unimodal and is a poor approximation for a multi-modal distribution. One approach to this problem is to utilize multi-modal Q distributions within the mean-field framework; for example, Jaakkola and Jordan (this volume) discuss the use of mixture models as approximating distributions.

These issues find a more satisfactory treatment in the context of directed graphs, as we see in the following section. In particular, the gradient for a directed graph (cf. Eq. (68)) does not require averages under the unconditional distribution.

Finally, let us consider the relationship between the mean field approximation and the lower bounds that we obtained via a sequential algorithm in Section 5.2. In fact, if we run the latter algorithm until all nodes are eliminated from the graph, we obtain a bound that is identical to the mean field bound (Jaakkola, 1997). To see this, note that for a Boltzmann machine in which all of the nodes have been eliminated there are no quadratic and linear terms; only the constant terms remain. Recall from Section 5.2 that the constant that arises when node i is removed is $\mu_i^L \hat{\theta}_{i0} + H(\mu_i^L)$, where $\hat{\theta}_{i0}$ refers to the value of θ_{i0} after it has been updated to absorb the linear terms from previously eliminated nodes $j < i$. (Recall that the latter update is given by $\tilde{\theta}_{i0} = \theta_{i0} + \mu_i^L \theta_{ij}$ for the removal of a particular node j). Collecting together such updates for $j < i$, and summing across all nodes i, we find that the resulting constant term is given as follows:

$$\sum_i \left\{ \hat{\theta}_{i0} \mu_i + H(\mu_i) \right\} = \sum_{i<j} \theta_{ij} \mu_i \mu_j + \sum_i \theta_{i0}^c \mu_i$$
$$- \sum_i \left[\mu_i \ln \mu_i + (1 - \mu_i) \ln(1 - \mu_i) \right] \tag{60}$$

This differs from the lower bound in Eq. (58) only by the term $\ln Z$, which disappears when we maximize with respect to μ_i.

6.3.2. *Neural networks*

As discussed in Section 3, the "sigmoid belief network" is essentially a (directed) neural network with graphical model semantics. We utilize the logistic function as the node probability function:

$$P(S_i = 1 | S_{\pi(i)}) = \frac{1}{1 + e^{-\sum_{j \in \pi(i)} \theta_{ij} S_j - \theta_{i0}}}, \tag{61}$$

where we assume that $\theta_{ij} = 0$ unless j is a parent of i. (In particular, $\theta_{ij} \neq 0 \Rightarrow \theta_{ji} = 0$). Noting that the probabilities for both the $S_i = 0$ case and the $S_i = 1$ case can be written in a single expression as follows:

$$P(S_i|S_{\pi(i)}) = \frac{e^{\left(\sum_{j \in \pi(i)} \theta_{ij} S_j + \theta_{i0}\right) S_i}}{1 + e^{\sum_{j \in \pi(i)} \theta_{ij} S_j + \theta_{i0}}}, \qquad (62)$$

we obtain the following representation for the joint distribution:

$$P(S|\theta) = \prod_i \left[\frac{e^{\left(\sum_{j \in \pi(i)} \theta_{ij} S_j + \theta_{i0}\right) S_i}}{1 + e^{\sum_{j \in \pi(i)} \theta_{ij} S_j + \theta_{i0}}} \cdot \right], \qquad (63)$$

We wish to calculate conditional probabilities under this joint distribution.

As we have seen (cf. Fig. 6), inference for general sigmoid belief networks is intractable, and thus it is sensible to consider variational approximations. Saul, Jaakkola, and Jordan (1996) and Saul and Jordan (this volume) have explored the viability of the simple completely factorized distribution. Thus once again we set:

$$Q(H|E,\mu) = \prod_{i \in H} \mu_i^{S_i} (1 - \mu_i)^{1-S_i}, \qquad (64)$$

and attempt to find the best such approximation by varying the parameters μ_i.

The computation of the KL divergence $D(Q\|P)$ proceeds much as it does in the case of the mean field Boltzmann machine. The entropy term $(Q \ln Q)$ is the same as before. The energy term $(Q \ln P)$ is found by taking the logarithm of Eq. (63) and averaging with respect to Q. Putting these results together, we obtain:

$$\begin{aligned}
\ln P(E|\theta) \geq &\sum_{i<j} \theta_{ij} \mu_i \mu_j + \sum_i \theta_{i0}^c \mu_i \\
&- \sum_i \left\langle \ln \left[1 + e^{\sum_{j \in \pi(i)} \theta_{ij} S_j + \theta_{i0}} \right] \right\rangle \\
&- \sum_i [\mu_i \ln(\mu_i) + (1 - \mu_i) \ln(1 - \mu_i)]
\end{aligned} \qquad (65)$$

where $\langle \cdot \rangle$ denotes an average with respect to the Q distribution. Note that, despite the fact that Q is factorized, we are unable to calculate the average of $\ln[1 + e^{z_i}]$, where z_i denotes $\sum_{j \in \pi(i)} \theta_{ij} S_j + \theta_{i0}$. This is an important term which arises directly from the directed nature of the sigmoid belief network (it arises from the denominator of the sigmoid, a factor which is necessary to define the sigmoid as a local conditional probability). To deal with this term, Saul et al. (1996) introduced additional variational parameters ξ_i. These parameters can be viewed as providing a tight form of Jensen's inequality. Note in particular that we require an upper bound on $\langle \ln[1 + e^{z_i}]\rangle$ (given that this term appears with a negative sign in Eq. (65)). Jensen's inequality provides such a bound, however Saul et al. found that this bound was not sufficiently tight and introduced a tighter bound due to Seung (1995). In particular:

$$
\begin{aligned}
\langle \ln[1 + e^{z_i}]\rangle &= \left\langle \ln[e^{\xi_i z_i} e^{-\xi_i z_i}(1 + e^{z_i})]\right\rangle \\
&= \xi_i \langle z_i \rangle + \left\langle \ln[e^{-\xi_i z_i} + e^{(1-\xi_i)z_i}]\right\rangle \\
&\leq \xi_i \langle z_i \rangle + \ln \left\langle e^{-\xi_i z_i} + e^{(1-\xi_i)z_i}\right\rangle,
\end{aligned}
\tag{66}
$$

which reduces to standard Jensen for $\xi_i = 0$. The final result can be utilized directly in Eq. (65) to provide a tractable lower bound on the log likelihood.

Saul and Jordan (this volume) show that in the limiting case of networks in which each hidden node has a large number of parents, so that a central limit theorem can be invoked, the parameter ξ_i has a probabilistic interpretation as the approximate expectation of $\sigma(z_i)$, where $\sigma(\cdot)$ is again the logistic function.

For fixed values of the parameters ξ_i, by differentiating the KL divergence with respect to the variational parameters μ_i, we obtain the following consistency equations:

$$
\mu_i = \sigma \left(\sum_j \theta_{ij}\mu_j + \theta_{i0} + \sum_j \theta_{ji}(\mu_j - \xi_j) + K_{ij} \right)
\tag{67}
$$

where K_{ij} is an expression that depends on node i, its child j, and the other parents (the "co-parents") of node j. Given that the first term is a sum over contributions from the parents of node i, and the second term is a sum over contributions from the children of node i, we see that the consistency equation for a given node again involves contributions from the Markov blanket of the node (see Fig. 21). Thus, as in the case of the Boltzmann machine, we find that the variational parameters are linked via their Markov blankets and the consistency equation (Eq. (67)) can be interpreted as a local message-passing algorithm.

Saul, Jaakkola, and Jordan (1996) and Saul and Jordan (this volume) also show how to update the variational parameters ξ_i. The two papers utilize these parameters in slightly different ways and obtain different update equations. Yet another variational approximation for the sigmoid belief network, including both upper and lower bounds, is presented in Jaakkola and Jordan (1996).

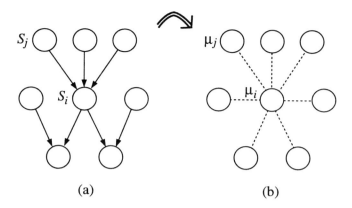

(a)   (b)

Figure 21.   (a) A node S_i in a sigmoid belief network machine with its Markov blanket. (b) The mean field equations yield a deterministic relationship, represented in the figure with the dotted lines, between the variational parameters μ_i and μ_j for nodes j in the Markov blanket of node i.

Finally, we can compute the gradient with respect to the parameters θ_{ij} for fixed variational parameters μ and ξ. The result obtained by Saul and Jordan (this volume) takes the following form:

$$\Delta \theta_{ij} \propto (\mu_i - \xi_i)\mu_j - \theta_{ij}\xi_i(1 - \xi_i)\mu_i(1 - \mu_i). \tag{68}$$

Note that there is no need to calculate variational parameters under the unconditional distribution, $P(S|\theta)$, as in the case of the Boltzmann machine (a fact first noted by Neal, 1992). Note also the interesting appearance of a regularization term—the second term in the equation is a "weight decay" term that is maximal for non-extreme values of the variational parameters (both of these parameters are bounded between zero and one).

Saul, et al. (1996) tested the sigmoid belief network on a handwritten digit recognition problem, obtaining results that were competitive with other supervised learning systems. An important advantage of the graphical model approach is its ability to deal with missing data. Indeed, Saul and Jordan (this volume) report that the degradation in performance with missing pixels in the digits is slight. For further comparative empirical work on sigmoid belief networks and related architectures, including comparisons with Gibbs sampling, see Frey, Hinton, and Dayan (1996).

6.3.3. *Factorial hidden Markov models*
The factorial hidden Markov model (FHMM) is a multiple chain structure (see Fig. 22(a)). Using the notation developed earlier (see Section 3.5), the joint probability distribution for the FHMM is given by:

$$P(\{X_t^{(m)}\}, \{Y_t\}|\theta) =$$

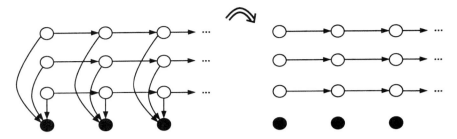

Figure 22. (a) The FHMM. (b) A variational approximation for the FHMM can be obtained by picking out a tractable substructure in the FHMM graph. Parameterizing this graph leads to a family of tractable approximating distributions.

$$\prod_{m=1}^{M} \left[\pi^{(m)}(X_1^{(m)}) \prod_{t=2}^{T} A^{(m)}(X_t^{(m)}|X_{t-1}^{(m)}) \right] \prod_{t=1}^{T} P(Y_t|\{X_t^{(m)}\}_{m=1}^{M}) \quad (69)$$

Computation under this probability distribution is generally infeasible, because, as we saw earlier, the clique size becomes unmanageably large when the FHMM chain structure is moralized and triangulated. Thus it is necessary to consider approximations.

For the FHMM there is a natural substructure on which to base a variational algorithm. In particular, the chains that compose the FHMM are individually tractable. Therefore, rather than removing all of the edges, as in the naive mean field approximation discussed in the previous two sections, it would seem more reasonable to remove only as many edges as are necessary to decouple the chains. In particular, we remove the edges that link the state nodes to the output nodes (see Fig. 22(b)). Without these edges the moralization process no longer links the state nodes and no longer creates large cliques. In fact, the moralization process on the delinked graph in Fig. 22(b) is vacuous, as is the triangulation. Thus the cliques on the delinked graph are of size N^2, where N is the number of states for a single chain. Inference in the approximate graph runs in time $O(MTN^2)$, where M is the number of chains and T is the length of the time series.

Let us now consider how to express a variational approximation using the delinked graph of Fig. 22(b) as an approximation. The idea is to introduce one free parameter into the approximating probability distribution, Q, for each edge that we have dropped. These free parameters, which we denote as $\lambda_t^{(m)}$, essentially serve as surrogates for the effect of the observation at time t on state component m. When we optimize the divergence $D(Q\|P)$ with respect to these parameters they become interdependent; this (deterministic) interdependence can be viewed as an approximation to the probabilistic dependence that is captured in an exact algorithm via the moralization process.

Referring to Fig. 22(b), we write the approximating Q distribution in the following factorized form:

$$Q(\{X_t^{(m)}\}|\{Y_t\},\theta,\lambda) = \prod_{m=1}^{M} \tilde{\pi}^{(m)}(X_1^{(m)}) \prod_{t=2}^{T} \tilde{A}^{(m)}(X_t^{(m)}|X_{t-1}^{(m)}), \qquad (70)$$

where λ is the vector of variational parameters $\lambda_t^{(m)}$. We define the transition matrix $\tilde{A}(m)$ to be the product of the exact transition matrix $A(m)$ and the variational parameter $\lambda_t^{(m)}$:

$$\tilde{A}^{(m)}(X_t^{(m)}|X_{t-1}^{(m)}) = A^{(m)}(X_t^{(m)}|X_{t-1}^{(m)})\lambda_t^{(m)}, \qquad (71)$$

and similarly for the initial state probabilities $\tilde{\pi}^{(m)}$:

$$\tilde{\pi}^{(m)}(X_1^{(m)}) = \pi^{(m)}(X_1^{(m)})\lambda_1^{(m)}. \qquad (72)$$

This family of distributions respects the conditional independence statements of the approximate graph in Fig. 22, and provides additional degrees of freedom via the variational parameters.

Ghahramani and Jordan (1997) present the equations that result from minimizing the KL divergence between the approximating probability distribution (Eq. (70)) and the true probability distribution (Eq. (69)). The result can be summarized as follows. As in the other architectures that we have discussed, the equation for a variational parameter $(\lambda_t^{(m)})$ is a function of terms that are in the Markov blanket of the corresponding delinked node (i.e., Y_t). In particular, the update for $\lambda_t^{(m)}$ depends on the parameters $\lambda_t^{(n)}$, for $n \neq m$, thus linking the variational parameters at time t. Moreover, the update for $\lambda_t^{(m)}$ depends on the expected value of the states $X_t^{(m)}$, where the expectation is taken under the distribution Q. Given that the chains are decoupled under Q, expectations are found by running one of the exact algorithms (for example, the forward-backward algorithm for HMMs), separately for each chain. These expectations of course depend on the current values of the parameters $\lambda_t^{(m)}$ (cf. Eq. (70)), and it is this dependence that effectively couples the chains.

To summarize, fitting the variational parameters for a FHMM is an iterative, two-phase procedure. In the first phase, an exact algorithm is run as a subroutine to calculate expectations for the hidden states. This is done independently for each of the M chains, making reference to the current values of the parameters $\lambda_t^{(m)}$. In the second phase, the parameters $\lambda_t^{(m)}$ are updated based on the expectations computed in the first phase. The procedure then returns to the first phase and iterates.

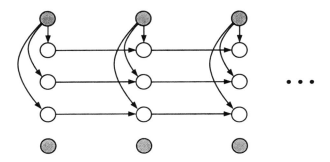

Figure 23.   The "forest of chains approximation" for the HMDT. Parameterizing this graph leads to an approximating family of Q distributions.

Ghahramani and Jordan (1997) reported results on fitting an FHMM to the Bach chorale data set (Merz & Murphy, 1996). They showed that significantly larger effective state spaces could be fit with the FHMM than with an unstructured HMM, and that performance in terms of probability of the test set was an order of magnitude larger for the FHMM. Moreover, evidence of overfitting was seen for the HMM for 35 states or more; no evidence of overfitting for the FHMM was seen for up to 1000 states.

6.3.4. *Hidden Markov decision trees*

As a final example we return to the hidden Markov decision tree (HMDT) described in the introduction and briefly discuss variational approximation for this architecture. As we have discussed, a HMDT is essentially a Markov time series model, where the probability model at each time step is a (probabilistic) decision tree with hidden decision nodes. The Markovian dependence is obtained via separate transition matrices at the different levels of the decision tree, giving the model a factorized structure.

The variational approach to fitting a HMDT is closely related to that of fitting a FHMM; however, there are additional choices as to the variational approximation. In particular, we have two substructures worth considering in the HMDT: (1) Dropping the vertical edges, we recover a decoupled set of chains. As in the FHMM, these chains can each be handled by the forward-backward algorithm. (2) Dropping the horizontal edges, we recover a decoupled set of decision trees. We can calculate probabilities in these trees using the posterior propagation algorithm described in Jordan (1994).

The first approach, which we refer to as the "forest of chains approximation," is shown in Fig. 23. As in the FHMM, we write a variational approximation for the forest of chains approximation by respecting the conditional independencies in the approximating graph and incorporating variational parameters to obtain extra degrees of freedom (see Jordan, et al., 1997, for the details).

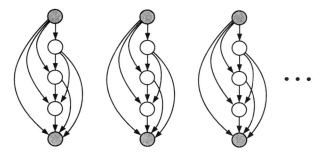

Figure 24. The "forest of trees approximation" for the HMDT. Parameterizing this graph leads to an approximating family of Q distributions.

We can also consider a "forest of trees approximation" in which the horizontal links are eliminated (see Fig. 24). Given that the decision tree is a fully connected graph, this is essentially a naive mean field approximation on a hypergraph.

Finally, it is also possible to develop a variational algorithm for the HMDT that is analogous to the Viterbi algorithm for HMMs. In particular, we utilize an approximation Q that assigns probability one to a single path in the state space. The KL divergence for this Q distribution is particularly easy to evaluate, given that the entropy contribution to the KL divergence (i.e., the $Q \ln Q$ term) is zero. Moreover, the evaluation of the energy (i.e., the $Q \ln P$ term) reduces to substituting the states along the chosen path into the P distribution.

The resulting algorithm involves a subroutine in which a standard Viterbi algorithm is run on a single chain, with the other chains held fixed. This subroutine is run on each chain in turn.

Jordan, et al. (1997) found that performance of the HMDT on the Bach chorales was essentially the same as that of the FHMM. The advantage of the HMDT was its greater interpretability; most of the runs resulted in a coarse-to-fine ordering of the temporal scales of the Markov processes from the top to the bottom of the tree.

7. Discussion

We have described a variety of applications of variational methods to problems of inference and learning in graphical models. We hope to have convinced the reader that variational methods can provide a powerful and elegant tool for graphical models, and that the algorithms that result are simple and intuitively appealing. It is important to emphasize, however, that research on variational methods for graphical models is of quite recent origin, and there are many open problems and unresolved issues. In this section we discuss a number of these issues. We also broaden the scope of the presentation and discuss a number of related strands of research.

7.1. RELATED RESEARCH

The methods that we have discussed all involve deterministic, iterative approximation algorithms. It is of interest to discuss related approximation schemes that are either non-deterministic or non-iterative.

7.1.1. *Recognition models and the Helmholtz machine*

All of the algorithms that we have presented have at their core a nonlinear optimization problem. In particular, after having introduced the variational parameters, whether sequentially or as a block, we are left with a bound such as that in Eq. (27) that must be optimized. Optimization of this bound is generally achieved via a fixed-point iteration or a gradient-based algorithm. This iterative optimization process induces interdependencies between the variational parameters which give us a "best" approximation to the marginal or conditional probability of interest.

Consider in particular a problem in which a directed graphical model is used for unsupervised learning. A common approach in unsupervised learning is to consider graphical models that are oriented in the "generative" direction; that is, they point from hidden variables to observables. In this case the "predictive" calculation of $P(E|H)$ is elementary. The calculation of $P(H|E)$, on the other hand, is a "diagnostic" calculation that proceeds backwards in the graph. Diagnostic calculations are generally non-trivial and require the full power of an inference algorithm.

An alternative approach to solving iteratively for an approximation to the diagnostic calculation is to learn both a generative model and a "recognition" model that approximates the diagnostic distribution $P(H|E)$. Thus we associate different parameters with the generative model and the recognition model and rely on the parameter estimation process to bring these parameterizations into register. This is the basic idea behind the "Helmholtz machine" (Dayan, et al., 1995; Hinton, et al., 1995).

The key advantage of the recognition-model approach is that the calculation of $P(H|E)$ is reduced to an elementary feedforward calculation that can be performed quickly.

There are some disadvantages to the approach as well. In particular, the lack of an iterative algorithm makes the Helmholtz machine unable to deal naturally with missing data, and with phenomena such as "explaining-away," in which the couplings between hidden variables change as a function of the conditioning variables. Moreover, although in some cases there is a clear natural parameterization for the recognition model that is induced from the generative model (in particular for linear models such as factor analysis), in general it is difficult to insure that the models are matched appropriately.[10] Some of these problems might be addressed by combining the recognition-model approach with the iterative variational approach; essentially treating the recognition-model as a "cache" for storing good initializations for the variational parameters.

7.1.2. *Sampling methods*

In this section we make a few remarks on the relationships between variational methods and stochastic methods, in particular the Gibbs sampler. In the setting of graphical models, both classes of methods rely on extensive message-passing. In Gibbs sampling, the message-passing is particularly simple: each node learns the current instantiation of its Markov blanket. With enough samples the node can estimate the distribution over its Markov blanket and (roughly speaking) determine its own statistics. The advantage of this scheme is that in the limit of very many samples, it is guaranteed to converge to the correct statistics. The disadvantage is that very many samples may be required.

The message-passing in variational methods is quite different. Its purpose is to couple the variational parameters of one node to those of its Markov blanket. The messages do not come in the form of samples, but rather in the form of approximate statistics (as summarized by the variational parameters). For example, in a network of binary nodes, while the Gibbs sampler is circulating messages of binary vectors that correspond to the *instantiations* of Markov blankets, the variational methods are circulating real-valued numbers that correspond to the *statistics* of Markov blankets. This may be one reason why variational methods often converge faster than Gibbs sampling. Of course, the disadvantage of these schemes is that they do not necessarily converge to the correct statistics. On the other hand, they can provide bounds on marginal probabilities that are quite difficult to estimate by sampling. Indeed, sampling-based methods—while well-suited to estimating the statistics of individual hidden nodes—are ill-equipped to compute marginal probabilities such as $P(E) = \sum_H P(H, E)$.

An interesting direction for future research is to consider combinations of sampling methods and variational methods. Some initial work in this direction has been done by Hinton, Sallans, and Ghahramani (this volume), who discuss brief Gibbs sampling from the point of view of variational approximation.

---

[10]The particular recognition model utilized in the Helmholtz machine is a layered graph, which makes weak conditional independence assumptions and thus makes it possible, in principle, to capture fairly general dependencies.

7.1.3. *Bayesian methods*

Variational inference can be applied to the general problem of Bayesian parameter estimation. Indeed we can quite generally treat parameters as additional nodes in a graphical model (cf. Heckerman, this volume) and thereby treat Bayesian inference on the same footing as generic probabilistic inference in a graphical model. This probabilistic inference problem is often intractable, and variational approximations can be useful.

A variational method known as "ensemble learning" was originally introduced as a way of fitting an "ensemble" of neural networks to data, where each setting of the parameters can be thought of as a different member of the ensemble (Hinton & van Camp, 1993). Let $Q(\theta|E)$ represent a variational approximation to the posterior distribution $P(\theta|E)$. The ensemble is fit by minimizing the appropriate KL divergence:

$$KL(Q\|P) = \int Q(\theta|E) \ln \frac{Q(\theta|E)}{P(\theta|E)} d\theta. \qquad (73)$$

Following the same line of argument as in Section 6, we know that this minimization must be equivalent to the maximization of a lower bound. In particular, copying the argument from Section 6, we find that minimizing the KL divergence yields the best lower bound on the following quantity:

$$\ln P(E) = \ln \int P(E|\theta) P(\theta) d\theta, \qquad (74)$$

which is the logarithm of the *marginal likelihood*; a key quantity in Bayesian model selection and model averaging.

More recently, the ensemble learning approach has been applied to mixture of experts architectures (Waterhouse, et al, 1996) and hidden Markov models (MacKay, 1997a). One interesting aspect of these applications is that they do not assume any particular parametric family for Q, just that Q factorizes in a specific way. The variational minimization itself determines the best family given this factorization and the prior on θ. In related work, MacKay (1997b) has described a connection between variational inference and Type II maximum likelihood inference.

Jaakkola and Jordan (1997b) have also developed variational methods for Bayesian inference, using a variational approach to find an analytically tractable approximation for logistic regression with a Gaussian prior on the parameters.

7.1.4. *Perspective and prospectives*

Perhaps the key issue that faces developers of variational methods is the issue of approximation accuracy. At the current state of development of variational methods for graphical models, we have little theoretical insight into conditions under which variational methods can be expected to be accurate and conditions under which they might be expected to be inaccurate. Moreover, there is little understanding of how to match variational transformations to architectures.

One can develop an intuition for when variational methods work by examining their properties in certain well-studied cases. For mean field methods, a good starting point is to understand the examples in the statistical mechanics literature where this approximation gives not only good, but indeed exact, results. These are densely connected graphs with uniformly weak (but non-negative) couplings between neighboring nodes (Parisi, 1988). The mean field equations for these networks have a unique solution that determines the statistics of individual nodes in the limit of very large graphs.

In more general graphical models, of course, the conditions for a mean field approximation may not be so favorable. Typically, this can be diagnosed by the presence of multiple solutions to the mean field equations. Roughly speaking, one can interpret each solution as corresponding to a mode of the posterior distribution; thus, multiple solutions indicate a multimodal posterior distribution. The simplest mean field approximations, in particular those that utilize a completely factorized approximating distribution, are poorly designed for such situations. However, they can succeed rather well in applications where the joint distribution $P(H, E)$ is multimodal, but the posterior distribution $P(H|E)$ is not. It is worth emphasizing this distinction between joint and posterior distributions. This is what allows simple variational methods—which make rather strong assumptions of conditional independence—to be used in the learning of nontrivial graphical models.

A second key issue has to do with broadening the scope of variational methods. In this paper we have presented a restricted set of variational techniques, those based on convexity transformations. For these techniques to be applicable the appropriate convexity properties need to be identified. While it is relatively easy to characterize small classes of models where these properties lead to simple approximation algorithms, such as the case in which the local conditional probabilities are log-concave generalized linear models, it is not generally easy to develop variational algorithms for other kinds of graphical models. A broader characterization of variational approximations is needed and a more systematic algebra is needed to match the approximations to models.

Other open problems include: (1) the problem of combining variational methods with sampling methods and with search based methods, (2) the problem of making more optimal choices of node ordering in the case of sequential methods, (3) the development of upper bounds within the block framework, (4) the combination of multiple variational approximations for the same model, and (5) the development of variational methods for architectures that combine continuous and discrete random variables.

Similar open problems exist for sampling methods and for methods based on incomplete or pruned versions of exact methods. The difficulty in providing solid theoretical foundations in all of these cases lies in the fact that accuracy is contingent to a large degree on the actual conditional probability values of the underlying probability model rather than on the discrete properties of the graph.

8. Acknowledgments

We wish to thank Brendan Frey, David Heckerman, Uffe Kjærulff, and (as always) Peter Dayan for helpful comments on the manuscript.

References

Bathe, K. J. (1996). *Finite Element Procedures*. Englewood Cliffs, NJ: Prentice-Hall.

Baum, L.E., Petrie, T., Soules, G., & Weiss, N. (1970). A maximization technique occurring in the statistical analysis of probabilistic functions of Markov chains. *The Annals of Mathematical Statistics, 41*, 164–171.

Cover, T., & Thomas, J. (1991). *Elements of Information Theory*. New York: John Wiley.

Cowell, R. (in press). Introduction to inference for Bayesian networks. In M. I. Jordan (Ed.), *Learning in Graphical Models*. Norwell, MA: Kluwer Academic Publishers.

Dagum, P., & Luby, M. (1993). Approximating probabilistic inference in Bayesian belief networks is NP-hard. *Artificial Intelligence, 60*, 141–153.

Dayan, P., Hinton, G. E., Neal, R., & Zemel, R. S. (1995). The Helmholtz Machine. *Neural Computation, 7*, 889–904.

Dean, T., & Kanazawa, K. (1989). A model for reasoning about causality and persistence. *Computational Intelligence, 5*, 142–150.

Dechter, R. (in press). Bucket elimination: A unifying framework for probabilistic inference. In M. I. Jordan (Ed.), *Learning in Graphical Models*. Norwell, MA: Kluwer Academic Publishers.

Dempster, A.P., Laird, N.M., & Rubin, D.B. (1977). Maximum-likelihood from incomplete data via the EM algorithm. *Journal of the Royal Statistical Society, B39*, 1-38.

Draper, D. L., & Hanks, S. (1994). Localized partial evaluation of belief networks. *Uncertainty and Artificial Intelligence: Proceedings of the Tenth Conference*. San Mateo, CA: Morgan Kaufmann.

Frey, B. Hinton, G. E., Dayan, P. (1996). Does the wake-sleep algorithm learn good density estimators? In D. S. Touretzky, M. C. Mozer, & M. E. Hasselmo (Eds.), *Advances in Neural Information Processing Systems 8*. Cambridge, MA: MIT Press.

Fung, R. & Favero, B. D. (1994). Backward simulation in Bayesian networks. *Uncertainty and Artificial Intelligence: Proceedings of the Tenth Conference*. San Mateo, CA: Morgan Kaufmann.

Galland, C. (1993). The limitations of deterministic Boltzmann machine learning. *Network, 4*, 355–379.

Ghahramani, Z., & Hinton, G. E. (1996). Switching state-space models. University of Toronto Technical Report CRG-TR-96-3, Department of Computer Science.

Ghahramani, Z., & Jordan, M. I. (1997). Factorial Hidden Markov models. *Machine Learning, 29*, 245–273.

Gilks, W., Thomas, A., & Spiegelhalter, D. (1994). A language and a program for complex Bayesian modelling. *The Statistician, 43*, 169–178.

Heckerman, D. (in press). A tutorial on learning with Bayesian networks. In M. I. Jordan (Ed.), *Learning in Graphical Models*. Norwell, MA: Kluwer Academic Publishers.

Henrion, M. (1991). Search-based methods to bound diagnostic probabilities in very large belief nets. *Uncertainty and Artificial Intelligence: Proceedings of the Seventh Conference*. San Mateo, CA: Morgan Kaufmann.

Hinton, G. E., & Sejnowski, T. (1986). Learning and relearning in Boltzmann machines. In D. E. Rumelhart & J. L. McClelland, (Eds.), *Parallel distributed processing: Volume 1*, Cambridge, MA: MIT Press.

Hinton, G.E. & van Camp, D. (1993). Keeping neural networks simple by minimizing the description length of the weights. In *Proceedings of the 6th Annual Workshop on Computational Learning Theory*, pp 5-13. New York, NY: ACM Press.

Hinton, G. E., Dayan, P., Frey, B., and Neal, R. M. (1995). The wake-sleep algorithm for unsupervised neural networks. *Science*, 268:1158–1161.

Hinton, G. E., Sallans, B., & Ghahramani, Z. (in press). A hierarchical community of experts. In M. I. Jordan (Ed.), *Learning in Graphical Models*. Norwell, MA: Kluwer Academic Publishers.

Horvitz, E. J., Suermondt, H. J., & Cooper, G.F. (1989). Bounded conditioning: Flexible inference for decisions under scarce resources. *Conference on Uncertainty in Artificial Intelligence: Proceedings of the Fifth Conference*. Mountain View, CA: Association for UAI.

Jaakkola, T. S., & Jordan, M. I. (1996). Computing upper and lower bounds on likelihoods in intractable networks. *Uncertainty and Artificial Intelligence: Proceedings of the Twelth Conference*. San Mateo, CA: Morgan Kaufmann.

Jaakkola, T. S. (1997). *Variational methods for inference and estimation in graphical models*. Unpublished doctoral dissertation, Massachusetts Institute of Technology.

Jaakkola, T. S., & Jordan, M. I. (1997a). Recursive algorithms for approximating probabilities in graphical models. In M. C. Mozer, M. I. Jordan, & T. Petsche (Eds.), *Advances in Neural Information Processing Systems 9*. Cambridge, MA: MIT Press.

Jaakkola, T. S., & Jordan, M. I. (1997b). Bayesian logistic regression: a variational approach. In D. Madigan & P. Smyth (Eds.), Proceedings of the 1997 Conference on Artificial Intelligence and Statistics, Ft. Lauderdale, FL.

Jaakkola, T. S., & Jordan. M. I. (1997c). Variational methods and the QMR-DT database. Submitted to: *Journal of Artificial Intelligence Research*.

Jaakkola, T. S., & Jordan. M. I. (in press). Improving the mean field approximation via the use of mixture distributions. In M. I. Jordan (Ed.), *Learning in Graphical Models*. Norwell, MA: Kluwer Academic Publishers.

Jensen, C. S., Kong, A., & Kjærulff, U. (1995). Blocking-Gibbs sampling in very large probabilistic expert systems. *International Journal of Human-Computer Studies, 42*, 647–666.

Jensen, F. V., & Jensen, F. (1994). Optimal junction trees. *Uncertainty and Artificial Intelligence: Proceedings of the Tenth Conference*. San Mateo, CA: Morgan Kaufmann.

Jensen, F. V. (1996). *An Introduction to Bayesian Networks*. London: UCL Press.

Jordan, M. I. (1994). A statistical approach to decision tree modeling. In M. Warmuth (Ed.), *Proceedings of the Seventh Annual ACM Conference on Computational Learning Theory*. New York: ACM Press.

Jordan, M. I., Ghahramani, Z., & Saul, L. K. (1997). Hidden Markov decision trees. In M. C. Mozer, M. I. Jordan, & T. Petsche (Eds.), *Advances in Neural Information Processing Systems 9*. Cambridge, MA: MIT Press.

Kanazawa, K., Koller, D., & Russell, S. (1995). Stochastic simulation algorithms for dynamic probabilistic networks. *Uncertainty and Artificial Intelligence: Proceedings of the Eleventh Conference*. San Mateo, CA: Morgan Kaufmann.

Kjærulff, U. (1990). Triangulation of graphs—algorithms giving small total state space. Research Report R-90-09, Department of Mathematics and Computer Science, Aalborg University, Denmark.

Kjærulff, U. (1994). Reduction of computational complexity in Bayesian networks through removal of weak dependences. *Uncertainty and Artificial Intelligence: Proceedings of the Tenth Conference.* San Mateo, CA: Morgan Kaufmann.

MacKay, D.J.C. (1997a). Ensemble learning for hidden Markov models. Unpublished manuscript. Department of Physics, University of Cambridge.

MacKay, D.J.C. (1997b). Comparison of approximate methods for handling hyperparameters. Submitted to *Neural Computation.*

MacKay, D.J.C. (1997b). Introduction to Monte Carlo methods. In M. I. Jordan (Ed.), *Learning in Graphical Models.* Norwell, MA: Kluwer Academic Publishers.

McEliece, R.J., MacKay, D.J.C., & Cheng, J.-F. (1996) Turbo decoding as an instance of Pearl's "belief propagation algorithm." Submitted to: *IEEE Journal on Selected Areas in Communication.*

Merz, C. J., & Murphy, P. M. (1996). *UCI repository of machine learning databases.* [http://www.ics.uci/~mlearn/MLRepository.html]. Irvine, CA: University of California, Department of Information and Computer Science.

Neal, R. (1992). Connectionist learning of belief networks, *Artificial Intelligence, 56,* 71-113.

Neal, R. (1993). Probabilistic inference using Markov chain Monte Carlo methods. University of Toronto Technical Report CRG-TR-93-1, Department of Computer Science.

Neal, R., & Hinton, G. E. (in press). A view of the EM algorithm that justifies incremental, sparse, and other variants. In M. I. Jordan (Ed.), *Learning in Graphical Models.* Norwell, MA: Kluwer Academic Publishers.

Parisi, G. (1988). *Statistical Field Theory.* Redwood City, CA: Addison-Wesley.

Pearl, J. (1988). *Probabilistic Reasoning in Intelligent Systems: Networks of Plausible Inference,* San Mateo, CA: Morgan Kaufmannn.

Peterson, C., & Anderson, J. R. (1987). A mean field theory learning algorithm for neural networks. *Complex Systems, 1,* 995-1019.

Rockafellar, R. (1972). *Convex Analysis.* Princeton University Press.

Rustagi, J. (1976). *Variational Methods in Statistics.* New York: Academic Press.

Sakurai, J. (1985). *Modern Quantum Mechanics.* Redwood City, CA: Addison-Wesley.

Saul, L. K., & Jordan, M. I. (1994). Learning in Boltzmann trees. *Neural Computation, 6,* 1173-1183.

Saul, L. K., Jaakkola, T. S., & Jordan, M. I. (1996). Mean field theory for sigmoid belief networks. *Journal of Artificial Intelligence Research, 4,* 61-76.

Saul, L. K., & Jordan, M. I. (1996). Exploiting tractable substructures in intractable networks. In D. S. Touretzky, M. C. Mozer, & M. E. Hasselmo (Eds.), *Advances in Neural Information Processing Systems 8.* Cambridge, MA: MIT Press.

Saul, L. K., & Jordan, M. I. (in press). A mean field learning algorithm for unsupervised neural networks. In M. I. Jordan (Ed.), *Learning in Graphical Models.* Norwell, MA: Kluwer Academic Publishers.

Seung, S. (1995). Annealed theories of learning. In J.-H Oh, C. Kwon, and S. Cho, (Eds.), *Neural Networks: The Statistical Mechanics Perspectives.* Singapore: World Scientific.

Shachter, R. D., Andersen, S. K., & Szolovits, P. (1994). Global conditioning for probabilistic inference in belief networks. *Uncertainty and Artificial Intelligence: Proceedings of the Tenth Conference.* San Mateo, CA: Morgan Kaufmann.

Shenoy, P. P. (1992). Valuation-based systems for Bayesian decision analysis. *Operations Research, 40,* 463-484.

Shwe, M. A., Middleton, B., Heckerman, D. E., Henrion, M., Horvitz, E. J., Lehmann, H. P., & Cooper, G. F. (1991). Probabilistic diagnosis using a reformulation of the INTERNIST-1/QMR knowledge base. *Meth. Inform. Med., 30,* 241-255.

Smyth, P., Heckerman, D., & Jordan, M. I. (1997). Probabilistic independence networks for hidden Markov probability models. *Neural Computation, 9,* 227-270.

Waterhouse, S., MacKay, D.J.C. & Robinson, T. (1996). Bayesian methods for mixtures of experts. In D. S. Touretzky, M. C. Mozer, & M. E. Hasselmo (Eds.), *Advances in Neural Information Processing Systems 8.* Cambridge, MA: MIT Press.

Williams, C. K. I., & Hinton, G. E. (1991). Mean field networks that learn to discriminate temporally distorted strings. In Touretzky, D. S., Elman, J., Sejnowski, T., & Hinton, G. E., (Eds.), *Proceedings of the 1990 Connectionist Models Summer School.* San Mateo, CA: Morgan Kaufmann.

9. Appendix

In this section, we calculate the conjugate functions for the logarithm function and the log logistic function.

For $f(x) = \ln x$, we have:

$$f^*(\lambda) = \min_x \{\lambda x - \ln x\}. \tag{75}$$

Taking the derivative with respect to x and setting to zero yields $x = \lambda^{-1}$. Substituting back in Eq. (75) yields:

$$f^*(\lambda) = \ln \lambda + 1, \tag{76}$$

which justifies the representation of the logarithm given in Eq. (14).

For the log logistic function $g(x) = -\ln(1 + e^{-x})$, we have:

$$g^*(\lambda) = \min_x \{\lambda x + \ln(1 + e^{-x})\}. \tag{77}$$

Taking the derivative with respect to x and setting to zero yields:

$$\lambda = \frac{e^{-x}}{1 + e^{-x}}, \tag{78}$$

from which we obtain:

$$x = \ln \frac{1 - \lambda}{\lambda} \tag{79}$$

and

$$\ln(1 + e^{-x}) = \frac{1}{1 - \lambda}. \tag{80}$$

Plugging these expressions back into Eq. (77) yields:

$$f^*(\lambda) = -\lambda \ln \lambda - (1 - \lambda) \ln(1 - \lambda), \tag{81}$$

which is the binary entropy function $H(\lambda)$. This justifies the representation of the logistic function given in Eq. (19).

IMPROVING THE MEAN FIELD APPROXIMATION VIA THE USE OF MIXTURE DISTRIBUTIONS

TOMMI S. JAAKKOLA
University of California
Santa Cruz, CA

AND

MICHAEL I. JORDAN
Massachusetts Institute of Technology
Cambridge, MA

Abstract. Mean field methods provide computationally efficient approximations to posterior probability distributions for graphical models. Simple mean field methods make a completely factorized approximation to the posterior, which is unlikely to be accurate when the posterior is multi-modal. Indeed, if the posterior is multi-modal, only one of the modes can be captured. To improve the mean field approximation in such cases, we employ mixture models as posterior approximations, where each mixture component is a factorized distribution. We describe efficient methods for optimizing the parameters in these models.

1. Introduction

Graphical models provide a convenient formalism in which to express and manipulate conditional independence statements. Inference algorithms for graphical models exploit these independence statements, using them to compute conditional probabilities while avoiding brute force marginalization over the joint probability table. Many inference algorithms, in particular the algorithms that construct a junction tree, make explicit their usage of conditional independence by constructing a data structure that captures the essential Markov properties underlying the graph. That is, the algorithm groups interacting variables into clusters, such that the hypergraph of clusters has Markov properties that allow simple local algorithms to be employed for inference. In the best case, in which the original graph is sparse and without long cycles, the clusters are small and inference is efficient. In the worst case, such as the case of a dense graph, the clusters are large and inference is inefficient (complexity scales exponentially in the size of the largest cluster). Architectures for which the complexity is prohibitive include the QMR database (Shwe, et al., 1991), the layered sigmoid belief network (Neal, 1992), and the factorial hidden Markov model (Ghahramani & Jordan, 1996).

Mean field theory (Parisi, 1988) provides an alternative perspective on the inference problem. The intuition behind mean field methods is that in dense graphs each node is subject to influences from many other nodes; thus, to the extent that each influence is weak and the total influence is roughly additive (on an appropriate scale), each node should roughly be characterized by its mean value. In particular this characterization is valid in situations in which the law of large numbers can be applied. The mean value is unknown, but it is related to the mean values of the other nodes. Mean field theory consists of finding consistency relations between the mean values for each of the nodes and solving the resulting equations (generally by iteration). For graphical models these equations generally have simple graphical interpretations; for example, Peterson and Anderson (1987) and Saul, Jaakkola, and Jordan (1996) found, in the cases of Markov networks and Bayesian networks, respectively, that the mean value of a given node is obtained additively (on a logit scale) from the mean values of the nodes in the Markov blanket of the node.

Exact methods and mean field methods might be said to be complementary in the sense that exact methods are best suited for sparse graphs and mean field methods are best suited for dense graphs. Both classes of methods have significant limitations, however, and the gap between their respective domains of application is large. In particular, the naive mean field methods that we have referred to above are based on the approximation that each node fluctuates independently about its mean value. If there are a strong interactions in the network, i.e. if higher-order moments are important, then mean field methods will generally fail. One way in which such higher-order interactions may manifest themselves is in the presence of multiple modes in the distribution; naive mean field theory, by assuming independent fluctuations, effectively assumes a unimodal distribution and will generally fail if there are multiple modes.

One approach to narrowing the gap between exact methods and mean field methods is the "structured mean field" methodology proposed by Saul and Jordan (1996). This approach involves deleting links in the graph and identifying a core graphical substructure that can be treated efficiently via exact methods (e.g., a forest of trees). Probabilistic dependencies not accounted for by the probability distribution on this core substructure are treated via a naive mean field approximation. For architectures with an obvious chain-like or tree-like substructure, such as the factorial hidden Markov model, this method is natural and successful. For architectures without such a readily identified substructure, however, such as the QMR database and the layered sigmoid belief network, it is not clear how to develop a useful structured mean field approximation.

The current paper extends the basic mean field methodology in a different direction. Rather than basing the approximation on the assumption of a unimodal approximating distribution,[1] we build in multimodality by allowing the approximating distribution to take the form of a mixture distribution. The components of the mixture are assumed to be simple factorized distributions, for reasons of computational efficiency. Thus, within a mode we assume independent fluctuations, and multiple modes are used to capture higher-order interactions.

In the following sections we describe our mixture-based approach that extends the basic mean field method. Section 2 describes the basics of mean field approximation, providing enough detail so as to make the paper self-contained. Section 3 then describes how to extend the mean field approximation by allowing mixture distributions in the posterior approximation. The following sections develop the machinery whereby this approximation can be carried out in practice.

2. Mean field approximation

Assume we have a probability model $P(S, S^*)$, where S^* is the set of instantiated or observed variables (the "evidence") and the variables S are hidden or unobserved. We wish to find a tractable approximation to the posterior probability $P(S|S^*)$.

In its simplest form mean field theory assumes that nodes fluctuate independently around their mean values. We make this assumption explicit by expressing the approximation in terms of a factorized distribution $Q_{mf}(S|S^*)$:

$$Q_{mf}(S|S^*) = \prod_i Q_i(S_i|S^*), \qquad (1)$$

where the parameters $Q_i(S_i|S^*)$ depend on each other and on the evidence S^* (i.e., we must refit the mean field approximation for each configuration of the evidence).

---

[1] By "unimodal distributions" we mean distributions that are log-concave. Mean field distributions that are products of exponential family distributions are unimodal in this sense.

The mean field approximation can be developed from several points of view, but a particularly useful perspective for applications to graphical models is the "variational" point of view. Within this approach we use the KL divergence as a measure of the goodness of the approximation and choose values of the parameters $Q_i(S_i|S^*)$ that minimize the KL divergence:

$$\text{KL}(\, Q_{mf}(S|S^*) \,||\, P(S|S^*) \,) = \sum_S Q_{mf}(S|S^*) \log \frac{Q_{mf}(S|S^*)}{P(S|S^*)}. \qquad (2)$$

Why do we use $\text{KL}(Q_{mf}||P)$ rather than $\text{KL}(P||Q_{mf})$? A pragmatic answer is that the use of $\text{KL}(Q_{mf}||P)$ implies that averages are taken using the tractable Q_{mf} distribution rather than the intractable P distribution (cf. Eq. (2)); only in the former case do we have any hope of finding the best approximation in practice. A more satisfying answer arises from considering the likelihood of the evidence, $P(S^*)$. Clearly calculation of the likelihood permits calculation of the conditional probability $P(S|S^*)$. Using Jensen's inequality we can lower bound the likelihood (cf. for example Saul, et al., 1996):

$$\begin{aligned}
\log P(S^*) &= \log \sum_S P(S, S^*) \\
&= \log \sum_S Q(S|S^*) \frac{P(S, S^*)}{Q(S|S^*)} \\
&\geq \sum_S Q(S|S^*) \log \frac{P(S, S^*)}{Q(S|S^*)},
\end{aligned}$$

for arbitrary $Q(S|S^*)$, in particular for the mean field distribution $Q_{mf}(S|S^*)$. It is easily verified that the difference between the left hand side and the right hand side of this inequality is the KL divergence $\text{KL}(Q||P)$; thus, minimizing this divergence is equivalent to maximizing a lower bound on the likelihood.

For graphical models, minimization of $\text{KL}(Q_{mf}||P)$ with respect to $Q_i(S_i|S^*)$ leads directly to an equation expressing $Q_i(S_i|S^*)$ in terms of the $Q_j(S_j|S^*)$ associated with the nodes in the Markov blanket of node i (Peterson & Anderson, 1987; Saul, et al., 1996). These equations are coupled nonlinear equations and are generally solved iteratively.

3. Mixture approximations

In this section we describe how to extend the mean field framework by utilizing mixture distributions rather than factorized distributions as the approximating distributions. For notational simplicity, we will drop the dependence of $Q(S|S^*)$ on S^* in this section and in the remainder of the paper, but it must be borne in mind that the approximation is optimized separately for each configuration of the evidence S^*. We also utilize the notation $\mathcal{F}(Q)$ to denote the lower bound on the right hand side of Eq. (3):

$$\mathcal{F}(Q) \equiv \sum_S Q(S) \log \frac{P(S, S^*)}{Q(S)} \tag{3}$$

When $Q(S)$ takes the factorized form $Q_{mf}(S)$ in Eq. (1), we will refer to the approximation as a "factorized mean field" approximation and will denote the corresponding bound as $\mathcal{F}(Q_{mf})$.

Our proposal is to utilize a mixture distribution as the approximating distribution:

$$Q_{mix}(S) = \sum_m \alpha_m Q_{mf}(S|m), \tag{4}$$

where each of the component distributions $Q_{mf}(S|m)$ are factorized distributions. The mixing proportions α_m, which are constrained to be positive and sum to one, are additional parameters to be fit via the minimization of the KL divergence.

In the remainder of this section we focus on the relationship between $\mathcal{F}(Q_{mix})$ – the mixture bound – and the factorized mean field bounds $\mathcal{F}(Q_{mf}|m)$ corresponding to the mixture components. To this end, consider:

$$
\begin{aligned}
\mathcal{F}(Q_{mix}) &= \sum_S Q_{mix}(S) \log \frac{P(S, S^*)}{Q_{mix}(S)} \\
&= \sum_{m,S} \alpha_m \left[Q_{mf}(S|m) \log \frac{P(S, S^*)}{Q_{mix}(S)} \right] \\
&= \sum_{m,S} \alpha_m \left[Q_{mf}(S|m) \log \frac{P(S, S^*)}{Q_{mf}(S|m)} + Q_{mf}(S|m) \log \frac{Q_{mf}(S|m)}{Q_{mix}(S)} \right] \\
&= \sum_m \alpha_m \mathcal{F}(Q_{mf}|m) + \sum_{m,S} \alpha_m Q_{mf}(S|m) \log \frac{Q_{mf}(S|m)}{Q_{mix}(S)} \\
&= \sum_m \alpha_m \mathcal{F}(Q_{mf}|m) + I(m; S) \tag{5}
\end{aligned}
$$

where $I(m; S)$ is the mutual information between the mixture index m and the variables S in the mixture distribution[2]. The first term in Eq. (5)

---

[2]Recall that the mutual information between any two random variables x and y is I(x;y) = $\sum_{x,y} P(x, y) \log P(y|x)/P(y)$.

is a convex combination of factorized mean field bounds and therefore it yields no gain over factorized mean field as far as the KL divergence is concerned. It is the second term, i.e., the mutual information, that characterizes the gain of using the mixture approximation.[3] As a non-negative quantity, $I(m; S)$ increases the likelihood bound and therefore improves the approximation. We note, however, that since $I(m; S) \leq \log M$, where M is the number of mixture components, the KL divergence between the mixture approximation and the true posterior can decrease at most logarithmically in the number of mixture components.

4. Computing the mutual information

To be able to use the mixture bound of Eq. (5) we need to be able to compute the mutual information term. The difficulty with the expression as it stands is the need to average the log of the mixture distribution over all configurations of the hidden variables. Given that there are an exponential number of such configurations, this computation is in general intractable. We will make use of a refined form of Jensen's inequality to make headway.

Let us first rewrite the mutual information as

$$
I(m; S) = \sum_{m,S} \alpha_m Q_{mf}(S|m) \log \frac{Q_{mf}(S|m)}{Q_{mix}(S)} \tag{6}
$$

$$
= \sum_{m,S} \alpha_m Q_{mf}(S|m) \left[-\log \frac{Q_{mix}(S)}{Q_{mf}(S|m)} \right] \tag{7}
$$

$$
= \sum_{m,S} \alpha_m Q_{mf}(S|m) \left[-\log \frac{\alpha_m R(S|m)}{\alpha_m R(S|m)} \frac{Q_{mix}(S)}{Q_{mf}(S|m)} \right] \tag{8}
$$

$$
= \sum_{m,S} \alpha_m Q_{mf}(S|m) \log R(S|m) - \sum_m \alpha_m \log \alpha_m
$$

$$
+ \sum_{m,S} \alpha_m Q_{mf}(S|m) \left[-\log \frac{R(S|m)}{\alpha_m} \frac{Q_{mix}(S)}{Q_{mf}(S|m)} \right] \tag{9}
$$

where we have introduced additional smoothing distributions $R(S|m)$ whose role is to improve the convexity bounds that we describe below.[4] With some foresight we have also introduced α_m into the expression; as will become

---

[3]Of course, this is only the potential gain to be realized from the mixture approximation. We cannot rule out the possibility that it will be harder to search for the best approximating distribution in the mixture approximation than in the factorized case. In particular the mixture approximation may introduce additional local minima into the KL divergence.

[4]In fact, if we use Jensen's inequality directly in Eq. (6), we obtain a vacuous bound of zero, as is easily verified.

apparent in the following section the forced appearance of α_m turns out to be convenient in updating the mixture coefficients.

To avoid the need to average over the logarithm of the mixture distribution, we make use of the following convexity bound:

$$-\log(x) \geq -\lambda\,x + \log(\lambda) + 1, \tag{10}$$

replacing the $-\log(\cdot)$ terms in Eq. (9) with linear functions, separately for each m. These substitutions imply a lower bound on the mutual information given by:

$$
\begin{aligned}
I(m;S) \;\geq\; & \sum_{m,S} \alpha_m Q_{mf}(S|m) \log R(S|m) - \sum_m \alpha_m \log \alpha_m \\
& - \sum_m \lambda_m \sum_S R(S|m) Q_{mix}(S) + \sum_m \alpha_m \log \lambda_m + 1 \quad (11) \\
\equiv\; & I_\lambda(m;S). \tag{12}
\end{aligned}
$$

The tightness of the convexity bound is controlled by the smoothing functions $R(S|m)$, which can be viewed as "flattening" the logarithm function such that Jensen's inequality is tightened. In particular, if we set $R(S|m) \propto Q_{mf}(S|m)/Q_{mix}(S)$ and maximize over the new variational parameters λ_m we recover the mutual information exactly. Such a choice would not reduce the complexity of our calculations, however. To obtain an efficient algorithm we will instead assume that the distributions R have simple factorized forms, and optimize the ensuing lower bound with respect to the parameters in these distributions. It will turn out that this assumption will permit all of the terms in our bound to be evaluated efficiently. We note finally that this bound is never vacuous. To see why, simply set $R(S|m)$ equal to a constant for all $\{S,m\}$ in which case $\max_\lambda I_\lambda(m;S) = 0$; optimization of R can only improve the bound.

5. Finding the mixture parameters

In order to find a reasonable mixture approximation we need to be able to optimize the bound in Eq. (5) with respect to the mixture model. Clearly a necessary condition for the feasibility of this optimization process is that the component factorized mean field distributions can be fit to the model tractably. That is, we must assume that the following mean field equations:

$$\frac{\partial \mathcal{F}(Q_{mf})}{\partial Q_j(S_j)} = constant \tag{13}$$

can be solved efficiently (not necessarily in closed form) for any of the marginals $Q_j(S_j)$ in the factorized mean field distribution Q_{mf}.[5] Examples of such mean field equations are provided by Peterson and Anderson (1987) and Saul, et al. (1996).

Let us first consider the updates for the factorized mean field components of the mixture model. We need to take derivatives of the lower bound:

$$\mathcal{F}(Q_{mix}) \geq \sum_m \alpha_m \mathcal{F}(Q_{mf}|m) + I_\lambda(m; S) \equiv \mathcal{F}_\lambda(Q_{mix}) \tag{14}$$

with respect to the parameters of the component factorized distributions. The important property of $I_\lambda(m; S)$ is that it is linear in any of the marginals $Q_j(S_j|k)$, where k indicates the mixture component (see Appendix A). As a result, we have:

$$\frac{\partial I_\lambda(m; S)}{\partial Q_j(S_j|k)} = constant \tag{15}$$

where the constant is independent of the marginal $Q_j(S_j|k)$ (and is generally dependent on the other marginals in the particular component mean field distribution). It follows from our assumption that the equations:

$$\frac{\partial \mathcal{F}_\lambda(Q_{mix})}{\partial Q_j(S_j|k)} = \alpha_k \frac{\partial \mathcal{F}_\lambda(Q_{mf}|k)}{\partial Q_j(S_j|k)} + \frac{\partial I_\lambda(m; S)}{\partial Q_j(S_j|k)} = 0 \tag{16}$$

can be solved efficiently for any specific marginal $Q_j(S_j|k)$. We can thus find the best fitting mixture components by iteratively optimizing each of the marginals in the model.

Let us now turn to the mixture coefficients α_k. We note first that, apart from the entropy term $-\sum_k \alpha_k \log \alpha_k$, these coefficients appear linearly in $I_\lambda(m; S)$. The same is therefore true for $\mathcal{F}_\lambda(Q_{mix})$ (see Eq. (14)), and we can write:

$$\mathcal{F}_\lambda(Q_{mix}) = \sum_k \alpha_k(-E(k)) - \sum_k \alpha_k \log \alpha_k + 1 \tag{17}$$

where $-E(k)$ is the collection of terms linear in α_k:

$$-E(k) \equiv \mathcal{F}(Q_{mf}|k) + \sum_S Q_{mf}(S|k) \log R(S|k)$$
$$+ \sum_m \lambda_m \sum_S R(S|m)Q_{mf}(S|k) + \log \lambda_k \tag{18}$$

---

[5]In the ordinary mean field equations the constant is zero, but for many probability models of interest this slight difference poses no additional difficulties.

Now Eq. (17) has the form of a free energy, and the mixture coefficients that maximize the lower bound $\mathcal{F}_\lambda(Q_{mix})$ therefore come from the Boltzmann distribution:

$$\alpha_k = \frac{e^{-E(k)}}{\sum_{k'} e^{-E(k')}}. \tag{19}$$

(This fact is easily verified using Lagrange multipliers to optimize Eq. (17) with respect to α_m).

Finally, we must optimize the bound with respect to the parameters λ_m and the parameters of the smoothing distribution. We discuss the latter updates in Appendix A. Differentiating the bound with respect to the parameters λ_m, we readily obtain:

$$\lambda_m = \frac{\alpha_m}{\sum_k \alpha_k \sum_S R(S|m) Q_{mf}(S|k)}, \tag{20}$$

where a simplified form for the expression in the denominator is presented in the Appendix.

6. Discussion

We have presented a general methodology for using mixture distributions in approximate probabilistic calculations. We have shown that the bound on the likelihood resulting from mixture-based approximations is composed of two terms, one a convex combination of simple factorized mean field bounds and the other the mutual information between the mixture labels and the hidden variables S. It is the latter term which represents the improvement available from the use of mixture models.

The basic mixture approximation utilizes parameters α_m (the mixing proportions), $Q_i(S_i|m)$ (the parameters of the factorized component distributions). These parameters are fit via Eq. (19) and Eq. (16), respectively. We also introduced variational parameters λ_m and $R_i(S_i|m)$ to provide tight approximations to the mutual information. Updates for these parameters were presented in Eq. (20) and Eq. (29).

Bishop, et al. (1998) have presented empirical results using the mixture approximation. In experiments with random sigmoid belief networks, they showed that the mixture approximation provides a better approximation than simple factorized mean field bounds, and moreover that the approximation improves monotonically with the number of components in the mixture.

An interesting direction for further research would involve the study of hybrids that combine the use of the mixture approximation with exact methods. Much as in the case of the structured mean field approximation of

Saul and Jordan (1996), it should be possible to utilize approximations that identify core substructures that are treated exactly, while the interactions between these substructures are treated via the mixture approach. This would provide a flexible model for dealing with a variety of forms of high-order interactions, while remaining tractable computationally.

References

Bishop, C., Lawrence, N., Jaakkola, T. S., & Jordan, M. I. Approximating posterior distributions in belief networks using mixtures. In M. I. Jordan, M. J. Kearns, & S. A. Solla, *Advances in Neural Information Processing Systems 10*, MIT Press, Cambridge MA (1998).

Ghahramani, Z. & Jordan, M. I. Factorial Hidden Markov models. In D. S. Touretzky, M. C. Mozer, & M. E. Hasselmo (Eds.), *Advances in Neural Information Processing Systems 8*, MIT Press, Cambridge MA (1996).

Neal, R. Connectionist learning of belief networks, *Artificial Intelligence, 56*: 71-113 (1992).

Parisi, G. *Statistical Field Theory*. Addison-Wesley: Redwood City (1988).

Peterson, C. & Anderson, J. R. A mean field theory learning algorithm for neural networks. *Complex Systems* 1:995–1019 (1987).

Saul, L. K., Jaakkola, T. S., & Jordan, M. I. Mean field theory for sigmoid belief networks. *Journal of Artificial Intelligence Research, 4*:61–76 (1996).

Saul, L. K. & Jordan, M. I. Exploiting tractable substructures in intractable networks. In D. S. Touretzky, M. C. Mozer, & M. E. Hasselmo (Eds.), *Advances in Neural Information Processing Systems 8*, MIT Press, Cambridge MA (1996).

Shwe, M. A., Middleton, B., Heckerman, D. E., Henrion, M., Horvitz, E. J., Lehmann, H. P., & Cooper, G. F. Probabilistic diagnosis using a reformulation of the INTERNIST-1/QMR knowledge base. *Meth. Inform. Med. 30*: 241-255 (1991).

A. Optimization of the smoothing distribution

Let us first adopt the following notation:

$$\pi_{R,Q}(m, m') \equiv \sum_S R(S|m)Q_{mf}(S|m') \tag{21}$$

$$= \prod_i \left[\sum_{S_i} R_i(S_i|m)Q_i(S_i|m') \right] \tag{22}$$

$$H(Q \parallel R \,|m) \equiv \sum_S Q_{mf}(S|m) \log R(S|m) \tag{23}$$

$$= \sum_i \sum_{S_i} Q_i(S_i|m) \log R_i(S_i|m) \tag{24}$$

$$H(m) \equiv -\sum_m \alpha_m \log \alpha_m \tag{25}$$

where we have evaluated the sums over S by making use of the assumption that $R(S|m)$ factorizes. We denote the marginals of these factorized forms by $R_i(S_i|m)$. Eq. (11) now reads as:

$$
\begin{aligned}
I_\lambda(m; S) \;=\;& \sum_m \alpha_m H(Q \parallel R \,|m) + H(m) \\
& - \sum_m \lambda_m \left[\sum_{m'} Q(m') \, \pi_{R,Q}(m, m') \right] + \sum_m \alpha_m \log \lambda_m + (26)
\end{aligned}
$$

To optimize the bound $I_\lambda(m; S)$ with respect to R, we need the following derivatives:

$$
\frac{\partial \, H(Q \parallel R \,|m)}{\partial \, R_j(S_j|k)} \;=\; \delta_{k,m} \, \frac{Q_j(S_j|k)}{R_j(S_j|k)} \tag{27}
$$

$$
\frac{\partial \, \pi_{R,Q}(m, m')}{\partial \, R_j(S_j|k)} \;=\; \delta_{k,m} \, Q_j(S_j|m') \prod_{i \neq j} \left[\sum_{S_i} R_i(S_i|m) Q_i(S_i|m') \right] . \tag{28}
$$

Denoting the product in Eq. (28) by $\pi_{R,Q}^j(m, m')$, we can now characterize the optimal R via the consistency equations:

$$
\frac{\partial \, I_\lambda(m; S)}{\partial \, R_j(S_j|k)} = \alpha_k \frac{Q_j(S_j|k)}{R_j(S_j|k)} - \lambda_k \left[\sum_{m'} Q(m') \, \pi_{R,Q}^j(k, m') Q_j(S_j|m') \right] = 0 \tag{29}
$$

Note that the second term does not depend on the smoothing marginal $R_j(S_j|k)$ and therefore these consistency equations are easily solved for any specific marginal. The best fitting R is found by iteratively optimizing each of its marginals. We note finally that the iterative solutions are not necessarily normalized. This is of no consequence, however, since the information bound of Eq. (11)—once maximized over the λ parameters—is invariant to the normalization of R.

INTRODUCTION TO MONTE CARLO METHODS

D.J.C. MACKAY

Department of Physics, Cambridge University.
Cavendish Laboratory, Madingley Road,
Cambridge, CB3 0HE. United Kingdom.

ABSTRACT

This chapter describes a sequence of Monte Carlo methods: **importance sampling**, **rejection sampling**, the **Metropolis method**, and **Gibbs sampling**. For each method, we discuss whether the method is expected to be useful for high–dimensional problems such as arise in inference with graphical models. After the methods have been described, the terminology of Markov chain Monte Carlo methods is presented. The chapter concludes with a discussion of advanced methods, including methods for reducing random walk behaviour.

For details of Monte Carlo methods, theorems and proofs and a full list of references, the reader is directed to Neal (1993), Gilks, Richardson and Spiegelhalter (1996), and Tanner (1996).

1. The problems to be solved

The aims of Monte Carlo methods are to solve one or both of the following problems.

Problem 1: to generate samples $\{\mathbf{x}^{(r)}\}_{r=1}^{R}$ from a given probability distribution $P(\mathbf{x})$.[1]

Problem 2: to estimate expectations of functions under this distribution, for example

$$\Phi = \langle \phi(\mathbf{x}) \rangle \equiv \int d^N \mathbf{x} \, P(\mathbf{x}) \phi(\mathbf{x}). \tag{1}$$

---

[1] Please note that I will use the word "sample" in the following sense: a sample from a distribution $P(\mathbf{x})$ is a single realization $\mathbf{x}$ whose probability distribution is $P(\mathbf{x})$. This contrasts with the alternative usage in statistics, where "sample" refers to a collection of realizations $\{\mathbf{x}\}$.

The probability distribution $P(\mathbf{x})$, which we will call the **target density**, might be a distribution from statistical physics or a conditional distribution arising in data modelling — for example, the posterior probability of a model's parameters given some observed data. We will generally assume that $\mathbf{x}$ is an N–dimensional vector with real components x_n, but we will sometimes consider discrete spaces also.

We will concentrate on the first problem (sampling), because if we have solved it, then we can solve the second problem by using the random samples $\{\mathbf{x}^{(r)}\}_{r=1}^R$ to give the estimator

$$\hat{\Phi} \equiv \frac{1}{R} \sum_r \phi(\mathbf{x}^{(r)}). \qquad (2)$$

Clearly if the vectors $\{\mathbf{x}^{(r)}\}_{r=1}^R$ are generated from $P(\mathbf{x})$ then the expectation of $\hat{\Phi}$ is Φ. Also, as the number of samples R increases, the variance of $\hat{\Phi}$ will decrease as $\frac{\sigma^2}{R}$, where σ^2 is the variance of ϕ,

$$\sigma^2 = \int d^N\mathbf{x} \, P(\mathbf{x})(\phi(\mathbf{x}) - \Phi)^2. \qquad (3)$$

This is one of the important properties of Monte Carlo methods.

The accuracy of the Monte Carlo estimate (equation (2)) is independent of the dimensionality of the space sampled. To be precise, the variance of $\hat{\Phi}$ goes as $\frac{\sigma^2}{R}$. So regardless of the dimensionality of $\mathbf{x}$, it may be that as few as a dozen independent samples $\{\mathbf{x}^{(r)}\}$ suffice to estimate Φ satisfactorily.

We will find later, however, that high dimensionality can cause other difficulties for Monte Carlo methods. Obtaining independent samples from a given distribution $P(\mathbf{x})$ is often not easy.

1.1. WHY IS SAMPLING FROM $P(\mathbf{x})$ HARD?

We will assume that the density from which we wish to draw samples, $P(\mathbf{x})$, can be evaluated, at least to within a multiplicative constant; that is, we can evaluate a function $P^*(\mathbf{x})$ such that

$$P(\mathbf{x}) = P^*(\mathbf{x})/Z. \qquad (4)$$

If we can evaluate $P^*(\mathbf{x})$, why can we not easily solve problem 1? Why is it in general difficult to obtain samples from $P(\mathbf{x})$? There are two difficulties. The first is that we typically do not know the normalizing constant

$$Z = \int d^N\mathbf{x} \, P^*(\mathbf{x}). \qquad (5)$$

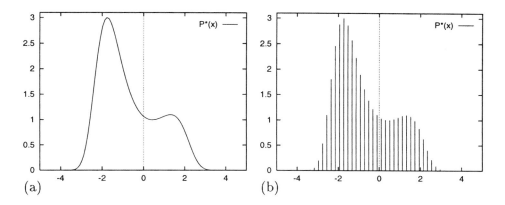

Figure 1. (a) The function $P^*(x) = \exp\left[0.4(x - 0.4)^2 - 0.08x^4\right]$. How to draw samples from this density? (b) The function $P^*(x)$ evaluated at a discrete set of uniformly spaced points $\{x_i\}$. How to draw samples from this discrete distribution?

The second is that, even if we did know Z, the problem of drawing samples from $P(\mathbf{x})$ is still a challenging one, especially in high–dimensional spaces. There are only a few high–dimensional densities from which it is easy to draw samples, for example the Gaussian distribution.[2]

Let us start from a simple one–dimensional example. Imagine that we wish to draw samples from the density $P(x) = P^*(x)/Z$ where

$$P^*(x) = \exp\left[0.4(x - 0.4)^2 - 0.08x^4\right], \;\; x \in (-\infty, \infty). \qquad (6)$$

We can plot this function (figure 1a). But that does not mean we can draw samples from it. To give ourselves a simpler problem, we could discretize the variable x and ask for samples from the discrete probability distribution over a set of uniformly spaced points $\{x_i\}$ (figure 1b). How could we solve this problem? If we evaluate $p_i^* = P^*(x_i)$ at each point x_i, we can compute

$$Z = \sum_i p_i^* \qquad (7)$$

and

$$p_i = p_i^*/Z \qquad (8)$$

and we can then sample from the probability distribution $\{p_i\}$ using various methods based on a source of random bits. But what is the cost of this procedure, and how does it scale with the dimensionality of the space,

---

[2]A sample from a univariate Gaussian can be generated by computing $\cos(2\pi u_1)\sqrt{2\log(1/u_2)}$, where u_1 and u_2 are uniformly distributed in $(0, 1)$.

N? Let us concentrate on the initial cost of evaluating Z. To compute Z (equation (7)) we have to visit every point in the space. In figure 1b there are 50 uniformly spaced points in one dimension. If our system had N dimensions, $N = 1000$ say, then the corresponding number of points would be 50^{1000}, an unimaginable number of evaluations of P^*. Even if each component x_n only took two discrete values, the number of evaluations of P^* would be 2^{1000}, a number that is still horribly huge, equal to the fourth power of the number of particles in the universe.

One system with 2^{1000} states is a collection of 1000 spins, for example, a 30×30 fragment of an Ising model (or 'Boltzmann machine' or 'Markov field') (Yeomans 1992) whose probability distribution is proportional to

$$P^*(\mathbf{x}) = \exp\left[-\beta E(\mathbf{x})\right] \tag{9}$$

where $x_n \in \{\pm 1\}$ and

$$E(\mathbf{x}) = -\left[\frac{1}{2}\sum_{m,n} J_{mn} x_m x_n + \sum_n H_n x_n\right]. \tag{10}$$

The energy function $E(\mathbf{x})$ is readily evaluated for any $\mathbf{x}$. But if we wish to evaluate this function at *all* states $\mathbf{x}$, the computer time required would be 2^{1000} function evaluations.

The Ising model is a simple model which has been around for a long time, but the task of generating samples from the distribution $P(\mathbf{x}) = P^*(\mathbf{x})/Z$ is still an active research area as evidenced by the work of Propp and Wilson (1996).

1.2. UNIFORM SAMPLING

Having agreed that we cannot visit every location $\mathbf{x}$ in the state space, we might consider trying to solve the second problem (estimating the expectation of a function $\phi(\mathbf{x})$) by drawing random samples $\{\mathbf{x}^{(r)}\}_{r=1}^R$ *uniformly* from the state space and evaluating $P^*(\mathbf{x})$ at those points. Then we could introduce Z_R, defined by

$$Z_R = \sum_{r=1}^R P^*(\mathbf{x}^{(r)}), \tag{11}$$

and estimate $\Phi = \int d^N\mathbf{x}\, \phi(\mathbf{x})P(\mathbf{x})$ by

$$\hat{\Phi} = \sum_{r=1}^R \phi(\mathbf{x}^{(r)}) \frac{P^*(\mathbf{x}^{(r)})}{Z_R}. \tag{12}$$

Is anything wrong with this strategy? Well, it depends on the functions $\phi(\mathbf{x})$ and $P^*(\mathbf{x})$. Let us assume that $\phi(\mathbf{x})$ is a benign, smoothly varying function and concentrate on the nature of $P^*(\mathbf{x})$. A high–dimensional distribution is often concentrated in a small region of the state space known as its typical set T, whose volume is given by $|T| \simeq 2^{H(\mathbf{X})}$, where $H(\mathbf{X})$ is the Shannon–Gibbs entropy of the probability distribution $P(\mathbf{x})$,

$$H(\mathbf{X}) = \sum_{\mathbf{x}} P(\mathbf{x}) \log_2 \frac{1}{P(\mathbf{x})}. \tag{13}$$

If almost all the probability mass is located in the typical set and $\phi(\mathbf{x})$ is a benign function, the value of $\Phi = \int d^N\mathbf{x}\, \phi(\mathbf{x}) P(\mathbf{x})$ will be principally determined by the values that $\phi(\mathbf{x})$ takes on in the typical set. So uniform sampling will only stand a chance of giving a good estimate of Φ if we make the number of samples R sufficiently large that we are likely to hit the typical set a number of times. So, how many samples are required? Let us take the case of the Ising model again. The total size of the state space is 2^N states, and the typical set has size 2^H. So each sample has a chance of $2^H/2^N$ of falling in the typical set. The number of samples required to hit the typical set once is thus of order

$$R_{\min} \simeq 2^{N-H}. \tag{14}$$

So, what is H? At high temperatures, the probability distribution of an Ising model tends to a uniform distribution and the entropy tends to $H_{\max} = N$ bits, so $R_{\min}$ is of order 1. Under these conditions, uniform sampling may well be a satisfactory technique for estimating Φ. But high temperatures are not of great interest. Considerably more interesting are intermediate temperatures such as the critical temperature at which the Ising model melts from an ordered phase to a disordered phase. At this temperature the entropy of an Ising model is roughly $N/2$ bits. For this probability distribution the number of samples required simply to hit the typical set once is of order

$$R_{\min} \simeq 2^{N-N/2} = 2^{N/2} \tag{15}$$

which for $N = 1000$ is about 10^{150}. This is roughly the square of the number of particles in the universe. Thus uniform sampling is utterly useless for the study of Ising models of modest size. And in most high–dimensional problems, if the distribution $P(\mathbf{x})$ is not actually uniform, uniform sampling is unlikely to be useful.

1.3. OVERVIEW

Having established that drawing samples from a high–dimensional distri-bution $P(\mathbf{x}) = P^*(\mathbf{x})/Z$ is difficult even if $P^*(\mathbf{x})$ is easy to evaluate, we will

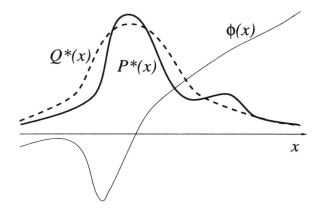

Figure 2. Functions involved in importance sampling. We wish to estimate the expectation of $\phi(x)$ under $P(x) \propto P^*(x)$. We can generate samples from the simpler distribution $Q(x) \propto Q^*(x)$. We can evaluate Q^* and P^* at any point.

now study a sequence of Monte Carlo methods: **importance sampling, rejection sampling,** the **Metropolis method,** and **Gibbs sampling.**

2. Importance sampling

Importance sampling is not a method for generating samples from $P(\mathbf{x})$ (problem 1); it is just a method for estimating the expectation of a function $\phi(\mathbf{x})$ (problem 2). It can be viewed as a generalization of the uniform sampling method.

For illustrative purposes, let us imagine that the target distribution is a one–dimensional density $P(x)$. It is assumed that we are able to evaluate this density, at least to within a multiplicative constant; thus we can evaluate a function $P^*(x)$ such that

$$P(x) = P^*(x)/Z. \tag{16}$$

But $P(x)$ is too complicated a function for us to be able to sample from it directly. We now assume that we have a simpler density $Q(x)$ which we can evaluate to within a multiplicative constant (that is, we can evaluate $Q^*(x)$, where $Q(x) = Q^*(x)/Z_Q$), and from which we can generate samples. An example of the functions P^*, Q^* and ϕ is shown in figure 2. We call Q the *sampler density.*

In importance sampling, we generate R samples $\{x^{(r)}\}_{r=1}^R$ from $Q(x)$. If these points were samples from $P(x)$ then we could estimate Φ by equation (2). But when we generate samples from Q, values of x where $Q(x)$ is greater than $P(x)$ will be over–represented in this estimator, and points

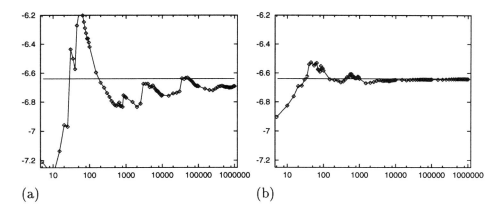

Figure 3. Importance sampling in action: a) using a Gaussian sampler density; b) using a Cauchy sampler density. Horizontal axis shows number of samples on a log scale. Vertical axis shows the estimate $\hat{\Phi}$. The horizontal line indicates the true value of Φ.

where $Q(x)$ is less than $P(x)$ will be under–represented. To take into account the fact that we have sampled from the wrong distribution, we introduce 'weights'

$$w_r \equiv \frac{P^*(x^{(r)})}{Q^*(x^{(r)})} \tag{17}$$

which we use to adjust the 'importance' of each point in our estimator thus:

$$\hat{\Phi} \equiv \frac{\sum_r w_r \phi(x^{(r)})}{\sum_r w_r}. \tag{18}$$

If $Q(x)$ is non–zero for all x where $P(x)$ is non–zero, it can be proved that the estimator $\hat{\Phi}$ converges to Φ, the mean value of $\phi(x)$, as R increases.

A practical difficulty with importance sampling is that it is hard to estimate how reliable the estimator $\hat{\Phi}$ is. The variance of $\hat{\Phi}$ is hard to estimate, because the empirical variances of the quantities w_r and $w_r\phi(x^{(r)})$ are not necessarily a good guide to the true variances of the numerator and denominator in equation (18). If the proposal density $Q(x)$ is small in a region where $|\phi(x)P^*(x)|$ is large then it is quite possible, even after many points $x^{(r)}$ have been generated, that none of them will have fallen in that region. This leads to an estimate of Φ that is drastically wrong, and no indication in the empirical variance that the true variance of the estimator $\hat{\Phi}$ is large.

2.1. CAUTIONARY ILLUSTRATION OF IMPORTANCE SAMPLING

In a toy problem related to the modelling of amino acid probability distributions with a one–dimensional variable x I evaluated a quantity of interest using importance sampling. The results using a Gaussian sampler and a Cauchy sampler are shown in figure 3. The horizontal axis shows the number of samples on a log scale. In the case of the Gaussian sampler, after about 500 samples had been evaluated one might be tempted to call a halt; but evidently there are infrequent samples that make a huge contribution to $\hat{\Phi}$, and the value of the estimate at 500 samples is wrong. Even after a million samples have been taken, the estimate has still not settled down close to the true value. In contrast, the Cauchy sampler does not suffer from glitches and converges (on the scale shown here) after about 5000 samples.

This example illustrates the fact that an importance sampler should have **heavy tails**.

2.2. IMPORTANCE SAMPLING IN MANY DIMENSIONS

We have already observed that care is needed in one–dimensional importance sampling problems. Is importance sampling a useful technique in spaces of higher dimensionality, say $N = 1000$?

Consider a simple case–study where the target density $P(\mathbf{x})$ is a uniform distribution inside a sphere,

$$P^*(\mathbf{x}) = \left\{ \begin{array}{ll} 1 & 0 \leq \rho(\mathbf{x}) \leq R_P \\ 0 & \rho(\mathbf{x}) > R_P \end{array} \right. , \tag{19}$$

where $\rho(\mathbf{x}) \equiv (\sum_i x_i^2)^{1/2}$, and the proposal density is a Gaussian centred on the origin,

$$Q(\mathbf{x}) = \prod_i \text{Normal}(x_i; 0, \sigma^2). \tag{20}$$

An importance sampling method will be in trouble if the estimator $\hat{\Phi}$ is dominated by a few large weights w_r. What will be the typical range of values of the weights w_r? By the central limit theorem, if ρ is the distance from the origin of a sample from Q, the quantity ρ^2 has a roughly Gaussian distribution with mean and standard deviation:

$$\rho^2 \sim N\sigma^2 \pm \sqrt{2N}\sigma^2. \tag{21}$$

Thus almost all samples from Q lie in a 'typical set' with distance from the origin very close to $\sqrt{N}\sigma$. Let us assume that σ is chosen such that the typical set of Q lies inside the sphere of radius R_P. [If it does not, then the law of large numbers implies that almost all the samples generated from Q

will fall outside R_P and will have weight zero.] Then we know that most samples from Q will have a value of Q that lies in the range

$$\frac{1}{(2\pi\sigma^2)^{N/2}} \exp\left(-\frac{N}{2} \pm \frac{\sqrt{2N}}{2}\right). \tag{22}$$

Thus the weights $w_r = P^*/Q$ will typically have values in the range

$$(2\pi\sigma^2)^{N/2} \exp\left(\frac{N}{2} \pm \frac{\sqrt{2N}}{2}\right). \tag{23}$$

So if we draw a hundred samples, what will the typical range of weights be? We can roughly estimate the ratio of the largest weight to the median weight by doubling the standard deviation in equation (23). The largest weight and the median weight will typically be in the ratio:

$$\frac{w_r^{\mathrm{max}}}{w_r^{\mathrm{med}}} = \exp\left(\sqrt{2N}\right). \tag{24}$$

In $N = 1000$ dimensions therefore, the largest weight after one hundred samples is likely to be roughly 10^{19} times greater than the median weight. Thus an importance sampling estimate for a high–dimensional problem will very likely be utterly dominated by a few samples with huge weights.

In conclusion, importance sampling in high dimensions often suffers from two difficulties. First, we clearly need to obtain samples that lie in the typical set of P, and this may take a long time unless Q is a good approximation to P. Second, even if we obtain samples in the typical set, the weights associated with those samples are likely to vary by large factors, because the probabilities of points in a typical set, although similar to each other, still differ by factors of order $\exp(\sqrt{N})$.

3. Rejection sampling

We assume again a one–dimensional density $P(x) = P^*(x)/Z$ that is too complicated a function for us to be able to sample from it directly. We assume that we have a simpler *proposal density* $Q(x)$ which we can evaluate (within a multiplicative factor Z_Q, as before), and which we can generate samples from. We further assume that we know the value of a constant c such that

$$\text{for all } x, \ cQ^*(x) > P^*(x). \tag{25}$$

A schematic picture of the two functions is shown in figure 4a.

We generate two random numbers. The first, x, is generated from the proposal density $Q(x)$. We then evaluate $cQ^*(x)$ and generate a uniformly

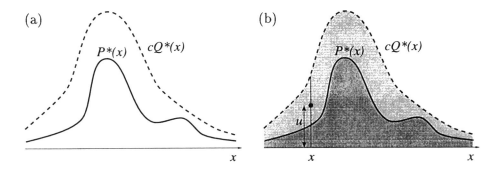

Figure 4. Rejection sampling. a) The functions involved in rejection sampling. We desire samples from $P(x) \propto P^*(x)$. We are able to draw samples from $Q(x) \propto Q^*(x)$, and we know a value c such that $cQ^*(x) > P^*(x)$ for all x. b) A point (x, u) is generated at random in the lightly shaded area under the curve $cQ^*(x)$. If this point also lies below $P^*(x)$ then it is accepted.

distributed random variable u from the interval $[0, cQ^*(x)]$. These two random numbers can be viewed as selecting a point in the two–dimensional plane as shown in figure 4b.

We now evaluate $P^*(x)$ and accept or reject the sample x by comparing the value of u with the value of $P^*(x)$. If $u > P^*(x)$ then x is rejected; otherwise it is accepted, which means that we add x to our set of samples $\{x^{(r)}\}$. The value of u is discarded.

Why does this procedure generate samples from $P(x)$? The proposed point (x, u) comes with uniform probability from the lightly shaded area underneath the curve $cQ^*(x)$ as shown in figure 4b. The rejection rule rejects all the points that lie above the curve $P^*(x)$. So the points (x, u) that are accepted are uniformly distributed in the heavily shaded area under $P^*(x)$. This implies that the probability density of the x–coordinates of the accepted points must be proportional to $P^*(x)$, so the samples must be independent samples from $P(x)$.

Rejection sampling will work best if Q is a good approximation to P. If Q is very different from P then c will necessarily have to be large and the frequency of rejection will be large.

3.1. REJECTION SAMPLING IN MANY DIMENSIONS

In a high–dimensional problem it is very likely that the requirement that cQ^* be an upper bound for P^* will force c to be so huge that acceptances will be very rare indeed. Finding such a value of c may be difficult too, since in many problems we don't know beforehand where the modes of P^* are located or how high they are.

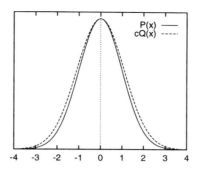

Figure 5. A Gaussian $P(x)$ and a slightly broader Gaussian $Q(x)$ scaled up by a factor c such that $cQ(x) \geq P(x)$.

As a case study, consider a pair of N–dimensional Gaussian distributions with mean zero (figure 5). Imagine generating samples from one with standard deviation σ_Q and using rejection sampling to obtain samples from the other whose standard deviation is σ_P. Let us assume that these two standard deviations are close in value — say, σ_Q is one percent larger than σ_P. [σ_Q must be larger than σ_P because if this is not the case, there is no c such that cQ upper–bounds P for all $\mathbf{x}$.] So, what is the value of c if the dimensionality is $N = 1000$? The density of $Q(\mathbf{x})$ at the origin is $1/(2\pi\sigma_Q^2)^{N/2}$, so for cQ to upper–bound P we need to set

$$c = \frac{(2\pi\sigma_Q^2)^{N/2}}{(2\pi\sigma_P^2)^{N/2}} = \exp\left(N \log \frac{\sigma_Q}{\sigma_P}\right). \tag{26}$$

With $N = 1000$ and $\frac{\sigma_Q}{\sigma_P} = 1.01$, we find $c = \exp(10) \simeq 20,000$. What will the rejection rate be for this value of c? The answer is immediate: since the acceptance rate is the ratio of the volume under the curve $P(\mathbf{x})$ to the volume under $cQ(\mathbf{x})$, the fact that P and Q are normalized implies that the acceptance rate will be $1/c$. For our case study, this is $1/20,000$. In general, c grows exponentially with the dimensionality N.

Rejection sampling, therefore, whilst a useful method for one–dimensional problems, is not a practical technique for generating samples from high–dimensional distributions $P(\mathbf{x})$.

4. The Metropolis method

Importance sampling and rejection sampling only work well if the proposal density $Q(x)$ is similar to $P(x)$. In large and complex problems it is difficult to create a single density $Q(x)$ that has this property.

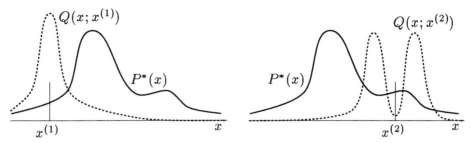

Figure 6.   Metropolis method in one dimension. The proposal distribution $Q(x'; x)$ is here shown as having a shape that changes as x changes, though this is not typical of the proposal densities used in practice.

The Metropolis algorithm instead makes use of a proposal density Q *which depends on the current state* $x^{(t)}$. The density $Q(x'; x^{(t)})$ might in the simplest case be a simple distribution such as a Gaussian centred on the current $x^{(t)}$. The proposal density $Q(x'; x)$ can be any fixed density. It is not necessary for $Q(x'; x^{(t)})$ to look at all similar to $P(x)$. An example of a proposal density is shown in figure 6; this figure shows the density $Q(x'; x^{(t)})$ for two different states $x^{(1)}$ and $x^{(2)}$.

As before, we assume that we can evaluate $P^*(x)$ for any x. A tentative new state x' is generated from the proposal density $Q(x'; x^{(t)})$. To decide whether to accept the new state, we compute the quantity

$$a = \frac{P^*(x')}{P^*(x^{(t)})} \frac{Q(x^{(t)}; x')}{Q(x'; x^{(t)})}. \tag{27}$$

If $a \geq 1$ then the new state is accepted.

Otherwise, the new state is accepted with probability a.   (28)

If the step is accepted, we set $x^{(t+1)} = x'$. If the step is rejected, then we set $x^{(t+1)} = x^{(t)}$. Note the difference from rejection sampling: in rejection sampling, rejected points are discarded and have no influence on the list of samples $\{x^{(r)}\}$ that we collected. Here, a rejection causes the current state to be written onto the list of points another time.

Notation: I have used the superscript $r = 1 \ldots R$ to label points that are *independent* samples from a distribution, and the superscript $t = 1 \ldots T$ to label the sequence of states in a Markov chain. It is important to note that a Metropolis simulation of T iterations does not produce T independent samples from the target distribution P. The samples are correlated.

To compute the acceptance probability we need to be able to compute the probability ratios $P(x')/P(x^{(t)})$ and $Q(x^{(t)}; x')/Q(x'; x^{(t)})$. If the proposal density is a simple symmetrical density such as a Gaussian centred on the current point, then the latter factor is unity, and the Metropolis

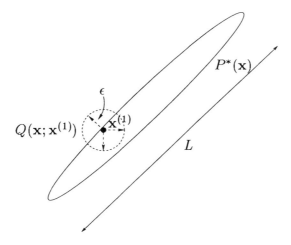

Figure 7. Metropolis method in two dimensions, showing a traditional proposal density that has a sufficiently small step size ϵ that the acceptance frequency will be about 0.5.

method simply involves comparing the value of the target density at the two points. The general algorithm for asymmetric Q, given above, is often called the Metropolis–Hastings algorithm.

It can be shown that for any positive Q (that is, any Q such that $Q(x';x) > 0$ for all x, x'), as $t \to \infty$, the probability distribution of $x^{(t)}$ tends to $P(x) = P^*(x)/Z$. [This statement should not be seen as implying that Q *has* to assign positive probability to every point x' — we will discuss examples later where $Q(x';x) = 0$ for some x, x'; notice also that we have said nothing about how rapidly the convergence to $P(x)$ takes place.]

The Metropolis method is an example of a '**Markov chain Monte Carlo**' method (abbreviated MCMC). In contrast to rejection sampling where the accepted points $\{x^{(r)}\}$ are independent samples from the desired distribution, Markov chain Monte Carlo methods involve a Markov process in which a sequence of states $\{x^{(t)}\}$ is generated, each sample $x^{(t)}$ having a probability distribution that depends on the previous value, $x^{(t-1)}$. Since successive samples are correlated with each other, the Markov chain may have to be run for a considerable time in order to generate samples that are effectively independent samples from P.

Just as it was difficult to estimate the variance of an importance sampling estimator, so it is difficult to assess whether a Markov chain Monte Carlo method has 'converged', and to quantify how long one has to wait to obtain samples that are effectively independent samples from P.

4.1. DEMONSTRATION OF THE METROPOLIS METHOD

The Metropolis method is widely used for high–dimensional problems. Many implementations of the Metropolis method employ a proposal distribution with a length scale ϵ that is short relative to the length scale L of the probable region (figure 7). A reason for choosing a small length scale is that for most high–dimensional problems, a large random step from a typical point (that is, a sample from $P(\mathbf{x})$) is very likely to end in a state which has very low probability; such steps are unlikely to be accepted. If ϵ is large, movement around the state space will only occur when a transition to a state which has very low probability is actually accepted, or when a large random step chances to land in another probable state. So the rate of progress will be slow, unless small steps are used.

The disadvantage of small steps, on the other hand, is that the Metropolis method will explore the probability distribution by a *random walk*, and random walks take a long time to get anywhere. Consider a one–dimensional random walk, for example, on each step of which the state moves randomly to the left or to the right with equal probability. After T steps of size ϵ, the state is only likely to have moved a distance about $\sqrt{T}\epsilon$. Recall that the first aim of Monte Carlo sampling is to generate a number of *independent* samples from the given distribution (a dozen, say). If the largest length scale of the state space is L, then we have to simulate a random–walk Metropolis method for a time $T \simeq (L/\epsilon)^2$ before we can expect to get a sample that is roughly independent of the initial condition — and that's assuming that every step is accepted: if only a fraction f of the steps are accepted on average, then this time is increased by a factor $1/f$.

Rule of thumb: lower bound on number of iterations of a Metropolis method. If the largest length scale of the space of probable states is L, a Metropolis method whose proposal distribution generates a random walk with step size ϵ must be run for at least $T \simeq (L/\epsilon)^2$ iterations to obtain an independent sample.

This rule of thumb only gives a lower bound; the situation may be much worse, if, for example, the probability distribution consists of several islands of high probability separated by regions of low probability.

To illustrate how slow the exploration of a state space by random walk is, figure 8 shows a simulation of a Metropolis algorithm for generating samples from the distribution:

$$P(x) = \left\{ \begin{array}{ll} \frac{1}{21} & x \in \{0, 1, 2 \ldots, 20\} \\ 0 & \text{otherwise} \end{array} \right. . \tag{29}$$

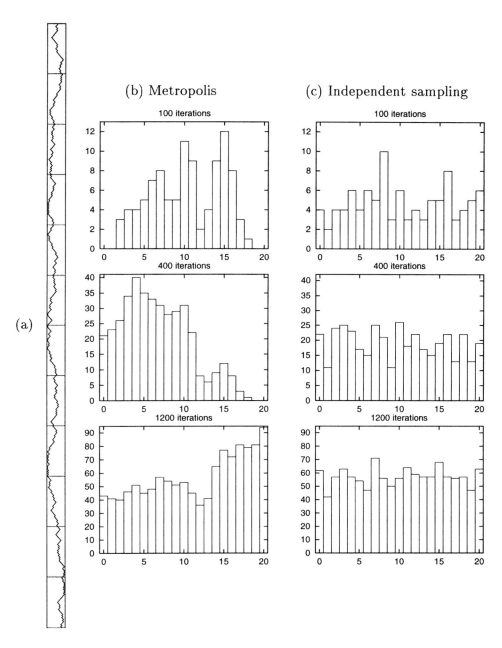

Figure 8. Metropolis method for a toy problem. (a) The state sequence for $t = 1 \ldots 600$. Horizontal direction = states from 0 to 20; vertical direction = time from 1 to 600; the cross bars mark time intervals of duration 50. (b) Histogram of occupancy of the states after 100, 400 and 1200 iterations. (c) For comparison, histograms resulting when successive points are drawn *independently* from the target distribution.

The proposal distribution is

$$Q(x'; x) = \left\{ \begin{array}{ll} \frac{1}{2} & x' = x \pm 1 \\ 0 & \text{otherwise} \end{array} \right. . \tag{30}$$

Because the target distribution $P(x)$ is uniform, rejections will occur only when the proposal takes the state to $x' = -1$ or $x' = 21$.

The simulation was started in the state $x_0 = 10$ and its evolution is shown in figure 8a. How long does it take to reach one of the end states $x = 0$ and $x = 20$? Since the distance is 10 steps the rule of thumb above predicts that it will typically take a time $T \simeq 100$ iterations to reach an end state. This is confirmed in the present example. The first step into an end state occurs on the 178th iteration. How long does it take to visit *both* end states? The rule of thumb predicts about 400 iterations are required to traverse the whole state space. And indeed the first encounter with the other end state takes place on the 540th iteration. Thus effectively independent samples are only generated by simulating for about four hundred iterations.

This simple example shows that it is important to try to abolish random walk behaviour in Monte Carlo methods. A systematic exploration of the toy state space $\{0, 1, 2, \ldots 20\}$ could get around it, using the same step sizes, in about twenty steps instead of four hundred!

4.2. METROPOLIS METHOD IN HIGH DIMENSIONS

The rule of thumb that we discussed above, giving a lower bound on the number of iterations of a random walk Metropolis method, also applies to higher dimensional problems. Consider the simplest case of a target distribution that is a Gaussian, and a proposal distribution that is a spherical Gaussian of standard deviation in each direction equal to ϵ. Without loss of generality, we can assume that the target distribution is a separable distribution aligned with the axes $\{x_n\}$, and that it has standard deviations $\{\sigma_n\}$ in the different directions n. Let $\sigma^{\max}$ and $\sigma^{\min}$ be the largest and smallest of these standard deviations. Let us assume that ϵ is adjusted such that the acceptance probability is close to 1. Under this assumption, each variable x_n evolves independently of all the others, executing a random walk with step sizes about ϵ. The time taken to generate effectively independent samples from the target distribution will be controlled by the largest lengthscale $\sigma^{\max}$; just as in the previous section, where we needed at least $T \simeq (L/\epsilon)^2$ iterations to obtain an independent sample, here we need $T \simeq (\sigma^{\max}/\epsilon)^2$.

Now how big can ϵ be? The bigger it is, the smaller this number T becomes, but if ϵ is too big — bigger than $\sigma^{\min}$ — then the acceptance rate will fall sharply. It seems plausible that the optimal ϵ must be similar to

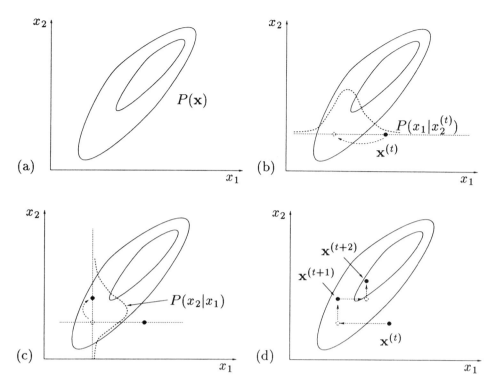

Figure 9. Gibbs sampling. (a) The joint density $P(\mathbf{x})$ from which samples are required. (b) Starting from a state $\mathbf{x}^{(t)}$, x_1 is sampled from the conditional density $P(x_1|x_2^{(t)})$. (c) A sample is then made from the conditional density $P(x_2|x_1)$. (d) A couple of iterations of Gibbs sampling.

$\sigma^{\min}$. Strictly, this may not be true; in special cases where the second smallest σ_n is significantly greater than $\sigma^{\min}$, the optimal ϵ may be closer to that second smallest σ_n. But our rough conclusion is this: where simple spherical proposal distributions are used, we will need at least $T \simeq (\sigma^{\max}/\sigma^{\min})^2$ iterations to obtain an independent sample, where $\sigma^{\max}$ and $\sigma^{\min}$ are the longest and shortest lengthscales of the target distribution.

This is good news and bad news. It is good news because, unlike the cases of rejection sampling and importance sampling, there is no catastrophic dependence on the dimensionality N. But it is bad news in that all the same, this quadratic dependence on the lengthscale ratio may force us to make very lengthy simulations.

Fortunately, there are methods for suppressing random walks in Monte Carlo simulations, which we will discuss later.

5. Gibbs sampling

We introduced importance sampling, rejection sampling and the Metropolis method using one–dimensional examples. Gibbs sampling, also known as the *heat bath method*, is a method for sampling from distributions over at least two dimensions. It can be viewed as a Metropolis method in which the proposal distribution Q is defined in terms of the *conditional* distributions of the joint distribution $P(\mathbf{x})$. It is assumed that whilst $P(\mathbf{x})$ is too complex to draw samples from directly, its conditional distributions $P(x_i|\{x_j\}_{j\neq i})$ are tractable to work with. For many graphical models (but not all) these one–dimensional conditional distributions are straightforward to sample from. Conditional distributions that are not of standard form may still be sampled from by adaptive rejection sampling if the conditional distribution satisfies certain convexity properties (Gilks and Wild 1992).

Gibbs sampling is illustrated for a case with two variables $(x_1, x_2) = \mathbf{x}$ in figure 9. On each iteration, we start from the current state $\mathbf{x}^{(t)}$, and x_1 is sampled from the conditional density $P(x_1|x_2)$, with x_2 fixed to $x_2^{(t)}$. A sample x_2 is then made from the conditional density $P(x_2|x_1)$, using the new value of x_1. This brings us to the new state $\mathbf{x}^{(t+1)}$, and completes the iteration.

In the general case of a system with K variables, a single iteration involves sampling one parameter at a time:

$$x_1^{(t+1)} \ \sim \ P(x_1|x_2^{(t)}, x_3^{(t)}, \ldots x_K^{(t)}) \tag{31}$$

$$x_2^{(t+1)} \ \sim \ P(x_2|x_1^{(t+1)}, x_3^{(t)}, \ldots x_K^{(t)}) \tag{32}$$

$$x_3^{(t+1)} \ \sim \ P(x_3|x_1^{(t+1)}, x_2^{(t+1)}, \ldots x_K^{(t)}), \text{etc.} \tag{33}$$

Gibbs sampling can be viewed as a Metropolis method which has the property that every proposal is always accepted. Because Gibbs sampling is a Metropolis method, the probability distribution of $\mathbf{x}^{(t)}$ tends to $P(\mathbf{x})$ as $t \to \infty$, as long as $P(\mathbf{x})$ does not have pathological properties.

5.1. GIBBS SAMPLING IN HIGH DIMENSIONS

Gibbs sampling suffers from the same defect as simple Metropolis algorithms — the state space is explored by a random walk, unless a fortuitous parameterization has been chosen which makes the probability distribution $P(\mathbf{x})$ separable. If, say, two variables x_1 and x_2 are strongly correlated, having marginal densities of width L and conditional densities of width ϵ, then it will take at least about $(L/\epsilon)^2$ iterations to generate an independent sample from the target density. However Gibbs sampling involves no adjustable parameters, so it is an attractive strategy when one wants to get a model running quickly. An excellent software package, BUGS, is available which makes it easy to set up almost arbitrary probabilistic models and simulate them by Gibbs sampling (Thomas, Spiegelhalter and Gilks 1992).

6. Terminology for Markov chain Monte Carlo methods

We now spend a few moments sketching the theory on which the Metropolis method and Gibbs sampling are based.

A **Markov chain** can be specified by an **initial** probability distribution $p^{(0)}(\mathbf{x})$ and a **transition probability** $T(\mathbf{x}'; \mathbf{x})$.

The probability distribution of the state at the $(t+1)$th iteration of the Markov chain is given by

$$p^{(t+1)}(\mathbf{x}') = \int d^N\mathbf{x}\, T(\mathbf{x}'; \mathbf{x})p^{(t)}(\mathbf{x}). \tag{34}$$

We construct the chain such that:

1. The desired distribution $P(\mathbf{x})$ is the **invariant distribution** of the chain.
   A distribution $\pi(\mathbf{x})$ is an invariant distribution of $T(\mathbf{x}'; \mathbf{x})$ if

$$\pi(\mathbf{x}') = \int d^N\mathbf{x}\, T(\mathbf{x}'; \mathbf{x})\pi(\mathbf{x}). \tag{35}$$

2. The chain must also be **ergodic**, that is,

$$p^{(t)}(\mathbf{x}) \to \pi(\mathbf{x}) \text{ as } t \to \infty, \text{ for any } p^{(0)}(\mathbf{x}). \tag{36}$$

It is often convenient to construct T by mixing or concatenating simple **base transitions** B all of which satisfy

$$P(\mathbf{x}') = \int d^N\mathbf{x}\, B(\mathbf{x}'; \mathbf{x})P(\mathbf{x}), \tag{37}$$

for the desired density $P(\mathbf{x})$. These base transitions need not be individually ergodic.

Many useful transition probabilities satisfy the **detailed balance** property:

$$T(\mathbf{x}'; \mathbf{x})P(\mathbf{x}) = T(\mathbf{x}; \mathbf{x}')P(\mathbf{x}'), \text{ for all } \mathbf{x} \text{ and } \mathbf{x}'. \tag{38}$$

This equation says that if we pick a state from the target density P and make a transition under T to another state, it is just as likely that we will pick $\mathbf{x}$ and go from $\mathbf{x}$ to $\mathbf{x}'$ as it is that we will pick $\mathbf{x}'$ and go from $\mathbf{x}'$ to $\mathbf{x}$. Markov chains that satisfy detailed balance are also called **reversible** Markov chains. The reason why the detailed balance property is of interest is that detailed balance implies invariance of the distribution $P(\mathbf{x})$ under the Markov chain T (the proof of this is left as an exercise for the reader). Proving that detailed balance holds is often a key step when proving that a Markov chain Monte Carlo simulation will converge to the desired distribution. The Metropolis method and Gibbs sampling method both satisfy detailed balance, for example. Detailed balance is not an essential condition, however, and we will see later that irreversible Markov chains can be useful in practice.

7. Practicalities

Can we predict how long a Markov chain Monte Carlo simulation will take to equilibrate? By considering the random walks involved in a Markov chain Monte Carlo simulation we can obtain simple *lower bounds* on the time required for convergence. But predicting this time more precisely is a difficult problem, and most of the theoretical results are of little practical use.

Can we diagnose or detect convergence in a running simulation? This is also a difficult problem. There are a few practical tools available, but none of them is perfect (Cowles and Carlin 1996).

Can we speed up the convergence time and time between independent samples of a Markov chain Monte Carlo method? Here, there is good news.

7.1. SPEEDING UP MONTE CARLO METHODS

7.1.1. *Reducing random walk behaviour in Metropolis methods*

The hybrid Monte Carlo method reviewed in Neal (1993) is a Metropolis method applicable to continuous state spaces which makes use of gradient information to reduce random walk behaviour.

For many systems, the probability $P(\mathbf{x})$ can be written in the form

$$P(\mathbf{x}) = \frac{e^{-E(\mathbf{x})}}{Z} \tag{39}$$

where not only $E(\mathbf{x})$, but also its gradient with respect to $\mathbf{x}$ can be readily evaluated. It seems wasteful to use a simple random–walk Metropolis method when this gradient is available — the gradient indicates which direction one should go in to find states with higher probability!

In the hybrid Monte Carlo method, the state space $\mathbf{x}$ is augmented by *momentum variables* $\mathbf{p}$, and there is an alternation of two types of proposal. The first proposal randomizes the momentum variable, leaving the state $\mathbf{x}$ unchanged. The second proposal changes both $\mathbf{x}$ and $\mathbf{p}$ using simulated Hamiltonian dynamics as defined by the Hamiltonian

$$H(\mathbf{x}, \mathbf{p}) = E(\mathbf{x}) + K(\mathbf{p}), \tag{40}$$

```
g = gradE ( x ) ;          # set gradient using initial x
E = findE ( x ) ;          # set objective function too

for l = 1:L                # loop L times
   p = randn ( size(x) ) ;  # initial momentum is Normal(0,1)
   H = p' * p / 2 + E ;     # evaluate H(x,p)

   xnew = x
   gnew = g ;
   for tau = 1:Tau          # make Tau 'leapfrog' steps

       p = p - epsilon * gnew / 2 ; # make half-step in p
       xnew = xnew + epsilon * p ;  # make step in x

       gnew = gradE ( xnew ) ;     # find new gradient
       p = p - epsilon * gnew / 2 ; # make half-step in p

   endfor

   Enew = findE ( xnew ) ;   # find new value of H
   Hnew = p' * p / 2 + Enew ;
   dH = Hnew - H ;           # Decide whether to accept

   if ( dH < 0 )                 accept = 1 ;
   elseif ( rand() < exp(-dH) ) accept = 1 ;
   else                          accept = 0 ;
   endif

   if ( accept )
      g = gnew ;   x = xnew ;   E = Enew ;
   endif
endfor
```

Figure 10. Octave source code for the hybrid Monte Carlo method.

where $K(\mathbf{p})$ is a 'kinetic energy' such as $K(\mathbf{p}) = \mathbf{p}^\mathsf{T}\mathbf{p}/2$. These two proposals are used to create (asymptotically) samples from the joint density

$$P_H(\mathbf{x}, \mathbf{p}) = \frac{1}{Z_H} \exp[-H(\mathbf{x}, \mathbf{p})] = \frac{1}{Z_H} \exp[-E(\mathbf{x})] \exp[-K(\mathbf{p})]. \qquad (41)$$

This density is separable, so it is clear that the marginal distribution of $\mathbf{x}$ is the desired distribution $\exp[-E(\mathbf{x})]/Z$. So, simply discarding the momen-

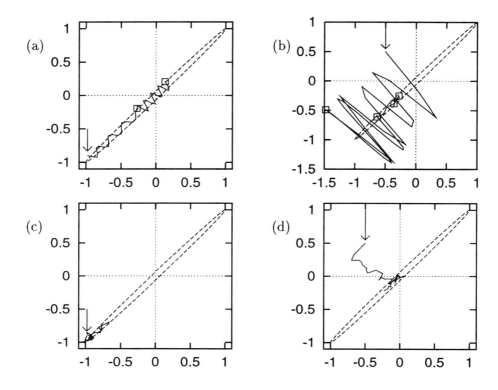

Figure 11. (a,b) Hybrid Monte Carlo used to generate samples from a bivariate Gaussian with correlation $\rho = 0.998$. (c,d) Random–walk Metropolis method for comparison. (a) Starting from the state indicated by the arrow, the continuous line represents two successive trajectories generated by the Hamiltonian dynamics. The squares show the endpoints of these two trajectories. Each trajectory consists of `Tau` = 19 'leapfrog' steps with `epsilon` = 0.055. After each trajectory, the momentum is randomized. Here, both trajectories are accepted; the errors in the Hamiltonian were +0.016 and −0.06 respectively. (b) The second figure shows how a sequence of four trajectories converges from an initial condition, indicated by the arrow, that is not close to the typical set of the target distribution. The trajectory parameters `Tau` and `epsilon` were randomized for each trajectory using uniform distributions with means 19 and 0.055 respectively. The first trajectory takes us to a new state, $(-1.5, -0.5)$, similar in energy to the first state. The second trajectory happens to end in a state nearer the bottom of the energy landscape. Here, since the potential energy E is smaller, the kinetic energy $K = \mathbf{p}^2/2$ is necessarily larger than it was at the start. When the momentum is randomized for the third trajectory, its magnitude becomes much smaller. After the fourth trajectory has been simulated, the state appears to have become typical of the target density. (c) A random–walk Metropolis method using a Gaussian proposal density with radius such that the acceptance rate was 58% in this simulation. The number of proposals was 38 so the total amount of computer time used was similar to that in (a). The distance moved is small because of random walk behaviour. (d) A random–walk Metropolis method given a similar amount of computer time to (b).

tum variables, we will obtain a sequence of samples $\{\mathbf{x}^{(t)}\}$ which asymptotically come from $P(\mathbf{x})$.

The first proposal draws a new momentum from the Gaussian density $\exp[-K(\mathbf{p})]/Z_K$. During the second, dynamical proposal, the momentum variable determines where the state $\mathbf{x}$ goes, and the *gradient* of $E(\mathbf{x})$ determines how the momentum $\mathbf{p}$ changes, in accordance with the equations

$$\dot{\mathbf{x}} = \mathbf{p} \qquad\qquad (42)$$

$$\dot{\mathbf{p}} = -\frac{\partial E(\mathbf{x})}{\partial \mathbf{x}}. \qquad\qquad (43)$$

Because of the persistent motion of $\mathbf{x}$ in the direction of the momentum $\mathbf{p}$, during each dynamical proposal, the state of the system tends to move a distance that goes *linearly* with the computer time, rather than as the square root.

If the simulation of the Hamiltonian dynamics is numerically perfect then the proposals are accepted every time, because the total energy $H(\mathbf{x}, \mathbf{p})$ is a constant of the motion and so a in equation (27) is equal to one. If the simulation is imperfect, because of finite step sizes for example, then some of the dynamical proposals will be rejected. The rejection rule makes use of the change in $H(\mathbf{x}, \mathbf{p})$, which is zero if the simulation is perfect. The occasional rejections ensure that asymptotically, we obtain samples $(\mathbf{x}^{(t)}, \mathbf{p}^{(t)})$ from the required joint density $P_H(\mathbf{x}, \mathbf{p})$.

The source code in figure 10 describes a hybrid Monte Carlo method which uses the 'leapfrog' algorithm to simulate the dynamics on the function findE(x), whose gradient is found by the function gradE(x). Figure 11 shows this algorithm generating samples from a bivariate Gaussian whose energy function is $E(\mathbf{x}) = \frac{1}{2}\mathbf{x}^\mathsf{T}\mathbf{A}\mathbf{x}$ with

$$\mathbf{A} = \begin{bmatrix} 250.25 & -249.75 \\ -249.75 & 250.25 \end{bmatrix}. \qquad\qquad (44)$$

7.1.2. *Overrelaxation*

The method of 'overrelaxation' is a similar method for reducing random walk behaviour in Gibbs sampling. Overrelaxation was originally introduced for systems in which all the conditional distributions are Gaussian. (There are joint distributions that are *not* Gaussian whose conditional distributions *are* all Gaussian, for example, $P(x, y) = \exp(-x^2 y^2)/Z$.)

In ordinary Gibbs sampling, one draws the new value $x_i^{(t+1)}$ of the current variable x_i from its conditional distribution, ignoring the old value $x_i^{(t)}$. This leads to lengthy random walks in cases where the variables are strongly correlated, as illustrated in the left hand panel of figure 12.

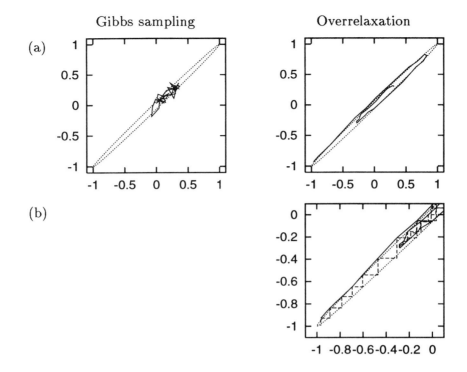

Figure 12. Overrelaxation contrasted with Gibbs sampling for a bivariate Gaussian with correlation $\rho = 0.998$. (a) The state sequence for 40 iterations, each iteration involving one update of both variables. The overrelaxation method had $\alpha = -0.98$. (This excessively large value is chosen to make it easy to see how the overrelaxation method reduces random walk behaviour.) The dotted line shows the contour $\mathbf{x}^T \Sigma^{-1} \mathbf{x} = 1$. (b) Detail of (a), showing the two steps making up each iteration. (After Neal (1995).)

In Adler's (1981) overrelaxation method, one instead samples $x_i^{(t+1)}$ from a Gaussian that is biased to the opposite side of the conditional distribution. If the conditional distribution of x_i is Normal(μ, σ^2) and the current value of x_i is $x_i^{(t)}$, then Adler's method sets x_i to

$$x_i^{(t+1)} = \mu + \alpha(x_i^{(t)} - \mu) + (1 - \alpha^2)^{1/2}\sigma\nu, \qquad (45)$$

where $\nu \sim$ Normal($0, 1$) and α is a parameter between -1 and 1, commonly set to a negative value.

The transition matrix $T(\mathbf{x}'; \mathbf{x})$ defined by this procedure does not satisfy detailed balance. The individual transitions for the individual coordinates just described *do* satisfy detailed balance, but when we form a chain by applying them in a fixed sequence, the overall chain is not reversible. If, say, two variables are positively correlated, then they will (on a short timescale) evolve in a directed manner instead of by random walk, as shown in figure 12. This may significantly reduce the time required to obtain effectively independent samples. This method is still a valid sampling strategy — it converges to the target density $P(\mathbf{x})$ — because it is made up of transitions that satisfy detailed balance.

The overrelaxation method has been generalized by Neal (1995, and this volume) whose 'ordered overrelaxation' method is applicable to any system where Gibbs sampling is used. For practical purposes this method may speed up a simulation by a factor of ten or twenty.

7.1.3. *Simulated annealing*

A third technique for speeding convergence is **simulated annealing**. In simulated annealing, a 'temperature' parameter is introduced which, when large, allows the system to make transitions which would be improbable at temperature 1. The temperature may be initially set to a large value and reduced gradually to 1. It is hoped that this procedure reduces the chance of the simulation's becoming stuck in an unrepresentative probability island.

We asssume that we wish to sample from a distribution of the form

$$P(\mathbf{x}) = \frac{e^{-E(\mathbf{x})}}{Z} \tag{46}$$

where $E(\mathbf{x})$ can be evaluated. In the simplest simulated annealing method, we instead sample from the distribution

$$P_T(\mathbf{x}) = \frac{1}{Z(T)} e^{-\frac{E(\mathbf{x})}{T}} \tag{47}$$

and decrease T gradually to 1.

Often the energy function can be separated into two terms,

$$E(\mathbf{x}) = E_0(\mathbf{x}) + E_1(\mathbf{x}), \tag{48}$$

of which the first term is 'nice' (for example, a separable function of $\mathbf{x}$) and the second is 'nasty'. In these cases, a better simulated annealing method might make use of the distribution

$$P'_T(\mathbf{x}) = \frac{1}{Z'(T)} e^{-E_0(\mathbf{x}) - \frac{E_1(\mathbf{x})}{T}} \tag{49}$$

with T gradually decreasing to 1. In this way, the distribution at high temperatures reverts to a well–behaved distribution defined by E_0.

Simulated annealing is often used as an optimization method, where the aim is to find an $\mathbf{x}$ that minimizes $E(\mathbf{x})$, in which case the temperature is decreased to zero rather than to 1. As a Monte Carlo method, simulated annealing as described above doesn't sample exactly from the right distribution; the closely related 'simulated tempering' methods (Marinari and Parisi 1992) correct the biases introduced by the annealing process by making the temperature itself a random variable that is updated in Metropolis fashion during the simulation.

7.2. CAN THE NORMALIZING CONSTANT BE EVALUATED?

If the target density $P(\mathbf{x})$ is given in the form of an unnormalized density $P^*(\mathbf{x})$ with $P(\mathbf{x}) = \frac{1}{Z}P^*(\mathbf{x})$, the value of Z may well be of interest. Monte Carlo methods do not readily yield an estimate of this quantity, and it is an area of active research to find ways of evaluating it. Techniques for evaluating Z include:

1. Importance sampling (reviewed by Neal (1993)).
2. 'Thermodynamic integration' during simulated annealing, the 'acceptance ratio' method, and 'umbrella sampling' (reviewed by Neal (1993)).
3. 'Reversible jump Markov chain Monte Carlo' (Green 1995).

Perhaps the best way of dealing with Z, however, is to find a solution to one's task that does not require that Z be evaluated. In Bayesian data modelling one can avoid the need to evaluate Z — which would be important for model comparison — by not having more than one model. Instead of using several models (differing in complexity, for example) and evaluating their relative posterior probabilities, one can make a single **hierarchical** model having, for example, various continuous hyperparameters which play a role similar to that played by the distinct models (Neal 1996).

7.3. THE METROPOLIS METHOD FOR BIG MODELS

Our original description of the Metropolis method involved a joint updating of all the variables using a proposal density $Q(\mathbf{x}'; \mathbf{x})$. For big problems it may be more efficient to use several proposal distributions $Q^{(b)}(\mathbf{x}'; \mathbf{x})$, each of which updates only some of the components of $\mathbf{x}$. Each proposal is individually accepted or rejected, and the proposal distributions are repeatedly run through in sequence.

In the Metropolis method, the proposal density $Q(\mathbf{x}'; \mathbf{x})$ typically has a number of parameters that control, for example, its 'width'. These parameters are usually set by trial and error with the rule of thumb being that one aims for a rejection frequency of about 0.5. It is *not* valid to have the width parameters be dynamically updated during the simulation in a way that depends on the history of the simulation. Such a modification of the proposal density would violate the detailed balance condition which guarantees that the Markov chain has the correct invariant distribution.

7.4. GIBBS SAMPLING IN BIG MODELS

Our description of Gibbs sampling involved sampling one parameter at a time, as described in equations (31–33). For big problems it may be more efficient to sample *groups* of variables jointly, that is to use several proposal distributions:

$$x_1^{(t+1)} \dots x_a^{(t+1)} \sim P(x_1 \dots x_a | x_{a+1}^{(t)} \dots x_K^{(t)}) \tag{50}$$

$$x_{a+1}^{(t+1)} \dots x_b^{(t+1)} \sim P(x_{a+1} \dots x_b | x_1^{(t+1)} \dots x_a^{(t+1)}, x_{b+1}^{(t)} \dots x_K^{(t)}), \text{ etc.} \tag{51}$$

7.5. HOW MANY SAMPLES ARE NEEDED?

At the start of this chapter, we observed that the variance of an estimator $\hat{\Phi}$ depends only on the number of independent samples R and the value of

$$\sigma^2 = \int d^N \mathbf{x} \, P(\mathbf{x}) (\phi(\mathbf{x}) - \Phi)^2. \tag{52}$$

We have now discussed a variety of methods for generating samples from $P(\mathbf{x})$. How many independent samples R should we aim for?

In many problems, we really only need about twelve independent samples from $P(\mathbf{x})$. Imagine that $\mathbf{x}$ is an unknown vector such as the amount of corrosion present in each of 10,000 underground pipelines around Sicily, and $\phi(\mathbf{x})$ is the total cost of repairing those pipelines. The distribution $P(\mathbf{x})$ describes the probability of a state $\mathbf{x}$ given the tests that have been carried out on some pipelines and the assumptions about the physics of corrosion. The quantity Φ is the expected cost of the repairs. The quantity σ^2 is the variance of the cost — σ measures by how much we should expect the actual cost to differ from the expectation Φ.

Now, how accurately would a manager like to know Φ? I would suggest there is little point in knowing Φ to a precision finer than about $\sigma/3$. After all, the true cost is likely to differ by $\pm\sigma$ from Φ. If we obtain $R = 12$ independent samples from $P(\mathbf{x})$, we can estimate Φ to a precision of $\sigma/\sqrt{12}$ — which is smaller than $\sigma/3$. So twelve samples suffice.

7.6. ALLOCATION OF RESOURCES

Assuming we have decided how many independent samples R are required, an important question is how one should make use of one's limited computer resources to obtain these samples.

A typical Markov chain Monte Carlo experiment involves an initial period in which control parameters of the simulation such as step sizes may be adjusted. This is followed by a 'burn in' period during which we hope the

Figure 13. Three possible Markov Chain Monte Carlo strategies for obtaining twelve samples using a fixed amount of computer time. Computer time is represented by horizontal lines; samples by white circles. (1) A single run consisting of one long 'burn in' period followed by a sampling period. (2) Four medium–length runs with different initial conditions and a medium–length burn in period. (3) Twelve short runs.

simulation 'converges' to the desired distribution. Finally, as the simulation continues, we record the state vector occasionally so as to create a list of states $\{\mathbf{x}^{(r)}\}_{r=1}^{R}$ that we hope are roughly independent samples from $P(\mathbf{x})$.

There are several possible strategies (figure 13).

1. Make one long run, obtaining all R samples from it.
2. Make a few medium length runs with different initial conditions, obtaining some samples from each.
3. Make R short runs, each starting from a different random initial condition, with the only state that is recorded being the final state of each simulation.

The first strategy has the best chance of attaining 'convergence'. The last strategy may have the advantage that the correlations between the recorded samples are smaller. The middle path appears to be popular with Markov chain Monte Carlo experts because it avoids the inefficiency of discarding burn–in iterations in many runs, while still allowing one to detect problems with lack of convergence that would not be apparent from a single run.

7.7. PHILOSOPHY

One curious defect of these Monte Carlo methods — which are widely used by Bayesian statisticians — is that they are all non–Bayesian. They involve computer experiments from which *estimators* of quantities of interest are derived. These estimators depend on the sampling distributions that were used to generate the samples. In contrast, an alternative Bayesian approach to the problem would use the results of our computer experiments to infer the properties of the target function $P(\mathbf{x})$ and generate predictive distributions for quantities of interest such as Φ. This approach would give answers which would depend only on the computed values of $P^*(\mathbf{x}^{(r)})$ at the points $\{\mathbf{x}^{(r)}\}$; the answers would not depend on how those points were chosen.

It remains an open problem to create a Bayesian version of Monte Carlo methods.

8. Summary

- Monte Carlo methods are a powerful tool that allow one to implement any probability distribution that can be expressed in the form $P(\mathbf{x}) = \frac{1}{Z}P^*(\mathbf{x})$.
- Monte Carlo methods can answer virtually any query related to $P(\mathbf{x})$ by putting the query in the form

$$\int \phi(\mathbf{x})P(\mathbf{x}) \simeq \frac{1}{R}\sum_r \phi(\mathbf{x}^{(r)}). \tag{53}$$

- In high–dimensional problems the only satisfactory methods are those based on Markov chain Monte Carlo: the Metropolis method and Gibbs sampling.
- Simple Metropolis algorithms, although widely used, perform poorly because they explore the space by a slow random walk. More sophisticated Metropolis algorithms such as hybrid Monte Carlo make use of proposal densities that give faster movement through the state space. The efficiency of Gibbs sampling is also troubled by random walks. The method of ordered overrelaxation is a general purpose technique for suppressing them.

ACKNOWLEDGEMENTS

This presentation of Monte Carlo methods owes a great deal to Wally Gilks and David Spiegelhalter. I thank Radford Neal for teaching me about Monte Carlo methods and for giving helpful comments on the manuscript.

References

Adler, S. L.: 1981, Over-relaxation method for the Monte-Carlo evaluation of the partition function for multiquadratic actions, *Physical Review D-Particles and Fields* **23**(12), 2901–2904.

Cowles, M. K. and Carlin, B. P.: 1996, Markov-chain Monte-Carlo convergence diagnostics — a comparative review, *Journal of the American Statistical Association* **91**(434), 883–904.

Gilks, W. and Wild, P.: 1992, Adaptive rejection sampling for Gibbs sampling, *Applied Statistics* **41**, 337–348.

Gilks, W. R., Richardson, S. and Spiegelhalter, D. J.: 1996, *Markov Chain Monte Carlo in Practice*, Chapman and Hall.

Green, P. J.: 1995, Reversible jump Markov chain Monte Carlo computation and Bayesian model determination, *Biometrika* **82**, 711–732.

Marinari, E. and Parisi, G.: 1992, Simulated tempering - a new Monte-Carlo scheme, *Europhysics Letters* **19**(6), 451–458.

Neal, R. M.: 1993, Probabilistic inference using Markov chain Monte Carlo methods, *Technical Report CRG-TR-93-1*, Dept. of Computer Science, University of Toronto.

Neal, R. M.: 1995, Suppressing random walks in Markov chain Monte Carlo using ordered overrelaxation, *Technical Report 9508*, Dept. of Statistics, University of Toronto.

Neal, R. M.: 1996, *Bayesian Learning for Neural Networks*, number 118 in *Lecture Notes in Statistics*, Springer, New York.

Propp, J. G. and Wilson, D. B.: 1996, Exact sampling with coupled Markov chains and applications to statistical mechanics, *Random Structures and Algorithms* **9**(1-2), 223–252.

Tanner, M. A.: 1996, *Tools for Statistical Inference: Methods for the Exploration of Posterior Distributions and Likelihood Functions*, Springer Series in Statistics, 3rd edn, Springer Verlag.

Thomas, A., Spiegelhalter, D. J. and Gilks, W. R.: 1992, BUGS: A program to perform Bayesian inference using Gibbs sampling, *in* J. M. Bernardo, J. O. Berger, A. P. Dawid and A. F. M. Smith (eds), *Bayesian Statistics 4*, Clarendon Press, Oxford, pp. 837–842.

Yeomans, J.: 1992, *Statistical mechanics of phase transitions*, Clarendon Press, Oxford.

For a full bibliography and a more thorough review of Monte Carlo methods, the reader is encouraged to consult Neal (1993), Gilks et al. (1996), and Tanner (1996).

SUPPRESSING RANDOM WALKS IN MARKOV CHAIN MONTE CARLO USING ORDERED OVERRELAXATION

RADFORD M. NEAL
Dept. of Statistics and Dept. of Computer Science
University of Toronto, Toronto, Ontario, Canada
`http://www.cs.toronto.edu/~radford/`

Abstract. Markov chain Monte Carlo methods such as Gibbs sampling and simple forms of the Metropolis algorithm typically move about the distribution being sampled via a random walk. For the complex, high-dimensional distributions commonly encountered in Bayesian inference and statistical physics, the distance moved in each iteration of these algorithms will usually be small, because it is difficult or impossible to transform the problem to eliminate dependencies between variables. The inefficiency inherent in taking such small steps is greatly exacerbated when the algorithm operates via a random walk, as in such a case moving to a point n steps away will typically take around n^2 iterations. Such random walks can sometimes be suppressed using "overrelaxed" variants of Gibbs sampling (a.k.a. the heatbath algorithm), but such methods have hitherto been largely restricted to problems where all the full conditional distributions are Gaussian. I present an overrelaxed Markov chain Monte Carlo algorithm based on order statistics that is more widely applicable. In particular, the algorithm can be applied whenever the full conditional distributions are such that their cumulative distribution functions and inverse cumulative distribution functions can be efficiently computed. The method is demonstrated on an inference problem for a simple hierarchical Bayesian model.

1. Introduction

Markov chain Monte Carlo methods are used to estimate the expectations of various functions of a state, $x = (x_1, \ldots, x_N)$, with respect to a distribution given by some density function, $\pi(x)$. Typically, the dimensionality, N, is large, and the density $\pi(x)$ is of a complex form, in which the components of x are highly dependent. The estimates are based on a (dependent) sample of states obtained by simulating an ergodic Markov chain that has $\pi(x)$ as its equilibrium distribution. Starting with the work of Metropolis, *et al.* (1953), Markov chain Monte Carlo methods have been widely used to solve problems in statistical physics and, more recently, Bayesian statistical inference. It is often the only approach known that is computationally feasible. Various Markov chain Monte Carlo methods and their applications are reviewed by Toussaint (1989), Neal (1993), and Smith and Roberts (1993).

For the difficult problems that are their primary domain, Markov chain Monte Carlo methods are limited in their efficiency by strong dependencies between components of the state, which force the Markov chain to move about the distribution in small steps. In the widely-used Gibbs sampling method (known to physicists as the heatbath method), the Markov chain operates by successively replacing each component of the state, x_i, by a value randomly chosen from its conditional distribution given the current values of the other components, $\pi(x_i \mid \{x_j\}_{j \neq i})$. When dependencies between variables are strong, these conditional distributions will be much narrower than the corresponding marginal distributions, $\pi(x_i)$, and many iterations of the Markov chain will be necessary for the state to visit the full range of the distribution defined by $\pi(x)$. Similar behaviour is typical when the Metropolis algorithm is used to update each component of the state in turn, and also when the Metropolis algorithm is used with a simple proposal distribution that changes all components of the state simultaneously.

This inefficiency due to dependencies between components is to a certain extent unavoidable. We might hope to eliminate the problem by transforming to a parameterization in which the components of the state are no longer dependent. If this can easily be done, it is certainly the preferred solution. Typically, however, finding and applying such a transformation is difficult or impossible. Even for a distribution as simple as a multivariate Gaussian, eliminating dependencies will not be easy if the state has millions of components, as it might for a problem in statistical physics or image processing.

However, in the Markov chain Monte Carlo methods that are most commonly used, this inherent inefficiency is greatly exacerbated by the random walk nature of the algorithm. Not only is the distribution explored by taking small steps, the direction of these steps is randomized in each iteration, with the result that on average it takes about n^2 steps to move to a point n steps away. This can greatly increase both the number of iterations required before equilibrium is approached, and the number of subsequent iterations that are needed to gather a sample of states from which accurate estimates for the quantities of interest can be obtained.

In the physics literature, this problem has been addressed in two ways

— by "overrelaxation" methods, introduced by Adler (1981), which are the main subject of this paper, and by dynamical methods, such as "hybrid Monte Carlo", which I briefly describe next.

The hybrid Monte Carlo method, due to Duane, Kennedy, Pendleton, and Roweth (1987), can be seen as an elaborate form of the Metropolis algorithm (in an extended state space) in which candidate states are found by simulating a trajectory defined by Hamiltonian dynamics. These trajectories will proceed in a consistent direction, until such time as they reach a region of low probability. By using states proposed by this deterministic process, random walk effects can be largely eliminated. In Bayesian inference problems for complex models based on neural networks, I have found (Neal 1995) that the hybrid Monte Carlo method can be hundreds or thousands of times faster than simple versions of the Metropolis algorithm.

Hybrid Monte Carlo can be applied to a wide variety of problems where the state variables are continuous, and derivatives of the probability density can be efficiently computed. The method does, however, require that careful choices be made both for the length of the trajectories and for the stepsize used in the discretization of the dynamics. Using too large a stepsize will cause the dynamics to become unstable, resulting in an extremely high rejection rate. This need to carefully select the stepsize in the hybrid Monte Carlo method is similar to the need to carefully select the width of the proposal distribution in simple forms of the Metropolis algorithm. (For example, if a candidate state is drawn from a Gaussian distribution centred at the current state, one must somehow decide what the standard deviation of this distribution should be). Gibbs sampling does not require that the user set such parameters. A Markov chain Monte Carlo method that shared this advantage while also suppressing random walk behaviour would therefore be of interest.

Markov chain methods based on "overrelaxation" show promise in this regard. The original overrelaxation method of Adler (1981) is similar to Gibbs sampling, except that the new value chosen for a component of the state is negatively correlated with the old value. In many circumstances, successive overrelaxation improves sampling efficiency by suppressing random walk behaviour. Like Gibbs sampling, Adler's overrelaxation method does not require that the user select a suitable value for a stepsize parameter. It is therefore significantly easier to use than hybrid Monte Carlo (although one does still need to set a parameter that plays a role analogous to the trajectory length in hybrid Monte Carlo). Overrelaxation methods also do not suffer from the growth in computation time with system size that results from the use of a global acceptance test in hybrid Monte Carlo. (On the other hand, although overrelaxation has been found to greatly improve sampling in a number of problems, there are distributions for which overrelaxation is ineffective, but hybrid Monte Carlo works well.)

Unfortunately, Adler's original overrelaxation method is applicable only to problems where all the full conditional distributions are Gaussian. Several proposals have been made for overrelaxation methods that are more generally applicable (see Section 3 below). Most of these methods employ occasional rejections to ensure that the correct distribution is invariant. As we will see, however, such rejections can undermine the ability of overrelaxation to suppress random walks. Moreover, the probability of rejection in these methods is determined by the distribution to be sampled, and cannot be reduced in any obvious way.

In this paper, I present a rejection-free overrelaxation method based on the use of order statistics. In principle, this "ordered overrelaxation" method can be used to sample from any distribution for which Gibbs sampling would produce an ergodic Markov chain. In practice, the method will be useful only if the required computations can be performed efficiently. I discuss in detail one strategy for performing these computations, which is applicable to problems where the full conditional distributions have forms for which the cumulative distribution functions and inverse cumulative distribution functions can be efficiently computed. I also mention several other strategies that may further widen the range of problems to which ordered overrelaxation can be applied.

In Section 2, which follows, I review Adler's Gaussian overrelaxation method. In Section 3, I discuss previous proposals for overrelaxation methods that are more generally applicable. The new method of ordered overrelaxation is introduced in Section 4, and strategies for its implementation are discussed in Section 5. In Section 6, the strategy employing cumulative distribution functions is used to demonstrate the ordered overrelaxation method on a Bayesian inference problem for a simple hierarchical model. I conclude by discussing how the method might be applied in practice, and some possibilities for future work.

2. Overrelaxation with Gaussian conditional distributions

Overrelaxation methods have long been used in the iterative solution of systems of linear equations (Young 1971), and hence also for the minimization of quadratic functions. The first Markov chain sampling method based on overrelaxation was introduced in the physics literature by Adler (1981), and later studied by Whitmer (1984). The same method was later found by Barone and Frigessi (1989), and discussed in a statistical context by Green and Han (1992). Though itself limited to problems with Gaussian conditional distributions, Adler's method is the starting point for the more general methods that have since been proposed.

2.1. ADLER'S GAUSSIAN OVERRELAXATION METHOD

Adler's overrelaxation method is applicable when the distribution for the state, $x = (x_1, \ldots, x_N)$, is such that all the full conditional densities, $\pi(x_i \mid \{x_j\}_{j \neq i})$, are Gaussian (in the terminology used by Adler, when the log probability density is "multiquadratic"). Note that this class includes distributions other than the multivariate Gaussians, such as $\pi(x_1, x_2) \propto \exp(-(1 + x_1^2)(1 + x_2^2))$. As in Gibbs sampling, the components of the state are updated in turn, using some fixed ordering. The new value chosen for component i will depend on its conditional mean, μ_i, and variance, σ_i^2, which in general are functions of the other components, x_j for $j \neq i$. In Adler's method, the old value, x_i, is replaced by the new value

$$x_i' \;=\; \mu_i + \alpha (x_i - \mu_i) + \sigma_i (1 - \alpha^2)^{1/2} n \qquad (1)$$

where n is a Gaussian random variate with mean zero and variance one. The parameter α controls the degree of overrelaxation (or underrelaxation); for the method to be valid, we must have $-1 \leq \alpha \leq +1$. Overrelaxation to the other side of the mean occurs when α is negative. When α is zero, the method is equivalent to Gibbs sampling. (In the literature, the method is often parameterized in terms of $\omega = 1 - \alpha$. I have not followed this convention, as it appears to me to make all the equations harder to understand.)

One can easily confirm that Adler's method leaves the desired distribution invariant — that is, if x_i has the desired distribution (Gaussian with mean μ_i and variance σ_i^2), then x_i' also has this distribution. Furthermore, it is clear that overrelaxed updates with $-1 < \alpha < +1$ produce an ergodic chain. When $\alpha = -1$ the method is not ergodic, though updates with $\alpha = -1$ can form part of an ergodic scheme in which other updates are performed as well, as in the "hybrid overrelaxation" method discussed by Wolff (1992).

2.2. HOW OVERRELAXATION CAN SUPPRESS RANDOM WALKS

The effect of overrelaxation is illustrated in Figure 1, in which both Gibbs sampling and the overrelaxation method are shown sampling from a bivariate Gaussian distribution with high correlation. Gibbs sampling undertakes a random walk, and in the 40 iterations shown (each consisting of an update of both variables) succeeds in moving only a small way along the long axis of the distribution. In the same number of iterations, Adler's Gaussian overrelaxation method with $\alpha = -0.98$ covers a greater portion of the distribution, since it tends to move consistently in one direction (subject to some random variation, and to "reflection" from the end of the distribution).

The manner in which overrelaxation avoids doing a random walk when sampling from this distribution is illustrated in the close-up view in Fig-

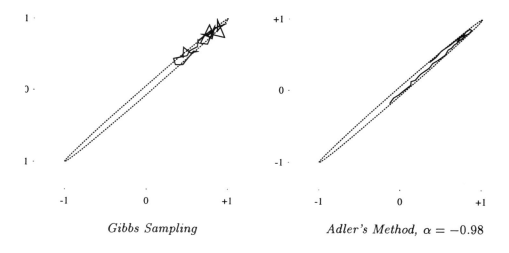

Gibbs Sampling   *Adler's Method,* $\alpha = -0.98$

Figure 1. Gibbs sampling and Adler's overrelaxation method applied to a bivariate Gaussian with correlation 0.998 (whose one-standard-deviation contour is plotted). The top left shows the progress of 40 Gibbs sampling iterations (each consisting of one update for each variable). The top right shows 40 overrelaxed iterations, with $\alpha = -0.98$. The close-up on the right shows how successive overrelaxed updates operate to avoid a random walk.

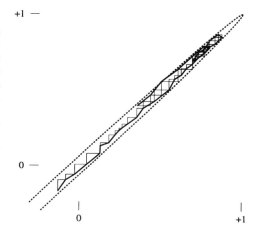

ure 1, which shows the changes in state after each variable is updated. When each of these updates is overrelaxed — tending to move to the other side of the conditional mean — the combined effect is to move in a consistent direction. The effect can be visualized most easily when $\alpha = -1$, in which case the state stays on a single elliptic contour of the probability density. Successive updates move the state along this contour until the end is reached, at which point the motion reverses. When α is close to, but not quite, -1, the small amount of randomness introduced will let the state move to different contours, and will also cause occasional reversals in direction of motion.

When α is chosen well, this randomization will occur on about the same time scale as is required for the state to move from one end of the distribution to the other. As the correlation of the bivariate Gaussian approaches

± 1, the optimal value of α approaches -1, and the benefit from using this optimal α rather than $\alpha = 0$ (Gibbs sampling) becomes arbitrarily large. This comes about because the number, n, of typical steps required to move from one end of the distribution to the other is proportional to the square root of the ratio of eigenvalues of the correlation matrix, which goes to infinity as the correlation goes to ± 1. The gain from moving to a nearly independent point in n step rather than the n^2 steps needed with a random walk therefore also goes to infinity.

2.3. THE BENEFIT FROM OVERRELAXATION

Figure 2 shows the benefit of overrelaxation in sampling from the bivariate Gaussian with $\rho = 0.998$ in terms of reduced autocorrelations for two functions of the state, x_1, and x_1^2. Here, a value of $\alpha = -0.89$ was used, which is close to optimal in terms of speed of convergence for this distribution. (The value of $\alpha = -0.98$ in Figure 1 was chosen to make the suppression of random walks visually clearer, but it is in fact somewhat too extreme for this value of ρ.)

The asymptotic efficiency of a Markov chain sampling method in estimating the expectation of a function of state is given by its "autocorrelation time" — the sum of the autocorrelations for that function of state at all lags, positive and negative (Hastings 1970). I obtained numerical estimates of the autocorrelation times for the quantities plotted in Figure 2 (using a series of 10,000 points, with truncation at the lags past which the estimated autocorrelations appeared to be approximately zero). These estimates show that the efficiency of estimation of $E[x_1]$ is a factor of about 22 better when using overrelaxation with $\alpha = -0.89$ than when using Gibbs sampling. For estimation of $E[x_1^2]$, the benefit from overrelaxation is a factor of about 16. In comparison with Gibbs sampling, using overrelaxation will reduce by these factors the variance of an estimate that is based on a run of given length, or alternatively, it will reduce by the same factors the length of run that is required to reduce the variance to some desired level.

Overrelaxation is not always beneficial, however. Some research has been done into when overrelaxation produces an improvement, but the results so far do not provide a complete answer, and in some cases, appear to have been mis-interpreted. Work in the physics literature has concentrated on systems of physical interest, and has primarily been concerned with scaling behaviour in the vicinity of a critical point. Two recent papers have addressed the question in the context of more general statistical applications.

Barone and Frigessi (1990) look at overrelaxation applied to multivariate Gaussian distributions, finding the rate of convergence in a number of interesting cases. In interpreting these results, however, one should keep in

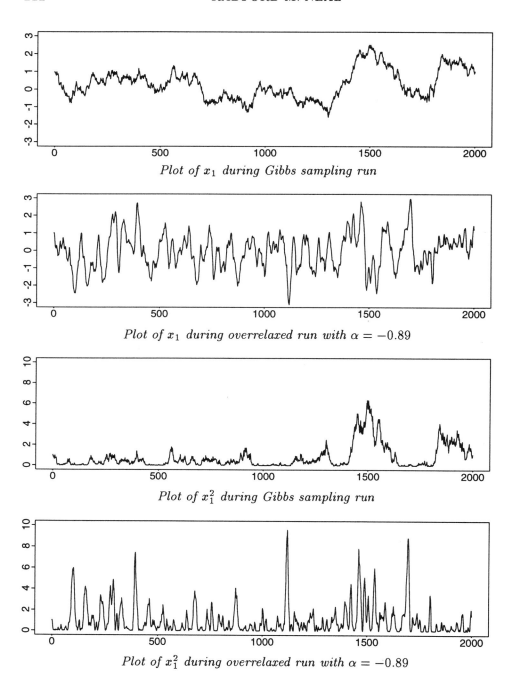

Figure 2. Sampling from a bivariate Gaussian with $\rho = 0.998$ using Gibbs sampling and Adler's overrelaxation method with $\alpha = -0.89$. The plots show the values of the first coordinate and of its square during 2000 iterations of the samplers (each iteration consisting of one update for each coordinate).

mind that if a method converges geometrically with rate ρ, the computation time required to reach some given level of accuracy is inversely proportional to $-\log(\rho)$. Hence, if two methods converge with rates ρ_1 and ρ_2, the relative advantage of method 2 is not ρ_1/ρ_2, but rather $\log(\rho_2)/\log(\rho_1)$, which for rates near one is approximately $(1-\rho_2)/(1-\rho_1)$. Seen in this light, the results of Barone and Frigessi confirm what was illustrated above — that overrelaxation can for some distributions be arbitrarily faster than Gibbs sampling. This is not always true, however; indeed, their results show that for some distributions with negative correlations, it can be better to underrelax (ie, to apply equation (1) with $0 < \alpha < 1$).

Green and Han (1992) look at the performance of overrelaxation as judged by the asymptotic variance of a Monte Carlo estimate for the expectation of a linear function of state. They show that this asymptotic variance goes to zero in the limit as α in equation (1) goes to -1. Recognizing that values for α very near -1 are not good from the point of view of convergence to equilibrium, since the state then remains for a long time on one contour of the joint probability density, they suggest that different chains be used during an initial period when equilibrium is being reached and during the subsequent generation of states for use in estimation.

In practice, however, we are usually interested in a non-linear function of state, and we require only a modest degree of accuracy. The results of Green and Han on asymptotic variance may therefore be of little relevance. In particular, for problems where Markov chain sampling is necessary, it is generally unrealistic to hope to find "antithetic" methods, in which negative autocorrelations produce estimation efficiencies greater than would be obtained with a sample of independent states. Fortunately, despite the locally-antithetic character of equation (1), the benefits of overrelaxation do not depend on negative autocorrelations carrying over to the functions of interest, but can come rather from the faster decay of autocorrelations to zero, as the chain moves more rapidly to a nearly independent state.

As remarked above, the benefits of overrelaxation are not universal, even within the class of multivariate Gaussian distributions (despite the results on asymptotic variance). More research into this matter is needed. In this work, however, I take it as given that in many contexts overrelaxation is beneficial — as is typically true when correlations between components of the state are positive, for example — and seek to extend these benefits to distributions where the conditional distributions are non-Gaussian.

3. Previous proposals for more general overrelaxation methods

Adler's overrelaxation method can be applied only when all the full conditional distributions are Gaussian. Although applications of this nature do exist, in both statistical physics and statistical inference, most problems to which Markov chain Monte Carlo methods are currently applied do not satisfy this constraint. A number of proposals have been made for more general overrelaxation methods, which I will review here before presenting the "ordered overrelaxation" method in the next section.

Brown and Woch (1987) make a rather direct proposal: To perform an overrelaxed update of a variable whose conditional distribution is not Gaussian, transform to a new parameterization of this variable in which the conditional distribution is Gaussian, do the update by Adler's method, and then transform back. This may sometimes be an effective strategy, but for many problems the required computations will be costly or infeasible.

A second proposal by Brown and Woch (1987), also made by Creutz (1987), is based on the Metropolis algorithm. To update component i, we first find a point, x_i^*, which is near the centre of the conditional distribution, $\pi(x_i \mid \{x_j\}_{j \neq i})$. We might, for example, choose x_i^* to be an approximation to the mode, though other choices are also valid, as long as they do not depend on the current x_i. We then take $x_i' = x_i^* - (x_i - x_i^*)$ as a candidate for the next state, which, in the usual Metropolis fashion, we accept with probability $\min[1, \, \pi(x_i' \mid \{x_j\}_{j \neq i}) \, / \, \pi(x_i \mid \{x_j\}_{j \neq i})]$. If x_i' is not accepted, the new state is the same as the old state.

If the conditional distribution is Gaussian, and x_i^* is chosen to be the exact mode, the state proposed with this method will always be accepted, since the Gaussian distribution is symmetrical. The result is then identical to Adler's method with $\alpha = -1$. Such a method can be combined with other updates to produce an ergodic chain. Alternatively, ergodicity can be ensured by adding some amount of random noise to the proposed states.

Green and Han (1992) propose a somewhat similar, but more general, method. To update component i, they find a Gaussian approximation to the conditional distribution, $\pi(x_i \mid \{x_j\}_{j \neq i})$, that does not depend on the current x_i. They then find a candidate state x_i' by overrelaxing from the current state according to equation (1), using the μ_i and σ_i that characterize this Gaussian approximation, along with some judiciously chosen α. This candidate state is then accepted or rejected using Hastings' (1970) generalization of the Metropolis algorithm, which allows for non-symmetric proposal distributions.

Fodor and Jansen (1994) propose a method that is applicable when the conditional distribution is unimodal, in which the candidate state is the point on the other side of the mode whose probability density is the same as that of the current state. This candidate state is accepted or rejected based on the derivative of the mapping from current state to candidate state. Ergodicity may again be ensured by mixing in other transitions, such as standard Metropolis updates.

The proposed generalizations in which detailed balance is achieved using accept-reject decisions all suffer from a potentially serious flaw: The rejection rate is determined by characteristics of the conditional distributions; if it is too high, there is no obvious way of reducing it. Moreover, even a quite small rejection rate may be too high. This point seems not to have been appreciated in the literature, but should be apparent from the discussion in Section 2. When sampling from a bivariate Gaussian, it is easy to see that when an overrelaxed update of one of the two variables is rejected, the effect is to reverse the direction of motion along the long axis of the distribution. Effective suppression of random walks therefore requires that the interval between such rejections be at least comparable to the time required for the method to move the length of the distribution, which can be arbitrarily long, depending on the degree of correlation of the variables.

4. Overrelaxation based on order statistics

In this section, I present a new form of overrelaxation, which can be applied (in theory) to any distribution over states with real-valued components, and in which changes are never rejected, thereby preserving the potential for the method to suppress random walks even in distributions with arbitrarily strong dependencies.

4.1. THE ORDERED OVERRELAXATION METHOD

As before, we aim to sample from a distribution over $x = (x_1, \ldots, x_N)$ with density $\pi(x)$, and we will proceed by updating the values of the components, x_i, repeatedly in turn, based on their full conditional distributions, whose densities are $\pi(x_i \mid \{x_j\}_{j \neq i})$.

In the new method, the old value, x_i, for component i is replaced by a new value, x_i', obtained as follows:

1) Generate K random values, independently, from the conditional distribution $\pi(x_i \mid \{x_j\}_{j \neq i})$.
2) Arrange these K values plus the old value, x_i, in non-decreasing order, labeling them as follows:

$$x_i^{(0)} \leq x_i^{(1)} \leq \cdots \leq x_i^{(r)} = x_i \leq \cdots \leq x_i^{(K)} \tag{2}$$

with r being the index in this ordering of the old value. (If several of the K generated values are equal to the old x_i, break the tie randomly.)
3) Let the new value for component i be $x_i' = x_i^{(K-r)}$.

Here, K is a parameter of the method, which plays a role analogous to that of α in Adler's Gaussian overrelaxation method. When K is one, the method is equivalent to Gibbs sampling; the behaviour as $K \to \infty$ is analogous to Gaussian overrelaxation with $\alpha = -1$.

As presented above, each step of this "ordered overrelaxation" method would appear to require computation time proportional to K. As discussed below, the method will provide a practical improvement in sampling efficiency only if an equivalent effect can be obtained using much less time. Strategies for accomplishing this are discussed in Section 5. First, however, I will show that the method is valid — that the update described above leaves the distribution $\pi(x)$ invariant — and that its behaviour is similar to that of Adler's method for Gaussian distributions.

4.2. VALIDITY OF ORDERED OVERRELAXATION

To show that ordered overrelaxation leaves $\pi(x)$ invariant, it suffices to show that each update for a component, i, satisfies "detailed balance" — ie, that the probability density for such an update replacing x_i by x_i' is the same as the probability density for x_i' being replaced by x_i, assuming that the starting state is distributed according to $\pi(x)$. It is well known that the detailed balance condition (also known as "reversibility") implies invariance of $\pi(x)$, and that invariance for each component update implies invariance for transitions in which each component is updated in turn. (Note, however, that the resulting sequential update procedure, considered as a whole, need not satisfy detailed balance; indeed, if random walks are to be suppressed as we wish, it must not.)

To see that detailed balance holds, consider the probability density that component i has a given value, x_i, to start, that x_i is in the end replaced by some given different value, x_i', and that along the way, a particular set of $K-1$ other values (along with x_i') are generated in step (1) of the update procedure. Assuming there are no tied values, this probability density is

$$\pi(x_i \mid \{x_j\}_{j \neq i}) \cdot K! \, \pi(x_i' \mid \{x_j\}_{j \neq i}) \prod_{r \neq t \neq s} \pi(x_i^{(t)} \mid \{x_j\}_{j \neq i}) \cdot I[s = K - r] \quad (3)$$

where r is the index of the old value, x_i, in the ordering found in step (2), and s is the index of the new value, x_i'. The final factor is zero or one, depending on whether the transition in question would actually occur with the particular set of $K-1$ other values being considered. The probability density for the reverse transition, from x_i' to x_i, with the same set of $K-1$ other values being involved, is readily seen to the identical to the above. Integrating over all possible sets of other values, we conclude that the probability density for a transition from x_i to x_i', involving any set of other values, is the same as the probability density for the reverse transition from x_i' to x_i. Allowing for the possibility of ties yields the same result, after a more detailed accounting.

4.3. BEHAVIOUR OF ORDERED OVERRELAXATION

In analysing ordered overrelaxation, it can be helpful to view it from a perspective in which the overrelaxation is done with respect to a uniform distribution. Let $F(x)$ be the cumulative distribution function for the conditional distribution $\pi(x_i \mid \{x_j\}_{j \neq i})$ (here assumed to be continuous), and let $F^{-1}(x)$ be the inverse of $F(x)$. Ordered overrelaxation for x_i is equivalent to the following procedure: First transform the current value to $u_i = F(x_i)$, then perform ordered overrelaxation for u_i, whose distribution is uniform over $[0, 1]$, yielding a new state u_i', and finally transform back to $x_i' = F^{-1}(u_i')$.

Overrelaxation for a uniform distribution, starting from u, may be analysed as follows. When K independent uniform variates are generated in step (1) of the procedure, the number of them that are less than u will be binomially distributed with mean Ku and variance $Ku(1-u)$. This number is the index, r, of $u = u^{(r)}$ found in step (2) of the procedure. Conditional on a value for r, which let us suppose is greater than $K/2$, the distribution of the new state, $u' = u^{(K-r)}$, will be that of the $K - r + 1$ order statistic of a sample of size r from a uniform distribution over $[0, u]$. As is well known (eg, David 1970, p. 11), the k'th order statistic of a sample of size n from a uniform distribution over $[0, 1]$ has a beta$(k, n-k+1)$ distribution, with density proportional to $u^{k-1}(1-u)^{n-k}$, mean $k/(n+1)$, and variance $k(n - k + 1)/(n+2)(n+1)^2$. Applying this result, u' for a given $r > K/2$ will have a rescaled beta$(K-r+1, 2r-K)$ distribution, with mean $\mu(r) = u(K-r+1)/(r+1)$ and variance $\sigma^2(r) = u^2(K-r+1)(2r-K)/(r+2)(r+1)^2$.

When K is large, we can get a rough idea of the behaviour of overrelaxation for a uniform distribution by considering the case where u (and hence likely r/K) is significantly greater than $1/2$. Behaviour when u is less than $1/2$ will of course be symmetrical, and we expect behaviour to smoothly interpolate between these regimes when u is within about $1/\sqrt{K}$ of $1/2$ (for which r/K might be either greater or less than $1/2$)

When $u \gg 1/2$, we can use the Taylor expansion

$$\mu(Ku + \delta) = \frac{Ku - Ku^2 + u}{Ku + 1} - \frac{Ku + 2u}{(Ku + 1)^2}\delta + \frac{Ku + 2u}{(Ku + 1)^3}\delta^2 + \cdots \quad (4)$$

to conclude that for large K, the expected value of u', averaging over possible values for $r = Ku + \delta$, with δ having mean zero and variance $Ku(1-u)$, is approximately

$$\frac{Ku - Ku^2 + u}{Ku + 1} + Ku(1 - u)\frac{Ku + 2u}{(Ku + 1)^3} \approx (1 - u) + 1/K \quad (5)$$

For $u \ll 1/2$, the bias will of course be opposite, with the expected value of u' being about $(1 - u) - 1/K$, and for $u \approx 1/2$, the expected value of u' will be approximately u.

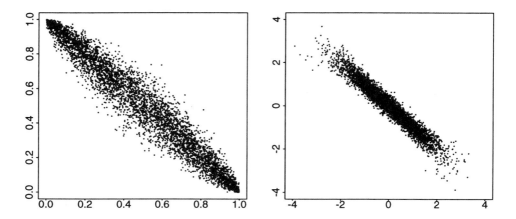

Figure 3. Points representing 5000 ordered overrelaxation updates. The plot on the left shows ordered overrelaxation for a uniform distribution. The horizontal axis gives the starting point, drawn uniformly from $[0,1]$; the vertical axis, the point found by ordered overrelaxation with $K = 100$ from that starting point. The plot on the right shows ordered overrelaxation for a Gaussian distribution. The points correspond to those on the left, but transformed by the inverse Gaussian cumulative distribution function.

The variance of u' will be, to order $1/K$, approximately $\sigma^2(Ku) + Ku(1-u)[\mu'(Ku)]^2$; that is, for $u \gg 1/2$:

$$\frac{(Ku^2 - Ku^3 + u^2)(2Ku - K)}{(Ku+2)(Ku+1)^2} + Ku(1-u)\frac{(Ku+2u)^2}{(Ku+1)^4} \approx \frac{2(1-u)}{K} \quad (6)$$

By symmetry, the variance of u' when $u \ll 1/2$ will be approximately $2u/K$. (Incidentally, the fact that u' has greater variance when u is near $1/2$ than when u is near 0 or 1 explains how it is possible for the method to leave the uniform distribution invariant even though u' is biased to be closer to $1/2$ than u is.)

The joint distribution for u and u' is illustrated on the left in Figure 3. The right of the figure shows how this translates to the joint distribution for the old and new state when ordered overrelaxation is applied to a Gaussian distribution.

4.4. COMPARISONS WITH ADLER'S METHOD AND GIBBS SAMPLING

For Gaussian overrelaxation by Adler's method, the joint distribution of the old and new state is Gaussian. As seen in Figure 3, this is clearly not the case for ordered overrelaxation. One notable difference is the way the tails of the joint distribution flare out with ordered overrelaxation, a reflection of the fact that if the old state is very far out in the tail, the new state will likely be much closer in. This effect is perhaps an advantage of the ordered overrelaxation method, as one might therefore expect convergence from a bad starting point to be faster with ordered overrelaxation than with Adler's method. (This is certainly true in the trivial case where the state consists of a single variable; further analysis is needed to establish whether it true in interesting cases.)

Although there is no exact equivalence between Adler's Gaussian overrelaxation method and ordered overrelaxation, it is of some interest to find a value of K for which ordered overrelaxation applied to a Gaussian distribution corresponds roughly to Adler's method with a given $\alpha < 0$. Specifically, we can try to equate the mean and variance of the new state, x', that results from an overrelaxed update of an old state, x, when x is one standard deviation away from its mean. Supposing without loss of generality that the mean is zero and the variance is one, we see from equations (5) and (6) that when $x = 1$, the expected value of x' using ordered overrelaxation is $\Phi^{-1}(\Phi(-1) + 1/K) \approx -1 + 1/K\phi(-1) \approx -1 + 4.13/K$ and the variance of x' is $2\,\Phi(-1)/K\phi(-1)^2 \approx 5.42/K$, where $\Phi(x)$ is the Gaussian cumulative distribution function, and $\phi(x)$ the Gaussian density function. Since the corresponding values for Adler's method are a mean of α and a variance of $1 - \alpha^2$, we can get a rough correspondence by setting $K \approx 3.5/(1 + \alpha)$.

For the example of Figure 2, showing overrelaxation by Adler's method with $\alpha = -0.89$, applied to a bivariate Gaussian with correlation 0.998, ordered overrelaxation should be roughly equivalent when $K = 32$. Figure 4 shows visually that this is indeed the case. Numerical estimates of autocorrelation times indicate that ordered overrelaxation with $K = 32$ is about a factor of 22 more efficient, in terms of the number of iterations required for a given level of accuracy, than is Gibbs sampling, when used to estimate $E[x_1]$. When used to estimate $E[x_1^2]$, ordered overrelaxation is about a factor of 14 more efficient. Measured by numbers of iterations, these efficiency advantages are virtually identical to those reported in Section 2.3 for Adler's method.

Of course, if it were implemented in the most obvious way, with K random variates being explicitly generated in step (1) of the procedure, ordered overrelaxation with $K = 32$ would required a factor of about 32 more computation time per iteration than would either Adler's overrelaxation method or Gibbs sampling. Adler's method would clearly be preferred in comparison to such an implementation of ordered overrelaxation. Interestingly, however, even with such a naive implementation, the computational efficiency of ordered overrelaxation is comparable to that of Gibbs sampling — the factor of about 32 slowdown per iteration being nearly cancelled by the factor of about 22 improvement from the elimination of random walks. This near equality of costs holds for smaller values of K as well — the improvement in efficiency (in terms of iterations) using ordered overrelaxation

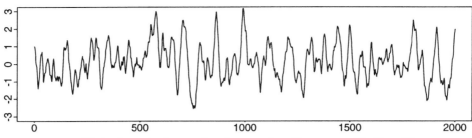

Plot of x_1 during ordered overrelaxation run with $K = 32$

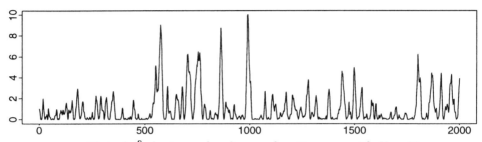

Plot of x_1^2 during ordered overrelaxation run with $K = 32$

Figure 4. Sampling from a bivariate Gaussian with $\rho = 0.998$ using ordered overrelaxation with $K = 32$. Compare with the results using Gibbs sampling and Adler's method shown in Figure 2.

with $K = 16$ is about a factor of 12 for $E[x_1]$ and 11 for $E[x_1^2]$, and with $K = 8$, the improvement is about a factor of 8 for $E[x_1]$ and 7 for $E[x_1^2]$.

We therefore see that any implementation of ordered overrelaxation whose computational cost is substantially less than that of the naive approach of explicitly generating K random variates will yield a method whose computational efficiency is greater than that of Gibbs sampling, when used with any value for K up to that which is optimal in terms of the number of iterations required for a given level of accuracy. Or rather, we see this for the case of a bivariate Gaussian distribution, and we may hope that it is true for many other distributions of interest as well, including those whose conditional distributions are non-Gaussian, for which Adler's overrelaxation method is not applicable.

5. Strategies for implementing ordered overrelaxation

In this section, I describe several approaches to implementing ordered overrelaxation, which are each applicable to some interesting class of distributions, and are more efficient than the obvious method of explicitly generating K random variates. In some cases, there is a bound on the time required for an overrelaxed update that is independent of K; in others the reduction in time is less dramatic (perhaps only a constant factor). As was seen in Section 4.4, any substantial reduction in time compared to the naive implementation will potentially provide an improvement over Gibbs sampling.

There will of course be some distributions for which none of these implementations is feasible; this will certainly be the case when Gibbs sampling itself is not feasible. Such distributions include, for example, the complex posterior distributions that arise with neural network models (Neal 1995). Hybrid Monte Carlo will likely remain the most efficient sampling method for such problems.

5.1. USING THE CUMULATIVE DISTRIBUTION FUNCTION

The most direct method for implementing ordered overrelaxation in bounded time (independently of K) is to transform the problem to one of performing overrelaxation for a uniform distribution on $[0, 1]$, as was done in the analysis of Section 4.3. This approach requires that we be able to efficiently compute the cumulative distribution function and its inverse for each of the conditional distributions for which overrelaxation is to be done. This requirement is somewhat restrictive, but reasonably fast methods for computing these functions are known for many standard distributions (Kennedy and Gentle 1980).

This implementation of ordered overrelaxation produces exactly the same effect as would a direct implementation of the steps in Section 4.1. As there, we aim to replace the current value, x_i, of component i, by a new value, x_i'. The conditional distribution for component i, $\pi(x_i \mid \{x_j\}_{j\neq i})$, is here assumed to be continuous, with cumulative distribution distribution function $F(x)$, whose inverse is $F^{-1}(x)$. We proceed as follows:

1) Compute $u = F(x_i)$, which will lie in $[0, 1]$.

2) Draw an integer r from the binomial(K, u) distribution. This r has the same distribution as the r in the direct procedure of Section 4.1.

3) If $r > K - r$, randomly generate v from the beta$(K - r + 1, 2r - K)$ distribution, and let $u' = uv$.

   If $r < K - r$, randomly generate v from the beta$(r + 1, K - 2r)$ distribution, and let $u' = 1 - (1 - u)v$.

   If $r = K - r$, let $u' = u$.

   Note that u' is the result of overrelaxing u with respect to the uniform distribution on $[0, 1]$.

4) Let the new value for component i be $x_i' = F^{-1}(u')$.

Step (3) is based on the fact (David 1970, p. 11) that the k'th order statistic in a sample of size n from a uniform distribution on $[0, 1]$ has a beta(k, $n - k + 1$) distribution. Efficient methods for generating random variates from beta and binomial distributions in bounded expected time are known (Devroye 1986, Sections IX.4 and X.4).

When feasible, this implementation allows ordered overrelaxation to be performed in time independent of K, though this time will exceed that required for a simple Gibbs sampling update. The implementation is similar in spirit and in likely computation time to the suggestion by Brown and Woch (1987) to perform a transformation that makes the conditional distribution Gaussian (see Section 3). The ordered overrelaxation framework admits other possible implementations, however, which may reduce the required computation time, or allow its application to distributions for which the cumulative distribution function or its inverse cannot be computed.

5.2. USING ECONOMIES OF SCALE

In some cases, an ordered overrelaxation update will quite naturally take less than K times as long as a Gibbs sampling update (and therefore be potentially advantageous). In the direct procedure of Section 4.1, the conditional distribution for x_i, from which K random variates are drawn in step (1), depends in general on the values of the other components, perhaps in a complex way. Since these other components are themselves being updated, this conditional distribution must be re-computed for each update of x_i. This need be done only once for an ordered overrelaxation update, however, even though K values will then be generated from the conditional distribution that is found. If the dominant contribution to the total computation time comes from this dependence on the values of the other components, rather than from the random variate generation itself, an ordered overrelaxation update could take much less than K times as long as a Gibbs sampling update.

Other situations can also lead to "economies of scale", in which generating K values from the same distribution takes less than K times as long as generating one value. This will occur whenever values are generated from some distribution in a parametric family using a method with some "setup cost" that is incurred whenever the parameters change (due to dependence on other components of state). The adaptive rejection sampling method of Gilks and Wild (1992) is another important example, as it is widely used to implement Gibbs sampling. In this scheme, a value is randomly drawn from a log-concave density using a succession of approximations to the density function. When more than one value is drawn from the same density, the approximations are continually refined, with the result that later values take much less time to generate than earlier values.

Further time savings can be obtained by noting that the exact numerical values of most of the K values generated are not needed. All that is required is that the number, r, of these values that are less than the current x_i be somehow determined, and that the single value $x_i^{(K-r)} = x_i'$ be found. In particular, the adaptive rejection sampling method can be modified in such a way that large groups of values are "generated" only to the extent that they are localized to regions where their exact values can be seen to be irrelevant. The cost of ordered overrelaxation can then be much less than K times the cost of a Gibbs sampling update. This is a somewhat complex procedure, however, which I will not present in detail here.

6. Demonstration: Inference for a hierarchical Bayesian model

In this section, I demonstrate the advantages of ordered overrelaxation over Gibbs sampling when both are applied to Bayesian inference for a simple hierarchical model. In this problem, the conditional distributions are non-Gaussian, so Adler's method cannot be applied. The implementation of ordered overrelaxation used is that based on the cumulative distribution function, described in Section 5.1.

For this demonstration, I used one of the models Gelfand and Smith (1990) use to illustrate Gibbs sampling. The data consist of p counts, $s_1, \ldots, s_p$. Conditional on a set of unknown parameters, $\lambda_1, \ldots, \lambda_p$, these counts are assumed to have independent Poisson distributions, with means of $\lambda_i t_i$, where the t_i are known quantities associated with the counts s_i. For example, s_i might be the number of failures of a device that has a failure rate of λ_i and that has been observed for a period of time t_i.

At the next level, a common hyperparameter β is introduced. Conditional on a value for β, the λ_i are assumed to be independently generated from a gamma distribution with a known shape parameter, α, and the scale factor β. The hyperparameter β is assumed to have an inverse gamma distribution with a known shape parameter, γ, and a known scale factor, δ.

The problem is to sample from the conditional distribution for β and the λ_i given the observed $s_1, \ldots, s_p$. The joint density of all unknowns is given by the following proportionality:

$$P(\beta, \lambda_1, \ldots, \lambda_p \mid s_1, \ldots, s_p)$$

$$\propto \quad P(\beta)\, P(\lambda_1, \ldots, \lambda_p \mid \beta)\, P(s_1, \ldots, s_p \mid \lambda_1, \ldots, \lambda_p) \qquad (7)$$

$$\propto \quad \beta^{-\gamma-1} e^{-\delta/\beta} \cdot \prod_{i=1}^{p} \beta^{-\alpha} \lambda_i^{\alpha-1} e^{-\lambda_i/\beta} \cdot \prod_{i=1}^{p} \lambda_i^{s_i} e^{-\lambda_i t_i} \qquad (8)$$

The conditional distribution for β given the other variables is thus inverse gamma:

$$P(\beta \mid \lambda_1, \ldots, \lambda_p, s_1, \ldots, s_p) \quad \propto \quad \beta^{-p\alpha-\gamma-1}e^{-(\delta+\Sigma_i\lambda_i)/\beta} \qquad (9)$$

However, I found it more convenient to work in terms of $\tau = 1/\beta$, whose conditional density is gamma:

$$P(\tau \mid \lambda_1, \ldots, \lambda_p, s_1, \ldots, s_p) \quad \propto \quad \tau^{p\alpha+\gamma-1}e^{-\tau(\delta+\Sigma_i\lambda_i)} \qquad (10)$$

The conditional distributions for the λ_i are also gamma:

$$P(\lambda_i \mid \{\lambda_j\}_{j\neq i}, \tau, s_1, \ldots, s_p) \quad \propto \quad \lambda_i^{s_i+\alpha-1}e^{-\lambda_i(t_i+\tau)} \qquad (11)$$

In each full iteration of Gibbs sampling or of ordered overrelaxation, these conditional distributions are used to update first the λ_i and then τ.

Gelfand and Smith (1990, Section 4.2) apply this model to a small data set concerning failures in ten pump systems, and find that Gibbs sampling essentially converges within ten iterations. Such rapid convergence does not always occur with this model, however. The λ_i and τ are mutually dependent, to a degree that increases as α and p increase. By adjusting α and p, one can arrange for Gibbs sampling to require arbitrarily many iterations to converge.

For the tests reported here, I set $p = 100$, $\alpha = 20$, $\delta = 1$, and $\gamma = 0.1$. The true value of τ was set to 5 (ie, $\beta = 0.2$). For each i from 1 to p, t_i was set to i/p, a value for λ_i was randomly generated from the gamma distribution with parameters α and β, and finally a synthetic observation, s_i, was randomly generated from the Poisson distribution with mean $\lambda_i t_i$. A single such set of 100 observations was used for all the tests, during which the true values of τ and the λ_i used to generate the data were of course ignored.

Figure 5 shows values of τ sampled from the posterior distribution by successive iterations of Gibbs sampling, and of ordered overrelaxation with $K = 5$, $K = 11$, and $K = 21$. Each of these methods was initialized with the λ_i set to s_i/t_i and τ set to α divided by the average of the initial λ_i: The ordered overrelaxation iterations took about 1.7 times as long as the Gibbs sampling iterations. (Although approximately in line with expectations, this timing figure should not be taken too seriously – since the methods were implemented in S-Plus, the times likely reflect interpretative overhead, rather than intrinsic computational difficulty.)

The figure clearly shows the reduction in autocorrelation for τ that can be achieved by using ordered overrelaxation rather than Gibbs sampling. Numerical estimates of the autocorrelations (with the first 50 points discarded) show that for Gibbs sampling, the autocorrelations do not approach

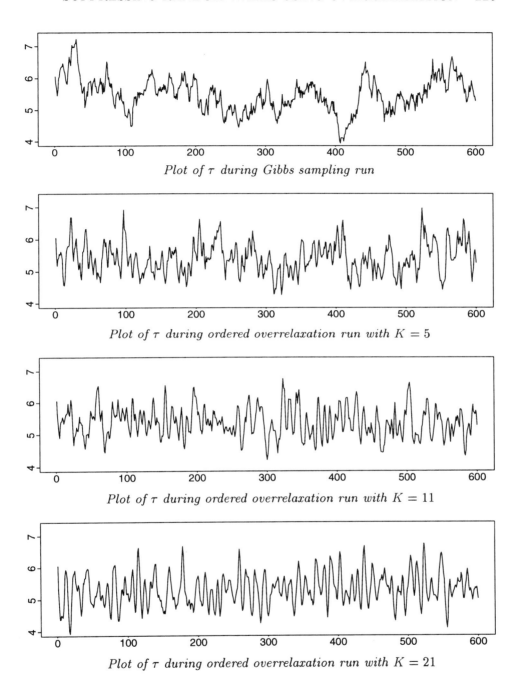

Plot of τ *during Gibbs sampling run*

Plot of τ *during ordered overrelaxation run with* K = 5

Plot of τ *during ordered overrelaxation run with* K = 11

Plot of τ *during ordered overrelaxation run with* K = 21

Figure 5.   Sampling from the posterior distribution for τ using Gibbs sampling and ordered overrelaxation with $K = 5$, $K = 11$, and $K = 21$. The plots show the progress of $τ = 1/β$ during runs of 600 full iterations (in which the $λ_i$ and τ are each updated once).

zero until around lag 28, whereas for ordered overrelaxation with $K = 5$, the autocorrelation is near zero by lag 11, and for $K = 11$, by lag 4. For ordered overrelaxation with $K = 21$, substantial negative autocorrelations are seen, which would increase the efficiency of estimation for the expected value of τ itself, but could be disadvantageous when estimating the expectations of other functions of state. The value $K = 11$ seems close to optimal in terms of speed of convergence.

7. Discussion

The results in this paper show that ordered overrelaxation should be able to speed the convergence of Markov chain Monte Carlo in a wide range of circumstances. Unlike the original overrelaxation method of Adler (1981), it is applicable when the conditional distributions are not Gaussian, and it avoids the rejections that can undermine the performance of other generalized overrelaxation methods. Compared to the alternative of suppressing random walks using hybrid Monte Carlo (Duane, *et al.* 1987), overrelaxation has the advantage that it does not require the setting of a stepsize parameter, making it potentially easier to apply on a routine basis.

An implementation of ordered overrelaxation based on the cumulative distribution function was described in Section 5.1, and used for the demonstration in Section 6. This implementation can be used for many problems, but it is not as widely applicable as Gibbs sampling. Natural economies of scale will allow ordered overrelaxation to provide at least some benefit in many other contexts, without any special effort. By modifying adaptive rejection sampling (Gilks and Wild 1992) to rapidly perform ordered overrelaxation, I believe that quite a wide range of problems will be able to benefit from ordered overrelaxation, which should often provide an order of magnitude or more speedup, with little effort on the part of the user.

To use overrelaxation, it is necessary for the user to set a time-constant parameter — α for Adler's method, K for ordered overrelaxation — which, roughly speaking, controls the number of iterations for which random walks are suppressed. Ideally, this parameter should be set so that random walks are suppressed over the time scale required for the whole distribution to be traversed, but no longer. Short trial runs could be used to select a value for this parameter; finding a precisely optimal value is not crucial. In favourable cases, an efficient implementation of ordered overrelaxation used with any value of K less than the optimal value will produce an advantage over Gibbs sampling of about a factor of K. Using a value of K that is greater than the optimum will still produce an advantage over Gibbs sampling, up to around the point where K is the square of the optimal value.

For routine use, a policy of simply setting K to around 20 may be reasonable. For problems with a high degree of dependency, this may give around an order of magnitude improvement in performance over Gibbs sampling, with no effort by the user. For problems with little dependency between variables, for which this value of K is too large, the result could be a slowdown compared with Gibbs sampling, but such problems are sufficiently easy anyway that this may cause little inconvenience. Of course, when convergence is very slow, or when many similar problems are to be solved, it will be well worthwhile to search for the optimal value of K.

There are problems for which overrelaxation (of whatever sort) is not advantageous, as can happen when variables are negatively correlated. Further research is needed to clarify when this occurs, and to determine how these situations are best handled. It can in fact be beneficial to underrelax in such a situation — eg, to use Adler's method with $\alpha > 0$ in equation (1). It is natural to ask whether there is an "ordered underrelaxation" method that could be used when the conditional distributions are non-Gaussian. I believe that there is. In the ordered overrelaxation method of Section 4.1, step (3) could be modified to randomly set x_i' to either $x_i^{(r+1)}$ or $x_i^{(r-1)}$ (with the change being rejected if the chosen $r \pm 1$ is out of range). This is a valid update (satisfying detailed balance), and should produce effects similar to those of Adler's method with $\alpha > 0$.

Acknowledgements.   I thank David MacKay for comments on the manuscript. This work was supported by the Natural Sciences and Engineering Research Council of Canada.

References

Adler, S. L. (1981) "Over-relaxation method for the Monte Carlo evaluation of the partition function for multiquadratic actions", *Physical Review D*, vol. 23, pp. 2901-2904.

Barone, P. and Frigessi, A. (1990) "Improving stochastic relaxation for Gaussian random fields", *Probability in the Engineering and Informational Sciences*, vol. 4, pp. 369-389.

Brown, F. R. and Woch, T. J. (1987) "Overrelaxed heat-bath and Metropolis algorithms for accelerating pure gauge Monte Carlo calculations", *Physical Review Letters*, vol. 58, pp. 2394-2396.

Creutz, M. (1987) "Overrelaxation and Monte Carlo simulation", *Physical Review D*, vol. 36, pp. 515-519.

David, H. A. (1970) *Order Statistics*, New York: John Wiley & Sons.

Devroye, L. (1986) *Non-uniform Random Variate Generation*, New York: Springer-Verlag.

Duane, S., Kennedy, A. D., Pendleton, B. J., and Roweth, D. (1987) "Hybrid Monte Carlo", *Physics Letters B*, vol. 195, pp. 216-222.

Fodor, Z. and Jansen, K. (1994) "Overrelaxation algorithm for coupled Gauge-Higgs systems", *Physics Letters B*, vol. 331, pp. 119-123.

Gilks, W. R. and Wild, P. (1992) "Adaptive rejection sampling for Gibbs sampling", *Applied Statistics*, vol. 41, pp. 337-348.

Gelfand, A. E. and Smith, A. F. M. (1990) "Sampling-based approaches to calculating marginal densities", *Journal of the American Statistical Association*, vol. 85, pp. 398-409.

Green, P. J. and Han, X. (1992) "Metropolis methods, Gaussian proposals and antithetic variables", in P. Barone, *et al.* (editors) *Stochastic Models, Statistical Methods, and Algorithms in Image Analysis*, Lecture Notes in Statistics, Berlin: Springer-Verlag.

Hastings, W. K. (1970) "Monte Carlo sampling methods using Markov chains and their applications", *Biometrika*, vol. 57, pp. 97-109.

Kennedy, W. J. and Gentle, J. E. (1980) *Statistical Computing*, New York: Marcel Dekker.

Metropolis, N., Rosenbluth, A. W., Rosenbluth, M. N., Teller, A. H., and Teller, E. (1953) "Equation of state calculations by fast computing machines", *Journal of Chemical Physics*, vol. 21, pp. 1087-1092.

Neal, R. M. (1993) "Probabilistic inference using Markov Chain Monte Carlo methods", Technical Report CRG-TR-93-1, Dept. of Computer Science, University of Toronto. Obtainable in compressed Postscript by anonymous ftp to ftp.cs.toronto.edu, directory pub/radford, file review.ps.Z.

Neal, R. M. (1995) *Bayesian Learning for Neural Networks*, Ph.D. thesis, Dept. of Computer Science, University of Toronto. Obtainable in compressed Postscript by anonymous ftp to ftp.cs.toronto.edu, directory pub/radford, file thesis.ps.Z.

Smith, A. F. M. and Roberts, G. O. (1993) "Bayesian computation via the Gibbs sampler and related Markov chain Monte Carlo methods", *Journal of the Royal Statistical Society B*, vol. 55, pp. 3-23. (See also the other papers and discussion in the same issue.)

Toussaint, D. (1989) "Introduction to algorithms for Monte Carlo simulations and their application to QCD", *Computer Physics Communications*, vol. 56, pp. 69-92.

Whitmer, C. (1984) "Over-relaxation methods for Monte Carlo simulations of quadratic and multiquadratic actions", *Physical Review D*, vol. 29, pp. 306-311.

Wolff, U. (1992) "Dynamics of hybrid overrelaxation in the gaussian model", *Physics Letters B*, vol. 288, pp. 166-170.

Young, D. M. (1971) *Iterative Solution of Large Linear Systems*, New York: Academic Press.

PART II : INDEPENDENCE

CHAIN GRAPHS AND SYMMETRIC ASSOCIATIONS

THOMAS S. RICHARDSON
Statistics Department
University of Washington
tsr@stat.washington.edu

Abstract. Graphical models based on chain graphs, which admit both directed and undirected edges, were introduced by by Lauritzen, Wermuth and Frydenberg as a generalization of graphical models based on undirected graphs, and acyclic directed graphs. More recently Andersson, Madigan and Perlman have given an alternative Markov property for chain graphs. This raises two questions: How are the two types of chain graphs to be interpreted? In which situations should chain graph models be used and with which Markov property?

The undirected edges in a chain graph are often said to represent 'symmetric' relations. Several different symmetric structures are considered, and it is shown that although each leads to a different set of conditional independences, none of those considered corresponds to either of the chain graph Markov properties.

The Markov properties of undirected graphs, and directed graphs, including latent variables and selection variables, are compared to those that have been proposed for chain graphs. It is shown that there are qualitative differences between these Markov properties. As a corollary, it is proved that there are chain graphs which do not correspond to any cyclic or acyclic directed graph, even with latent or selection variables.

1. Introduction

The use of acyclic directed graphs (often called 'DAG's) to simultaneously represent causal hypotheses and to encode independence and conditional independence constraints associated with those hypotheses has proved fruitful in the construction of expert systems, in the development of efficient updating algorithms (Pearl [22]; Lauritzen and Spiegelhalter [19]), and in inferring causal structure (Pearl and Verma [25]; Cooper and Herskovits [5]; Spirtes, Glymour and Scheines [31]).

Likewise, graphical models based on undirected graphs, also known as Markov random fields, have been used in spatial statistics to analyze data from field trials, image processing, and a host of other applications (Hammersley and Clifford [13]; Besag [4]; Speed [29]; Darroch *et al.* [8]). More recently, chain graphs, which admit both directed and undirected edges have been proposed as a natural generalization of both undirected graphs and acyclic directed graphs (Lauritzen and Wermuth [20]; Frydenberg [11]). Since acyclic directed graphs and undirected graphs can both be regarded as special cases of chain graphs it is undeniable that chain graphs are a generalization in this sense.

The introduction of chain graphs has been justified on the grounds that this admits the modelling of 'simultaneous responses' (Frydenberg [11]), 'symmetric associations' (Lauritzen and Wermuth [20]) or simply 'associative relations', as distinct from causal relations (Andersson, Madigan and Perlman [1]). The existence of two different Markov properties for chain graphs raises the question of what *sort* of symmetric relation is represented by a chain graph under a given Markov property, since the two properties are clearly different. A second related question concerns whether or not there are modelling applications for which chain graphs are particularly well suited, and if there are, which Markov property is most appropriate.

One possible approach to clarifying this issue is to begin by considering causal systems, or data generating processes, which have a symmetric structure. Three simple, though distinct, ways in which two variables, X and Y, could be related symmetrically are: (a) there is an unmeasured, 'confounding', or 'latent' variable that is a common cause of both X and Y; (b) X and Y are both causes of some 'selection' variable (conditioned on in the sample); (c) there is feedback between X and Y, so that X is a cause of Y, and Y is a cause of X. In fact situations (a) and (b) can easily be represented by DAGs through appropriate extensions of the formalism (Spirtes, Glymour and Scheines [31]; Cox and Wermuth [7]; Spirtes, Meek and Richardson [32]). In addition, certain kinds of linear feedback can also be modelled with directed cyclic graphs (Spirtes [30]; Koster [16]; Richardson [26, 27, 28]; Pearl and Dechter [24]). Each of these situations leads to a different set of conditional independences. However, perhaps surprisingly, none of these situations, nor any combination of them, lead in general to either of the Markov properties associated with chain graphs.

The remainder of the paper is organized as follows: Section 2 contains definitions of the various graphs considered and their associated Markov properties. Section 3 considers two simple chain graphs, under both the original Markov property proposed by Lauritzen, Wermuth and Frydenberg, and the alternative given by Andersson, Madigan and Perlman. These are compared to the corresponding directed graphs obtained by replacing the undirected edges with directed edges in accordance with situations (a), (b) and (c) above. Section 4 generalizes the results of the previous section: two properties are presented, motivated by causal and spatial intuitions, that the set of conditional independences entailed by a graphical model might satisfy. It is shown that the sets of independences entailed by (i) an undirected graph via separation, and (ii) a (cyclic or acyclic) directed graph (possibly with latent and/or selection variables) via d-separation, satisfy both properties. By contrast neither of these properties, in general, will hold in a chain graph under the Lauritzen-Wermuth-Frydenberg (LWF) interpretation. One property holds for chain graphs under the Andersson-Madigan-Perlman (AMP) interpretation, the other does not. Section 5 contains a discussion of data-generating processes associated with different graphical models, together with a brief sketch of the causal intervention theory that has been developed for directed graphs. Section 6 is the conclusion, while proofs not contained in the main text are given in Section 7.

2. Graphs and Probability Distributions

This section introduces the various kinds of graph considered in this paper, together with their associated Markov properties.

2.1. UNDIRECTED AND DIRECTED GRAPHS

An *undirected graph*, UG, is an ordered pair $(\mathbf{V}, \mathbf{U})$, where $\mathbf{V}$ is a set of vertices and $\mathbf{U}$ is a set of undirected edges $X - Y$ between vertices.[1]

Similarly, a *directed graph*, DG, is an ordered pair $(\mathbf{V}, \mathbf{D})$ where $\mathbf{D}$ is a set of directed edges $X \to Y$ between vertices in $\mathbf{V}$. A *directed cycle* consists of a sequence of n distinct edges $X_1 \to X_2 \to \cdots \to X_n \to X_1$ $(n \geq 2)$. If a directed graph, DG, contains no directed cycles it is said to be *acyclic*, otherwise it is *cyclic*. An edge $X \to Y$ is said to be *out of* X and *into* Y; X and Y are the *endpoints* of the edge. Note that if cycles are permitted there may be more than one edge between a given pair of vertices e.g. $X \leftarrow Y \leftarrow X$. Figure 1 gives examples of undirected and directed graphs.

2.2. DIRECTED GRAPHS WITH LATENT VARIABLES AND SELECTION VARIABLES

Cox and Wermuth [7] and Spirtes *et al.* [32] introduce directed graphs in which $\mathbf{V}$ is partitioned into three disjoint sets $\mathbf{O}$ (Observed), $\mathbf{S}$ (Selection)

---

[1]Bold face $(\mathbf{X})$ denote sets; italics (X) denote individual vertices; greek letters (π) denote paths.

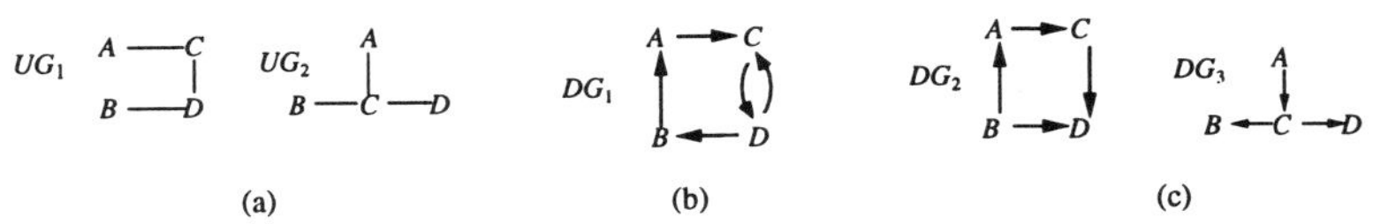

Figure 1. (a) undirected graphs; (b) a cyclic directed graph; (c) acyclic directed graphs

and **L** (Latent), written $DG(\mathbf{O}, \mathbf{S}, \mathbf{L})$ (where DG may be cyclic). The interpretation of this definition is that DG represents a causal or data-generating mechanism; **O** represents the subset of the variables that are observed; **S** represents a set of *selection* variables which, due to the nature of the mechanism selecting the sample, are conditioned on in the subpopulation from which the sample is drawn; the variables in **L** are not observed and for this reason are called *latent*.[2]

Example: Randomized Trial of an Ineffective Drug with Unpleasant Side-Effects[3]

A simple causal mechanism containing latent and selection variables is given in Figure 2. The graph represents a randomized trial of an ineffective drug with unpleasant side-effects. Patients are randomly assigned to the treatment or control group (A). Those in the treatment group suffer unpleasant side-effects, the severity of which is influenced by the patient's general level of health (H), with sicker patients suffering worse side-effects. Those patients who suffer sufficiently severe side-effects are likely to drop out of the study. The selection variable (Sel) records whether or not a patient remains in the study, thus for all those remaining in the study $Sel = Stay\ In$. Since unhealthy patients who are taking the drug are more likely to drop out, those patients in the treatment group who remain in the study tend to be healthier than those in the control group. Finally health status (H) influences how rapidly the patient recovers. This example is of interest because, as should be intuitively clear, a simple comparison of the recovery time of the patients still in the treatment and control groups at the end of the study will indicate faster recovery among those in the treatment group. This comparison falsely indicates that the drug has a beneficial effect, whereas in fact, this difference is due entirely to the side-effects causing the sicker patients in the treatment group to drop out of the study.[4] (The only difference between the two graphs in Figure 2 is that in $DG_1(\mathbf{O_1}, \mathbf{S_1}, \mathbf{L_1})$

---

[2]Note that the terms *variable* and *vertex* are used interchangeably.

[3]I am indebted to Chris Meek for this example.

[4]For precisely these reasons, in real drug trials investigators often go to great lengths to find out why patients dropped out of the study.

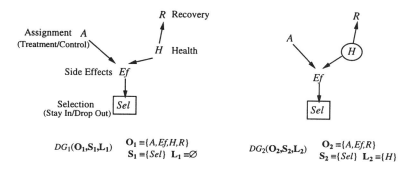

$$DG_1(\mathbf{O_1,S_1,L_1}) \qquad \begin{array}{l} \mathbf{O_1} \equiv \{A, Ef, H, R\} \\ \mathbf{S_1} \equiv \{Sel\} \ \mathbf{L_1} \equiv \varnothing \end{array}$$

$$DG_2(\mathbf{O_2,S_2,L_2}) \qquad \begin{array}{l} \mathbf{O_2} \equiv \{A, Ef, R\} \\ \mathbf{S_2} \equiv \{Sel\} \ \mathbf{L_2} \equiv \{H\} \end{array}$$

Figure 2. Randomized trial of an ineffective drug with unpleasant side effects leading to drop out. In $DG_1(\mathbf{O_1, S_1, L_1})$, $H \in \mathbf{O_1}$, and is observed, while in $DG_2(\mathbf{O_2, S_2, L_2})$ $H \in \mathbf{L_2}$ and is unobserved (variables in $\mathbf{L}$ are circled; variables in $\mathbf{S}$ are boxed; variables in $\mathbf{O}$ are not marked).

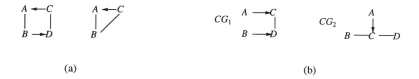

(a)   (b)

Figure 3. (a) mixed graphs containing partially directed cycles; (b) chain graphs.

health status (H) is observed so $H \in \mathbf{O_1}$, while in $DG_2(\mathbf{O_2, S_2, L_2})$ it is not observed so $H \in \mathbf{L_2}$.)

2.3. MIXED GRAPHS AND CHAIN GRAPHS

In a *mixed graph* a pair of vertices may be connected by a directed edge or an undirected edge (but not both). A *partially directed cycle* in a mixed graph G is a sequence of n distinct edges $\langle E_1, \ldots, E_n \rangle$, $(n \geq 3)$, with endpoints X_i, X_{i+1} respectively, such that:

(a) $X_1 \equiv X_{n+1}$,
(b) $\forall i \ (1 \leq i \leq n)$ either $X_i - X_{i+1}$ or $X_i \to X_{i+1}$, and
(c) $\exists j \ (1 \leq j \leq n)$ such that $X_j \to X_{j+1}$.

A *chain graph CG* is a mixed graph in which there are no partially directed cycles (see Figure 3). Koster [16] considers classes of reciprocal graphs containing directed and undirected edges in which partially directed cycles are allowed. Such graphs are not considered separately here, though many of the comments which apply to LWF chain graphs also apply to reciprocal graphs since the former are a subclass of the latter.

To make clear which kind of graph is being referred to UG will denote undirected graphs, DG directed graphs, CG chain graphs, and G a graph which may be any one of these. A *path* between X and Y in a graph G (of whatever type) consists of a sequence of edges $\langle E_1, \ldots, E_n \rangle$ such that there exists a sequence of distinct vertices $\langle X \equiv X_1, \ldots, X_{n+1} \equiv Y \rangle$ where E_i has *endpoints*, X_i and X_{i+1} $(1 \leq i \leq n)$, i.e. E_i is $X_i - X_{i+1}, X_i \to X_{i+1}$, or $X_i \leftarrow X_{i+1}$ $(1 \leq i \leq n)$.[5] If no vertex occurs more than once on the path then the path is *acyclic*, otherwise it is *cyclic*. A directed path from X to Y is a path of the form $X \to \cdots \to Y$.

2.4. THE GLOBAL MARKOV PROPERTY ASSOCIATED WITH UNDIRECTED GRAPHS

A *global Markov property* associates a set of conditional independence relations with a graph G.[6] In an undirected graph UG, for disjoint sets of vertices $\mathbf{X}$, $\mathbf{Y}$ and $\mathbf{Z}$, ($\mathbf{Z}$ may be empty), if there is no path from a variable $X \in \mathbf{X}$, to a variable $Y \in \mathbf{Y}$, that does not include some variable in $\mathbf{Z}$, then $\mathbf{X}$ and $\mathbf{Y}$ are said to be *separated* by $\mathbf{Z}$.

Undirected Global Markov Property; separation $(\models_U)$

$UG \models_U \mathbf{X} \perp\!\!\!\perp \mathbf{Y} \mid \mathbf{Z}$ if $\mathbf{X}$ and $\mathbf{Y}$ are separated by $\mathbf{Z}$ in UG.[7]

Thus the undirected graphs in Figure 1(a) entail the following conditional independences via separation:

$$UG_1 \quad \models_U \quad A \perp\!\!\!\perp D \mid C; \ A \perp\!\!\!\perp D \mid \{B, C\}; \ B \perp\!\!\!\perp C \mid D; \ B \perp\!\!\!\perp C \mid \{A, D\};$$
$$A \perp\!\!\!\perp B \mid C \ A \perp\!\!\!\perp B \mid D; \ A \perp\!\!\!\perp B \mid \{C, D\}$$

$$UG_2 \quad \models_U \quad A \perp\!\!\!\perp B \mid C; \ A \perp\!\!\!\perp B \mid \{C, D\}; \ A \perp\!\!\!\perp D \mid C; \ A \perp\!\!\!\perp D \mid \{B, C\};$$
$$B \perp\!\!\!\perp D \mid C; \ B \perp\!\!\!\perp D \mid \{A, C\}.$$

Here, and throughout, all and only 'elementary' independence relations of the form $\{X\} \perp\!\!\!\perp \{Y\} \mid \mathbf{Z}$ ($\mathbf{Z}$ may be empty) are listed. For instance, note that UG_1 also entails $\{A\} \perp\!\!\!\perp \{B, D\} \mid \{C\}$.

---

[5]'Path' is defined here as a sequence of edges, rather than vertices; in a directed cyclic graph a sequence of vertices does not in general define a unique path, since there may be more than one edge between a given pair of vertices. (Note that in a chain graph there is at most one edge between each pair of vertices.)

[6]Often global Markov conditions are introduced as a means for deriving the consequences of a set of local Markov conditions. Here the global property is defined directly in terms of the relevant graphical criterion.

[7]'$\mathbf{X} \perp\!\!\!\perp \mathbf{Y} \mid \mathbf{Z}$' means that '$\mathbf{X}$ is independent of $\mathbf{Y}$ given $\mathbf{Z}$'; if $\mathbf{Z} = \emptyset$, the abbreviation $\mathbf{X} \perp\!\!\!\perp \mathbf{Y}$ is used. When convenient braces are omitted from singleton sets $\{V\}$, e.g. $V \perp\!\!\!\perp \mathbf{Y} \mid \mathbf{Z}$ instead of $\{V\} \perp\!\!\!\perp \mathbf{Y} \mid \mathbf{Z}$

2.5. THE GLOBAL MARKOV PROPERTY ASSOCIATED WITH DIRECTED GRAPHS

In a directed graph DG, X is a *parent* of Y, (and Y is a *child* of X) if there is a directed edge $X \to Y$ in G. X is an *ancestor* of Y (and Y is a *descendant* of X) if there is a directed path $X \to \cdots \to Y$ from X to Y, or $X \equiv Y$. Thus 'ancestor' ('descendant') is the transitive, reflexive closure of the 'parent' ('child') relation. A pair of consecutive edges on a path π in DG are said to *collide at vertex* A if both edges are into A, i.e. $\to A \leftarrow$, in this case A is called a *collider on* π, otherwise A is a *non-collider on* π. Thus every vertex on a path in a directed graph is either a collider, a non-collider, or an endpoint. For distinct vertices X and Y, and set $\mathbf{Z} \subseteq \mathbf{V} \backslash \{X, Y\}$, a path π between X and Y is said to *d-connect* X and Y given $\mathbf{Z}$ if every collider on π is an ancestor of a vertex in $\mathbf{Z}$, and no non-collider on π is in $\mathbf{Z}$. For disjoint sets $\mathbf{X}$, $\mathbf{Y}$, $\mathbf{Z}$, if there is an $X \in \mathbf{X}$, and $Y \in \mathbf{Y}$, such that there is a path which d-connects X and Y given $\mathbf{Z}$ then $\mathbf{X}$ and $\mathbf{Y}$ are said to be *d-connected* given $\mathbf{Z}$. If no such path exists then $\mathbf{X}$ and $\mathbf{Y}$ are said to be *d-separated* given $\mathbf{Z}$ (see Pearl [22]).

Directed Global Markov Property; d-separation $(\models_{DS})$

$DG \models_{DS} \mathbf{X} \perp\!\!\!\perp \mathbf{Y} \mid \mathbf{Z}$ if $\mathbf{X}$ and $\mathbf{Y}$ are d-separated by $\mathbf{Z}$ in DG.

Thus the directed graphs in Figure 1(b,c) entail the following conditional independences via d-separation:

$$DG_1 \quad \models_{DS} \quad B \perp\!\!\!\perp C \mid \{A, D\};$$

$$DG_2 \quad \models_{DS} \quad B \perp\!\!\!\perp C \mid A; \ A \perp\!\!\!\perp D \mid \{B, C\};$$

$$DG_3 \quad \models_{DS} \quad A \perp\!\!\!\perp B \mid C; \ A \perp\!\!\!\perp B \mid \{C, D\}; \ A \perp\!\!\!\perp D \mid C; \ A \perp\!\!\!\perp D \mid \{B, C\};$$
$$B \perp\!\!\!\perp D \mid C; \ B \perp\!\!\!\perp D \mid \{A, C\}.$$

Note that the conditional independences entailed by DG_3 under d-separation are precisely those entailed by UG_2 under separation.

2.6. THE GLOBAL MARKOV PROPERTY ASSOCIATED WITH DIRECTED GRAPHS WITH LATENT AND SELECTION VARIABLES

The global Markov property for a directed graph with latent and/or selection variables is a natural extension of the global Markov property for directed graphs. For $DG(\mathbf{O}, \mathbf{S}, \mathbf{L})$, and $\mathbf{X} \dot\cup \mathbf{Y} \dot\cup \mathbf{Z} \subseteq \mathbf{O}$ define:

$$DG(\mathbf{O}, \mathbf{S}, \mathbf{L}) \models_{DS} \mathbf{X} \perp\!\!\!\perp \mathbf{Y} \mid \mathbf{Z} \text{ if and only if } DG \models_{DS} \mathbf{X} \perp\!\!\!\perp \mathbf{Y} \mid \mathbf{Z} \cup \mathbf{S}.$$

In other words, the set of conditional independence relations entailed by $DG(\mathbf{O}, \mathbf{S}, \mathbf{L})$ is exactly the subset of those independence relations entailed by the directed graph DG, in which no latent variables occur, and the conditioning set always includes (implicitly) all the selection variables in $\mathbf{S}$. Since, under the interpretation of $DG(\mathbf{O}, \mathbf{S}, \mathbf{L})$, the only observed variables are in $\mathbf{O}$, conditional independence relations involving variables in $\mathbf{L}$ are not observed. Similarly, samples are drawn from a subpopulation in which all variables in $\mathbf{S}$ are conditioned on, e.g. in the example in Section 2.2, the only patients observed were those for which $Sel = Stay\ In$. Thus the variables in $\mathbf{S}$ will be conditioned upon in every conditional independence relation observed to hold in the sample. Hence $DG(\mathbf{O}, \mathbf{S}, \mathbf{L})$ entails a set of conditional independences which hold in the observed distribution $\mathrm{P}(\mathbf{O} \mid \mathbf{S} = \mathbf{In})$. (See Spirtes and Richardson [33]; Spirtes, Meek and Richardson [32]; Cox and Wermuth [7].) Thus the graph $DG_1(\mathbf{O_1}, \mathbf{S_1}, \mathbf{L_1})$, shown in Figure 2, entails the following conditional independences:

$$DG_1(\mathbf{O_1}, \mathbf{S_1}, \mathbf{L_1}) \models_{DS} A \perp\!\!\!\perp R \mid H;\ A \perp\!\!\!\perp R \mid \{H, Ef\},$$

since $DG_1 \models_{DS} A \perp\!\!\!\perp R \mid \{H, Sel\};\ A \perp\!\!\!\perp R \mid \{H, Ef, Sel\}$.

However, the graph $DG_2(\mathbf{O_2}, \mathbf{S_2}, \mathbf{L_2})$ does not entail any independences, since health status is unobserved, $H \notin \mathbf{O_2}$, so neither of the above mentioned independences entailed by the graph $DG_1(\mathbf{O_1}, \mathbf{S_1}, \mathbf{L_1})$ is entailed by $DG_2(\mathbf{O_2}, \mathbf{S_2}, \mathbf{L_2})$.

2.7. GLOBAL MARKOV PROPERTIES ASSOCIATED WITH CHAIN GRAPHS

There are two different global Markov properties which have been proposed for chain graphs. In both definitions a conditional independence relation is entailed if sets $\mathbf{X}$ and $\mathbf{Y}$ are separated by $\mathbf{Z}$ in an undirected graph the vertices of which are a subset of those in the chain graph, while the edges are a superset of those occurring between these vertices in the original chain graph.[8]

2.7.1. *The Lauritzen-Wermuth-Frydenberg chain graph Markov property*

A vertex V in a chain graph is said to be *anterior* to a set $\mathbf{W}$ if there is a path π from V to some $W \in \mathbf{W}$ in which all directed edges $(X \to Y)$ on the path (if any) are such that Y is between X and W on π, $Ant(\mathbf{W}) = \{V \mid V \text{ is anterior to } W\}$. Let $CG(\mathbf{W})$ denote the *induced subgraph* of CG obtained by removing all vertices in $\mathbf{V} \backslash \mathbf{W}$ and all edges with an endpoint

---

[8]More recently, both of these Markov properties have been re-formulated in terms of a separation criteria that may be applied to the original chain graph, rather than an undirected graph derived from it (see Studený and Bouckaert [36], Andersson *et al.* [2]).

Figure 4. Contrast between the LWF and AMP Markov properties. Undirected graphs used to test $A \perp\!\!\!\perp D \mid \{B, C\}$ in CG_1 under (a) the LWF property, (b) the AMP property. Undirected graphs used to test $B \perp\!\!\!\perp D \mid C$ in CG_2 under (c) the LWF property, (d) the AMP property.

in $\mathbf{V} \backslash \mathbf{W}$. A *complex* in CG is an induced subgraph with the following form: $X \rightarrow V_1 - \cdots - V_n \leftarrow Y$ $(n \geq 1)$. A complex is *moralized* by adding the undirected edge $X - Y$. $Moral(CG)$ is the undirected graph formed by moralizing all complexes in CG, and then replacing all directed edges with undirected edges.

LWF Global Markov Property for Chain Graphs ($\models_{LWF}$)

$CG \models_{LWF} \mathbf{X} \perp\!\!\!\perp \mathbf{Y} \mid \mathbf{Z}$ if $\mathbf{X}$ is separated from $\mathbf{Y}$ by $\mathbf{Z}$ in the undirected graph $Moral(CG(Ant(\mathbf{X} \cup \mathbf{Y} \cup \mathbf{Z})))$.

Hence the chain graphs in Figure 3(b) entail the following conditional independences under the LWF Markov property:

$CG_1 \models_{LWF} A \perp\!\!\!\perp B;\ A \perp\!\!\!\perp D \mid \{B, C\};\ B \perp\!\!\!\perp C \mid \{A, D\};$

$CG_2 \models_{LWF} A \perp\!\!\!\perp B \mid C;\ A \perp\!\!\!\perp B \mid \{C, D\};\ A \perp\!\!\!\perp D \mid C;\ A \perp\!\!\!\perp D \mid \{B, C\};$
$\qquad\qquad B \perp\!\!\!\perp D \mid C;\ B \perp\!\!\!\perp D \mid \{A, C\}.$

Notice that the conditional independences entailed by CG_2 under the LWF Markov property are the same as those entailed by DG_3 under d-separation, and UG_2 under separation (see Figure 1).

2.7.2. *The Andersson-Madigan-Perlman chain graph Markov property*

In a chain graph vertices V and W are said to be *connected* if there is a path containing only undirected edges between V and W, $Con(\mathbf{W}) = \{V \mid V$ is connected to some $W \in \mathbf{W}\}$. The extended subgraph, $Ext(CG, \mathbf{W})$, has vertex set $Con(\mathbf{W})$ and contains all directed edges in $CG(\mathbf{W})$, and all undirected edges in $CG(Con(\mathbf{W}))$. A vertex V in a chain graph is said to be an *ancestor* of a set $\mathbf{W}$ if there is a path π from V to some $W \in \mathbf{W}$ in which all edges on the path are directed $(X \rightarrow Y)$ and are such that Y is between X and W on π.[9] (See Figure 5.) Now let

[9]Note that other authors, e.g. Lauritzen [17], have used 'ancestral' to refer to the set named 'anterior' in Section 3.

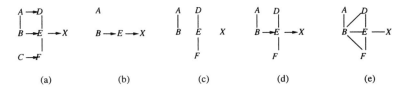

Figure 5. Constructing an augmented and extended chain graph: (a) a chain graph CG; (b) directed edges in $\mathrm{Anc}(\{A, E, X\})$; (c) undirected edges in $\mathrm{Con}(\mathrm{Anc}(\{A, E, X\}))$ (d) $\mathrm{Ext}(CG, \mathrm{Anc}(\{A, E, X\}))$; (e) $\mathrm{Aug}(\mathrm{Ext}(CG, \mathrm{Anc}(\{A, E, X\})))$.

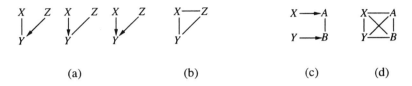

Figure 6. (a) Triplexes $\langle X, Y, Z \rangle$ and (b) the corresponding augmented triplex. (c) A chain graph with a bi-flag $\langle X, A, B, Y \rangle$ and two triplexes $\langle A, B, Y \rangle$, $\langle X, A, B \rangle$; (d) the corresponding augmented chain graph.

$$Anc(\mathbf{W}) = \{V \mid V \text{ is an ancestor of some } W \in \mathbf{W}\}.$$

A triple of vertices $\langle X, Y, Z \rangle$ is said to form a *triplex* in CG if the induced subgraph $CG(\{X, Y, Z\})$ is either $X \to Y - Z$, $X \to Y \leftarrow Z$, or $X - Y \leftarrow Z$. A triplex is *augmented* by adding the $X - Z$ edge. A set of four vertices $\langle X, A, B, Y \rangle$ is said to form a *bi-flag* if the edges $X \to A$, $Y \to B$, and $A - B$ are present in the induced subgraph over $\{X, A, B, Y\}$. A bi-flag is *augmented* by adding the edge $X - Y$. $Aug(CG)$ is the undirected graph formed by augmenting all triplexes and bi-flags in CG and replacing all directed edges with undirected edges (see Figure 6). Now let

$$Aug[CG; \mathbf{X}, \mathbf{Y}, \mathbf{Z}] = Aug(Ext(CG, Anc(\mathbf{X} \cup \mathbf{Y} \cup \mathbf{Z}))).$$

AMP Global Markov Property ($\models_{AMP}$)

$CG \models_{AMP} \mathbf{X} \perp\!\!\!\perp \mathbf{Y} \mid \mathbf{Z}$ if $\mathbf{X}$ is separated from $\mathbf{Y}$ by $\mathbf{Z}$ in the undirected graph $Aug[CG; \mathbf{X}, \mathbf{Y}, \mathbf{Z}]$.

Hence the conditional independence relations associated with the chain graphs in Figure 3(b) under the AMP global Markov property are:

$CG_1 \models_{AMP}$ $A \perp\!\!\!\perp B$; $A \perp\!\!\!\perp B \mid C$; $A \perp\!\!\!\perp B \mid D$; $A \perp\!\!\!\perp D$; $A \perp\!\!\!\perp D \mid B$; $B \perp\!\!\!\perp C$; $B \perp\!\!\!\perp C \mid A$;

$CG_2 \models_{AMP}$ $A \perp\!\!\!\perp B$; $A \perp\!\!\!\perp B \mid D$; $A \perp\!\!\!\perp D$; $A \perp\!\!\!\perp D \mid B$; $B \perp\!\!\!\perp D \mid \{A, C\}$.

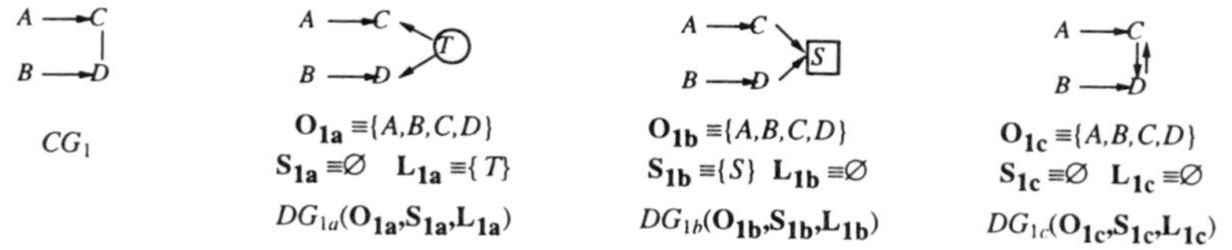

CG_1

$O_{1a} \equiv \{A,B,C,D\}$
$S_{1a} \equiv \varnothing$ $L_{1a} \equiv \{T\}$
$DG_{1a}(O_{1a}, S_{1a}, L_{1a})$

$O_{1b} \equiv \{A,B,C,D\}$
$S_{1b} \equiv \{S\}$ $L_{1b} \equiv \varnothing$
$DG_{1b}(O_{1b}, S_{1b}, L_{1b})$

$O_{1c} \equiv \{A,B,C,D\}$
$S_{1c} \equiv \varnothing$ $L_{1c} \equiv \varnothing$
$DG_{1c}(O_{1c}, S_{1c}, L_{1c})$

Figure 7. A chain graph and directed graphs in which C and D are symmetrically related.

Both LWF and AMP properties coincide with separation (d-separation) for the special case of a chain graph which is an undirected (acyclic, directed) graph. Thus chain graphs with either property are a generalization of both acyclic, directed graphs and undirected graphs. Cox and Wermuth [7] distinguish between the LWF and AMP Markov properties by using dashed lines, $X \dashrightarrow Y$, in chain graphs under the AMP property.

2.8. MARKOV EQUIVALENCE AND COMPLETENESS

Two graphs G_1, G_2 under global Markov properties R_1, R_2 respectively are said to be *Markov equivalent* if $G_1 \models_{R_1} X \perp\!\!\!\perp Y \mid Z$ if and only if $G_2 \models_{R_2} X \perp\!\!\!\perp Y \mid Z$. Thus CG_2 under the LWF Markov property, DG_3 under d-separation, and UG_2 under separation are all Markov equivalent. For a given global Markov property R, and graph G with vertex set $\mathbf{V}$, a distribution P is said to be G-*Markovian$_R$* if for disjoint subsets $\mathbf{X}$, $\mathbf{Y}$ and $\mathbf{Z}$, $G \models_R X \perp\!\!\!\perp Y \mid Z$ implies $X \perp\!\!\!\perp Y \mid Z$ in P. A global Markov property is said to be *weakly complete* if for all disjoint sets $\mathbf{X}$, $\mathbf{Y}$ and $\mathbf{Z}$, such that $G \not\models_R X \perp\!\!\!\perp Y \mid Z$ there is a G-Markovian$_R$ distribution P in which $X \not\!\perp\!\!\!\perp Y \mid Z$. The property R is said to be *strongly complete* if there is a G-*Markovian$_R$* distribution P in which $G \models_R X \perp\!\!\!\perp Y \mid Z$ if and only if $X \perp\!\!\!\perp Y \mid Z$ in P. All of the global Markov properties here are known to be strongly (and hence weakly) complete (Geiger [12]; Frydenberg [11]; Spirtes [30]; Meek [21]; Spirtes *et al.* [31]; Studený and Bouckaert [36]; Andersson *et al.* [2]).

3. Directed Graphs with Symmetric Relations

In this section the Markov properties of simple directed graphs with symmetrically related variables are compared to those of the corresponding chain graphs. In particular, the following symmetric relations between variables X and Y are considered: (a) X and Y have a latent common cause; (b) X and Y are both causes of some selection variable; (c) X is a cause of Y, and Y is a cause of X, as occurs in a feedback system.

The conditional independences relations entailed by the directed graphs

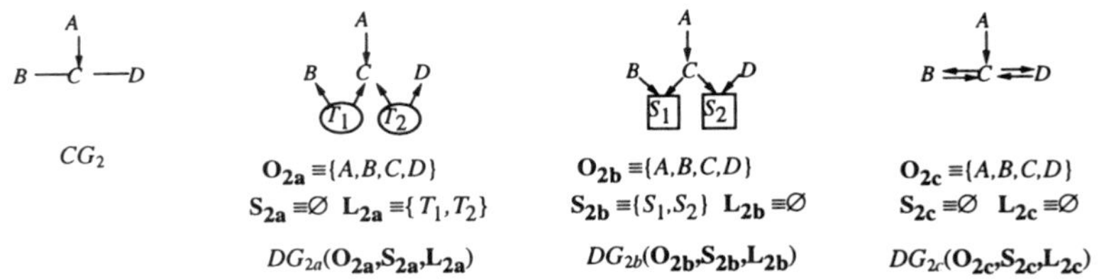

$O_{2a} \equiv \{A,B,C,D\}$
$S_{2a} \equiv \varnothing$ $L_{2a} \equiv \{T_1, T_2\}$
$DG_{2a}(O_{2a}, S_{2a}, L_{2a})$

$O_{2b} \equiv \{A,B,C,D\}$
$S_{2b} \equiv \{S_1, S_2\}$ $L_{2b} \equiv \varnothing$
$DG_{2b}(O_{2b}, S_{2b}, L_{2b})$

$O_{2c} \equiv \{A,B,C,D\}$
$S_{2c} \equiv \varnothing$ $L_{2c} \equiv \varnothing$
$DG_{2c}(O_{2c}, S_{2c}, L_{2c})$

Figure 8. A chain graph and directed graphs in which the pairs of vertices B and C, and C and D, are symmetrically related.

in Figure 7 are:

$DG_{1a}(\mathbf{O_{1a}}, \mathbf{S_{1a}}, \mathbf{L_{1a}}) \models_{DS} A \perp\!\!\!\perp B; \ A \perp\!\!\!\perp B \mid C; \ A \perp\!\!\!\perp B \mid D; \ A \perp\!\!\!\perp D;$
$\qquad\qquad\qquad\qquad\qquad\quad A \perp\!\!\!\perp D \mid B; \ B \perp\!\!\!\perp C; \ B \perp\!\!\!\perp C \mid A;$

$DG_{1b}(\mathbf{O_{1b}}, \mathbf{S_{1b}}, \mathbf{L_{1b}}) \models_{DS} A \perp\!\!\!\perp B \mid C; \ A \perp\!\!\!\perp B \mid D; \ B \perp\!\!\!\perp C \mid D; \ A \perp\!\!\!\perp D \mid C;$
$\qquad\qquad\qquad\qquad\qquad\quad A \perp\!\!\!\perp B \mid \{C, D\}; A \perp\!\!\!\perp D \mid \{B, C\}; B \perp\!\!\!\perp C \mid \{A, D\};$

$DG_{1c}(\mathbf{O_{1c}}, \mathbf{S_{1c}}, \mathbf{L_{1c}}) \models_{DS} A \perp\!\!\!\perp B; \ A \perp\!\!\!\perp B \mid \{C, D\}.$

It follows that none of these directed graphs is Markov equivalent to CG_1 under the LWF Markov property. However, $DG_{1a}(\mathbf{O_{1a}}, \mathbf{S_{1a}}, \mathbf{L_{1a}})$ is Markov equivalent to CG_1 under the AMP Markov property. Turning now to the directed graphs shown in Figure 8, the following conditional independence relations are entailed:

$DG_{2a}(\mathbf{O_{2a}}, \mathbf{S_{2a}}, \mathbf{L_{2a}}) \models_{DS} A \perp\!\!\!\perp B; \ A \perp\!\!\!\perp B \mid D; \ A \perp\!\!\!\perp D; \ A \perp\!\!\!\perp D \mid B; \ B \perp\!\!\!\perp D;$
$\qquad\qquad\qquad\qquad\qquad\quad B \perp\!\!\!\perp D \mid A;$

$DG_{2b}(\mathbf{O_{2b}}, \mathbf{S_{2b}}, \mathbf{L_{2b}}) \models_{DS} A \perp\!\!\!\perp B \mid C; \ A \perp\!\!\!\perp B \mid \{C, D\}; \ A \perp\!\!\!\perp D \mid C;$
$\qquad\qquad\qquad\qquad\qquad\quad A \perp\!\!\!\perp D \mid \{B, C\}; \ B \perp\!\!\!\perp D \mid C; \ B \perp\!\!\!\perp D \mid \{A, C\};$

$DG_{2c}(\mathbf{O_{2c}}, \mathbf{S_{2c}}, \mathbf{L_{2c}})$ does not entail any conditional independences.

It follows that none of these directed graphs is Markov equivalent to CG_2 under the AMP Markov property. However, $DG_{2b}(\mathbf{O_{2b}}, \mathbf{S_{2b}}, \mathbf{L_{2b}})$ is Markov equivalent to CG_2 under the LWF Markov property. Further, note that $DG_{2b}(\mathbf{O_{2b}}, \mathbf{S_{2b}}, \mathbf{L_{2b}})$ is also Markov equivalent to UG_2 (under separation) and DG_3 (under d-separation) in Figure 1(a).

There are two other simple symmetric relations that might be considered: (d) X and Y have a common child that is a latent variable; (e) X and Y have a common parent that is a selection variable. However, without additional edges X and Y are entailed to be independent (given $\mathbf{S}$)

in these configurations, whereas this is clearly not the case if there is an edge between X and Y in a chain graph.

Hence none of the simple directed graphs with symmetric relations corresponding to CG_1 are Markov equivalent to CG_1 under the LWF Markov property, and likewise none of those corresponding to CG_2 are Markov equivalent to CG_2 under the AMP Markov property. In the next section a stronger result is proved: in fact there are no directed graphs, however complicated, with or without latent and selection variables, that are Markov equivalent to CG_1 and CG_2 under the LWF and AMP Markov properties, respectively.

4. Inseparability and Related Properties

In this section two Markov properties, motivated by spatial and causal intuitions, are introduced. It is then shown that these Markov properties hold for all undirected graphs, and all directed graphs (under d-separation) possibly with latent and selection variables. Distinct vertices X and Y are *inseparable$_R$* in G under Markov Property R if there is no set $\mathbf{W}$ such that $G \models_R X \perp\!\!\!\perp Y \mid \mathbf{W}$. If X and Y are not inseparable$_R$, they are *separable$_R$*. Let $[G]_R^{\text{Ins}}$ be the undirected graph in which there is an edge $X - Y$ if and only if X and Y are inseparable$_R$ in G under R. Note that in accord with the definition of $\models_{DS}$ for $DG(\mathbf{O}, \mathbf{S}, \mathbf{L})$, only vertices $X, Y \in \mathbf{O}$ are separable$_{DS}$ or inseparable$_{DS}$, thus $[DG(\mathbf{O}, \mathbf{S}, \mathbf{L})]_{DS}^{\text{Ins}}$ is defined to have vertex set $\mathbf{O}$.

For an undirected graph model $[UG]_S^{\text{Ins}}$ is just the undirected graph UG. For an acyclic, directed graph (without latent or selection variables) under d-separation, or a chain graph under either Markov property $[G]_R^{\text{Ins}}$ is simply the undirected graph formed by replacing all directed edges with undirected edges, hence for any chain graph CG, $[CG]_{AMP}^{\text{Ins}} = [CG]_{LWF}^{\text{Ins}}$.

In any graphical model, if there is an edge (directed or undirected) between a pair of variables then those variables are inseparable$_R$. For undirected graphs, acyclic directed graphs, and chain graphs (under either Markov property), inseparability$_R$ is both a necessary and a sufficient condition for the existence of an edge between a pair of variables. However, in a directed graph with cycles, or in a (cyclic or acyclic) directed graph with latent and/or selection variables, inseparability$_{DS}$ is not a sufficient condition for there to be an edge between a pair of variables (recall that in $DG(\mathbf{O}, \mathbf{S}, \mathbf{L})$, the entailed conditional independences are restricted to those that are observable).

An *inducing path* between X and Y in $DG(\mathbf{O}, \mathbf{S}, \mathbf{L})$ is a path π between X and Y on which (i) every vertex in $\mathbf{O} \cup \mathbf{S}$ is a collider on π, and (ii) every collider is an ancestor of X, Y or $\mathbf{S}$.[10] In a directed graph, $DG(\mathbf{O}, \mathbf{S}, \mathbf{L})$,

---

[10]The notion of an inducing path was first introduced for acyclic directed graphs with

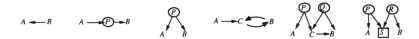

Figure 9. Examples of directed graphs $DG(\mathbf{O}, \mathbf{S}, \mathbf{L})$ in which A and B are inseparable$_{DS}$.

variables $X, Y \in \mathbf{O}$, are inseparable$_{DS}$ if and only if there is an inducing path between X and Y in $DG(\mathbf{O}, \mathbf{S}, \mathbf{L})$.[11] For example, C and D were inseparable$_{DS}$ in $DG_{1a}(\mathbf{O_{1a}}, \mathbf{S_{1a}}, \mathbf{L_{1a}})$, and $DG_{1b}(\mathbf{O_{1b}}, \mathbf{S_{1b}}, \mathbf{L_{1b}})$, while in $DG_{1c}(\mathbf{O_{1c}}, \mathbf{S_{1c}}, \mathbf{L_{1c}})$ A and B were the only separable$_{DS}$ variables. Figure 9 contains further examples of graphs in which vertices are inseparable$_{DS}$.

4.1. 'BETWEEN SEPARATED' MODELS

A vertex B will be said to be *between*$_R$ X and Y in G under Markov property R, if and only if there exists a sequence of *distinct* vertices $\langle X \equiv X_0, X_1, \ldots, X_n \equiv B, X_{n+1}, \ldots, X_{n+m} \equiv Y \rangle$ in $[G]_R^{\text{Ins}}$ such that each consecutive pair of vertices X_i, X_{i+1} in the sequence are inseparable$_R$ in G under R. Clearly B will be between$_R$ X and Y in G if and only if B lies on a path between X and Y in $[G]_R^{\text{Ins}}$. The set of vertices between X and Y under property R in graph G is denoted $Between_R(G; X, Y)$, abbreviated to $Between_R(X, Y)$, when G is clear from context. Note that for any chain graph CG, $\text{Between}_{LWF}(CG; X, Y) = \text{Between}_{AMP}(CG; X, Y)$, for all vertices X and Y.

Between$_R$ Separated Models

A model G is *between*$_R$ *separated*, if for all pairs of vertices X, Y and sets $\mathbf{W}$ ($X, Y \notin \mathbf{W}$):
$G \models_R X \perp\!\!\!\perp Y \mid \mathbf{W} \implies G \models_R X \perp\!\!\!\perp Y \mid \mathbf{W} \cap \text{Between}_R(G; X, Y)$
(where $\{X, Y\} \cup \mathbf{W}$ is a subset of the vertices in $[G]_R^{\text{Ins}}$).

It follows that if G is between$_R$ separated, then in order to make some (separable) pair of vertices X and Y conditionally independent, it is always sufficient to condition on a subset (possibly empty) of the vertices that lie on paths between X and Y.

The intuition that only vertices on paths between X and Y are relevant to making X and Y independent is related to the idea, fundamental to much

---

latent variables in Verma and Pearl [37]; it was subsequently extended to include selection variables in Spirtes, Meek and Richardson [32].

[11] Inseparability$_{DS}$ is a necessary and sufficient condition for there to be an edge between a pair of variables in a Partial Ancestral Graph (PAG), (Richardson [26, 27]; Spirtes *et al.* [32, 31]), which represents structural features common to a Markov equivalence class of directed graphs.

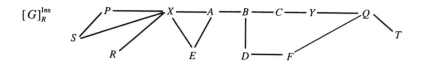

$[G]_R^{\text{Ins}}$

Figure 10. Between$_R(G; X, Y) = \{A, B, C, D, E, F, Q\}$, CoCon$_R(G; X, Y) = \{A, B, C, D, E, F, Q, T\}$, while P, R and S, are vertices not in CoCon$_R(G; X, Y)$

of graphical modelling, that if vertices are *dependent* then they should be *connected* in some way graphically. This is a natural correspondence, present in the spatial intuition that only contiguous regions interact directly, and also in causal principles which state that if two quantities are dependent then they are causally connected (Hausman [14]).[12]

Theorem 1 **(i)** *All undirected graphs H are between$_S$ separated.*
(ii) *All directed graphs $DG(\mathbf{O}, \mathbf{S}, \mathbf{L})$ are between$_{DS}$ separated.*

Proof: The proof for undirected graph models is given here. It is easy to see that the proof carries over directly to directed graphs without selection or latent variables (i.e. $\mathbf{V} = \mathbf{O}$, $\mathbf{S} = \mathbf{L} = \emptyset$) replacing 'separated' by 'd-separated', and 'connected' by 'd-connected'. The proof for directed graphs with latent and/or selection variables is in the appendix.

Suppose, for a contradiction, $UG \models_S X \perp\!\!\!\perp Y \mid \mathbf{W}$, but $UG \not\models_S X \perp\!\!\!\perp Y \mid \mathbf{W} \cap \text{Between}_S(X, Y)$. Then there is a path π in UG connecting X and Y given $\mathbf{W} \cap \text{Between}_S(X, Y)$. Since this path does not connect given $\mathbf{W}$, it follows that there is some vertex V on π, and $V \in \mathbf{W} \backslash \text{Between}_S(X, Y)$. But if V is on π, then π constitutes a sequence of vertices $\langle X \equiv X_0, X_1, \ldots, X_n \equiv V, X_{n+1}, \ldots, X_{n+m} \equiv Y \rangle$ such that consecutive pairs of vertices are inseparable$_S$ (because there is an edge between each pair of variables). Hence $V \in \text{Between}_S(X, Y)$, which is a contradiction. $\square$

In general, chain graphs are not between$_{LWF}$ separated or between$_{AMP}$ separated. This is shown by CG_1 and CG_2 in Figure 3:

$$CG_1 \models_{LWF} A \perp\!\!\!\perp D \mid \{B, C\},$$

so A and D are separable$_{LWF}$, but Between$_{LWF}(CG_1; A, D) = \{C\}$ and

$$CG_1 \not\models_{LWF} A \perp\!\!\!\perp D \mid \{C\}.$$

For the AMP property note that

$$CG_2 \models_{AMP} B \perp\!\!\!\perp D \mid \{A, C\},$$

[12]Where 'A and B are causally connected' means that either A is a cause of B, B is a cause of A, or they share some common cause (or some combination of these).

but $\text{Between}_{AMP}(CG_2; B, D) = \{C\}$, and yet

$$CG_2 \not\models_{AMP} B \perp\!\!\!\perp D \mid \{C\}.$$

4.2. 'CO-CONNECTION DETERMINED' MODELS

A vertex W will be said to be *co-connected$_R$* to X and Y in G if X, Y and W are vertices in $[G]_R^{\text{Ins}}$ satisfying:

(i) There is a sequence of vertices $\langle X, A_1, A_2, \ldots, A_n, W \rangle$ in $[G]_R^{\text{Ins}}$ which does not contain Y and consecutive pairs of variables in the sequence are inseparable$_R$ in G under R.

(ii) There is a sequence of vertices $\langle W, B_1, B_2, \ldots, B_m, Y \rangle$ in $[G]_R^{\text{Ins}}$ which does not contain X and consecutive pairs of variables in the sequence are inseparable$_R$ in G under R.

Let $CoCon_R(G; X, Y) = \{V \mid V \text{ is co-connected}_R \text{ to } X \text{ and } Y \text{ in } [G]_R^{\text{Ins}}\}$.

It is easy to see that B will be co-connected$_R$ to X and Y in G if and only if (a) B is not separated from Y by X in $[G]_R^{\text{Ins}}$, and (b) B is not separated from X by Y in $[G]_R^{\text{Ins}}$. Note that for any chain graph CG, and vertices X, Y, $CoCon_{LWF}(CG; X, Y) = CoCon_{AMP}(CG; X, Y)$.

Clearly $\text{Between}_R(G; X, Y) \subseteq CoCon_R(G; X, Y)$, so being co-connected$_R$ to X and Y is a weaker requirement than being between$_R$ X and Y. Both $\text{Between}_R(G; X, Y)$ and $CoCon_R(G; X, Y)$ are sets of vertices which are topologically 'in between' X and Y in $[G]_R^{\text{Ins}}$.

Co-Connection$_R$ Determined Models

A model G will be said to be *co-connection$_R$ determined*, if for all pairs of vertices X, Y and sets $\mathbf{W}$ ($X, Y \notin \mathbf{W}$):
$G \models_R X \perp\!\!\!\perp Y \mid \mathbf{W} \iff G \models_R X \perp\!\!\!\perp Y \mid \mathbf{W} \cap CoCon_R(G; X, Y)$
(where $\{X, Y\} \cup \mathbf{W}$ is a subset of the vertices in $[G]_R^{\text{Ins}}$).

This principle states that the inclusion or exclusion of vertices that are not in $CoCon_R(X, Y)$ from some set $\mathbf{W}$ is irrelevant to whether X and Y are entailed to be independent given $\mathbf{W}$.

Theorem 2 (i) *Undirected graph models are co-connection$_S$ determined.*

    (ii) *Directed graphs, possibly with latent and/or selection variables, are co-connection$_{DS}$ determined.*

    (iii) *Chain graphs are co-connection$_{AMP}$ determined.*

Proof: Again the proof for undirected graphs is given here. The proofs for directed graphs and AMP chain graphs are given in the appendix.

Since $\text{Between}_S(X,Y) \subseteq \text{CoCon}_S(X,Y)$, an argument similar to that used in the proof of Theorem 1 (replacing 'Between_S' with 'CoCon_S') shows that if $UG \models_S X \perp\!\!\!\perp Y \mid \mathbf{W}$ then $UG \models_S X \perp\!\!\!\perp Y \mid \mathbf{W} \cap \text{CoCon}_S(X,Y)$. Conversely, if $UG \models_S X \perp\!\!\!\perp Y \mid \mathbf{W} \cap \text{CoCon}_S(X,Y)$ then X and Y are separated by $\mathbf{W} \cap \text{CoCon}_S(X,Y)$ in UG. Since $\mathbf{W} \cap \text{CoCon}_S(X,Y) \subseteq \mathbf{W}$, it follows that X and Y are separated by $\mathbf{W}$ in UG.[13]   □

For undirected graphs $UG \models_S X \perp\!\!\!\perp Y \mid \mathbf{W} \implies UG \models_S X \perp\!\!\!\perp Y \mid \mathbf{W} \cap \text{Between}_S(X,Y)$, i.e. undirected graphs could be said to be between$_S$ *determined*. Chain graphs are not co-connection$_{LWF}$ determined. In CG_1 B and C are separable$_{LWF}$, since $CG_1 \models_{LWF} B \perp\!\!\!\perp C \mid \{A, D\}$, but $CG_1 \not\models_{LWF} B \perp\!\!\!\perp C \mid \{D\}$ and $\text{CoCon}_{LWF}(CG_1; B, C) = \{D\}$. In contrast, chain graphs *are* co-connection$_{AMP}$ determined.

5. Discussion

The two Markov properties presented in the previous section are based on the intuition that only vertices which, in some sense, come 'between' X and Y should be relevant as to whether or not X and Y are entailed to be independent. Both of these properties are satisfied by undirected graphs and by all forms of directed graph model. Since chain graphs are not between$_R$ separated under either Markov property, this captures a qualitative difference between undirected and directed graphs, and chain graphs. On the other hand since chain graphs are co-connection$_{AMP}$ determined, in this respect, at least, AMP chain graphs are more similar to directed and undirected graphs.

5.1. DATA GENERATING PROCESSES

Since the pioneering work of Sewall Wright [38] in genetics, statistical models based on directed graphs have been used to model causal relations, and data generating processes. Models allowing directed graphs with cycles have been used for over 50 years in econometrics, and allow the possibility of representing linear feedback systems which reach a deterministic equilibrium subject to stochastic boundary conditions (Fisher [10]; Richardson [27]). Besag [3] gives several spatial-temporal data generating processes whose limiting spatial distributions satisfy the Markov property with respect to a naturally associated undirected graph. These data generating processes are time-reversible and temporally stationary. Thus there are data generating mechanisms known to give rise to the distributions described by undirected and directed graphs.

---

[13]This is the 'Strong Union Property' of separation in undirected graphs (Pearl [22]).

Cox [6] states that chain graphs under the LWF Markov property "do not satisfy the requirement of specifying a direct mode of data generation." However, Lauritzen[14] has recently sketched out, via an example, a dynamic data generating process for LWF chain graphs in which a pair of vertices joined by an undirected edge, $X - Y$, arrive at a stochastic equilibrium, as $t \to \infty$; the equilibrium distribution being determined by the parents of X and Y in the chain graph.

A data generation process corresponding to a Gaussian AMP chain graph may be constructed via a set of linear equations with correlated errors (Andersson *et al.* [1]). Each variable is given as a linear function of its parents in the chain graph, together with an error term. The distribution over the error terms is given by the undirected edges in the graph, as in a Gaussian undirected graphical model or 'covariance selection model' (Dempster [9]), for which Besag [3] specifies a data generating process. The linear model constructed in this way differs from a standard linear structural equation model (SEM): a SEM model usually specifies zeroes in the covariance matrix for the error terms, while the covariance selection model sets to zero elements of the *inverse* error covariance matrix.

The existence of a data generating process for a particular chain graph (under either Markov property) is important since it provides a full justification for using this structure. As has been shown in this paper, the mere fact that two variables are 'symmetrically related' does not, on its own, justify the use of a chain graph model.

5.2. A THEORY OF INTERVENTION IN DIRECTED GRAPHS

Strotz and Wold [35], Spirtes *et al.* [31] and Pearl [23] develop a theory of causal intervention for directed graph models which makes it sometimes possible to calculate the effect of an ideal intervention in a causal system. Space does not permit a detailed account of the theory here, however, the central idea is very simple: manipulating a variable, say X, modifies the structure of the graph, removing the edges between X and its parents, and instead making a 'policy' variable the sole parent of X. The relationships between all other variables and their parents are not affected; it is in this sense that the intervention is 'ideal', only one variable is directly affected.[15]

Example: Returning to the example considered in section 2.2, hypothetically a researcher could intervene to directly determine whether or not the patient suffers the side-effects, e.g. by giving all of the patients (in both the

---

[14]Personal communication.

[15]It should also be noted that for obvious physical reasons it may not make sense to speak of manipulating certain variables, e.g. the age or sex of an individual.

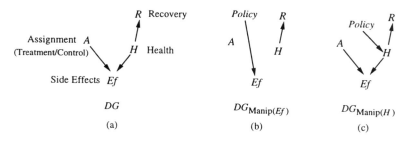

Figure 11. Intervening in a causal system: (a) before intervention; (b) intervening to directly control side-effects; (c) intervening to directly control health status.

treatment and control groups) something which either prevents or precipitates the side-effects. The graph in Figure 11(b) shows the result of such an intervention. After the intervention, which group the patient was assigned to initially (treatment/control) becomes independent of whether the patient suffers side-effects, as would be expected. The graph in Figure 11(c) shows the result of intervening to control the patient's health status directly.

One common objection to this intervention theory is that it makes a distinction between models that are statistically equivalent,[16] and hence which could not be differentiated purely on the basis of observational data. For example the graphs $A \rightarrow B$ and $A \leftarrow B$, are statistically equivalent,[17] and yet the effect on B of intervening to manipulate A will clearly be different. This is true, but misses the point: scientists are often able to control certain variables directly, and to perform controlled experiments, thus certain models can often be ruled out on the basis of background knowledge. This objection is also over-simplistic: when there are more than two variables it is often the case that all Markov equivalent models share certain structural features in common, even when latent and/or selection variables may be present (Verma and Pearl [37]; Frydenberg [11]; Spirtes and Verma [34]; Richardson [28]; Spirtes and Richardson [33]). Thus knowing that the data was generated by a model in a particular Markov equivalence class, even if which particular model is unknown, may be enough to predict the results of certain interventions (see Spirtes *et al.* [31]; Pearl [23]). A theory of intervention constitutes an important part of a causal data generating mechansim; specification of the dynamic behaviour of the system is another element, which may be of great importance in settings where feedback is present (Richardson [27, Ch. 2];).

In the absence of a theory of intervention for chain graphs, a resear-

---

[16]In the sense that they represent the same set of distributions.

[17]This observation is the basis for the slogan "Correlation is not Causation."

cher would be unable to answer questions concerning the consequences of intervening in a system with the structure of a chain graph. However, Lauritzen[18] has recently given, in outline, a theory of intervention for LWF chain graphs, which is compatible with the data generating process he has proposed. Such an intervention theory would appear to be of considerable use in applied settings when the substantive research hypotheses are causal in nature.

6. Conclusion

The examples given in this paper make clear that there are many ways in which a pair of variables may be symmetrically related. Further, different symmetric relationships, in general, will lead to quite different Markov properties. In particular, as has been shown, there are qualitative differences between the Markov properties associated with undirected and directed graphs (possibly with latent and/or selection variables), and either of those associated with chain graphs. Consequently, the Markov structure of a chain graph does not, in general, correspond to any symmetric relationship that can be described by a directed graph model via marginalizing or conditioning. For this reason, the inclusion of an undirected edge, rather than a directed edge, in a hypothesized chain graph model, should not be regarded as being 'weaker' or 'safer', substantively, than the inclusion of a directed edge.

This paper has shown that there are many symmetric relations which do *not* correspond to chain graphs. However, this leaves open the interesting question of which symmetric relations chain graphs *do* correspond to. A full answer to this question would involve the specification, in general, of a data generating process for chain graphs (under a given Markov property), together with an associated theory of intervention.

Acknowledgements

I would like to thank Julian Besag, David Cox, Clark Glymour, Steffen Lauritzen, David Madigan, Chris Meek, Michael Perlman, Richard Scheines, Peter Spirtes, Milan Studený, and Nanny Wermuth for helpful conversations on this topic. I am also grateful to three anonymous reviewers for useful comments and suggestions. Finally, I would like to gratefully acknowledge the Isaac Newton Institute for Mathematical Sciences, Cambridge, England, UK, where the revised version of this paper was prepared.

---

[18]Personal communication.

7. Proofs

In $DG(\mathbf{O}, \mathbf{S}, \mathbf{L})$ suppose that μ is a path that d-connects X and Y given $\mathbf{Z} \cup \mathbf{S}$, C is a collider on μ, and C is not an ancestor of $\mathbf{S}$. Let $length(C, \mathbf{Z})$ be 0 if C is a member of $\mathbf{Z}$; otherwise it is the length of a shortest directed path δ from C to a member of $\mathbf{Z}$. Let

$$Coll(\mu) = \{C \mid C \text{ is a collider on } \mu, \text{ and } C \text{ is not an ancestor of } \mathbf{S}\}.$$

Then let

$$size(\mu, \mathbf{Z}) = |\mathrm{Coll}(\mu)| + \sum_{C \in \mathrm{Coll}(\mu)} length(C, \mathbf{Z})$$

where $|\mathrm{Coll}(\mu)|$ is the cardinality of $\mathrm{Coll}(\mu)$. A path μ is a *minimal* acyclic d-connecting path between X and Y given $\mathbf{Z} \cup \mathbf{S}$, if μ is acyclic, d-connects X and Y given $\mathbf{Z} \cup \mathbf{S}$, and there is no other acyclic path μ' that d-connects X and Y given $\mathbf{Z} \cup \mathbf{S}$ such that $size(\mu', \mathbf{Z}) < size(\mu, \mathbf{Z})$. If there is a path that d-connects X and Y given $\mathbf{Z}$ then there is at least one minimal acyclic d-connecting path between X and Y given $\mathbf{Z}$.[19]

In the following proofs $\mu(A, B)$ denotes the subpath of μ between vertices A and B.

Lemma 1 *If μ is a minimal acyclic d-connecting path between X and Y given $\mathbf{Z} \cup \mathbf{S}$ in $DG(\mathbf{O}, \mathbf{S}, \mathbf{L})$, $\mathbf{Z} \cup \{X, Y\} \subseteq \mathbf{O}$, then for each collider C_i on μ that is not an ancestor of $\mathbf{S}$, there is a directed path δ_i from C_i to some vertex in $\mathbf{Z}$, such that δ_i intersects μ only at C_i, δ_i and δ_j do not intersect $(i \neq j)$ and no vertex on any path δ_i is in $\mathbf{S}$.*

Proof: Let δ_i be a shortest acyclic directed path from a collider C_i on μ to a member of $\mathbf{Z}$, where C_i is not an ancestor of $\mathbf{S}$, and hence no vertex on δ_i is in $\mathbf{S}$. We will now be prove that δ_i does not intersect μ except at C_i by showing that if such a point of intersection exists, then μ is not minimal, contrary to the assumption.

Form a path μ' in the following way: if δ_i intersects μ at a vertex other than C_i then let W_X be the vertex closest to X on μ that is on both δ_i and μ, and let W_Y be the vertex closest to Y on μ that is on both δ_i and μ. Suppose without loss of generality that W_X is after W_Y on δ_i. Let μ' be the concatenation of $\mu(X, W_X)$, $\delta_i(W_X, W_Y)$, and $\mu(W_Y, Y)$. It is now easy to show that μ' d-connects X and Y given $\mathbf{Z} \cup \mathbf{S}$. (See Figure 12.) Moreover $size(\mu', \mathbf{Z}) < size(\mu, \mathbf{Z})$ because μ' contains no more colliders than μ and a

---

[19]It is not hard to prove that in a DG, if there is a path (cyclic or acyclic) d-connecting X and Y given $\mathbf{Z}$, then there is an *acyclic* path d-connecting X and Y given $\mathbf{Z}$.

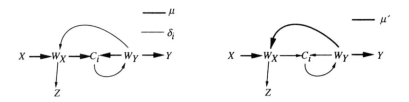

Figure 12. Finding a d-connecting path μ' of smaller size than μ, in the case where μ intersects with a directed path δ_i from a collider C_i to a vertex in **Z**.

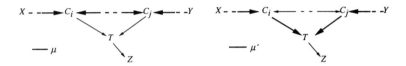

Figure 13. Finding a d-connecting path μ' of smaller size than μ, in the case where two directed paths, δ_i and δ_j, intersect.

shortest directed path from W_X to a member of **Z** is shorter than δ_i. Hence μ is not minimal, contrary to the assumption.

It remains to be shown that if μ is minimal, then δ_i and δ_j $(i \neq j)$ do not intersect. Suppose this is false. (See Figure 13.)

Let the vertex on δ_i closest to C_i that is also on δ_j be T. Let μ' be the concatenation of $\mu(X, C_i)$, $\delta_i(C_i, T)$, $\delta_j(T, C_j)$, and $\mu(C_j, Y)$. It is now easy to show that μ' d-connects X and Y given **Z**$\cup$**S** and size$(\mu', \mathbf{Z}) <$ size$(\mu, \mathbf{Z})$ because C_i and C_j are not colliders on μ', the only collider on μ' that may not be on μ is T, and the length of a shortest path from T to a member of **Z** is less than the length of a shortest path from C_i to a member of **Z**. Hence μ is not minimal, contrary to the assumption. $\square$

Lemma 2 *If μ is a minimal d-connecting path between X and Y, given* **Z**$\cup$**S** *in* $DG(\mathbf{O}, \mathbf{S}, \mathbf{L})$, *$B$ is a vertex on μ, and* **Z**$\cup\{X, Y, B\} \subseteq \mathbf{O}$, *then there is a sequence of vertices* $\langle X \equiv X_0, X_1, \ldots, X_n \equiv B, X_{n+1}, \ldots, X_{n+m} \equiv Y \rangle$ *in* **O**, *such that X_i and X_{i+1} $(0 \leq i < n + m)$ are* inseparable$_{DS}$ *in* $DG(\mathbf{O}, \mathbf{S}, \mathbf{L})$.

Proof: Since μ is a d-connecting path given $\mathbf{S} \cup \mathbf{Z}$ every collider on μ that is not an ancestor of **S** is an ancestor of a vertex in **Z**. Denote the colliders on μ that are not ancestors of **S** as $C_1, \ldots, C_k$. Let δ_j be a shortest directed path from C_j to some vertex $Z_j \in \mathbf{Z}$. It follows by Lemma 1 that δ_j and μ intersect only at C_j, and that δ_j and $\delta_{j'}$ $(j \neq j')$ do not intersect, and no vertex on some path δ_j is in **S**. A sequence of vertices X_i in **O**, such that each X_i is either on μ or is on a directed path δ_j from C_j to Z_j can now be constructed:

Base Step: Let $X_0 \equiv X$.

Inductive Step: If X_i is on some path δ_j then define W_{i+1} to be C_j; otherwise, if X_i is on μ, then let W_{i+1} be X_i. Let V_{i+1} be the next vertex on μ, after W_{i+1}, such that $V_{i+1} \in \mathbf{O}$. If there is no vertex $C_{j'}$ between W_{i+1} and V_{i+1} on μ, then let $X_{i+1} \equiv V_{i+1}$. Otherwise let C_{j^*} be the first collider on μ, after W_{i+1}, that is not an ancestor of $\mathbf{S}$, and let X_{i+1} be the first vertex in $\mathbf{O}$ on the directed path δ_{j^*} (such a vertex is guaranteed to exist since Z_{j^*}, the endpoint of δ_{j^*}, is in $\mathbf{O}$). It follows from the construction that if B is on μ, and $B \in \mathbf{O}$, then for some i, $X_i \equiv B$.

Claim: X_i and X_{i+1} are inseparable$_{DS}$ in $DG(\mathbf{O}, \mathbf{S}, \mathbf{L})$ under d-separation. If X_i and X_{i+1} are both on μ, then $\mu(X_i, X_{i+1})$ is a path on which every non-collider is in $\mathbf{L}$, and every collider is an ancestor of $\mathbf{S}$. Thus $\mu(X_i, X_{i+1})$ d-connects X_i and X_{i+1} given $\mathbf{Z} \cup \mathbf{S}$ for any $\mathbf{Z} \subseteq \mathbf{O} \backslash \{X_i, X_{i+1}\}$. So X_i and X_{i+1} are inseparable$_{DS}$. If X_i lies on some path δ_j, but X_{i+1} is on μ, then the path π formed by concatenating the directed path $X_i \leftarrow \cdots \leftarrow C_j$ and $\mu(C_j, X_{i+1})$ again is such that every non-collider on π is in $\mathbf{L}$, and every collider is an ancestor of $\mathbf{S}$, hence again X_i and X_{i+1} are inseparable$_{DS}$. The cases in which either X_{i+1} alone, or both X_i and X_{i+1} are not on μ can be handled similarly. □

Corollary 1 *If B is a vertex on a minimal d-connecting path π between X and Y given $\mathbf{Z} \cup \mathbf{S}$ in $DG(\mathbf{O}, \mathbf{S}, \mathbf{L})$, $\mathbf{Z} \cup \{X, Y, B\} \subseteq \mathbf{O}$, then $B \in$ Between$_{DS}(X, Y)$.*

Proof: This follows directly from Lemma 2 □

Corollary 2 *If μ is a minimal d-connecting path between X and Y given $\mathbf{Z} \cup \mathbf{S}$ in $DG(\mathbf{O}, \mathbf{S}, \mathbf{L})$, C is a collider on μ that is an ancestor of $\mathbf{Z}$ but not $\mathbf{S}$, δ is a shortest directed path from C to some $Z \in \mathbf{Z}$, and $\mathbf{Z} \cup \{X, Y, C\} \subseteq \mathbf{O}$, then $Z \in$ CoCon$_{DS}(X, Y)$.*

Proof: By Lemma 1, δ does not intersect μ except at C. Let the sequence of vertices on δ that are in $\mathbf{O}$ be $\langle V_1, \ldots, V_r \equiv Z \rangle$. It follows from the construction in Lemma 1 that there is a sequence of vertices $\langle X \equiv X_0, X_1, \ldots, X_n \equiv V_1, X_{n+1}, \ldots, X_{n+m} \equiv Y \rangle$ in $\mathbf{O}$ such that consecutive pairs of vertices are inseparable$_{DS}$. Since, by hypothesis, C is not an ancestor of $\mathbf{S}$, it follows that no vertex on δ is in $\mathbf{S}$. Hence $\delta(V_i, V_{i+1})$ is a directed path from V_i to V_{i+1} on which, with the exception of the endpoints, every vertex is in $\mathbf{L}$ and is a non-collider on δ, it follows that V_i and V_{i+1} are inseparable$_{DS}$ in $DG(\mathbf{O}, \mathbf{S}, \mathbf{L})$. Thus the sequences $\langle X \equiv X_0, X_1, \ldots, X_n \equiv V_1, \ldots, V_r \equiv Z \rangle$ and $\langle Y \equiv$

$X_{n+m}, \ldots, X_n \equiv V_1, \ldots, V_r \equiv Z\rangle$ establish that $Z \in \mathrm{CoCon}_{DS}(X, Y)$ in $DG(\mathbf{O}, \mathbf{S}, \mathbf{L})$.   □

Theorem 1 (i) *A directed graph $DG(\mathbf{O}, \mathbf{S}, \mathbf{L})$ is between$_{DS}$ separated under d-separation.*

Proof: Suppose, for a contradiction, that $DG(\mathbf{O}, \mathbf{S}, \mathbf{L}) \models_{DS} X \perp\!\!\!\perp Y \mid \mathbf{W}$, $(\mathbf{W} \cup \{X, Y\} \subseteq \mathbf{O})$, but $DG(\mathbf{O}, \mathbf{S}, \mathbf{L}) \not\models_{DS} X \perp\!\!\!\perp Y \mid \mathbf{W} \cap \mathrm{Between}_{DS}(X, Y)$. In this case there is some minimal path π d-connecting X and Y given $\mathbf{S} \cup (\mathbf{W} \cap \mathrm{Between}_{DS}(X, Y))$ in $DG(\mathbf{O}, \mathbf{S}, \mathbf{L})$, but this path is not d-connecting given $\mathbf{S} \cup \mathbf{W}$. It is not possible for a collider on π to have a descendant in $\mathbf{S} \cup (\mathbf{W} \cap \mathrm{Between}_{DS}(X, Y))$, but not in $\mathbf{S} \cup \mathbf{W}$. Hence there is some non-collider B on π, s.t. $B \in \mathbf{S} \cup \mathbf{W}$, but $B \notin \mathbf{S} \cup (\mathbf{W} \cap \mathrm{Between}_{DS}(X, Y))$. This implies $B \in \mathbf{W} \backslash \mathrm{Between}_{DS}(X, Y)$, and since $\mathbf{W} \subseteq \mathbf{O}$, it follows that $B \in \mathbf{O}$. But in this case by Corollary 1, $B \in \mathrm{Between}_{DS}(X, Y)$, which is a contradiction.   □

Theorem 2 (ii) *A directed graph $DG(\mathbf{O}, \mathbf{S}, \mathbf{L})$ is co-connection$_{DS}$ determined.*

Proof: Since $\mathrm{Between}_{DS}(X, Y) \subseteq \mathrm{CoCon}_{DS}(X, Y)$, the proof of Theorem 1 above, replacing 'between$_{DS}$' with 'co-connected$_{DS}$', suffices to show that if $DG(\mathbf{O}, \mathbf{S}, \mathbf{L}) \models_{DS} X \perp\!\!\!\perp Y \mid \mathbf{W}$ then $DG(\mathbf{O}, \mathbf{S}, \mathbf{L}) \models_{DS} X \perp\!\!\!\perp Y \mid \mathbf{W} \cap \mathrm{CoCon}_{DS}(X, Y)$.

To prove the converse, suppose, for a contradiction, $DG(\mathbf{O}, \mathbf{S}, \mathbf{L}) \models_{DS} X \perp\!\!\!\perp Y \mid \mathbf{W} \cap \mathrm{CoCon}_{DS}(X, Y)$, but $DG(\mathbf{O}, \mathbf{S}, \mathbf{L}) \not\models_{DS} X \perp\!\!\!\perp Y \mid \mathbf{W}$, where $\mathbf{W} \cup \{X, Y\} \subseteq \mathbf{O}$. It then follows that there is some minimal d-connecting path π between X and Y in $DG(\mathbf{O}, \mathbf{S}, \mathbf{L})$ given $\mathbf{W} \cup \mathbf{S}$. Clearly it is not possible for there to be a non-collider on π which is in $\mathbf{S} \cup (\mathbf{W} \cap \mathrm{CoCon}_{DS}(X, Y))$, but not in $\mathbf{S} \cup \mathbf{W}$. Hence it follows that there is some collider C on π which has a descendant in $\mathbf{S} \cup \mathbf{W}$, but not in $\mathbf{S} \cup (\mathbf{W} \cap \mathrm{CoCon}_{DS}(X, Y))$. Hence C is an ancestor of $\mathbf{W} \backslash \mathrm{CoCon}_{DS}(X, Y)$, but not $\mathbf{S}$. Consider a shortest directed path δ from C to some vertex W in $\mathbf{W}$. It follows from Lemma 1, and the minimality of π that δ does not intersect π except at C. It now follows by Corollary 2, that $W \in \mathrm{CoCon}_{DS}(X, Y)$. Therefore if C is an ancestor of a vertex in $\mathbf{S} \cup \mathbf{W}$, then C is also an ancestor of a vertex in $\mathbf{S} \cup (\mathbf{W} \cap \mathrm{CoCon}_{DS}(X, Y))$. Hence π d-connects X and Y given $\mathbf{S} \cup (\mathbf{W} \cap \mathrm{CoCon}_{DS}(X, Y))$, which is a contradiction.   □

Lemma 3 *Let CG be a chain graph with vertex set $\mathbf{V}$; $X, Y \in \mathbf{V}$ and $\mathbf{W} \subseteq \mathbf{V} \backslash \{X, Y\}$. Let H be the undirected graph $\mathrm{Aug}[CG; X, Y, \mathbf{W}]$. If there*

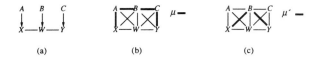

(a) (b) (c)

Figure 14. (a) A chain graph CG with $\mathrm{CoCon}_{AMP}(CG; X, Y) = \{B, W\}$; (b) a path μ in $\mathrm{Aug}[CG; X, Y, \{W\}]$; (c) a path μ' in $\mathrm{Aug}[CG; X, Y, \{W\}]$ every vertex of which occurs on μ and is in $\mathrm{CoCon}_{AMP}(CG; X, Y)$.

is a path μ connecting X and Y in H, then there is a path μ' connecting X and Y in H such that if V is a vertex on μ' then V is on μ, and $V \in \mathrm{CoCon}_{AMP}(X, Y) \cup \{X, Y\}$.

Proof: If X and Y are adjacent in H then the claim is trivial since $\mu' \equiv \langle X, Y \rangle$ satisfies the lemma. Suppose then that X and Y are not adjacent in H.

Let the vertices on μ be $\langle X \equiv X_1, \ldots, X_n \equiv Y \rangle$. Let α be the greatest j such that X_j is adjacent to X in H. Let β be the smallest $k > \alpha$ such that X_k is adjacent to Y in H. (Since X and Y are not adjacent $\alpha, \beta < n$.)

It is sufficient to prove that $\{X_\alpha, \ldots, X_\beta\} \subseteq \mathrm{CoCon}_{AMP}(X, Y)$, since then the path $\mu' \equiv \langle X, X_\alpha, \ldots, X_\beta, Y \rangle$ satisfies the conditions of the lemma.

This can be proved by showing that there is a path in $[CG]^{Ins}_{AMP}$ from X to each X_i ($\alpha \leq i \leq \beta$) which does not contain Y. A symmetric argument shows that there is also a path from Y to X_i ($\alpha \leq i \leq \beta$) in $[CG]^{Ins}_{AMP}$, which does not contain X. The proof is by induction on i.

Base case: $i = \alpha$. Since X is adjacent to X_α in H, either there is a (directed or undirected) edge between X and X_i in CG, or the edge was added via augmentation of a triplex or bi-flag in $\mathrm{Ext}(CG, \mathrm{Anc}(\{X, Y\} \cup \mathbf{W}))$. In the former case there is nothing to prove since X and X_i are adjacent in $[CG]^{Ins}_{AMP}$. If the edge was added via augmentation of a triplex then there is a vertex T such that $\langle X, T, X_i \rangle$ is a triplex in CG, hence T is adjacent to X and X_i in $[CG]^{Ins}_{AMP}$. Since X and Y are not adjacent in H, $T \not\equiv Y$, so $\langle X, T, X_i \rangle$ is a path which satisfies the claim. If the edge was added via augmentation of a bi-flag then there are two vertices T_0, T_1, forming a bi-flag $\langle X, T_0, T_1, X_i \rangle$. From the definition of augmentation it then follows that T_0 and T_1 are adjacent to X and X_i in H. Since we suppose that X and Y are not adjacent in H it follows that neither T_0 nor T_1 can be Y. Hence $\langle X, T_0, T_1, X_i \rangle$ is a path in $[CG]^{Ins}_{AMP}$ satisfying the claim.

Inductive case: $i > \alpha$; suppose that there is a path from X to X_{i-1} in $[CG]^{Ins}_{AMP}$ which does not contain Y.

Since $i - 1 < \beta$, X_{i-1} is not adjacent to Y in H. By a similar proof to that in the base case it can easily be shown that there is a path from X_{i-1} to X_i in $[CG]^{Ins}_{AMP}$ which does not contain Y. This path may then be

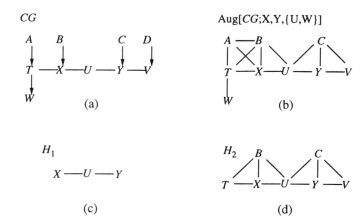

Figure 15. (a) A chain graph, CG, in which $\mathrm{CoCon}_{AMP}(CG; X, Y) = \{U\}$; (b) the undirected graph $\mathrm{Aug}[CG; X, Y, \{U, W\}]$; (c) H_1, the induced subgraph of $\mathrm{Aug}[CG; X, Y, \{U, W\}]$ over $\mathrm{CoCon}_{AMP}(X, Y) \cup \{X, Y\} = \{U, X, Y\}$; (d) the undirected graph H_2, $\mathrm{Aug}[CG; X, Y, \{U, W\} \cap \mathrm{CoCon}_{AMP}(X, Y)]$.

concatenated with the path from X to X_{i-1} (whose existence is guaranteed by the induction hypothesis) to form a path connecting X and X_{i-1} in $[CG]_{AMP}^{Ins}$ which does not contain Y. □

Lemma 4 *Let CG be a chain graph, and let H_1 be the induced subgraph of $\mathrm{Aug}[CG; X, Y, \mathbf{W}]$ over $\mathrm{CoCon}_{AMP}(X, Y) \cup \{X, Y\}$. Let H_2 be the undirected graph $\mathrm{Aug}[CG; X, Y, \mathbf{W} \cap \mathrm{CoCon}_{AMP}(X, Y)]$. H_1 is a subgraph of H_2.*

Proof: We first prove that if a vertex V is in H_1 then V is in H_2. If V occurs in H_1 then $V \in \mathrm{CoCon}_{AMP}(X, Y) \cup \{X, Y\}$. Clearly X and Y occur in both H_1 and H_2, so suppose that $V \in \mathrm{CoCon}_{AMP}(X, Y)$.

It follows from the definition of the extended graph that if V is a vertex in $\mathrm{Ext}(CG, \mathbf{T})$ then there is a path consisting of undirected edges from V to some vertex in $\mathbf{T}$. Since V is in $\mathrm{Ext}(CG, \mathrm{Anc}(\{X, Y\} \cup \mathbf{W}))$ there is a path π of the form $\langle V \equiv X_0 - \cdots - X_n \to \cdots \to X_{n+m} \equiv W \rangle$ in CG, where $W \in \{X, Y\} \cup \mathbf{W}$, and $n, m \geq 0$. Let X_k be the first vertex on π which is in $\{X, Y\} \cup \mathbf{W}$, i.e. $\forall i \; (0 \leq i < k) \; X_i \notin \{X, Y\} \cup \mathbf{W}$. Now, if $X_k \in \mathbf{W}$ then since $V \in \mathrm{CoCon}_{AMP}(X, Y)$, and $\pi(V, X_k)$ is a path from V to X_k which does not contain X or Y, it follows that $X_k \in \mathbf{W} \cap \mathrm{CoCon}_{AMP}(X, Y)$. Hence V occurs in $\mathrm{Ext}(CG, \mathrm{Anc}(\mathbf{W} \cap \mathrm{CoCon}_{AMP}(X, Y)))$, and so also in H_2. Alternatively, if $X_k \in \{X, Y\}$, then again X_k occurs in $\mathrm{Ext}(CG, \mathrm{Anc}(\{X, Y\}))$, and thus in H_2.

Hence, if there is an edge $A - B$ in H_1, then A and B occur in H_2. There are three reasons why there may be an edge in H_1:

(a) There is an edge (directed or undirected) between A and B in CG. It then follows immediately that there is an edge between A and B in H_2.

(b) The edge between A and B in H_1 is the result of augmenting a triplex in $\text{Ext}(CG, \text{Anc}(\{X, Y\} \cup \mathbf{W}))$. Then there is some vertex T such that $\langle A, T, B \rangle$ forms a triplex in $\text{Ext}(CG, \text{Anc}(\{X, Y\} \cup \mathbf{W}))$. Since, by hypothesis, $A, B \in \text{CoCon}_{AMP}(X, Y)$, it follows that $T \in \text{CoCon}_{AMP}(X, Y) \cup \{X, Y\}$, and hence T occurs in H_1. It then follows by the previous reasoning that T is in H_2, and so the triplex is also present in $\text{Ext}(CG, \text{Anc}(\{X, Y\} \cup (\mathbf{W} \cap \text{CoCon}_{AMP}(X, Y))))$. Hence there is an edge between A and B in H_2.

(c) The edge between A and B in H_1 is the result of augmenting a bi-flag in $\text{Ext}(CG, \text{Anc}(\{X, Y\} \cup \mathbf{W}))$. This case is identical to the previous one, except that there are two vertices T_0, T_1, such that $\langle A, T_0, T_1, B \rangle$ forms a bi-flag in $\text{Ext}(CG, \text{Anc}(\{X, Y\} \cup \mathbf{W}))$. As before, it follows from the hypothesis that $A, B \in \text{CoCon}_{AMP}(X, Y)$, that $T_0, T_1 \in \text{CoCon}_{AMP}(X, Y) \cup \{X, Y\}$, hence T_0 and T_1 occur in H_2 and the bi-flag is in $\text{Ext}(CG, \text{Anc}(\{X, Y\} \cup (\mathbf{W} \cap \text{CoCon}_{AMP}(X, Y))))$. Thus the $A-B$ edge is also present in H_2. $\square$

Theorem 2 (iii) *Chain graphs are co-connection$_{AMP}$ determined.*

Proof: $(CG \models_{AMP} X \perp\!\!\!\perp Y \mid \mathbf{W} \Rightarrow CG \models_{AMP} X \perp\!\!\!\perp Y \mid \mathbf{W} \cap \text{CoCon}_{AMP}(X, Y))$
Let H be $\text{Aug}[CG; X, Y, \mathbf{W}]$. Since $CG \models_{AMP} X \perp\!\!\!\perp Y \mid \mathbf{W}$, X and Y are separated given $\mathbf{W}$ in H.
Claim: X and Y are separated in H by $\mathbf{W} \cap \text{CoCon}_{AMP}(X, Y)$. Suppose, for a contradiction, that there is some path μ in H, connecting X and Y on which there is no vertex in $\mathbf{W} \cap \text{CoCon}_{AMP}(X, Y)$. It then follows from Lemma 3 that there is a path μ' in H composed only of vertices on μ which are in $\text{CoCon}_{AMP}(X, Y)$. Since no vertex on μ is in $\mathbf{W} \cap \text{CoCon}_{AMP}(X, Y)$, it then follows that no vertex on μ' is in $\mathbf{W}$. So X and Y are not separated by $\mathbf{W}$ in H, contradicting the hypothesis.

However, $\text{Aug}[CG; X, Y, \mathbf{W} \cap \text{CoCon}_{AMP}(X, Y)]$ is a subgraph of H, so X and Y are separated by $\mathbf{W} \cap \text{CoCon}_{AMP}(X, Y)$ in $\text{Aug}[CG; X, Y, \mathbf{W} \cap \text{CoCon}_{AMP}(X, Y)]$. Thus $CG \models_{AMP} X \perp\!\!\!\perp Y \mid \mathbf{W} \cap \text{CoCon}_{AMP}(X, Y)$.

$(CG \models_{AMP} X \perp\!\!\!\perp Y \mid \mathbf{W} \cap \text{CoCon}_{AMP}(X, Y) \Rightarrow CG \models_{AMP} X \perp\!\!\!\perp Y \mid \mathbf{W})$
The proof is by contraposition. Suppose that there is a path μ from X to Y in $\text{Aug}[CG; X, Y, \mathbf{W}]$. Lemma 3 implies that there is a path μ' from X to Y in $\text{Aug}[CG; X, Y, \mathbf{W}]$ every vertex of which is in $\{X, Y\} \cup \text{CoCon}_{AMP}(X, Y)$. It then follows from Lemma 4 that this path exists in $\text{Aug}[CG; X, Y, \mathbf{W} \cap \text{CoCon}_{AMP}(X, Y)]$. $\square$

References

1. S. A. Andersson, D. Madigan, and M. D. Perlman. An alternative Markov property for chain graphs. In F. V. Jensen and E. Horvitz, editors, *Uncertainty in Artificial Intelligence: Proceedings of the 12th Conference*, pages 40–48, San Francisco, 1996. Morgan Kaufmann.

2. S. A. Andersson, D. Madigan, and M. D. Perlman. A new pathwise separation criterion for chain graphs. In preparation, 1997.

3. J. Besag. On spatial-temporal models and Markov fields. In *Transactions of the 7th Prague Conference on Information Theory, Statistical Decision Functions and Random Processes*, pages 47–55. Academia, Prague, 1974.

4. J. Besag. Spatial interaction and the statistical analysis of lattice systems (with discussion). *J. Royal Statist. Soc. Ser. B*, 36:302–309, 1974.

5. G. F. Cooper and E. Herskovits. A Bayesian method for the induction of probabilistic networks from data. *Machine Learning*, 9:309–347, 1992.

6. D. R. Cox. Causality and graphical models. In *Proceedings, 49th Session*, volume 1 of *Bulletin of the International Statistical Institute*, pages 363–372, 1993.

7. D. R. Cox and N. Wermuth. *Multivariate Dependencies: Models, Analysis and Interpretation*. Chapman and Hall, London, 1996.

8. J. N. Darroch, S. L. Lauritzen, and T. P. Speed. Markov fields and log-linear models for contingency tables. *Ann. Statist.*, 8:522–539, 1980.

9. A. Dempster. Covariance selection. *Biometrics*, 28:157–175, 1972.

10. F. M. Fisher. A correspondence principle for simultaneous equation models. *Econometrica*, 38(1):73–92, 1970.

11. M. Frydenberg. The chain graph Markov property. *Scandin. J. Statist.*, 17:333–353, 1990.

12. D. Geiger. *Graphoids: a qualitative framework for probabilistic inference*. PhD thesis, UCLA, 1990.

13. J. M. Hammersley and P. Clifford. Markov fields on finite graphs and lattices. Unpublished manuscript, 1971.

14. D. Hausman. Causal priority. *Nous*, 18:261–279, 1984.

15. D. Heckerman, D. Geiger, and D. M. Chickering. Learning Bayesian networks: the combination of knowledge and statistical data. In B. Lopez de Mantaras and D. Poole, editors, *Uncertainty in Artificial Intelligence: Proceedings of the 10th Conference*, pages 293–301, San Francisco, 1994. Morgan Kaufmann.

16. J. T. A. Koster. Markov properties of non-recursive causal models. *Ann. Statist.*, 24:2148–2178, October 1996.

17. S. L. Lauritzen. *Graphical Models*. Number 81 in Oxford Statistical Science Series. Springer-Verlag, 1993.

18. S. L. Lauritzen, A. P. Dawid, B. Larsen, and H.-G. Leimer. Independence properties of directed Markov fields. *Networks*, 20:491–505, 1990.

19. S. L. Lauritzen and D. J. Spiegelhalter. Local computation with probabilities in graphical structures and their application to expert systems (with discussion). *J. Royal Statist. Soc. Ser. B*, 50(2):157–224, 1988.

20. S. L. Lauritzen and N. Wermuth. Graphical models for association between variables, some of which are qualitative and some quantitative. *Ann. Statist.*, 17:31–57, 1989.

21. C. Meek. Strong completeness and faithfulness in Bayesian networks. In P. Besnard and S. Hanks, editors, *Uncertainty in Artificial Intelligence: Proceedings of the 11th Conference*, pages 403–410, San Francisco, 1995. Morgan Kaufmann.

22. J. Pearl. *Probabilistic Reasoning in Intelligent Systems*. Morgan Kaufman, 1988.

23. J. Pearl. Causal diagrams for empirical research (with discussion). *Biometrika*, 82:669–690, 1995.

24. J. Pearl and R. Dechter. Identifying independencies in causal graphs with feedback. In F. V. Jensen and E. Horvitz, editors, *Uncertainty in Artificial Intelligence:*

Proceedings of the 12th *Conference*, pages 454–461, San Francisco, 1996. Morgan Kaufmann.

25. J. Pearl and T. Verma. A theory of inferred causation. In J. A. Allen, R. Fikes, and E. Sandewall, editors, *Principles of Knowledge Representation and Reasoning: Proceedings of the Second International Conference*, pages 441–452, San Mateo, CA, 1991. Morgan Kaufmann.

26. T. S. Richardson. A discovery algorithm for directed cyclic graphs. In F. V. Jensen and E. Horvitz, editors, *Uncertainty in Artificial Intelligence: Proceedings of the* 12th *Conference*, pages 454–461, San Francisco, 1996. Morgan Kaufmann.

27. T. S. Richardson. *Models of feedback: interpretation and discovery.* PhD thesis, Carnegie-Mellon University, 1996.

28. T. S. Richardson. A polynomial-time algorithm for deciding Markov equivalence of directed cyclic graphical models. In F. V. Jensen and E. Horvitz, editors, *Uncertainty in Artificial Intelligence: Proceedings of the* 12th *Conference*, pages 462–469, San Francisco, 1996. Morgan Kaufmann.

29. T. P. Speed. A note on nearest-neighbour Gibbs and Markov distributions over graphs. *Sankhya Ser. A*, 41:184–197, 1979.

30. P. Spirtes. Directed cyclic graphical representations of feedback models. In P. Besnard and S. Hanks, editors, *Uncertainty in Artificial Intelligence: Proceedings of the* 11th *Conference*, pages 491–498, San Francisco, 1995. Morgan Kaufmann.

31. P. Spirtes, C. Glymour, and R. Scheines. *Causation, Prediction and Search.* Lecture Notes in Statistics. Oxford University Press, 1996.

32. P. Spirtes, C. Meek, and T.S. Richardson. Causal inference in the presence of latent variables and selection bias. In P. Besnard and S. Hanks, editors, *Uncertainty in Artificial Intelligence: Proceedings of the* 11th *Conference*, pages 403–410, San Francisco, 1995. Morgan Kaufmann.

33. P. Spirtes and T. S. Richardson. A polynomial-time algorithm for determining dag equivalence in the presence of latent variables and selection bias. In D. Madigan and P. Smyth, editors, *Preliminary papers of the Sixth International Workshop on AI and Statistics, January 4-7, Fort Lauderdale, Florida*, pages 489–501, 1997.

34. P. Spirtes and T. Verma. Equivalence of causal models with latent variables. Technical Report CMU-PHIL-33, Department of Philosophy, Carnegie Mellon University, October 1992.

35. R. H. Strotz and H. O. A. Wold. Recursive versus non-recursive systems: an attempt at synthesis. *Econometrica*, 28:417–427, 1960. (Also in Causal Models in the Social Sciences, H.M. Blalock Jr. ed., Chicago: Aldine Atherton, 1971).

36. M. Studený and R. Bouckaert. On chain graph models for description of conditional independence structures. *Ann. Statist.*, 1996. Accepted for publication.

37. T. Verma and J. Pearl. Equivalence and synthesis of causal models. In M. Henrion, R. Shachter, L. Kanal, and J. Lemmer, editors, *Uncertainty in Artificial Intelligence: Proceedings of the* 12th *Conference*, pages 220–227, San Francisco, 1996. Morgan Kaufmann.

38. S. Wright. Correlation and Causation. *J. Agricultural Research*, 20:557–585, 1921.

THE MULTIINFORMATION FUNCTION AS A TOOL FOR MEASURING STOCHASTIC DEPENDENCE

M. STUDENÝ AND J. VEJNAROVÁ

Institute of Information Theory and Automation
Academy of Sciences of Czech Republic
Pod vodárenskou věží 4, 182 08 Prague
AND
Laboratory of Intelligent Systems
University of Economics
Ekonomická 957, 148 00 Prague
Czech Republic

Abstract. Given a collection of random variables $[\xi_i]_{i \in N}$ where N is a finite nonempty set, the corresponding *multiinformation function* assigns to each subset $A \subset N$ the relative entropy of the joint distribution of $[\xi_i]_{i \in A}$ with respect to the product of distributions of individual random variables ξ_i for $i \in A$. We argue that it is a useful tool for problems concerning stochastic (conditional) dependence and independence (at least in the discrete case).

First, the multiinformation function makes it possible to express the *conditional mutual information* between $[\xi_i]_{i \in A}$ and $[\xi_i]_{i \in B}$ given $[\xi_i]_{i \in C}$ (for every disjoint $A, B, C \subset N$), which can be considered as a good measure of conditional stochastic dependence. Second, one can introduce reasonable measures of dependence of level r among variables $[\xi_i]_{i \in A}$ (where $A \subset N$, $1 \le r < \operatorname{card} A$) which are expressible by means of the multiinformation function. Third, it enables one to derive theoretical results on (nonexistence of an) axiomatic characterization of stochastic conditional independence models.

1. Introduction

Information theory provides a good measure of stochastic dependence between two random variables, namely the *mutual information* [7, 3]. It is always nonnegative and vanishes if the corresponding two random variables are stochastically independent. On the other hand it achieves its maximal value iff one random variable is a function of the other variable [28].

Perez [15] wanted also to express numerically the degree of stochastic dependence among any finite number of random variables and proposed a numerical characteristic called "dependence tightness." Later he changed the terminology, calling the characteristic *multiinformation* and encouraging research on asymptotic properties of an estimator of multiinformation [18]. Note that multiinformation also appeared in various guises in earlier information-theoretical papers. For example, Watanabe [24] called it "total correlation" and Csiszár [2] showed that the IPFP procedure converges to the probability distribution minimizing multiinformation within the considered family of distributions having prescribed marginals.

Further prospects occur when one considers multiinformation as a set function. That means if $[\xi_i]_{i \in N}$ is a collection of random variables indexed by a finite set N then the *multiinformation function* (corresponding to $[\xi_i]_{i \in N}$) assigns the multiinformation of the subcollection $[\xi_i]_{i \in A}$ to every $A \subset N$. Such a function was mentioned already in sixties by Watanabe [25] under the name "total cohesion function." Some pleasant properties of the multiinformation function were utilized by Perez [15] in probabilistic decision-making. Malvestuto named the multiinformation function "entaxy" and applied it in the theory of relational databases [9]. The multiinformation function plays an important role in the problem of finding "optimal dependence structure simplification" solved in thesis [21], too. Finally, it has appeared to be a very useful tool for studying of formal properties of conditional independence.

The first author in modern statistics to deal with those formal properties of conditional independence was probably Dawid [5]. He characterized certain statistical concepts (e.g. the concept of sufficient statistics) in terms of generalized stochastic conditional independence. Spohn [17] studied stochastic conditional independence from the viewpoint of philosophical logic and formulated the same properties as Dawid. The importance of conditional independence in probabilistic reasoning was explicitly discerned and highlighted by Pearl and Paz [13]. They interpreted Dawid's formal properties in terms of axioms for irrelevance models and formulated a natural conjecture that these properties characterize stochastic conditional independence models. This conjecture was refuted in [19] by substantial use of the multiinformation function and this result was later strengthened by showing that stochastic conditional independence models cannot be characterized by a finite number of formal properties of that type [20].

However, as we have already mentioned, the original prospect of multiinformation was to express quantitatively the strength of dependence among random variables. An abstract view on measures of dependence was brought by Rényi [16] who formulated a few reasonable requirements on measures of dependence of two real-valued random variables. Zvárová [28] studied in more detail information-theoretical measures of dependence including mutual information. The idea of measuring dependence appeared also in nonprobabilistic calculi for dealing with uncertainty in artificial intelligence [22, 23].

This article is basically an overview paper, but it brings several minor new results which (as we hope) support our claims about the usefulness of the multiinformation function. The basic fact here is that the multiinformation function is related to *conditional mutual information*. In the first part of the paper we show that the conditional mutual information complies with several reasonable requirements (analogous to Rényi's conditions) which should be satisfied by a measure of degree of stochastic conditional dependence.

The second part of the paper responds to an interesting suggestion from Naftali Tishby and Joachim Buhmann. Is it possible to decompose multiinformation (which is considered to be a measure of global dependence) into level-specific measures of dependence among variables? That means one would like to measure the strength of interactions of the "first level" by a special measure of *pairwise dependence*, and similarly for interactions of "higher levels." We show that the multiinformation can indeed be viewed as a sum of such level-specific measures of dependence. Nevertheless, we have found recently that such a formula is not completely new: similar level-specific measures of dependence were already considered by Han [8].

Finally, in the third part of the paper, as an example of theoretical use of the multiinformation function we recall the results about nonexistence of an axiomatic characterization of conditional independence models. Unlike the original paper [20] we present a long didactic proof emphasizing the essential steps.

Note that all results of the paper are formulated for random variables taking a finite number of values although the multiinformation function can be used also in the case of continuous variables. The reason is that we wish to present really elementary proofs which are not complicated by measure-theoretical technicalities.

2. Basic concepts

We recall well-known information-theoretical concepts in this section; most of them can be found in textbooks, e.g. [3]. The reader who is familiar with information theory can skip the section.

Throughout the paper N denotes a finite nonempty set of factors or in short a *factor set*. In the sequel, whenever $A, B \subset N$ the juxtaposition AB

will be used to shorten the notation for the set union $A \cup B$ and for any $i \in N$, the singleton will be sometimes denoted by i instead of $\{i\}$.

2.1. DISCRETE PROBABILITY DISTRIBUTIONS

The factors should correspond to discrete random variables. A discrete random variable ξ_i corresponding to a factor $i \in N$ has to take values in a nonempty finite set $\mathbf{X}_i$ called the *frame* for i. In the situation when a fixed frame $\mathbf{X}_i$ is assigned to every factor $i \in N$ and $\emptyset \neq A \subset N$ the symbol $\mathbf{X}_A$ denotes the Cartesian product $\prod_{i \in A} \mathbf{X}_i$, that is the frame for A. Whenever $\emptyset \neq B \subset A \subset N$ and $x \in \mathbf{X}_A$, then its coordinate projection to $\mathbf{X}_B$ will be denoted by x_B.

By a *probability distribution on* a nonempty finite set $\mathbf{Y}$ we understand every nonnegative real function P on $\mathbf{Y}$ with $\sum\{P(y); y \in \mathbf{Y}\} = 1$. By a (discrete) *probability distribution over* a factor set N is understood any probability distribution on $\mathbf{X}_N$ where $\{\mathbf{X}_i; i \in N\}$ is an arbitrary collection of frames. Or equivalently, any particular joint distribution of a discrete random vector $[\xi_i]_{i \in N}$.

Having $\emptyset \neq A \subset N$ and a probability distribution P over N the *marginal distribution* P^A is a probability distribution over A defined as follows:

$$P^A(a) = \sum\{P(a, b); b \in \mathbf{X}_{N \setminus A}\} \quad \text{for every } a \in \mathbf{X}_A .$$

It describes the distribution of the random subvector $[\xi_i]_{i \in A}$. In the sequel we adopt the natural convention $P^{\emptyset} \equiv 1$.

Having $\emptyset \neq B \subset N$ and $b \in \mathbf{X}_B$ such that $P^B(b) > 0$ the *conditional distribution* $P^{|b}$ is a probability distribution over $N \setminus B$ defined by:

$$P^{|b}(a) = \frac{P(a, b)}{P^B(b)} \quad \text{for every } a \in \mathbf{X}_{N \setminus B} .$$

It describes the (conditional) distribution of $[\xi_i]_{i \in N \setminus B}$ under the condition $[\xi_i]_{i \in B} \equiv b$. For disjoint $A, B \subset N$ one can use the symbol $P^{A|b}$ to denote $(P^{AB})^{|b} = (P^{|b})^A$.

Every mapping between frames induces a transformation of distributions. Supposing P is a probability distribution on $\mathbf{Y}$ and $f : \mathbf{Y} \to \mathbf{Z}$ is a mapping into a nonempty finite set $\mathbf{Z}$, the formula

$$Q(z) = \sum\{P(y); y \in \mathbf{Y} \,\&\, f(y) = z\} \quad \text{for every } z \in \mathbf{Z},$$

defines a probability distribution on $\mathbf{Z}$. In such a case we say that Q is an *image* of P (by f). Provided P is the distribution of a random vector ξ, Q is the distribution of the transformed vector $f(\xi)$.

Supposing $A, B \subset N$ are disjoint and P is a distribution over N we say that A is *functionally dependent* on B with respect to P and write $B \to A\,(P)$ if there exists a mapping $f : \mathbf{X}_B \to \mathbf{X}_A$ such that

$$P^{AB}(a, b) = P^B(b) \qquad \text{for } a = f(b),\ b \in \mathbf{X}_B,$$
$$P^{AB}(a, b) = 0 \qquad \text{for remaining } a \in \mathbf{X}_A,\ b \in \mathbf{X}_B.$$

It reflects the situation when P is the distribution of a random vector $[\xi_i]_{i \in N}$ whose random subvector $[\xi_i]_{i \in A}$ is a deterministic function of another random subvector $[\xi_i]_{i \in B}$. Note that the function f is uniquely determined on the set $\{b \in \mathbf{X}_B;\ P^B(b) > 0\}$; outside that set it can take arbitrary values.

Supposing $A, B, C \subset N$ are disjoint and P is a distribution over N we say that A is *conditionally independent* of B given C with respect to P and we write $A \perp\!\!\!\perp B | C\,(P)$ if the equality

$$P^{ABC}(a, b, c) \cdot P^C(c) = P^{AC}(a, c) \cdot P^{BC}(b, c)$$

holds for every $a \in \mathbf{X}_A$, $b \in \mathbf{X}_B$, $c \in \mathbf{X}_C$. It describes the situation when P is the distribution of a random vector $[\xi_i]_{i \in N}$ and in every situation when the values of $[\xi_i]_{i \in C}$ are known the values of $[\xi_i]_{i \in A}$ and $[\xi_i]_{i \in B}$ are completely unrelated (from a stochastic point of view).

2.2. INDEPENDENCY MODELS

The symbol $\mathcal{T}(N)$ will denote the collection of ordered triplets $\langle A, B | C \rangle$ of pairwise disjoint subsets of a factor set N, where $A \neq \emptyset \neq B$. These triplets will serve for identification of conditional independence statements within the factor set N.

In general, an *independency model* over N is a subset of the class $\mathcal{T}(N)$. Supposing $\langle A, B | C \rangle \in \mathcal{T}(N)$, its symmetric image is the triplet $\langle B, A | C \rangle \in \mathcal{T}(N)$. The *symmetric closure* of an independency model $\mathcal{I} \subset \mathcal{T}(N)$ is the class of triplets in $\mathcal{I}$ and their symmetric images.

The independency model *induced by a probability distribution* P over N consists just of those triplets $\langle A, B | C \rangle \in \mathcal{T}(N)$ such that $A \perp\!\!\!\perp B | C\,(P)$. A *probabilistic independency model* (over N) is an independency model induced by some probability distribution over N.

Lemma 2.1 *Supposing* $\mathcal{I}, \mathcal{J} \subset \mathcal{T}(N)$ *are probabilistic independency models the class* $\mathcal{I} \cap \mathcal{J}$ *is also a probabilistic independency model.*

Proof. Let P be a probability distribution on $\mathbf{X}_N$ inducing $\mathcal{I}$ and Q be a probability distribution on $\mathbf{Y}_N \equiv \prod_{i \in N} \mathbf{Y}_i$ inducing $\mathcal{J}$. Put $\mathbf{Z}_i = \mathbf{X}_i \times \mathbf{Y}_i$ for every $i \in N$ and define

$$R([x_i, y_i]_{i \in N}) = P([x_i]_{i \in N}) \cdot Q([y_i]_{i \in N}) \quad \text{for } [x_i, y_i]_{i \in N} \in \mathbf{Z}_N.$$

It is easy to verify that for every $\langle A, B|C \rangle \in \mathcal{T}(N)$ one has $A \perp\!\!\!\perp B|C\,(R)$ iff $[\,A \perp\!\!\!\perp B|C\,(P)$ & $A \perp\!\!\!\perp B|C\,(Q)\,]$. □

2.3. RELATIVE ENTROPY

Supposing Q and R are probability distributions on a nonempty finite set $\mathbf{Y}$ we say that Q is *absolutely continuous* with respect to R iff $R(y) = 0$ implies $Q(y) = 0$ for every $y \in \mathbf{Y}$. In that case we can define the *relative entropy* of Q with respect to R as

$$\mathcal{H}(Q|R) = \sum \{\, Q(y) \cdot \ln \frac{Q(y)}{R(y)} \; ; \; y \in \mathbf{Y} \,\&\, Q(y) > 0 \,\} \,.$$

Lemma 2.2 *Suppose that Q and R are probability distributions on a nonempty finite set $\mathbf{Y}$ such that Q is absolutely continuous with respect to R. Then*
(a) $\mathcal{H}(Q|R) \geq 0$,
(b) $\mathcal{H}(Q|R) = 0$ *iff* $Q = R$.

Proof: Consider the real function φ on the interval $[0, \infty)$ defined by
$\varphi(z) = z \cdot \ln z$ for $z > 0$, $\varphi(0) = 0$,
and the function $h : \mathbf{Y} \to [0, \infty)$ defined by
$h(y) = Q(y)/R(y)$ if $R(y) > 0$, $h(y) = 0$ otherwise.
Since φ is a continuous strictly convex function, one can use the well-known Jensen's inequality [3] with respect to R and write:

$$0 = \varphi(1) = \varphi(\sum_{y \in \mathbf{Y}} h(y) \cdot R(y)) \leq \sum_{y \in \mathbf{Y}} \varphi(h(y)) \cdot R(y) = \mathcal{H}(Q|R).$$

Owing to strict convexity of φ the equality holds iff h is constant on the set $\{y \in \mathbf{Y}; R(y) > 0\}$. That means $h \equiv 1$ there, i.e. $Q = R$. □

Supposing that $\langle A, B|C \rangle \in \mathcal{T}(N)$ and P is a probability distribution over N the formula

$$
\begin{aligned}
\hat{P}(x) &= \frac{P^{AC}(x_{AC}) \cdot P^{BC}(x_{BC})}{P^C(x_C)} && \text{for } x \in \mathbf{X}_{ABC} \text{ with } P^C(x_C) > 0, \\
\hat{P}(x) &= 0 && \text{for remaining } x \in \mathbf{X}_{ABC}\,.
\end{aligned}
\tag{1}
$$

defines a probability distribution on $\mathbf{X}_{ABC}$. Evidently, P^{ABC} is absolutely continuous with respect to $\hat{P}$. The *conditional mutual information* between A and B given C with respect to P, denoted by $I(A; B|C \parallel P)$ is the relative entropy of P^{ABC} with respect to $\hat{P}$. In case that P is known from the context we write just $I(A; B|C)$.

Consequence 2.1 *Supposing that $\langle A, B|C \rangle \in \mathcal{T}(N)$ and P is a probability distribution over N one has*

(a) $I(A; B|C \| P) \geq 0$,

(b) $I(A; B|C \| P) = 0$ iff $A \perp\!\!\!\perp B|C\,(P)$.

Proof: Owing to Lemma 2.2 it suffices to realize that $P^{ABC} = \hat{P}$ means nothing but the corresponding conditional independence statement. $\square$

2.4. MULTIINFORMATION FUNCTION

The *multiinformation function* induced by a probability distribution P (over a factor set N) is a real function on the power set of N defined as follows:

$$M(D \| P) = \mathcal{H}(P^D | \prod_{i \in D} P^{\{i\}}) \text{ for } \emptyset \neq D \subset N, \quad M(\emptyset \| P) = 0.$$

We again omit the symbol of P when the probability distribution is clear from the context. It follows from Lemma 2.2(b) that $M(D) = 0$ whenever card $D = 1$.

Lemma 2.3 *Let $\langle A, B|C \rangle \in \mathcal{T}(N)$ and P be a probability distribution over N. Then*

$$I(A; B|C) = M(ABC) + M(C) - M(AC) - M(BC). \qquad (2)$$

Proof: Let us write $\mathcal{H}(P^{ABC}|\hat{P})$ as

$$\sum \{P^{ABC}(x) \cdot \ln \frac{P^{ABC}(x) \cdot P^C(x_C)}{P^{AC}(x_{AC}) \cdot P^{BC}(x_{BC})}; \ x \in \mathbf{X}_{ABC} \ \& \ P^{ABC}(x) > 0\}.$$

Now we can artificially multiply both the numerator and the denominator of the ratio in the argument of the logarithm by a special product $\prod_{i \in A} P^{\{i\}}(x_i) \cdot \prod_{i \in B} P^{\{i\}}(x_i) \cdot \prod_{i \in C} P^{\{i\}}(x_i) \cdot \prod_{i \in C} P^{\{i\}}(x_i)$ which is always strictly positive for any considered configuration x. Using well-known properties of logarithm one can write it as a sum of four terms:

$$\sum \{ P^{ABC}(x) \cdot \ln \frac{P^{ABC}(x)}{\prod_{i \in ABC} P^{\{i\}}(x_i)}; \ x \in \mathbf{X}_{ABC} \ \& \ P^{ABC}(x) > 0 \}$$

$$+ \quad \sum \{ P^{ABC}(x) \cdot \ln \frac{P^C(x_C)}{\prod_{i \in C} P^{\{i\}}(x_i)}; \ x \in \mathbf{X}_{ABC} \ \& \ P^{ABC}(x) > 0 \}$$

$$- \quad \sum \{ P^{ABC}(x) \cdot \ln \frac{P^{AC}(x_{AC})}{\prod_{i \in AC} P^{\{i\}}(x_i)}; \ x \in \mathbf{X}_{ABC} \ \& \ P^{ABC}(x) > 0 \}$$

$$- \quad \sum \{ P^{ABC}(x) \cdot \ln \frac{P^{BC}(x_{BC})}{\prod_{i \in BC} P^{\{i\}}(x_i)}; \ x \in \mathbf{X}_{ABC} \ \& \ P^{ABC}(x) > 0 \}.$$

The first term is nothing but the value of the multiinformation function for ABC. To see that the second term is $M(C)$ one can sum there in groups of configurations for which the corresponding logarithm has the same value, that is groups of xs having the same projection to C:

$$\sum_{\substack{x_C \in \mathbf{X}_C \\ P^C(x_C) > 0}} \sum_{\substack{y \in \mathbf{X}_{AB} \\ P^{ABC}(y,x_C) > 0}} P^{ABC}(y,x_C) \cdot \ln \frac{P^C(x_C)}{\prod_{i \in C} P^{\{i\}}(x_i)} =$$

$$= \sum_{\substack{x_C \in \mathbf{X}_C \\ P^C(x_C) > 0}} \ln \frac{P^C(x_C)}{\prod_{i \in C} P^{\{i\}}(x_i)} \cdot \sum_{\substack{y \in \mathbf{X}_{AB} \\ P^{ABC}(y,x_C) > 0}} P^{ABC}(y,x_C) =$$

$$= \sum_{\substack{x_C \in \mathbf{X}_C \\ P^C(x_C) > 0}} \ln \frac{P^C(x_C)}{\prod_{i \in C} P^{\{i\}}(x_i)} \cdot P^C(x_C) .$$

Similarly for the other two terms.   □

2.5. ENTROPY AND CONDITIONAL ENTROPY

If Q is a discrete probability distribution on a nonempty finite set $\mathbf{Y}$ the *entropy* of Q is defined by the formula

$$\mathcal{H}(Q) = \sum \{ Q(y) \cdot \ln \frac{1}{Q(y)} \; ; \; y \in \mathbf{Y} \ \& \ Q(y) > 0 \} .$$

Lemma 2.4 *Suppose that Q is a discrete probability distribution on a nonempty finite set $\mathbf{Y}$. Then*
(a) $\mathcal{H}(Q) \geq 0$,
(b) $\mathcal{H}(Q) = 0$ iff there exists $y \in \mathbf{Y}$ such that $Q(y) = 1$.

Proof. Since logarithm is an increasing real function one has $\ln Q(y)^{-1} \geq 0$ for every $y \in \mathbf{Y}$ with $Q(y) > 0$. Hence $Q(y) \cdot \ln Q(y)^{-1} \geq 0$ for every such y; the equality occurs here only if $Q(y) = 1$. It gives both (a) and (b).   □

The *entropic function* induced by a probability distribution P over a factor set N is a real function on the power set of N defined as follows:

$$H(D \,\|\, P) = \mathcal{H}(P^D) \quad \text{for } \emptyset \neq D \subset N, \qquad H(\emptyset \,\|\, P) = 0 .$$

We will often omit the symbol of P when it is clear from the context. By using the same procedure as in the proof of Lemma 2.3 it is not difficult to see that

$$M(D) = -H(D) + \sum_{i \in D} H(\{i\}) \quad \text{for every } D \subset N .$$

Hence, using the formula (2) from Lemma 2.3 one derives

$$I(A; B|C) = -H(ABC) - H(C) + H(AC) + H(BC).\qquad(3)$$

Supposing $A, B \subset N$ are disjoint the *conditional entropy* of A given B is defined as a simple difference

$$H(A|B) = H(AB) - H(B).$$

We use the symbol $H(A|B \| P)$ to indicate the corresponding probability distribution P.

Lemma 2.5 *Let P be a probability distribution over N, $A, B \subset N$ are disjoint. Then*

$$H(A|B \| P) = \sum \{ P^B(b) \cdot H(A \| P^{|b}) ; \ b \in \mathbf{X}_B \ \& \ P^B(b) > 0 \}.\qquad(4)$$

Proof. One can easily see using the method used in the proof of Lemma 2.3 that the expression

$$\sum \{ P^{AB}(ab) \cdot \ln \frac{P^B(b)}{P^{AB}(ab)} ; \ a \in \mathbf{X}_A \ \& \ b \in \mathbf{X}_B \ \& \ P^{AB}(ab) > 0 \}$$

is nothing but $H(A|B \| P)$. On the other hand, one can utilize the definition of $P^{A|b}$ and write it in the form

$$\sum_{\substack{b \in \mathbf{X}_B \\ P^B(b) > 0}} P^B(b) \cdot \sum_{\substack{a \in \mathbf{X}_A \\ P^{A|b}(a) > 0}} P^{A|b}(a) \cdot \ln \frac{1}{P^{A|b}(a)},$$

which gives the expression from (4). $\qquad\qquad\square$

3. Measure of conditional stochastic dependence

In this section we give several arguments why conditional mutual information should be considered as a suitable quantitative measure of degree of conditional stochastic dependence.

To motivate this topic let us consider the following specific task. Suppose that ξ_A, ξ_B, and ξ_C are discrete random vectors and the joint distributions of ξ_{AC} and ξ_{BC} are already known (fixed or prescribed). What then are possible values for the conditional mutual information $I(A; B|C)$? By Consequence 2.1 zero is a lower bound for those values, and it is the precise bound since one can always find a distribution having prescribed marginals for AC and BC such that $I(A; B|C) = 0$ (namely the "conditional product" $\hat{P}$ given by the formula (1)).

3.1. MAXIMAL DEGREE OF CONDITIONAL DEPENDENCE

But one can also find an upper bound.

Lemma 3.1 *Let* $\langle A, B|C \rangle \in \mathcal{T}(N)$ *and* P *be a probability distribution over* N. *Then*

$$I(A; B|C) \leq \min \{ H(A|C),\, H(B|C) \}.$$

Proof: It follows from (3) with help of the definition of conditional entropy that:
$$I(A; B|C) = H(A|C) - H(A|BC).$$
Moreover, $0 \leq H(A|BC)$ follows from (4) with Lemma 2.4(a). This implies $I(A; B|C) \leq H(A|C)$, the other estimate with $H(B|C)$ is analogous.   □

The following proposition generalizes an analogous result obtained in the unconditional case by Zvárová ([28], Theorem 5) and loosely corresponds to the condition E) mentioned by Rényi [16].

Proposition 3.1 *Supposing* $\langle A, B|C \rangle \in \mathcal{T}(N)$ *and* P *is a probability distribution over* N *one has*

$$I(A; B|C \,\|\, P) = H(A|C \,\|\, P) \quad iff \quad BC \to A\,(P).$$

Proof: By the formula mentioned in the proof of Lemma 3.1 the considered equality occurs just in case $H(A|BC \,\|\, P) = 0$. Owing to the formula (4) and Lemma 2.4(a) this is equivalent to the requirement $H(A \,\|\, P^{|\,bc}) = 0$ for every $(b, c) \in \mathbf{X}_{BC}$ with $P^{BC}(b, c) > 0$. By Lemma 2.4(b) it means just that for every such a pair $(b, c) \in \mathbf{X}_{BC}$ there exists $a \in \mathbf{X}_A$ with $P^{A|\,bc}(a) = 1$. Of course, this $a \in \mathbf{X}_A$ is uniquely determined. This enables us to define the required function from $\mathbf{X}_{BC}$ to $\mathbf{X}_A$.   □

A natural question that arises is how tight is the upper bound for $I(A; B|C)$ from Lemma 3.1? More exactly, we ask whether one can always find a distribution having prescribed marginals for AC and BC with $I(A; B|C) = \min\{H(A|C), H(B|C)\}$. In general, the answer is negative as shown by the following example.

Example 3.1 Let us put $\mathbf{X}_A = \mathbf{X}_B = \mathbf{X}_C = \{0,1\}$ and define P_{AC} and P_{BC} as follows

$$P_{AC}(0,0) = \tfrac{1}{3}, \; P_{AC}(0,1) = P_{AC}(1,1) = \tfrac{1}{4}, \; P_{AC}(1,0) = \tfrac{1}{6},$$

$$P_{BC}(0,0) = P_{BC}(0,1) = P_{BC}(1,0) = P_{BC}(1,1) = \tfrac{1}{4}.$$

Since $(P_{AC})^C = (P_{BC})^C$ there exists a distribution on $\mathbf{X}_{ABC}$ having them as marginals. In fact, any such distribution P can be expressed as follows

$$
\begin{aligned}
P(0,0,0) &= \alpha, \\
P(0,0,1) &= \beta, \\
P(0,1,0) &= \tfrac{1}{3} - \alpha, \\
P(0,1,1) &= \tfrac{1}{4} - \beta, \\
P(1,0,0) &= \tfrac{1}{4} - \alpha, \\
P(1,0,1) &= \tfrac{1}{4} - \beta, \\
P(1,1,0) &= \alpha - \tfrac{1}{12}, \\
P(1,1,1) &= \beta,
\end{aligned}
$$

where $\alpha \in [\tfrac{1}{12}, \tfrac{1}{4}], \beta \in [0, \tfrac{1}{4}]$. It is easy to show that $H(A|C) < H(B|C)$. On the other hand, for every parameter α either $P(0,0,0)$ and $P(1,0,0)$ are simultaneously nonzero or $P(0,1,0)$ and $P(1,1,0)$ are simultaneously nonzero. Therefore A is not functionally dependent on BC with respect to P and by Proposition 3.1 the upper bound $H(A|C)$ is not achieved. $\diamond$

However, the upper bound given in Lemma 3.1 can be precise for specific prescribed marginals. Let us provide a general example.

Example 3.2 Suppose that P_{BC} is given, consider an arbitrary function $g : \mathbf{X}_B \to \mathbf{X}_A$ and define P_{AC} by the formula

$$P_{AC}(a,c) = \sum \{ P_{BC}(b,c) \; ; \; b \in \mathbf{X}_B \; \& \; g(b) = a \} \quad \text{for } a \in \mathbf{X}_A, \, c \in \mathbf{X}_C.$$

One can always find a distribution P over ABC having such a pair of distributions P_{AC}, P_{BC} as marginals and satisfying $I(A; B|C \parallel P) = H(A|C \parallel P)$. Indeed, define P over ABC as follows:

$$
\begin{aligned}
P(a,b,c) &= P_{BC}(b,c) && \text{if } g(b) = a, \\
P(a,b,c) &= 0 && \text{otherwise.}
\end{aligned}
$$

This ensures that $BC \to A \, (P)$, then use Proposition 3.1. $\diamond$

3.2. MUTUAL COMPARISON OF DEPENDENCE DEGREES

A natural intuitive requirement on a quantitative characteristic of degree of dependence is that a higher degree of dependence among variables should be reflected by a higher value of that characteristic. Previous results on conditional mutual information are in agreement with this wish: its minimal value characterizes independence, while its maximal values more or less correspond to the maximal degree of dependence.

Well, what about the behavior "between" these "extreme" cases? One can imagine two "comparable" nonextreme cases when one case represents evidently a higher degree of dependence among variables than the other case. For example, let us consider two random vectors ξ_{AB} resp. η_{AB} (take $C = \emptyset$) having distributions P_{AB} resp. Q_{AB} depicted by the following diagrams.

P_{AB}	0	$\frac{1}{7}$	$\frac{1}{7}$
	$\frac{1}{7}$	$\frac{1}{7}$	$\frac{1}{7}$
	$\frac{1}{7}$	$\frac{1}{7}$	0

Q_{AB}	0	0	$\frac{2}{7}$
	$\frac{1}{7}$	$\frac{2}{7}$	0
	$\frac{1}{7}$	$\frac{1}{7}$	0

Clearly, $(P_{AB})^A = (Q_{AB})^A$ and $(P_{AB})^B = (Q_{AB})^B$. But intuitively, Q_{AB} expresses a higher degree of stochastic dependence between $\eta_A = \xi_A$ and $\eta_B = \xi_B$ than P_{AB}. The distribution Q_{AB} is more "concentrated" than P_{AB}: Q_{AB} is an image of P_{AB}. Therefore, we can anticipate $I(A; B|\emptyset \| P) \leq I(A; B|\emptyset \| Q)$, which is indeed the case.

The following proposition says that conditional mutual information has the desired property. Note that the property is not derivable from other properties of measures of dependence mentioned either by Rényi [16] or by Zvárová [28] (in the unconditional case).

Proposition 3.2 *Suppose that $\langle A, B|C \rangle \in \mathcal{T}(N)$ and P, Q are probability distributions over N such that $P^{AC} = Q^{AC}$, $P^{BC} = Q^{BC}$ and Q^{ABC} is an image of P^{ABC}. Then*

$$I(A; B|C \| P) \leq I(A; B|C \| Q).$$

Proof: Let us write P instead of P^{ABC} throughout the proof and similarly for Q. Suppose that Q is an image of P by $f : \mathbf{X}_{ABC} \to \mathbf{X}_{ABC}$. For every

$x \in \mathbf{X}_{ABC}$ with $Q(x) > 0$ put $T = \{y \in \mathbf{X}_{ABC}\, ; f(y) = x\, \& \, P(y) > 0\}$ and write (owing to the fact that the logarithm is an increasing function):

$$\sum_{y \in T} P(y) \cdot \ln P(y) \leq \sum_{y \in T} P(y) \cdot \ln \left(\sum_{z \in T} P(z) \right) = Q(x) \cdot \ln Q(x).$$

We can sum it over all such xs and derive

$$\sum_{\substack{y \in \mathbf{X}_{ABC} \\ P(y) > 0}} P(y) \cdot \ln P(y) \leq \sum_{\substack{x \in \mathbf{X}_{ABC} \\ Q(x) > 0}} Q(x) \cdot \ln Q(x).$$

Hence

$$-H(ABC \,\|\, P) \leq -H(ABC \,\|\, Q).$$

Owing to the assumptions $P^{AC} = Q^{AC}$, $P^{BC} = Q^{BC}$ one has $H(AC \,\|\, P) = H(AC \,\|\, Q)$, $H(BC \,\|\, P) = H(BC \,\|\, Q)$ and $H(C \,\|\, P) = H(C \,\|\, Q)$. The formula (3) then gives the desired claim.   □

Nevertheless, the mentioned inequality from Proposition 3.2 may not hold when the assumption that marginals for AC and BC coincide is relaxed, as demonstrated by the following example.

Example 3.3 Take $C = \emptyset$ and consider the distributions P_{AB} and Q_{AB} depicted by the following diagrams:

Evidently, Q_{AB} is an image of P_{AB}, but $I(A; B|\emptyset \,\|\, P) > I(A; B|\emptyset \,\|\, Q)$.   ◇

Remark One can imagine more general transformations of distributions: instead of "functional" transformations introduced in subsection 2.1 one can consider transformations by Markov kernels. However, Proposition 3.2 cannot be generalized to such a case. In fact, the distribution P_{AB} from the motivational example starting this subsection can be obtained from Q_{AB} by an "inverse" transformation realized by a Markov kernel.

3.3. TRANSFORMED DISTRIBUTIONS

Rényi's condition F) in [16] states that a one-to-one transformation of a random variable does not change the value of a measure of dependence. Similarly, Zvárová [28] requires that restrictions to sub-σ-algebras (which somehow correspond to separate simplifying transformations of variables) decrease the value of the measure of dependence.

The above mentioned requirements can be generalized to the "conditional" case as shown in the following proposition. Note that the assumption of the proposition means (under the situation when P is the distribution of a random vector $[\xi_i]_{i \in N}$) simply that the random subvector $[\xi_i]_{i \in A}$ is transformed while the other variables ξ_i, $i \in BC$ are preserved.

Proposition 3.3 *Let $\langle A, B|C \rangle$, $\langle D, B|C \rangle \in \mathcal{T}(N)$, P, Q be probability distributions over N. Suppose that there exists a mapping $g : \mathbf{X}_A \to \mathbf{X}_D$ such that Q^{DBC} is an image of P^{ABC} by the mapping $f : \mathbf{X}_{ABC} \to \mathbf{X}_{DBC}$ defined by*

$$f(a, b, c) = [\, g(a), b, c \,] \quad \text{for } a \in \mathbf{X}_A \,, \ (b, c) \in \mathbf{X}_{BC} \,.$$

Then

$$I(A; B|C \parallel P) \geq I(D; B|C \parallel Q) \,.$$

Proof: Throughout the proof we write P instead of P^{ABC} and Q instead of Q^{DBC}. Let us denote by $\mathbf{Y}$ the class of all $(c, d) \in \mathbf{X}_{CD}$ such that $P(g_{-1}(d) \times \mathbf{X}_B \times \{c\}) > 0$ where $g_{-1}(d) = \{a \in \mathbf{X}_A; g(a) = d\}$. For every $(c, d) \in \mathbf{Y}$ introduce a probability distribution R_{cd} on $g_{-1}(d) \times \mathbf{X}_B$ by the formula:

$$R_{cd}(a, b) = \frac{P(a, b, c)}{P(g_{-1}(d) \times \mathbf{X}_B \times \{c\})} \quad \text{for } a \in g_{-1}(d), \ b \in \mathbf{X}_B \,.$$

It can be formally considered as a distribution on $\mathbf{X}_A \times \mathbf{X}_B$. Thus, by Consequence 2.1(a) we have

$$0 \leq I(A; B|\emptyset \parallel R_{cd}) \quad \text{for every } (c, d) \in \mathbf{Y} \,.$$

One can multiply this inequality by $P(g_{-1}(d) \times \mathbf{X}_B \times \{c\})$, sum over $\mathbf{Y}$ and obtain by simple cancellation of $P(g_{-1}(d) \times \mathbf{X}_B \times \{c\})$:

$$0 \leq \sum_{(c,d) \in \mathbf{Y}} \ \sum_{\substack{(a,b) \in g_{-1}(d) \times \mathbf{X}_B \\ P(abc) > 0}}$$

$$P(abc) \cdot \ln \frac{P(abc) \cdot P(g_{-1}(d) \times \mathbf{X}_B \times \{c\})}{P(\{a\} \times \mathbf{X}_B \times \{c\}) \cdot P(g_{-1}(d) \times \{b\} \times \{c\})} \,.$$

One can apply basic properties of the logarithm and write the right-hand side of the obtained inequality as a sum of four terms (as in the proof of Lemma 2.3). We leave it to the reader to verify that each of these terms is a certain entropy (possibly with the minus sign). We just give hints indicating formally the way of summation:

$$\sum_c \sum_d \sum_b \sum_a P(abc) \cdot \ln P(abc) = \sum_c \sum_b \sum_d \sum_a \cdots = \sum_c \sum_b \sum_a \cdots = -H(ABC \,\|\, P)$$

$$-\sum_c \sum_d \sum_a \sum_b P(abc) \cdot \ln P(\{a\} \times \mathbf{X}_B \times \{c\}) = \sum_c \sum_d \sum_a \cdots = \sum_c \sum_a \cdots = H(AC \,\|\, P)$$

$$-\sum_c \sum_d \sum_b \sum_a P(abc) \cdot \ln P(g_{-1}(d) \times \{b\} \times \{c\}) = \sum_c \sum_d \sum_b \cdots = H(DBC \,\|\, Q)$$

$$\sum_c \sum_d \sum_a \sum_b P(abc) \cdot \ln P(g_{-1}(d) \times \mathbf{X}_B \times \{c\}) = \sum_c \sum_d \cdots = -H(DC \,\|\, Q)$$

Thus, one can derive:

$$0 \le -H(ABC \,\|\, P) + H(AC \,\|\, P) + H(DBC \,\|\, Q) - H(DC \,\|\, Q) \,. \tag{5}$$

Since $P^{BC} = Q^{BC}$ one also has

$$0 = H(BC \,\|\, P) - H(BC \,\|\, Q) - H(C \,\|\, P) + H(C \,\|\, Q) \,. \tag{6}$$

Hence by summing (5) and (6) and using the formula (3)

$$0 \le I(A; B|C \,\|\, P) - I(D; B|C \,\|\, Q) \,,$$

which concludes the proof. $\qquad\qquad\qquad\qquad\qquad\qquad\qquad\qquad\qquad\qquad\square$

If g is a one-to one mapping, one can apply Proposition 3.3 both to g and g^{-1}, from which the following consequence immediately follows (it corresponds exactly to the Rényi's requirement F)).

Consequence 3.1 *Supposing the mapping g in Proposition 3.3 is a one-to-one mapping one has*

$$I(A; B|C \,\|\, P) = I(D; B|C \,\|\, Q) \,.$$

Nevertheless, Proposition 3.3 cannot be strengthened to transformations involving variables in C (more exactly transformations of the subvector $[\xi_i]_{i \in AC}$), as the following example shows.

Example 3.4 Let us put $\mathbf{X}_A = \mathbf{X}_B = \mathbf{X}_C = \mathbf{X}_D = \{0, 1\}$, $\mathbf{X}_E = \{0\}$ and define a distribution P on $\mathbf{X}_{ABC}$ as follows

$$P(0, 0, 0) = P(1, 0, 0) = P(0, 1, 1) = P(1, 1, 1) = \frac{1}{4} \,,$$

where the remaining values of P zero. Since $A \perp\!\!\!\perp B | C \, (P)$ one has by Consequence 2.1(b) $I(A; B | C \, \| \, P) = 0$. Let us consider a mapping $g : \mathbf{X}_{AC} \to \mathbf{X}_{DE}$ defined by

$$g(0,0) = g(1,0) = (0,0) \quad g(0,1) = g(1,1) = (1,0) \, .$$

Then the image of P by the mapping $f : \mathbf{X}_{ABC} \to \mathbf{X}_{DBE}$ defined by

$$f(a,b,c) = [\, g(a,c), b \,] \quad \text{for } (a,c) \in \mathbf{X}_{AC} \, , \ b \in \mathbf{X}_B \, ,$$

is the following distribution Q on $\mathbf{X}_{DBE}$:

$$Q(0,0,0) = Q(1,1,0) = \frac{1}{2} \, , \quad Q(0,1,0) = Q(1,0,0) = 0 \, .$$

Evidently $I(D; B | E \, \| \, Q) = \ln 2 \, .$ $\qquad\qquad\qquad\qquad\qquad\qquad\qquad\qquad$ $\diamond$

4. Different levels of stochastic dependence

Let us start this section with some motivation. A quite common "philosophical" point of view on stochastic dependence is the following: The global strength of dependence among variables $[\xi_i]_{i \in N}$ is considered as a result of various *interactions* among factors in N.

For example, in hierarchical log-linear models for contingency tables [4] one can distinguish the first-order interactions, i.e. interactions of pairs of factors, the second-order interactions, i.e. interactions of triplets of factors, etc. In substance, the first-order interactions correspond to pairwise dependence relationships, i.e. to (unconditional) dependences between ξ_i and ξ_j for $i, j \in N$, $i \neq j$. Similarly, one can (very loosely) imagine that the second-order interactions correspond to conditional dependences with one conditioning variable, i.e. to conditional dependences between ξ_i and ξ_j given ξ_k where $i, j, k \in N$ are distinct. An analogous principle holds for higher-order interactions. Note that we have used the example with log-linear models just for motivation – to illustrate informally the aim of this section. In fact, one can interpret only special hierarchical log-linear models in terms of conditional (in)dependence.

This leads to the idea of distinguishing different "levels" of stochastic dependence. Thus, the first level could "involve" pairwise (unconditional) dependences. The second level could correspond to pairwise conditional dependences between two variables given a third one, the third level to pairwise conditional dependences given a pair of variables, etc. Let us give a simple example of a probability distribution which exhibits different behavior for different levels. The following construction will be used in the next section, too.

Construction A Supposing $A \subset N$, card $A \geq 2$, there exists a probability distribution P over N such that

$$M(B \parallel P) = \ln 2 \qquad \text{whenever } A \subset B \subset N,$$
$$M(B \parallel P) = 0 \qquad \text{otherwise.}$$

Proof: Let us put $\mathbf{X}_i = \{0, 1\}$ for $i \in A$, $\mathbf{X}_i = \{0\}$ for $i \in N \setminus A$. Define P on $\mathbf{X}_N$ as follows

$$P([x_i]_{i \in N}) = 2^{1-\text{card } A} \qquad \text{whenever } \sum_{i \in N} x_i \text{ is even,}$$
$$P([x_i]_{i \in N}) = 0 \qquad \text{otherwise.}$$

$\square$

The distribution P from Construction A exhibits only the highest-level dependences within the factor set A. Indeed, for every pair $i, j \in A$, $i \neq j$, one can easily verify (by Consequence 2.1 and Lemma 2.3) that i is conditionally independent of j given any proper subset C of $A \setminus \{i, j\}$ (with respect to P) but i is *not* conditionally independent of j given $A \setminus \{i, j\}$. Or equivalently, supposing $[\xi_i]_{i \in N}$ has the distribution P, the variables $[\xi_i]_{i \in A}$ are "collectively dependent" although the variables $[\xi_i]_{i \in D}$, where D is arbitrary proper subset of A, are "completely independent." Such distributions are called in [26] *pseudo-independent models*. The main conclusion of [26] is that in the case of such an underlying model standard algorithms for learning Bayesian network approximations fail to find a suitable network. This perhaps justifies a wish to measure the strength of each level of dependence separately. Good quantitative level-specific measures of dependence may help one to recognize whether a considered distribution is similar to the fearful pseudo-independent model. They can provide a good theoretical basis for necessary statistical tests.

Thus, we wish to have an analogue of the above mentioned classification of interactions by order in log-linear models together with the possibility of expressing numerically the degree of dependence for each level.

4.1. LEVEL-SPECIFIC MEASURES OF DEPENDENCE

In the previous section we argued that the conditional mutual information $I(A; B \mid C)$ is a good measure of stochastic conditional dependence between $[\xi_i]_{i \in A}$ and $[\xi_j]_{j \in B}$ given $[\xi_k]_{k \in C}$ where $A, B, C \subset N$ are pairwise disjoint subsets of N. In the special case when A and B are singletons, we will get a measure $I(i; j \mid K)$ of conditional dependence between ξ_i and ξ_j given $[\xi_k]_{k \in K}$, where $K \subset N \setminus \{i, j\}$. This leads directly to our proposal of how to measure the degree of dependence for a specific level.

Suppose that P is a probability distribution over N, $A \subset N$ with card $A \geq 2$. Then for each $r = 1, \ldots,$ card $A - 1$ we put:

$$\Delta(r, A \| P) = \sum \{ I(a; b | K \| P) \, ; \, \{a, b\} \subset A, \ K \subset A \setminus \{a, b\}, \ \text{card} \, K = r - 1 \}.$$

If the distribution P is known from the context, we write $\Delta(r, A)$ instead of $\Delta(r, A \| P)$. Moreover, we will occasionally write just $\Delta(r)$ as a shorthand for $\Delta(r, N)$. We regard this number as a basis of a measure of dependence of level r among factors from A. Consequence 2.1 directly implies:

Proposition 4.1 *Let P be a probability distribution over N, $A \subset N$, card $A \geq 2$, $1 \leq r \leq$ card $A - 1$. Then*
(a) $\Delta(r, A \| P) \geq 0$,
(b) $\Delta(r, A \| P) = 0$ iff $[\forall \langle a, b | K \rangle \in \mathcal{T}(A) \ \text{card} \, K = r - 1 \quad a \perp\!\!\!\perp b | K \, (P)]$.

So, the number $\Delta(r)$ is nonnegative and vanishes just in case when there are no stochastic dependences of level r. Particularly, $\Delta(1)$ can be regarded as a measure of degree of pairwise unconditional dependence. The reader can ask whether there are different measures of the strength of level-specific interactions. Of course, one can find many such information-theoretical measures. However, if one is interested only in symmetric measures (i.e. measures whose values are not changed by a permutation of variables) based on entropy, then (in our opinion) the corresponding measure must be nothing but a multiple of $\Delta(r)$. We base our conjecture on the result of Han [8]: he introduced certain level-specific measures which are positive multiples of $\Delta(r)$ and proved that every entropy-based measure of multivariate "symmetric" correlation is a linear combination of his measures with nonnegative coefficients.

Of course, owing to Lemma 2.3 the number $\Delta(r)$ can be expressed by means of the multiinformation function. To get a neat formula we introduce a provisional notation for sums of the multiinformation function over sets of the same cardinality. We denote for every $A \subset N$, card $A \geq 2$:

$$\sigma(i, A) = \sum \{ M(D \| P) \, ; \, D \subset A, \ \text{card} \, D = i \} \quad \text{for } i = 0, \ldots, \text{card} \, A.$$

Of course $\sigma(i)$ will be a shorthand for $\sigma(i, N)$. Let us mention that $\sigma(0) = \sigma(1) = 0$.

Lemma 4.1 *For every $r = 1, \ldots, n - 1$ (where $n =$ card $N \geq 2$)*

$$\Delta(r) = \binom{r + 1}{2} \cdot \sigma(r + 1) - r \cdot (n - r) \cdot \sigma(r) + \binom{n - r + 1}{2} \cdot \sigma(r - 1).$$

Proof. Let us fix $1 \leq r \leq n-1$ and write by Lemma 2.3

$$2\Delta(r) = \sum_{\langle a,b|K\rangle \in \mathcal{L}} \{\, M(abK) + M(K) - M(aK) - M(bK)\,\}, \qquad (7)$$

where $\mathcal{L}$ is the class of all $\langle a, b|K\rangle \in \mathcal{T}(N)$ where a, b are singletons and card $K = r-1$. Note that in $\mathcal{L}$ the triplets $\langle a, b|K\rangle$ and $\langle b, a|K\rangle$ are distinguished: hence the term $2\Delta(r)$ in (7). Evidently, the sum contains only the terms $M(D)$ such that $r - 1 \leq \text{card } D \leq r + 1$, and one can write

$$\Delta(r) = \sum \{\, k(D) \cdot M(D)\,;\; D \subset N,\; r-1 \leq \text{card } D \leq r+1\,\},$$

where $k(D)$ are suitable coefficients. However, since every permutation π of factors in N transforms $\langle a, b|K\rangle \in \mathcal{L}$ into $\langle \pi(a), \pi(b)|\pi(K)\rangle \in \mathcal{L}$ the coefficient $k(D)$ depends only on card D. Thus, if one divides the number of overall occurrences of terms $M(E)$ with card $E = \text{card } D$ in (7) by the number of sets E with card $E = \text{card } D$, the absolute value of $2k(D)$ is obtained. Since card $\mathcal{L} = n \cdot (n-1) \cdot \binom{n-2}{r-1}$ one can obtain for card $D = r+1$ that $k(D) = \frac{1}{2} \cdot n(n-1)\binom{n-2}{r-1}/\binom{n}{r+1} = \binom{r+1}{2}$. Similarly, in case card $D = r-1$ one has $k(D) = \frac{1}{2} \cdot n(n-1)\binom{n-2}{r-1}/\binom{n}{r-1} = \binom{n-r+1}{2}$. Finally, in case card $D = r$ one derives $-k(D) = \frac{1}{2} \cdot 2n(n-1)\binom{n-2}{r-1}/\binom{n}{r} = r(n-r)$. To get the desired formula it suffices to utilize the definitions of $\sigma(r-1)$, $\sigma(r)$, $\sigma(r+1)$. $\square$

Lemma 4.1 provides a neat formula for $\Delta(r)$, but in the case when a great number of conditional independence statements are known to hold, the definition formula is better from the computational complexity viewpoint.

4.2. DECOMPOSITION OF MULTIINFORMATION

Thus, for a factor set N, card $N \geq 2$, the number $M(N)$ quantifies global dependence among factors in N and the numbers $\Delta(r, N)$ quantify level-specific dependences. So, one expects that the multiinformation is at least a weighted sum of these numbers. This is indeed the case, but as the reader can expect, the coefficients depend on card N.

For every $n \geq 2$ and $r \in \{1, \ldots, n-1\}$ we put

$$\beta(r, n) = 2 \cdot r^{-1} \cdot \binom{n}{r}^{-1}.$$

Evidently, $\beta(r, n)$ is always a strictly positive rational number.

Proposition 4.2 Let P be a probability distribution over N, card $N \geq 2$.
Then
$$M(N \parallel P) = \sum_{r=1}^{n-1} \beta(r, n) \cdot \Delta(r, N \parallel P).$$

Proof: Using Lemma 4.1 we write (note that the superfluous symbol of P
is omitted throughout the proof and $\beta(r)$ is used instead of $\beta(r, n)$)

$$\sum_{r=1}^{n-1} \beta(r) \cdot \Delta(r) = \sum_{r=1}^{n-1} \beta(r) \cdot \binom{r+1}{2} \cdot \sigma(r+1)$$

$$- \sum_{r=1}^{n-1} \beta(r) \cdot r \cdot (n-r) \cdot \sigma(r) + \sum_{r=1}^{n-1} \beta(r) \cdot \binom{n-r+1}{2} \cdot \sigma(r-1).$$

Let us rewrite this into a more convenient form:

$$\sum_{j=2}^{n} \beta(j-1) \cdot \binom{j}{2} \cdot \sigma(j) - \sum_{j=1}^{n-1} \beta(j) \cdot j \cdot (n-j) \cdot \sigma(j) + \sum_{j=0}^{n-2} \beta(j+1) \cdot \binom{n-j}{2} \cdot \sigma(j).$$

This is, in fact, $\sum_{j=0}^{n} l(j) \cdot \sigma(j)$, where $l(j)$ are suitable coefficients. Thus,
$l(n) = \beta(n-1) \cdot \binom{n}{2} = 1$,
$l(n-1) = \beta(n-2) \cdot \binom{n-1}{2} - \beta(n-1) \cdot (n-1) = \frac{2}{n} - \frac{2}{n} = 0$,
and moreover, for every $2 \leq j \leq n-2$ one can write
$l(j) = \beta(j-1) \cdot \binom{j}{2} - \beta(j) \cdot j \cdot (n-j) + \beta(j+1) \cdot \binom{n-j}{2} =$
$= \binom{n}{j}^{-1} \cdot \{(n-j+1) - 2(n-j) + (n-j-1)\} = 0$.
Hence, owing to $\sigma(0) = \sigma(1) = 0$ and $n \geq 2$ we obtain

$$\sum_{r=1}^{n-1} \beta(r) \cdot \Delta(r) = \sum_{j=2}^{n} l(j) \cdot \sigma(j) = \sigma(n) = M(N).$$

$\square$

If one considers a subset $A \subset N$ in the role of N in the preceding
statement, then one obtains

$$M(A \parallel P) = \sum_{r=1}^{\text{card } A - 1} \beta(r, \text{card } A) \cdot \Delta(r, A \parallel P) \tag{8}$$

for every $A \subset N$, card $A \geq 2$. One can interpret this in the following
way. Whenever $[\xi_i]_{i \in A}$ is a random subvector of $[\xi_i]_{i \in N}$, then $M(A \parallel P)$
is a measure of global dependence among factors in A, and the value
$\beta(r, \text{card } A) \cdot \Delta(r, A \parallel P)$ expresses the contribution of dependences of level

r among factors in A. In this sense, the coefficient $\beta(r, \operatorname{card} A)$ then reflects the relationship between the level r and the number of factors. Thus, the "weights" of different levels (and their mutual ratios, too) depend on the number of factors in consideration.

The formula (8) leads to the following proposal. We propose to measure the strength of stochastic dependence among factors $A \subset N$ ($\operatorname{card} A \geq 2$) of level r ($1 \leq r \leq \operatorname{card} A - 1$) by means of the number:

$$\lambda(r, A \| P) = \beta(r, \operatorname{card} A) \cdot \Delta(r, A \| P).$$

The symbol of P is omitted whenever it is suitable. By Proposition 4.1 $\lambda(r, A)$ is nonnegative and vanishes just in case of absence of interactions of degree r within A. The formula (8) says that $M(A)$ is just the sum of $\lambda(r, A)$s. To have a direct formula one can rewrite the definition of $\lambda(r, A)$ using Lemma 4.1 as follows:

$$\lambda(r, A) = (a - r) \cdot \binom{a}{r+1}^{-1} \cdot \sigma(r+1, A)$$

$$- 2 \cdot (a - r) \cdot \binom{a}{r}^{-1} \cdot \sigma(r, A) + (a - r) \cdot \binom{a}{r-1}^{-1} \cdot \sigma(r-1, A),$$

where $a = \operatorname{card} A$, $1 \leq r \leq a - 1$.

Let us clarify the relation to Han's measure [8] $\Delta^2 e_r^{(n)}$ of level r among $n = \operatorname{card} N$ variables. We have:

$$\lambda(r, N) = (n - r) \cdot \Delta^2 e_r^{(n)} \quad \text{for every } 1 \leq r \leq n - 1, \ n \geq 2.$$

We did not study the computational complexity of calculating the particular characteristics introduced in this section — this can be a subject of future, more applied research.

5. Axiomatic characterization

The aim of this section is to demonstrate that the multiinformation function can be used to derive theoretical results concerning formal properties of conditional independence. For this purpose we recall the proof of the result from [20]. Moreover, we enrich the proof by introducing several concepts which (as we hope) clarify the proof and indicate which steps are substantial. The reader may surmise that our proof is based on Consequence 2.1 and the formula from Lemma 2.3. However, these facts by themselves are not sufficient, one needs something more.

Let us describe the structure of this long section. Since the mentioned result says that probabilistic independency models cannot be characterized

by means of a finite number of formal properties of (= axioms for) independency models one has to clarify thoroughly what is meant by such a formal
property. This is done in subsection 5.1: first (in 5.1.1) syntactic records
of those properties are introduced and illustrated by examples, and then
(in 5.1.2) their meaning is explained. The aim to get rid of superfluous formal properties motivates the rest of the subsection 5.1: the situation when
a formal property of independency models is a consequence of other such
formal properties is analyzed in 5.1.3; "pure" formal properties having in
every situation a nontrivial meaning are treated in 5.1.4.

The subsection 5.2 is devoted to specific formal properties of probabilistic independency models. We show by an example that their validity (=
probabilistic soundness) can be sometimes derived by means of the multiinformation function. The analysis in 5.2.1 leads to the proposal to limit
attention to certain "perfect" formal properties of probabilistic independency models in 5.2.2.

Finally, the subsection 5.3 contains the proof of the nonaxiomatizability
result. The method of the proof is described in 5.3.1: one has to find an
infinite collection of perfect probabilistically sound formal properties of
independency models. Their probabilistic soundness is verified in 5.3.2, their
perfectness in 5.3.3.

5.1. FORMAL PROPERTIES OF INDEPENDENCY MODELS

We have already introduced the concept of an independency model over N
as a subset of the class $\mathcal{T}(N)$ (see subsection 2.2.). This is too general a concept to be of much use. One needs to restrict oneself to special independency
models which satisfy certain reasonable properties. Many authors dealing
with probabilistic independency models have formulated certain reasonable
properties in the form of formal schemata which they named *axioms*. Since
we want to prove that probabilistic independency models cannot be characterized by means of a finite number of such axioms we have to specify
meticulously what is the exact meaning of such formal schemata. Thus, we
both describe the syntax of those schemata and explain their semantics.

Let us start with an example. A *semigraphoid* [14] is an independency
model which satisfies four formal properties expressed by the following
schemata having the form of inference rules.

$$\langle A, B|C \rangle \ \rightarrow \ \langle B, A|C \rangle \qquad\qquad \text{symmetry}$$
$$\langle A, BC|D \rangle \ \rightarrow \ \langle A, C|D \rangle \qquad\qquad \text{decomposition}$$
$$\langle A, BC|D \rangle \ \rightarrow \ \langle A, B|CD \rangle \qquad\qquad \text{weak union}$$
$$[\langle A, B|CD \rangle \ \wedge \ \langle A, C|D \rangle] \ \rightarrow \ \langle A, BC|D \rangle \qquad\qquad \text{contraction.}$$

Roughly, the schemata should be understood as follows: if an independency model contains the triplets before the arrow, then it contains the triplet after the arrow. Thus, we are interested in formal properties of independency models of such a type.

5.1.1. *Syntax of an inference rule*

Let us start with a few technical definitions. Supposing S is a given fixed nonempty finite set of symbols, the formulas $\langle \mathcal{K}_1, \mathcal{K}_2 | \mathcal{K}_3 \rangle$, where $\mathcal{K}_1, \mathcal{K}_2, \mathcal{K}_3$ are disjoint subsets of S represented by juxtapositions of their elements, will be called *terms* over S.

We write $\mathcal{K} \approx \mathcal{L}$ to denote that $\mathcal{K}$ and $\mathcal{L}$ are juxtapositions of all elements of the same subset of S (they can differ in their order). We say that a term $\langle \mathcal{K}_1, \mathcal{K}_2 | \mathcal{K}_3 \rangle$ over S is an *equivalent version* of the term $\langle \mathcal{L}_1, \mathcal{L}_2 | \mathcal{L}_3 \rangle$ over S if $\mathcal{K}_i \approx \mathcal{L}_i$ for every $i = 1, 2, 3$. We say that $\langle \mathcal{K}_1, \mathcal{K}_2 | \mathcal{K}_3 \rangle$ is a *symmetric version* of $\langle \mathcal{L}_1, \mathcal{L}_2 | \mathcal{L}_3 \rangle$ if $\mathcal{K}_1 \approx \mathcal{L}_2$, $\mathcal{K}_2 \approx \mathcal{L}_1$, $\mathcal{K}_3 \approx \mathcal{L}_3$. For example, the term $\langle AE, BC | D \rangle$ over $S = \{A, B, C, D, E, F\}$ is an equivalent version of the term $\langle AE, CB | D \rangle$ and a symmetric version of the term $\langle BC, EA | D \rangle$.

A *regular inference rule* with r antecedents and s consequents is specified by

(a) positive integers r, s,

(b) a finite set of symbols S, possibly including a special symbol $\emptyset$,

(c) a sequence of ordered triplets $[\mathcal{S}_1^k, \mathcal{S}_2^k, \mathcal{S}_3^k]$, $k = 1, \ldots, r + s$ of nonempty subsets of S such that for every k the sets $\mathcal{S}_1^k$, $\mathcal{S}_2^k$, $\mathcal{S}_3^k$ are pairwise disjoint.

Moreover, we have several technical requirements:

- S has at least three symbols,

- if $\mathcal{S}_i^k$ contains the symbol $\emptyset$, then no other symbol from S is involved in $\mathcal{S}_i^k$ (for every $k = 1, \ldots, r + s$ and every $i = 1, 2, 3$),

- if $k, l \in \{1, \ldots, r + s\}$, $k \neq l$, then $\mathcal{S}_i^k \neq \mathcal{S}_i^l$ for some $i \in \{1, 2, 3\}$,

- every $\sigma \in S$ belongs to some $\mathcal{S}_i^k$,

- there is no pair of different symbols $\sigma, \tau \in S$ such that
  $\forall k = 1, \ldots, r + s \ \ \forall i = 1, 2, 3 \ \ [\sigma \in \mathcal{S}_i^k \Rightarrow \tau \in \mathcal{S}_i^k]$.

A *syntactic record* of the corresponding inference rule is then

$$[\langle \mathcal{S}_1^1, \mathcal{S}_2^1 | \mathcal{S}_3^1 \rangle \wedge \ldots \wedge \langle \mathcal{S}_1^r, \mathcal{S}_2^r | \mathcal{S}_3^r \rangle] \rightarrow [\langle \mathcal{S}_1^{r+1}, \mathcal{S}_2^{r+1} | \mathcal{S}_3^{r+1} \rangle \vee \ldots \vee \langle \mathcal{S}_1^{r+s}, \mathcal{S}_2^{r+s} | \mathcal{S}_3^{r+s} \rangle]$$

where each $\mathcal{S}_i^k$ is represented by a juxtaposition of involved symbols. Here the terms $\langle \mathcal{S}_1^k, \mathcal{S}_2^k | \mathcal{S}_3^k \rangle$ for $k = 1, \ldots, r$ are the *antecedent terms*, while $\langle \mathcal{S}_1^k, \mathcal{S}_2^k | \mathcal{S}_3^k \rangle$ for $k = r + 1, \ldots, r + s$ are the *consequent terms*.

Example 5.1 Take $r = 2$, $s = 1$, and $\mathcal{S} = \{A, B, C, D\}$. Moreover, let us put $[\mathcal{S}_1^1, \mathcal{S}_2^1, \mathcal{S}_3^1] = [\{A\}, \{B\}, \{C, D\}]$, $[\mathcal{S}_1^2, \mathcal{S}_2^2, \mathcal{S}_3^2] = [\{A\}, \{C\}, \{D\}]$, $[\mathcal{S}_1^3, \mathcal{S}_2^3, \mathcal{S}_3^3] = [\{A\}, \{B, C\}, \{D\}]$. All our technical requirements are satisfied. One possible corresponding syntactic record was already mentioned under the label "contraction" in the definition of semigraphoid. Thus, contraction is a regular inference rule with two antecedents and one consequent. Note that another possible syntactic record can be obtained for example by replacing the first antecedent term by its equivalent version:
$[\langle A, B|DC\rangle \wedge \langle A, C|D\rangle] \rightarrow \langle A, BC|D\rangle.$ ◇

Of course, the remaining semigraphoid schemata are also regular inference rules in the sense of our definition.

Remark Our technical requirements in the above definition anticipate the semantics of the symbols. The symbols from $\mathcal{S}$ are interpreted as (disjoint) subsets of a factor set N and the special symbol $\emptyset$ is reserved for the empty set. Terms are interpreted as elements of $\mathcal{T}(N)$. The third requirement ensures that no term in a syntactic record of an inference rule is an equivalent version of another (different) term. Further requirements avoid redundancy of symbols in $\mathcal{S}$: the fourth one means that no symbol is unused, while the fifth one prevents their doubling, as for example in the "rule": $[\langle A, BE|CD\rangle \wedge \langle A, C|D\rangle] \rightarrow \langle A, EBC|D\rangle$
where the symbol B is doubled by the symbol E.

5.1.2. *Semantics of an inference rule*

Let us consider a regular inference rule α with r antecedents and s consequents. What is its meaning for a fixed nonempty factor set N? A *substitution mapping* (for N) is a mapping m which assigns a set $m(\sigma) \subset N$ to every symbol $\sigma \in \mathcal{S}$ in such a way that:

— $m(\emptyset)$ is the empty set,

— $\{m(\sigma)\,;\,\sigma \in \mathcal{S}\}$ is a disjoint collection of subsets of N,

— $\bigcup_{\sigma \in \mathcal{S}_1^k} m(\sigma) \neq \emptyset$ for every $k = 1, \ldots, r + s$,

— $\bigcup_{\sigma \in \mathcal{S}_2^k} m(\sigma) \neq \emptyset$ for every $k = 1, \ldots, r + s$.

Of course, it may happen that no such substitution mapping exists for a factor set N; for example in case of contraction for N with $\operatorname{card} N = 2$. However, in case such a mapping m exists an *inference instance* of the considered inference rule (induced by m) is $(r + s)$-tuple $[t_1, \ldots, t_{r+s}]$ of elements of $\mathcal{T}(N)$ defined as follows:

$$t_k = \langle \bigcup_{\sigma \in \mathcal{S}_1^k} m(\sigma),\ \bigcup_{\sigma \in \mathcal{S}_2^k} m(\sigma)\ |\ \bigcup_{\sigma \in \mathcal{S}_3^k} m(\sigma)\rangle \quad \text{for } k = 1, \ldots, r + s\,.$$

The $(r+s)$-tuple $[t_1, \ldots, t_r \,|\, t_{r+1}, \ldots, t_{r+s}]$ is formally divided into the r-tuple made of the triplets $t_1, \ldots, t_r$ which are called *antecedents*, and the s-tuple made of the triplets $t_{r+1}, \ldots, t_{r+s}$ which are called *consequents*.

Example 5.2 Let us continue with Example 5.1 and consider contraction and $N = \{1, 2, 3\}$. Put $m(A) = \{1\}$, $m(B) = \{2\}$, $m(C) = \{3\}$, $m(D) = \emptyset$. It is a substitution mapping for N. The corresponding inference instance (induced by m) is then $[t_1, t_2 \,|\, t_3]$ where

$t_1 = \langle\{1\}, \{2\}|\{3\}\rangle$, $\quad t_2 = \langle\{1\}, \{3\}|\emptyset\rangle$, $\quad t_3 = \langle\{1\}, \{2, 3\}|\emptyset\rangle$.

Here t_1, t_2 are the antecedents and t_3 is the consequent. However, there are other inference instances, induced by other possible substitution mappings for N. In this case one finds 5 other ones:

$\tilde{t}_1 = \langle\{1\}, \{3\}|\{2\}\rangle$, $\quad \tilde{t}_2 = \langle\{1\}, \{2\}|\emptyset\rangle$, $\quad \tilde{t}_3 = \langle\{1\}, \{2, 3\}|\emptyset\rangle$,
$\hat{t}_1 = \langle\{2\}, \{1\}|\{3\}\rangle$, $\quad \hat{t}_2 = \langle\{2\}, \{3\}|\emptyset\rangle$, $\quad \hat{t}_3 = \langle\{2\}, \{1, 3\}|\emptyset\rangle$,
$\check{t}_1 = \langle\{2\}, \{3\}|\{1\}\rangle$, $\quad \check{t}_2 = \langle\{2\}, \{1\}|\emptyset\rangle$, $\quad \check{t}_3 = \langle\{2\}, \{1, 3\}|\emptyset\rangle$,
$\bar{t}_1 = \langle\{3\}, \{1\}|\{2\}\rangle$, $\quad \bar{t}_2 = \langle\{3\}, \{2\}|\emptyset\rangle$, $\quad \bar{t}_3 = \langle\{3\}, \{1, 2\}|\emptyset\rangle$,
$\ddot{t}_1 = \langle\{3\}, \{2\}|\{1\}\rangle$, $\quad \ddot{t}_2 = \langle\{3\}, \{1\}|\emptyset\rangle$, $\quad \ddot{t}_3 = \langle\{3\}, \{1, 2\}|\emptyset\rangle$. $\qquad \diamond$

Of course, the number of possible substitution mappings is finite for a fixed regular inference rule and a fixed factor set. Therefore, the number of all inference instances of a regular inference rule for a given factor set is always finite and the following definition is sensible.

Having a fixed factor set N we say that an independency model $\mathcal{I} \subset \mathcal{T}(N)$ is *closed under* a regular inference rule α with r antecedents and s consequents iff for every inference instance $[t_1, \ldots, t_{r+s}] \in \mathcal{T}(N)^{r+s}$ (of α for N) $\{t_1, \ldots, t_r\} \subset \mathcal{I}$ implies $\{t_{r+1}, ..., t_{r+s}\} \cap \mathcal{I} \neq \emptyset$.

Example 5.3 Let us continue with Example 5.2. The independency model $\mathcal{I}$ over $N = \{1, 2, 3\}$ consisting of the triplet $\langle\{1\}, \{2\}|\emptyset\rangle$ only is closed under contraction since no inference instance for N has both antecedents in $\mathcal{I}$. On the other hand, the model $\mathcal{M} = \{\langle\{1\}, \{2\}|\emptyset\rangle, \langle\{1\}, \{3\}|\{2\}\rangle\}$ is not closed under contraction. Indeed, one has $\tilde{t}_1, \tilde{t}_2 \in \mathcal{M}$ but $\tilde{t}_3 \notin \mathcal{M}$ for the inference instance $[\tilde{t}_1, \tilde{t}_2 \,|\, \tilde{t}_3]$ $\qquad \diamond$

5.1.3. *Logical implication of inference rules*

The aim of regular inference rules is to sketch formal properties of independency models, especially probabilistic independency models. In fact, one can have in mind another reasonable class of independency models instead of the class of probabilistic independency models. For example the class of graph-isomorphic independency models [14] or the class of EMVD-models [20, 9] or various classes of possibilistic independency models [1, 6]. Such an approach hides a deeper wish or hope to characterize the respective class

of independency models as the class of those closed under a collection of
regular inference rules. We can speak about the *axiomatic characterization*
of the respective class of independency models.

For example, in the case of probabilistic independency models such a
characterization would make it possible to recognize them without laborious
construction of an inducing probability distribution. Indeed, the process
of verification of whether a given independency model is closed under a
finite number of known inference rules is completely automatic and can be
done by a computer. Of course such a desired collection of inference rules
should be minimal (a finite collection would be an ideal solution). One
needs a criterion for removing superfluous regular inference rules from such
a desired collection. Therefore, we are interested in the following relation
among inference rules.

We say that a collection of regular inference rules Υ *logically implies* a
regular inference ω and write $\Upsilon \models \omega$ if for every (nonempty finite) factor
set N and for every independency model $\mathcal{M}$ over N the following holds:
whenever $\mathcal{M}$ is closed under every inference rule $\upsilon \in \Upsilon$, then $\mathcal{M}$ is closed
under ω.

Usually, an easy sufficient condition for logical implication is (syntactic)
derivability. We give an illustrative example to explain what we have in
mind. We hope that it gives better insight than a pedantic definition, which
would be too complicated.

Example 5.4 Let us consider the following regular inference rule ω with
three antecedents and one consequent:
$[\langle A, B \mid E \rangle \ \wedge \ \langle A, C \mid BE \rangle \ \wedge \ \langle A, D \mid CE \rangle] \ \rightarrow \ \langle A, D \mid E \rangle.$
This inference rule is logically implied by the semigraphoid inference rules.
To show it we construct a special *derivation sequence* of terms over the
corresponding set of symbols $\mathcal{S} = \{A, B, C, D, E\}$. Here is the derivation
sequence:

1. $\langle A, B \mid E \rangle$,

2. $\langle A, C \mid BE \rangle$,

3. $\langle A, D \mid CE \rangle$,

4. $\langle A, BC \mid E \rangle$ is directly derived from 2. and 1. by contraction,

5. $\langle A, C \mid E \rangle$ is directly derived from 4. by decomposition,

6. $\langle A, CD \mid E \rangle$ is directly derived from 3. and 5. by contraction,

7. $\langle A, D \mid E \rangle$ is directly derived from 6. by decomposition.

The last term is the consequent term of ω. Every term in the derivation
sequence is either an antecedent term of ω, or it is "directly derived" from

preceding terms (in the derivation sequence) by virtue of a semigraphoid inference rule.

Now, let us consider a fixed factor set N and a semigraphoid $\mathcal{M} \subset \mathcal{T}(N)$ (i.e. an independency model over N closed under all semigraphoid inference rules). To show that $\mathcal{M}$ is closed under ω let us consider an inference instance $[t_1, t_2, t_3 \mid t_4]$ of ω for N induced by a substitution mapping m. So, we can construct a sequence $u_1, \ldots, u_7$ of elements of $\mathcal{T}(N)$ which "copies" the derivation sequence:

$$u_1 = \langle m(A), m(B) \mid m(E) \rangle \equiv t_1 ,$$

$$u_2 = \langle m(A), m(C) \mid m(B) \cup m(E) \rangle \equiv t_2 ,$$

$$u_3 = \langle m(A), m(D) \mid m(C) \cup m(E) \rangle \equiv t_3 ,$$

$$u_4 = \langle m(A), m(B) \cup m(C) \mid m(E) \rangle ,$$

$$u_5 = \langle m(A), m(C) \mid m(E) \rangle ,$$

$$u_6 = \langle m(A), m(C) \cup m(D) \mid m(E) \rangle ,$$

$$u_7 = \langle m(A), m(D) \mid m(E) \rangle \equiv t_4 .$$

Owing to the fact that $\mathcal{M}$ is closed under every semigraphoid inference rule one can derive from the assumption $\{t_1, t_2, t_3\} \subset \mathcal{M}$ by induction on $j = 1, \ldots, 7$ that $\{u_1, \ldots, u_j\} \subset \mathcal{M}$. Especially, $t_4 \in \mathcal{M}$, which was the desired conclusion. Thus, $\mathcal{M}$ is closed under ω.   ◇

5.1.4. *Pure inference rules*

It may happen that an inference instance of a regular inference rule is trivial in the sense that it has as a consequent one of its antecedents (for example in the case of decomposition for a substitution mapping m with $m(B) = \emptyset$). Thus, we wish to concentrate on a class of "pure" inference rules which have only "informative" inference instances. For technical reasons (which will become clear later - see 5.2.2) we would also like to avoid those inference rules which possibly may have an inference instance whose consequent is the symmetric image of an antecedent, as demonstrated by the following example.

Example 5.5 Let us consider the following regular inference rule:
$[\langle A, BC \mid D \rangle \wedge \langle B, D \mid AC \rangle] \rightarrow \langle B, A \mid D \rangle$.
Take $N = \{1, 2\}$ and put $m(A) = \{1\}$, $m(B) = \{2\}$, $m(C) = \emptyset$, $m(D) = \{3\}$. It induces the inference instance $[t_1, t_2 \mid t_3]$ with $t_1 = \langle \{1\}, \{2\} \mid \{3\} \rangle$, $t_2 = \langle \{2\}, \{3\} \mid \{1\} \rangle$, $t_3 = \langle \{2\}, \{1\} \mid \{3\} \rangle$. Here the consequent t_3 is the symmetric image of the antecedent t_1.   ◇

Thus, we say that a regular inference rule ω is *pure* if there is no inference instance of ω (for arbitrary factor set N) in which a consequent either coincides with an antecedent or with the symmetric image of an antecedent.

Such a definition is not suitable for verification. We need a sufficient condition formulated by means of syntactic concepts from 5.1.1. To formulate it we give two definitions. Suppose that ω is a regular inference rule with a syntactic record having $\mathcal{S}$ as the set of symbols. We say that the symbol sets $\mathcal{K}, \mathcal{L} \subset \mathcal{S}$ are *distinguished* in ω if $\exists\, k \in \{1, \ldots, r+s\}\ \exists\, j \in \{1,2\}\ \ \mathcal{S}_j^k \subset (\mathcal{K} \setminus \mathcal{L}) \cup (\mathcal{L} \setminus \mathcal{K})$. A term $\langle \mathcal{K}_1, \mathcal{K}_2 | \mathcal{K}_3 \rangle$ over $\mathcal{S}$ is *distinguished* in ω from a term $\langle \mathcal{L}_1, \mathcal{L}_2 | \mathcal{L}_3 \rangle$ over $\mathcal{S}$ if $\mathcal{K}_i$ and $\mathcal{L}_i$ are distinguished in ω for some $i = 1, 2, 3$.

Lemma 5.1 *A regular inference rule ω is pure if every consequent term of ω is distinguished in ω both from all antecedent terms of ω and from their symmetric versions.*

Proof. First note the following: whenever symbol sets $\mathcal{K}$ and $\mathcal{L}$ are distinguished in ω, then for every substitution mapping m one has
$$\emptyset \neq m(\mathcal{S}_j^k) \subset m(\mathcal{K} \setminus \mathcal{L}) \cup m(\mathcal{L} \setminus \mathcal{K}) \subset (m(\mathcal{K}) \setminus m(\mathcal{L})) \cup (m(\mathcal{L}) \setminus m(\mathcal{K})),$$
which implies $m(\mathcal{K}) \neq m(\mathcal{L})$. Hence, terms distinguished in ω are transformed to distinct elements of $\mathcal{T}(N)$ by any substitution mapping. Therefore, under the mentioned assumption, no consequent of a respective inference instance can coincide either with an antecedent or with its symmetric image. $\square$

We leave it to the reader to verify by means of Lemma 5.1 that contraction is a pure inference rule. On the other hand one can easily see that decomposition and weak union are not pure rules.

5.2. PROBABILISTICALLY SOUND INFERENCE RULES

We say that a regular inference rule ω is *probabilistically sound* if every probabilistic independency model is closed under ω.

That means, every probabilistically sound inference rule expresses a formal property which is shared by all probabilistic independency models. Is it difficult to verify probabilistic soundness of a given regular inference rule? The multiinformation function is a good tool for this purpose, although perhaps not universal. In the effort to characterize all probabilistic independency models over four factors [10, 11] a lot of probabilistically sound inference rules were found whose soundness was not verified with help of the multiinformation function. However, it has appeared lately that at least some of them can be regarded as a consequence of deeper properties of the multiinformation function, namely of certain "conditional" inequalities for the multiinformation (or entropic) function [27, 12]. Thus, the question whether every probabilistically sound inference rule can be derived by means of the multiinformation function remains open. However, to support our arguments about its usefulness we give an illustrative example. We believe that an example is more didactic than a technical description of the method.

Example 5.6 To show the probabilistic soundness of weak union one has to verify for arbitrary factor set N, for any probability distribution P over N, and for any collection of disjoint sets $A, B, C, D \subset N$ which are nonempty with the possible exceptions of C and D, that

$$A \perp\!\!\!\perp BC|D\,(P) \;\Rightarrow\; A \perp\!\!\!\perp B|CD\,(P)\,.$$

The assumption $A \perp\!\!\!\perp BC|D\,(P)$ can be rewritten by Consequence 2.1(b) and Lemma 2.3 in terms of the multiinformation function M induced by the distribution P:

$$0 = M(ABCD) + M(D) - M(AD) - M(BCD)\,.$$

Then one can "artificially" add and subtract the terms $M(CD) - M(ACD)$ and by Lemma 2.3 derive:

$$
\begin{aligned}
0 &= \{M(ABCD) + M(CD) - M(ACD) - M(BCD)\} \\
&\quad + \{M(ACD) + M(D) - M(AD) - M(CD)\} \\
&= I(A;B|CD) + I(A;C|D)\,.
\end{aligned}
$$

By Consequence 2.1(a) both $I(A;B|CD)$ and $I(A;C|D)$ are nonnegative, and therefore they vanish! But that implies by Consequence 2.1(b) that $A \perp\!\!\!\perp B|CD\,(P)$.   ◇

Note that one can easily see using the method shown in the preceding example that every semigraphoid inference rule is probabilistically sound.

5.2.1. *Redundant rules*
However, some probabilistically sound inference rules are superfluous for the purposes of providing an axiomatic characterization of probabilistic independency models. The following consequence follows directly from given definitions.

Consequence 5.1 *If ω is a regular inference rule which is logically implied by a collection of probabilistically sound inference rules, then ω is probabilistically sound.*

A clear example of a superfluous rule is an inference rule with redundant antecedent terms.

Example 5.7 The inference rule
$$[\langle A, BC \,|\, D\rangle \,\wedge\, \langle C, B \,|\, A\rangle] \,\rightarrow\, \langle A, B \,|\, CD\rangle$$
is a probabilistically sound regular inference rule. But it can be ignored since it is evidently logically implied by weak union.   ◇

Therefore we should limit ourselves to "minimal" probabilistically sound inference rules, i.e. to probabilistically sound inference rules such that no antecedent term can be removed without violating the probabilistic soundness of the resulting reduced inference rule. However, even such a rule can be logically implied by probabilistically sound rules with fewer antecedents. We need the following auxiliary construction of a probability distribution to give an easy example.

Construction B Supposing $A \subset N$, card $A \geq 2$, there exists a probability distribution P over N such that

$$M(B \,\|\, P) = \max\{0, \operatorname{card}(A \cap B) - 1\} \cdot \ln 2 \quad \text{for } B \subset N.$$

Proof: Let us put $\mathbf{X}_i = \{0, 1\}$ for $i \in A$, $\mathbf{X}_i = \{0\}$ for $i \in N \setminus A$. Define P on $\mathbf{X}_N$ as follows:

$$P([x_i]_{i \in N}) = \tfrac{1}{2} \qquad \text{whenever } [\forall i, j \in A \ \ x_i = x_j],$$
$$P([x_i]_{i \in N}) = 0 \qquad \text{otherwise.}$$

                                                                                      □

Example 5.8 We have already verified earlier that the inference rule $\boldsymbol{\omega}$ from Example 5.4 is logically implied by the semigraphoid inference rules. Hence, $\boldsymbol{\omega}$ is probabilistically sound by Consequence 5.1.

Let us consider a "reduced" inference rule made by a removal of an antecedent term:
$$[\langle A, B|E\rangle \,\wedge\, \langle A, C|BE\rangle] \,\rightarrow\, \langle A, D|E\rangle.$$
This is a regular inference rule with 2 antecedents and one consequent. To disprove its probabilistic soundness one has to find a probabilistic independency model over a factor set N which is not closed under this rule. Use Construction B with $N = \{1, 2, 3, 4\}$ and $A = \{1, 4\}$. By Consequence 2.1 one verifies that $\{1\} \perp\!\!\!\perp \{2\}|\emptyset\,(P)$, $\{1\} \perp\!\!\!\perp \{3\}|\{2\}\,(P)$, but $\neg[\{1\} \perp\!\!\!\perp \{4\}|\emptyset\,(P)]$ for the constructed distribution P. As concerns an alternative "reduced" inference rule
$$[\langle A, B\,|\,E\rangle \,\wedge\, \langle A, D\,|\,CE\rangle] \,\rightarrow\, \langle A, D\,|\,E\rangle$$
use Construction B with $A = \{1, 3, 4\}$ and a distribution P over N such

that $\{1\} \perp\!\!\!\perp \{2\}|\emptyset\,(P)$, $\{1\} \perp\!\!\!\perp \{4\}|\{3\}\,(P)$, but $\neg[\{1\} \perp\!\!\!\perp \{4\}|\emptyset\,(P)]$. As concerns the third possible "reduced" inference rule
$$[\langle A, C\,|\,BE\rangle \wedge \langle A, D\,|\,CE\rangle] \rightarrow \langle A, D\,|\,E\rangle$$
use again Construction B with $A = \{1, 2, 3, 4\}$. Thus, one has a distribution P with $\{1\} \perp\!\!\!\perp \{3\}|\{2\}\,(P)$, $\{1\} \perp\!\!\!\perp \{4\}|\{3\}\,(P)$, but $\neg[\{1\} \perp\!\!\!\perp \{4\}|\emptyset\,(P)]$. $\Diamond$

5.2.2. *Perfect rules*

Thus, one should search for conditions which ensure that an inference rule is not logically implied by probabilistically sound inference rules with fewer antecedents. We propose the following condition.

We say that a probabilistically sound regular inference rule with r antecedents (and s consequents) is *perfect* if there exists a factor set N and an inference instance $[t_1, \ldots, t_r\,|\,t_{r+1}, \ldots, t_{r+s}] \in \mathcal{T}(N)^{r+s}$ such that the symmetric closure of every proper subset of $\{t_1, \ldots, t_r\}$ is a probabilistic independency model over N.

Lemma 5.2 *Let ω be a perfect, probabilistically sound, pure inference rule with r antecedents, $r \geq 1$. Then there exists a factor set N and an independency model $\mathcal{M}$ over N such that*

- *$\mathcal{M}$ is closed under every probabilistically sound regular inference rule with at most $r - 1$ antecedents,*

- *$\mathcal{M}$ is not closed under ω.*

Proof: Let $[t_1, \ldots, t_{r+s}] \in \mathcal{T}(N)$ be the inference instance of ω mentioned in the definition of perfectness. Define $\mathcal{M} \subset \mathcal{T}(N)$ as the symmetric closure of the set of antecedents $\{t_1, \ldots, t_r\}$. Let us show that $\mathcal{M}$ is closed under all probabilistically sound inference rules with at most $r - 1$ antecedents.

Suppose for a contradiction that $[\tilde{t}_1, \ldots, \tilde{t}_{\tilde{r}+\tilde{s}}] \in \mathcal{T}(N)^{\tilde{r}+\tilde{s}}$ is an inference instance of such an inference rule υ (with $\tilde{r} \leq r - 1$ antecedents and $\tilde{s}$ consequents) for N with $\{\tilde{t}_1, \ldots, \tilde{t}_{\tilde{r}}\} \subset \mathcal{M}$ and $\{\tilde{t}_{\tilde{r}+1}, \ldots, \tilde{t}_{\tilde{r}+\tilde{s}}\} \cap \mathcal{M} = \emptyset$. However, owing to the fact that $\tilde{r} < r$ and the assumption (of perfectness) the symmetric closure $\mathcal{I}$ of $\{\tilde{t}_1, \ldots, \tilde{t}_{\tilde{r}}\}$ is a probabilistic independency model. So, (by the definition of probabilistic soundness) $\mathcal{I}$ is closed under υ, and therefore $\{\tilde{t}_{\tilde{r}+1}, \ldots, \tilde{t}_{\tilde{r}+\tilde{s}}\} \cap \mathcal{I} \neq \emptyset$ which contradicts the fact that $\mathcal{I} \subset \mathcal{M}$. Therefore $\mathcal{M}$ has to be closed under any such inference rule υ.

Owing to the assumption that the inference rule ω is pure by definition one has $\{t_{r+1}, \ldots, t_{r+s}\} \cap \mathcal{M} = \emptyset$. Since $\mathcal{M}$ was defined to contain $\{t_1, \ldots, t_r\}$, it is not closed under ω. $\qquad\square$

The preceding lemma implies the following consequence with help of the definition of logical implication.

Consequence 5.2 *No perfect probabilistically sound pure inference rule is logically implied by a collection of probabilistically sound inference rules with fewer antecedents.*

Contraction is an example of a perfect pure regular inference rule.

5.3. NO FINITE AXIOMATIC CHARACTERIZATION

5.3.1. *Method of the proof*

It is clear in the light of Consequence 5.2 how to disprove the existence of a finite system of regular inference rules characterizing probabilistic independency models.

Lemma 5.3 *Let us suppose that we have found for every $r \geq 3$ a perfect, probabilistically sound, pure inference rule with at least r antecedents. Then every system Υ of regular inference rules characterizing probabilistic independency models as independency models closed under rules in Υ is infinite.*

Proof: Let us suppose for a contradiction that there exists a finite system Υ of regular inference rules such that for every factor set N an independency model $\mathcal{M} \subset \mathcal{T}(N)$ is a probabilistic independency model (over N) iff it is closed under all rules in Υ. Hence, every rule in Υ must be probabilistically sound. We choose $\tilde{r} \geq 3$ which exceeds the maximal number of antecedents of rules in Υ. According to the assumption there exists a perfect, probabilistically sound, pure inference rule ω with r antecedents, where $r \geq \tilde{r}$.

By Lemma 5.2 we find a factor set N and an independency model $\mathcal{M}$ over N which is closed under every probabilistically sound inference rule with at most $r - 1$ antecedents but not under ω. Since every inference rule from Υ has at most $r - 1$ antecedents, $\mathcal{M}$ is closed under every inference rule from Υ. Therefore $\mathcal{M}$ is a probabilistic independency model over N. However, $\mathcal{M}$ is not closed under ω which contradicts the fact that ω is probabilistically sound. $\square$

Thus, we need to verify the assumptions of the preceding lemma. Let us consider for each $n \geq 3$ the following inference rule $\gamma(n)$ with n antecedents and one consequent:

$$[\langle A, B_1 | B_2 \rangle \wedge \ldots \wedge \langle A, B_{n-1} | B_n \rangle \wedge \langle A, B_n | B_1 \rangle] \rightarrow \langle A, B_2 | B_1 \rangle . \quad \gamma(n)$$

It is no problem to verify that each $\gamma(n)$ is indeed a regular inference rule. Moreover, one can verify easily using Lemma 5.1 that each $\gamma(n)$ is a pure rule.

5.3.2. *Soundness*

To show their probabilistic soundness we use the properties of the multiinformation function.

Lemma 5.4 *Each above mentioned rule $\gamma(n)$ is probabilistically sound.*

Proof: Let us fix $n \geq 3$. We have to show for arbitrary factor set N, any distribution P over N, and any collection of nonempty disjoint subsets $A, B_1, \ldots, B_n \subset N$ that (under convention $B_{n+1} \equiv B_1$) the assumption

$$[\forall j = 1, \ldots, n \quad A \perp\!\!\!\perp B_j | B_{j+1} \, (P) \,]$$

implies that $A \perp\!\!\!\perp B_2 | B_1 \, (P)$. By Consequence 2.1(b) with Lemma 2.3 one has for every $j = 1, \ldots, n$ (M is the corresponding multiinformation function):

$$M(AB_j B_{j+1}) + M(B_{j+1}) - M(AB_{j+1}) - M(B_j B_{j+1}) = 0 \, .$$

Hence we get by summing, the above mentioned convention and Lemma 2.3:

$$
\begin{aligned}
0 &= \sum_{j=1}^{n} \{ \, M(AB_j B_{j+1}) + M(B_{j+1}) - M(AB_{j+1}) - M(B_j B_{j+1}) \, \} \\
&= \sum_{j=1}^{n} M(AB_j B_{j+1}) + \sum_{j=1}^{n} M(B_{j+1}) - \sum_{j=1}^{n} M(AB_{j+1}) - \sum_{j=1}^{n} M(B_j B_{j+1}) \\
&= \sum_{j=1}^{n} M(AB_j B_{j+1}) + \sum_{j=1}^{n} M(B_j) - \sum_{j=1}^{n} M(AB_j) - \sum_{j=1}^{n} M(B_j B_{j+1}) \\
&= \sum_{j=1}^{n} \{ \, M(AB_j B_{j+1}) + M(B_j) - M(AB_j) - M(B_j B_{j+1}) \, \} \\
&= \sum_{j=1}^{n} I(A; B_{j+1} | B_j) \, .
\end{aligned}
$$

Owing to Consequence 2.1(a) necessarily $I(A; B_{j+1} | B_j \, \| \, P) = 0$ for every $j = 1, \ldots, n$. Hence by Consequence 2.1(b) $A \perp\!\!\!\perp B_2 | B_1 \, (P)$. $\square$

5.3.3. *Perfectness*

To verify perfectness of a rule one needs some method for showing that an independency model is a probabilistic independency model. We again use Constructions A and B.

Lemma 5.5 *Suppose that $N = \{0, 1, \ldots, n\}$, $n \geq 3$ and $\mathcal{M} \subset \mathcal{T}(N)$ be the symmetric closure of the set $\{ \langle \, \{0\}, \{i\} \, | \, \{i+1\} \, \rangle; \; i = 1, \ldots, n-1 \}$. Then $\mathcal{M}$ is a probabilistic independency model over N.*

Proof: It suffices to find a probabilistic independency model $\mathcal{M}_t$ with $\mathcal{M} \subset \mathcal{M}_t$ and $t \notin \mathcal{M}_t$ for every $t \in \mathcal{T}(N) \setminus \mathcal{M}$. Indeed, then $\mathcal{M} \equiv \bigcap_{t \in \mathcal{T}(N) \setminus \mathcal{M}} \mathcal{M}_t$, and by Lemma 2.1 $\mathcal{M}$ is a probabilistic independency model.

Moreover, one can limit oneself to the triplets of the form $\langle a, b | C \rangle \in \mathcal{T}(N) \setminus \mathcal{M}$ where a, b are singletons. Indeed, for a given general $\langle A, B | C \rangle \in \mathcal{T}(N) \setminus \mathcal{M}$ choose $a \in A$, $b \in B$ and find the respective probabilistic independency model $\mathcal{M}_t$ for $t = \langle a, b | C \rangle$. Since $\mathcal{M}_t$ is a semigraphoid, $t \notin \mathcal{M}_t$ implies $\langle A, B | C \rangle \notin \mathcal{M}_t$.

In the sequel we distinguish 5 cases for a given fixed $\langle a, b | C \rangle \in \mathcal{T}(N) \setminus \mathcal{M}$. Each case requires a different construction of the respective probabilistic independency model $\mathcal{M}_t$, that is a different construction of a probability distribution P over N such that $\{0\} \perp\!\!\!\perp \{i\} \mid \{i+1\} \, (P)$ for $i = 1, \ldots, n-1$, but $\neg [\, \{a\} \perp\!\!\!\perp \{b\} \mid C \, (P) \,]$. One can verify these statements about P through the multiinformation function induced by P. If the multiinformation function is known (as it is in the case of our constructions) one can use Consequence 2.1(b) and Lemma 2.3 for this purpose. We leave this to the reader. Here is the list of cases.

I. $\forall i = 1, \ldots, n-1 \quad \{a, b\} \neq \{0, i\}$ (C arbitrary).
   In this case use Construction A where $A = \{a, b\}$.

II. $[\exists j \in \{1, \ldots, n-1\} \quad \{a, b\} = \{0, j\}]$ and $C \setminus \{j-1, j+1\} \neq \emptyset$.
   In this case choose $r \in C \setminus \{j-1, j+1\}$ and use Construction A where $A = \{0, j, r\}$.

III. $[\exists j \in \{2, \ldots, n-1\} \quad \{a, b\} = \{0, j\}]$ and $C = \{j-1, j+1\}$.
   In this case use Construction A where $A = \{0, j-1, j, j+1\}$.

IV. $[\exists j \in \{2, \ldots, n-1\} \quad \{a, b\} = \{0, j\}]$ and $C = \{j-1\}$.
   Use Construction B where $A = \{0, j, j+1, \ldots, n\}$.

V. $[\exists j \in \{1, \ldots, n-1\} \quad \{a, b\} = \{0, j\}]$ and $C = \emptyset$.
   Use Construction B where $A = N$.

$\square$

Consequence 5.3 *Each above mentioned rule $\gamma(n)$ is perfect.*

Proof: Let us fix $n \geq 3$, put $N = \{0, 1, \ldots, n\}$ and $t_j = \langle \{0\}, \{j\} | \{j+1\} \rangle$ for $j = 1, \ldots, n$ (convention $n + 1 \equiv 1$), $t_{n+1} = \langle \{0\}, \{2\} | \{1\} \rangle$. Evidently, $[t_1, \ldots, t_n \mid t_{n+1}]$ is an inference instance of $\gamma(n)$. To show that the symmetric closure of every proper subset of $\{t_1, \ldots, t_n\}$ is a probabilistic independency model it suffices to verify it only for every subset of cardinality $n - 1$ (use Lemma 2.1). However, owing to possible cyclic re-indexing of N it suffices to prove (only) that the symmetric closure $\mathcal{M}$ of $\{t_1, \ldots, t_{n-1}\}$ is a probabilistic independency model. This follows from Lemma 5.5. $\square$

Proposition 5.1 *There is no finite system* Υ *of regular inference rules characterizing probabilistic independency models as independency models closed under rules in* Υ .

Proof. An easy consequence of Lemmas 5.3, 5.4 and Consequence 5.3.   □

Conclusions

Let us summarize the paper. Several results support our claim that conditional mutual information $I(A; B|C)$ is a good measure of stochastic conditional dependence between random vectors ξ_A and ξ_B given ξ_C. The value of $I(A; B|C)$ is always nonnegative and vanishes iff ξ_A is conditionally independent of ξ_B given ξ_C. On the other hand, the upper bound for $I(A; B|C)$ is $\min\{H(A|C), H(B|C)\}$, and the value $H(A|C)$ is achieved just in case ξ_A is a function of ξ_{BC}. A transformation of ξ_{ABC} which saves ξ_{AC} and ξ_{BC} increases the value of $I(A; B|C)$. On the other hand, if ξ_A is transformed while ξ_{BC} is saved, then $I(A; B|C)$ decreases. Note that the paper [29] deals with a more practical use of conditional mutual information: it is applied to the problem of finding relevant factors in medical decision-making.

Special level-specific measures of dependence were introduced. While the value $M(A)$ of the multiinformation function is viewed as a measure of global stochastic dependence within $[\xi_i]_{i\in A}$, the value of $\lambda(r, A)$ (for $1 \le r \le \operatorname{card} A-1$) is interpreted as a measure of the strength of dependence of level r among variables $[\xi_i]_{i\in A}$. The value of $\lambda(r, A)$ is always nonnegative and vanishes iff ξ_i is conditionally independent of ξ_j given ξ_K for arbitrary distinct $i, j \in A$, $K \subset A$, $\operatorname{card} K = r-1$. And of course, the sum of $\lambda(r, A)$s is just $M(A)$. Note that measures $\lambda(r, A)$ are certain multiples of Han's [8] measures of multivariate symmetric correlation.

Finally, we have used the multiinformation function as a tool to show that conditional independence models have no finite axiomatic characterization. A didactic proof of this result, originally shown in [20], is given. We analyze thoroughly syntax and semantics of inference rule schemata (= axioms) which characterize formal properties of conditional independence models. The result of the analysis is that two principal features of such schemata are pointed out: the inference rules should be (probabilistically) *sound* and *perfect*. To derive the nonaxiomatizability result one has to find an infinite collection of sound and perfect inference rules. In the verification of both soundness and perfectness the multiinformation function proved to be an effective tool.

Let us add a remark concerning the concept of a perfect rule. We have used this concept only in the proof of the nonaxiomatizability result. However, our aim is a bit deeper, in fact. We (vaguely) guess that probabilistic independency models have a certain uniquely determined "minimal" ax-iomatic characterization, which is of course infinite. In particular, we con-jecture that the semigraphoid inference rules and perfect probabilistically sound pure inference rules form together the desired axiomatic characteri-zation of probabilistic independency models.

Acknowledgments

We would like to express our gratitude to our colleague František Matúš who directed our attention to the paper [8]. We also thank to both review-ers for their valuable comments and correction of grammatical errors. This work was partially supported by the grant VŠ 96008 of the Ministry of Ed-ucation of the Czech Republic and by the grant 201/98/0478 "Conditional independence structures: information theoretical approach" of the Grant Agency of Czech Republic.

References

1. de Campos, L.M. (1995) Independence relationships in possibility theory and their application to learning in belief networks, in G. Della Riccia, R. Kruse and R. Viertl (eds.), *Mathematical and Statistical Methods in Artificial Intelligence*, Springer-Verlag, 119–130.
2. Csiszár, I. (1975) *I*-divergence geometry of probability distributions and minimazi-tion problems, *Ann. Probab.*, **3**, 146–158.
3. Cover, T.M., and Thomas, J.A. (1991) *Elements of Information Theory*, John Wiley, New York.
4. Darroch, J.N., Lauritzen, S.L., and Speed, T.P. (1980) Markov fields and log-linear interaction models for contingency tables, *Ann. Statist.*, **8**, 522–539.
5. Dawid, A.P. (1979) Conditional independence in statistical theory, *J. Roy. Stat. Soc. B*, **41**, 1–31.
6. Fonck P. (1994) Conditional independence in possibility theory, in R.L. de Mantaras and D. Poole (eds.), *Uncertainty in Artificial Intelligence: proceedings of the 10th conference*, Morgan Kaufman, San Francisco, 221–226.
7. Gallager, R.G. (1968) *Information Theory and Reliable Communication*, John Wi-ley, New York.
8. Han T.S. (1978) Nonnegative entropy of multivariate symmetric correlations, *Infor-mation and Control*, **36**, 113–156.
9. Malvestuto, F.M. (1983) Theory of random observables in relational data bases, *Inform. Systems*, **8**, 281–289.
10. Matúš, F., and Studený, M. (1995) Conditional independencies among four random variables I., *Combinatorics, Probability and Computing*, **4**, 269–278.
11. Matúš, F. (1995) Conditional independencies among four random variables II., *Com-binatorics, Probability and Computing*, **4**, 407–417.
12. Matúš, F. (1998) Conditional independencies among four random variables III., submitted to *Combinatorics, Probability and Computing*.
13. Pearl, J., and Paz, A. (1987) Graphoids: graph-based logic for reasoning about relevance relations, in B. Du Boulay, D. Hogg and L. Steels (eds.), *Advances in Artificial Intelligence - II*, North Holland, Amsterdam, pp. 357–363.
14. Pearl, J. (1988) *Probabilistic Reasoning in Intelligent Systems: networks of plausible inference*, Morgan Kaufmann, San Mateo.

15. Perez, A. (1977) ε-admissible simplifications of the dependence structure of a set of random variables, *Kybernetika*, **13**, 439–449.
16. Rényi, A. (1959) On measures of dependence, *Acta Math. Acad. Sci. Hung.*, **10**, 441–451.
17. Spohn, W. (1980) Stochastic independence, causal independence and shieldability, *J. Philos. Logic*, **9**, 73–99.
18. Studený, M. (1987) Asymptotic behaviour of empirical multiinformation, *Kybernetika*, **23**, 124–135.
19. Studený, M. (1989) Multiinformation and the problem of characterization of conditional independence relations, *Problems of Control and Information Theory*, **18**, 3–16.
20. Studený, M. (1992) Conditional independence relations have no finite complete characterization, in S. Kubík and J.Á. Víšek (eds.), *Information Theory, Statistical Decision Functions and Random Processes: proceedings of the 11th Prague conference - B*, Kluwer, Dordrecht (also Academia, Prague), pp. 377–396.
21. Studený, M. (1987) The concept of multiinformation in probabilistic decision-making (in Czech), PhD. thesis, Institute of Information Theory and Automation, Czechoslovak Academy of Sciences, Prague.
22. Vejnarová, J. (1994) A few remarks on measures of uncertainty in Dempster-Shafer theory, *Int. J. General Systems*, **22**, pp. 233–243.
23. Vejnarová J. (1997) Measures of uncertainty and independence concept in different calculi, accepted to *EPIA'97*.
24. Watanabe, S. (1960) Information theoretical analysis of multivariate correlation, *IBM Journal of research and development*, **4**, pp. 66–81.
25. Watanabe, S. (1969) *Knowing and Guessing: a qualitative study of inference and information*, John Wiley, New York.
26. Xiang, Y., Wong, S.K.M., and Cercone, N. (1996) Critical remarks on single link search in learning belief networks, in E. Horvitz and F. Jensen (eds.), *Uncertainty in Artificial Intelligence: proceedings of 12th conference*, Morgan Kaufman, San Francisco, 564–571.
27. Zhang, Z., and Yeung, R. (1997) A non-Shannon type conditional information inequality, to appear in *IEEE Transactions on Information Theory*.
28. Zvárová, J. (1974) On measures of statistical dependence, *Časopis pro pěstování matematiky*, **99**, 15–29.
29. Zvárová, J., and Studený, M. (1997) Information-theoretical approach to constitution and reduction of medical data, *Int. J. Medical Informatics*, **45**, 65–74.

PART III : FOUNDATIONS FOR LEARNING

A TUTORIAL ON LEARNING WITH BAYESIAN NETWORKS

DAVID HECKERMAN
Microsoft Research, Bldg 9S
Redmond WA, 98052-6399
heckerma@microsoft.com

Abstract. A Bayesian network is a graphical model that encodes probabilistic relationships among variables of interest. When used in conjunction with statistical techniques, the graphical model has several advantages for data analysis. One, because the model encodes dependencies among all variables, it readily handles situations where some data entries are missing. Two, a Bayesian network can be used to learn causal relationships, and hence can be used to gain understanding about a problem domain and to predict the consequences of intervention. Three, because the model has both a causal and probabilistic semantics, it is an ideal representation for combining prior knowledge (which often comes in causal form) and data. Four, Bayesian statistical methods in conjunction with Bayesian networks offer an efficient and principled approach for avoiding the overfitting of data. In this paper, we discuss methods for constructing Bayesian networks from prior knowledge and summarize Bayesian statistical methods for using data to improve these models. With regard to the latter task, we describe methods for learning both the parameters and structure of a Bayesian network, including techniques for learning with incomplete data. In addition, we relate Bayesian-network methods for learning to techniques for supervised and unsupervised learning. We illustrate the graphical-modeling approach using a real-world case study.

1. Introduction

A Bayesian network is a graphical model for probabilistic relationships among a set of variables. Over the last decade, the Bayesian network has become a popular representation for encoding uncertain expert knowledge in expert systems (Heckerman et al., 1995a). More recently, researchers

301

have developed methods for learning Bayesian networks from data. The techniques that have been developed are new and still evolving, but they have been shown to be remarkably effective for some data-analysis problems.

In this paper, we provide a tutorial on Bayesian networks and associated Bayesian techniques for extracting and encoding knowledge from data. There are numerous representations available for data analysis, including rule bases, decision trees, and artificial neural networks; and there are many techniques for data analysis such as density estimation, classification, regression, and clustering. So what do Bayesian networks and Bayesian methods have to offer? There are at least four answers.

One, Bayesian networks can readily handle incomplete data sets. For example, consider a classification or regression problem where two of the explanatory or input variables are strongly anti-correlated. This correlation is not a problem for standard supervised learning techniques, provided all inputs are measured in every case. When one of the inputs is not observed, however, most models will produce an inaccurate prediction, because they do not encode the correlation between the input variables. Bayesian networks offer a natural way to encode such dependencies.

Two, Bayesian networks allow one to learn about causal relationships. Learning about causal relationships are important for at least two reasons. The process is useful when we are trying to gain understanding about a problem domain, for example, during exploratory data analysis. In addition, knowledge of causal relationships allows us to make predictions in the presence of interventions. For example, a marketing analyst may want to know whether or not it is worthwhile to increase exposure of a particular advertisement in order to increase the sales of a product. To answer this question, the analyst can determine whether or not the advertisement is a cause for increased sales, and to what degree. The use of Bayesian networks helps to answer such questions even when no experiment about the effects of increased exposure is available.

Three, Bayesian networks in conjunction with Bayesian statistical techniques facilitate the combination of domain knowledge and data. Anyone who has performed a real-world analysis knows the importance of prior or domain knowledge, especially when data is scarce or expensive. The fact that some commercial systems (i.e., expert systems) can be built from prior knowledge alone is a testament to the power of prior knowledge. Bayesian networks have a causal semantics that makes the encoding of causal prior knowledge particularly straightforward. In addition, Bayesian networks encode the strength of causal relationships with probabilities. Consequently, prior knowledge and data can be combined with well-studied techniques from Bayesian statistics.

Four, Bayesian methods in conjunction with Bayesian networks and other types of models offers an efficient and principled approach for avoiding the over fitting of data. As we shall see, there is no need to hold out some of the available data for testing. Using the Bayesian approach, models can be "smoothed" in such a way that all available data can be used for training.

This tutorial is organized as follows. In Section 2, we discuss the Bayesian interpretation of probability and review methods from Bayesian statistics for combining prior knowledge with data. In Section 3, we describe Bayesian networks and discuss how they can be constructed from prior knowledge alone. In Section 4, we discuss algorithms for probabilistic inference in a Bayesian network. In Sections 5 and 6, we show how to learn the probabilities in a fixed Bayesian-network structure, and describe techniques for handling incomplete data including Monte-Carlo methods and the Gaussian approximation. In Sections 7 through 12, we show how to learn both the probabilities and structure of a Bayesian network. Topics discussed include methods for assessing priors for Bayesian-network structure and parameters, and methods for avoiding the overfitting of data including Monte-Carlo, Laplace, BIC, and MDL approximations. In Sections 13 and 14, we describe the relationships between Bayesian-network techniques and methods for supervised and unsupervised learning. In Section 15, we show how Bayesian networks facilitate the learning of causal relationships. In Section 16, we illustrate techniques discussed in the tutorial using a real-world case study. In Section 17, we give pointers to software and additional literature.

2. The Bayesian Approach to Probability and Statistics

To understand Bayesian networks and associated learning techniques, it is important to understand the Bayesian approach to probability and statistics. In this section, we provide an introduction to the Bayesian approach for those readers familiar only with the classical view.

In a nutshell, the Bayesian probability of an event x is a person's *degree of belief* in that event. Whereas a classical probability is a physical property of the world (e.g., the probability that a coin will land heads), a Bayesian probability is a property of the person who assigns the probability (e.g., your degree of belief that the coin will land heads). To keep these two concepts of probability distinct, we refer to the classical probability of an event as the true or physical probability of that event, and refer to a degree of belief in an event as a Bayesian or personal probability. Alternatively, when the meaning is clear, we refer to a Bayesian probability simply as a probability.

One important difference between physical probability and personal probability is that, to measure the latter, we do not need repeated trials. For example, imagine the repeated tosses of a sugar cube onto a wet surface. Every time the cube is tossed, its dimensions will change slightly. Thus, although the classical statistician has a hard time measuring the probability that the cube will land with a particular face up, the Bayesian simply restricts his or her attention to the next toss, and assigns a probability. As another example, consider the question: What is the probability that the Chicago Bulls will win the championship in 2001? Here, the classical statistician must remain silent, whereas the Bayesian can assign a probability (and perhaps make a bit of money in the process).

One common criticism of the Bayesian definition of probability is that probabilities seem arbitrary. Why should degrees of belief satisfy the rules of probability? On what scale should probabilities be measured? In particular, it makes sense to assign a probability of one (zero) to an event that will (not) occur, but what probabilities do we assign to beliefs that are not at the extremes? Not surprisingly, these questions have been studied intensely.

With regards to the first question, many researchers have suggested different sets of properties that should be satisfied by degrees of belief (e.g., Ramsey 1931, Cox 1946, Good 1950, Savage 1954, DeFinetti 1970). It turns out that each set of properties leads to the same rules: the rules of probability. Although each set of properties is in itself compelling, the fact that different sets all lead to the rules of probability provides a particularly strong argument for using probability to measure beliefs.

The answer to the question of scale follows from a simple observation: people find it fairly easy to say that two events are equally likely. For example, imagine a simplified wheel of fortune having only two regions (shaded and not shaded), such as the one illustrated in Figure 1. Assuming everything about the wheel as symmetric (except for shading), you should conclude that it is equally likely for the wheel to stop in any one position. From this judgment and the sum rule of probability (probabilities of mutually exclusive and collectively exhaustive sum to one), it follows that your probability that the wheel will stop in the shaded region is the percent area of the wheel that is shaded (in this case, 0.3).

This *probability wheel* now provides a reference for measuring your probabilities of other events. For example, what is your probability that Al Gore will run on the Democratic ticket in 2000? First, ask yourself the question: Is it more likely that Gore will run or that the wheel when spun will stop in the shaded region? If you think that it is more likely that Gore will run, then imagine another wheel where the shaded region is larger. If you think that it is more likely that the wheel will stop in the shaded region, then imagine another wheel where the shaded region is smaller. Now, repeat this process until you think that Gore running and the wheel stopping in the

Figure 1.   The probability wheel: a tool for assessing probabilities.

shaded region are equally likely. At this point, your probability that Gore will run is just the percent surface area of the shaded area on the wheel.

In general, the process of measuring a degree of belief is commonly referred to as a *probability assessment*. The technique for assessment that we have just described is one of many available techniques discussed in the Management Science, Operations Research, and Psychology literature. One problem with probability assessment that is addressed in this literature is that of precision. Can one really say that his or her probability for event x is 0.601 and not 0.599? In most cases, no. Nonetheless, in most cases, probabilities are used to make decisions, and these decisions are not sensitive to small variations in probabilities. Well-established practices of *sensitivity analysis* help one to know when additional precision is unnecessary (e.g., Howard and Matheson, 1983). Another problem with probability assessment is that of accuracy. For example, recent experiences or the way a question is phrased can lead to assessments that do not reflect a person's true beliefs (Tversky and Kahneman, 1974). Methods for improving accuracy can be found in the decision-analysis literature (e.g, Spetzler et al. (1975)).

Now let us turn to the issue of learning with data. To illustrate the Bayesian approach, consider a common thumbtack—one with a round, flat head that can be found in most supermarkets. If we throw the thumbtack up in the air, it will come to rest either on its point (*heads*) or on its head (*tails*).[1] Suppose we flip the thumbtack $N + 1$ times, making sure that the physical properties of the thumbtack and the conditions under which it is flipped remain stable over time. From the first N observations, we want to determine the probability of heads on the $N + 1$th toss.

In the classical analysis of this problem, we assert that there is some physical probability of heads, which is unknown. We *estimate* this physical probability from the N observations using criteria such as low bias and low variance. We then use this estimate as our probability for heads on the $N + 1$th toss. In the Bayesian approach, we also assert that there is

---

[1]This example is taken from Howard (1970).

some physical probability of heads, but we encode our uncertainty about this physical probability using (Bayesian) probabilities, and use the rules of probability to compute our probability of heads on the $N + 1$th toss.[2]

To examine the Bayesian analysis of this problem, we need some notation. We denote a variable by an upper-case letter (e.g., X, Y, X_i, Θ), and the state or value of a corresponding variable by that same letter in lower case (e.g., x, y, x_i, θ). We denote a set of variables by a bold-face upper-case letter (e.g., $\mathbf{X}, \mathbf{Y}, \mathbf{X}_i$). We use a corresponding bold-face lower-case letter (e.g., $\mathbf{x}, \mathbf{y}, \mathbf{x}_i$) to denote an assignment of state or value to each variable in a given set. We say that variable set $\mathbf{X}$ is in *configuration* $\mathbf{x}$. We use $p(X = x|\xi)$ (or $p(x|\xi)$ as a shorthand) to denote the probability that $X = x$ of a person with state of information ξ. We also use $p(x|\xi)$ to denote the probability distribution for X (both mass functions and density functions). Whether $p(x|\xi)$ refers to a probability, a probability density, or a probability distribution will be clear from context. We use this notation for probability throughout the paper. A summary of all notation is given at the end of the chapter.

Returning to the thumbtack problem, we define Θ to be a variable[3] whose values θ correspond to the possible true values of the physical probability. We sometimes refer to θ as a *parameter*. We express the uncertainty about Θ using the probability density function $p(\theta|\xi)$. In addition, we use X_l to denote the variable representing the outcome of the lth flip, $l = 1, \ldots, N + 1$, and $D = \{X_1 = x_1, \ldots, X_N = x_N\}$ to denote the set of our observations. Thus, in Bayesian terms, the thumbtack problem reduces to computing $p(x_{N+1}|D, \xi)$ from $p(\theta|\xi)$.

To do so, we first use Bayes' rule to obtain the probability distribution for Θ given D and background knowledge ξ:

$$p(\theta|D, \xi) = \frac{p(\theta|\xi)\, p(D|\theta, \xi)}{p(D|\xi)} \tag{1}$$

where

$$p(D|\xi) = \int p(D|\theta, \xi)\, p(\theta|\xi)\, d\theta. \tag{2}$$

Next, we expand the term $p(D|\theta, \xi)$. Both Bayesians and classical statisticians agree on this term: it is the likelihood function for binomial sampling.

---

[2]Strictly speaking, a probability belongs to a single person, not a collection of people. Nonetheless, in parts of this discussion, we refer to "our" probability to avoid awkward English.

[3]Bayesians typically refer to Θ as an *uncertain variable*, because the value of Θ is uncertain. In contrast, classical statisticians often refer to Θ as a *random variable*. In this text, we refer to Θ and all uncertain/random variables simply as variables.

In particular, given the value of Θ, the observations in D are mutually independent, and the probability of heads (tails) on any one observation is θ $(1 - \theta)$. Consequently, Equation 1 becomes

$$p(\theta|D, \xi) = \frac{p(\theta|\xi)\; \theta^h\; (1 - \theta)^t}{p(D|\xi)} \tag{3}$$

where h and t are the number of heads and tails observed in D, respectively. The probability distributions $p(\theta|\xi)$ and $p(\theta|D, \xi)$ are commonly referred to as the *prior* and *posterior* for Θ, respectively. The quantities h and t are said to be *sufficient statistics* for binomial sampling, because they provide a summarization of the data that is sufficient to compute the posterior from the prior. Finally, we average over the possible values of Θ (using the expansion rule of probability) to determine the probability that the $N+1$th toss of the thumbtack will come up heads:

$$
\begin{aligned}
p(X_{N+1} = heads|D, \xi) &= \int p(X_{N+1} = heads|\theta, \xi)\; p(\theta|D, \xi)\; d\theta \\
&= \int \theta\; p(\theta|D, \xi)\; d\theta \equiv \mathrm{E}_{p(\theta|D,\xi)}(\theta) \tag{4}
\end{aligned}
$$

where $\mathrm{E}_{p(\theta|D,\xi)}(\theta)$ denotes the expectation of θ with respect to the distribution $p(\theta|D, \xi)$.

To complete the Bayesian story for this example, we need a method to assess the prior distribution for Θ. A common approach, usually adopted for convenience, is to assume that this distribution is a *beta* distribution:

$$p(\theta|\xi) = \mathrm{Beta}(\theta|\alpha_h, \alpha_t) \equiv \frac{\Gamma(\alpha)}{\Gamma(\alpha_h)\Gamma(\alpha_t)}\theta^{\alpha_h-1}(1 - \theta)^{\alpha_t-1} \tag{5}$$

where $\alpha_h > 0$ and $\alpha_t > 0$ are the parameters of the beta distribution, $\alpha = \alpha_h + \alpha_t$, and $\Gamma(\cdot)$ is the *Gamma* function which satisfies $\Gamma(x+1) = x\Gamma(x)$ and $\Gamma(1) = 1$. The quantities α_h and α_t are often referred to as *hyperparameters* to distinguish them from the parameter θ. The hyperparameters α_h and α_t must be greater than zero so that the distribution can be normalized. Examples of beta distributions are shown in Figure 2.

The beta prior is convenient for several reasons. By Equation 3, the posterior distribution will also be a beta distribution:

$$p(\theta|D, \xi) = \frac{\Gamma(\alpha + N)}{\Gamma(\alpha_h + h)\Gamma(\alpha_t + t)}\theta^{\alpha_h+h-1}(1-\theta)^{\alpha_t+t-1} = \mathrm{Beta}(\theta|\alpha_h+h, \alpha_t+t) \tag{6}$$

We say that the set of beta distributions is a *conjugate family of distributions* for binomial sampling. Also, the expectation of θ with respect to this

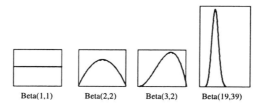

Figure 2.   Several beta distributions.

distribution has a simple form:

$$\int \theta \ \text{Beta}(\theta|\alpha_h, \alpha_t) \ d\theta = \frac{\alpha_h}{\alpha} \tag{7}$$

Hence, given a beta prior, we have a simple expression for the probability of heads in the $N + 1$th toss:

$$p(X_{N+1} = heads|D, \xi) = \frac{\alpha_h + h}{\alpha + N} \tag{8}$$

Assuming $p(\theta|\xi)$ is a beta distribution, it can be assessed in a number of ways. For example, we can assess our probability for heads in the first toss of the thumbtack (e.g., using a probability wheel). Next, we can imagine having seen the outcomes of k flips, and reassess our probability for heads in the next toss. From Equation 8, we have (for $k = 1$)

$$p(X_1 = heads|\xi) = \frac{\alpha_h}{\alpha_h + \alpha_t} \quad p(X_2 = heads|X_1 = heads, \xi) = \frac{\alpha_h + 1}{\alpha_h + \alpha_t + 1}$$

Given these probabilities, we can solve for α_h and α_t. This assessment technique is known as the method of *imagined future data*.

Another assessment method is based on Equation 6. This equation says that, if we start with a Beta$(0, 0)$ prior[4] and observe α_h heads and α_t tails, then our posterior (i.e., new prior) will be a Beta(α_h, α_t) distribution. Recognizing that a Beta$(0, 0)$ prior encodes a state of minimum information, we can assess α_h and α_t by determining the (possibly fractional) number of observations of heads and tails that is equivalent to our actual knowledge about flipping thumbtacks. Alternatively, we can assess $p(X_1 = heads|\xi)$ and α, which can be regarded as an *equivalent sample size* for our current knowledge. This technique is known as the method of *equivalent samples*.

---

[4]Technically, the hyperparameters of this prior should be small positive numbers so that $p(\theta|\xi)$ can be normalized.

Other techniques for assessing beta distributions are discussed by Winkler (1967) and Chaloner and Duncan (1983).

Although the beta prior is convenient, it is not accurate for some problems. For example, suppose we think that the thumbtack may have been purchased at a magic shop. In this case, a more appropriate prior may be a mixture of beta distributions—for example,

$$p(\theta|\xi) = 0.4 \text{ Beta}(20, 1) + 0.4 \text{ Beta}(1, 20) + 0.2 \text{ Beta}(2, 2)$$

where 0.4 is our probability that the thumbtack is heavily weighted toward heads (tails). In effect, we have introduced an additional *hidden* or unobserved variable H, whose states correspond to the three possibilities: (1) thumbtack is biased toward heads, (2) thumbtack is biased toward tails, and (3) thumbtack is normal; and we have asserted that θ conditioned on each state of H is a beta distribution. In general, there are simple methods (e.g., the method of imagined future data) for determining whether or not a beta prior is an accurate reflection of one's beliefs. In those cases where the beta prior is inaccurate, an accurate prior can often be assessed by introducing additional hidden variables, as in this example.

So far, we have only considered observations drawn from a binomial distribution. In general, observations may be drawn from any physical probability distribution:

$$p(x|\boldsymbol{\theta}, \xi) = f(x, \boldsymbol{\theta})$$

where $f(x, \boldsymbol{\theta})$ is the likelihood function with parameters $\boldsymbol{\theta}$. For purposes of this discussion, we assume that the number of parameters is finite. As an example, X may be a continuous variable and have a Gaussian physical probability distribution with mean μ and variance v:

$$p(x|\boldsymbol{\theta}, \xi) = (2\pi v)^{-1/2}\, e^{-(x-\mu)^2/2v}$$

where $\boldsymbol{\theta} = \{\mu, v\}$.

Regardless of the functional form, we can learn about the parameters given data using the Bayesian approach. As we have done in the binomial case, we define variables corresponding to the unknown parameters, assign priors to these variables, and use Bayes' rule to update our beliefs about these parameters given data:

$$p(\boldsymbol{\theta}|D, \xi) = \frac{p(D|\boldsymbol{\theta}, \xi)\, p(\boldsymbol{\theta}|\xi)}{p(D|\xi)} \qquad (9)$$

We then average over the possible values of Θ to make predictions. For example,

$$p(x_{N+1}|D, \xi) = \int p(x_{N+1}|\boldsymbol{\theta}, \xi)\, p(\boldsymbol{\theta}|D, \xi)\, d\boldsymbol{\theta} \qquad (10)$$

For a class of distributions known as the *exponential family*, these computations can be done efficiently and in closed form.[5] Members of this class include the binomial, multinomial, normal, Gamma, Poisson, and multivariate-normal distributions. Each member of this family has sufficient statistics that are of fixed dimension for any random sample, and a simple conjugate prior.[6] Bernardo and Smith (pp. 436–442, 1994) have compiled the important quantities and Bayesian computations for commonly used members of the exponential family. Here, we summarize these items for multinomial sampling, which we use to illustrate many of the ideas in this paper.

In multinomial sampling, the observed variable X is discrete, having r possible states $x^1, \ldots, x^r$. The likelihood function is given by

$$p(X = x^k | \boldsymbol{\theta}, \xi) = \theta_k, \quad k = 1, \ldots, r$$

where $\boldsymbol{\theta} = \{\theta_2, \ldots, \theta_r\}$ are the parameters. (The parameter θ_1 is given by $1 - \sum_{k=2}^{r} \theta_k$.) In this case, as in the case of binomial sampling, the parameters correspond to physical probabilities. The sufficient statistics for data set $D = \{X_1 = x_1, \ldots, X_N = x_N\}$ are $\{N_1, \ldots, N_r\}$, where N_i is the number of times $X = x^k$ in D. The simple conjugate prior used with multinomial sampling is the Dirichlet distribution:

$$p(\boldsymbol{\theta}|\xi) = \text{Dir}(\boldsymbol{\theta}|\alpha_1, \ldots, \alpha_r) \equiv \frac{\Gamma(\alpha)}{\prod_{k=1}^{r} \Gamma(\alpha_k)} \prod_{k=1}^{r} \theta_k^{\alpha_k - 1} \quad (11)$$

where $\alpha = \sum_{i=1}^{r} \alpha_k$, and $\alpha_k > 0, k = 1, \ldots, r$. The posterior distribution $p(\boldsymbol{\theta}|D, \xi) = \text{Dir}(\boldsymbol{\theta}|\alpha_1 + N_1, \ldots, \alpha_r + N_r)$. Techniques for assessing the beta distribution, including the methods of imagined future data and equivalent samples, can also be used to assess Dirichlet distributions. Given this conjugate prior and data set D, the probability distribution for the next observation is given by

$$p(X_{N+1} = x^k | D, \xi) = \int \theta_k \, \text{Dir}(\boldsymbol{\theta}|\alpha_1 + N_1, \ldots, \alpha_r + N_r) \, d\boldsymbol{\theta} = \frac{\alpha_k + N_k}{\alpha + N} \quad (12)$$

As we shall see, another important quantity in Bayesian analysis is the *marginal likelihood* or *evidence* $p(D|\xi)$. In this case, we have

$$p(D|\xi) = \frac{\Gamma(\alpha)}{\Gamma(\alpha + N)} \cdot \prod_{k=1}^{r} \frac{\Gamma(\alpha_k + N_k)}{\Gamma(\alpha_k)} \quad (13)$$

---

[5] Recent advances in Monte-Carlo methods have made it possible to work efficiently with many distributions outside the exponential family. See, for example, Gilks et al. (1996).

[6] In fact, except for a few, well-characterized exceptions, the exponential family is the only class of distributions that have sufficient statistics of fixed dimension (Koopman, 1936; Pitman, 1936).

We note that the explicit mention of the state of knowledge ξ is useful, because it reinforces the notion that probabilities are subjective. Nonetheless, once this concept is firmly in place, the notation simply adds clutter. In the remainder of this tutorial, we shall not mention ξ explicitly.

In closing this section, we emphasize that, although the Bayesian and classical approaches may sometimes yield the same prediction, they are fundamentally different methods for learning from data. As an illustration, let us revisit the thumbtack problem. Here, the Bayesian "estimate" for the physical probability of heads is obtained in a manner that is essentially the opposite of the classical approach.

Namely, in the classical approach, θ is fixed (albeit unknown), and we imagine all data sets of size N that *may be* generated by sampling from the binomial distribution determined by θ. Each data set D will occur with some probability $p(D|\theta)$ and will produce an estimate $\theta^*(D)$. To evaluate an estimator, we compute the expectation and variance of the estimate with respect to all such data sets:

$$\mathrm{E}_{p(D|\theta)}(\theta^*) \;=\; \sum_D p(D|\theta) \; \theta^*(D)$$
$$\mathrm{Var}_{p(D|\theta)}(\theta^*) \;=\; \sum_D p(D|\theta) \; (\theta^*(D) - \mathrm{E}_{p(D|\theta)}(\theta^*))^2 \qquad (14)$$

We then choose an estimator that somehow balances the bias $(\theta - \mathrm{E}_{p(D|\theta)}(\theta^*))$ and variance of these estimates over the possible values for θ.[7] Finally, we apply this estimator to the data set that we actually observe. A commonly-used estimator is the maximum-likelihood (ML) estimator, which selects the value of θ that maximizes the likelihood $p(D|\theta)$. For binomial sampling, we have

$$\theta^*_{\mathrm{ML}}(D) = \frac{N_k}{\sum_{k=1}^{r} N_k}$$

For this (and other types) of sampling, the ML estimator is *unbiased*. That is, for all values of θ, the ML estimator has zero bias. In addition, for all values of θ, the variance of the ML estimator is no greater than that of any other unbiased estimator (see, e.g., Schervish, 1995).

In contrast, in the Bayesian approach, D is fixed, and we imagine all possible values of θ from which this data set *could have been* generated. Given θ, the "estimate" of the physical probability of heads is just θ itself. Nonetheless, we are uncertain about θ, and so our final estimate is the expectation of θ with respect to our posterior beliefs about its value:

$$\mathrm{E}_{p(\theta|D,\xi)}(\theta) = \int \theta \; p(\theta|D,\xi) \; d\theta \qquad (15)$$

---

[7]Low bias and variance are not the only desirable properties of an estimator. Other desirable properties include consistency and robustness.

The expectations in Equations 14 and 15 are different and, in many cases, lead to different "estimates". One way to frame this difference is to say that the classical and Bayesian approaches have different definitions for what it means to be a good estimator. Both solutions are "correct" in that they are self consistent. Unfortunately, both methods have their drawbacks, which has lead to endless debates about the merit of each approach. For example, Bayesians argue that it does not make sense to consider the expectations in Equation 14, because we only see a single data set. If we saw more than one data set, we should combine them into one larger data set. In contrast, classical statisticians argue that sufficiently accurate priors can not be assessed in many situations. The common view that seems to be emerging is that one should use whatever method that is most sensible for the task at hand. We share this view, although we also believe that the Bayesian approach has been under used, especially in light of its advantages mentioned in the introduction (points three and four). Consequently, in this paper, we concentrate on the Bayesian approach.

3. Bayesian Networks

So far, we have considered only simple problems with one or a few variables. In real learning problems, however, we are typically interested in looking for relationships among a large number of variables. The Bayesian network is a representation suited to this task. It is a graphical model that efficiently encodes the joint probability distribution (physical or Bayesian) for a large set of variables. In this section, we define a Bayesian network and show how one can be constructed from prior knowledge.

A Bayesian network for a set of variables $\mathbf{X} = \{X_1, \ldots, X_n\}$ consists of (1) a network structure S that encodes a set of conditional independence assertions about variables in $\mathbf{X}$, and (2) a set P of local probability distributions associated with each variable. Together, these components define the joint probability distribution for $\mathbf{X}$. The network structure S is a directed acyclic graph. The nodes in S are in one-to-one correspondence with the variables $\mathbf{X}$. We use X_i to denote both the variable and its corresponding node, and $\mathbf{Pa}_i$ to denote the parents of node X_i in S as well as the variables corresponding to those parents. The *lack* of possible arcs in S encode conditional independencies. In particular, given structure S, the joint probability distribution for $\mathbf{X}$ is given by

$$p(\mathbf{x}) = \prod_{i=1}^{n} p(x_i | \mathbf{pa}_i) \tag{16}$$

The local probability distributions P are the distributions corresponding to the terms in the product of Equation 16. Consequently, the pair (S, P)

encodes the joint distribution $p(\mathbf{x})$.

The probabilities encoded by a Bayesian network may be Bayesian or physical. When building Bayesian networks from prior knowledge alone, the probabilities will be Bayesian. When learning these networks from data, the probabilities will be physical (and their values may be uncertain). In subsequent sections, we describe how we can learn the structure and probabilities of a Bayesian network from data. In the remainder of this section, we explore the construction of Bayesian networks from prior knowledge. As we shall see in Section 10, this procedure can be useful in learning Bayesian networks as well.

To illustrate the process of building a Bayesian network, consider the problem of detecting credit-card fraud. We begin by determining the variables to model. One possible choice of variables for our problem is *Fraud* (*F*), *Gas* (*G*), *Jewelry* (*J*), *Age* (*A*), and *Sex* (*S*), representing whether or not the current purchase is fraudulent, whether or not there was a gas purchase in the last 24 hours, whether or not there was a jewelry purchase in the last 24 hours, and the age and sex of the card holder, respectively. The states of these variables are shown in Figure 3. Of course, in a realistic problem, we would include many more variables. Also, we could model the states of one or more of these variables at a finer level of detail. For example, we could let *Age* be a continuous variable.

This initial task is not always straightforward. As part of this task we must (1) correctly identify the goals of modeling (e.g., prediction versus explanation versus exploration), (2) identify many possible observations that may be relevant to the problem, (3) determine what subset of those observations is worthwhile to model, and (4) organize the observations into variables having mutually exclusive and collectively exhaustive states. Difficulties here are not unique to modeling with Bayesian networks, but rather are common to most approaches. Although there are no clean solutions, some guidance is offered by decision analysts (e.g., Howard and Matheson, 1983) and (when data are available) statisticians (e.g., Tukey, 1977).

In the next phase of Bayesian-network construction, we build a directed acyclic graph that encodes assertions of conditional independence. One approach for doing so is based on the following observations. From the chain rule of probability, we have

$$p(\mathbf{x}) = \prod_{i=1}^{n} p(x_i | x_1, \ldots, x_{i-1}) \qquad (17)$$

Now, for every X_i, there will be some subset $\Pi_i \subseteq \{X_1, \ldots, X_{i-1}\}$ such that X_i and $\{X_1, \ldots, X_{i-1}\} \setminus \Pi_i$ are conditionally independent given Π_i. That is, for any $\mathbf{x}$,

$$p(x_i | x_1, \ldots, x_{i-1}) = p(x_i | \pi_i) \qquad (18)$$

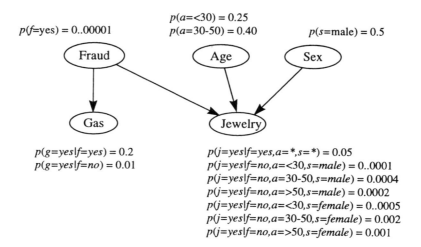

$p(f{=}yes) = 0..00001$

$p(a{=}{<}30) = 0.25$
$p(a{=}30\text{-}50) = 0.40$

$p(s{=}male) = 0.5$

$p(g{=}yes|f{=}yes) = 0.2$
$p(g{=}yes|f{=}no) = 0.01$

$p(j{=}yes|f{=}yes,a{=}{*},s{=}{*}) = 0.05$
$p(j{=}yes|f{=}no,a{=}{<}30,s{=}male) = 0..0001$
$p(j{=}yes|f{=}no,a{=}30\text{-}50,s{=}male) = 0.0004$
$p(j{=}yes|f{=}no,a{=}{>}50,s{=}male) = 0.0002$
$p(j{=}yes|f{=}no,a{=}{<}30,s{=}female) = 0..0005$
$p(j{=}yes|f{=}no,a{=}30\text{-}50,s{=}female) = 0.002$
$p(j{=}yes|f{=}no,a{=}{>}50,s{=}female) = 0.001$

Figure 3. A Bayesian-network for detecting credit-card fraud. Arcs are drawn from cause to effect. The local probability distribution(s) associated with a node are shown adjacent to the node. An asterisk is a shorthand for "any state."

Combining Equations 17 and 18, we obtain

$$p(\mathbf{x}) = \prod_{i=1}^{n} p(x_i|\pi_i) \qquad (19)$$

Comparing Equations 16 and 19, we see that the variables sets $(\Pi_1, \ldots, \Pi_n)$ correspond to the Bayesian-network parents $(\mathbf{Pa}_1, \ldots, \mathbf{Pa}_n)$, which in turn fully specify the arcs in the network structure S.

Consequently, to determine the structure of a Bayesian network we (1) order the variables somehow, and (2) determine the variables sets that satisfy Equation 18 for $i = 1, \ldots, n$. In our example, using the ordering (F, A, S, G, J), we have the conditional independencies

$$
\begin{aligned}
p(a|f) &= p(a) \\
p(s|f,a) &= p(s) \\
p(g|f,a,s) &= p(g|f) \\
p(j|f,a,s,g) &= p(j|f,a,s)
\end{aligned}
\qquad (20)
$$

Thus, we obtain the structure shown in Figure 3.

This approach has a serious drawback. If we choose the variable order carelessly, the resulting network structure may fail to reveal many conditional independencies among the variables. For example, if we construct a Bayesian network for the fraud problem using the ordering (J, G, S, A, F), we obtain a fully connected network structure. Thus, in the worst case, we have to explore $n!$ variable orderings to find the best one. Fortunately, there is another technique for constructing Bayesian networks that does not require an ordering. The approach is based on two observations: (1) people can often readily assert causal relationships among variables, and (2) causal relationships typically correspond to assertions of conditional dependence. In particular, to construct a Bayesian network for a given set of variables, we simply draw arcs from cause variables to their immediate effects. In almost all cases, doing so results in a network structure that satisfies the definition *Equation* 16. For example, given the assertions that *Fraud* is a direct cause of *Gas*, and *Fraud*, *Age*, and *Sex* are direct causes of *Jewelry*, we obtain the network structure in Figure 3. The causal semantics of Bayesian networks are in large part responsible for the success of Bayesian networks as a representation for expert systems (Heckerman et al., 1995a). In Section 15, we will see how to learn causal relationships from data using these causal semantics.

In the final step of constructing a Bayesian network, we assess the local probability distribution(s) $p(x_i|\mathbf{pa}_i)$. In our fraud example, where all variables are discrete, we assess one distribution for X_i for every configuration of $\mathbf{Pa}_i$. Example distributions are shown in Figure 3.

Note that, although we have described these construction steps as a simple sequence, they are often intermingled in practice. For example, judgments of conditional independence and/or cause and effect can influence problem formulation. Also, assessments of probability can lead to changes in the network structure. Exercises that help one gain familiarity with the practice of building Bayesian networks can be found in Jensen (1996).

4. Inference in a Bayesian Network

Once we have constructed a Bayesian network (from prior knowledge, data, or a combination), we usually need to determine various probabilities of interest from the model. For example, in our problem concerning fraud detection, we want to know the probability of fraud given observations of the other variables. This probability is not stored directly in the model, and hence needs to be computed. In general, the computation of a probability of interest given a model is known as *probabilistic inference*. In this section we describe probabilistic inference in Bayesian networks.

Because a Bayesian network for $\mathbf{X}$ determines a joint probability distribution for $\mathbf{X}$, we can—in principle—use the Bayesian network to compute any probability of interest. For example, from the Bayesian network in Figure 3, the probability of fraud given observations of the other variables can be computed as follows:

$$p(f|a,s,g,j) = \frac{p(f,a,s,g,j)}{p(a,s,g,j)} = \frac{p(f,a,s,g,j)}{\sum_{f'} p(f',a,s,g,j)} \qquad (21)$$

For problems with many variables, however, this direct approach is not practical. Fortunately, at least when all variables are discrete, we can exploit the conditional independencies encoded in a Bayesian network to make this computation more efficient. In our example, given the conditional independencies in Equation 20, Equation 21 becomes

$$\begin{aligned}
p(f|a,s,g,j) &= \frac{p(f)p(a)p(s)p(g|f)p(j|f,a,s)}{\sum_{f'} p(f')p(a)p(s)p(g|f')p(j|f',a,s)} \qquad (22)\\
&= \frac{p(f)p(g|f)p(j|f,a,s)}{\sum_{f'} p(f')p(g|f')p(j|f',a,s)}
\end{aligned}$$

Several researchers have developed probabilistic inference algorithms for Bayesian networks with discrete variables that exploit conditional independence roughly as we have described, although with different twists. For example, Howard and Matheson (1981), Olmsted (1983), and Shachter (1988) developed an algorithm that reverses arcs in the network structure until the answer to the given probabilistic query can be read directly from the graph. In this algorithm, each arc reversal corresponds to an application of Bayes' theorem. Pearl (1986) developed a message-passing scheme that updates the probability distributions for each node in a Bayesian network in response to observations of one or more variables. Lauritzen and Spiegelhalter (1988), Jensen et al. (1990), and Dawid (1992) created an algorithm that first transforms the Bayesian network into a tree where each node in the tree corresponds to a subset of variables in **X**. The algorithm then exploits several mathematical properties of this tree to perform probabilistic inference. Most recently, D'Ambrosio (1991) developed an inference algorithm that simplifies sums and products symbolically, as in the transformation from Equation 21 to 22. The most commonly used algorithm for discrete variables is that of Lauritzen and Spiegelhalter (1988), Jensen et al (1990), and Dawid (1992).

Methods for exact inference in Bayesian networks that encode multivariate-Gaussian or Gaussian-mixture distributions have been developed by Shachter and Kenley (1989) and Lauritzen (1992), respectively. These methods also use assertions of conditional independence to simplify inference. Approximate methods for inference in Bayesian networks with other distributions, such as the generalized linear-regression model, have also been developed (Saul et al., 1996; Jaakkola and Jordan, 1996).

Although we use conditional independence to simplify probabilistic inference, exact inference in an arbitrary Bayesian network for discrete variables is NP-hard (Cooper, 1990). Even approximate inference (for example, Monte-Carlo methods) is NP-hard (Dagum and Luby, 1993). The source of the difficulty lies in undirected cycles in the Bayesian-network structure—cycles in the structure where we ignore the directionality of the arcs. (If we add an arc from *Age* to *Gas* in the network structure of Figure 3, then we obtain a structure with one undirected cycle: $F - G - A - J - F$.) When a Bayesian-network structure contains many undirected cycles, inference is intractable. For many applications, however, structures are simple enough (or can be simplified sufficiently without sacrificing much accuracy) so that inference is efficient. For those applications where generic inference methods are impractical, researchers are developing techniques that are custom tailored to particular network topologies (Heckerman 1989; Suermondt and Cooper, 1991; Saul et al., 1996; Jaakkola and Jordan, 1996) or to particular inference queries (Ramamurthi and Agogino, 1988; Shachter et al., 1990; Jensen and Andersen, 1990; Darwiche and Provan, 1996).

5. Learning Probabilities in a Bayesian Network

In the next several sections, we show how to refine the structure and local probability distributions of a Bayesian network given data. The result is set of techniques for data analysis that combines prior knowledge with data to produce improved knowledge. In this section, we consider the simplest version of this problem: using data to update the probabilities of a given Bayesian network structure.

Recall that, in the thumbtack problem, we do not learn the probability of heads. Instead, we update our posterior distribution for the variable that represents the physical probability of heads. We follow the same approach for probabilities in a Bayesian network. In particular, we assume—perhaps from causal knowledge about the problem—that the physical joint probability distribution for $\mathbf{X}$ can be encoded in some network structure S. We write

$$p(\mathbf{x}|\boldsymbol{\theta}_s, S^h) = \prod_{i=1}^{n} p(x_i|\mathbf{pa}_i, \boldsymbol{\theta}_i, S^h) \qquad (23)$$

where $\boldsymbol{\theta}_i$ is the vector of parameters for the distribution $p(x_i|\mathbf{pa}_i, \boldsymbol{\theta}_i, S^h)$, $\boldsymbol{\theta}_s$ is the vector of parameters $(\boldsymbol{\theta}_1, \ldots, \boldsymbol{\theta}_n)$, and S^h denotes the event (or "hypothesis" in statistics nomenclature) that the physical joint probability distribution can be factored according to S.[8] In addition, we assume

---

[8] As defined here, network-structure hypotheses overlap. For example, given $\mathbf{X} = \{X_1, X_2\}$, any joint distribution for $\mathbf{X}$ that can be factored according the network

that we have a random sample $D = \{\mathbf{x}_1, \ldots, \mathbf{x}_N\}$ from the physical joint probability distribution of $\mathbf{X}$. We refer to an element $\mathbf{x}_l$ of D as a *case*. As in Section 2, we encode our uncertainty about the parameters $\boldsymbol{\theta}_s$ by defining a (vector-valued) variable Θ_s, and assessing a prior probability density function $p(\boldsymbol{\theta}_s | S^h)$. The problem of learning probabilities in a Bayesian network can now be stated simply: Given a random sample D, compute the posterior distribution $p(\boldsymbol{\theta}_s | D, S^h)$.

We refer to the distribution $p(x_i | \mathbf{pa}_i, \boldsymbol{\theta}_i, S^h)$, viewed as a function of $\boldsymbol{\theta}_i$, as a *local distribution function*. Readers familiar with methods for supervised learning will recognize that a local distribution function is nothing more than a probabilistic classification or regression function. Thus, a Bayesian network can be viewed as a collection of probabilistic classification/regression models, organized by conditional-independence relationships. Examples of classification/regression models that produce probabilistic outputs include linear regression, generalized linear regression, probabilistic neural networks (e.g., MacKay, 1992a, 1992b), probabilistic decision trees (e.g., Buntine, 1993; Friedman and Goldszmidt, 1996), kernel density estimation methods (Book, 1994), and dictionary methods (Friedman, 1995). In principle, any of these forms can be used to learn probabilities in a Bayesian network; and, in most cases, Bayesian techniques for learning are available. Nonetheless, the most studied models include the unrestricted multinomial distribution (e.g., Cooper and Herskovits, 1992), linear regression with Gaussian noise (e.g., Buntine, 1994; Heckerman and Geiger, 1996), and generalized linear regression (e.g., MacKay, 1992a and 1992b; Neal, 1993; and Saul et al., 1996).

In this tutorial, we illustrate the basic ideas for learning probabilities (and structure) using the unrestricted multinomial distribution. In this case, each variable $X_i \in \mathbf{X}$ is discrete, having r_i possible values $x_i^1, \ldots, x_i^{r_i}$, and each local distribution function is collection of multinomial distributions, one distribution for each configuration of $\mathbf{Pa}_i$. Namely, we assume

$$p(x_i^k | \mathbf{pa}_i^j, \boldsymbol{\theta}_i, S^h) = \theta_{ijk} > 0 \qquad (24)$$

where $\mathbf{pa}_i^1, \ldots, \mathbf{pa}_i^{q_i}$ ($q_i = \prod_{X_i \in \mathbf{Pa}_i} r_i$) denote the configurations of $\mathbf{Pa}_i$, and $\boldsymbol{\theta}_i = ((\theta_{ijk})_{k=2}^{r_i})_{j=1}^{q_i}$ are the parameters. (The parameter θ_{ij1} is given by $1 - \sum_{k=2}^{r_i} \theta_{ijk}$.) For convenience, we define the vector of parameters

$$\boldsymbol{\theta}_{ij} = (\theta_{ij2}, \ldots, \theta_{ijr_i})$$

structure containing no arc, can also be factored according to the network structure $X_1 \longrightarrow X_2$. Such overlap presents problems for model averaging, described in Section 7. Therefore, we should add conditions to the definition to insure no overlap. Heckerman and Geiger (1996) describe one such set of conditions.

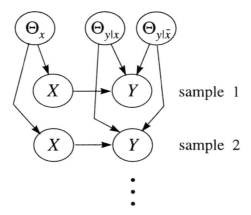

Figure 4. A Bayesian-network structure depicting the assumption of parameter independence for learning the parameters of the network structure $X \to Y$. Both variables X and Y are binary. We use x and $\bar{x}$ to denote the two states of X, and y and $\bar{y}$ to denote the two states of Y.

for all i and j. We use the term "unrestricted" to contrast this distribution with multinomial distributions that are low-dimensional functions of $\mathbf{Pa}_i$— for example, the generalized linear-regression model.

Given this class of local distribution functions, we can compute the posterior distribution $p(\boldsymbol{\theta}_s|D, S^h)$ efficiently and in closed form under two assumptions. The first assumption is that there are no missing data in the random sample D. We say that the random sample D is *complete*. The second assumption is that the parameter vectors $\boldsymbol{\theta}_{ij}$ are mutually independent.[9] That is,

$$p(\boldsymbol{\theta}_s|S^h) = \prod_{i=1}^{n} \prod_{j=1}^{q_i} p(\boldsymbol{\theta}_{ij}|S^h)$$

We refer to this assumption, which was introduced by Spiegelhalter and Lauritzen (1990), as *parameter independence.*

Given that the joint physical probability distribution factors according to some network structure S, the assumption of parameter independence can itself be represented by a larger Bayesian-network structure. For example, the network structure in Figure 4 represents the assumption of parameter independence for $\mathbf{X} = \{X, Y\}$ (X, Y binary) and the hypothesis that the network structure $X \to Y$ encodes the physical joint probability distribution for $\mathbf{X}$.

[9]The computation is also straightforward if two or more parameters are equal. For details, see Thiesson (1995).

Under the assumptions of complete data and parameter independence, the parameters remain independent given a random sample:

$$p(\boldsymbol{\theta}_s | D, S^h) = \prod_{i=1}^{n} \prod_{j=1}^{q_i} p(\boldsymbol{\theta}_{ij} | D, S^h) \tag{25}$$

Thus, we can update each vector of parameters $\boldsymbol{\theta}_{ij}$ independently, just as in the one-variable case. Assuming each vector $\boldsymbol{\theta}_{ij}$ has the prior distribution $\mathrm{Dir}(\boldsymbol{\theta}_{ij} | \alpha_{ij1}, \ldots, \alpha_{ijr_i})$, we obtain the posterior distribution

$$p(\boldsymbol{\theta}_{ij} | D, S^h) = \mathrm{Dir}(\boldsymbol{\theta}_{ij} | \alpha_{ij1} + N_{ij1}, \ldots, \alpha_{ijr_i} + N_{ijr_i}) \tag{26}$$

where N_{ijk} is the number of cases in D in which $X_i = x_i^k$ and $\mathbf{Pa}_i = \mathbf{pa}_i^j$.

As in the thumbtack example, we can average over the possible configurations of $\boldsymbol{\theta}_s$ to obtain predictions of interest. For example, let us compute $p(\mathbf{x}_{N+1} | D, S^h)$, where $\mathbf{x}_{N+1}$ is the next case to be seen after D. Suppose that, in case $\mathbf{x}_{N+1}$, $X_i = x_i^k$ and $\mathbf{Pa}_i = \mathbf{pa}_i^j$, where k and j depend on i. Thus,

$$p(\mathbf{x}_{N+1} | D, S^h) = \mathrm{E}_{p(\boldsymbol{\theta}_s | D, S^h)} \left(\prod_{i=1}^{n} \theta_{ijk} \right)$$

To compute this expectation, we first use the fact that the parameters remain independent given D:

$$p(\mathbf{x}_{N+1} | D, S^h) = \int \prod_{i=1}^{n} \theta_{ijk} \; p(\boldsymbol{\theta}_s | D, S^h) \; d\boldsymbol{\theta}_s = \prod_{i=1}^{n} \int \theta_{ijk} \; p(\boldsymbol{\theta}_{ij} | D, S^h) \; d\boldsymbol{\theta}_{ij}$$

Then, we use Equation 12 to obtain

$$p(\mathbf{x}_{N+1} | D, S^h) = \prod_{i=1}^{n} \frac{\alpha_{ijk} + N_{ijk}}{\alpha_{ij} + N_{ij}} \tag{27}$$

where $\alpha_{ij} = \sum_{k=1}^{r_i} \alpha_{ijk}$ and $N_{ij} = \sum_{k=1}^{r_i} N_{ijk}$.

These computations are simple because the unrestricted multinomial distributions are in the exponential family. Computations for linear regression with Gaussian noise are equally straightforward (Buntine, 1994; Heckerman and Geiger, 1996).

6. Methods for Incomplete Data

Let us now discuss methods for learning about parameters when the random sample is incomplete (i.e., some variables in some cases are not observed). An important distinction concerning missing data is whether or not the absence of an observation is dependent on the actual states of the variables. For example, a missing datum in a drug study may indicate that a patient became too sick—perhaps due to the side effects of the drug—to continue in the study. In contrast, if a variable is hidden (i.e., never observed in any case), then the absence of this data is independent of state. Although Bayesian methods and graphical models are suited to the analysis of both situations, methods for handling missing data where absence is independent of state are simpler than those where absence and state are dependent. In this tutorial, we concentrate on the simpler situation only. Readers interested in the more complicated case should see Rubin (1978), Robins (1986), and Pearl (1995).

Continuing with our example using unrestricted multinomial distributions, suppose we observe a single incomplete case. Let $\mathbf{Y} \subset \mathbf{X}$ and $\mathbf{Z} \subset \mathbf{X}$ denote the observed and unobserved variables in the case, respectively. Under the assumption of parameter independence, we can compute the posterior distribution of $\boldsymbol{\theta}_{ij}$ for network structure S as follows:

$$
\begin{aligned}
p(\boldsymbol{\theta}_{ij}|\mathbf{y}, S^h) &= \sum_{\mathbf{z}} p(\mathbf{z}|\mathbf{y}, S^h)\, p(\boldsymbol{\theta}_{ij}|\mathbf{y}, \mathbf{z}, S^h) \qquad\qquad (28) \\
&= (1 - p(\mathbf{pa}_i^j|\mathbf{y}, S^h))\left\{ p(\boldsymbol{\theta}_{ij}|S^h) \right\} + \\
&\quad \sum_{k=1}^{r_i} p(x_i^k, \mathbf{pa}_i^j|\mathbf{y}, S^h)\left\{ p(\boldsymbol{\theta}_{ij}|x_i^k, \mathbf{pa}_i^j, S^h) \right\}
\end{aligned}
$$

(See Spiegelhalter and Lauritzen (1990) for a derivation.) Each term in curly brackets in Equation 28 is a Dirichlet distribution. Thus, unless both X_i and all the variables in $\mathbf{Pa}_i$ are observed in case $\mathbf{y}$, the posterior distribution of $\boldsymbol{\theta}_{ij}$ will be a linear combination of Dirichlet distributions— that is, a Dirichlet mixture with mixing coefficients $(1 - p(\mathbf{pa}_i^j|\mathbf{y}, S^h))$ and $p(x_i^k, \mathbf{pa}_i^j|\mathbf{y}, S^h), k = 1, \ldots, r_i$.

When we observe a second incomplete case, some or all of the Dirichlet components in Equation 28 will again split into Dirichlet mixtures. That is, the posterior distribution for $\boldsymbol{\theta}_{ij}$ we become a mixture of Dirichlet mixtures. As we continue to observe incomplete cases, each missing values for $\mathbf{Z}$, the posterior distribution for $\boldsymbol{\theta}_{ij}$ will contain a number of components that is exponential in the number of cases. In general, for any interesting set of local likelihoods and priors, the exact computation of the posterior distribution for $\boldsymbol{\theta}_s$ will be intractable. Thus, we require an approximation for incomplete data.

6.1. MONTE-CARLO METHODS

One class of approximations is based on Monte-Carlo or sampling methods. These approximations can be extremely accurate, provided one is willing to wait long enough for the computations to converge.

In this section, we discuss one of many Monte-Carlo methods known as *Gibbs sampling*, introduced by Geman and Geman (1984). Given variables $\mathbf{X} = \{X_1, \ldots, X_n\}$ with some joint distribution $p(\mathbf{x})$, we can use a Gibbs sampler to approximate the expectation of a function $f(\mathbf{x})$ with respect to $p(\mathbf{x})$ as follows. First, we choose an initial state for each of the variables in $\mathbf{X}$ somehow (e.g., at random). Next, we pick some variable X_i, unassign its current state, and compute its probability distribution given the states of the other $n - 1$ variables. Then, we sample a state for X_i based on this probability distribution, and compute $f(\mathbf{x})$. Finally, we iterate the previous two steps, keeping track of the average value of $f(\mathbf{x})$. In the limit, as the number of cases approach infinity, this average is equal to $E_{p(\mathbf{x})}(f(\mathbf{x}))$ provided two conditions are met. First, the Gibbs sampler must be *irreducible*: The probability distribution $p(\mathbf{x})$ must be such that we can eventually sample any possible configuration of $\mathbf{X}$ given any possible initial configuration of $\mathbf{X}$. For example, if $p(\mathbf{x})$ contains no zero probabilities, then the Gibbs sampler will be irreducible. Second, each X_i must be chosen infinitely often. In practice, an algorithm for deterministically rotating through the variables is typically used. Introductions to Gibbs sampling and other Monte-Carlo methods—including methods for initialization and a discussion of convergence—are given by Neal (1993) and Madigan and York (1995).

To illustrate Gibbs sampling, let us approximate the probability density $p(\boldsymbol{\theta}_s | D, S^h)$ for some particular configuration of $\boldsymbol{\theta}_s$, given an incomplete data set $D = \{\mathbf{y}_1, \ldots, \mathbf{y}_N\}$ and a Bayesian network for discrete variables with independent Dirichlet priors. To approximate $p(\boldsymbol{\theta}_s | D, S^h)$, we first initialize the states of the unobserved variables in each case somehow. As a result, we have a complete random sample D_c. Second, we choose some variable X_{il} (variable X_i in case l) that is not observed in the original random sample D, and reassign its state according to the probability distribution

$$p(x'_{il} | D_c \setminus x_{il}, S^h) = \frac{p(x'_{il}, D_c \setminus x_{il} | S^h)}{\sum_{x''_{il}} p(x''_{il}, D_c \setminus x_{il} | S^h)}$$

where $D_c \setminus x_{il}$ denotes the data set D_c with observation x_{il} removed, and the sum in the denominator runs over all states of variable X_{il}. As we shall see in Section 7, the terms in the numerator and denominator can be computed efficiently (see Equation 35). Third, we repeat this reassignment for all unobserved variables in D, producing a new complete random sample

D'_c. Fourth, we compute the posterior density $p(\boldsymbol{\theta}_s|D'_c, S^h)$ as described in Equations 25 and 26. Finally, we iterate the previous three steps, and use the average of $p(\boldsymbol{\theta}_s|D'_c, S^h)$ as our approximation.

6.2. THE GAUSSIAN APPROXIMATION

Monte-Carlo methods yield accurate results, but they are often intractable—for example, when the sample size is large. Another approximation that is more efficient than Monte-Carlo methods and often accurate for relatively large samples is the *Gaussian approximation* (e.g., Kass et al., 1988; Kass and Raftery, 1995).

The idea behind this approximation is that, for large amounts of data, $p(\boldsymbol{\theta}_s|D, S^h)$
$\propto p(D|\boldsymbol{\theta}_s, S^h) \cdot p(\boldsymbol{\theta}_s|S^h)$ can often be approximated as a multivariate-Gaussian distribution. In particular, let

$$g(\boldsymbol{\theta}_s) \equiv \log(p(D|\boldsymbol{\theta}_s, S^h) \cdot p(\boldsymbol{\theta}_s|S^h)) \tag{29}$$

Also, define $\tilde{\boldsymbol{\theta}}_s$ to be the configuration of $\boldsymbol{\theta}_s$ that maximizes $g(\boldsymbol{\theta}_s)$. This configuration also maximizes $p(\boldsymbol{\theta}_s|D, S^h)$, and is known as the *maximum a posteriori* (MAP) configuration of $\boldsymbol{\theta}_s$. Using a second degree Taylor polynomial of $g(\boldsymbol{\theta}_s)$ about the $\tilde{\boldsymbol{\theta}}_s$ to approximate $g(\boldsymbol{\theta}_s)$, we obtain

$$g(\boldsymbol{\theta}_s) \approx g(\tilde{\boldsymbol{\theta}}_s) - \frac{1}{2}(\boldsymbol{\theta}_s - \tilde{\boldsymbol{\theta}}_s)A(\boldsymbol{\theta}_s - \tilde{\boldsymbol{\theta}}_s)^t \tag{30}$$

where $(\boldsymbol{\theta}_s - \tilde{\boldsymbol{\theta}}_s)^t$ is the transpose of row vector $(\boldsymbol{\theta}_s - \tilde{\boldsymbol{\theta}}_s)$, and A is the negative Hessian of $g(\boldsymbol{\theta}_s)$ evaluated at $\tilde{\boldsymbol{\theta}}_s$. Raising $g(\boldsymbol{\theta}_s)$ to the power of e and using Equation 29, we obtain

$$
\begin{aligned}
p(\boldsymbol{\theta}_s|D, S^h) &\propto p(D|\boldsymbol{\theta}_s, S^h)\, p(\boldsymbol{\theta}_s|S^h) \\
&\approx p(D|\tilde{\boldsymbol{\theta}}_s, S^h)\, p(\tilde{\boldsymbol{\theta}}_s|S^h)\, \exp\{-\frac{1}{2}(\boldsymbol{\theta}_s - \tilde{\boldsymbol{\theta}}_s)A(\boldsymbol{\theta}_s - \tilde{\boldsymbol{\theta}}_s)^t\}
\end{aligned}
\tag{31}
$$

Hence, $p(\boldsymbol{\theta}_s|D, S^h)$ is approximately Gaussian.

To compute the Gaussian approximation, we must compute $\tilde{\boldsymbol{\theta}}_s$ as well as the negative Hessian of $g(\boldsymbol{\theta}_s)$ evaluated at $\tilde{\boldsymbol{\theta}}_s$. In the following section, we discuss methods for finding $\tilde{\boldsymbol{\theta}}_s$. Meng and Rubin (1991) describe a numerical technique for computing the second derivatives. Raftery (1995) shows how to approximate the Hessian using likelihood-ratio tests that are available in many statistical packages. Thiesson (1995) demonstrates that, for unrestricted multinomial distributions, the second derivatives can be computed using Bayesian-network inference.

6.3. THE MAP AND ML APPROXIMATIONS AND THE EM ALGORITHM

As the sample size of the data increases, the Gaussian peak will become sharper, tending to a delta function at the MAP configuration $\tilde{\boldsymbol{\theta}}_s$. In this limit, we do not need to compute averages or expectations. Instead, we simply make predictions based on the MAP configuration.

A further approximation is based on the observation that, as the sample size increases, the effect of the prior $p(\boldsymbol{\theta}_s|S^h)$ diminishes. Thus, we can approximate $\tilde{\boldsymbol{\theta}}_s$ by the maximum *maximum likelihood* (ML) configuration of $\boldsymbol{\theta}_s$:

$$\hat{\boldsymbol{\theta}}_s = \arg\max_{\boldsymbol{\theta}_s} \left\{ p(D|\boldsymbol{\theta}_s, S^h) \right\}$$

One class of techniques for finding a ML or MAP is gradient-based optimization. For example, we can use gradient ascent, where we follow the derivatives of $g(\boldsymbol{\theta}_s)$ or the likelihood $p(D|\boldsymbol{\theta}_s, S^h)$ to a local maximum. Russell et al. (1995) and Thiesson (1995) show how to compute the derivatives of the likelihood for a Bayesian network with unrestricted multinomial distributions. Buntine (1994) discusses the more general case where the likelihood function comes from the exponential family. Of course, these gradient-based methods find only local maxima.

Another technique for finding a local ML or MAP is the expectation–maximization (EM) algorithm (Dempster et al., 1977). To find a local MAP or ML, we begin by assigning a configuration to $\boldsymbol{\theta}_s$ somehow (e.g., at random). Next, we compute the *expected sufficient statistics* for a complete data set, where expectation is taken with respect to the joint distribution for $\mathbf{X}$ conditioned on the assigned configuration of $\boldsymbol{\theta}_s$ and the known data D. In our discrete example, we compute

$$\mathrm{E}_{p(\mathbf{x}|D,\boldsymbol{\theta}_s,S^h)}(N_{ijk}) = \sum_{l=1}^{N} p(x_i^k, \mathbf{pa}_i^j | \mathbf{y}_l, \boldsymbol{\theta}_s, S^h) \tag{32}$$

where $\mathbf{y}_l$ is the possibly incomplete lth case in D. When X_i and all the variables in $\mathbf{Pa}_i$ are observed in case $\mathbf{x}_l$, the term for this case requires a trivial computation: it is either zero or one. Otherwise, we can use any Bayesian network inference algorithm to evaluate the term. This computation is called the *expectation step* of the EM algorithm.

Next, we use the expected sufficient statistics as if they were actual sufficient statistics from a complete random sample D_c. If we are doing an ML calculation, then we determine the configuration of $\boldsymbol{\theta}_s$ that maximize $p(D_c|\boldsymbol{\theta}_s, S^h)$. In our discrete example, we have

$$\theta_{ijk} = \frac{\mathrm{E}_{p(\mathbf{x}|D,\boldsymbol{\theta}_s,S^h)}(N_{ijk})}{\sum_{k=1}^{r_i} \mathrm{E}_{p(\mathbf{x}|D,\boldsymbol{\theta}_s,S^h)}(N_{ijk})}$$

If we are doing a MAP calculation, then we determine the configuration of $\boldsymbol{\theta}_s$ that maximizes $p(\boldsymbol{\theta}_s|D_c, S^h)$. In our discrete example, we have[10]

$$\theta_{ijk} = \frac{\alpha_{ijk} + E_{p(\mathbf{x}|D,\boldsymbol{\theta}_s,S^h)}(N_{ijk})}{\sum_{k=1}^{r_i}(\alpha_{ijk} + E_{p(\mathbf{x}|D,\boldsymbol{\theta}_s,S^h)}(N_{ijk}))}$$

This assignment is called the *maximization step* of the EM algorithm. Dempster et al. (1977) showed that, under certain regularity conditions, iteration of the expectation and maximization steps will converge to a local maximum. The EM algorithm is typically applied when sufficient statistics exist (i.e., when local distribution functions are in the exponential family), although generalizations of the EM algroithm have been used for more complicated local distributions (see, e.g., Saul et al. 1996).

7. Learning Parameters and Structure

Now we consider the problem of learning about both the structure and probabilities of a Bayesian network given data.

Assuming we think structure can be improved, we must be uncertain about the network structure that encodes the physical joint probability distribution for $\mathbf{X}$. Following the Bayesian approach, we encode this uncertainty by defining a (discrete) variable whose states correspond to the possible network-structure hypotheses S^h, and assessing the probabilities $p(S^h)$. Then, given a random sample D from the physical probability distribution for $\mathbf{X}$, we compute the posterior distribution $p(S^h|D)$ and the posterior distributions $p(\boldsymbol{\theta}_s|D, S^h)$, and use these distributions in turn to compute expectations of interest. For example, to predict the next case after seeing D, we compute

$$p(\mathbf{x}_{N+1}|D) = \sum_{S^h} p(S^h|D) \int p(\mathbf{x}_{N+1}|\boldsymbol{\theta}_s, S^h) \, p(\boldsymbol{\theta}_s|D, S^h) \, d\boldsymbol{\theta}_s \qquad (33)$$

In performing the sum, we assume that the network-structure hypotheses are mutually exclusive. We return to this point in Section 9.

---

[10]The MAP configuration $\tilde{\boldsymbol{\theta}}_s$ depends on the coordinate system in which the parameter variables are expressed. The expression for the MAP configuration given here is obtained by the following procedure. First, we transform each variable set $\boldsymbol{\theta}_{ij} = (\theta_{ij2}, \ldots, \theta_{ijr_i})$ to the new coordinate system $\boldsymbol{\phi}_{ij} = (\phi_{ij2}, \ldots, \phi_{ijr_i})$, where $\phi_{ijk} = \log(\theta_{ijk}/\theta_{ij1}), k = 2, \ldots, r_i$. This coordinate system, which we denote by $\boldsymbol{\phi}_s$, is sometimes referred to as the *canonical* coordinate system for the multinomial distribution (see, e.g., Bernardo and Smith, 1994, pp. 199–202). Next, we determine the configuration of $\boldsymbol{\phi}_s$ that maximizes $p(\boldsymbol{\phi}_s|D_c, S^h)$. Finally, we transform this MAP configuration to the original coordinate system. Using the MAP configuration corresponding to the coordinate system $\boldsymbol{\phi}_s$ has several advantages, which are discussed in Thiesson (1995b) and MacKay (1996).

The computation of $p(\boldsymbol{\theta}_s|D, S^h)$ is as we have described in the previous two sections. The computation of $p(S^h|D)$ is also straightforward, at least in principle. From Bayes' theorem, we have

$$p(S^h|D) = p(S^h)\, p(D|S^h)/p(D) \qquad (34)$$

where $p(D)$ is a normalization constant that does not depend upon structure. Thus, to determine the posterior distribution for network structures, we need to compute the marginal likelihood of the data ($p(D|S^h)$) for each possible structure.

We discuss the computation of marginal likelihoods in detail in Section 9. As an introduction, consider our example with unrestricted multinomial distributions, parameter independence, Dirichlet priors, and complete data. As we have discussed, when there are no missing data, each parameter vector $\boldsymbol{\theta}_{ij}$ is updated independently. In effect, we have a separate multi-sided thumbtack problem for every i and j. Consequently, the marginal likelihood of the data is the just the product of the marginal likelihoods for each i–j pair (given by Equation 13):

$$p(D|S^h) = \prod_{i=1}^{n}\prod_{j=1}^{q_i} \frac{\Gamma(\alpha_{ij})}{\Gamma(\alpha_{ij} + N_{ij})} \cdot \prod_{k=1}^{r_i} \frac{\Gamma(\alpha_{ijk} + N_{ijk})}{\Gamma(\alpha_{ijk})} \qquad (35)$$

This formula was first derived by Cooper and Herskovits (1992).

Unfortunately, the full Bayesian approach that we have described is often impractical. One important computation bottleneck is produced by the average over models in Equation 33. If we consider Bayesian-network models with n variables, the number of possible structure hypotheses is more than exponential in n. Consequently, in situations where the user can not exclude almost all of these hypotheses, the approach is intractable.

Statisticians, who have been confronted by this problem for decades in the context of other types of models, use two approaches to address this problem: *model selection* and *selective model averaging*. The former approach is to select a "good" model (i.e., structure hypothesis) from among all possible models, and use it as if it were the correct model. The latter approach is to select a manageable number of good models from among all possible models and pretend that these models are exhaustive. These related approaches raise several important questions. In particular, do these approaches yield accurate results when applied to Bayesian-network structures? If so, how do we search for good models? And how do we decide whether or not a model is "good"?

The question of accuracy is difficult to answer in theory. Nonetheless, several researchers have shown experimentally that the selection of a single good hypothesis often yields accurate predictions (Cooper and Herskovits

1992; Aliferis and Cooper 1994; Heckerman et al., 1995b) and that model averaging using Monte-Carlo methods can sometimes be efficient and yield even better predictions (Madigan et al., 1996). These results are somewhat surprising, and are largely responsible for the great deal of recent interest in learning with Bayesian networks. In Sections 8 through 10, we consider different definitions of what is means for a model to be "good", and discuss the computations entailed by some of these definitions. In Section 11, we discuss model search.

We note that model averaging and model selection lead to models that generalize well to *new* data. That is, these techniques help us to avoid the overfitting of data. As is suggested by Equation 33, Bayesian methods for model averaging and model selection are efficient in the sense that all cases in D can be used to both smooth and train the model. As we shall see in the following two sections, this advantage holds true for the Bayesian approach in general.

8.   Criteria for Model Selection

Most of the literature on learning with Bayesian networks is concerned with model selection. In these approaches, some *criterion* is used to measure the degree to which a network structure (equivalence class) fits the prior knowledge and data. A search algorithm is then used to find an equivalence class that receives a high score by this criterion. Selective model averaging is more complex, because it is often advantageous to identify network structures that are significantly different. In many cases, a single criterion is unlikely to identify such complementary network structures. In this section, we discuss criteria for the simpler problem of model selection. For a discussion of selective model averaging, see Madigan and Raftery (1994).

8.1.   RELATIVE POSTERIOR PROBABILITY

A criterion that is often used for model selection is the log of the relative posterior probability $\log p(D, S^h) = \log p(S^h) + \log p(D|S^h)$.[11] The logarithm is used for numerical convenience. This criterion has two components: the log prior and the log marginal likelihood. In Section 9, we examine the computation of the log marginal likelihood. In Section 10.2, we discuss the assessment of network-structure priors. Note that our comments about these terms are also relevant to the full Bayesian approach.

---

[11]An equivalent criterion that is often used is $\log(p(S^h|D)/p(S_0^h|D)) = \log(p(S^h)/p(S_0^h)) + \log(p(D|S^h)/p(D|S_0^h))$. The ratio $p(D|S^h)/p(D|S_0^h)$ is known as a *Bayes' factor*.

The log marginal likelihood has the following interesting interpretation described by Dawid (1984). From the chain rule of probability, we have

$$\log p(D|S^h) = \sum_{l=1}^{N} \log p(\mathbf{x}_l|\mathbf{x}_1, \ldots, \mathbf{x}_{l-1}, S^h) \tag{36}$$

The term $p(\mathbf{x}_l|\mathbf{x}_1, \ldots, \mathbf{x}_{l-1}, S^h)$ is the prediction for $\mathbf{x}_l$ made by model S^h after averaging over its parameters. The log of this term can be thought of as the utility or reward for this prediction under the utility function $\log p(\mathbf{x})$.[12] Thus, a model with the highest log marginal likelihood (or the highest posterior probability, assuming equal priors on structure) is also a model that is the best sequential predictor of the data D under the log utility function.

Dawid (1984) also notes the relationship between this criterion and cross validation. When using one form of cross validation, known as *leave-one-out* cross validation, we first train a model on all but one of the cases in the random sample—say, $V_l = \{\mathbf{x}_1, \ldots, \mathbf{x}_{l-1}, \mathbf{x}_{l+1}, \ldots, \mathbf{x}_N\}$. Then, we predict the omitted case, and reward this prediction under some utility function. Finally, we repeat this procedure for every case in the random sample, and sum the rewards for each prediction. If the prediction is probabilistic and the utility function is $\log p(\mathbf{x})$, we obtain the cross-validation criterion

$$\mathrm{CV}(S^h, D) = \sum_{l=1}^{N} \log p(\mathbf{x}_l|V_l, S^h) \tag{37}$$

which is similar to Equation 36. One problem with this criterion is that training and test cases are interchanged. For example, when we compute $p(\mathbf{x}_1|V_1, S^h)$ in Equation 37, we use $\mathbf{x}_2$ for training and $\mathbf{x}_1$ for testing. Whereas, when we compute $p(\mathbf{x}_2|V_2, S^h)$, we use $\mathbf{x}_1$ for training and $\mathbf{x}_2$ for testing. Such interchanges can lead to the selection of a model that over fits the data (Dawid, 1984). Various approaches for attenuating this problem have been described, but we see from Equation 36 that the log-marginal-likelihood criterion avoids the problem altogether. Namely, when using this criterion, we never interchange training and test cases.

8.2. LOCAL CRITERIA

Consider the problem of diagnosing an ailment given the observation of a set of findings. Suppose that the set of ailments under consideration are

---

[12]This utility function is known as a *proper scoring rule*, because its use encourages people to assess their true probabilities. For a characterization of proper scoring rules and this rule in particular, see Bernardo (1979).

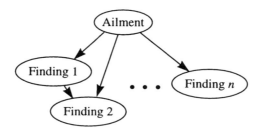

Figure 5.   A Bayesian-network structure for medical diagnosis.

mutually exclusive and collectively exhaustive, so that we may represent these ailments using a single variable A. A possible Bayesian network for this classification problem is shown in Figure 5.

The posterior-probability criterion is *global* in the sense that it is equally sensitive to all possible dependencies. In the diagnosis problem, the posterior-probability criterion is just as sensitive to dependencies among the finding variables as it is to dependencies between ailment and findings. Assuming that we observe all (or perhaps all but a few) of the findings in D, a more reasonable criterion would be *local* in the sense that it ignores dependencies among findings and is sensitive only to the dependencies among the ailment and findings. This observation applies to all classification and regression problems with complete data.

One such local criterion, suggested by Spiegelhalter et al. (1993), is a variation on the sequential log-marginal-likelihood criterion:

$$\text{LC}(S^h, D) = \sum_{l=1}^{N} \log p(a_l | \mathbf{F}_l, D_l, S^h) \tag{38}$$

where a_l and $\mathbf{F}_l$ denote the observation of the ailment A and findings $\mathbf{F}$ in the lth case, respectively. In other words, to compute the lth term in the product, we train our model S with the first $l - 1$ cases, and then determine how well it predicts the ailment given the findings in the lth case. We can view this criterion, like the log-marginal-likelihood, as a form of cross validation where training and test cases are never interchanged.

The log utility function has interesting theoretical properties, but it is sometimes inaccurate for real-world problems. In general, an appropriate reward or utility function will depend on the decision-making problem or problems to which the probabilistic models are applied. Howard and Matheson (1983) have collected a series of articles describing how to construct utility models for specific decision problems. Once we construct such utility models, we can use suitably modified forms of Equation 38 for model selection.

9. Computation of the Marginal Likelihood

As mentioned, an often-used criterion for model selection is the log relative posterior probability $\log p(D, S^h) = \log p(S^h) + \log p(D|S^h)$. In this section, we discuss the computation of the second component of this criterion: the log marginal likelihood.

Given (1) local distribution functions in the exponential family, (2) mutual independence of the parameters $\boldsymbol{\theta}_i$, (3) conjugate priors for these parameters, and (4) complete data, the log marginal likelihood can be computed efficiently and in closed form. Equation 35 is an example for unrestricted multinomial distributions. Buntine (1994) and Heckerman and Geiger (1996) discuss the computation for other local distribution functions. Here, we concentrate on approximations for incomplete data.

The Monte-Carlo and Gaussian approximations for learning about parameters that we discussed in Section 6 are also useful for computing the marginal likelihood given incomplete data. One Monte-Carlo approach, described by Chib (1995) and Raftery (1996), uses Bayes' theorem:

$$p(D|S^h) = \frac{p(\boldsymbol{\theta}_s|S^h) \; p(D|\boldsymbol{\theta}_s, S^h)}{p(\boldsymbol{\theta}_s|D, S^h)} \tag{39}$$

For any configuration of $\boldsymbol{\theta}_s$, the prior term in the numerator can be evaluated directly. In addition, the likelihood term in the numerator can be computed using Bayesian-network inference. Finally, the posterior term in the denominator can be computed using Gibbs sampling, as we described in Section 6.1. Other, more sophisticated Monte-Carlo methods are described by DiCiccio et al. (1995).

As we have discussed, Monte-Carlo methods are accurate but computationally inefficient, especially for large databases. In contrast, methods based on the Gaussian approximation are more efficient, and can be as accurate as Monte-Carlo methods on large data sets.

Recall that, for large amounts of data, $p(D|\boldsymbol{\theta}_s, S^h) \cdot p(\boldsymbol{\theta}_s|S^h)$ can often be approximated as a multivariate-Gaussian distribution. Consequently,

$$p(D|S^h) = \int p(D|\boldsymbol{\theta}_s, S^h) \; p(\boldsymbol{\theta}_s|S^h) \; d\boldsymbol{\theta}_s \tag{40}$$

can be evaluated in closed form. In particular, substituting Equation 31 into Equation 40, integrating, and taking the logarithm of the result, we obtain the approximation:

$$\log p(D|S^h) \approx \log p(D|\tilde{\boldsymbol{\theta}}_s, S^h) + \log p(\tilde{\boldsymbol{\theta}}_s|S^h) + \frac{d}{2}\log(2\pi) - \frac{1}{2}\log|A| \tag{41}$$

where d is the dimension of $g(\boldsymbol{\theta}_s)$. For a Bayesian network with unrestricted multinomial distributions, this dimension is typically given by $\sum_{i=1}^{n} q_i(r_i - 1)$. Sometimes, when there are hidden variables, this dimension is lower. See Geiger et al. (1996) for a discussion of this point.

This approximation technique for integration is known as *Laplace's method*, and we refer to Equation 41 as the *Laplace approximation*. Kass et al. (1988) have shown that, under certain regularity conditions, relative errors in this approximation are $O(1/N)$, where N is the number of cases in D. Thus, the Laplace approximation can be extremely accurate. For more detailed discussions of this approximation, see—for example—Kass et al. (1988) and Kass and Raftery (1995).

Although Laplace's approximation is efficient relative to Monte-Carlo approaches, the computation of $|A|$ is nevertheless intensive for large-dimension models. One simplification is to approximate $|A|$ using only the diagonal elements of the Hessian A. Although in so doing, we incorrectly impose independencies among the parameters, researchers have shown that the approximation can be accurate in some circumstances (see, e.g., Becker and Le Cun, 1989, and Chickering and Heckerman, 1996). Another efficient variant of Laplace's approximation is described by Cheeseman and Stutz (1995), who use the approximation in the AutoClass program for data clustering (see also Chickering and Heckerman, 1996.)

We obtain a very efficient (but less accurate) approximation by retaining only those terms in Equation 41 that increase with N: $\log p(D|\tilde{\boldsymbol{\theta}}_s, S^h)$, which increases linearly with N, and $\log|A|$, which increases as $d \log N$. Also, for large N, $\tilde{\boldsymbol{\theta}}_s$ can be approximated by the ML configuration of $\boldsymbol{\theta}_s$. Thus, we obtain

$$\log p(D|S^h) \approx \log p(D|\hat{\boldsymbol{\theta}}_s, S^h) \; - \frac{d}{2} \log N \qquad (42)$$

This approximation is called the *Bayesian information criterion* (BIC), and was first derived by Schwarz (1978).

The BIC approximation is interesting in several respects. First, it does not depend on the prior. Consequently, we can use the approximation without assessing a prior.[13] Second, the approximation is quite intuitive. Namely, it contains a term measuring how well the parameterized model predicts the data ($\log p(D|\hat{\boldsymbol{\theta}}_s, S^h)$) and a term that punishes the complexity of the model ($d/2 \; log N$). Third, the BIC approximation is exactly minus the Minimum Description Length (MDL) criterion described by Rissanen (1987). Thus, recalling the discussion in Section 9, we see that the marginal likelihood provides a connection between cross validation and MDL.

---

[13] One of the technical assumptions used to derive this approximation is that the prior is non-zero around $\hat{\boldsymbol{\theta}}_s$.

10. Priors

To compute the relative posterior probability of a network structure, we must assess the structure prior $p(S^h)$ and the parameter priors $p(\boldsymbol{\theta}_s|S^h)$ (unless we are using large-sample approximations such as BIC/MDL). The parameter priors $p(\boldsymbol{\theta}_s|S^h)$ are also required for the alternative scoring functions discussed in Section 8. Unfortunately, when many network structures are possible, these assessments will be intractable. Nonetheless, under certain assumptions, we can derive the structure and parameter priors for many network structures from a manageable number of direct assessments. Several authors have discussed such assumptions and corresponding methods for deriving priors (Cooper and Herskovits, 1991, 1992; Buntine, 1991; Spiegelhalter et al., 1993; Heckerman et al., 1995b; Heckerman and Geiger, 1996). In this section, we examine some of these approaches.

10.1. PRIORS ON NETWORK PARAMETERS

First, let us consider the assessment of priors for the parameters of network structures. We consider the approach of Heckerman et al. (1995b) who address the case where the local distribution functions are unrestricted multinomial distributions and the assumption of parameter independence holds.

Their approach is based on two key concepts: independence equivalence and distribution equivalence. We say that two Bayesian-network structures for $\mathbf{X}$ are *independence equivalent* if they represent the same set of conditional-independence assertions for $\mathbf{X}$ (Verma and Pearl, 1990). For example, given $\mathbf{X} = \{X, Y, Z\}$, the network structures $X \to Y \to Z$, $X \leftarrow Y \to Z$, and $X \leftarrow Y \leftarrow Z$ represent only the independence assertion that X and Z are conditionally independent given Y. Consequently, these network structures are equivalent. As another example, a *complete network structure* is one that has no missing edge—that is, it encodes no assertion of conditional independence. When $\mathbf{X}$ contains n variables, there are $n!$ possible complete network structures: one network structure for each possible ordering of the variables. All complete network structures for $p(\mathbf{x})$ are independence equivalent. In general, two network structures are independence equivalent if and only if they have the same structure ignoring arc directions and the same v-structures (Verma and Pearl, 1990). A *v-structure* is an ordered tuple (X, Y, Z) such that there is an arc from X to Y and from Z to Y, but no arc between X and Z.

The concept of distribution equivalence is closely related to that of independence equivalence. Suppose that all Bayesian networks for $\mathbf{X}$ under consideration have local distribution functions in the family $\mathcal{F}$. This is not a restriction, per se, because $\mathcal{F}$ can be a large family. We say that two

Bayesian-network structures S_1 and S_2 for $\mathbf{X}$ are *distribution equivalent with respect to (wrt)* $\mathcal{F}$ if they represent the same joint probability distributions for $\mathbf{X}$—that is, if, for every $\boldsymbol{\theta}_{s1}$, there exists a $\boldsymbol{\theta}_{s2}$ such that $p(\mathbf{x}|\boldsymbol{\theta}_{s1}, S_1^h) = p(\mathbf{x}|\boldsymbol{\theta}_{s2}, S_2^h)$, and vice versa.

Distribution equivalence wrt some $\mathcal{F}$ implies independence equivalence, but the converse does not hold. For example, when $\mathcal{F}$ is the family of generalized linear-regression models, the complete network structures for $n \geq 3$ variables do not represent the same sets of distributions. Nonetheless, there are families $\mathcal{F}$—for example, unrestricted multinomial distributions and linear-regression models with Gaussian noise—where independence equivalence implies distribution equivalence wrt $\mathcal{F}$ (Heckerman and Geiger, 1996).

The notion of distribution equivalence is important, because if two network structures S_1 and S_2 are distribution equivalent wrt to a given $\mathcal{F}$, then the hypotheses associated with these two structures are identical—that is, $S_1^h = S_2^h$. Thus, for example, if S_1 and S_2 are distribution equivalent, then their probabilities must be equal in any state of information. Heckerman et al. (1995b) call this property *hypothesis equivalence*.

In light of this property, we should associate each hypothesis with an equivalence class of structures rather than a single network structure, and our methods for learning network structure should actually be interpreted as methods for learning equivalence classes of network structures (although, for the sake of brevity, we often blur this distinction). Thus, for example, the sum over network-structure hypotheses in Equation 33 should be replaced with a sum over equivalence-class hypotheses. An efficient algorithm for identifying the equivalence class of a given network structure can be found in Chickering (1995).

We note that hypothesis equivalence holds provided we interpret Bayesian-network structure simply as a representation of conditional independence. Nonetheless, stronger definitions of Bayesian networks exist where arcs have a causal interpretation (see Section 15). Heckerman et al. (1995b) and Heckerman (1995) argue that, although it is unreasonable to assume hypothesis equivalence when working with causal Bayesian networks, it is often reasonable to adopt a weaker assumption of *likelihood equivalence,* which says that the observations in a database can not help to discriminate two equivalent network structures.

Now let us return to the main issue of this section: the derivation of priors from a manageable number of assessments. Geiger and Heckerman (1995) show that the assumptions of parameter independence and likelihood equivalence imply that the parameters for any *complete* network structure S_c must have a Dirichlet distribution with constraints on the hyperparameters given by

$$\alpha_{ijk} = \alpha \; p(x_i^k, \mathbf{pa}_i^j | S_c^h) \tag{43}$$

where α is the user's equivalent sample size,[14], and $p(x_i^k, \mathbf{pa}_i^j | S_c^h)$ is computed from the user's joint probability distribution $p(\mathbf{x} | S_c^h)$. This result is rather remarkable, as the two assumptions leading to the constrained Dirichlet solution are qualitative.

To determine the priors for parameters of *incomplete* network structures, Heckerman et al. (1995b) use the assumption of *parameter modularity*, which says that if X_i has the same parents in network structures S_1 and S_2, then

$$p(\boldsymbol{\theta}_{ij} | S_1^h) = p(\boldsymbol{\theta}_{ij} | S_2^h)$$

for $j = 1, \ldots, q_i$. They call this property parameter modularity, because it says that the distributions for parameters $\boldsymbol{\theta}_{ij}$ depend only on the structure of the network that is local to variable X_i—namely, X_i and its parents.

Given the assumptions of parameter modularity and parameter independence,[15] it is a simple matter to construct priors for the parameters of an arbitrary network structure given the priors on complete network structures. In particular, given parameter independence, we construct the priors for the parameters of each node separately. Furthermore, if node X_i has parents $\mathbf{Pa}_i$ in the given network structure, we identify a complete network structure where X_i has these parents, and use Equation 43 and parameter modularity to determine the priors for this node. The result is that all terms α_{ijk} for all network structures are determined by Equation 43. Thus, from the assessments α and $p(\mathbf{x} | S_c^h)$, we can derive the parameter priors for all possible network structures. Combining Equation 43 with Equation 35, we obtain a model-selection criterion that assigns equal marginal likelihoods to independence equivalent network structures.

We can assess $p(\mathbf{x} | S_c^h)$ by constructing a Bayesian network, called a *prior network*, that encodes this joint distribution. Heckerman et al. (1995b) discuss the construction of this network.

10.2. PRIORS ON STRUCTURES

Now, let us consider the assessment of priors on network-structure hypotheses. Note that the alternative criteria described in Section 8 can incorporate prior biases on network-structure hypotheses. Methods similar to those discussed in this section can be used to assess such biases.

The simplest approach for assigning priors to network-structure hypotheses is to assume that every hypothesis is equally likely. Of course,

---

[14]Recall the method of equivalent samples for assessing beta and Dirichlet distributions discussed in Section 2.

[15]This construction procedure also assumes that every structure has a non-zero prior probability.

this assumption is typically inaccurate and used only for the sake of convenience. A simple refinement of this approach is to ask the user to exclude various hypotheses (perhaps based on judgments of of cause and effect), and then impose a uniform prior on the remaining hypotheses. We illustrate this approach in Section 12.

Buntine (1991) describes a set of assumptions that leads to a richer yet efficient approach for assigning priors. The first assumption is that the variables can be ordered (e.g., through a knowledge of time precedence). The second assumption is that the presence or absence of possible arcs are mutually independent. Given these assumptions, $n(n-1)/2$ probability assessments (one for each possible arc in an ordering) determines the prior probability of every possible network-structure hypothesis. One extension to this approach is to allow for multiple possible orderings. One simplification is to assume that the probability that an arc is absent or present is independent of the specific arc in question. In this case, only one probability assessment is required.

An alternative approach, described by Heckerman et al. (1995b) uses a prior network. The basic idea is to penalize the prior probability of any structure according to some measure of deviation between that structure and the prior network. Heckerman et al. (1995b) suggest one reasonable measure of deviation.

Madigan et al. (1995) give yet another approach that makes use of imaginary data from a domain expert. In their approach, a computer program helps the user create a hypothetical set of complete data. Then, using techniques such as those in Section 7, they compute the posterior probabilities of network-structure hypotheses given this data, assuming the prior probabilities of hypotheses are uniform. Finally, they use these posterior probabilities as priors for the analysis of the real data.

11. Search Methods

In this section, we examine search methods for identifying network structures with high scores by some criterion. Consider the problem of finding the best network from the set of all networks in which each node has no more than k parents. Unfortunately, the problem for $k > 1$ is NP-hard even when we use the restrictive prior given by Equation 43 (Chickering et al. 1995). Thus, researchers have used heuristic search algorithms, including greedy search, greedy search with restarts, best-first search, and Monte-Carlo methods.

One consolation is that these search methods can be made more efficient when the model-selection criterion is separable. Given a network structure for domain $\mathbf{X}$, we say that a criterion for that structure is *separable* if it can be written as a product of variable-specific criteria:

$$C(S^h, D) = \prod_{i=1}^{n} c(X_i, \mathbf{Pa}_i, D_i) \qquad (44)$$

where D_i is the data restricted to the variables X_i and $\mathbf{Pa}_i$. An example of a separable criterion is the BD criterion (Equations 34 and 35) used in conjunction with any of the methods for assessing structure priors described in Section 10.

Most of the commonly used search methods for Bayesian networks make successive arc changes to the network, and employ the property of separability to evaluate the merit of each change. The possible changes that can be made are easy to identify. For any pair of variables, if there is an arc connecting them, then this arc can either be reversed or removed. If there is no arc connecting them, then an arc can be added in either direction. All changes are subject to the constraint that the resulting network contains no directed cycles. We use E to denote the set of eligible changes to a graph, and $\Delta(e)$ to denote the change in log score of the network resulting from the modification $e \in E$. Given a separable criterion, if an arc to X_i is added or deleted, only $c(X_i, \mathbf{Pa}_i, D_i)$ need be evaluated to determine $\Delta(e)$. If an arc between X_i and X_j is reversed, then only $c(X_i, \mathbf{Pa}_i, D_i)$ and $c(X_j, \Pi_j, D_j)$ need be evaluated.

One simple heuristic search algorithm is greedy search. First, we choose a network structure. Then, we evaluate $\Delta(e)$ for all $e \in E$, and make the change e for which $\Delta(e)$ is a maximum, provided it is positive. We terminate search when there is no e with a positive value for $\Delta(e)$. When the criterion is separable, we can avoid recomputing all terms $\Delta(e)$ after every change. In particular, if neither X_i, X_j, nor their parents are changed, then $\Delta(e)$ remains unchanged for all changes e involving these nodes as long as the resulting network is acyclic. Candidates for the initial graph include the empty graph, a random graph, a graph determined by one of the polynomial algorithms described previously in this section, and the prior network.

A potential problem with any local-search method is getting stuck at a local maximum. One method for escaping local maxima is greedy search with random restarts. In this approach, we apply greedy search until we hit a local maximum. Then, we randomly perturb the network structure, and repeat the process for some manageable number of iterations.

Another method for escaping local maxima is simulated annealing. In this approach, we initialize the system at some temperature T_0. Then, we pick some eligible change e at random, and evaluate the expression $p = \exp(\Delta(e)/T_0)$. If $p > 1$, then we make the change e; otherwise, we make the change with probability p. We repeat this selection and evaluation process α times or until we make β changes. If we make no changes in α repetitions, then we stop searching. Otherwise, we lower the temperature by multiplying the current temperature T_0 by a decay factor $0 < \gamma < 1$, and continue the search process. We stop searching if we have lowered the temperature more than δ times. Thus, this algorithm is controlled by five parameters: $T_0, \alpha, \beta, \gamma$ and δ. To initialize this algorithm, we can start with the empty graph, and make T_0 large enough so that almost every eligible change is made, thus creating a random graph. Alternatively, we may start with a lower temperature, and use one of the initialization methods described for local search.

Another method for escaping local maxima is best-first search (e.g., Korf, 1993). In this approach, the space of all network structures is searched systematically using a heuristic measure that determines the next best structure to examine. Chickering (1996) has shown that, for a fixed amount of computation time, greedy search with random restarts produces better models than does either simulated annealing or best-first search.

One important consideration for any search algorithm is the search space. The methods that we have described search through the space of Bayesian-network structures. Nonetheless, when the assumption of hypothesis equivalence holds, one can search through the space of network-structure equivalence classes. One benefit of the latter approach is that the search space is smaller. One drawback of the latter approach is that it takes longer to move from one element in the search space to another. Work by Spirtes and Meek (1995) and Chickering (1996)) confirm these observations experimentally. Unfortunately, no comparisons are yet available that determine whether the benefits of equivalence-class search outweigh the costs.

12. A Simple Example

Before we move on to other issues, let us step back and look at our overall approach. In a nutshell, we can construct both structure and parameter priors by constructing a Bayesian network (the prior network) along with additional assessments such as an equivalent sample size and causal constraints. We then use either Bayesian model selection, selective model averaging, or full model averaging to obtain one or more networks for prediction and/or explanation. In effect, we have a procedure for using data to improve the structure and probabilities of an initial Bayesian network.

Here, we present two artificial examples to illustrate this process. Consider again the problem of fraud detection from Section 3. Suppose we are given the database D in Table 12, and we want to predict the next case— that is, compute $p(\mathbf{x}_{N+1}|D)$. Let us assert that only two network-structure hypotheses have appreciable probability: the hypothesis corresponding to the network structure in Figure 3 (S_1), and the hypothesis corresponding

TABLE 1. An imagined database for the fraud problem.

Case	Fraud	Gas	Jewelry	Age	Sex
1	no	no	no	30-50	female
2	no	no	no	30-50	male
3	yes	yes	yes	>50	male
4	no	no	no	30-50	male
5	no	yes	no	<30	female
6	no	no	no	<30	female
7	no	no	no	>50	male
8	no	no	yes	30-50	female
9	no	yes	no	<30	male
10	no	no	no	<30	female

to the same structure with an arc added from *Age* to *Gas* (S_2). Furthermore, let us assert that these two hypotheses are equally likely—that is, $p(S_1^h) = p(S_2^h) = 0.5$. In addition, let us use the parameter priors given by Equation 43, where $\alpha = 10$ and $p(\mathbf{x}|S_c^h)$ is given by the prior network in Figure 3. Using Equations 34 and 35, we obtain $p(S_1^h|D) = 0.26$ and $p(S_2^h|D) = 0.74$. Because we have only two models to consider, we can model average according to Equation 33:

$$p(\mathbf{x}_{N+1}|D) = 0.26\ p(\mathbf{x}_{N+1}|D, S_1^h) + 0.74\ p(\mathbf{x}_{N+1}|D, S_2^h)$$

where $p(\mathbf{x}_{N+1}|D, S^h)$ is given by Equation 27. (We don't display these probability distributions.) If we had to choose one model, we would choose S_2, assuming the posterior-probability criterion is appropriate. Note that the data favors the presence of the arc from *Age* to *Gas* by a factor of three. This is not surprising, because in the two cases in the database where fraud is absent and gas was purchased recently, the card holder was less than 30 years old.

An application of model selection, described by Spirtes and Meek (1995), is illustrated in Figure 6. Figure 6a is a hand-constructed Bayesian network for the domain of ICU ventilator management, called the Alarm network (Beinlich et al., 1989). Figure 6c is a random sample from the Alarm network of size 10,000. Figure 6b is a simple prior network for the domain. This network encodes mutual independence among the variables, and (not shown) uniform probability distributions for each variable.

Figure 6d shows the most likely network structure found by a two-pass greedy search in equivalence-class space. In the first pass, arcs were added until the model score did not improve. In the second pass, arcs were deleted until the model score did not improve. Structure priors were uniform; and parameter priors were computed from the prior network using Equation 43 with $\alpha = 10$.

The network structure learned from this procedure differs from the true network structure only by a single arc deletion. In effect, we have used the data to improve dramatically the original model of the user.

13. Bayesian Networks for Supervised Learning

As we discussed in Section 5, the local distribution functions $p(x_i|\mathbf{pa}_i, \boldsymbol{\theta}_i, S^h)$ are essentially classification/regression models. Therefore, if we are doing supervised learning where the explanatory (input) variables cause the outcome (target) variable and data is complete, then the Bayesian-network and classification/regression approaches are identical.

When data is complete but input/target variables do not have a simple cause/effect relationship, tradeoffs emerge between the Bayesian-network approach and other methods. For example, consider the classification problem in Figure 5. Here, the Bayesian network encodes dependencies between findings and ailments as well as among the findings, whereas another classification model such as a decision tree encodes only the relationships between findings and ailment. Thus, the decision tree may produce more accurate classifications, because it can encode the necessary relationships with fewer parameters. Nonetheless, the use of local criteria for Bayesian-network model selection mitigates this advantage. Furthermore, the Bayesian network provides a more natural representation in which to encode prior knowledge, thus giving this model a possible advantage for sufficiently small sample sizes. Another argument, based on bias–variance analysis, suggests that neither approach will dramatically outperform the other (Friedman, 1996).

Singh and Provan (1995) compare the classification accuracy of Bayesian networks and decision trees using complete data sets from the University of California, Irvine Repository of Machine Learning databases. Specifically, they compare C4.5 with an algorithm that learns the structure and probabilities of a Bayesian network using a variation of the Bayesian methods we have described. The latter algorithm includes a model-selection phase that discards some input variables. They show that, overall, Bayesian networks and decisions trees have about the same classification error. These results support the argument of Friedman (1996).

When the input variables cause the target variable and data is incomplete, the dependencies between input variables becomes important, as we discussed in the introduction. Bayesian networks provide a natural framework for learning about and encoding these dependencies. Unfortunately, no studies have been done comparing these approaches with other methods

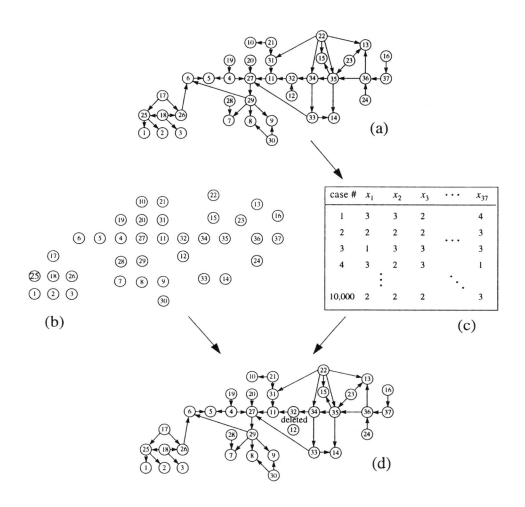

Figure 6. (a) The Alarm network structure. (b) A prior network encoding a user's beliefs about the Alarm domain. (c) A random sample of size 10,000 generated from the Alarm network. (d) The network learned from the prior network and the random sample. The only difference between the learned and true structure is an arc deletion as noted in (d). Network probabilities are not shown.

for handling missing data.

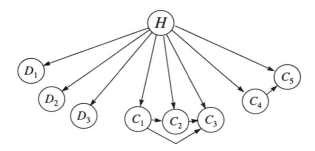

Figure 7.   A Bayesian-network structure for AutoClass. The variable H is hidden. Its possible states correspond to the underlying classes in the data.

14. Bayesian Networks for Unsupervised Learning

The techniques described in this paper can be used for unsupervised learning. A simple example is the AutoClass program of Cheeseman and Stutz (1995), which performs data clustering. The idea behind AutoClass is that there is a single hidden (i.e., never observed) variable that causes the observations. This hidden variable is discrete, and its possible states correspond to the underlying classes in the data. Thus, AutoClass can be described by a Bayesian network such as the one in Figure 7. For reasons of computational efficiency, Cheeseman and Stutz (1995) assume that the discrete variables (e.g., D_1, D_2, D_3 in the figure) and user-defined sets of continuous variables (e.g., $\{C_1, C_2, C_3\}$ and $\{C_4, C_5\}$) are mutually independent given H. Given a data set D, AutoClass searches over variants of this model (including the number of states of the hidden variable) and selects a variant whose (approximate) posterior probability is a local maximum.

AutoClass is an example where the user presupposes the existence of a hidden variable. In other situations, we may be unsure about the presence of a hidden variable. In such cases, we can score models with and without hidden variables to reduce our uncertainty. We illustrate this approach on a real-world case study in Section 16. Alternatively, we may have little idea about what hidden variables to model. The search algorithms of Spirtes et al. (1993) provide one method for identifying possible hidden variables in such situations. Martin and VanLehn (1995) suggest another method.

Their approach is based on the observation that if a set of variables are mutually dependent, then a simple explanation is that these variables have a single hidden common cause rendering them mutually independent. Thus, to identify possible hidden variables, we first apply some learning technique to select a model containing no hidden variables. Then, we look for sets of mutually dependent variables in this learned model. For each

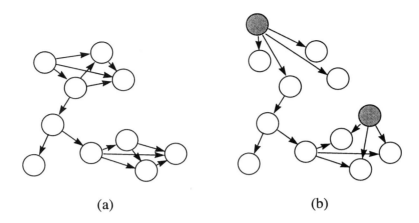

Figure 8.   (a) A Bayesian-network structure for observed variables. (b) A Bayesian-network structure with hidden variables (shaded) suggested by the network structure in (a).

such set of variables (and combinations thereof), we create a new model containing a hidden variable that renders that set of variables conditionally independent. We then score the new models, possibly finding one better than the original. For example, the model in Figure 8a has two sets of mutually dependent variables. Figure 8b shows another model containing hidden variables suggested by this model.

15. Learning Causal Relationships

As we have mentioned, the causal semantics of a Bayesian network provide a means by which we can learn causal relationships. In this section, we examine these semantics, and provide a basic discussion on how causal relationships can be learned. We note that these methods are new and controversial. For critical discussions on both sides of the issue, see Spirtes et al. (1993), Pearl (1995), and Humphreys and Freedman (1995).

For purposes of illustration, suppose we are marketing analysts who want to know whether or not we should increase, decrease, or leave alone the exposure of a particular advertisement in order to maximize our profit from the sales of a product. Let variables *Ad* (*A*) and *Buy* (*B*) represent whether or not an individual has seen the advertisement and has purchased the product, respectively. In one component of our analysis, we would like to learn the physical probability that $B = true$ given that we *force* A to be true, and the physical probability that $B = true$ given that we force A

to be false.[16] We denote these probabilities $p(b|\hat{a})$ and $p(b|\hat{\bar{a}})$, respectively. One method that we can use to learn these probabilities is to perform a randomized experiment: select two similar populations at random, force A to be true in one population and false in the other, and observe B. This method is conceptually simple, but it may be difficult or expensive to find two similar populations that are suitable for the study.

An alternative method follows from causal knowledge. In particular, suppose A causes B. Then, whether we force A to be true or simply observe that A is true in the current population, the advertisement should have the same causal influence on the individual's purchase. Consequently, $p(b|\hat{a}) = p(b|a)$, where $p(b|a)$ is the physical probability that $B = true$ given that we observe $A = true$ in the current population. Similarly, $p(b|\hat{\bar{a}}) = p(b|\bar{a})$. In contrast, if B causes A, forcing A to some state should not influence B at all. Therefore, we have $p(b|\hat{a}) = p(b|\hat{\bar{a}}) = p(b)$. In general, knowledge that X causes Y allows us to equate $p(y|x)$ with $p(y|\hat{x})$, where $\hat{x}$ denotes the intervention that forces X to be x. For purposes of discussion, we use this rule as an operational definition for cause. Pearl (1995) and Heckerman and Shachter (1995) discuss versions of this definition that are more complete and more precise.

In our example, knowledge that A causes B allows us to learn $p(b|\hat{a})$ and $p(b|\hat{\bar{a}})$ from observations alone—no randomized experiment is needed. But how are we to determine whether or not A causes B? The answer lies in an assumption about the connection between causal and probabilistic dependence known as the *causal Markov condition*, described by Spirtes et al. (1993). We say that a directed acyclic graph $\mathcal{C}$ is a *causal graph for variables* $\mathbf{X}$ if the nodes in $\mathcal{C}$ are in a one-to-one correspondence with $\mathbf{X}$, and there is an arc from node X to node Y in $\mathcal{C}$ if and only if X is a direct cause of Y. The causal Markov condition says that if $\mathcal{C}$ is a causal graph for $\mathbf{X}$, then $\mathcal{C}$ is also a Bayesian-network structure for the joint physical probability distribution of $\mathbf{X}$. In Section 3, we described a method based on this condition for constructing Bayesian-network structure from causal assertions. Several researchers (e.g., Spirtes et al., 1993) have found that this condition holds in many applications.

Given the causal Markov condition, we can infer causal relationships from conditional-independence and conditional-dependence relationships that we learn from the data.[17] Let us illustrate this process for the marketing example. Suppose we have learned (with high Bayesian probability)

---

[16]It is important that these interventions do not interfere with the normal effect of A on B. See Heckerman and Shachter (1995) for a discussion of this point.

[17]Spirtes et al. (1993) also require an assumption known as *faithfulness*. We do not need to make this assumption explicit, because it follows from our assumption that $p(\boldsymbol{\theta}_s|S^h)$ is a probability density function.

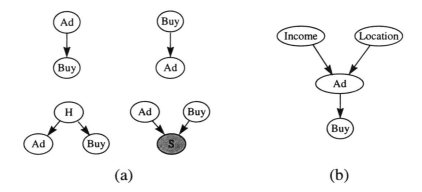

Figure 9.   (a) Causal graphs showing for explanations for an observed dependence between *Ad* and *Buy*. The node *H* corresponds to a hidden common cause of *Ad* and *Buy*. The shaded node *S* indicates that the case has been included in the database. (b) A Bayesian network for which *A* causes *B* is the only causal explanation, given the causal Markov condition.

that the physical probabilities $p(b|a)$ and $p(b|\bar{a})$ are not equal. Given the causal Markov condition, there are four simple causal explanations for this dependence: (1) A is a cause for B, (2) B is a cause for A, (3) there is a hidden common cause of A and B (e.g., the person's income), and (4) A and B are causes for data selection. This last explanation is known as *selection bias*. Selection bias would occur, for example, if our database failed to include instances where A and B are false. These four causal explanations for the presence of the arcs are illustrated in Figure 9a. Of course, more complicated explanations—such as the presence of a hidden common cause and selection bias—are possible.

So far, the causal Markov condition has not told us whether or not A causes B. Suppose, however, that we observe two additional variables: *Income* (I) and *Location* (L), which represent the income and geographic location of the possible purchaser, respectively. Furthermore, suppose we learn (with high probability) the Bayesian network shown in Figure 9b. Given the causal Markov condition, the *only* causal explanation for the conditional-independence and conditional-dependence relationships encoded in this Bayesian network is that *Ad* is a cause for *Buy*. That is, none of the other explanations described in the previous paragraph, or combinations thereof, produce the probabilistic relationships encoded in Figure 9b. Based on this observation, Pearl and Verma (1991) and Spirtes et al. (1993) have created algorithms for inferring causal relationships from dependence relationships for more complicated situations.

TABLE 2. Sufficient statistics for the Sewall and Shah (1968) study.

4	349	13	64	9	207	33	72	12	126	38	54	10	67	49	43
2	232	27	84	7	201	64	95	12	115	93	92	17	79	119	59
8	166	47	91	6	120	74	110	17	92	148	100	6	42	198	73
4	48	39	57	5	47	123	90	9	41	224	65	8	17	414	54
5	454	9	44	5	312	14	47	8	216	20	35	13	96	28	24
11	285	29	61	19	236	47	88	12	164	62	85	15	113	72	50
7	163	36	72	13	193	75	90	12	174	91	100	20	81	142	77
6	50	36	58	5	70	110	76	12	48	230	81	13	49	360	98

16. A Case Study: College Plans

Real-world applications of techniques that we have discussed can be found in Madigan and Raftery (1994), Lauritzen et al. (1994), Singh and Provan (1995), and Friedman and Goldszmidt (1996). Here, we consider an application that comes from a study by Sewell and Shah (1968), who investigated factors that influence the intention of high school students to attend college. The data have been analyzed by several groups of statisticians, including Whittaker (1990) and Spirtes et al. (1993), all of whom have used non-Bayesian techniques.

Sewell and Shah (1968) measured the following variables for 10,318 Wisconsin high school seniors: *Sex* (SEX): male, female; *Socioeconomic Status* (SES): low, lower middle, upper middle, high; *Intelligence Quotient* (IQ): low, lower middle, upper middle, high; *Parental Encouragement* (PE): low, high; and *College Plans* (CP): yes, no. Our goal here is to understand the (possibly causal) relationships among these variables.

The data are described by the sufficient statistics in Table 16. Each entry denotes the number of cases in which the five variables take on some particular configuration. The first entry corresponds to the configuration SEX=male, SES=low, IQ=low, PE=low, and CP=yes. The remaining entries correspond to configurations obtained by cycling through the states of each variable such that the last variable (CP) varies most quickly. Thus, for example, the upper (lower) half of the table corresponds to male (female) students.

As a first pass, we analyzed the data assuming no hidden variables. To generate priors for network parameters, we used the method described in Section 10.1 with an equivalent sample size of 5 and a prior network where

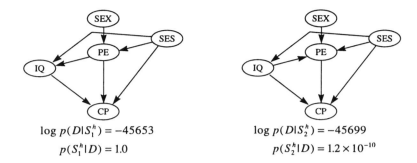

$$\log p(D|S_1^h) = -45653 \qquad\qquad \log p(D|S_2^h) = -45699$$
$$p(S_1^h|D) = 1.0 \qquad\qquad\qquad p(S_2^h|D) = 1.2 \times 10^{-10}$$

Figure 10. The a posteriori most likely network structures without hidden variables.

$p(\mathbf{x}|S_c^h)$ is uniform. (The results were not sensitive to the choice of parameter priors. For example, none of the results reported in this section changed qualitatively for equivalent sample sizes ranging from 3 to 40.) For structure priors, we assumed that all network structures were equally likely, except we excluded structures where SEX and/or SES had parents, and/or CP had children. Because the data set was complete, we used Equations 34 and 35 to compute the posterior probabilities of network structures. The two most likely network structures that we found after an exhaustive search over all structures are shown in Figure 10. Note that the most likely graph has a posterior probability that is extremely close to one.

If we adopt the causal Markov assumption and also assume that there are no hidden variables, then the arcs in both graphs can be interpreted causally. Some results are not surprising—for example the causal influence of socioeconomic status and IQ on college plans. Other results are more interesting. For example, from either graph we conclude that sex influences college plans only indirectly through parental influence. Also, the two graphs differ only by the orientation of the arc between PE and IQ. Either causal relationship is plausible. We note that the second most likely graph was selected by Spirtes et al. (1993), who used a non-Bayesian approach with slightly different assumptions.

The most suspicious result is the suggestion that socioeconomic status has a direct influence on IQ. To question this result, we considered new models obtained from the models in Figure 10 by replacing this direct influence with a hidden variable pointing to both SES and IQ. We also considered models where the hidden variable pointed to SES, IQ, and PE, and none, one, or both of the connections $SES—PE$ and $PE—IQ$ were removed. For each structure, we varied the number of states of the hidden variable from two to six.

We computed the posterior probability of these models using the

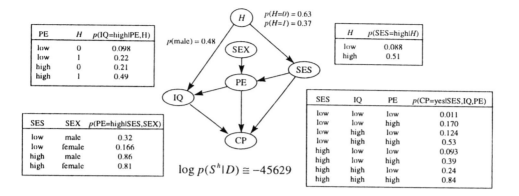

Figure 11.   The a posteriori most likely network structure with a hidden variable. Probabilities shown are MAP values. Some probabilities are omitted for lack of space.

Cheeseman-Stutz (1995) variant of the Laplace approximation. To find the MAP $\tilde{\theta}_s$, we used the EM algorithm, taking the largest local maximum from among 100 runs with different random initializations of θ_s. Among the models we considered, the one with the highest posterior probability is shown in Figure 11. This model is $2 \cdot 10^{10}$ times more likely that the best model containing no hidden variable. The next most likely model containing a hidden variable, which has one additional arc from the hidden variable to PE, is $5 \cdot 10^{-9}$ times less likely than the best model. Thus, if we again adopt the causal Markov assumption and also assume that we have not omitted a reasonable model from consideration, then we have strong evidence that a hidden variable is influencing both socioeconomic status and IQ in this population—a sensible result. An examination of the probabilities in Figure 11 suggests that the hidden variable corresponds to some measure of "parent quality".

17. Pointers to Literature and Software

Like all tutorials, this one is incomplete. For those readers interested in learning more about graphical models and methods for learning them, we offer the following additional references and pointers to software. Buntine (1996) provides another guide to the literature.

Spirtes et al. (1993) and Pearl (1995) use methods based on large-sample approximations to learn Bayesian networks. In addition, as we have discussed, they describe methods for learning causal relationships from observational data.

In addition to directed models, researchers have explored network structures containing undirected edges as a knowledge representation. These representations are discussed (e.g.) in Lauritzen (1982), Verma and Pearl (1990), Frydenberg (1990), Whittaker (1990), and Richardson (1997). Bayesian methods for learning such models from data are described by Dawid and Lauritzen (1993) and Buntine (1994).

Finally, several research groups have developed software systems for learning graphical models. For example, Scheines et al. (1994) have developed a software program called TETRAD II for learning about cause and effect. Badsberg (1992) and Højsgaard et al. (1994) have built systems that can learn with mixed graphical models using a variety of criteria for model selection. Thomas, Spiegelhalter, and Gilks (1992) have created a system called BUGS that takes a learning problem specified as a Bayesian network and compiles this problem into a Gibbs-sampler computer program.

Acknowledgments

I thank Max Chickering, Usama Fayyad, Eric Horvitz, Chris Meek, Koos Rommelse, and Padhraic Smyth for their comments on earlier versions of this manuscript. I also thank Max Chickering for implementing the software used to analyze the Sewall and Shah (1968) data, and Chris Meek for bringing this data set to my attention.

Notation

$X, Y, Z, \ldots$ Variables or their corresponding nodes in a Bayesian network

$\mathbf{X}, \mathbf{Y}, \mathbf{Z}, \ldots$ Sets of variables or corresponding sets of nodes

$X = x$ Variable X is in state x

$\mathbf{X} = \mathbf{x}$ The set of variables $\mathbf{X}$ is in configuration $\mathbf{x}$

$\mathbf{x}, \mathbf{y}, \mathbf{z}$ Typically refer to a complete case, an incomplete case, and missing data in a case, respectively

$\mathbf{X} \setminus \mathbf{Y}$ The variables in X that are not in Y

D A data set: a set of cases

D_l The first $l - 1$ cases in D

$p(\mathbf{x}|\mathbf{y})$ The probability that $\mathbf{X} = \mathbf{x}$ given $\mathbf{Y} = \mathbf{y}$ (also used to describe a probability density, probability distribution, and probability density)

$\mathrm{E}_{p(\cdot)}(x)$ The expectation of x with respect to $p(\cdot)$

S A Bayesian network structure (a directed acyclic graph)

$\mathbf{Pa}_i$ The variable or node corresponding to the parents of node X_i in a Bayesian network structure

$\mathbf{pa}_i$ A configuration of the variables $\mathbf{Pa}_i$

r_i The number of states of discrete variable X_i

q_i The number of configurations of $\mathbf{Pa}_i$

S_c A complete network structure

S^h The hypothesis corresponding to network structure S

θ_{ijk} The multinomial parameter corresponding to the probability $p(X_i = x_i^k | \mathbf{Pa}_i = \mathbf{pa}_i^j)$

$\boldsymbol{\theta}_{ij} = (\theta_{ij2}, \ldots, \theta_{ijr_i})$

$\boldsymbol{\theta}_i = (\boldsymbol{\theta}_{i1}, \ldots, \boldsymbol{\theta}_{iq_i})$

$\boldsymbol{\theta}_s = (\boldsymbol{\theta}_1, \ldots, \boldsymbol{\theta}_n)$

α An equivalent sample size

α_{ijk} The Dirichlet hyperparameter corresponding to θ_{ijk}

$\alpha_{ij} = \sum_{k=1}^{r_i} \alpha_{ijk}$

N_{ijk} The number of cases in data set D where $X_i = x_i^k$ and $\mathbf{Pa}_i = \mathbf{pa}_i^j$

$N_{ij} = \sum_{k=1}^{r_i} N_{ijk}$

References

Aliferis, C. and Cooper, G. (1994). An evaluation of an algorithm for inductive learning of Bayesian belief networks using simulated data sets. In *Proceedings of Tenth Conference on Uncertainty in Artificial Intelligence,* Seattle, WA, pages 8–14. Morgan Kaufmann.

Badsberg, J. (1992). Model search in contingency tables by CoCo. In Dodge, Y. and Whittaker, J., editors, *Computational Statistics*, pages 251–256. Physica Verlag, Heidelberg.

Becker, S. and LeCun, Y. (1989). Improving the convergence of back-propagation learning with second order methods. In *Proceedings of the 1988 Connectionist Models Summer School*, pages 29–37. Morgan Kaufmann.

Beinlich, I., Suermondt, H., Chavez, R., and Cooper, G. (1989). The ALARM monitoring system: A case study with two probabilistic inference techniques for belief networks. In *Proceedings of the Second European Conference on Artificial Intelligence in Medicine,* London, pages 247–256. Springer Verlag, Berlin.

Bernardo, J. (1979). Expected information as expected utility. *Annals of Statistics*, 7:686–690.

Bernardo, J. and Smith, A. (1994). *Bayesian Theory*. John Wiley and Sons, New York.

Buntine, W. (1991). Theory refinement on Bayesian networks. In *Proceedings of Seventh Conference on Uncertainty in Artificial Intelligence,* Los Angeles, CA, pages 52–60. Morgan Kaufmann.

Buntine, W. (1993). Learning classification trees. In *Artificial Intelligence Frontiers in Statistics: AI and statistics III*. Chapman and Hall, New York.

Buntine, W. (1996). A guide to the literature on learning graphical models. *IEEE Transactions on Knowledge and Data Engineering*, 8:195–210.

Chaloner, K. and Duncan, G. (1983). Assessment of a beta prior distribution: PM elicitation. *The Statistician*, 32:174–180.

Cheeseman, P. and Stutz, J. (1995). Bayesian classification (AutoClass): Theory and results. In Fayyad, U., Piatesky-Shapiro, G., Smyth, P., and Uthurusamy, R., editors, *Advances in Knowledge Discovery and Data Mining*, pages 153–180. AAAI Press, Menlo Park, CA.

Chib, S. (1995). Marginal likelihood from the Gibbs output. *Journal of the American Statistical Association*, 90:1313–1321.

Chickering, D. (1995). A transformational characterization of equivalent Bayesian network structures. In *Proceedings of Eleventh Conference on Uncertainty in Artificial Intelligence,* Montreal, QU, pages 87–98. Morgan Kaufmann.

Chickering, D. (1996). Learning equivalence classes of Bayesian-network structures. In *Proceedings of Twelfth Conference on Uncertainty in Artificial Intelligence,* Portland, OR. Morgan Kaufmann.

Chickering, D., Geiger, D., and Heckerman, D. (1995). Learning Bayesian networks: Search methods and experimental results. In *Proceedings of Fifth Conference on Artificial Intelligence and Statistics,* Ft. Lauderdale, FL, pages 112–128. Society for Artificial Intelligence in Statistics.

Chickering, D. and Heckerman, D. (Revised November, 1996). Efficient approximations for the marginal likelihood of incomplete data given a Bayesian network. Technical Report MSR-TR-96-08, Microsoft Research, Redmond, WA.

Cooper, G. (1990). Computational complexity of probabilistic inference using Bayesian belief networks (Research note). *Artificial Intelligence*, 42:393–405.

Cooper, G. and Herskovits, E. (1992). A Bayesian method for the induction of probabilistic networks from data. *Machine Learning*, 9:309–347.

Cooper, G. and Herskovits, E. (January, 1991). A Bayesian method for the induction of probabilistic networks from data. Technical Report SMI-91-1, Section on Medical Informatics, Stanford University.

Cox, R. (1946). Probability, frequency and reasonable expectation. *American Journal of Physics*, 14:1–13.

Dagum, P. and Luby, M. (1993). Approximating probabilistic inference in bayesian belief networks is np-hard. *Artificial Intelligence*, 60:141–153.

D'Ambrosio, B. (1991). Local expression languages for probabilistic dependence. In *Proceedings of Seventh Conference on Uncertainty in Artificial Intelligence*, Los Angeles, CA, pages 95–102. Morgan Kaufmann.

Darwiche, A. and Provan, G. (1996). Query DAGs: A practical paradigm for implementing belief-network inference. In *Proceedings of Twelfth Conference on Uncertainty in Artificial Intelligence*, Portland, OR, pages 203–210. Morgan Kaufmann.

Dawid, P. (1984). Statistical theory. The prequential approach (with discussion). *Journal of the Royal Statistical Society A*, 147:178–292.

Dawid, P. (1992). Applications of a general propagation algorithm for probabilistic expert systmes. *Statistics and Computing*, 2:25–36.

de Finetti, B. (1970). *Theory of Probability*. Wiley and Sons, New York.

Dempster, A., Laird, N., and Rubin, D. (1977). Maximum likelihood from incomplete data via the EM algorithm. *Journal of the Royal Statistical Society*, B 39:1–38.

DiCiccio, T., Kass, R., Raftery, A., and Wasserman, L. (July, 1995). Computing Bayes factors by combining simulation and asymptotic approximations. Technical Report 630, Department of Statistics, Carnegie Mellon University, PA.

Friedman, J. (1995). Introduction to computational learning and statistical prediction. Technical report, Department of Statistics, Stanford University.

Friedman, J. (1996). On bias, variance, 0/1-loss, and the curse of dimensionality. *Data Mining and Knowledge Discovery*, 1.

Friedman, N. and Goldszmidt, M. (1996). Building classifiers using Bayesian networks. In *Proceedings AAAI-96 Thirteenth National Conference on Artificial Intelligence*, Portland, OR, pages 1277–1284. AAAI Press, Menlo Park, CA.

Frydenberg, M. (1990). The chain graph Markov property. *Scandinavian Journal of Statistics*, 17:333–353.

Geiger, D. and Heckerman, D. (Revised February, 1995). A characterization of the Dirichlet distribution applicable to learning Bayesian networks. Technical Report MSR-TR-94-16, Microsoft Research, Redmond, WA.

Geiger, D., Heckerman, D., and Meek, C. (1996). Asymptotic model selection for directed networks with hidden variables. In *Proceedings of Twelfth Conference on Uncertainty in Artificial Intelligence*, Portland, OR, pages 283–290. Morgan Kaufmann.

Geman, S. and Geman, D. (1984). Stochastic relaxation, Gibbs distributions and the Bayesian restoration of images. *IEEE Transactions on Pattern Analysis and Machine Intelligence*, 6:721–742.

Gilks, W., Richardson, S., and Spiegelhalter, D. (1996). *Markov Chain Monte Carlo in Practice*. Chapman and Hall.

Good, I. (1950). *Probability and the Weighing of Evidence*. Hafners, New York.

Heckerman, D. (1989). A tractable algorithm for diagnosing multiple diseases. In *Proceedings of the Fifth Workshop on Uncertainty in Artificial Intelligence*, Windsor, ON, pages 174–181. Association for Uncertainty in Artificial Intelligence, Mountain View, CA. Also in Henrion, M., Shachter, R., Kanal, L., and Lemmer, J., editors, *Uncertainty in Artificial Intelligence 5*, pages 163–171. North-Holland, New York, 1990.

Heckerman, D. (1995). A Bayesian approach for learning causal networks. In *Proceedings of Eleventh Conference on Uncertainty in Artificial Intelligence*, Montreal, QU, pages 285–295. Morgan Kaufmann.

Heckerman, D. and Geiger, D. (Revised, November, 1996). Likelihoods and priors for Bayesian networks. Technical Report MSR-TR-95-54, Microsoft Research, Redmond, WA.

Heckerman, D., Geiger, D., and Chickering, D. (1995a). Learning Bayesian networks: The combination of knowledge and statistical data. *Machine Learning*, 20:197–243.

Heckerman, D., Mamdani, A., and Wellman, M. (1995b). Real-world applications of Bayesian networks. *Communications of the ACM*, 38.

Heckerman, D. and Shachter, R. (1995). Decision-theoretic foundations for causal reasoning. *Journal of Artificial Intelligence Research*, 3:405–430.

Højsgaard, S., Skjøth, F., and Thiesson, B. (1994). User's guide to BIOFROST. Technical report, Department of Mathematics and Computer Science, Aalborg, Denmark.

Howard, R. (1970). Decision analysis: Perspectives on inference, decision, and experimentation. *Proceedings of the IEEE*, 58:632–643.

Howard, R. and Matheson, J. (1981). Influence diagrams. In Howard, R. and Matheson, J., editors, *Readings on the Principles and Applications of Decision Analysis*, volume II, pages 721–762. Strategic Decisions Group, Menlo Park, CA.

Howard, R. and Matheson, J., editors (1983). *The Principles and Applications of Decision Analysis*. Strategic Decisions Group, Menlo Park, CA.

Humphreys, P. and Freedman, D. (1996). The grand leap. *British Journal for the Philosphy of Science*, 47:113–118.

Jaakkola, T. and Jordan, M. (1996). Computing upper and lower bounds on likelihoods in intractable networks. In *Proceedings of Twelfth Conference on Uncertainty in Artificial Intelligence,* Portland, OR, pages 340–348. Morgan Kaufmann.

Jensen, F. (1996). *An Introduction to Bayesian Networks*. Springer.

Jensen, F. and Andersen, S. (1990). Approximations in Bayesian belief universes for knowledge based systems. Technical report, Institute of Electronic Systems, Aalborg University, Aalborg, Denmark.

Jensen, F., Lauritzen, S., and Olesen, K. (1990). Bayesian updating in recursive graphical models by local computations. *Computational Statisticals Quarterly*, 4:269–282.

Kass, R. and Raftery, A. (1995). Bayes factors. *Journal of the American Statistical Association*, 90:773–795.

Kass, R., Tierney, L., and Kadane, J. (1988). Asymptotics in Bayesian computation. In Bernardo, J., DeGroot, M., Lindley, D., and Smith, A., editors, *Bayesian Statistics 3*, pages 261–278. Oxford University Press.

Koopman, B. (1936). On distributions admitting a sufficient statistic. *Transactions of the American Mathematical Society*, 39:399–409.

Korf, R. (1993). Linear-space best-first search. *Artificial Intelligence*, 62:41–78.

Lauritzen, S. (1982). *Lectures on Contingency Tables*. University of Aalborg Press, Aalborg, Denmark.

Lauritzen, S. (1992). Propagation of probabilities, means, and variances in mixed graphical association models. *Journal of the American Statistical Association*, 87:1098–1108.

Lauritzen, S. and Spiegelhalter, D. (1988). Local computations with probabilities on graphical structures and their application to expert systems. *J. Royal Statistical Society B*, 50:157–224.

Lauritzen, S., Thiesson, B., and Spiegelhalter, D. (1994). Diagnostic systems created by model selection methods: A case study. In Cheeseman, P. and Oldford, R., editors, *AI and Statistics IV*, volume Lecture Notes in Statistics, 89, pages 143–152. Springer-Verlag, New York.

MacKay, D. (1992a). Bayesian interpolation. *Neural Computation*, 4:415–447.

MacKay, D. (1992b). A practical Bayesian framework for backpropagation networks. *Neural Computation*, 4:448–472.

MacKay, D. (1996). Choice of basis for the Laplace approximation. Technical report, Cavendish Laboratory, Cambridge, UK.

Madigan, D., Garvin, J., and Raftery, A. (1995). Eliciting prior information to enhance the predictive performance of Bayesian graphical models. *Communications in Statistics: Theory and Methods*, 24:2271–2292.

Madigan, D. and Raftery, A. (1994). Model selection and accounting for model uncertainty in graphical models using Occam's window. *Journal of the American Statistical*

Association, 89:1535–1546.

Madigan, D., Raftery, A., Volinsky, C., and Hoeting, J. (1996). Bayesian model averaging. In *Proceedings of the AAAI Workshop on Integrating Multiple Learned Models*, Portland, OR.

Madigan, D. and York, J. (1995). Bayesian graphical models for discrete data. *International Statistical Review*, 63:215–232.

Martin, J. and VanLehn, K. (1995). Discrete factor analysis: Learning hidden variables in bayesian networks. Technical report, Department of Computer Science, University of Pittsburgh, PA. Available at http://bert.cs.pitt.edu/ vanlehn.

Meng, X. and Rubin, D. (1991). Using EM to obtain asymptotic variance-covariance matrices: The SEM algorithm. *Journal of the American Statistical Association*, 86:899–909.

Neal, R. (1993). Probabilistic inference using Markov chain Monte Carlo methods. Technical Report CRG-TR-93-1, Department of Computer Science, University of Toronto.

Olmsted, S. (1983). *On representing and solving decision problems*. PhD thesis, Department of Engineering-Economic Systems, Stanford University.

Pearl, J. (1986). Fusion, propagation, and structuring in belief networks. *Artificial Intelligence*, 29:241–288.

Pearl, J. (1995). Causal diagrams for empirical research. *Biometrika*, 82:669–710.

Pearl, J. and Verma, T. (1991). A theory of inferred causation. In Allen, J., Fikes, R., and Sandewall, E., editors, *Knowledge Representation and Reasoning: Proceedings of the Second International Conference*, pages 441–452. Morgan Kaufmann, New York.

Pitman, E. (1936). Sufficient statistics and intrinsic accuracy. *Proceedings of the Cambridge Philosophy Society*, 32:567–579.

Raftery, A. (1995). Bayesian model selection in social research. In Marsden, P., editor, *Sociological Methodology*. Blackwells, Cambridge, MA.

Raftery, A. (1996). *Hypothesis testing and model selection*, chapter 10. Chapman and Hall.

Ramamurthi, K. and Agogino, A. (1988). Real time expert system for fault tolerant supervisory control. In Tipnis, V. and Patton, E., editors, *Computers in Engineering*, pages 333–339. American Society of Mechanical Engineers, Corte Madera, CA.

Ramsey, F. (1931). Truth and probability. In Braithwaite, R., editor, *The Foundations of Mathematics and other Logical Essays*. Humanities Press, London. Reprinted in Kyburg and Smokler, 1964.

Richardson, T. (1997). Extensions of undirected and acyclic, directed graphical models. In *Proceedings of Sixth Conference on Artificial Intelligence and Statistics*, Ft. Lauderdale, FL, pages 407–419. Society for Artificial Intelligence in Statistics.

Rissanen, J. (1987). Stochastic complexity (with discussion). *Journal of the Royal Statistical Society, Series B*, 49:223–239 and 253–265.

Robins, J. (1986). A new approach to causal interence in mortality studies with sustained exposure results. *Mathematical Modelling*, 7:1393–1512.

Rubin, D. (1978). Bayesian inference for causal effects: The role of randomization. *Annals of Statistics*, 6:34–58.

Russell, S., Binder, J., Koller, D., and Kanazawa, K. (1995). Local learning in probabilistic networks with hidden variables. In *Proceedings of the Fourteenth International Joint Conference on Artificial Intelligence*, Montreal, QU, pages 1146–1152. Morgan Kaufmann, San Mateo, CA.

Saul, L., Jaakkola, T., and Jordan, M. (1996). Mean field theory for sigmoid belief networks. *Journal of Artificial Intelligence Research*, 4:61–76.

Savage, L. (1954). *The Foundations of Statistics*. Dover, New York.

Schervish, M. (1995). *Theory of Statistics*. Springer-Verlag.

Schwarz, G. (1978). Estimating the dimension of a model. *Annals of Statistics*, 6:461–464.

Sewell, W. and Shah, V. (1968). Social class, parental encouragement, and educational aspirations. *American Journal of Sociology*, 73:559–572.

Shachter, R. (1988). Probabilistic inference and influence diagrams. *Operations Research*,

36:589–604.

Shachter, R., Andersen, S., and Poh, K. (1990). Directed reduction algorithms and decomposable graphs. In *Proceedings of the Sixth Conference on Uncertainty in Artificial Intelligence,* Boston, MA, pages 237–244. Association for Uncertainty in Artificial Intelligence, Mountain View, CA.

Shachter, R. and Kenley, C. (1989). Gaussian influence diagrams. *Management Science,* 35:527–550.

Silverman, B. (1986). *Density Estimation for Statistics and Data Analysis.* Chapman and Hall, New York.

Singh, M. and Provan, G. (November, 1995). Efficient learning of selective Bayesian network classifiers. Technical Report MS-CIS-95-36, Computer and Information Science Department, University of Pennsylvania, Philadelphia, PA.

Spetzler, C. and Stael von Holstein, C. (1975). Probability encoding in decision analysis. *Management Science,* 22:340–358.

Spiegelhalter, D., Dawid, A., Lauritzen, S., and Cowell, R. (1993). Bayesian analysis in expert systems. *Statistical Science,* 8:219–282.

Spiegelhalter, D. and Lauritzen, S. (1990). Sequential updating of conditional probabilities on directed graphical structures. *Networks,* 20:579–605.

Spirtes, P., Glymour, C., and Scheines, R. (1993). *Causation, Prediction, and Search.* Springer-Verlag, New York.

Spirtes, P. and Meek, C. (1995). Learning Bayesian networks with discrete variables from data. In *Proceedings of First International Conference on Knowledge Discovery and Data Mining,* Montreal, QU. Morgan Kaufmann.

Suermondt, H. and Cooper, G. (1991). A combination of exact algorithms for inference on Bayesian belief networks. *International Journal of Approximate Reasoning,* 5:521–542.

Thiesson, B. (1995a). Accelerated quantification of Bayesian networks with incomplete data. In *Proceedings of First International Conference on Knowledge Discovery and Data Mining,* Montreal, QU, pages 306–311. Morgan Kaufmann.

Thiesson, B. (1995b). Score and information for recursive exponential models with incomplete data. Technical report, Institute of Electronic Systems, Aalborg University, Aalborg, Denmark.

Thomas, A., Spiegelhalter, D., and Gilks, W. (1992). Bugs: A program to perform Bayesian inference using Gibbs sampling. In Bernardo, J., Berger, J., Dawid, A., and Smith, A., editors, *Bayesian Statistics 4,* pages 837–842. Oxford University Press.

Tukey, J. (1977). *Exploratory Data Analysis.* Addison–Wesley.

Tversky, A. and Kahneman, D. (1974). Judgment under uncertainty: Heuristics and biases. *Science,* 185:1124–1131.

Verma, T. and Pearl, J. (1990). Equivalence and synthesis of causal models. In *Proceedings of Sixth Conference on Uncertainty in Artificial Intelligence,* Boston, MA, pages 220–227. Morgan Kaufmann.

Whittaker, J. (1990). *Graphical Models in Applied Multivariate Statistics.* John Wiley and Sons.

Winkler, R. (1967). The assessment of prior distributions in Bayesian analysis. *American Statistical Association Journal,* 62:776–800.

A VIEW OF THE EM ALGORITHM THAT JUSTIFIES INCREMENTAL, SPARSE, AND OTHER VARIANTS

RADFORD M. NEAL

Dept. of Statistics and Dept. of Computer Science
University of Toronto, Toronto, Ontario, Canada
http://www.cs.toronto.edu/~radford/

GEOFFREY E. HINTON

Department of Computer Science
University of Toronto, Toronto, Ontario, Canada
http://www.cs.toronto.edu/~hinton/

Abstract. The EM algorithm performs maximum likelihood estimation for data in which some variables are unobserved. We present a function that resembles negative free energy and show that the M step maximizes this function with respect to the model parameters and the E step maximizes it with respect to the distribution over the unobserved variables. From this perspective, it is easy to justify an incremental variant of the EM algorithm in which the distribution for only one of the unobserved variables is recalculated in each E step. This variant is shown empirically to give faster convergence in a mixture estimation problem. A variant of the algorithm that exploits sparse conditional distributions is also described, and a wide range of other variant algorithms are also seen to be possible.

1. Introduction

The Expectation-Maximization (EM) algorithm finds maximum likelihood parameter estimates in problems where some variables were unobserved. Special cases of the algorithm date back several decades, and its use has grown even more since its generality and widespread applicability were discussed by Dempster, Laird, and Rubin (1977). The scope of the algorithm's applications are evident in the book by McLachlan and Krishnan (1997).

The EM algorithm estimates the parameters of a model iteratively, starting from some initial guess. Each iteration consists of an Expectation (E) step, which finds the distribution for the unobserved variables, given the known values for the observed variables and the current estimate of the parameters, and a Maximization (M) step, which re-estimates the parameters to be those with maximum likelihood, under the assumption that the distribution found in the E step is correct. It can be shown that each such iteration improves the true likelihood, or leaves it unchanged (if a local maximum has already been reached, or in uncommon cases, before then).

The M step of the algorithm may be only partially implemented, with the new estimate for the parameters improving the likelihood given the distribution found in the E step, but not necessarily maximizing it. Such a partial M step always results in the true likelihood improving as well. Dempster, *et al* refer to such variants as "generalized EM (GEM)" algorithms. A sub-class of GEM algorithms of wide applicability, the "Expectation-Conditional Maximization (ECM)" algorithms, have been developed by Meng and Rubin (1992), and further generalized by Meng and van Dyk (1997).

In many cases, partial implementation of the E step is also natural. The unobserved variables are commonly independent, and influence the likelihood of the parameters only through simple sufficient statistics. If these statistics can be updated incrementally when the distribution for one of the variables is re-calculated, it makes sense to immediately re-estimate the parameters before performing the E step for the next unobserved variable, as this utilizes the new information immediately, speeding convergence. An incremental algorithm along these general lines was investigated by Nowlan (1991). However, such incremental variants of the EM algorithm have not previously received any formal justification.

We present here a view of the EM algorithm in which it is seen as maximizing a joint function of the parameters and of the distribution over the unobserved variables that is analogous to the "free energy" function used in statistical physics, and which can also be viewed in terms of a Kullback-Liebler divergence. The E step maximizes this function with respect to the distribution over unobserved variables; the M step with respect to the parameters. Csiszàr and Tusnàdy (1984) and Hathaway (1986) have also viewed EM in this light.

In this paper, we use this viewpoint to justify variants of the EM algorithm in which the joint maximization of this function is performed by other means — a process which must also lead to a maximum of the true likelihood. In particular, we can now justify incremental versions of the algorithm, which in effect employ a partial E step, as well as "sparse" versions, in which most iterations update only that part of the distribution for an unobserved variable pertaining to its most likely values, and "winner-take-all" versions, in which, for early iterations, the distributions over unobserved variables are restricted to those in which a single value has probability one.

We include a brief demonstration showing that use of an incremental algorithm speeds convergence for a simple mixture estimation problem.

2. General theory

Suppose that we have observed the value of some random variable, Z, but not the value of another variable, Y, and that based on this data, we wish to find the maximum likelihood estimate for the parameters of a model for Y and Z. We assume that this problem is not easily solved directly, but that the corresponding problem in which Y is also known would be more tractable. For simplicity, we assume here that Y has a finite range, as is often the case, but the results can be generalized.

Assume that the joint probability for Y and Z is parameterized using θ, as $P(y, z \mid \theta)$. The marginal probability for Z is then $P(z \mid \theta) = \sum_y P(y, z \mid \theta)$. Given observed data, z, we wish to find the value of θ that maximizes the log likelihood, $L(\theta) = \log P(z \mid \theta)$.

The EM algorithm starts with some initial guess at the maximum likelihood parameters, $\theta^{(0)}$, and then proceeds to iteratively generate successive estimates, $\theta^{(1)}, \theta^{(2)}, \ldots$ by repeatedly applying the following two steps, for $t = 1, 2, \ldots$

$$
\left.
\begin{array}{ll}
\textbf{E Step:} & \text{Compute a distribution } \widetilde{P}^{(t)} \text{ over the range of } Y \text{ such} \\
& \text{that } \widetilde{P}^{(t)}(y) = P(y \mid z, \theta^{(t-1)}). \\[2ex]
\textbf{M Step:} & \text{Set } \theta^{(t)} \text{ to the } \theta \text{ that maximizes } E_{\widetilde{P}^{(t)}}[\log P(y, z \mid \theta)].
\end{array}
\right\} \quad (1)
$$

Here, $E_{\widetilde{P}}[\,\cdot\,]$ denotes expectation with respect to the distribution over the range of Y given by $\widetilde{P}$. Note that in preparation for the later generalization, the standard algorithm has here been expressed in a slightly non-standard fashion.

The E step of the algorithm can be seen as representing the unknown value for Y by a distribution of values, and the M step as then performing maximum likelihood estimation for the joint data obtained by combining this with the known value of Z, an operation that is assumed to be feasible. As shown by Dempster, *et al*, each EM iteration increases the true log likelihood, $L(\theta)$, or leaves it unchanged. Indeed, for most models, the algorithm will converge to a local maximum of $L(\theta)$ (though there are exceptions to this). Such monotonic improvement in $L(\theta)$ is also guaranteed for any

GEM algorithm, in which only a partial maximization is performed in the
M step, with $\theta^{(t)}$ simply set to some value such that $E_{\widetilde{P}^{(t)}}[\log P(z, y \mid \theta^{(t)})]$
is greater than $E_{\widetilde{P}^{(t)}}[\log P(y, z \mid \theta^{(t-1)})]$ (or is equal if convergence has been
reached).

In order to make sense of the corresponding idea of partially performing
the E step, we use a view of the EM algorithm and its variants in which
both the E and the M steps are seen as maximizing, or at least increasing,
the same function, $F(\widetilde{P}, \theta)$. We will show that if a local maximum of F
occurs at θ^* and $\widetilde{P}^*$, then a local maximum of L occurs at θ^* as well. We
can therefore contemplate a wide variety of algorithms for maximizing L
by means of maximizing F, among which are incremental algorithms, in
which each E step updates only one factor of $\widetilde{P}$, corresponding to one data
item.

The function $F(\widetilde{P}, \theta)$ is defined as follows:

$$F(\widetilde{P}, \theta) \;=\; E_{\widetilde{P}}[\log P(y, z \mid \theta)] \;+\; H(\widetilde{P}) \tag{2}$$

where $H(\widetilde{P}) = -E_{\widetilde{P}}[\log \widetilde{P}(y)]$ is the entropy of the distribution $\widetilde{P}$. Note
that F is defined with respect to a particular value for the observed data,
z, which is fixed throughout. For simplicity, we will assume here that
$P(y, z \mid \theta)$ is never zero, so that F is always finite, but this restriction
is not essential. We also need to assume that $P(y, z \mid \theta)$ is a continuous
function of θ, from which we can conclude that F is a continuous function
of both θ and $\widetilde{P}$.

Apart from a change of sign, the function F is analogous to the "variational free energy" of statistical physics, provided that the physical states
are taken to be values of Y, and the "energy" of a state is $-\log P(y, z \mid \theta)$.
One can also relate F to the Kullback-Liebler divergence between $\widetilde{P}(y)$ and
$P_\theta(y) = P(y \mid z, \theta)$, as follows:

$$F(\widetilde{P}, \theta) \;=\; -D(\widetilde{P} \| P_\theta) \;+\; L(\theta) \tag{3}$$

The following two lemmas state properties of F corresponding to well-
known facts from statistical physics — that the "Boltzmann" distribution
over states minimizes the variational free energy, and that the free energy
is related to the log of the "partition function". They also correspond to
the properties that the Kullback-Liebler divergence is non-negative and is
zero between identical distributions.

Lemma 1 *For a fixed value of θ, there is a unique distribution, P_θ, that
maximizes $F(\widetilde{P}, \theta)$, given by $P_\theta(y) = P(y \mid z, \theta)$. Furthermore, this P_θ
varies continuously with θ.*

PROOF. In maximizing F with respect to $\widetilde{P}$, we are constrained by the requirement that $\widetilde{P}(y) \geq 0$ for all y. Solutions with $\widetilde{P}(y) = 0$ for some y are not possible, however — one can easily show that the slope of the entropy is infinite at such points, so that moving slightly away from the boundary will increase F. Any maximum of F must therefore occur at a critical point subject to the constraint that $\sum_y \widetilde{P}(y) = 1$, and can be found using a Lagrange multiplier. At such a maximum, P_θ, the gradient of F with respect to the components of $\widetilde{P}$ will be normal to the constraint surface, i.e. for some λ and for all y,

$$\lambda = \frac{\partial F}{\partial \widetilde{P}(y)}(P_\theta) = \log P(y, z \,|\, \theta) - \log P_\theta(y) - 1 \qquad (4)$$

From this, it follows that $P_\theta(y)$ must be proportional to $P(y, z \,|\, \theta)$. Normalizing so that $\sum_y P_\theta(y) = 1$, we have $P_\theta(y) = P(y \,|\, z, \theta)$ as the unique solution. That P_θ varies continuously with θ follows immediately from our assumption that $P(y, z \,|\, \theta)$ does.

Lemma 2 *If* $\widetilde{P}(y) = P(y \,|\, z, \theta) = P_\theta(y)$ *then* $F(\widetilde{P}, \theta) = \log P(z \,|\, \theta) = L(\theta)$.

PROOF. If $\widetilde{P}(y) = P(y \,|\, z, \theta)$, then

$$
\begin{aligned}
F(\widetilde{P}, \theta) &= E_{\widetilde{P}}[\log P(y, z \,|\, \theta)] + H(\widetilde{P}) \\
&= E_{\widetilde{P}}[\log P(y, z \,|\, \theta)] - E_{\widetilde{P}}[\log P(y \,|\, z, \theta)] \\
&= E_{\widetilde{P}}[\log P(y, z \,|\, \theta) - \log P(y \,|\, z, \theta)] \\
&= E_{\widetilde{P}}[\log P(z \,|\, \theta)] \\
&= \log P(z \,|\, \theta)
\end{aligned}
$$

An iteration of the the standard EM algorithm can therefore be expressed in terms of the function F as follows:

> **E Step:** Set $\widetilde{P}^{(t)}$ to the $\widetilde{P}$ that maximizes $F(\widetilde{P}, \theta^{(t-1)})$.
>
> **M Step:** Set $\theta^{(t)}$ to the θ that maximizes $F(\widetilde{P}^{(t)}, \theta)$.

$$(5)$$

Theorem 1 *The iterations given by (1) and by (5) are equivalent.*

PROOF. That the E steps of the iterations are equivalent follows directly from Lemma 1. That the M steps are equivalent follows from the fact that the entropy term in the definition of F in equation (2) does not depend on θ.

Once the EM iterations have been expressed in the form (5), it is clear that the algorithm converges to values $\widetilde{P}^*$ and θ^* that locally maximize

$F(\widetilde{P}, \theta)$ (ignoring the possibility of convergence to a saddle point). The following theorem shows that, in general, finding a local maximum for $F(\widetilde{P}, \theta)$ will also yield a local maximum for $L(\theta)$, justifying not only the standard algorithm of (5), but variants of it in which the E and M steps are performed partially, as well as algorithms in which the maximization is done with respect to $\widetilde{P}$ and θ simultaneously.

Theorem 2 *If $F(\widetilde{P}, \theta)$ has a local maximum at $\widetilde{P}^*$ and θ^*, then $L(\theta)$ has a local maximum at θ^* as well. Similarly, if F has a global maximum at $\widetilde{P}^*$ and θ^*, then L has a global maximum at θ^*.*

PROOF. By combining Lemmas 1 and 2, we see that $L(\theta) = \log P(z \mid \theta) = F(P_\theta, \theta)$, for any θ, and that, in particular, $L(\theta^*) = F(P_{\theta^*}, \theta^*) = F(\widetilde{P}^*, \theta^*)$. To show that θ^* is a local maximum of L, we need to show that there is no $\theta^\dagger$ near to θ^* for which $L(\theta^\dagger) > L(\theta^*)$. To see this, note that if such a $\theta^\dagger$ existed, then we would also have $F(\widetilde{P}^\dagger, \theta^\dagger) > F(\widetilde{P}^*, \theta^*)$, where $\widetilde{P}^\dagger = P_{\theta^\dagger}$. But since P_θ varies continuously with θ, $\widetilde{P}^\dagger$ must be near to $\widetilde{P}^*$, contradicting the assumption that F has a local maximum at $\widetilde{P}^*$ and θ^*. The proof for global maxima is analogous, but without the restriction to nearby values of θ. The assumptions of continuity are unnecessary for this latter result.

3. Incremental algorithms

In typical applications, we wish to find the maximum likelihood parameter estimate given a number of independent data items. The observed variable, Z, can then be decomposed as $(Z_1, \ldots, Z_n)$, and the unobserved variable, Y, as $(Y_1, \ldots, Y_n)$. The joint probability for Y and Z can be factored as $P(y, z \mid \theta) = \prod_i P(y_i, z_i \mid \theta)$. Often, the data items are also identically distributed, but we will not need to assume that here.

An incremental variant of the EM algorithm that exploits this structure can be justified on the basis of Theorem 2. Note that since the Y_i are independent, we can restrict the search for a maximum of F to distributions $\widetilde{P}$ that factor as $\widetilde{P}(y) = \prod_i \widetilde{P}_i(y_i)$, since $\widetilde{P}$ will have this form at the maximum. We can then write F in the form $F(\widetilde{P}, \theta) = \sum_i F_i(\widetilde{P}_i, \theta)$, where

$$F_i(\widetilde{P}_i, \theta) = E_{\widetilde{P}_i}[\log P(y_i, z_i \mid \theta)] + H(\widetilde{P}_i) \tag{6}$$

An incremental algorithm using the following iteration can then be used to maximize F, and hence L, starting from some guess at the parameters, $\theta^{(0)}$, and some guess at the distribution, $\widetilde{P}_i^{(0)}$, which might or might not be consistent with $\theta^{(0)}$:

E Step: Choose some data item, i, to be updated.

Set $P_j^{(t)} = P_j^{(t-1)}$ for $j \neq i$. (This takes no time).

Set $P_i^{(t)}$ to the $\tilde{P}_i$ that maximizes $F_i(\tilde{P}_i, \theta^{(t-1)})$, given by $\tilde{P}_i^{(t)}(y_i) = P(y_i \mid z_i, \theta^{(t-1)})$. $\qquad$ (7)

M Step: Set $\theta^{(t)}$ to the θ that maximizes $F(\tilde{P}^{(t)}, \theta)$, or, equivalently, that maximizes $E_{\tilde{P}^{(t)}}[\log P(y, z \mid \theta)]$.

Data items might be selected for updating in the E step cyclicly, or by some scheme that gives preference to data items for which $\tilde{P}_i$ has not yet stabilized.

Each E step of the above algorithm requires looking at only a single data item, but, as written, it appears that the M step requires looking at all components of $\tilde{P}$. This can be avoided in the common case where the inferential import of the complete data can be summarized by a vector of sufficient statistics that can be incrementally updated, as is the case with models in the exponential family.

Letting this vector of sufficient statistics be $s(y, z) = \sum_i s_i(y_i, z_i)$, the standard EM iteration of (1) can be implemented as follows:

E Step: Set $\tilde{s}^{(t)} = E_{\tilde{P}}[s(y, z)]$, where $\tilde{P}(y) = P(y \mid z, \theta^{(t-1)})$.

(In detail, set $\tilde{s}^{(t)} = \sum_i \tilde{s}_i^{(t)}$, with $\tilde{s}_i^{(t)} = E_{\tilde{P}_i}[s_i(y_i, z_i)]$, where $\tilde{P}_i(y_i) = P(y_i \mid z_i, \theta^{(t-1)})$.) $\qquad$ (8)

M Step: Set $\theta^{(t)}$ to the θ with maximum likelihood given $\tilde{s}^{(t)}$.

Similarly, the iteration of (7) can be implemented using sufficient statistics that are maintained incrementally, starting with an initial guess, $\tilde{s}_i^{(0)}$, which may or may not be consistent with $\theta^{(0)}$. Subsequent iterations proceed as follows:

E Step: Choose some data item, i, to be updated.

Set $\tilde{s}_j^{(t)} = \tilde{s}_j^{(t-1)}$ for $j \neq i$. (This takes no time.)

Set $\tilde{s}_i^{(t)} = E_{\tilde{P}_i}[s_i(y_i, z_i)]$, for $\tilde{P}_i(y_i) = P(y_i \mid z_i, \theta^{(t-1)})$. $\qquad$ (9)

Set $\tilde{s}^{(t)} = \tilde{s}^{(t-1)} - \tilde{s}_i^{(t-1)} + \tilde{s}_i^{(t)}$.

M Step: Set $\theta^{(t)}$ to the θ with maximum likelihood given $s^{(t)}$.

In iteration (9), both the E and the M steps take constant time, independent of the number of data items. A cycle of n such iterations, visiting each data item once, will sometimes take only slightly more time than one iteration of the standard algorithm, and should make more progress, since the distributions for each variable found in the partial E steps are utilized immediately, instead of being held until the distributions for all the unobserved variables have been found. Nearly as fast convergence may be obtained with an intermediate variant of the algorithm, in which each E step recomputes the distributions for several data items (but many fewer than n). Use of this intermediate variant rather than the pure incremental algorithm reduces the amount of time spent in performing the M steps.

Note that an algorithm based on iteration (9) must save the last value computed for each $\tilde{s}_i$, so that its contribution to $\tilde{s}$ may be removed when a new value for $\tilde{s}_i$ is computed. This requirement will generally not be onerous. The incremental update of $\tilde{s}$ could potentially lead to problems with cumulative round-off error. If necessary, this accumulation can be avoided in several ways — one could use a fixed-point representation of $\tilde{s}$, in which addition and subtraction is exact, for example, or recompute $\tilde{s}$ non-incrementally at infrequent intervals.

An incremental variant of the EM algorithm somewhat similar to that of (9) was investigated by Nowlan (1991). His variant does not maintain strictly accurate sufficient statistics, however. Rather, it uses statistics computed as an exponentially decaying average of recently-visited data points, with iterations of the following form:

E Step: Select the next data item, i, for updating.

$$\left. \begin{array}{l} \text{Set } \tilde{s}_i^{(t)} \;=\; E_{\tilde{P}_i}[s_i(y_i, z_i)], \text{ for } \tilde{P}_i(y_i) = P(y_i \,|\, z_i,\, \theta^{(t-1)}). \\[6pt] \text{Set } \tilde{s}^{(t)} \;=\; \gamma \tilde{s}^{(t-1)} + \tilde{s}_i^{(t)}. \end{array} \right\} \quad (10)$$

M Step: Set $\theta^{(t)}$ to the θ with maximum likelihood given $s^{(t)}$.

where $0 < \gamma < 1$ is a decay constant.

The above algorithm will not converge to the exact answer, at least not if γ is kept at some fixed value. It is found empirically, however, that it can converge to the vicinity of the correct answer more rapidly than the standard EM algorithm. When the data set is large and redundant, one might expect that, with an appropriate value for γ, this algorithm could be faster than the incremental algorithm of (9), since it can forget out-of-date statistics more rapidly.

4. Demonstration for a mixture model

In order to demonstrate that the incremental algorithm of (9) can speed convergence, we have applied it to a simple mixture of Gaussians problem. The algorithm using iteration (10) was also tested.

In the Gaussian mixture model, the observed variables, Z_i, are real-valued, and the unobserved variables, Y_i, are binary, indicating from which of two Gaussian distributions the corresponding observed variable was generated. The joint probability (density) for Y_i and Z_i given parameters $\theta = (\alpha, \mu_0, \sigma_0, \mu_1, \sigma_1)$ is as follows:

$$P(y_i, z_i \mid \alpha, \mu_0, \sigma_0, \mu_1, \sigma_1)$$

$$= \begin{cases} (1 - \alpha)\,(2\pi\sigma_0^2)^{-\frac{1}{2}} \exp\left(-\tfrac{1}{2}(z_i - \mu_0)^2/\sigma_0^2\right) & \text{if } y_i = 0 \\[2ex] \alpha\,(2\pi\sigma_1^2)^{-\frac{1}{2}} \exp\left(-\tfrac{1}{2}(z_i - \mu_1)^2/\sigma_1^2\right) & \text{if } y_i = 1 \end{cases} \tag{11}$$

For this problem, the vector of sufficient statistics for data item i is

$$s_i(y_i, z_i) \;=\; [\,(1-y_i),\; (1-y_i)z_i,\; (1-y_i)z_i^2,\; y_i,\; y_i z_i,\; y_i z_i^2\,] \tag{12}$$

Given $s(y, z) = \sum_i s_i(y_i, z_i) = (n_0, m_0, q_0, n_1, m_1, q_1)$, the maximum likelihood parameter estimates are given by $\alpha = n_1/(n_0 + n_1)$, $\mu_0 = m_0/n_0$, $\sigma_0^2 = q_0/n_0 - (m_0/n_0)^2$, $\mu_1 = m_1/n_1$, and $\sigma_1^2 = q_1/n_1 - (m_1/n_1)^2$.

We synthetically generated a sample of 1000 points, z_i, from this distribution with $\alpha = 0.3$, $\mu_0 = 0$, $\sigma_0 = 1$, $\mu_1 = -0.2$, and $\sigma_1 = 0.1$. We then applied the standard algorithm of (8) and the incremental algorithm of (9) to this data. As initial parameter values, we used $\alpha^{(0)} = 0.5$, $\mu_0^{(0)} = +1.0$, $\sigma_0^{(0)} = 1$, $\mu_1^{(0)} = -1$, and $\sigma_1^{(0)} = 1$. For the incremental algorithm, a single iteration of the standard algorithm was then performed to initialize the distributions for the unobserved variables. This is not necessarily the best procedure, but was done to avoid any arbitrary selection for the starting distributions, which would affect the comparison with the standard algorithm. The incremental algorithm visited data points cyclicly.

Both algorithms converged to identical maxima of L, at which $\alpha^* = 0.269$, $\mu_0^* = -0.016$, $\sigma_0^* = 0.959$, $\mu_1^* = -0.193$, and $\sigma_1^* = 0.095$. Special measures to control round-off error in the incremental algorithm were found to be unnecessary in this case (using 64-bit floating-point numbers). The rates of convergence of the two algorithms are shown in Figure 1, in which the log likelihood, L, is plotted as a function of the number of "passes" — a pass being one iteration for the standard algorithm, and n iterations for the incremental algorithm. (In both case, a pass visits each data point once.) As can be seen, the incremental algorithm reached any given level of L in about half as many passes as the standard algorithm.

Unfortunately, each pass of the incremental algorithm required about twice as much computation time as did a pass of the standard algorithm, due primarily to the computation required to perform an M step after visiting every data point. This cost can be greatly reduced by using an

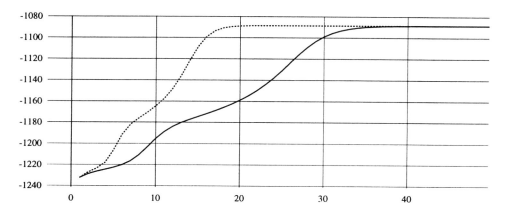

Figure 1. Comparison of convergence rates for the standard EM algorithm (solid line) and the incremental algorithm (dotted line). The log likelihood is shown on the vertical axis, the number of passes of the algorithm on the horizontal axis.

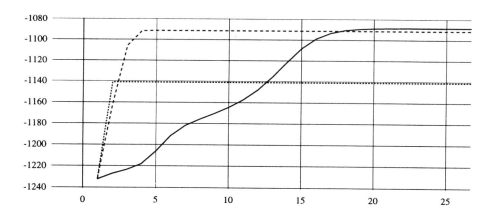

Figure 2. Convergence rates of the algorithm using exponentially decayed statistics with $\gamma = 0.99$ (dashed line) and $\gamma = 0.95$ (dotted line). For comparison, the performance of the incremental algorithm (solid line) is reproduced as well (as in Figure 1).

intermediate algorithm in which each E step recomputes the distributions for the next ten data points. The rate of convergence with this algorithm is virtually indistinguishable from that of the pure incremental algorithm, while the time required for each pass is only about 10% greater than for the standard algorithm, producing a substantial net gain in speed.

The algorithm of iteration (10) was also tested. The same initialization procedure was used, with the elaboration that the decayed statistics were computed, but not used, during the initial standard iteration, in order to initialize them for use in later iterations.

Two runs of this algorithm are shown in Figure 2, done with $\gamma = 0.99$ and with $\gamma = 0.95$. Also shown is the run of the incremental algorithm (as in Figure 1). The run with $\gamma = 0.99$ converged to a good (but not optimal) point more rapidly than the incremental algorithm, but the run with $\gamma = 0.95$ converged to a rather poor point. These results indicate that there may be scope for improved algorithms that combine such fast convergence with the guarantees of stability and convergence to a true maximum that the incremental algorithm provides.

5. A sparse algorithm

A "sparse" variant of the EM algorithm may be advantageous when the unobserved variable, Y, can take on many possible values, but only a small set of "plausible" values have non-negligible probability (given the observed data and the current parameter estimate). Substantial computation may sometimes be saved in this case by "freezing" the probabilities of the implausible values for many iterations, re-computing only the relative probabilities of the plausible values. At infrequent intervals, the probabilities for all values are recomputed, and a new set of plausible values selected (which may differ from the old set due to the intervening change in the parameter estimate). This procedure can be designed so that F is guaranteed to increase with every iteration, ensuring stability, even though some iterations may decrease L.

In detail, the sparse algorithm represents $\tilde{P}^{(t)}$ as follows:

$$\tilde{P}^{(t)}(y) = \begin{cases} q_y^{(t)} & \text{if } y \notin S^{(t)} \\ Q^{(t)} r_y^{(t)} & \text{if } y \in S^{(t)} \end{cases} \tag{13}$$

Here, $S^{(t)}$ is the set of plausible values for Y, the $q_y^{(t)}$ are the frozen probabilities for implausible values, $Q^{(t)}$ is the frozen total probability for plausible values, and the $r_y^{(t)}$ are the relative probabilities for the plausible values, which are updated every iteration.

Most iterations of the sparse algorithm go as follows:

$$
\left.
\begin{aligned}
&\textbf{E Step:} \quad \text{Set } S^{(t)} = S^{(t-1)}, \; Q^{(t)} = Q^{(t-1)}, \text{ and } q_y^{(t)} = q_y^{(t-1)} \\
&\qquad\qquad \text{for all } y \notin S^{(t)}. \text{ (This takes no time.)} \\
&\qquad\qquad \text{Set } r_y^{(t)} = P(y \,|\, z, \theta^{(t-1)}) \,/\, P(y \in S^{(t)} \,|\, z, \theta^{(t-1)}) \\
&\qquad\qquad \text{for all } y \in S^{(t)}. \\[4pt]
&\textbf{M Step:} \quad \text{Set } \theta^{(t)} \text{ to the } \theta \text{ that maximizes } F(\widetilde{P}^{(t)}, \theta).
\end{aligned}
\right\} \quad (14)
$$

It can easily be shown that the above E step selects those $r_y^{(t)}$ that maximize $F(\widetilde{P}^{(t)}, \theta^{(t-1)})$. For suitable models, this restricted E step will take time proportional only to the size of $S^{(t)}$, independent of how many values are in the full range for Y. For the method to be useful, the model must also be such that the M step above can be done efficiently, as is discussed below.

On occasion, the sparse algorithm performs a full iteration, as follows:

$$
\left.
\begin{aligned}
&\textbf{E Step:} \quad \text{Set } S^{(t)} \text{ to those } y \text{ for which } P(y \,|\, z, \theta^{(t-1)}) \\
&\qquad\qquad \text{is non-negligible.} \\
&\qquad\qquad \text{For all } y \notin S^{(t)}, \text{ set } q_y^{(t)} = P(y \,|\, z, \theta^{(t-1)}). \\
&\qquad\qquad \text{Set } Q^{(t)} = P(y \in S^{(t)} \,|\, z, \theta^{(t-1)}). \\
&\qquad\qquad \text{For all } y \in S^{(t)}, \text{ set } r_y^{(t)} = P(y \,|\, z, \theta^{(t-1)}) \,/\, Q^{(t)}. \\[4pt]
&\textbf{M Step:} \quad \text{Set } \theta^{(t)} \text{ to the } \theta \text{ that maximizes } F(\widetilde{P}^{(t)}, \theta).
\end{aligned}
\right\} \quad (15)
$$

The decisions as to which values have "non-negligible" probability can be made using various heuristics. One could take the N most probable values, for some predetermined N, or one could take as many values as are needed to account for some predetermined fraction of the total probability. The choice made will affect only the speed of convergence, not the stability of the algorithm — even with a bad choice for $S^{(t)}$, subsequent iterations cannot decrease F.

For problems with independent observations, where $Y = (Y_1, \ldots, Y_n)$, each data item, i, can be treated independently, with a separate set of "plausible" values, $S_i^{(t)}$, and with distributions $P_i^{(t)}$ expressed in terms of quantities $q_{i,y}^{(t)}$, $Q_i^{(t)}$, and $r_{i,y}^{(t)}$. For efficient implementation of the M step in (14), it is probably necessary for the model to have simple sufficient statistics. The contribution to these of values with frozen probabilities can then be computed once when the full iteration of (15) is performed, and saved for use in the M step of (14), in combination with the statistics for the plausible values in $S_i^{(t)}$.

The Gaussian mixture problem provides an example of the potential usefulness of the sparse algorithm. If there are many components in the mixture, each data point will typically have a non-negligible probability of having come from only a few components whose means are nearby. Freezing the small probabilities for the distant components avoids the continual recomputation of quantities that have negligible effect on the course of the algorithm.

Note that the sparse and incremental variants of EM can easily be applied in combination.

6. Other variants

The incremental and sparse algorithms are not the only variants of EM that can be justified by viewing it in terms of maximizing F. One could, for example, employ any of a wide variety of standard optimization methods to find the maximum of $F(\tilde{P}, \theta)$ with respect to $\tilde{P}$ and θ jointly. This view can also provide insight into other EM-like procedures.

For example, a "winner-take-all" variant of the EM algorithm may be obtained by constraining the distribution $\tilde{P}$ to assign zero probability to all but one value. Such a distribution can, of course, be represented by the single value that is assigned probability one. Obviously, such a variant of the algorithm cannot, in general, converge to the unconstrained maximum of $F(\tilde{P}, \theta)$, and hence need not find a value of θ that maximizes L. There might, however, be computational advantages to using this variant in the early stages of maximizing F, switching to a variant capable of finding the true maximum only when the winner-take-all variant has converged.

The well-known "K-means" clustering algorithm can be seen in this light as an incremental, winner-take-all version of the EM algorithm as applied to the Gaussian mixture problem (with variances and mixing proportions fixed). The winner-take-all method is also often used in estimating Hidden Markov Models for speech recognition. In neither instance is L guaranteed to increase with each iteration, which might lead one to regard these methods as completely *ad hoc*, but they appear more sensible when seen in terms of maximizing F, even though they don't find the unconstrained maximum.

ACKNOWLEDGEMENTS

We thank Wray Buntine, Bill Byrne, Mike Jordan, Jim Kay, Andreas Stolcke, and Mike Titterington for comments on an earlier version of this paper. This work was supported by the Natural Sciences and Engineering Research Council of Canada and by the Ontario Information Technology Research Centre. Geoffrey Hinton is the Nesbitt-Burns fellow of the Canadian Institute for Advanced Research.

REFERENCES

Csiszàr I. and Tusnàdy, G. (1984) "Information geometry and alternating minimization procedures", in E. J. Dudewicz, *et al* (editors) *Recent Results in Estimation Theory and Related Topics* (Statistics and Decisions, Supplement Issue No. 1, 1984).

Dempster, A. P., Laird, N. M., and Rubin, D. B. (1977) "Maximum likelihood from incomplete data via the EM algorithm" (with discussion), *Journal of the Royal Statistical Society B*, vol. 39, pp. 1-38.

Hathaway, R. J. (1986) "Another interpretation of the EM algorithm for mixture distributions", *Statistics and Probability Letters*, vol. 4, pp. 53-56.

McLachlan, G. J. and Krishnan, T. (1997) *The EM Algorithm and Extensions*, New York: Wiley.

Meng, X. L. and Rubin, D. B. (1992) "Recent extensions of the EM algorithm (with discussion)", in J. M. Bernardo, J. O. Berger, A. P. Dawid, and A. F. M. Smith (editors), *Bayesian Statistics 4*, Oxford: Clarendon Press.

Meng, X. L. and van Dyk, D. (1997) "The EM algorithm — an old folksong sung to a fast new tune" (with discussion), *Journal of the Royal Statistical Society B*, vol. 59, pp. 511-567.

Nowlan, S. J. (1991) *Soft Competitive Adaptation: Neural Network Learning Algorithms based on Fitting Statistical Mixtures*, Ph. D. thesis, School of Computer Science, Carnegie Mellon University, Pittsburgh.

PART IV : LEARNING FROM DATA

LATENT VARIABLE MODELS

CHRISTOPHER M. BISHOP

Microsoft Research
St. George House
1 Guildhall Street
Cambridge CB2 3NH, U.K.

Abstract. A powerful approach to probabilistic modelling involves supplementing a set of observed variables with additional latent, or hidden, variables. By defining a joint distribution over visible and latent variables, the corresponding distribution of the observed variables is then obtained by marginalization. This allows relatively complex distributions to be expressed in terms of more tractable joint distributions over the expanded variable space. One well-known example of a hidden variable model is the mixture distribution in which the hidden variable is the discrete component label. In the case of continuous latent variables we obtain models such as factor analysis. The structure of such probabilistic models can be made particularly transparent by giving them a graphical representation, usually in terms of a directed acyclic graph, or Bayesian network. In this chapter we provide an overview of latent variable models for representing continuous variables. We show how a particular form of linear latent variable model can be used to provide a *probabilistic* formulation of the well-known technique of principal components analysis (PCA). By extending this technique to mixtures, and hierarchical mixtures, of probabilistic PCA models we are led to a powerful interactive algorithm for data visualization. We also show how the probabilistic PCA approach can be generalized to non-linear latent variable models leading to the Generative Topographic Mapping algorithm (GTM). Finally, we show how GTM can itself be extended to model temporal data.

1. Density Modelling

One of the central problems in pattern recognition and machine learning is that of density estimation, in other words the construction of a model of a probability distribution given a finite sample of data drawn from that distribution. Throughout this chapter we will consider the problem of modelling the distribution of a set of continuous variables $t_1, \ldots, t_d$ which we will collectively denote by the vector $\mathbf{t}$.

A standard approach to the problem of density estimation involves parametric models in which a specific form for the density is proposed which contains a number of adaptive parameters. Values for these parameters are then determined from an observed data set $D = \{\mathbf{t}_1, \ldots, \mathbf{t}_N\}$ consisting of N data vectors. The most widely used parametric model is the normal, or Gaussian, distribution given by

$$p(\mathbf{t}|\boldsymbol{\mu}, \boldsymbol{\Sigma}) = (2\pi)^{-d/2}|\boldsymbol{\Sigma}|^{-1/2} \exp\left\{-\frac{1}{2}(\mathbf{t} - \boldsymbol{\mu})\boldsymbol{\Sigma}^{-1}(\mathbf{t} - \boldsymbol{\mu})^{\mathrm{T}}\right\} \quad (1)$$

where $\boldsymbol{\mu}$ is the mean, $\boldsymbol{\Sigma}$ is the covariance matrix, and $|\boldsymbol{\Sigma}|$ denotes the determinant of $\boldsymbol{\Sigma}$. One technique for setting the values of these parameters is that of maximum likelihood which involves consideration of the log probability of the observed data set given the parameters, i.e.

$$\mathcal{L}(\boldsymbol{\mu}, \boldsymbol{\Sigma}) = \ln p(D|\boldsymbol{\mu}, \boldsymbol{\Sigma}) = \sum_{n=1}^{N} \ln p(\mathbf{t}_n|\boldsymbol{\mu}, \boldsymbol{\Sigma}) \quad (2)$$

in which it is assumed that the data vectors $\mathbf{t}_n$ are drawn independently from the distribution. When viewed as a function of $\boldsymbol{\mu}$ and $\boldsymbol{\Sigma}$, the quantity $p(D|\boldsymbol{\mu}, \boldsymbol{\Sigma})$ is called the *likelihood* function. Maximization of the likelihood (or equivalently the log likelihood) with respect to $\boldsymbol{\mu}$ and $\boldsymbol{\Sigma}$ leads to the set of parameter values which are most likely to have given rise to the observed data set. For the normal distribution (1) the log likelihood (2) can be maximized analytically, leading to the intuitive result [1] that the maximum likelihood solutions $\widehat{\boldsymbol{\mu}}$ and $\widehat{\boldsymbol{\Sigma}}$ are given by

$$\widehat{\boldsymbol{\mu}} = \frac{1}{N} \sum_{n=1}^{N} \mathbf{t}_n \quad (3)$$

$$\widehat{\boldsymbol{\Sigma}} = \frac{1}{N} \sum_{n=1}^{N} (\mathbf{t}_n - \widehat{\boldsymbol{\mu}})(\mathbf{t}_n - \widehat{\boldsymbol{\mu}})^{\mathrm{T}} \quad (4)$$

corresponding to the sample mean and sample covariance respectively.

As an alternative to maximum likelihood, we can define priors over $\boldsymbol{\mu}$ and $\boldsymbol{\Sigma}$ use Bayes' theorem, together with the observed data, to determine the posterior distribution. An introduction to Bayesian inference for the normal distribution is given in [5].

While the simple normal distribution (1) is widely used, it suffers from some significant limitations. In particular, it can often prove to be too flexible in that the number of independent parameters in the model can be excessive. This problem is addressed through the introduction of continuous latent variables. On the other hand, the normal distribution can also be insufficiently flexible since it can only represent uni-modal distributions. A more general family of distributions can be obtained by considering mixtures of Gaussians, corresponding to the introduction of a discrete latent variable. We consider each of these approaches in turn.

1.1. LATENT VARIABLES

Consider the number of free parameters in the normal distribution (1). Since Σ is symmetric, it contains $d(d+1)/2$ independent parameters. There are a further d independent parameters in μ, making $d(d+3)/2$ parameters in total. For large d this number grows like d^2, and excessively large numbers of data points may be required to ensure that the maximum likelihood solution for Σ is well determined. One way to reduce the number of free parameters in the model is to consider a diagonal covariance matrix, which has just d free parameters. This, however, corresponds to a very strong assumption, namely that the components of $\mathbf{t}$ are statistically independent, and such a model is therefore unable to capture the correlations between different components.

We now show how the number of degrees of freedom within the model can be controlled, while still allowing correlations to be captured, by introducing *latent* (or 'hidden') variables. The goal of a latent variable model is to express the distribution $p(\mathbf{t})$ of the variables $t_1, \ldots, t_d$ in terms of a smaller number of latent variables $\mathbf{x} = (x_1, \ldots, x_q)$ where $q < d$. This is achieved by first decomposing the joint distribution $p(\mathbf{t}, \mathbf{x})$ into the product of the marginal distribution $p(\mathbf{x})$ of the latent variables and the conditional distribution $p(\mathbf{t}|\mathbf{x})$ of the data variables given the latent variables. It is often convenient to assume that the conditional distribution factorizes over the data variables, so that the joint distribution becomes

$$p(\mathbf{t}, \mathbf{x}) = p(\mathbf{x})p(\mathbf{t}|\mathbf{x}) = p(\mathbf{x}) \prod_{i=1}^{d} p(t_i|\mathbf{x}). \tag{5}$$

This factorization property can be expressed graphically in terms of a Bayesian network, as shown in Figure 1.

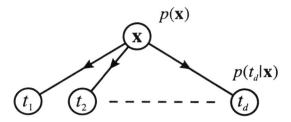

Figure 1. Bayesian network representation of the latent variable distribution given by (5), in which the data variables $t_1, \ldots, t_d$ are independent given the latent variables $\mathbf{x}$.

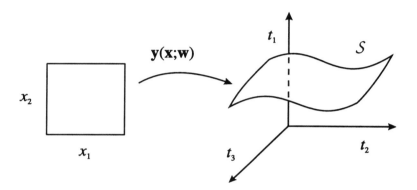

Figure 2. The non-linear function $\mathbf{y}(\mathbf{x}; \mathbf{w})$ defines a manifold S embedded in data space given by the image of the latent space under the mapping $\mathbf{x} \to \mathbf{y}$.

We next express the conditional distribution $p(\mathbf{t}|\mathbf{x})$ in terms of a mapping from latent variables to data variables, so that

$$\mathbf{t} = \mathbf{y}(\mathbf{x}; \mathbf{w}) + \mathbf{u} \tag{6}$$

where $\mathbf{y}(\mathbf{x}; \mathbf{w})$ is a function of the latent variable $\mathbf{x}$ with parameters $\mathbf{w}$, and $\mathbf{u}$ is an $\mathbf{x}$-independent noise process. If the components of $\mathbf{u}$ are uncorrelated, the conditional distribution for $\mathbf{t}$ will factorize as in (5). Geometrically the function $\mathbf{y}(\mathbf{x}; \mathbf{w})$ defines a manifold in data space given by the image of the latent space, as shown in Figure 2.

The definition of the latent variable model is completed by specifying the distribution $p(\mathbf{u})$, the mapping $\mathbf{y}(\mathbf{x}; \mathbf{w})$, and the marginal distribution $p(\mathbf{x})$. As we shall see later, it is often convenient to regard $p(\mathbf{x})$ as a *prior* distribution over the latent variables.

The desired model for the distribution $p(\mathbf{t})$ of the data is obtained by marginalizing over the latent variables

$$p(\mathbf{t}) = \int p(\mathbf{t}|\mathbf{x})p(\mathbf{x})\,d\mathbf{x}. \tag{7}$$

This integration will, in general, be analytically intractable except for specific forms of the distributions $p(\mathbf{t}|\mathbf{x})$ and $p(\mathbf{x})$.

One of the simplest latent variable models is called *factor analysis* [3, 4] and is based on a linear mapping $\mathbf{y}(\mathbf{x}; \mathbf{w})$ so that

$$\mathbf{t} = \mathbf{W}\mathbf{x} + \boldsymbol{\mu} + \mathbf{u}, \tag{8}$$

in which $\mathbf{W}$ and $\boldsymbol{\mu}$ are adaptive parameters. The distribution $p(\mathbf{x})$ is chosen to be a zero-mean unit covariance Gaussian distribution $\mathcal{N}(\mathbf{0}, \mathbf{I})$, while the noise model for $\mathbf{u}$ is also a zero mean Gaussian with a covariance matrix $\boldsymbol{\Psi}$ which is diagonal. Using (7) it is easily shown that the distribution $p(\mathbf{t})$ is also Gaussian, with mean $\boldsymbol{\mu}$ and a covariance matrix given by $\boldsymbol{\Psi} + \mathbf{W}\mathbf{W}^{\mathrm{T}}$.

The parameters of the model, comprising $\mathbf{W}$, $\boldsymbol{\Psi}$ and $\boldsymbol{\mu}$, can again be determined by maximum likelihood. There is, however, no longer a closed-form analytic solution, and so their values must be determined by iterative procedures. For q latent variables, there are $q \times d$ parameters in $\mathbf{W}$ together with d in $\boldsymbol{\Psi}$ and d in $\boldsymbol{\mu}$. There is some redundancy between these parameters, and a more careful analysis shows that the number of independent degrees of freedom in this model is given by

$$(d + 1)(q + 1) - q(q + 1)/2. \tag{9}$$

The number of independent parameters in this model therefore only grows linearly with d, and yet the model can still capture the dominant correlations between the data variables. We consider the nature of such models in more detail in Section 2.

1.2. MIXTURE DISTRIBUTIONS

The density models we have considered so far are clearly very limited in terms of the variety of probability distributions which they can model since they can only represent distributions which are uni-modal. However, they can form the basis of a very general framework for density modelling, obtained by considering probabilistic *mixtures* of M simpler parametric distributions. This leads to density models of the form

$$p(\mathbf{t}) = \sum_{i=1}^{M} \pi_i p(\mathbf{t}|i) \tag{10}$$

in which the $p(\mathbf{t}|i)$ represent the individual components of the mixture and might consist, for example, of normal distributions of the form (1) each with its own independent mean $\boldsymbol{\mu}_i$ and covariance matrix $\boldsymbol{\Sigma}_i$. The parameters π_i in (10) are called *mixing coefficients* and satisfy the requirements $0 \le \pi_i \le 1$ and $\sum_i \pi_i = 1$ so that $p(\mathbf{t})$ will be non-negative and will integrate to unity (assuming the individual component densities also have these properties). We can represent the mixture distribution (10) as a simple Bayesian network, as shown in Figure 3.

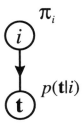

Figure 3. Bayesian network representation of a simple mixture distribution.

The mixing coefficients can be interpreted as *prior* probabilities for the values of the label i. For a given data point $\mathbf{t}_n$ we can then use Bayes' theorem to evaluate the corresponding posterior probabilities, given by

$$R_{ni} \equiv p(i|\mathbf{t}_n) = \frac{\pi_i p(\mathbf{t}_n|i)}{\sum_j \pi_j p(\mathbf{t}_n|j)}. \tag{11}$$

The value of $p(i|\mathbf{t}_n)$ can be regarded as the *responsibility* which component i takes for 'explaining' data point $\mathbf{t}_n$. Effectively this is using Bayes' theorem to reverse the direction of the arrow in Figure 3.

The log likelihood for the mixture distribution takes the form

$$\mathcal{L}(\{\pi_i, \boldsymbol{\mu}_i, \boldsymbol{\Sigma}_i\}) = \sum_{n=1}^{N} \ln \left\{ \sum_{i=1}^{M} \pi_i p(\mathbf{t}|i) \right\}. \tag{12}$$

Maximization of this log likelihood is more complex than for a single component due to the presence of the sum inside the logarithm. An elegant and powerful technique for performing this optimization called the expectation-maximization (EM) algorithm [11], and an introductory account of EM in the context of mixture distributions is given in [5]. The EM algorithm is based on the observation that, if we were given a set of indicator variables z_{ni} specifying which component i was responsible for generating each data point $\mathbf{t}_n$, then the log likelihood would take the form

$$\mathcal{L}_{\text{comp}}(\{\pi_i, \boldsymbol{\mu}_i, \boldsymbol{\Sigma}_i\}) = \sum_{n=1}^{N} \sum_{i=1}^{M} z_{ni} \ln \left\{ \pi_i p(\mathbf{t}|i) \right\} \tag{13}$$

and its optimization would be straightforward, with the result that each component is fitted independently to the corresponding group of data points, and the mixing coefficients are given by the fractions of points in each group.

The $\{z_{ni}\}$ are regarded as 'missing data', and the data set $\{t_n\}$ is said to be 'incomplete'. Combining $\{t_n\}$ and $\{z_{ni}\}$ we obtain the corresponding 'complete' data set, with a log likelihood given by (13). Of course, the values of $\{z_{ni}\}$ are unknown, but their posterior distribution can be computed using Bayes' theorem, and the expectation of z_{ni} under this distribution is just the set of responsibilities R_{ni} given by (11). The EM algorithm is based on the maximization of the expected complete-data log likelihood given from (13) by

$$\langle \mathcal{L}_{\text{comp}}(\{\pi_i, \boldsymbol{\mu}_i, \boldsymbol{\Sigma}_i\}) \rangle = \sum_{n=1}^{N} \sum_{i=1}^{M} R_{ni} \ln \{\pi_i p(\mathbf{t}|i)\}. \tag{14}$$

It alternates between the E-step, in which the R_{ni} are evaluated using (11), and the M-step in which (14) is maximized with respect to the model parameters to give a revised set of parameter values. At each cycle of the EM algorithm the true log likelihood is guaranteed to increase unless it is already at a local maximum [11].

The EM algorithm can also be applied to the problem of maximizing the likelihood for a single latent variable model of the kind discussed in Section 1.1. We note that the log likelihood for such a model takes the form

$$\mathcal{L}(\mathbf{W}, \boldsymbol{\mu}, \boldsymbol{\Psi}) = \sum_{n=1}^{N} \ln p(\mathbf{t}_n) = \sum_{n=1}^{N} \ln \left\{ \int p(\mathbf{t}_n|\mathbf{x}_n) p(\mathbf{x}_n) \, d\mathbf{x}_n \right\}. \tag{15}$$

Again, this is difficult to treat because of the integral inside the logarithm. In this case the values of $\mathbf{x}_n$ are regarded as the missing data. Given the prior distribution $p(\mathbf{x})$ we can consider the corresponding posterior distribution obtained through Bayes' theorem

$$p(\mathbf{x}_n|\mathbf{t}_n) = \frac{p(\mathbf{t}_n|\mathbf{x}_n) p(\mathbf{x}_n)}{p(\mathbf{t}_n)} \tag{16}$$

and the sufficient statistics for this distribution are evaluated in the E-step. The M-step involves maximization of the expected complete-data log likelihood and is generally much simpler than the direct maximization of the true log likelihood. For simple models such as the factor analysis model discussed in Section 1.1 this maximization can be performed analytically. The EM (expectation-maximization) algorithm for maximizing the likelihood function for standard factor analysis was derived by Rubin and Thayer [23].

We can combine the technique of mixture modelling with that of latent variables, and consider a mixture of latent-variable models. The corresponding Bayesian network is shown in Figure 4. Again, the EM algorithm

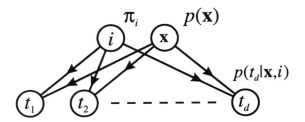

Figure 4. Bayesian network representation of a mixture of latent variable models. Given the values of i and $\mathbf{x}$, the variables $t_1, \ldots, t_d$ are conditionally independent.

provides a natural framework for determination of the model parameters, and allows both the values of the component label i and of the latent variable $\mathbf{x}$ to be treated together as missing data.

In the subsequent sections of this chapter we shall see how the concepts of latent variables and mixture distributions can be used in a fruitful partnership to obtain a range of powerful algorithms for density modelling, pattern classification and data visualization.

2. Probabilistic Principal Component Analysis

Principal component analysis is a well-established technique for dimensionality reduction, and a chapter on the subject may be found in practically every text on multivariate analysis. Examples of its many applications include data compression, image processing, data visualization, exploratory data analysis, and pattern recognition.

The most common derivation of PCA is in terms of a standardized linear projection which maximizes the variance in the projected space [14]. For a set of observed d-dimensional data vectors $\{\mathbf{t}_n\}$, $n \in \{1 \ldots N\}$, the q *principal axes* $\mathbf{v}_j$, $j \in \{1, \ldots, q\}$, are those orthonormal axes onto which the retained variance under projection is maximal. It can be shown that the vectors $\mathbf{v}_j$ are given by the q dominant eigenvectors (i.e. those with the largest associated eigenvalues λ_j) of the sample covariance matrix

$$\mathbf{S} = \frac{1}{N} \sum_{n=1}^{N} (\mathbf{t}_n - \widehat{\boldsymbol{\mu}})(\mathbf{t}_n - \widehat{\boldsymbol{\mu}})^{\mathrm{T}} \tag{17}$$

such that $\mathbf{S}\mathbf{v}_j = \lambda_j \mathbf{v}_j$. Here $\widehat{\boldsymbol{\mu}}$ is the sample mean, given by (3). The q principal components of the observed vector $\mathbf{t}_n$ are given by the vector

$\mathbf{u}_n = \mathbf{V}^{\mathrm{T}}(\mathbf{t}_n - \widehat{\boldsymbol{\mu}})$, where $\mathbf{V}^{\mathrm{T}} = (\mathbf{v}_1, \ldots, \mathbf{v}_q)^{\mathrm{T}}$, in which the variables u_j are decorellated such that the covariance matrix for $\mathbf{u}$ is diagonal with elements $\{\lambda_j\}$.

A complementary property of PCA, and that most closely related to the original discussions of Pearson [20], is that, of all orthogonal linear projections $\mathbf{x}_n = \mathbf{V}^{\mathrm{T}}(\mathbf{t}_n - \widehat{\boldsymbol{\mu}})$, the principal component projection minimizes the squared reconstruction error $\sum_n \|\mathbf{t}_n - \widehat{\mathbf{t}}_n\|^2$, where the optimal linear reconstruction of $\mathbf{t}_n$ is given by $\widehat{\mathbf{t}}_n = \mathbf{V}\mathbf{x}_n + \widehat{\boldsymbol{\mu}}$.

One serious disadvantage of both these definitions of PCA is the absence of a probability density model and associated likelihood measure. Deriving PCA from the perspective of density estimation would offer a number of important advantages, including the following:

- The corresponding likelihood measure would permit comparison with other density–estimation techniques and would facilitate statistical testing.
- Bayesian inference methods could be applied (e.g. for model comparison) by combining the likelihood with a prior.
- If PCA were used to model the class–conditional densities in a classification problem, the posterior probabilities of class membership could be computed.
- The value of the probability density function would give a measure of the novelty of a new data point.
- The single PCA model could be extended to a mixture of such models.

In this section we review the key result of Tipping and Bishop [25], which shows that principal component analysis may indeed be obtained from a probability model. In particular we show that the maximum-likelihood estimator of $\mathbf{W}$ in (8) for a specific form of latent variable models is given by the matrix of (scaled and rotated) principal axes of the data.

2.1. RELATIONSHIP TO LATENT VARIABLES

Links between principal component analysis and latent variable models have already been noted by a number of authors. For instance Anderson [2] observed that principal components emerge when the data is assumed to comprise a systematic component, plus an independent error term for each variable having common variance σ^2. Empirically, the similarity between the columns of $\mathbf{W}$ and the principal axes has often been observed in situations in which the elements of $\boldsymbol{\Psi}$ are approximately equal [22]. Basilevsky [4] further notes that when the model $\mathbf{W}\mathbf{W}^{\mathrm{T}} + \sigma^2\mathbf{I}$ is exact, and therefore equal to $\mathbf{S}$, the matrix $\mathbf{W}$ is identifiable and can be determined analytically through eigen-decomposition of $\mathbf{S}$, without resort to iteration.

As well as assuming that the model is exact, such observations do not consider the maximum-likelihood context. By considering a particular case of the factor analysis model in which the noise covariance is isotropic so that $\mathbf{\Psi} = \sigma^2 \mathbf{I}$, we now show that even when the data covariance matrix cannot be expressed exactly using the form $\mathbf{WW}^{\mathrm{T}} + \sigma^2 \mathbf{I}$, the maximum-likelihood estimator $\mathbf{W}_{\mathrm{ML}}$ is that matrix whose columns are the scaled and rotated principal eigenvectors of the sample covariance matrix $\mathbf{S}$ [25]. An important consequence of this derivation is that PCA may be expressed in terms of a probability density model, which we shall refer to as probabilistic principal component analysis (PPCA).

2.2. THE PROBABILITY MODEL

For the isotropic noise model $\mathbf{u} \sim N(\mathbf{0}, \sigma^2 \mathbf{I})$, equations (6) and (8) imply a probability distribution over $\mathbf{t}$-space for a given $\mathbf{x}$ given by

$$p(\mathbf{t}|\mathbf{x}) = (2\pi\sigma^2)^{-d/2} \exp\left\{-\frac{1}{2\sigma^2}\|\mathbf{t} - \mathbf{Wx} - \boldsymbol{\mu}\|^2\right\}. \qquad (18)$$

In the case of an isotropic Gaussian prior over the latent variables defined by

$$p(\mathbf{x}) = (2\pi)^{-q/2} \exp\left\{-\frac{1}{2}\mathbf{x}^{\mathrm{T}}\mathbf{x}\right\} \qquad (19)$$

we then obtain the marginal distribution of $\mathbf{t}$ in the form

$$p(\mathbf{t}) \;=\; \int p(\mathbf{t}|\mathbf{x})p(\mathbf{x})d\mathbf{x} \qquad (20)$$

$$=\; (2\pi)^{-d/2}|\mathbf{C}|^{-1/2} \exp\left\{-\frac{1}{2}(\mathbf{t} - \boldsymbol{\mu})^{\mathrm{T}}\mathbf{C}^{-1}(\mathbf{t} - \boldsymbol{\mu})\right\} \qquad (21)$$

where the model covariance is

$$\mathbf{C} = \sigma^2 \mathbf{I} + \mathbf{WW}^{\mathrm{T}}. \qquad (22)$$

Using Bayes' theorem, the *posterior* distribution of the latent variables $\mathbf{x}$ given the observed $\mathbf{t}$ is given by

$$p(\mathbf{x}|\mathbf{t}) \;=\; (2\pi)^{-q/2}|\sigma^2\mathbf{M}|^{-1/2} \times$$
$$\exp\left\{-\frac{1}{2}(\mathbf{x} - \langle\mathbf{x}\rangle)^{\mathrm{T}}(\sigma^2\mathbf{M})^{-1}(\mathbf{x} - \langle\mathbf{x}\rangle)\right\} \qquad (23)$$

where the posterior covariance matrix is given by

$$\sigma^2 \mathbf{M} = \sigma^2(\sigma^2 \mathbf{I} + \mathbf{W}^{\mathrm{T}}\mathbf{W})^{-1} \qquad (24)$$

and the mean of the distribution is given by

$$\langle \mathbf{x} \rangle = \mathbf{M}^{-1}\mathbf{W}^{\mathrm{T}}(\mathbf{t} - \boldsymbol{\mu}). \tag{25}$$

Note that $\mathbf{M}$ has dimension $q \times q$ while $\mathbf{C}$ has dimension $d \times d$.

The log-likelihood for the observed data under this model is given by

$$
\begin{aligned}
\mathcal{L} &= \sum_{n=1}^{N} \ln\{p(\mathbf{t}_n)\} \\
&= -\frac{Nd}{2}\ln(2\pi) - \frac{N}{2}\ln|\mathbf{C}| - \frac{N}{2}\mathrm{Tr}\left\{\mathbf{C}^{-1}\mathbf{S}\right\}
\end{aligned} \tag{26}
$$

where the sample covariance matrix $\mathbf{S}$ of the observed $\{\mathbf{t}_n\}$ is given by (17).

In principle, we could determine the parameters for this model by maximizing the log-likelihood $\mathcal{L}$ using the EM algorithm of Rubin and Thayer [23]. However, we now show that, for the case of an isotropic noise covariance of the form we are considering, there is an exact analytical solution for the model parameters.

2.3. PROPERTIES OF THE MAXIMUM-LIKELIHOOD SOLUTION

Our key result is that the log-likelihood (26) is maximized when the columns of $\mathbf{W}$ span the principal subspace of the data. To show this we consider the derivative of (26) with respect to $\mathbf{W}$:

$$\frac{\partial \mathcal{L}}{\partial \mathbf{W}} = N(\mathbf{C}^{-1}\mathbf{S}\mathbf{C}^{-1}\mathbf{W} - \mathbf{C}^{-1}\mathbf{W}) \tag{27}$$

which may be obtained from standard matrix differentiation results (see [19], pp 133). In [25] it is shown that, with $\mathbf{C}$ given by (22), the only non-zero stationary points of (27) occur for:

$$\mathbf{W} = \mathbf{U}_q(\boldsymbol{\Lambda}_q - \sigma^2\mathbf{I})^{1/2}\mathbf{R} \tag{28}$$

where the q column vectors in $\mathbf{U}_q$ are eigenvectors of $\mathbf{S}$, with corresponding eigenvalues in the diagonal matrix $\boldsymbol{\Lambda}_q$, and $\mathbf{R}$ is an arbitrary $q \times q$ orthogonal rotation matrix. Furthermore, it is also shown that the stationary point corresponding to the *global maximum* of the likelihood occurs when $\mathbf{U}_q$ comprises the *principal* eigenvectors of $\mathbf{S}$ (i.e. the eigenvectors corresponding to the q largest eigenvalues) and that all other combinations of eigenvectors represent saddle-points of the likelihood surface. Thus, from (28), the columns of the maximum-likelihood estimator $\mathbf{W}_{\mathrm{ML}}$ contain the principal eigenvectors of $\mathbf{S}$, with scalings determined by the corresponding eigenvalues together with the parameter σ^2, and with arbitrary rotation.

It may also be shown that for $\mathbf{W} = \mathbf{W}_{\mathrm{ML}}$, the maximum-likelihood estimator for σ^2 is given by

$$\sigma_{\mathrm{ML}}^2 = \frac{1}{d-q} \sum_{j=q+1}^{d} \lambda_j \tag{29}$$

which has a clear interpretation as the variance 'lost' in the projection, averaged over the lost dimensions. Note that the columns of $\mathbf{W}_{\mathrm{ML}}$ are not orthogonal since

$$\mathbf{W}_{\mathrm{ML}}^{\mathrm{T}} \mathbf{W}_{\mathrm{ML}} = \mathbf{R}^{\mathrm{T}}(\boldsymbol{\Lambda}_q - \sigma^2 \mathbf{I})\mathbf{R}, \tag{30}$$

which in general is not diagonal. However, the columns of $\mathbf{W}$ will be orthogonal for the particular choice $\mathbf{R} \neq \mathbf{I}$.

In summary, we can obtain a probabilistic principal components model by finding the q principal eigenvectors and eigenvalues of the sample covariance matrix. The density model is then given by a Gaussian distribution with mean $\boldsymbol{\mu}$ given by the sample mean, and a covariance matrix $\mathbf{W}\mathbf{W}^{\mathrm{T}} + \sigma^2 \mathbf{I}$ in which $\mathbf{W}$ is given by (28) and σ^2 is given by (29).

3. Mixtures of Probabilistic PCA

We now extend the latent variable model of Section 2 by considering a mixture of probabilistic principal component analysers [24], in which the model distribution is given by (10) with component densities given by (22). It is straightforward to obtain an EM algorithm to determine the parameters π_i, $\boldsymbol{\mu}_i$, $\mathbf{W}_i$ and σ_i^2. The E-step of the EM algorithm involves the use of the current parameter estimates to evaluate the responsibilities of the mixture components i for the data points $\mathbf{t}_n$, given from Bayes' theorem by

$$R_{ni} = \frac{p(\mathbf{t}_n|i)\pi_i}{p(\mathbf{t}_n)}. \tag{31}$$

In the M-step, the mixing coefficients and component means are re-estimated using

$$\widetilde{\pi}_i = \frac{1}{N} \sum_{n=1}^{N} R_{ni} \tag{32}$$

$$\widetilde{\boldsymbol{\mu}}_i = \frac{\sum_{n=1}^{N} R_{ni} \mathbf{t}_n}{\sum_{n=1}^{N} R_{ni}} \tag{33}$$

while the parameters $\mathbf{W}_i$ and σ_i^2 are obtained by first evaluating the weighted covariance matrices given by

$$\mathbf{S}_i = \frac{\sum_{n=1}^{N} R_{ni}(\mathbf{t}_n - \widetilde{\boldsymbol{\mu}})(\mathbf{t}_n - \widetilde{\boldsymbol{\mu}})^{\mathrm{T}}}{\sum_{n=1}^{N} R_{ni}} \tag{34}$$

and then applying (28) and (29).

3.1. EXAMPLE APPLICATION: HAND-WRITTEN DIGIT CLASSIFICATION

One potential application for high-dimensional density models is handwritten digit recognition. Examples of gray-scale pixel images of a given digit will generally lie on a lower-dimensional smooth continuous manifold, the geometry of which is determined by properties of the digit such as rotation, scaling and thickness of stroke. One approach to the classification of such digits (although not necessarily the best) is to build a model of each digit separately, and classify unseen digits according to the model to which they are most 'similar'.

Hinton *et al.* [12] discussed the problem of handwritten digit problem, and applied a 'mixture' of conventional PCA models, using soft reconstruction-based clustering, to the classification of scaled and smoothed 8-by-8 gray-scale images taken from the CEDAR U.S. postal service database [15]. The models were constructed using an 11,000-digit subset of the '*br*' data set (which was further split into training and validation sets), and the '*bs*' test set was classified according to which model best reconstructed each digit. We repeated the experiment with the same data using the probabilistic PCA mixture approach utilizing the same choice of parameter values ($M = 10$ and $q = 10$). The same method of classification was used, and the best model on the validation set misclassified 4.64% of the digits in the test set, while Hinton *et al.* [12] reported an error of 4.91%. We would expect the improvement to be a result partly of the localized clustering of the PPCA model, but also the use of individually-estimated values of σ_i^2 for each component, rather than a single, arbitrarily-chosen, global value used in [12].

One of the advantages of the PPCA methodology is that the definition of the density model permits the posterior probabilities of class membership to be computed for each digit and utilized for subsequent classification. After optimizing the parameters M and q for each model to obtain the best performance on the validation set, the model misclassified 4.61% of the test set. An advantage of the use of posterior probabilities is that it is possible to reject (using an optimal criterion) a proportion of the test samples about which the classifier is most 'unsure', and thus improve the classification performance on the remaining data. Using this approach to reject 5% of the test examples resulted in a misclassification rate of 2.50%.

4. Hierarchical Mixtures for Data Visualization

An interesting application for the PPCA model, and mixtures of PPCA models, is to the problem of data visualization. By considering a further extension to a hierarchical mixture model, we are led to a powerful interactive algorithm for visualization which retains a probabilistic framework and which can provide considerable insight into the structure of data in spaces of high dimensionality [10].

4.1. VISUALIZATION USING PROBABILISTIC PCA

Consider first the use of a single PPCA model for data visualization. In standard principal component analysis, the data points are visualized by orthogonal projection onto the principal components plane (spanned by the two leading eigenvectors). For our probabilistic PCA model this projection is modified slightly. From (23) and (25) it may be seen that the *posterior mean* projection of $\mathbf{t}_n$ is given by $\langle \mathbf{x}_n \rangle = \mathbf{M}^{-1}\mathbf{W}^{\mathrm{T}}(\mathbf{t}_n - \hat{\boldsymbol{\mu}})$. When $\sigma^2 \to 0$, $\mathbf{M}^{-1} \to (\mathbf{W}^{\mathrm{T}}\mathbf{W})^{-1}$ and $\mathbf{W}\mathbf{M}^{-1}\mathbf{W}^{\mathrm{T}}$ then becomes an orthogonal projection, and so PCA is recovered (although the density model then becomes singular, and thus undefined). For $\sigma^2 > 0$, the projection onto the manifold is shrunk towards the origin as a result of the prior over $\mathbf{x}$. Because of this, $\mathbf{W}\langle \mathbf{x}_n \rangle$ is *not* an orthogonal projection of $\mathbf{t}_n$. We note, however, that information is not lost because of this shrinkage, since each data point may still be optimally reconstructed from the latent variable by taking the shrinkage into account. With $\mathbf{W} = \mathbf{W}_{\mathrm{ML}}$ the required reconstruction is given by

$$\hat{\mathbf{t}}_n = \mathbf{W}_{\mathrm{ML}}\{\mathbf{W}_{\mathrm{ML}}^{\mathrm{T}}\mathbf{W}_{\mathrm{ML}}\}^{-1}\mathbf{M}\langle \mathbf{x}_n \rangle, \tag{35}$$

and is derived in [25]. Thus the latent variables convey the necessary information to reconstruct the original data vector optimally, even in the case of $\sigma^2 > 0$.

The data set can therefore be visualized by mapping each data point onto the corresponding posterior mean $\langle \mathbf{x}_n \rangle$ in the two-dimensional latent space, as illustrated in Figure 5. Note that this type of visualization plot satisfies a topographic property in that points in data space which are sufficiently close will map to points in latent space which are also close.

We illustrate the visualization properties of this model using a toy data set consisting of 450 data points generated from a mixture of three Gaussians in three-dimensional space. Each Gaussian is relatively flat (has small variance) in one dimension, and two of these clusters are closely spaced with their principal planes parallel to each other, while the third is well separated from the first two. The structure of this data set has been chosen order to demonstrate the benefits of the interactive hierarchical approach developed in Section 4.3. A single two-dimensional latent variable model is

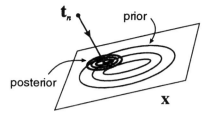

Figure 5. Illustration of the projection of a data vector $\mathbf{t}_n$ onto the point on the principal subspace corresponding to the posterior mean.

trained on this data set, and the result of plotting the posterior means of the data points is shown in Figure 6.

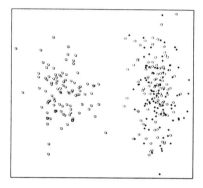

Figure 6. Plot of the posterior means of the data points from the toy data set, obtained from the probabilistic PCA model, indicating the presence of (at least) two distinct clusters.

4.2. MIXTURE MODELS FOR DATA VISUALIZATION

Next we consider the application of a simple mixture of PPCA models to data visualization. Once a mixture of probabilistic PCA models has been fitted to the data set, the procedure for visualizing the data points involves plotting each data point $\mathbf{t}_n$ on each of the two-dimensional latent spaces at the corresponding posterior mean position $\langle \mathbf{x}_{ni} \rangle$ given by

$$\langle \mathbf{x}_{ni} \rangle = (\mathbf{W}_i^{\mathrm{T}} \mathbf{W}_i + \sigma_i^2 \mathbf{I})^{-1} \mathbf{W}_i^{\mathrm{T}} (\mathbf{t}_n - \boldsymbol{\mu}_i) \tag{36}$$

as illustrated in Figure 7.

As a further refinement, the density of 'ink' for each data point $\mathbf{t}_n$ is weighted by the corresponding responsibility R_{ni} of model i for that data point, so that the total density of 'ink' is distributed by a partition of

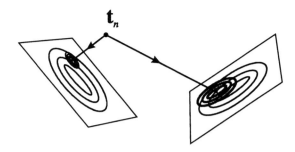

Figure 7. Illustration of the projection of a data vector onto two principal surfaces in a probabilistic PCA mixture model.

unity across the plots. Thus, each data point is plotted on every component model projection, while if a particular model takes nearly all of the posterior probability for a particular data point, then that data point will effectively be visible only on the corresponding latent space plot.

We shall regard the single PPCA plot introduced in Section 4.1 as the top level in a hierarchical visualization model, in which the mixture model forms the second level. Extensions to further levels of the hierarchy will be developed in Section 4.3.

The model can be extended to provide an interactive data exploration tool as follows. On the basis of the single top-level plot the user decides on an appropriate number of models to fit at the second level, and selects points $\mathbf{x}^{(i)}$ on the plot, corresponding, for example, to the centres of apparent clusters. The resulting points $\mathbf{y}^{(i)}$ in data space, obtained from $\mathbf{y}^{(i)} = \mathbf{W}\mathbf{x}^{(i)} + \boldsymbol{\mu}$, are then used to initialize the means $\boldsymbol{\mu}_i$ of the respective sub-models. To initialize the matrices $\mathbf{W}_i$ we first assign the data points to their nearest mean vector $\boldsymbol{\mu}_i$ and then compute the corresponding sample covariance matrices. This is a hard clustering analogous to K-means and represents an approximation to the posterior probabilities R_{ni} in which the largest posterior probability is replaced by 1 and the remainder by 0. For each of these clusters we then find the eigenvalues and eigenvectors of the sample covariance matrix and hence determine the probabilistic PCA density model. This initialization is then used as the starting point for the EM algorithm.

Consider the application of this procedure to the toy data set introduced in Section 4.1. At the top level we observed two apparent clusters, and so we might select a mixture of two models for the second level, with centres initialized somewhere near the centres of the two clusters seen at the top level. The result of fitting this mixture by EM leads to the two-level visualization plot shown in Figure 8.

The visualization process can be enhanced further by providing infor-

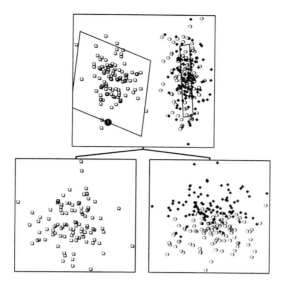

Figure 8. The result of applying the two-level visualization algorithm to the toy data set. At the second level a mixture of two latent variable models has been fitted and the data plotted on each latent space using the approach described in the text. In addition, the two latent planes have been visualized by projection back onto the top-level model. The left-hand plane at the second level is almost perpendicular to the top-level plane (as can be seen by its projection) giving further insight into why the two clusters which appear well separated on the left-hand second-level model appear to be overlapping at the top level.

mation at the top level on the location and orientation of the latent spaces corresponding to the second level, as shown in Figure 8. This is achieved by considering the orthogonal projection of the latent plane in data space onto the corresponding plane of the parent model.

4.3. HIERARCHICAL MIXTURE MODELS

We now extend the mixture representation of Section 1.2 to give a hierarchical mixture model. Our formulation will be quite general and can be applied to hierarchical mixtures of any parametric density. So far we have considered a two-level system consisting of a single latent variable model at the top level and a mixture of M_0 such models at the second level. We can now extend the hierarchy to a third level by associating a group $\mathcal{G}_i$ of latent variable models with each model i in the second level. The corresponding probability density can be written in the form

$$p(\mathbf{t}) = \sum_{i=1}^{M_0} \pi_i \sum_{j \in \mathcal{G}_i} \pi_{j|i} p(\mathbf{t}|i,j) \tag{37}$$

where $p(\mathbf{t}|i,j)$ again represent independent latent variable models, and $\pi_{j|i}$ correspond to sets of mixing coefficients, one set for each i, which satisfy $0 \leq \pi_{j|i} \leq 1$ and $\sum_j \pi_{j|i} = 1$. Thus each level of the hierarchy corresponds to a generative model, with lower levels giving more refined and detailed representations. This model is illustrated in Figure 9.

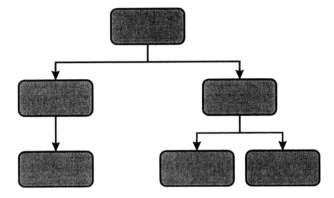

Figure 9.   An example structure for the hierarchical mixture model.

Hierarchical mixtures of *conditional* density estimators were introduced by Jordan and Jacobs [16] in which all of the component distributions, as well as the various mixing coefficients, are conditioned on an observed 'input' vector. However, we are interested in hierarchical mixtures of unconditional density models. In this case a mixture of mixtures would be equivalent to a simple flat mixture and nothing would be gained from the hierarchy. In order to achieve the goal of hierarchical modelling we need to constrain the parameters of the model.

To see the appropriate form for the constraint, we note that the determination of the parameters of the models at the third level can again be viewed as a missing data problem in which the missing information corresponds to labels specifying which model generated each data point. When no information about the labels is provided the log likelihood for the model (37) would take the form

$$\mathcal{L} = \sum_{n=1}^{N} \ln \left\{ \sum_{i=1}^{M_0} \pi_i \sum_{j \in \mathcal{G}_i} \pi_{j|i} p(\mathbf{t}|i,j) \right\} \tag{38}$$

and the model would collapse to a simple mixture model. If, however, we were given a set of indicator variables z_{ni} specifying which model i at the second level generated each data point $\mathbf{t}_n$ then the log likelihood would become

$$\mathcal{L} = \sum_{n=1}^{N} \sum_{i=1}^{M_0} z_{ni} \ln \left\{ \pi_i \sum_{j \in \mathcal{G}_i} \pi_{j|i} p(\mathbf{t}|i, j) \right\}. \tag{39}$$

In fact we only have partial, probabilistic, information in the form of the posterior responsibilities R_{ni} for each model i having generated the data points $\mathbf{t}_n$, obtained from the second level of the hierarchy. The corresponding log likelihood is obtained by taking the expectation of (39) with respect to the posterior distribution of the z_{ni} to give

$$\mathcal{L} = \sum_{n=1}^{N} \sum_{i=1}^{M_0} R_{ni} \ln \left\{ \pi_i \sum_{j \in \mathcal{G}_i} \pi_{j|i} p(\mathbf{t}|i, j) \right\} \tag{40}$$

in which the R_{ni} are treated as constants. In the particular case in which the R_{ni} are all 0 or 1, corresponding to complete certainty about which model in the second level is responsible for each data point, the log likelihood (40) reduces to the form (39).

Maximization of (40) can again be performed using the EM algorithm, as shown in [10]. This has the same form as the EM algorithm for a simple mixture, discussed in Section 1.2, except that in the E-step, the posterior probability that model (i, j) generated data point $\mathbf{t}_n$ is given by

$$R_{ni,j} = R_{ni} R_{nj|i} \tag{41}$$

in which

$$R_{nj|i} = \frac{\pi_{j|i} p(\mathbf{t}_n|i, j)}{\sum_{j'} \pi_{j'|i} p(\mathbf{t}_n|i, j')}. \tag{42}$$

This result automatically satisfies the relation

$$\sum_{j \in \mathcal{G}_i} R_{ni,j} = R_{ni} \tag{43}$$

so that the responsibility of each model at the second level for a given data point n is shared by a partition of unity between the corresponding group of offspring models at the third level. It is straightforward to extend this hierarchical approach to any desired number of levels.

The result of applying this approach to the toy data set is shown in Figure 10.

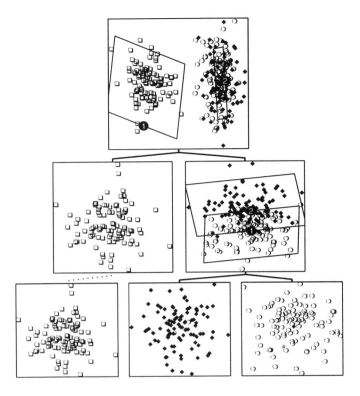

Figure 10. Plot of the complete three-level hierarchy for the toy data set. At the third level the three clusters have been almost perfectly separated. The structure of this particular hierarchical model is as shown in Figure 9.

4.4. EXAMPLE: OIL FLOW DATA

We now illustrate the application of the hierarchical visualization algorithm by considering an example data set arising from a non-invasive monitoring system used to determine the quantity of oil in a multi-phase pipeline containing a mixture of oil, water and gas [7]. The diagnostic data is collected from a set of three horizontal and three vertical beam-lines along which gamma rays at two different energies are passed. By measuring the degree of attenuation of the gammas, the fractional path length through oil and water (and hence gas) can readily be determined, giving 12 diagnostic measurements in total. In practice the aim is to solve the inverse problem of determining the fraction of oil in the pipe. The complexity of the problem arises from the possibility of the multi-phase mixture adopting one of a number of different geometrical configurations. Our goal is to visualize the structure of the data in the original 12-dimensional space. A data set consisting of 1000 points is obtained synthetically by simulating the physical processes in the pipe, including the presence of noise determined by photon statistics. Locally, the data is expected to have an intrinsic dimensionality of 2 corresponding to the 2 degrees of freedom given by the fraction of oil and the fraction of water (the fraction of gas being redundant). However, the presence of different configurations, as well as the geometrical interaction between phase boundaries and the beam paths, leads to numerous distinct clusters. It would appear that a hierarchical approach of the kind discussed here should be capable of discovering this structure. Results from fitting the oil flow data using a 3-level hierarchical model are shown in Figure 11.

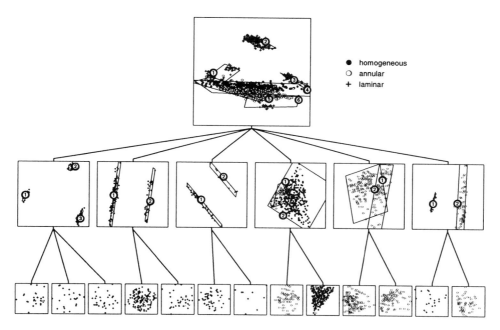

Figure 11. Results of fitting the oil data. The symbols denote different multi-phase flow configurations corresponding to homogeneous (•), annular (o) and laminar (+). Note, for example, how the apparently single cluster, number 2, in the top level plot is revealed to be two quite distinct clusters at the second level.

In the case of the toy data, the optimal choice of clusters and subclusters is relatively unambiguous and a single application of the algorithm is sufficient to reveal all of the interesting structure within the data. For more complex data sets, it is appropriate to adopt an exploratory perspective and investigate alternative hierarchies through the selection of differing numbers of clusters and their respective locations. The example shown in Figure 11 has clearly been highly successful. Note how the apparently single cluster, number 2, in the top-level plot is revealed to be two quite distinct clusters at the second level. Also, data points from the 'homogeneous' configuration have been isolated and can be seen to lie on a two-dimensional triangular structure in the third level. Inspection of the corresponding value of σ^2 confirms that this cluster is confined to a nearly planar sub-space, as expected from the physics of the diagnostic data for the homogeneous configurations.

5. Non-linear Models: The Generative Topographic Mapping

The latent variable models we have considered so far are based on a mapping from latent variables to data variables of the form (6) in which the function $\mathbf{y}(\mathbf{x}; \mathbf{w})$ is linear in $\mathbf{x}$. Thus the manifold $\mathcal{S}$ in data space, shown in Figure 2 is a hyperplane. Data living on a manifold which is not hyperplanar (for example the hand-written digits data considered in Section 3.1) can then be approximated using a mixture of linear latent variable models. An alternative approach, however, would be to consider a latent variable model which is *non-linear*.

The difficulty with using a non-linear mapping function $\mathbf{y}(\mathbf{x}; \mathbf{w})$ in (6) is that in general the integration over $\mathbf{x}$ in (7) will become analytically intractable. However, by making careful model choices a tractable, non-linear model, called the *Generative Topographic Mapping* or GTM, can be derived [8].

The central concept is to introduce a prior distribution $p(\mathbf{x})$ given by a sum of delta functions centred on the nodes of a regular grid in latent space

$$p(\mathbf{x}) = \frac{1}{K} \sum_{i=1}^{K} \delta(\mathbf{x} - \mathbf{x}_i) \tag{44}$$

in which case the integral in (7) can be performed analytically even for non-linear functions $\mathbf{y}(\mathbf{x}; \mathbf{w})$. The conditional distribution $p(\mathbf{t}|\mathbf{x})$ is chosen to be an isotropic Gaussian with variance σ^2. (Note that this is easily generalized to deal with mixed continuous and categorical data by considering the corresponding product of Gaussian and multinomial distributions.) Each latent point $\mathbf{x}_i$ is then mapped to a corresponding point $\mathbf{y}(\mathbf{x}_i; \mathbf{w})$ in data space, which forms the centre of a Gaussian density function, as illustrated in Figure 12. From (7) and (44) we see that the distribution function in data space then takes the form

$$p(\mathbf{t}|\mathbf{W}, \sigma^2) = \frac{1}{K} \sum_{i=1}^{K} p(\mathbf{t}|\mathbf{x}_i, \mathbf{W}, \sigma^2) \tag{45}$$

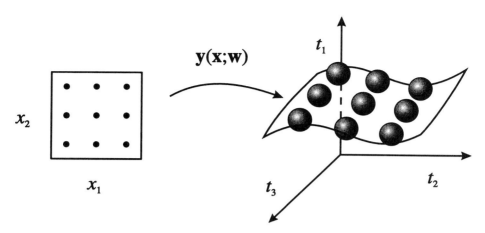

Figure 12. In order to formulate a tractable non-linear latent variable model, we consider a prior distribution $p(\mathbf{x})$ consisting of a superposition of delta functions, located at the nodes of a regular grid in latent space. Each node $\mathbf{x}_i$ is mapped to a corresponding point $\mathbf{y}(\mathbf{x}_i; \mathbf{w})$ in data space, and forms the centre of a corresponding Gaussian distribution.

which corresponds to a *constrained* Gaussian mixture model [13] since the centres of the Gaussians, given by $\mathbf{y}(\mathbf{x}_i; \mathbf{w})$, cannot move independently but are related through the function $\mathbf{y}(\mathbf{x}; \mathbf{w})$. Note that, provided the mapping function $\mathbf{y}(\mathbf{x}; \mathbf{w})$ is smooth and continuous, the projected points $\mathbf{y}(\mathbf{x}_i; \mathbf{w})$ will necessarily have a *topographic* ordering in the sense that any two points $\mathbf{x}_A$ and $\mathbf{x}_B$ which are close in latent space will map to points $\mathbf{y}(\mathbf{x}_A; \mathbf{w})$ and $\mathbf{y}(\mathbf{x}_B; \mathbf{w})$ which are close in data space.

5.1. AN EM ALGORITHM FOR GTM

Since GTM is a form of mixture model it is natural to seek an EM algorithm for maximizing the corresponding log likelihood. By choosing a particular form for the mapping $\mathbf{y}(\mathbf{x}; \mathbf{w})$ we can obtain an EM algorithm in which the M-step has a simple form. In particular we shall choose $\mathbf{y}(\mathbf{x}; \mathbf{w})$ to be given by a generalized linear regression model of the form

$$\mathbf{y}(\mathbf{x}; \mathbf{w}) = \mathbf{W}\boldsymbol{\phi}(\mathbf{x}) \tag{46}$$

where the elements of $\boldsymbol{\phi}(\mathbf{x})$ consist of M fixed basis functions $\phi_j(\mathbf{x})$, and $\mathbf{W}$ is a $d \times M$ matrix. Generalized linear regression models possess the same universal approximation capabilities as multi-layer adaptive networks, provided the basis functions $\phi_j(\mathbf{x})$ are chosen appropriately. The usual limitation of such models, however, is that the number of basis functions must typically grow exponentially with the dimensionality q of the input space [5]. In the present context this is not a significant problem since the dimensionality is governed by the number of latent variables which will typically be small. In fact for data visualization applications we generally use $q = 2$.

In the E-step of the EM algorithm we evaluate the posterior probabilities for each of the latent points i for every data point $\mathbf{t}_n$ using

$$R_{in} \quad = \quad p(\mathbf{x}_i|\mathbf{t}_n, \mathbf{W}, \sigma^2) \tag{47}$$

$$= \quad \frac{p(\mathbf{t}_n|\mathbf{x}_i, \mathbf{W}, \sigma^2)}{\sum_{i'=1}^{K} p(\mathbf{t}_n|\mathbf{x}_{i'}, \mathbf{W}, \sigma^2)}. \tag{48}$$

Then in the M-step we obtain a revised value for $\mathbf{W}$ by solving a set of coupled *linear* equations of the form

$$\mathbf{\Phi}^{\mathrm{T}}\mathbf{G}\mathbf{\Phi}\mathbf{W}^{\mathrm{T}} = \mathbf{\Phi}^{\mathrm{T}}\mathbf{R}\mathbf{T} \tag{49}$$

where $\mathbf{\Phi}$ is a $K \times M$ matrix with elements $\Phi_{ij} = \phi_j(\mathbf{x}_i)$, $\mathbf{T}$ is a $N \times d$ matrix with elements t_{nk}, $\mathbf{R}$ is a $K \times N$ matrix with elements R_{in}, and $\mathbf{G}$ is a $K \times K$ diagonal matrix with elements

$$G_{ii} = \sum_{n=1}^{N} R_{in}(\mathbf{W}, \sigma^2). \tag{50}$$

We can now solve (49) for $\mathbf{W}$ using singular value decomposition to allow for possible ill-conditioning. Also in the M-step we update σ^2 using the following re-estimation formula

$$\sigma^2 = \frac{1}{Nd} \sum_{n=1}^{N} \sum_{i=1}^{K} R_{in}(\mathbf{W}, \sigma^2) \|\mathbf{W}\phi(\mathbf{x}_i) - \mathbf{t}_n\|^2. \tag{51}$$

Note that the matrix $\mathbf{\Phi}$ is constant throughout the algorithm, and so need only be evaluated once at the start.

When using GTM for data visualization we can again plot each data point at the point on latent space corresponding to the mean of the posterior distribution, given by

$$\langle \mathbf{x}|\mathbf{t}_n, \mathbf{W}, \sigma^2 \rangle \quad = \quad \int \mathbf{x} p(\mathbf{x}|\mathbf{t}_n, \mathbf{W}, \sigma^2) \, d\mathbf{x} \tag{52}$$

$$= \quad \sum_{i=1}^{K} R_{in}\mathbf{x}_i. \tag{53}$$

It should be borne in mind, however, that as a consequence of the non-linear mapping from latent space to data space the posterior distribution can be multi-modal in which case the posterior mean can potentially give a very misleading summary of the true distribution. An alternative approach is therefore to evaluate the mode of the distribution, given by

$$i^{\max} = \arg\max_{\{i\}} R_{in}. \tag{54}$$

In practice it is often convenient to plot both the mean and the mode for each data point, as significant differences between them can be indicative of a multi-modal distribution.

One of the motivations for the development of the GTM algorithm was to provide a principled alternative to the widely used 'self-organizing map' (SOM) algorithm [17] in which a set of unlabelled data vectors $\mathbf{t}_n$ ($n = 1, \ldots, N$) in a d-dimensional data space is summarized in terms of a set of reference vectors having a spatial organization corresponding to a (generally) two-dimensional sheet. These reference vectors are analogous to the projections of the latent points into data space given by $\mathbf{y}(\mathbf{x}_i; \mathbf{w})$. While the SOM algorithm has achieved many successes in practical applications, it also suffers from some significant deficiencies, many of which are highlighted in [18]. These include: the absence of a cost function, the lack of any guarantee of topographic ordering, the absence of any general proofs of convergence, and the fact that the model does not define a probability density. These problems are all absent in GTM. The computational complexities of the GTM and SOM algorithms are similar, since the dominant cost in each case is the evaluation of the Euclidean distanced between each data point and each reference point in data space, and is the same for both algorithms.

Clearly, we can easily formulate a density model consisting of a mixture of GTM models, and obtain the corresponding EM algorithm, in a principled manner. The development of an analogous algorithm for the SOM would necessarily be somewhat ad-hoc.

5.2. GEOMETRY OF THE MANIFOLD

An additional advantage of the GTM algorithm (compared with the SOM) is that the non-linear manifold in data space is defined explicitly in terms of the analytic function $\mathbf{y}(\mathbf{x}; \mathbf{w})$. This allows a whole variety of geometrical properties of the manifold to be evaluated [9]. For example, local magnification factors can be expressed in terms of derivatives of the basis functions appearing in (46). Magnification factors specify the extent to which the area of a small patch of the latent space of a topographic mapping is magnified on projection to the data space, and are of considerable interest in both neuro-biological and data analysis contexts. Previous attempts to consider magnification factors for the SOM were been hindered because the manifold is only defined at discrete points (given by the reference vectors).

We can determine the properties of the manifold, including magnification factors, using techniques of differential geometry as follows [9]. Consider a standard set of Cartesian coordinates x^i in the latent space. Since each point P in latent space is mapped by a continuous function to a corresponding point P' in data space, the mapping defines a set of curvilinear coordinates ξ^i in the manifold in which each point P' is labelled with the coordinate values $\xi^i = x^i$ of P, as illustrated in Figure 13. Throughout this

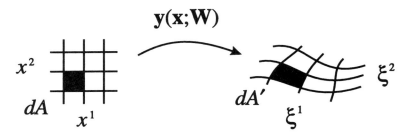

Figure 13. This diagram shows the mapping of the Cartesian coordinate system x^i in latent space onto a curvilinear coordinate system ξ^i in the q-dimensional manifold $\mathcal{S}$.

section we shall use the standard notation of differential geometry in which raised indices denote contravariant components and lowered indices denote covariant components, with an implicit summation over pairs of repeated covariant-contravariant indices.

We first discuss the metric properties of the manifold $\mathcal{S}$. Consider a local transformation, at some point P' in $\mathcal{S}$, to a set of rectangular Cartesian coordinates $\zeta^i = \zeta^i(\boldsymbol{\xi})$. Then the squared length element in these coordinates is given by

$$ds^2 = \delta_{\mu\nu}d\zeta^\mu d\zeta^\nu = \delta_{\mu\nu}\frac{\partial\zeta^\mu}{\partial\xi^i}\frac{\partial\zeta^\nu}{\partial\xi^j}d\xi^i d\xi^j = g_{ij}d\xi^i d\xi^j \tag{55}$$

where g_{ij} is the metric tensor, which is therefore given by

$$g_{ij} = \delta_{\mu\nu}\frac{\partial\zeta^\mu}{\partial\xi^i}\frac{\partial\zeta^\nu}{\partial\xi^j}. \tag{56}$$

We now seek an expression for g_{ij} in terms of the non-linear mapping $\mathbf{y}(\mathbf{x})$. Consider again the squared length element ds^2 lying within the manifold $\mathcal{S}$. Since $\mathcal{S}$ is embedded within the Euclidean data space, this also corresponds to the squared length element of the form

$$ds^2 = \delta_{kl}dy^k dy^l = \delta_{kl}\frac{\partial y^k}{\partial x^i}\frac{\partial y^l}{\partial x^j}dx^i dx^j = g_{ij}dx^i dx^j \tag{57}$$

and so we have

$$g_{ij} = \delta_{kl} \frac{\partial y^k}{\partial x^i} \frac{\partial y^l}{\partial x^j}. \tag{58}$$

Using (46) the metric tensor can be expressed in terms of the derivatives of the basis functions $\phi_j(\mathbf{x})$ in the form

$$\mathbf{g} = \mathbf{\Omega}^{\mathrm{T}} \mathbf{W}^{\mathrm{T}} \mathbf{W} \mathbf{\Omega} \tag{59}$$

where $\mathbf{\Omega}$ has elements $\Omega_{ji} = \partial \phi_j / \partial x^i$. It should be emphasized that, having obtained the metric tensor as a function of the latent space coordinates, many other geometrical properties are easily evaluated, such as the local curvatures of the manifold.

Our goal is to find an expression for the area dA' of the region of $\mathcal{S}$ corresponding to an infinitesimal rectangle in latent space with area $dA = \prod_i dx^i$ as shown in Figure 13. The area element in the manifold $\mathcal{S}$ can be related to the corresponding area element in the latent space by the Jacobian of the transformation $\xi \to \zeta$

$$dA' = \prod_\mu d\zeta^\mu = J \prod_i d\xi^i = J \prod_i dx^i = J dA \tag{60}$$

where the Jacobian J is given by

$$J = \det \left(\frac{\partial \zeta^\mu}{\partial \xi^i} \right) = \det \left(\frac{\partial \zeta^\mu}{\partial x^i} \right). \tag{61}$$

We now introduce the determinant g of the metric tensor which we can write in the form

$$g = \det(g_{ij}) = \det \left(\delta_{\mu\nu} \frac{\partial \zeta^\mu}{\partial x^i} \frac{\partial \zeta^\nu}{\partial x^j} \right) = \det \left(\frac{\partial \zeta^\mu}{\partial x^i} \right) \det \left(\frac{\partial \zeta^\nu}{\partial x^j} \right) = J^2 \tag{62}$$

and so, using (60), we obtain an expression for the local magnification factor in the form

$$\frac{dA'}{dA} = J = \det{}^{1/2} \mathbf{g}. \tag{63}$$

Although the magnification factor represents the extent to which areas are magnified on projection to the data space, it gives no information about which directions in latent space correspond to the stretching. We can recover this information by considering the decomposition of the metric tensor $\mathbf{g}$ in terms of its eigenvectors and eigenvalues. This information can be conveniently displayed by selecting a regular grid in latent space (which could correspond to the reference vector grid, but could also be much finer) and plotting at each grid point an ellipse with principal axes oriented according to the eigenvectors, with principal radii given by the square roots of the eigenvalues. The standard area magnification factor is given from (63) by the square root of the product of the eigenvalues, and so corresponds to the area of the ellipse.

As an illustration of the GTM algorithm and the evaluation of magnification factors we consider a data set of measurements taken from the genus *Leptograpsus* of rock crabs[1]. Measurements were taken from two species classified by their colour (orange or blue) with the aim of discovering morphological differences which would allow preserved specimens (which have lost their colour) to be distinguished. The data set contains 50 examples of each sex from each species, and the measurements correspond to length of frontal lip, rear width, length along mid-line, maximum width of carapace, and body length. Since all of the variables correspond to length measurements, the dominant feature of the crabs data is an overall scaling of the data vector in relation to the size of the crab. To remove this effect each data vector $\mathbf{t}_n = (t_{1n}, \ldots, t_{dn})^\mathrm{T}$ is normalized to unit mean, so that

$$\widetilde{t}_{kn} = t_{kn} \Big/ \sum_{k'=1}^{d} t_{k'n}. \tag{64}$$

The latent space visualization of the crabs data is shown in Figure 14 together with the local magnification factor. It can be seen that the two

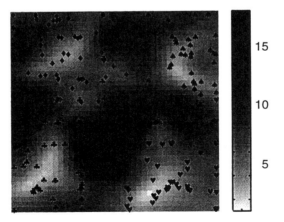

Figure 14. Plot of the latent-space distribution of the crabs data, in which ♣ denotes blue males, ♦ denotes blue females, ♥ denotes orange males, and ♠ denotes orange females. The grey-scale background shows the corresponding magnification factor as a function of the latent space coordinates, in which darker shades indicate larger values of the magnification factor.

species form distinct clusters, with the manifold undergoing a relatively large stretching in the region between them. Within each cluster there is a partial separation of males from females.

The corresponding plot of the local eigenvector decomposition of the metric is given in Figure 15, and shows both the direction and magnitude of the stretching.

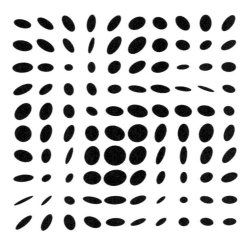

Figure 15.   Plots of the local stretching of the latent space, corresponding to the example in Figure 14, using the ellipse representation discussed in the text.

6. Temporal Models: GTM Through Time

In all of the models we have considered so far, it has been assumed that the data vectors are independent and identically distributed. One common situation in which this assumption is generally violated in where the data vectors are successive samples in a time series, with neighbouring vectors having typically a high correlation. As our final example of the use of latent variables, we consider an extension of the GTM algorithm to deal with temporal data [6]. The key observation is that the hidden states of the GTM model are discrete, as a result of the choice of latent distribution $p(\mathbf{x})$, which allows the machinery of hidden Markov models to be combined with GTM to give a non-linear temporal latent variable model.

The structure of the model is illustrated in Figure 16, in which the hidden states of the model at each time step n are labelled by the index i_n corresponding to the latent points $\{\mathbf{x}_{i_n}\}$. We introduce a set of transition probabilities $p(i_{n+1}|i_n)$ corresponding to the probability of making a transition to state i_{n+1} given that the current state is i_n. The emission density for the hidden Markov model is then given by the GTM density model (45). It should be noted that both the transition probabilities $p(i_{n+1}|i_n)$

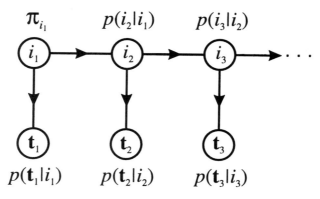

Figure 16.   The temporal version of GTM consists of a hidden Markov model in which the hidden states are given by the latent points of the GTM model, and the emission probabilities are governed by the GTM mixture distribution. Note that the parameters of the GTM model, as well as the transition probabilities between states, are tied to common values across all time steps. For clarity we have simplified the graph and not made the factorization property of the conditional distribution $p(\mathbf{t}|i)$ explicit.

and the parameters $\mathbf{W}$ and σ^2 governing the GTM model are common to all time steps, so that the number of adaptive parameters in the model is independent of the length of the time series. We also introduce separate prior probabilities π_{i_1} on each of the latent points at the first time step of the algorithm.

Again we can obtain an EM algorithm for maximizing the likelihood for the temporal GTM model. In the context of hidden Markov models, the EM algorithm is often called the Baum-Welch algorithm, and is reviewed in [21]. The E-step involves the evaluation of the posterior probabilities of the hidden states at each time step, and can be accomplished efficiently using a technique called the *forward-backward* algorithm since it involves two counter-directional propagations along the Markov chain. The M-step equations again take the form given in Section 5.1.

As an illustration of the temporal GTM algorithm we consider a data set obtained from a series of helicopter test flights. The motivation behind this application is to determine the accumulated stress on the helicopter airframe. Different flight modes, and transitions between flight modes, cause different levels of stress, and at present maintenance intervals are determined using an *assumed* usage spectrum. The ultimate goal in this application would be to segment each flight into its distinct regimes, together with the transitions between those regimes, and hence evaluate the overall integrated stress with greater accuracy.

The data used in this simulation was gathered from the flight recorder over four test flights, and consists of 9 variables (sampled every two seconds) measuring quantities such as acceleration, rate of change of heading, speed, altitude and engine torque. A sample of the data is shown in Figure 17.

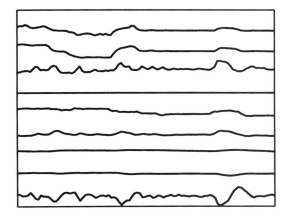

Figure 17.   Sample of the helicopter data showing the evolution of 9 different dynamical quantities such as acceleration, speed, and engine torque as a function of time.

Figure 18 shows the posterior probability distribution in latent space for a trained temporal GTM model, in which the posterior probabilities for a given temporal sequence have been evaluated using the forward-backward algorithm as described earlier.

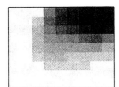 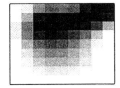 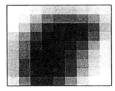 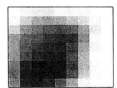

Figure 18.   Plots of the posterior probability distribution in latent space at 4 time steps, corresponding to a transition from one flight regime to another.

7. Discussion

In this chapter we have surveyed a number of hidden variable models for representing the distributions of continuous variables. We considered examples involving discrete, continuous and mixed hidden variables, together with linear and non-linear models for the distribution of observed variables conditioned on the hidden variables.

These models can conveniently be expressed in terms of probabilistic graphical structures, which provides insight into the corresponding inference and learning algorithms. For example, we saw that two key operations are the inference of the posterior distribution of the hidden variables given the observed variables (corresponding to the E-step of the EM algorithm) and the evaluation of the likelihood function which involves summing or integrating over all possible configurations of the hidden variables. For the models considered in this chapter, the integration over continuous hidden variables was possible because of simple (linear and Gaussian) choices for the model structure. In the case of discrete hidden variables we considered models in which only one of the hidden states can be active at any one time, giving rise to the standard mixture distribution.

The graphical viewpoint, however, also helps to motivate the development of new classes of probabilistic model. For instance, more general representations for discrete hidden states can be considered in which there are multiple hidden variables. However, for many models this leads to intractable algorithms since the number of *configurations* of hidden states may grow exponentially with the number of hidden variables. The development of controlled approximations to deal with such models is currently the focus of extensive research within the graphical modelling and neural computing communities.

ACKNOWLEDGEMENTS

The author would like to thank the following for their contributions to the work reported in this chapter: Geoffrey Hinton, Iain Strachan, Markus Svensén, Michael Tipping and Chris Williams.

References

1. Anderson, T. W. (1958). *An Introduction to Multivariate Statistical Analysis*. New York: John Wiley.
2. Anderson, T. W. (1963). Asymptotic theory for principal component analysis. *Annals of Mathematical Statistics 34*, 122–148.
3. Bartholomew, D. J. (1987). *Latent Variable Models and Factor Analysis*. London: Charles Griffin & Co. Ltd.
4. Basilevsky, A. (1994). *Statistical Factor Analysis and Related Methods*. New York: Wiley.
5. Bishop, C. M. (1995). *Neural Networks for Pattern Recognition*. Oxford University Press.
6. Bishop, C. M., G. E. Hinton, and I. G. D. Strachan (1997). GTM through time. In *Proceedings IEE Fifth International Conference on Artificial Neural Networks, Cambridge, U.K.*, pp. 111–116.
7. Bishop, C. M. and G. D. James (1993). Analysis of multiphase flows using dual-energy gamma densitometry and neural networks. *Nuclear Instruments and Methods in Physics Research A327*, 580–593.
8. Bishop, C. M., M. Svensén, and C. K. I. Williams (1997a). GTM: the generative topographic mapping. Accepted for publication in Neural Computation. To appear in volume 10, number 1. Available as NCRG/96/015 from http://www.ncrg.aston.ac.uk/.

9.   Bishop, C. M., M. Svensén, and C. K. I. Williams (1997b). Magnification factors for the GTM algorithm. In *Proceedings IEE Fifth International Conference on Artificial Neural Networks, Cambridge, U.K.*, pp. 64–69.

10. Bishop, C. M. and M. E. Tipping (1996). A hierarchical latent variable model for data visualization. Technical Report NCRG/96/028, Neural Computing Research Group, Aston University, Birmingham, UK. Accepted for publication in IEEE PAMI.

11. Dempster, A. P., N. M. Laird, and D. B. Rubin (1977). Maximum likelihood from incomplete data via the EM algorithm. *Journal of the Royal Statistical Society, B 39*(1), 1–38.

12. Hinton, G. E., P. Dayan, and M. Revow (1997). Modeling the manifolds of images of handwritten digits. *IEEE Transactions on Neural Networks 8*(1), 65–74.

13. Hinton, G. E., C. K. I. Williams, and M. D. Revow (1992). Adaptive elastic models for hand-printed character recognition. In J. E. Moody, S. J. Hanson, and R. P. Lippmann (Eds.), *Advances in Neural Information Processing Systems*, Volume 4, pp. 512–519. Morgan Kauffmann.

14. Hotelling, H. (1933). Analysis of a complex of statistical variables into principal components. *Journal of Educational Psychology 24*, 417–441.

15. Hull, J. J. (1994). A database for handwritten text recognition research. *IEEE Transactions on Pattern Analysis and Machine Intelligence 16*, 550–554.

16. Jordan, M. I. and R. A. Jacobs (1994). Hierarchical mixtures of experts and the EM algorithm. *Neural Computation 6*(2), 181–214.

17. Kohonen, T. (1982). Self-organized formation of topologically correct feature maps. *Biological Cybernetics 43*, 59–69.

18. Kohonen, T. (1995). *Self-Organizing Maps*. Berlin: Springer-Verlag.

19. Krzanowski, W. J. and F. H. C. Marriott (1994). *Multivariate Analysis Part I: Distributions, Ordination and Inference*. London: Edward Arnold.

20. Pearson, K. (1901). On lines and planes of closest fit to systems of points in space. *The London, Edinburgh and Dublin Philosophical Magazine and Journal of Science, Sixth Series 2*, 559–572.

21. Rabiner, L. R. (1989). A tutorial on hidden Markov models and selected applications in speech recognition. *Proceedings of the IEEE 77*(2), 257–285.

22. Rao, C. R. (1955). Estimation and tests of significance in factor analysis. *Psychometrika 20*, 93–111.

23. Rubin, D. B. and D. T. Thayer (1982). EM algorithms for ML factor analysis. *Psychometrika 47*(1), 69–76.

24. Tipping, M. E. and C. M. Bishop (1997a). Mixtures of probabilistic principal component analysers. Technical Report NCRG/97/003, Neural Computing Research Group, Aston University, Birmingham, UK. Submitted to Neural Computation.

25. Tipping, M. E. and C. M. Bishop (1997b). Probabilistic principal component analysis. Technical report, Neural Computing Research Group, Aston University, Birmingham, UK. Submitted to Journal of the Royal Statistical Society, B.

STOCHASTIC ALGORITHMS FOR EXPLORATORY DATA ANALYSIS:
DATA CLUSTERING AND DATA VISUALIZATION

JOACHIM M. BUHMANN
Institut für Informatik III,
Rheinische Friedrich-Wilhelms-Universität
D-53117 Bonn, Germany
jb@informatik.uni-bonn.de
http://www-dbv.informatik.uni-bonn.de

Abstract. Iterative, EM-type algorithms for data clustering and data visualization are derived on the basis of the maximum entropy principle. These algorithms allow the data analyst to detect structure in vectorial or relational data. Conceptually, the clustering and visualization procedures are formulated as combinatorial or continuous optimization problems which are solved by stochastic optimization.

1. INTRODUCTION

Exploratory Data Analysis addresses the question of how to discover and model structure hidden in a data set. Data clustering (JD88) and data visualization are important algorithmic tools in this quest for explanation of data relations. The structural relationships between data points, e.g., pronounced similarity of groups of data vectors, have to be detected in an unsupervised fashion. This search for prototypes poses a delicate tradeoff: a sufficiently rich modelling approach should be able to capture the essential structure in a data set but we should restrain ourselves from imposing too much structure which is absent in the data. Analogously, visualization techniques should not create structure which is caused by the visualization methodology rather than by data properties.

In the first part of this article we discuss the topic of grouping vectorial and relational data. Conceptually, there exist two different approaches to data clustering:

— *Parameter estimation of mixture models* by parametric statistics.
— *Vector quantization* of a data set by combinatorial optimization.

Parametric statistics assumes that noisy data have been generated by an unknown number of qualitatively similar, stochastic processes. Each individual process is characterized by a unimodal probability density. The density of the full data set is modelled by a parametrized *mixture model*, e.g., Gaussian mixtures are used most frequently (MB88). This model-based approach to data clustering requires estimating the mixture parameters, e.g., the mean and variance of four Gaussians for the data set depicted in Fig. 1a. Bayesian statistics provides a unique conceptual framework to compare and validate different mixture models.

The second approach to data clustering which has been popularized as vector quantization in information and communication theory, aims at finding a partition of a data set according to an optimization principle. Clustering as a data partitioning problem arises in two different forms depending on the data format [1]:

— *Central clustering* of vectorial data $\Xi = \{\mathbf{x}_i \in \mathbb{R}^d : 1 \leq i \leq N\}$;
— *Pairwise clustering* of proximity data $\mathcal{D} = \{\mathcal{D}_{ik} \in \mathbb{R} : 1 \leq i, k \leq N\}$.

The goal of data clustering is to determine a partitioning of a data set which either minimizes the average distance of data points to their cluster centers for central clustering or the average distance between data points of the same cluster for pairwise clustering. Note that the dissimilarities $\mathcal{D}_{ik}$ do not necessarily respect the requirements of a distance measure, e.g., dissimilarities or confusion values of protein, genetic, psychometric or linguistic data frequently violate the triangle inequality and the self-dissimilarity $\mathcal{D}_{ii}$ is not necessarily zero. For Sect. 3 we only assume symmetry $\mathcal{D}_{ik} = \mathcal{D}_{ki}$.

The second main topic of this paper addresses the question how relational data can be represented by points in a low-dimensional Euclidian space. A class of algorithms known as *Multidimensional Scaling* (Sect. 4) determine coordinates in a two- or three-dimensional Euclidian space such that pairwise distances $\|\mathbf{x}_i - \mathbf{x}_k\|$ match as close as possible the pairwise dissimilarities $\mathcal{D}$. A combination of data visualization and data clustering is discussed in Sect. 5. This algorithm preserves the grouping structure of relational data during the visualization procedure.

2. Central Clustering

The most widely used nonparametric technique to find data prototypes is central clustering or vector quantization. Given a set of d-dimensional data

---

[1]In principle, it is possible to consider triple or even more complicated data relations in an analogous fashion but the discussion in this paper is restricted to vectorial and relational data.

vectors $\Xi = \{\mathbf{x}_i \in \mathbb{R}^d : 1 \leq i \leq N\}$, central clustering poses the problem to determine an optimal set of d-dimensional reference vectors $\Upsilon = \{\mathbf{y}_\nu \in \mathbb{R}^d : 1 \leq \nu \leq K\}$ according to an optimality criterion. A data partition is specified by Boolean assignment variables $\mathbf{M}$ and a configuration space $\mathcal{M}$,

$$\mathbf{M} = (M_{i\nu})\Big|_{\substack{i=1,\ldots,N \\ \nu=1,\ldots,K}} \in \{0,1\}^{N \times K}, \tag{1}$$

$$\mathcal{M} = \left\{ \mathbf{M} \in \{0,1\}^{N \times K} : \sum_{\nu=1}^{K} M_{i\nu} = 1, \ \forall i \right\}. \tag{2}$$

$M_{i\nu} \equiv 1(0)$ denotes that the data point $\mathbf{x}_i$ is (not) assigned to reference vector $\mathbf{y}_\nu$. The solution space is defined as the set of admissible configurations in Eq. (2). Admissibility requires a unique assignment of data to clusters expressed by the constraint $\sum_{\nu=1}^{K} M_{i\nu} = 1$, $\forall i$.

2.1. COST FUNCTION FOR CENTRAL CLUSTERING

The quality of a set of reference vectors is assessed by an objective function which favors assignment solutions with high intra cluster compactness. Furthermore, we require superadditivity of clustering costs $\mathcal{H}$, i.e., splitting a cluster α into two clusters α', α'' should always be favorable $\mathcal{H}(\alpha) \geq \mathcal{H}(\alpha') + \mathcal{H}(\alpha'')$. Without this design principle a spurious bias could favor a specific "optimal" number of clusters. The cost function for central clustering

$$\mathcal{H}^{cc}(\mathbf{M}) = \sum_{i=1}^{N} \sum_{\nu=1}^{K} M_{i\nu} \mathcal{D}(\mathbf{x}_i, \mathbf{y}_\nu). \tag{3}$$

fulfills these requirements by summing up the average distortion error $\mathcal{D}(\mathbf{x}_i, \mathbf{y}_\nu)$ between a data vector $\mathbf{x}_i$ and the corresponding reference vector $\mathbf{y}_\nu$. An appropriate distortion measure $\mathcal{D}(\mathbf{x}_i, \mathbf{y}_\nu)$ depends on the application domain with the most common choice being the squared Euclidian distance $\mathcal{D}(\mathbf{x}_i, \mathbf{y}_\nu) \equiv \|\mathbf{x}_i - \mathbf{y}_\nu\|^2$ between the data vector and its reference vector. The standard algorithm for minimizing (3), known as K-means algorithm (Mac67), iteratively assigns data to the closest cluster centers and reestimates these centers according to the data assignments until convergence.

A generalization of the objective function (3) has been discussed in the context of source-channel-coding. Noisy channels with a significant confusion probability between cluster index α and γ make it preferable to place code vector $\mathbf{y}_\alpha$ close to $\mathbf{y}_\gamma$. The following diagram displays the communication setup:

$$\{\mathbf{x}_i\} \rightarrow \boxed{\text{Encoder } \mathbf{x}_i \rightarrow \mathbf{y}_\alpha} \overset{\alpha}{\rightarrow} \boxed{\text{Channel}} \overset{\gamma}{\rightarrow} \boxed{\text{Decoder}} \rightarrow \{\mathbf{y}_\gamma\}$$

with $\boxed{\text{noise } \mathbf{T}_{\alpha\gamma}}$ feeding into the Channel.

In addition to the quantization error $\mathcal{D}(\mathbf{x}_i, \mathbf{y}_\alpha)$ we have to take the channel distortion due to index corruption into account. An appropriate cost function for the total distortions between sender and receiver

$$\mathcal{D}(\mathbf{x}_i, \mathbf{y}_\alpha) \equiv \sum_{\nu=1}^{K} \mathbf{T}_{\alpha\nu} \|\mathbf{x}_i - \mathbf{y}_\nu\|^2 \tag{4}$$

favors the topological organization of code vectors according to the closeness measure $\mathbf{T}_{\alpha\nu}$ which specifies the probability of confusing index α with index ν due to transmission noise. Distortions with a low-dimensional, topological arrangement of clusters defining a chain or a two-dimensional grid are very popular as selforganizing topological maps in "*neural computation*" (Koh84; Lut89; RMS92; BSW97).

2.2. STOCHASTIC OPTIMIZATION OF $\mathcal{H}^{cc}(\mathbf{M})$

Throughout this paper, we advocate a stochastic optimization principle to find optimized centroids and assignments of data to clusters. The assignments are considered to be random variables. Stochastic optimization of the cost function $\mathcal{H}^{cc}(\mathbf{M})$ (3) requires determining the probability distribution over assignments $\mathbf{M}$. Since many assignments might yield the same expected costs, we have to break this ambiguity by introducing an unbiased uniqueness constraint, e.g., the maximum entropy principle. The maximum entropy principle, originally suggested for central clustering by Rose et al. (RGF90), states that assignments are distributed according to the Gibbs distribution

$$\mathbf{P}^{\text{Gibbs}}(\mathcal{H}^{cc}(\mathbf{M})) = \exp\left(-(\mathcal{H}^{cc}(\mathbf{M}) - \mathcal{F}(\mathcal{H}^{cc}))/T\right), \tag{5}$$

$$\mathcal{F}(\mathcal{H}^{cc}) = -T \log \sum_{\mathbf{M} \in \mathcal{M}} \exp\left(-\mathcal{H}^{cc}(\mathbf{M})/T\right) \tag{6}$$

The "computational temperature" T serves as a Lagrange parameter for the expected costs. As pointed out in (HB97), the free energy $\mathcal{F}(\mathcal{H}^{cc})$ in Eq. (6) can be interpreted as a smoothed version of the original cost function $\mathcal{H}^{cc}$. The factor $\exp(\mathcal{F}(\mathcal{H}^{cc})/T)$ normalizes the exponential terms $\exp\left(-\mathcal{H}^{cc}(\mathbf{M})/T\right)$. Constraining the assignments by $\sum_{\nu=1}^{K} M_{i\nu} = 1$ the term $\exp(-\mathcal{F}(\mathcal{H}^{cc})/T)$ can be rewritten as

$$\sum_{\mathbf{M} \in \mathcal{M}} \exp\left(-\sum_{i=1}^{N} \sum_{\nu=1}^{K} M_{i\nu} \mathcal{D}(\mathbf{x}_i, \mathbf{y}_\nu)/T\right) = \prod_{i=1}^{N} \sum_{\nu=1}^{K} \exp\left(-\mathcal{D}(\mathbf{x}_i, \mathbf{y}_\nu)/T\right) \tag{7}$$

The cost function $\mathcal{H}^{cc}$ which is linear in $M_{i\nu}$ yields a factorized Gibbs distribution

$$\mathbf{P}^{\text{Gibbs}}(\mathcal{H}^{cc}(\mathbf{M})) = \prod_{i=1}^{N} \frac{\exp(-\sum_{\nu=1}^{K} M_{i\nu} \mathcal{D}(\mathbf{x}_i, \mathbf{y}_\nu)/T)}{\sum_{\mu=1}^{K} \exp(-\mathcal{D}(\mathbf{x}_i, \mathbf{y}_\mu)/T)} \tag{8}$$

for predefined reference vectors $\Upsilon = \{\mathbf{y}_\nu\}$. This Gibbs distribution can also be interpreted as the complete data likelihood for mixture models with parameters Υ. Basically, the distribution (8) describes a mixture model with equal priors for each component and equal, isotropic covariances.

The optimal reference vectors $\{\mathbf{y}_\nu^*\}$ are derived by maximizing the entropy of the Gibbs distribution, keeping the average costs $\langle \mathcal{H}^{cc} \rangle$ fixed, i.e.,

$$
\begin{aligned}
\Upsilon^* &= \arg\max_\Upsilon \left(-\sum_{\mathbf{M} \in \mathcal{M}} \mathbf{P}^{\text{Gibbs}}(\mathcal{H}^{cc}(\mathbf{M})) \log \mathbf{P}^{\text{Gibbs}}(\mathcal{H}^{cc}(\mathbf{M})) \right) \\
&= \arg\max_\Upsilon \left(\sum_{\mathbf{M} \in \mathcal{M}} \mathcal{H}^{cc}(\mathbf{M}) \mathbf{P}^{\text{Gibbs}}(\mathcal{H}^{cc}(\mathbf{M}))/T \right. \\
&\qquad \left. + \sum_{i=1}^{N} \log \sum_{\mu=1}^{K} \exp(-\mathcal{D}(\mathbf{x}_i, \mathbf{y}_\mu)/T) \right).
\end{aligned}
\tag{9}
$$

$\mathbf{P}^{\text{Gibbs}}(\mathbf{M})$ is the Gibbs distribution of the assignments for a set Υ of fixed reference vectors. To determine closed equations for the optimal reference vectors $\mathbf{y}_\nu^*$ we differentiate the argument in Eq. (9) with the expected costs being kept constant. The resulting equation

$$
0 = \sum_{i=1}^{N} \langle M_{i\nu} \rangle \frac{\partial}{\partial \mathbf{y}_\nu} \mathcal{D}(\mathbf{x}_i, \mathbf{y}_\nu) \quad \text{with} \tag{10}
$$

$$
\langle M_{i\nu} \rangle \equiv \frac{\exp(-\mathcal{D}(\mathbf{x}_i, \mathbf{y}_\nu)/T)}{\sum_\mu \exp(-\mathcal{D}(\mathbf{x}_i, \mathbf{y}_\mu)/T)} \quad \forall \nu \in \{1, \ldots, K\} \tag{11}
$$

is known as the centroid equation in signal processing which are optimal in the sense of rate distortion theory (CT91). The angular brackets denote Gibbs expectation values, i.e., $\langle f(\mathbf{M}) \rangle \equiv \sum_{\mathbf{M} \in \mathcal{M}} f(\mathbf{M}) \mathbf{P}^{\text{Gibbs}}(\mathbf{M})$. The equations (10,11) are efficiently solved in an iterative fashion using the expectation maximization (EM) algorithm (DLR77):

The EM algorithm alternates an estimation step to determine the expected assignments $\langle M_{i\nu} \rangle$ with a maximization step to estimate maximum likelihood values for the cluster centers $\mathbf{y}_\nu$. Dempster et al. (DLR77) have proven that the likelihood increases monotonically under this alternation scheme. The algorithm converges towards a local maximum of the likelihood function. The log-likelihood is up to a factor $(-T)$ equivalent to the free energy for central clustering. The function $f(.)$ denotes an appropriate annealing schedule, e.g., $f(T) = T/2$.

The size K of the cluster set, i.e., the complexity of the clustering solution, has to be determined by a problem-dependent complexity measure

---

EM Algorithm I for Centroid Estimation

INITIALIZE $\mathbf{y}_\nu^{(0)} \in \mathbb{R}^d$ randomly and $\langle M_{i\nu}\rangle^{(0)} \in (0,1)$ arbitrarily;
    temperature $T \leftarrow T_0$;
WHILE $T > T_{\text{FINAL}}$
    $t \leftarrow 0$;
    REPEAT
        E-step: estimate $\langle M_{i\nu}\rangle^{(t+1)}$ as a function of $\mathbf{y}_\nu^{(t)}$;
        M-step: calculate $\mathbf{y}_\nu^{(t+1)}$ for given $\langle M_{i\nu}\rangle^{(t+1)}$;
        $t \leftarrow t+1$;
    UNTIL all $\{\langle M_{i\nu}\rangle^{(t)}, \mathbf{y}_\nu^{(t)}\}$ satisfy Eqs. (10,11)
    $T \leftarrow f(T)$;

(BK93) which monotonically grows with the number of clusters. Simultaneous minimization of the distortion costs and the complexity costs yields an optimal number K^* of clusters. Constant complexity costs per cluster or logarithmic complexity costs $-\log(\sum_{i=1}^N M_{i\nu}/N)$ (Shannon information) are utilized in various applications like signal processing, image compression or speech recognition. A clustering result with logarithmic complexity costs is shown in Fig. 1c. It is important to emphasize that the vector quantization approach to clustering optimizes a data partitioning and, therefore, is not suited to detect univariate components of a data distribution. The splitting of the four Gaussians in Fig. 1a into 45 clusters (Fig. 1c) results from low complexity costs and is not a defect of the method. Note also, that the distortion costs as well as the complexity costs determine the position of the prototypes $\{\mathbf{y}_\nu\}$. For example, the density of clusters in Fig. 1c is asymptotically independent of the density of data (in the area of non-vanishing data density), which is a consequence of the logarithmic complexity costs.

3. Pairwise Clustering

3.1. COST FUNCTION FOR PAIRWISE CLUSTERING

The second important class of data are relational data which are encoded by a proximity or dissimilarity matrix. Clustering these non-metric data which are characterized by relations and not by explicit Euclidian coordinates is usually formulated as an optimization problem with quadratic assignment costs. A suggestion what measure we should use to evaluate a clustering solution for relational data is provided by the identity

$$\sum_{i=1}^N M_{i\nu}\|\mathbf{x}_i - \mathbf{y}_\nu\|^2 = \frac{1}{2}\sum_{i=1}^N M_{i\nu}\frac{\sum_{k=1}^N M_{k\nu}\|\mathbf{x}_i - \mathbf{x}_k\|^2}{\sum_{k=1}^N M_{k\nu}} \qquad (12)$$

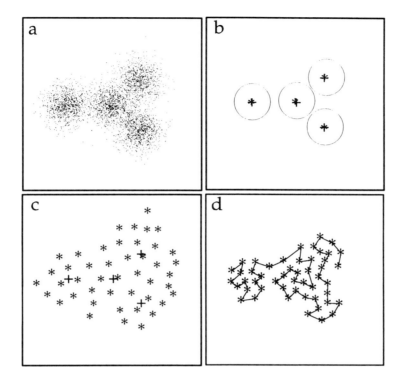

Figure 1. Clustering of multivariate data (a) generated by four Gaussian sources: The estimated Gaussian mixture model is depicted in (b), the plus signs (+) are the centers of the Gaussian sources and stars ($\star$) are cluster centers. The circles denote the covariance estimates. Figure (c) shows a data partitioning using a logarithmic complexity measure. Data clustering by a self-organizing chain is shown in (d), neighboring clusters being connected.

with $\mathbf{y}_\nu = \sum_{k=1}^N M_{k\nu}\mathbf{x}_k / \sum_{k=1}^N M_{k\nu}$. For squared Euclidian distances $\mathcal{D}_{ik} = \|\mathbf{x}_i - \mathbf{x}_k\|^2$ pairwise clustering with normalized average intra-cluster distances is identical to central clustering with cluster means as prototypes. This identity strongly motivates the objective function for pairwise clustering

$$\mathcal{H}^{\mathrm{pc}}(\{M_{i\nu}\}) = \frac{1}{2} \sum_{i,k=1}^N \sum_{\nu=1}^K \frac{M_{i\nu} M_{k\nu} \mathcal{D}_{ik}}{\sum_{l=1}^N M_{l\nu}} \qquad (13)$$

with $M_{i\nu} \in \{0,1\}$ and $\sum_{\nu=1}^K M_{i\nu} = 1$. Whenever two data items i and k are assigned to the same cluster ν the costs are increased by the amount $\mathcal{D}_{ik}/\sum_{l=1}^N M_{l\nu}$. The objective function has the important invariance property that a constant shift of all dissimilarities $\mathcal{D}_{ik} \rightarrow \mathcal{D}_{ik} + \mathcal{D}_0$ does not effect the assignments of data to clusters (for a rigorous axiomatic frame-

---

Algorithm II for Pairwise Clustering

INITIALIZE $\mathcal{E}_{i\nu}{}^{(0)}$ and $\langle M_{i\nu}\rangle^{(0)} \in (0,1)$ randomly;
         temperature $T \leftarrow T_0$;
WHILE $T > T_{\text{FINAL}}$
     $t \leftarrow 0$;
     REPEAT
         E-like step: estimate $\langle M_{i\nu}\rangle^{(t+1)}$ as a function of $\mathcal{E}_{i\nu}{}^{(t)}$;
         M-like step: calculate $\mathcal{E}_{i\nu}{}^{(t+1)}$ for given $\langle M_{i\nu}\rangle^{(t+1)}$
         $t \leftarrow t + 1$;
     UNTIL all $\{\langle M_{i\nu}\rangle^{(t)}, \mathcal{E}_{i\nu}{}^{(t)}\}$ satisfy (14)
     $T \leftarrow f(T)$;

---

work, see (Hof97)) which dispenses the data analyst from estimating absolute dissimilarity values instead of (relative) dissimilarity differences.

3.2. MEANFIELD APPROXIMATION OF PAIRWISE CLUSTERING

Minimization of the quadratic cost function (13) turns out to be algorithmically complicated due to pairwise, potentially conflicting interactions between assignments. The deterministic annealing technique, which produces robust reestimation equations for central clustering in the maximum entropy framework, is not directly applicable to pairwise clustering since there is no analytical technique known to capture correlations between assignments $M_{i\nu}$ and $M_{k\nu}$ in an exact fashion. The expected assignments $\langle M_{i\nu}\rangle$, however, can be approximated by calculating the average influence $\mathcal{E}_{i\nu}$ exerted by all $M_{k\nu}, k \neq i$ on the assignment $M_{i\nu}$ (pp. 29, (HKP91)), thereby neglecting pair-correlations ($\langle M_{i\nu}M_{k\nu}\rangle = \langle M_{i\nu}\rangle\langle M_{k\nu}\rangle$). A maximum entropy estimate of $\mathcal{E}_{i\nu}$ yields the transcendental equations

$$\langle M_{i\nu}\rangle = \frac{\exp(-\mathcal{E}_{i\nu}/T)}{\sum_{\mu=1}^{K}\exp(-\mathcal{E}_{i\mu}/T)}, \tag{14}$$

$$\mathcal{E}_{i\nu}(\{\langle M_{i\nu}\rangle\}|\mathcal{D}) = \sum_{k=1}^{N}\frac{\langle M_{k\nu}\rangle}{\sum_{\substack{j=1\\j\neq i}}^{N}\langle M_{j\nu}\rangle + 1}\left(\mathcal{D}_{ik} - \frac{\sum_{j=1}^{N}\langle M_{j\nu}\rangle\mathcal{D}_{jk}}{2\sum_{\substack{j=1\\j\neq i}}^{N}\langle M_{j\nu}\rangle}\right). \tag{15}$$

The partial assignment costs $\mathcal{E}_{i\nu}$ of object i to cluster ν measure the average dissimilarity in cluster ν weighted by its cluster size. The second summand in the bracket in (15) can be interpreted as a reactive term which takes the increased size of cluster ν after assignment of object i into account. Equation (14) suggests an algorithm for learning the optimized cluster assignments which resembles the EM algorithm: In the E-step, the assignments $\{M_{i\nu}\}$ are estimated for given $\{\mathcal{E}_{i\nu}\}$. In the M-step the $\{\mathcal{E}_{i\nu}\}$ are reestimated on the basis of new assignment estimates. This iterative algorithm converges to a consistent solution of assignments for the pairwise data clustering problem (HB97).

3.3. TOPOLOGICAL PAIRWISE CLUSTERING

Central clustering with cost function (3) has been generalized to a topological clustering problem with distortions (4). These generalized distortions break the permutation symmetry between clusters and favor a data partitioning according to neighborhood in index space, e.g., a linear chain as in Fig. 1d. The same generalization can be introduced for pairwise clustering, i.e., to break the permutation symmetry of clusters. We introduce a pairwise clustering cost function which coincides with topological central clustering for quadratic Euclidian distances as dissimilarities. This design criterion yields the cost function

$$\mathcal{H}^{\text{tpc}}(\{M_{i\nu}\}) = \frac{1}{2}\sum_{i,k=1}^{N}\sum_{\nu=1}^{K}\tilde{M}_{i\nu}\tilde{M}_{k\nu}\frac{\mathcal{D}_{ik}}{\sum_{l=1}^{N}\tilde{M}_{l\nu}} \tag{16}$$

$$\tilde{M}_{i\nu} = \sum_{\mu=1}^{K}\mathbf{T}_{\mu\nu}M_{i\mu}. \tag{17}$$

The effective assignments $\tilde{M}_{i\nu}$ can be interpreted as transformed assignments which encode the neighborhood structure of clusters. To find the maximum entropy estimates of the assignments for topological pairwise clustering we apply the inverse transformation to the cost function (17) and transform the solution of the resulting costs (13) which yields

$$\langle M_{i\alpha}\rangle = \frac{\exp(-\tilde{\mathcal{E}}_{i\alpha}/T)}{\sum_{\mu=1}^{K}\exp(-\tilde{\mathcal{E}}_{i\mu}/T)}, \tag{18}$$

$$\tilde{\mathcal{E}}_{i\alpha} = \sum_{\nu=1}^{K}\mathbf{T}_{\alpha\nu}\mathcal{E}_{i\nu}(\{\langle\tilde{M}_{i\nu}\rangle\}|\mathcal{D}), \tag{19}$$

where $\mathcal{E}_{i\nu}$ in r.h.s. of (19) are the assignment costs (15) with $M_{i\nu}$ being replaced by $\tilde{M}_{i\nu}$.

4. Data Visualization by Multidimensional Scaling

Grouping data into clusters is an important concept in discovering structure. Apart from partitioning a data set, the data analyst often explores data by visual inspection to discover correlations and deviations from randomness. The task of embedding given dissimilarity data $\mathcal{D}$ in a d-dimensional

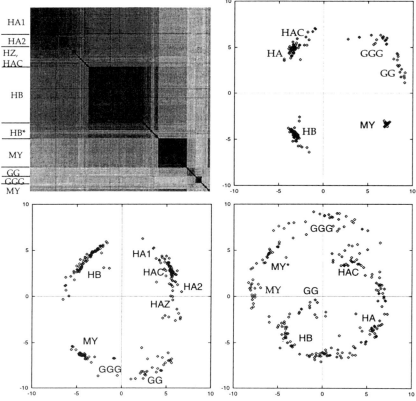

Figure 2. Similarity matrix (a) of 226 protein sequences of the globin family. Dark grey levels correspond to high similarity values. (b)-(d) show the embeddings derived by deterministic annealing algorithm: (b) global (c) intermediate and (d) local normalization of the cost function (see text).

Euclidian space, a prerequisite for visual inspection, is known as multidimensional scaling (DH73; Sam69). The quality of an embedding $\mathcal{X} = \{\mathbf{x}_i \in \mathbb{R}^d : 1 \leq i \leq n\}$ is measured by the difference of the squared Euclidian distances $\|\mathbf{x}_i - \mathbf{x}_k\|^2$ and the dissimilarity values $\mathcal{D}_{ik}$, i.e.,

$$\mathcal{H}^{\mathrm{mds}}(\{\mathbf{x}_i\}) = \sum_{i=1}^{N} \sum_{k=1}^{N} w_{ik} \left(\|\mathbf{x}_i - \mathbf{x}_k\|^2 - \mathcal{D}_{ik} \right)^2 \qquad (20)$$

with squared Euclidian distances for computational simplicity. Cost function $\mathcal{H}^{\mathrm{mds}}(\{\mathbf{x}_i\})$ is known as SSTRESS (CC94; TY77) in the literature. The weighting factors w_{ik} are introduced to weight the disparities individually and, thereby, to gauge the scale of the stress function, i.e., to normalize out the absolute values of the disparities $\mathcal{D}_{ij}$. Dependent on the data analysis task at hand, it might be appropriate to use a local, a global or an intermediate normalization

$$w_{ik}^{(l)} = \frac{1}{N(N-1)\mathcal{D}_{ik}^2}; \; w_{ik}^{(g)} = \frac{1}{\sum_{i,k=1}^{N} \mathcal{D}_{ik}^2}; \; w_{ik}^{(m)} = \frac{1}{D_{ik} \sum_{l,m=1}^{N} \mathcal{D}_{lm}^2} \quad (21)$$

which corresponds to the minimization of relative, absolute or intermediate error (DH73).

We pursue the same optimization strategy to minimize (20) as in the pairwise clustering case, i.e., we derive the maximum entropy estimate of the expected coordinates $\langle \mathbf{x}_i \rangle$ using the approximation that the distribution of the embedding coordinates $\mathcal{X}$ factors according to

$$P^0(\mathcal{X}|\Phi_i) = \prod_{i=1}^{N} \frac{\exp(-f_i(\mathbf{x}_i)/T)}{\int\limits_{-\infty}^{\infty} d\mathbf{x}_i \exp(-f_i(\mathbf{x}_i)/T)} \quad (22)$$

$$f_i(\mathbf{x}_i) = \alpha_i^0 \|\mathbf{x}_i\|^4 + \|\mathbf{x}_i\|^2 \mathbf{x}_i^T \hat{\mathbf{h}}_i + Tr\left[\mathbf{x}_i \mathbf{x}_i^T \mathbf{H}_i\right] + \mathbf{x}_i^T \mathbf{h}_i . \quad (23)$$

Utilizing the symmetry $\mathcal{D}_{ik} = \mathcal{D}_{ki}$ and neglecting constant terms an expansion of $\mathcal{H}^{\mathrm{mds}}$ yields the expected costs (expectations w.r.t. 22)

$$\langle \mathcal{H}^{\mathrm{mds}} \rangle = \sum_{i,k=1}^{N} w_{ik} \left[2\langle \|\mathbf{x}_i\|^4 \rangle - 8\langle \|\mathbf{x}_i\|^2 \mathbf{x}_i \rangle^T \langle \mathbf{x}_k \rangle + 2\langle \|\mathbf{x}_i\|^2 \rangle \langle \|\mathbf{x}_k\|^2 \rangle \right.$$
$$\left. + 4 Tr\left[\langle \mathbf{x}_i \mathbf{x}_i^T \rangle \langle \mathbf{x}_k \mathbf{x}_k^T \rangle \right] - 4 \mathcal{D}_{ik} (\langle \|\mathbf{x}_i\|^2 \rangle - \langle \mathbf{x}_i \rangle^T \langle \mathbf{x}_k \rangle) \right], \quad (24)$$

$Tr[A]$ denoting the trace of matrix $\mathbf{A}$. A detailed derivation is in (KB97).

The statistics $\Phi_i = (\alpha_i^0, \mathbf{h}_i, \mathbf{H}_i, \hat{\mathbf{h}}_i)$, $1 \le i \le N$ are defined as $\alpha_i^0 = 2\sum_{k=1}^{N} w_{ik}$, $\hat{\mathbf{h}}_i = -8\sum_{k=1}^{N} w_{ik}\langle \mathbf{x}_k \rangle$, $\mathbf{h}_i = 8\sum_{k=1}^{N} w_{ik}(\mathcal{D}_{ik}\langle \mathbf{x}_k \rangle - \langle |\mathbf{x}_k|^2 \mathbf{x}_k \rangle)$ and $\mathbf{H}_i = \sum_{k=1}^{N} w_{ik}(8\langle \mathbf{x}_k \mathbf{x}_k^T \rangle + 4\mathbf{I}(\langle |\mathbf{x}_k|^2 \rangle - \mathcal{D}_{ik}))$. We propose a deterministic annealing algorithm (sketched in the box for Algorithm III) to compute the statistics $\Phi = (\Phi_1, \ldots, \Phi_N)$ in an iterative fashion. Fig. 2 gives an idea of how MDS might be used in practice. Starting with the dissimilarity matrix (a) of 226 protein sequences from the globin family (dark grey levels correspond to small dissimilarities), embeddings are derived by minimizing (20) with global (b), intermediate (c) or local (d) weighting. The embeddings clearly reveal the cluster structure of the data with different accuracy in the representation of inter- and intra-cluster dissimilarities.

5. Simultaneous Pairwise Clustering and Embedding

Multidimensional scaling allows the experimentalist to visualize data. There exists, however, no guarantee that the visualized structure is indeed supported by the information in the data set rather than being generated by

---

Algorithm III: MDS by Deterministic Annealing

INITIALIZE the parameters Φ^0 of $P^0(\mathcal{X}|\Phi^0)$ randomly.
WHILE $T > T_{\text{FINAL}}$
    REPEAT
        E-like step:
            Calculate $\langle \mathbf{x}_i \rangle^{(t+1)}$, $\langle \mathbf{x}_i \mathbf{x}_i^T \rangle^{(t+1)}$, $\langle \|\mathbf{x}_i\|^2 \mathbf{x}_i \rangle^{(t+1)}$
              w.r.t. $P^{(t)}(\mathcal{X}|\Phi^{(t)})$
        M-like step:
            compute $\Phi_k^{(t+1)}$, $1 \leq k \leq N, k \neq i$
        $t \leftarrow t+1$;
    UNTIL convergence
    $T \leftarrow f(T)$;

---

the visualization process. We, therefore, have proposed a combination of pairwise clustering and visualization with an emphasis on preservation of the grouping statistics (HB97). The coordinates of data points in the embedding space are estimated in such a way that the statistics of the resulting cluster structure matches the statistics of the original pairwise clustering solution. The relation of this new principle for structure preserving data embedding to standard multidimensional scaling is summarized in the following diagram:

$$
\begin{array}{ccccc}
\{\mathcal{D}_{ik}\} & \longrightarrow & \mathcal{H}^{\text{pc}}(\mathbf{M}|\{\mathcal{D}_{ik}\}) & \longrightarrow & \mathbf{P}^{\text{Gibbs}}(\mathcal{H}^{\text{pc}}(\mathbf{M}|\{\mathcal{D}_{ik}\})) \\
\downarrow \mathcal{H}^{\text{mds}} & & & & \downarrow \mathcal{I}(\mathcal{H}^{\text{cc}}\|\mathcal{H}^{\text{pc}}) \\
\{\|\mathbf{x}_i - \mathbf{x}_k\|^2\} & \longrightarrow & \mathcal{H}^{\text{cc}}(\mathbf{M}|\{\mathbf{x}_i\}) & \longrightarrow & \mathbf{P}^{\text{Gibbs}}(\mathcal{H}^{\text{cc}}(\mathbf{M}|\{\mathbf{x}_i\})).
\end{array}
$$

Multidimensional scaling provides the left/bottom path for structure detection, i.e., how to discover cluster structure in dissimilarity data. The dissimilarity data are first embedded in a Euclidian space and clusters are derived by a subsequent grouping procedure as K-means clustering. In contrast to this strategy for visualization, we advocate the top/right path, i.e., the pairwise clustering statistic is measured and afterwards, the points are positioned in the embedding space to match this statistic by minimizing the Kullback-Leibler divergence $\mathcal{I}(\cdot)$ between the two Gibbs distributions $\mathbf{P}^{\text{Gibbs}}(\mathcal{H}^{\text{cc}}(\mathbf{M}|\{\mathbf{x}_i\}))$ and $\mathbf{P}^{\text{Gibbs}}(\mathcal{H}^{\text{pc}}(\mathbf{M}|\{\mathcal{D}_{ik}\}))$. This approach is motivated by the identity (12) which yields an exact solution ($\mathcal{I}(\mathbf{P}^{\text{Gibbs}}(\mathcal{H}^{\text{cc}})\|\mathbf{P}^{\text{Gibbs}}(\mathcal{H}^{\text{pc}})) = 0$) for pairwise clustering instances with $\mathcal{D}_{ik} = \|\mathbf{x}_i - \mathbf{x}_k\|^2$.

Suppose we have found a stationary solution of the mean–field equations (14). For the clustering problem it suffices to consider the mean assignments $\langle M_{i\nu} \rangle$ with the parameters $\mathcal{E}_{i\nu}$ being auxiliary variables. The identity (12) allows us to interpret these variables as the squared distance to the cluster centroid under the assumption of Euclidian data. In the multidimensional scaling problem the coordinates $\mathbf{x}_i$ are the unknown quantities. If the potentials $\mathcal{E}_{i\nu}$ are restricted to be of the form $\|\mathbf{x}_i - \mathbf{y}_\nu\|^2$ with the centroid definition $\mathbf{y}_\nu = \sum_{i=1}^N M_{i\nu}\mathbf{x}_k / \sum_{i=1}^N M_{i\nu}$, then the following reestimation equations for the embedding coordinates are fulfilled:

$$\mathbf{K}_i\mathbf{x}_i \approx \frac{1}{2}\sum_{\nu=1}^K \langle M_{i\nu}\rangle \left(\|\mathbf{y}_\nu\|^2 - \mathcal{E}_{i\nu}(\{\langle M_{i\nu}\rangle\}|\mathcal{D})\right)\left(\mathbf{y}_\nu - \sum_{\mu=1}^K \langle M_{i\mu}\rangle\mathbf{y}_\mu\right), \quad (25)$$

$$\mathbf{K}_i = \langle\mathbf{y}\mathbf{y}^T\rangle_i - \langle\mathbf{y}\rangle_i\langle\mathbf{y}\rangle_i^T \quad \text{with} \quad \langle\mathbf{y}\rangle_i = \sum_{\nu=1}^K \langle M_{i\nu}\rangle\mathbf{y}_\nu. \quad (26)$$

The dissimilarity values determine the coordinates $\mathbf{x}_i$ through the potentials $\mathcal{E}_{i\nu}$ which are defined in (15). Details of the derivation can be found in Appendix C of (HB97). The coordinates $\{\mathbf{x}_i\}$ and $\{\mathbf{y}_\nu\}$ are calculated by iteratively solving the equations (25) according to the Algorithm IV.

Algorithm IV: Structure Preserving MDS

INITIALIZE $\hat{\mathbf{x}}_i^{(0)}$ randomly and $\langle M_{i\nu}\rangle^{(0)} \in (0,1)$ arbitrarily;
      temperature $T \leftarrow T_0$;
WHILE $T > T_{\text{FINAL}}$
   $t \leftarrow 0$;
   REPEAT
      E-like step: estimate $\langle M_{i\nu}\rangle^{(t+1)}$ as a function of $\{\hat{\mathbf{x}}_i^{(t)}, \hat{\mathbf{y}}_\nu^{(t)}\}$
      M-like step:
         REPEAT
            calculate $\hat{\mathbf{x}}_i^{(t+1)}$ given $\langle M_{i\nu}\rangle^{(t+1)}$ and $\hat{\mathbf{y}}_\nu^{(t)}$
            update $\hat{\mathbf{y}}_\nu^{(t+1)}$ to fulfill the centroid condition
         UNTIL convergence
      $t \leftarrow t + 1$
   UNTIL convergence
   $T \leftarrow f(T)$;

The derived system of transcendental equations given by (11) with quadratic distortions, by (25) and by the centroid condition explicitly reflects the dependencies between the clustering procedure and the Euclidian representation. Simultaneous solution of these equations leads to an efficient algorithm which interleaves the multidimensional scaling process and the clustering process, and which avoids an artificial separation into two uncorrelated data processing steps. The advantages of this algorithm are convincingly demonstrated in the case of dimension reduction. 20-dimensional

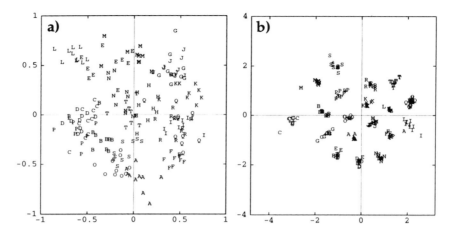

Figure 3.   Embedding of 20-dimensional data into two dimensions: (a) projection of the data onto the first two principal components; (b) cluster preserving embedding with Algorithm IV. Only 10% of the data are shown.

data generated by 20 Gaussians located on the unit sphere are projected onto a two-dimensional plane in Fig. 3 either by **P**rincipal **C**omponent **A**nalysis (a) or by **S**tructure **P**reserving **MDS** (b). Clearly the cluster structure is only well preserved in case (b).

6. Discussion

Exploratory data analysis aims at the discovery of hidden structure in data sets. Standard methods to achieve this goal encompasses data clustering methods and visualization. A rich framework for deriving algorithms in a probabilistic setting has been discussed both for data clustering as well as data visualization. The deterministic annealing methodology yields robust algorithms which can be tuned in precision by selecting an appropriate temperature value and which have been shown to perform well on real-world data. Extensions of clustering algorithms to hierarchical clustering (HB95; HB96b) or clustering approaches with K-winner-take-all rules (HB96a) are conceptually straightforward and have been published elsewhere.

References

J. Buhmann and H. Kühnel. Vector quantization with complexity costs. *IEEE Transactions on Information Theory*, 39(4):1133–1145, July 1993.

C. M. Bishop, M. Svensén, and C. K. I. Williams. GTM: A principled alternative to the self-organizing map. *Neural Computation*, (in press), 1997.

T. F. Cox and M.A.A. Cox. *Multidimensional Scaling.* Number 59 in Monographs on Statistics and Applied Probability. Chapman & Hall, London, 1994.

T. M. Cover and J. A. Thomas. *Elements of Information Theory*. John Wiley & Sons, New York, 1991.

R. O. Duda and P. E. Hart. *Pattern Classification and Scene Analysis*. Wiley, New York, 1973. Sect. 3.2.

A. P. Dempster, N. M Laird, and D. B. Rubin. Maximum likelihood from incomplete data via the EM algorithm. *J. Royal Statist. Soc. Ser. B*, 39:1–38, 1977.

Thomas Hofmann and Joachim M. Buhmann. Hierarchical pairwise data clustering by mean–field annealing. In *Proceedings of ICANN'95, NEURONÎMES'95*, volume II, pages 197–202. EC2 & Cie, 1995.

Thomas Hofmann and Joachim M. Buhmann. An annealed "neural gas" network for robust vector quantization. In *Proceedings of ICANN'96*, pages 151–156, Berlin, Heidelberg, New York, 1996. Springer.

Thomas Hofmann and Joachim M. Buhmann. Infering hierarchical clustering structures by deterministic annealing. In *Proceedings of the Knowledge Discovery and Data Mining Conference 1996*, Portland, Redwood City, CA, USA, 1996. AAAI Press. (in press).

Thomas Hofmann and Joachim M. Buhmann. Pairwise data clustering by deterministic annealing. *IEEE Transactions on Pattern Analysis and Machine Intelligence*, 19(1):1–14, 1997.

J. Hertz, A. Krogh, and R. G. Palmer. *Introduction to the Theory of Neural Computation*. Addison Wesley, New York, 1991.

Thomas Hofmann. *Data Clustering and Beyond: A Deterministic Annealing Framework for Exploratory Data Analysis*. PhD thesis, Mathematisch-Naturwissenschaftliche Fakultät, Rheinische Friedrich-Wilhelms-Universität Bonn, D-53117 Bonn, Fed. Rep. Germany, 1997.

A. K. Jain and R. C. Dubes. *Algorithms for Clustering Data*. Prentice Hall, Englewood Cliffs, NJ 07632, 1988.

Hansjörg Klock and Joachim M. Buhmann. Multidimensional scaling by deterministic annealing. In M.Pellilo and E.R.Hancock, editors, *Proceedings EMMCVPR'97*, Lecture Notes In Computer Science. Springer Verlag, 1997.

T. Kohonen. *Self-organization and Associative Memory*. Springer, Berlin, 1984.

S.P. Luttrell. Hierarchical vector quantizations. *IEE Proceedings*, 136:405–413, 1989.

J. MacQueen. Some methods for classification and analysis of multivariate observations. In *Proceedings of the 5th Berkeley Symposium on Mathematical Statistics and Probability*, pages 281–297, 1967.

G. J. McLachlan and K. E. Basford. *Mixture Models*. Marcel Dekker, INC, New York, Basel, 1988.

K. Rose, E. Gurewitz, and G. Fox. A deterministic annealing approach to clustering. *Pattern Recognition Letters*, 11(11):589–594, 1990.

H. Ritter, T. Martinetz, and K. Schulten. *Neural Computation and Self-organizing Maps*. Addison Wesley, New York, 1992.

J. W. Sammon Jr. A non-linear mapping for data structure analysis. *IEEE Transactions on Computers*, 18:401–409, 1969.

Yoshio Takane and Forest W. Young. Nonmetric individul differences multidimensional scaling: An alternating least squares method with optimal scaling features. *Psychometrika*, 42(1):7–67, March 1977.

LEARNING BAYESIAN NETWORKS WITH LOCAL STRUCTURE

NIR FRIEDMAN

Computer Science Division, 387 Soda Hall, University of California, Berkeley, CA 94720. nir@cs.berkeley.edu

AND

MOISES GOLDSZMIDT

SRI International, 333 Ravenswood Avenue, EK329, Menlo Park, CA 94025. moises@erg.sri.com

Abstract.

We examine a novel addition to the known methods for learning Bayesian networks from data that improves the quality of the learned networks. Our approach explicitly represents and learns the *local structure* in the *conditional probability distributions* (CPDs) that quantify these networks. This increases the space of possible models, enabling the representation of CPDs with a variable number of parameters. The resulting learning procedure induces models that better emulate the interactions present in the data. We describe the theoretical foundations and practical aspects of learning local structures and provide an empirical evaluation of the proposed learning procedure. This evaluation indicates that learning curves characterizing this procedure converge faster, in the number of training instances, than those of the standard procedure, which ignores the local structure of the CPDs. Our results also show that networks learned with local structures tend to be more complex (in terms of arcs), yet require fewer parameters.

1. Introduction

Bayesian networks are graphical representations of probability distributions; they are arguably the representation of choice for uncertainty in artificial intelligence. These networks provide a compact and natural representation, effective inference, and efficient learning. They have been suc-

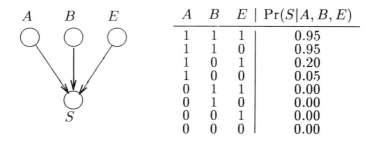

A	B	E	Pr($S\mid A, B, E$)
1	1	1	0.95
1	1	0	0.95
1	0	1	0.20
1	0	0	0.05
0	1	1	0.00
0	1	0	0.00
0	0	1	0.00
0	0	0	0.00

Figure 1. A simple network structure and the associated CPD for variable S (showing the probability values for $S = 1$).

cessfully applied in expert systems, diagnostic engines, and optimal decision making systems.

A Bayesian network consists of two components. The first is a directed acyclic graph (DAG) in which each vertex corresponds to a random variable. This graph describes conditional independence properties of the represented distribution. It captures the *structure* of the probability distribution, and is exploited for efficient inference and decision making. Thus, while Bayesian networks can represent arbitrary probability distributions, they provide computational advantage to those distributions that can be represented with a sparse DAG. The second component is a collection of *conditional probability distributions* (CPDs) that describe the conditional probability of each variable given its parents in the graph. Together, these two components represent a unique probability distribution (Pearl, 1988).

In recent years there has been growing interest in learning Bayesian networks from data; see, for example, Cooper and Herskovits (1992); Buntine (1991b); Heckerman (1995); and Lam and Bacchus (1994). Most of this research has focused on learning the *global* structure of the network, that is, the edges of the DAG. Once this structure is fixed, the parameters in the CPDs quantifying the network are learned by estimating a locally exponential number of parameters from the data. In this article we introduce methods and algorithms for learning *local structures* to represent the CPDs as a part of the process of learning the network. Using these structures, we can model various degrees of complexity in the CPD representations. As we will show, this approach considerably improves the quality of the learned networks.

In its most naive form, a CPD is encoded by means of a tabular representation that is locally exponential in the number of parents of a variable X: for each possible assignment of values to the parents of X, we need to specify a distribution over the values X can take. For example, consider the simple network in Figure 1, where the variables A, B, E and S correspond to the events "alarm armed," "burglary," "earthquake," and "loud alarm sound," respectively. Assuming that all variables are binary, a tabular representation of the CPD for S requires eight parameters, one for each possible state of the parents. One possible quantification of this CPD is given in Figure 1. Note, however, that when the alarm is not armed (i.e., when $A = 0$) the probability of $S = 1$ is zero, regardless of the values B and E. Thus, the interaction between S and its parents is simpler than the eight-way situation that is assumed in the tabular representation of the CPD.

The locally exponential size of the tabular representation of the CPDs is a major problem in learning Bayesian networks. As a general rule, learning many parameters is a liability, since a large number of parameters requires a large training set to be assessed reliably. Thus learning procedures generally encode a bias against structures that involve many parameters. For example, given a training set with instances sampled from the network in Figure 1, the learning procedure might choose a simpler network structure than that of the original network. When the tabular representation is used, the CPD for S requires eight parameters. However, a network with only two parents for S, say A and B, would require only four parameters. Thus, for a small training set, such a network may be preferred, even though it ignores the effect of E on S. This example illustrates that by taking into account the number of parameters, the learning procedure may penalize a large CPD, even if the interactions between the variable and its parents are relatively benign.

Our strategy is to address this problem by explicitly representing the *local structure* of the CPDs. This representation often requires fewer parameters to encode CPDs. This enables the learning procedure to weight each CPD according to the number of parameters it actually requires to capture the interaction between a variable and its parents, rather than the maximal number required by the tabular representation. In other words, this explicit representation of local structure in the network's CPD allows us to adjust the *penalty* incurred by the network to reflect the real complexity of the interactions described by the network.

There are different types of local structures for CPDs, a prominent example is the *noisy-or* gate and its generalizations (Heckerman and Breese, 1994; Pearl, 1988; Srinivas, 1993). In this article, we focus on learning local structures that are motivated by properties of *context-specific* independence (CSI) (Boutilier et al., 1996). These independence statements imply that in some *contexts*, defined by an assignment to variables in the network, the conditional probability of variable X is independent of some of its parents. For example, in the network of Figure 1, when the the alarm is not set

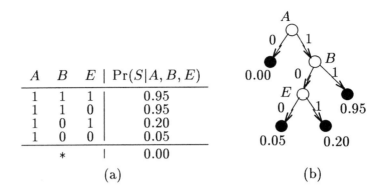

A	B	E	Pr(S|A, B, E)
1	1	1	0.95
1	1	0	0.95
1	0	1	0.20
1	0	0	0.05
	*		0.00

(a)   (b)

Figure 2. Two representations of a local CPD structure: (a) a *default table*, and (b) a *decision tree*.

(i.e., the context defined by $A = 0$), the conditional probability does not depend on the value of B and E; $P(S \mid A = 0, B = b, E = e)$ is the same for all values b and e of B and E. As we can see, CSI properties induce equality constraints among the conditional probabilities in the CPDs. In this article, we concentrate on two different representations for capturing the local structure that follows from such equality constraints. These representations, shown in Figure 2, in general require fewer parameters than a tabular representation. Figure 2(a) describes a *default table*, which is similar to the usual tabular representation, except that it does not list all of the possible values of S's parents. Instead, the table provides a *default* probability assignment to all the values of the parents that are not explicitly listed. In this example, the default table requires five parameters instead of the eight parameters required by the tabular representation. Figure 2(b) describes another possible representation based on *decision trees* (Quinlan and Rivest, 1989). Each leaf in the decision tree describes a probability for S, and the internal nodes and arcs encode the necessary information to decide how to choose among leaves, based on the values of S's parents. For example, in the tree of Figure 2(b) the probability of $S = 1$ is 0 when $A = 0$, regardless of the state of B and E; and the probability of $S = 1$ is 0.95 when $A = 1$ and $B = 1$, regardless of the state of E. In this example, the decision tree requires four parameters instead of eight.

Our main hypothesis is that incorporating local structure representations into the learning procedure leads to two important improvements in the quality of the induced models. First, the induced parameters are more reliable. Since these representations usually require less parameters, the frequency estimation for each parameter takes, on average, a larger number of samples into account and thus is more robust. Second, the global structure of the induced network is a better approximation to the real (in)dependencies in the underlying distribution. The use of local structure enables the learning procedure to explore networks that would have incurred an exponential penalty (in terms of the number of parameters required) and thus would have not been taken into consideration. We cannot stress enough the importance of this last point. Finding better estimates of the parameters for a global structure that makes unrealistic independence assumptions will not overcome the deficiencies of the model. Thus, it is crucial to obtain a good approximation of the global structure.

The experiments described in Section 5 confirm our main hypothesis. Moreover, the results in that section show that the use of local representations for the CPDs significantly affects the learning process itself: The learning procedures require fewer data samples in order to induce a network that better approximates the target distribution.

The main contributions of this article are: the derivation of the scoring functions and algorithms for learning the local representations; the formulation of the hypothesis introduced above, which uncovers the benefits of having an explicit local representation for CPDs; and the empirical investigation that validates this hypothesis.

CPDs with local structure have often been used and exploited in tasks of knowledge acquisition from experts; as we already mentioned above, the *noisy-or* gate and its generalizations are well known examples (Heckerman and Breese, 1994; Pearl, 1988; Srinivas, 1993). In the context of learning, several authors have noted that CPDs can be represented via logistic regression, noisy-or, and neural networks (Buntine, 1991b; Diez, 1993; Musick, 1994; Neal, 1992; Spiegelhalter and Lauritzen, 1990). With the exception of Buntine, these authors have focused on the case where the network structure is fixed in advance, and motivate the use of local structure for learning reliable parameters. The method proposed by Buntine (1991b) is not limited to the case of a fixed structure; he also points to the use of decision trees for representing CPDs. Yet, in that paper, he does not provide empirical or theoretical evidence for the benefits of using local structured representations with regards to a more accurate induction of the global structure of the network. To the best of our knowledge, the benefits that relate to that, as well as to the convergence speed of the learning procedure (in terms of the number of training instances), have been unknown in the literature prior to our work.

The reminder of this article is organized as follows: In Section 2 we review the definition of Bayesian networks, and the scores used for learning these networks. In Section 3 we describe the two forms of local structured CPDs we consider in this article. In Section 4 we formally derive the score for learning networks with CPDs represented as default tables and decision trees, and describe the procedures for learning these structures. In Section 5 we describe the experimental results. We present our conclusions in Section 6.

2. Learning Bayesian Networks

Consider a finite set $\mathbf{U} = \{X_1, \ldots, X_n\}$ of discrete random variables where each variable X_i may take on values from a finite domain. We use capital letters such as X, Y, Z to denote variable names, and lowercase letters such as x, y, z to denote specific values taken by those variables. The set of values X can attain is denoted as $Val(X)$; the cardinality of this set is denoted as $||X|| = |Val(X)|$. Sets of variables are denoted by boldface capital letters such as $\mathbf{X}, \mathbf{Y}, \mathbf{Z}$, and assignments of values to the variables in these sets are denoted by boldface lowercase letters such as $\mathbf{x}, \mathbf{y}, \mathbf{z}$ (we use $Val(\mathbf{X})$ and $||\mathbf{X}||$ in the obvious way).

Let P be a joint probability distribution over the variables in $\mathbf{U}$, and let $\mathbf{X}, \mathbf{Y}, \mathbf{Z}$ be subsets of $\mathbf{U}$. $\mathbf{X}$ and $\mathbf{Y}$ are *conditionally independent*, given $\mathbf{Z}$, if for all $\mathbf{x} \in Val(\mathbf{X}), \mathbf{y} \in Val(\mathbf{Y})$, and $\mathbf{z} \in Val(\mathbf{Z})$, we have that $P(\mathbf{x} \mid \mathbf{z}, \mathbf{y}) = P(\mathbf{x} \mid \mathbf{z})$ whenever $P(\mathbf{y}, \mathbf{z}) > 0$.

A *Bayesian network* is an annotated DAG that encodes a joint probability distribution of a domain composed of a set of random variables. Formally, a Bayesian network for $\mathbf{U}$ is the pair $B = \langle G, \mathcal{L} \rangle$. G is a DAG whose nodes correspond to the random variables $X_1, \ldots, X_n$, and whose edges represent direct dependencies between the variables. The graph structure G encodes the following set of independence statements: each variable X_i is independent of its nondescendants, given its parents in G. The set composed of a variable and its parents is usually referred to as a *family*.

Standard arguments (Pearl, 1988) show that any distribution P that satisfies the independence statements encoded in the graph G can be *factored* as

$$P(X_1, \ldots, X_n) = \prod_{i=1}^{n} P(X_i \mid \mathbf{Pa}_i), \qquad (1)$$

where $\mathbf{Pa}_i$ denote the parents of X_i in G. Note that to completely specify a distribution of this form, we only need to provide the conditional probabilities on the right hand side. This is precisely the second component of the Bayesian network, namely $\mathcal{L}$. This set of CPDs specify the conditional probability $P(X_i \mid \mathbf{Pa}_i)$ for all variables X_i. It immediately follows that there is exactly one distribution that has the form of Equation 1 with the conditional probabilities specified in $\mathcal{L}$.

When we deal with discrete variables, we usually represent the CPDs in $\mathcal{L}$ as conditional probability tables such as the one in Figure 1. These tables contain a parameter $\theta_{x_i|\mathbf{pa}_i}$ for each value $x_i \in \mathit{Val}(X_i)$ and $\mathbf{pa}_i \in \mathit{Val}(\mathbf{Pa}_i)$.

The problem of learning a Bayesian network can be now stated as follows. Given a *training set* $D = \{\mathbf{u}_1, \ldots, \mathbf{u}_N\}$ of instances of $\mathbf{U}$, find a network $B = \langle G, \mathcal{L} \rangle$ that *best matches* D.[1] To formalize the notion of goodness of fit of a network with respect to the data, we normally introduce a scoring function, and to solve the optimization problem we usually rely on heuristic search techniques over the space of possible networks (Heckerman, 1995). Several different scoring functions have been proposed in the literature. In this article we focus our attention on the ones that are most frequently used: the *Minimal Description Length* (MDL) score (Lam and Bacchus, 1994) and the BDe score (Heckerman et al., 1995a).

2.1. THE MDL SCORE

The MDL principle (Rissanen, 1989) is motivated by *universal coding*. Suppose that we are given a set D of instances, which we would like to store in our records. Naturally, we would like to conserve space and save a compressed version of D. One way of compressing the data is to find a suitable model for D that the encoder can use to produce a compact version of D. Moreover, as we want to be able to recover D, we must also store the model used by the encoder to compress D. The *total description length* is then defined as the sum of the length of the compressed version of D and the length of the description of the model used in the compression. The MDL principle dictates that the optimal model is the one (from a particular class of interest) that minimizes the total description length.

In the context of learning Bayesian networks, the model is a network. Such a network, B, describes a probability distribution, P_B, over the instances appearing in the data. Using this distribution, we can build an encoding scheme that assigns shorter code words to more probable instances (e.g., using Shannon encoding or a Huffman code; see Cover and Thomas (1991)). According to the MDL principle, we should choose a network, B, such that the combined length of the network description and the encoded data (with respect to P_B) is minimized. This implies that the learning procedure balances the complexity of the induced network with the degree of accuracy with which the network represents the frequencies in D.

We now describe in detail the representation length required for the storage of both the network and the coded data. The MDL score of a candidate network is defined as the total description length. To store a

---

[1] Throughout this article we will assume that the training data is *complete*, i.e., that each $\mathbf{u}_i$ assigns values to all variables in $\mathbf{U}$. Existing solutions to the problem of missing values apply to the approaches we discuss below; see Heckerman (1995).

network $B = \langle G, \mathcal{L} \rangle$, we need to describe $\mathbf{U}$, G, and $\mathcal{L}$.

To describe $\mathbf{U}$, we store the the number of variables, n, and the cardinality of each variable X_i. Since $\mathbf{U}$ is the same for all candidate networks, we can ignore the description length of $\mathbf{U}$ in the comparisons between networks.

To describe the DAG G, it is sufficient to store for each variable X_i a description of $\mathbf{Pa}_i$ (namely, its parents in G). This description consists of the number of parents, k, followed by the index of the set $\mathbf{Pa}_i$ in some (agreed upon) enumeration of all $\binom{n}{k}$ sets of this cardinality. Since we can encode the number k using $\log n$ bits, and we can encode the index using $\log \binom{n}{k}$ bits, the description length of the graph structure is[2]

$$DL_{graph}(G) = \sum_i \left(\log n + \log \binom{n}{|\mathbf{Pa}_i|} \right).$$

To describe the CPDs in $\mathcal{L}$, we must store the parameters in each conditional probability table. For the table associated with X_i, we need to store $||\mathbf{Pa}_i||(||X_i|| - 1)$ parameters. The representation length of these parameters depends on the number of bits we use for each numeric parameter. The usual choice in the literature is $1/2 \log N$ (see Friedman and Yakhini (1996) for a thorough discussion of this point). Thus, the encoding length of X_i's CPD is

$$DL_{tab}(X_i, \mathbf{Pa}_i) = \frac{1}{2}||\mathbf{Pa}_i||(||X_i|| - 1) \log N.$$

To encode the training data, we use the probability measure defined by the network B to construct a Huffman code for the instances in D. In this code, the exact length of each codeword depends on the probability assigned to that particular instance. There is no closed-form description of this length. However, it is known (Cover and Thomas, 1991) that we can approximate the optimal encoding length using $-\log P_B(\mathbf{u})$ as the encoding length of each instance $\mathbf{u}$. Thus, the description length of the data is approximated by

$$DL_{data}(D \mid B) = - \sum_{i=1}^{N} \log P_B(\mathbf{u}_i).$$

We can rewrite this expression in a more convenient form. We start by introducing some notation. Let $\hat{P}_D$ be the empirical probability measure

---

[2]Since description lengths are measured in terms of bits, we use logarithms of base 2 throughout this article.

induced by the data set D. More precisely, we define

$$\hat{P}_D(A) = \frac{1}{N}\sum_{i=1}^{N} 1_A(\mathbf{u}_i) \text{ where } 1_A(\mathbf{u}) = \left\{ \begin{array}{ll} 1 & \text{if } \mathbf{u} \in A \\ 0 & \text{if } \mathbf{u} \notin A \end{array} \right.$$

for all events of interest, i.e., $A \subseteq Val(\mathbf{U})$. Let $N_{\mathbf{X}}^D(\mathbf{x})$ be the number of instances in D where $\mathbf{X} = \mathbf{x}$ (from now on, we omit the subscript from $\hat{P}_D$, and the superscript and the subscript from $N_{\mathbf{X}}^D$, whenever they are clear from the context). Clearly, $N(\mathbf{x}) = N \cdot \hat{P}(\mathbf{x})$. We use Equation 1 to rewrite the representation length of the data as

$$
\begin{aligned}
DL_{data}(D \mid B) &= -\sum_{j=1}^{N} \log P_B(\mathbf{u}_j) \\
&= -N \sum_{u} \hat{P}(u) \log \prod_{i} P(x_i \mid \mathbf{pa}_i) \\
&= -\sum_{i} \sum_{x_i, \mathbf{pa}_i} N(x_i, \mathbf{pa}_i) \log P(x_i \mid \mathbf{pa}_i).
\end{aligned}
\tag{2}
$$

Thus, the encoding of the data can be decomposed as a sum of terms that are "local" to each CPD: these terms depend only on the counts $N(x_i, \mathbf{pa}_i)$. Standard arguments show the following.

Proposition 2.1: *If $P(X_i \mid \mathbf{Pa}_i)$ is represented as a table, then the parameter values that minimize $DL_{data}(D \mid B)$ are $\theta_{x_i \mid \mathbf{pa}_i} = \hat{P}(x_i \mid \mathbf{pa}_i)$.*

Thus, given a fixed network structure G, learning the parameters that minimize the description length is straightforward: we simply compute the appropriate long-run fractions from the data.

Assuming that we assign parameters in the manner prescribed by this proposition, we can rewrite $DL_{data}(D \mid B)$ in a more convenient way in terms of conditional entropy: $N \sum_i H(X_i \mid \mathbf{Pa}_i)$, where $H(X \mid Y) = -\sum_{x,y} \hat{P}(x,y) \log \hat{P}(x \mid y)$ is the *conditional entropy* of X, given Y. This formula provides an information-theoretic interpretation to the representation of the data: it measures how many bits are necessary to encode the value of X_i, once we know the value of $\mathbf{Pa}_i$.

Finally, the MDL score of a candidate network structure G, assuming that we choose parameters as prescribed above, is defined as the total description length

$$
\begin{aligned}
DL(G, D) &= DL_{graph}(G) + \sum_{i} DL_{tab}(X_i, \mathbf{Pa}_i) + \\
& \quad N \sum_{i} H(X_i \mid \mathbf{Pa}_i).
\end{aligned}
\tag{3}
$$

According to the MDL principle, we should strive to find the network structure that minimizes this description length. In practice, this is usually done
by searching over the space of possible networks.

2.2. THE BDE SCORE

Scores for learning Bayesian networks can also be derived from methods
of Bayesian statistics. A prime example of such scores is the BDe score,
proposed by Heckerman et al. (1995a). This score is based on earlier work
by Cooper and Herskovits (1992) and Buntine (1991b). The BDe score is
(proportional to) the posterior probability of each network structure, given
the data. Learning amounts to searching for the network(s) that maximize
this probability.

Let G^h denote the hypothesis that the underlying distribution satisfies
the independencies encoded in G (see Heckerman et al. (1995a) for a more
elaborate discussion of this hypothesis). For a given structure G, let Θ_G
represent the vector of parameters for the CPDs quantifying G. The posterior probability we are interested in is $\Pr(G^h \mid D)$. Using Bayes' rule we
write this term as

$$\Pr(G^h \mid D) = \alpha \Pr(D \mid G^h) \Pr(G^h), \qquad (4)$$

where α is a normalization constant that does not depend on the choice of
G. The term $\Pr(G^h)$ is the prior probability of the network structure, and
the term $\Pr(D \mid G^h)$ is the probability of the data, given that the network
structure is G.

There are several ways of choosing a prior over network structures. Heck-
erman et al. suggest choosing a prior $\Pr(G^h) \propto a^{\Delta(G,G')}$, where $\Delta(G, G')$,
is the difference in edges between G and a *prior* network structure G', and
$0 < a < 1$ is penalty for each such edge. In this article, we use a prior based
on the MDL encoding of G. We let $\Pr(G^h) \propto 2^{DL_{graph}(G)}$.

To evaluate the $\Pr(D \mid G^h)$ we must consider all possible parameter
assignments to G. Thus,

$$\Pr(D \mid G^h) = \int \Pr(D \mid \Theta_G, G^h) \Pr(\Theta_G \mid G^h) d\Theta_G, \qquad (5)$$

where $\Pr(D \mid \Theta_G, G^h)$ is defined by Equation 1, and $\Pr(\Theta_G \mid G^h)$ is the
prior density over parameter assignments to G. Heckerman et al. (following
Cooper and Herskovits (1992)) identify a set of assumptions that justify
decomposing this integral. Roughly speaking, they assume that each distribution $P(X_i \mid \mathbf{pa}_i)$ can be learned independently of all other distributions.

Using this assumption, they rewrite $\Pr(D \mid G^h)$ as

$$\Pr(D \mid G^h) = \prod_i \prod_{\mathbf{pa}_i} \int \prod_{x_i} \theta_{x_i|\mathbf{pa}_i}^{N(x_i,\mathbf{pa}_i)} \Pr(\Theta_{X_i|\mathbf{pa}_i} \mid G^h) d\Theta_{X_i|\mathbf{pa}_i}. \quad (6)$$

(This decomposition is analogous to the decomposition in Equation 2.) When the prior on each multinomial distribution $\Theta_{X_i|\mathbf{pa}_i}$ is a *Dirichlet prior*, the integrals in Equation 6 have a closed-form solution (Heckerman, 1995).

We briefly review the properties of Dirichlet priors. For more detailed description, we refer the reader to DeGroot (1970). A Dirichlet prior for a multinomial distribution of a variable X is specified by a set of *hyperparameters* $\{N'_x : x \in Val(X)\}$. We say that

$$\Pr(\Theta_X) \sim Dirichlet(\{N'_x : x \in Val(X)\})$$

if

$$\Pr(\Theta_X) = \alpha \prod_x \theta_x^{N'_x},$$

where α is a normalization constant. If the prior is a Dirichlet prior, the probability of observing a sequence of values of X with counts $N(x)$ is

$$\int \prod_x \theta_x^{N(x)} \Pr(\Theta_X \mid G^h) d\Theta_X = \frac{\Gamma(\sum_x N'_x)}{\Gamma(\sum_x (N'_x + N(x)))} \prod_x \frac{\Gamma(N'_x + N(x))}{\Gamma(N'_x)},$$

where $\Gamma(x) = \int_0^\infty t^{x-1} e^{-t} dt$ is the *Gamma* function that satisfies the properties $\Gamma(1) = 1$ and $\Gamma(x+1) = x\Gamma(x)$.

Returning to the BDe score, if we assign to each $\Theta_{X_i|\mathbf{pa}_i}$ a Dirichlet prior with hyperparameters $N'_{x_i|\mathbf{pa}_i}$, then

$$\Pr(D \mid G^h) = \prod_i \prod_{\mathbf{pa}_i} \frac{\Gamma(\sum_{x_i} N'_{x_i|\mathbf{pa}_i})}{\Gamma(\sum_{x_i} N'_{x_i|\mathbf{pa}_i} + N(\mathbf{pa}_i))} \prod_{x_i} \frac{\Gamma(N'_{x_i|\mathbf{pa}_i} + N(x_i,\mathbf{pa}_i))}{\Gamma(N'_{x_i|\mathbf{pa}_i})}.$$

$$(7)$$

There still remains a problem with the direct application of this method. For each possible network structure we would have to assign priors on the parameter values. This is clearly infeasible, since the number of possible structures is extremely large. Heckerman et al. propose a set of assumptions that justify a method by which, given a prior network B^p and an equivalent sample size N', we can assign prior probabilities to parameters in every possible network structure. The prior assigned to $\Theta_{X_i|\mathbf{pa}_i}$ in a structure G is computed from the prior distribution represented in B^p. In this method, we assign $N'_{x_i|\mathbf{pa}_i} = N' \cdot P_{B^p}(x_i, \mathbf{pa}_i)$. (Note that $\mathbf{Pa}_i$ are the parents of

X_i in G, but not necessarily in B^p.) Thus, their proposal essentially uses the conditional probability of X_i, given $\mathbf{pa}_i$, in the prior network B^p as the expected probability. Similarly, the confidence in the prior (e.g., the magnitude of the hyperparameters) is proportional to the expected number of occurrences of the values of $\mathbf{Pa}_i$.

The exposition above shows how to score a network structure G. In order to make predictions about the probability distribution over the set of variables $\mathbf{u}$, given a structure G, we need to compute the set of parameters to quantify the G. According to the Bayesian methodology, we should average over all possible assignments to Θ_G. Thus,

$$\Pr(\mathbf{u} \mid D, G^h) = \int \Pr(\mathbf{u} \mid \Theta_G, G^h) \Pr(\Theta_G \mid D, G^h) d\Theta_G.$$

Once again we can decompose this term using the structure of the G. Using the assumptions stated above of completely observable data, and parameter independence, we get that $\Pr(\mathbf{u} \mid D, G^h) = \prod_i \Pr(x_i \mid \mathbf{pa}_i, D, G^h)$ where

$$\Pr(x_i \mid \mathbf{pa}_i, D, G^h) = \int \theta_{X_i \mid \mathbf{pa}_i} \Pr(\theta_{X_i \mid \mathbf{pa}_i} \mid \mathbf{pa}_i, D, G^h) d\theta_{X_i \mid \mathbf{pa}_i}.$$

If we use Dirichlet priors, then these integrals have the closed-form solution

$$\Pr(x_i \mid \mathbf{pa}_i, D, G^h) = \frac{N'_{x_i \mid \mathbf{pa}_i} + N(x_i, \mathbf{pa}_i)}{\sum_{x_i} N'_{x_i \mid \mathbf{pa}_i} + N(\mathbf{pa}_i)}.$$

When we consider large data sets, the MDL score and the BDe score tend to score candidate structures similarly. More precisely, these two scores are asymptotically equivalent. This equivalence can be derived by using asymptotic approximations to the $\Gamma(\cdot)$ function in Equation 7, as done by Bouckaert (1994), or by using a general result of Schwarz (1978). Schwarz shows that, given some regularity constraints on the prior,

$$log \Pr(D \mid G^h) \approx log \Pr(D \mid \hat{\Theta}_G, G^h) - \frac{d}{2} \log N, \qquad (8)$$

where $\hat{\Theta}_G$ are the maximum likelihood parameters for G, given D, and d is the *dimension* of G, which in our setting is the number of free parameters in G.

Note that the term on the right-hand side of Equation 8 (which one attempts to maximize) is the negative of the MDL score of Equation 3 (which one attempts to minimize), when we ignore the description of G, which corresponds to the logarithm of the prior $\Pr(G^h)$. Note also that this term is negligible in the asymptotic analysis, since it does not depend on N.

3. Local Structure

In the discussion above, we have assumed the standard tabular representation of the CPDs quantifying the networks. This representation requires that for each variable X_i we encode a locally exponential number, $\|\mathbf{Pa}_i\|(\|X_i\| - 1)$, of parameters. In practice, however, the interaction between X_i and its parents $\mathbf{Pa}_i$ can be more benign, and some regularities can be exploited to represent the same information with fewer parameters. In the example of Figure 1, the the CPD for S can be encoded with four parameters, by means of the decision tree of Figure 2(b), in contrast to the eight parameters required by the tabular representation.

A formal foundation for representing and reasoning with such regularities is provided in the notion of *context-specific independence* (CSI) (Boutilier et al., 1996). Formally, we say that $\mathbf{X}$ and $\mathbf{Y}$ are *contextually independent*, given $\mathbf{Z}$ and the *context* $\mathbf{c} \in Val(\mathbf{C})$, if

$$P(\mathbf{X} \mid \mathbf{Z}, \mathbf{c}, \mathbf{Y}) = P(\mathbf{X} \mid \mathbf{Z}, \mathbf{c}) \text{ whenever } P(\mathbf{Y}, \mathbf{Z}, \mathbf{c}) > 0. \tag{9}$$

CSI statements are more specific than the conditional independence statements captured by the Bayesian network structure. CSI implies the independence of X and Y, given a specific value of the context variable(s), while conditional independence applies for all value assignments to the conditioning variable. As shown by Boutilier et al. (1996), the representation of CSI leads to several benefits in knowledge elicitation, compact representation, and computational efficiency. As we show here, CSI is also beneficial to learning, since models can be quantified with fewer parameters.

As we can see from Equation 9, CSI statements force equivalence relations between certain conditional probabilities. If X_i is contextually independent of $\mathbf{Y}$ given $\mathbf{Z}$ and $\mathbf{c} \in Val(\mathbf{C})$, then $P(X_i \mid \mathbf{Z}, \mathbf{c}, \mathbf{y}) = P(X_i \mid \mathbf{Z}, \mathbf{c}, \mathbf{y}')$ for $\mathbf{y}, \mathbf{y}' \in Val(\mathbf{Y})$. Thus, if the parent set $\mathbf{Pa}_i$ of X_i is equal to $\mathbf{Y} \cup \mathbf{Z} \cup \mathbf{C}$, such CSI statements will induce equality constraints among the conditional probability of X_i given its parents. This observation suggests an alternative way of thinking of local structure in terms of the partitions they induce on the possible values of the parents of each variable X_i. We note that while CSI properties imply such partitions, not all partitions can be characterized by CSI properties.

These partitions impose a structure over the CPDs for each X_i. In this article we are interested in representations that explicitly capture this structure that reduces the number of parameters to be estimated by the learning procedure. We focus on two representations that are relatively straightforward to learn. The first one, called *default tables*, represent a set of singleton partitions with one additional partition that can contain several values of $\mathbf{Pa}_i$. Thus, the savings it will introduce depends on how many values in

$Val(\mathbf{Pa}_i)$ can be grouped together. The second representation is based on decision trees and can represent more complex partitions. Consequently it can reduce the number of parameters even further. Yet the induction algorithm for decision trees is somewhat more complex than that of default tables.

We introduce a notation that simplifies the presentation below. Let L be a representation for the CPD for X_i. We capture the partition structure represented by L using a *characteristic* random variable Υ_L. This random variable maps each value of $\mathbf{Pa}_i$ to the partition that contains it. Formally, $\Upsilon_L(\mathbf{pa}_i) = \Upsilon_L(\mathbf{pa}_i')$ for two values $\mathbf{pa}_i$ and $\mathbf{pa}_i'$ of $\mathbf{Pa}_i$, if and only if these two values are in the same partition in L. It is easy to see that from the definition of Υ_L, we get $\mathcal{P}(X_i \mid \Upsilon_L) = \mathcal{P}(X_i \mid \mathbf{Pa}_i)$, since if $\mathbf{Pa}_i$ and $\mathbf{Pa}_i'$ are in the same partition, it must be that $P(X_i \mid \mathbf{pa}_i) = P(X_i \mid \mathbf{pa}_i')$. This means that we can describe the parameterization of the structure L in terms of the characteristic random variable Υ_L as follows: $\Theta_L = \{\theta_{x_i \mid v} : x_i \in Val(X_i), v \in Val(\Upsilon_L)\}$.

As an example, consider the tabular CPD representation, in which no CSI properties are taken into consideration. This implies that the corresponding partitions contain exactly one value for $\mathbf{Pa}_i$. Thus, in this case, $Val(\Upsilon_L)$ is isomorphic to $Val(\mathbf{Pa}_i)$. CPD representations that specify CSI relations will have fewer partitions, and thus will require fewer parameters.

In the sections below we formally describe default tables and decision trees, and the partition structures they represent.

3.1. DEFAULT TABLES

A default table is similar to a standard tabular representation of a CPD, except that only a subset of the possible values of the parents of a variable are explicitly represented as rows in the table. The values of the parents that are not explicitly represented as individual rows are mapped to a special row called the *default row*. The underlying idea is that the probability of a node X is the same for all the values of the parents that are mapped to the default row; therefore, there is no need to represent these values separately in several entries. Consequently, the number of parameters explicitly represented in a default table can be smaller than the number of parameters in a tabular representation of a CPD. In the example showing in Figure 2(a), all the values of the parents of S, where $A = 0$ (the alarm is not armed), are mapped to the default row in the table, since the probability of $S = 1$ is the same in all of these situations, regardless of the values of B and E.

Formally, a default table is an object $\mathcal{D} = (S_{\mathcal{D}}, \Theta_{\mathcal{D}})$. $S_{\mathcal{D}}$ describes the *structure* of the table, namely, which *rows* are represented explicitly, and which are represented via the default row. We define $Rows(\mathcal{D}) \subseteq Val(\mathbf{Pa}_i)$

to be the set of rows in $\mathcal{D}$ that are represented explicitly. This structure defines the following characteristic random variable. If $\mathbf{pa}_i \in Rows(\mathcal{D})$, then the value $\Upsilon(\mathbf{pa}_i)$ is the partition that contains only $\mathbf{pa}_i$. If $\mathbf{pa}_i \notin Rows(\mathcal{D})$, then the value $\Upsilon(\mathbf{pa}_i)$ is the default partition that contains all the values that are not explicitly represented, that is $Val(\mathbf{Pa}_i) - Rows(\mathcal{D})$. Thus, the partitions defined by the default table correspond to the rows in the explicit representation of the table (e.g., as in Figure 2(a)).

The set of parameters, $\Theta_{\mathcal{D}}$, constitutes the parameterization for $\mathcal{D}$. It contains parameters $\theta_{x_i|v}$ for each value $x_i \in Val(\Upsilon_{\mathcal{D}})$. To determine $P(x_i \mid \mathbf{pa}_i)$ from this representation we need to consider two cases. If $\mathbf{pa}_i \in Rows(\mathcal{D})$, then $P(x_i \mid \mathbf{pa}_i) = \theta_{x_i|\Upsilon_{\mathcal{D}}=\{\mathbf{pa}_i\}}$. If $\mathbf{pa}_i \notin Rows(\mathcal{D})$, then $P(x_i \mid \mathbf{pa}_i) = \theta_{x_i|\Upsilon_{\mathcal{D}}=D}$, where $D = Val(\mathbf{Pa}_i) = Rows(\mathcal{D})$ is the partition that corresponds to the default row.

3.2. DECISION TREES

A *decision tree* for variable X is a tree in which each internal node is annotated with a parent variable, outgoing edges from a particular node are annotated with the values that the variable represented by that node can take, and leaves are annotated with a probability distribution over X. The process of retrieving the probability of X, given a value of its parents, is as follows. We start at the root node and traverse the tree until we reach a leaf. At each internal node, we choose which subtree to traverse by testing the value of the parent that annotates that node and following the outgoing edge that corresponds to that value. Thus, suppose that we would like to know $\Pr(S = 1 \mid A = 1, B = 0, E = 1)$ in the tree shown in Figure 2(b). We follow the edge to the right subtree at A, since this edge is annotated with the value 1 for A. Similarly, we follow the left edge at B (annotated with 0), and again the right edge at E, till we reach the appropriate leaf.

Formally, we denote a tree as an object $\mathcal{T} = (S_{\mathcal{T}}, \Theta_{\mathcal{T}})$. The first component, $S_{\mathcal{T}}$ represents the structure of the tree, and is defined recursively. A tree can be either a leaf or a composite tree. A leaf is represented by a structure equal to a special constant $S_{\mathcal{T}} = \Lambda$. A composite tree is represented by a structure of the form $S_{\mathcal{T}} = \langle Y, \{S_{\mathcal{T}_y} : y \in Val(Y)\} \rangle$, where Y is the test variable at the root of the tree, and $S_{\mathcal{T}_y}$ is a tree structure, for each value y of Y. We denote by $Label(\mathcal{T})$ the variable tested at the root of $\mathcal{T}$, and by $Sub(\mathcal{T}, v)$ the subtree associated with the value v of $Label(\mathcal{T})$.

Finally, we need to describe the partitions induced by this representation. Let a *path* be the set of arcs lying between the root and a leaf. A path is *consistent* with $\mathbf{pa}_i$ if the labeling of the path is consistent with the assignment of values in $\mathbf{pa}_i$. It is easy to verify that for every $\mathbf{pa}_i \in Val(\mathbf{Pa}_i)$ there is a unique consistent path in the tree. The partitions induced by a decision tree correspond to the set of paths in the tree, where the partition that correspond to a particular path p consists of all the value assignments that p is consistent with. Again, we define the set of parameters, $\Theta_{\mathcal{T}}$, to contain parameters $\theta_{x_i|v}$ for each value $x_i \in \mathit{Val}(\Upsilon_{\mathcal{D}})$. That is, we associate with each (realizable) path in the tree a distribution over X_i. To determine $P(x_i \mid \mathbf{pa}_i)$ from this representation, we simply choose $\theta_{x_i|v}$, where $v = \{\mathbf{pa}'_i \mid \mathbf{pa}'_i$ is consistent with $p\}$, where p is the (unique) path that is consistent with $\mathbf{pa}_i$.

4. Learning Local Structure

We start this section by deriving both the MDL and BDe scoring functions for default table and decision tree representations. We then describe the procedures for searching for high scoring networks. Note that the material in this section can be easily generalized to derive a score and produce a learning procedure for any structured representation of the CPDs that represents a partition over the values of the parent variables. (See Boutilier et al. (1996) for a discussion of such representations.)

4.1. SCORING FUNCTIONS

We introduce some notations necessary for our derivations. Let L denote a local representation of $P(X_i \mid \mathbf{Pa}_i)$, e.g., a default table, a tree, or a (complete) table. We denote by S_L the structure of the local representation L, and by Θ_L, the parameterization of L. We assume that $\Theta_L = \{\theta_{x_i|v} : x_i \in \mathit{Val}(X_i), v \in \mathit{Val}(\Upsilon_L)\}$.

4.1.1. MDL Score for Local Structure

Let $B = \langle G, \{L_i\} \rangle$ be a Bayesian network, where L_i is the local representation of $P(X_i \mid \mathbf{Pa}_i)$. The MDL encoding of the DAG G remains the same as in Section 2.1. Changes occur in the encoding of L_i. We now have to encode the structure S_{L_i} and the parameters Θ_{L_i}. Additionally, the choice of optimal parameters, given the data, now depends on the choice of local structure.

First, we describe the encoding of S_L for both default table and tree representations.

When L is a default table $\mathcal{D}$, we need to describe the set of rows that are represented explicitly in the table, that is, $\mathit{Rows}(\mathcal{D})$. We start by encoding the number $k = |\mathit{Rows}(\mathcal{D})|$; then we describe $\mathit{Rows}(\mathcal{D})$ by encoding its index in some (agreed upon) enumeration of all $\binom{\|\mathbf{Pa}_i\|}{k}$ sets of this cardinality.

Thus, the description length of the structure $\mathcal{D}$ is

$$DL_{local\text{-}struct}(\mathcal{D}) = \log ||\mathbf{Pa}_i|| + \log \binom{||\mathbf{Pa}_i||}{k}.$$

When L is a tree $\mathcal{T}$, we need to encode the structure of the tree, and the labeling of internal nodes in the tree. We use the encoding proposed by Quinlan and Rivest (1989).[3] A tree is encoded recursively as follows: a leaf is encoded by a single bit with value equal to 0. The encoding of a composite tree starts with a bit set to the value 1, to differentiate it from a leaf, followed by a description of the associated test variable and the description of all the immediate subtrees. The encoding of the test variable depends on the position of the node in the tree. At the root, the test variable can be any of X_i's parents. In contrast, at the a subtree, the choice of a test variable is more restricted, since along a single path we test each variable at most once. In general, if there are k variables that have not been tested yet in the path from the root to the current node in the tree, then we need to store only $\log(k)$ bits to describe the test variable. The total description length of the tree structure is described by the following recurring formula:

$$DL_{\mathcal{T}}(\mathcal{T}, k) = \begin{cases} 1 & \text{if } \mathcal{T} \text{ is a leaf,} \\ 1 + \log(k) + \sum_i DL_{\mathcal{T}}(\mathcal{T}_i, k-1) & \text{if } \mathcal{T} \text{ is a composite tree} \\ & \text{with subtrees } \mathcal{T}_1, \ldots, \mathcal{T}_m. \end{cases}$$

Using this formula, we define $DL_{local\text{-}struct}(\mathcal{T}) = DL_{\mathcal{T}}(\mathcal{T}, |\mathbf{Pa}_i|)$.

Next, we encode the $(||X_i|| - 1)||\Upsilon_L||$ parameters for L with description length

$$DL_{param}(L) = \frac{1}{2}(||X_i|| - 1)||\Upsilon_L|| \log N.$$

Finally, as we did in Section 2.1, we describe the encoding of the data given the model using Equation 2.

We now generalize Proposition 2.1 to describe the optimal choice of parameters for a network when CPDs are represented using local structure.

Proposition 4.1: *If $P(X_i \mid \mathbf{Pa}_i)$ is represented by local representation L_i, for $i = 1, \ldots, n$, then we can rewrite $DL_{data}(D \mid B)$ as*

$$DL_{data}(D \mid B) = -N \sum_i \sum_{v \in Val(\Upsilon_{L_i})} \sum_{x_i} \hat{P}(x_i, \Upsilon_{L_i} = v) \log \theta_{x_i|v}.$$

---

[3] Wallace and Patrick (1993) note that this encoding is inefficient, in the sense that the number of legal tree structures that can be described by n-bit strings, is significantly smaller than 2^n. Their encoding, which is more efficient, can be easily incorporated into our MDL encoding. For clarity of presentation, we use the Quinlan and Rivest encoding in this article.

Moreover, the parameter values for L that minimize $DL_{data}(D \mid B)$ are

$$\theta_{x_i \mid \Upsilon_{L_i} = v} = \hat{P}(x_i \mid \Upsilon_{L_i} = v).$$

As in the case of tabular CPD representation, DL_{data} is minimized when the parameters correspond to the appropriate frequencies in the training data. As a consequence of this result, we find that for a fixed local structure L, the minimal representation length of the data is simply $N \cdot H(X \mid \Upsilon_L)$. Thus, once again we derive an information-theoretic interpretation of $DL_{data}(\Theta_L, D)$. This interpretation shows that the encoding of X depends only on the values of Υ_L. From the *data processing inequality* (Cover and Thomas, 1991) it follows that $H(X_i \mid \Upsilon_L) \geq H(X_i \mid \mathbf{Pa}_i)$. This implies that a local structure cannot fit the data better than a tabular CPD. Nevertheless, as our experiments confirm, the reduction in the number of parameters can compensate for the potential loss in information.

To summarize, the MDL score for a graph structure augmented with a local structure L_i for each X_i is

$$
\begin{aligned}
DL(G, L_1, \ldots, L_n, D) \quad = \quad & DL_{graph}(G) + \sum_i (DL_{local\text{-}struct}(L_i) + DL_{param}(L_i)) \\
& + N \sum_i H(X \mid \Upsilon_{L_i}).
\end{aligned}
$$

4.1.2. *BDe Score for Local Structure*

We now describe how to extend the BDe score for learning local structure. Given the hypothesis G^h, we denote by $\mathcal{L}_G^h$ the hypothesis that the underlying distribution satisfies the constraints of a set of local structures $\mathcal{L} = \{L_i : 1 \leq i \leq n\}$, where L_i is a local structure for the CPD of X_i in G.

Using Bayes' rule, it follows that

$$\Pr(G^h, L_G^h \mid D) \propto \Pr(D \mid L_G^h, G^h) \Pr(L_G^h \mid G^h) \Pr(G^h).$$

The specification of priors on local structures presents no additional complications other than the specification of priors for the structure of the network G^h. Buntine (1991a, 1993), for example, suggests several possible priors on decision trees. A natural prior over local structures is defined via the MDL description length, by setting $\Pr(\mathcal{L}_G^h \mid G^h) \propto 2^{-\sum_i DL_{local\text{-}struct}(L_i)}$.

For the term $\Pr(D \mid L_G^h, G^h)$, we make an assumption of parameter independence, similar to the one made by Heckerman et al. (1995a) and by Buntine (1991b): the parameter values for each possible value of the characteristic variable Υ_{L_i} are independent of each other. Thus, each multinomial sample is independent of the others, and we can derive the analogue of Equation 6:

$$\Pr(D \mid \mathcal{L}_G^h, G^h) = \prod_i \prod_{v \in Val(\Upsilon_{L_i})} \int \prod_{x_i} \theta_{x_i|v}^{N(x_i, v)} \Pr(\Theta_{X_i|v} \mid L_i^h, G^h) d\Theta_{X_i|v}$$

(10)

(This decomposition is analogous to the one described in Proposition 4.1.) As before, we assume that the priors $\Pr(\Theta_{X_i|v} \mid \mathcal{L}_G^h, G^h)$ are Dirichlet, and thus we get a closed-form solution for Equation 10,

$$\Pr(D \mid \mathcal{L}_G^h, G^h) = \prod_i \prod_{v \in Val(\Upsilon_{L_i})} \frac{\Gamma(\sum_{x_i} N'_{x_i|v})}{\Gamma(\sum_{x_i} N'_{x_i|v} + N(v))} \prod_{x_i} \frac{\Gamma(N'_{x_i|v} + N(x_i, v))}{\Gamma(N'_{x_i|v})}.$$

Once more we are faced with the problem of specifying a multitude of priors, that is, specifying $\Pr(\Theta_{X_i|v} \mid \mathcal{L}_G^h, G^h)$ for each possible combination of global and local structures. Our objective, as in the case tabular CPDs, is to set these priors from a prior distribution represented by a specific network B^P.

Recall that the values of the characteristic random variable are the partitions imposed by the local structure over $Val(\mathbf{Pa}_i)$. We make two assumptions regarding the priors and the groupings generated by this partition.

First, we assume that the prior for a value of the characteristic variable does not depend on the local structure. It depends only on the set of instances of the parents that are grouped by this particular value of the characteristic random variable. For example, consider two possible trees for the same CPD, one that tests first on Y and then on Z, and another that tests first on Z and then on Y. Our assumption requires that the leaves that correspond to $Y = y, Z = z$, be assigned the same prior in both trees.

Second, we assume that the vector of Dirichlet hyperparameters assigned to an element of the partition that corresponds to a union of several smaller partitions in another local structure is simply the sum of the vectors of Dirichlet hyperparameters assigned to these smaller partitions. Again, consider two trees, one that consists of a single leaf, and another that has one test at the root. This assumption requires that for each $x_i \in Val(X_i)$, the Dirichlet hyperparameter $N'_{x_i|v}$, where v is the root in the first tree, is the sum of the $N'_{x_i|v'}$ for all the leaves in the second tree.

It is straightforward to show that if a prior distribution over structures, local structures, and parameters satisfies these assumptions and the assumptions of Heckerman et al. (1995a), then there must be a distribution P' and a positive real N' such that for any structure G and any choice of local structure $\mathcal{L}_G$ for G

$$\Pr(\Theta_{X_i|v} \mid \mathcal{L}_G^h, G^h) \sim Dirichlet(\{N' \cdot P'(x_i, \Upsilon_i^L = v) : x_i \in Val(X_i)\}) \,.$$
(11)

This result allows us to represent the prior information using a Bayesian network B' (that specifies the prior distribution P') and a positive real N'. From these two, we compute the Dirichlet hyperparameters for every hypothesis we need to evaluate during learning.

Finally, we note that we can use Schwarz's result (1978) to show that the MDL and BDe scores for local structure are asymptotically equivalent.

4.2. LEARNING PROCEDURES

Once we define the appropriate score, the learning task reduces to finding the network that maximizes the score, given the data. Unfortunately, this is an intractable problem. Chickering (1996) shows that finding the network (quantified with tabular CPDs) that maximizes the BDe score is NP-hard. Similar arguments also apply to learning with the MDL score. Moreover, there are indications that finding the optimal decision tree for a given family also is an NP-hard problem; see Quinlan and Rivest (1989). Thus, we suspect that finding a graph G and a set of local structures $\{L_1, \ldots, L_n\}$ that jointly maximize the MDL or BDe score is also an intractable problem.

A standard approach to dealing with hard optimization problems is heuristic search. Many search strategies can be applied. For clarity, we focus here on one of the simplest, namely *greedy hillclimbing*. In this strategy, we initialize the search with some network (e.g., the empty network) and repeatedly apply to the "current" candidate the local change (e.g., adding and removing edges) that leads to the largest improvement in the score. This "upward" step is repeated until a local maxima is reached, that is, no modification of the current candidate improves the score. Heckerman et al. (1995a) compare this greedy procedure with several more sophisticated search procedures. Their results indicate that greedy hillclimbing can be quite effective for learning Bayesian networks in practice.

The greedy hillclimbing procedure for learning network structure can be summarized as follows.

> procedure LearnNetwork(G_0)
>   Let $G_{current} \leftarrow G_0$
>   do
>   Generate all successors $S = \{G_1, \ldots, G_n\}$ of $G_{current}$
> $\Delta Score = \max_{G \in S} Score(G) - Score(G_{current})$
>   If $\Delta Score > 0$ then
>   Let $G_{current} \leftarrow \arg\max_{G \in S} Score(G)$

while($\Delta Score > 0$ **)**
return $G_{current}$

The successors of the current structure are generated by adding an arc, removing an arc, and reversing the direction of an arc. (We consider only legal successors that do not involve a cycle.)

This greedy procedure is particularly efficient for learning Bayesian networks since the scores we use *decompose*. That is, both the MDL score and the (logarithm of the) BDe score have the the form $\sum_i Score(X_i \mid \mathbf{Pa}_i)$. Since the successors considered during the search modify at most two parent sets, we only need to recompute few terms to evaluate each successor. Moreover, we can cache these computations to get additional savings; see Bouckaert (1994) and Buntine (1991b).

When allowing local structured representations, we modify this loop by adding a learning operation before scoring each successor of G. This modification invokes a local search procedure that attempts to find (an approximation to) the best local structure for the each CPD. Since only one or two parent sets are modified in each successor, we invoke this procedure only for these CPDs.

The specific procedures used for learning default tables and decision trees are described next. Since these procedures are applied independently to each CPD, we fix the choice of X_i and of its parents $\mathbf{Pa}_i$ in the discussion below. Both procedures rely on additional decomposability properties of the score functions, in terms of the underlying partitions defined by the characteristic random variable. More precisely, the score of the data, given the local structure (i.e., , DL_{data} for MDL, and $\log \Pr(D \mid G^h, \mathcal{L}_G^h)$ for BDe), can be written as a sum

$$\sum_i \sum_{v \in Val(\Upsilon_{L_i})} Score(X_i \mid v),$$

where $Score(X_i \mid v)$ is a function of counts of the possible values X_i takes in these instances where $\Upsilon_{L_i} = v$. This decomposition implies that if we consider refining the local structure by replacing one partition (that corresponds to one value of Υ_{L_i}) by the union of several partitions, then we only need to reevaluate the terms that correspond to these new subpartitions.

We use a greedy strategy for inducing default tables. The procedure starts with a trivial default table containing only the default row. Then, it iteratively refines the default row, by finding the single row (i.e., assignment of values to the parents) that when represented explicitly leads to the biggest improvement in the score. This refinement can be done efficiently, since we need only to replace the term that corresponded to the previous default row with the sum of the terms that correspond to the new row and

the new default row. This greedy expansion is repeated until no improvement in the score can be gained by adding another row. The procedure is
summarized as follows.

procedure LearnDefault()
   Let $Rows(\mathcal{D}) \leftarrow \emptyset$
   do
      Let $r = \arg\max_{r \in Val(\mathbf{Pa}_i) - Rows(\mathcal{D})} Score(Rows(\mathcal{D}) \cup \{r\})$
      if $Score(Rows(\mathcal{D}) \cup \{r\}) < Score(Rows(\mathcal{D}))$ then
         return $Rows(\mathcal{D})$
      $Rows(\mathcal{D}) \leftarrow Rows(\mathcal{D}) \cup \{r\}$
end

For inducing decision trees, we adopt the approach outlined by Quinlan
and Rivest (1989). The common wisdom in the decision-tree learning literature (e.g., Quinlan (1993)), is that greedy search of decision trees tends to
become stuck at bad local minima. The approach of Quinlan and Rivest attempts to circumvent this problem using a two-phased approach. In the first
phase we "grow" the tree in a top-down fashion. We start with the trivial
tree consisting of one leaf, and add branches to it in a greedy fashion, until
a maximal tree is learned. Note that in some stages of this growing phase,
adding branches can lower the score: the rationale is that if we continue to
grow these branches, we might improve the score. In the second phase, we
remove harmful branches by "trimming" the tree in a bottom-up fashion.
We now describe the two phases in more details.

In the first phase we grow a tree in a top-down fashion. We repeatedly
replace a leaf with a subtree that has as its root some parent of X, say Y;
and whose children are leaves, one for each value of Y. In order to decide on
which parent Y we should *split* the tree, we compute the score of the tree
associated with each parent, and select the parent that induces the best
scoring tree. Since the scores we use are decomposable, we can compute
the split in a *local* fashion by evaluating on the instances with respect to
the training data that are compatible with the path from the root of the
tree to the node that is being split. This recursive growing of the tree stops
when the node has no training instances associated with it, the value of X
is constant in the associated training set, or all the parents of X have been
tested along the path leading to that node.

In the second phase, we trim the tree in a bottom-up manner. At each
node we consider whether score of the subtree rooted at that node is better
or equal to the score replacing that subtree by a leaf. If this is the case,
then the subtree is trimmed and replaced with a leaf.

These two phases can be implemented by a simple recursive procedure,
LearnTree, that receives a set of instances and returns the "best" tree for

this set of instances.

```
procedure SimpleTree(Y)
    For y ∈ Val(Y), let l_y ← Λ (i.e., a leaf)
    return ⟨Y, {l_y : y ∈ Val(Y)}⟩
end
procedure LearnTree(D)
    if D = ∅ or X_i is homogeneous in D then
        return Λ.
    // Growing phase
    Let Y_split = arg max_{Y ∈ Pa_i} Score(SimpleTree(Y) | D)
    for y ∈ Val(Y_split)
        Let D_y = {u_i ∈ D : Y_split = y in u_i}
        Let T_y = ExpandTree( Λ, D_y)
    let T = ⟨Y_split, {T_y : y ∈ Val(Y)}⟩
    // Trimming phase
    if Score(Λ | D) > Score(T | D) then
        return Λ
    else
        return T
end
```

5. Experimental Results

The main purpose of our experiments is to confirm and quantify the hypothesis stated in the introduction: A learning procedure that learns local structures for the CPDs will induce more accurate models for two reasons: 1) fewer parameters will lead to a more reliable estimation, and 2) flexible penalty for larger families will result in network structures that are better approximations to the real (in)dependencies in the underlying distribution.

The experiments compared networks induced with table-based, tree-based, and default-based procedures, where an X-based procedure learns networks with X as the representation of CPDs. We ran experiments using both the MDL score and the BDe score. When using the BDe score, we also needed to provide a prior distribution and equivalent sample size. In all of our experiments, we used a uniform prior distribution, and examined several settings of the equivalent sample size N'. All learning procedures were based on the same search method discussed in Section 4.2.

We ran experiments with several variations, including different settings of the BDe prior equivalent size and different initialization points for the search procedures. These experiments involved learning approximately 15,000 networks. The results are summarized below.

TABLE 1. Description of the networks used in the experiments.

Name	Description	n	$\|\mathbf{U}\|$	$\|\Theta\|$
Alarm	A network by medical experts for monitoring patients in intensive care (Beinlich et al., 1989).	37	$2^{53.95}$	509
Hailfinder	A network for modeling summer hail in northeastern Colorado (http://www.lis.pitt.edu/~dsl/hailfinder).	56	$2^{106.56}$	2656
Insurance	A network for classifying insurance applications (Russell et al., 1995).	27	$2^{44.57}$	1008

5.1. METHODOLOGY

The data sets used in the experiments were sampled from three Bayesian networks whose main characteristics are described in Table 1. From each of these networks we sampled training sets of sizes—250, 500, 1000, 2000, 4000, 8000, 16000, 24000, and 32000 instances—and ran the learning procedures on them. The learning procedures received only the data sets, and did not have access to the generating network. In order to increase the accuracy of the results, we repeated the experiment with 10 (independently sampled) sets of training data. In all of the experiments, the methods we compared received as input the same training data.

By virtue of having a golden model in each experiment, represented by the original networks, we could precisely quantify the error between the induced models and the original model. We were also able to quantify the effect of the local structures on the parameter estimation and the structure selection.

5.2. MEASURES OF ERROR

As the main measurement of error we use the *entropy distance* (also known as *Kullbak-Leibler divergence* and *relative entropy*) from the generating distribution to the induced distribution. The entropy distance from a distribution P to an approximation Q is defined as

$$D(P\|Q) = \sum_x P(x) \log \frac{P(x)}{Q(x)}.$$

This quantity is a measure of the inefficiency incurred by assuming that the distribution is Q when the real distribution is P. Note that the entropy distance is not symmetric, i.e., $D(P\|Q)$ is not equal in general to $D(Q\|P)$. Another important property of the entropy distance function is that $D(P\|Q) \geq 0$, where equality holds if and only if $P = Q$.

There are several possible justifications for using the entropy distance. On the axiomatic side, Shore and Johnson (1980) suggest several desirable properties of approximation measures, and show that entropy distance is the only function that satisfies all of them. There are also motivating examples from data compression and gambling. In both examples, the entropy distance measures the *loss* incurred by using the distribution Q instead of the true distribution P (e.g., additional bits needed or expected monetary losses). We refer the reader to Cover and Thomas (1991) for a discussion and a detailed analysis of these examples.

Measuring the entropy distance of the induced networks allows us to compare the generalization error of the different procedures. We are also interested in assessing the separate influences of the parameter estimation and the induced network structure on this error.

Let G be a network structure. We define the *inherent error* of G with respect to a target distribution P^* as

$$D_{\text{struct}}(P^*\|G) = \min_{\mathcal{L}} D(P^*\|(G, \mathcal{L})).$$

The inherent error of G is the smallest error achievable by any possible choice of CPDs $\mathcal{L}$ for G. Thus, even if we can find the "best" possible parameters for G, we still cannot hope to get a smaller error than $D_{\text{struct}}(P^*\|G)$.

As it turns out, this measure of error can be evaluated by means of a closed-form equation. As we might expect, the best CPDs for G are those where the conditional distribution of X_i, given $\mathbf{Pa}_i$, is identical to $P^*(X_i \mid \mathbf{Pa}_i)$.

Proposition 5.1: *Let G be a network structure and let P^* be a distribution. Then $D_{\text{struct}}(P^*\|G) = D(P^*\|(G, \mathcal{L}^*))$, where $\mathcal{L}^*$ is such that $P(X_i \mid \mathbf{Pa}_i) = P^*(X_i \mid \mathbf{Pa}_i)$ for all i.*

An alternative way of thinking about the inherent error of a network structure G, is as a measure of how "reasonable" are the independence assumptions encoded in G. We can attempt to measure the error of the network structure by estimating to what degree each of these independencies is violated in P^*. One way of measuring the strength of the dependency between variables is the measure of *conditional mutual information*. Let $\mathbf{X}, \mathbf{Y}, \mathbf{Z}$ be three sets of variables; the conditional mutual information between $\mathbf{X}$ and $\mathbf{Y}$, given $\mathbf{Z}$, is defined as

$$I_P(\mathbf{X}; \mathbf{Y} \mid \mathbf{Z}) = H_P(\mathbf{X} \mid \mathbf{Z}) - H_P(\mathbf{X} \mid \mathbf{Y}, \mathbf{Z}).$$

Intuitively, this term measures how much the knowledge of $\mathbf{Y}$ helps us compress $\mathbf{X}$ when we already know $\mathbf{Z}$. It well known that $I_P(\mathbf{X}; \mathbf{Y} \mid \mathbf{Z}) \geq 0$, and that $I_P(\mathbf{X}; \mathbf{Y} \mid \mathbf{Z}) = 0$, if and only if $\mathbf{X}$ is independent of $\mathbf{Y}$, given $\mathbf{Z}$ (Cover and Thomas, 1991).

Using the mutual information as a quantitative measure of strength of dependencies, we can measure the extent to which the independence assumptions represented in G are violated in the real distribution. This suggests that we evaluate this measure for all conditional independencies represented by G. However, many of these independence assumptions "overlap" in the sense that they imply each other. Thus, we need to find a minimal set of independencies that imply all the other independencies represented by G. Pearl (1988) shows how to construct such a minimal sets of independence. Assume that the variable ordering $X_1, \ldots, X_n$ is consistent with the arc direction in G (i.e., if X_i is a parent of X_j, then $i < j$). If, for every i, X_i is independent of $\{X_1, \ldots X_{i-1}\} - \mathbf{Pa}_i$, given $\mathbf{Pa}_i$, then using the chain rule we find that P can be factored as in Equation 1. As a consequence, we find that this set of independence assumptions implies all the independence assumptions that are represented by G. Starting with different consistent orderings, we get different minimal sets of assumptions. However, the next proposition shows that evaluating the error of the model with respect to any of these sets leads to the same answer.

Proposition 5.2: *Let G be a network structure, $X_1, \ldots, X_n$ be a variable ordering consistent with arc direction in G, and P^* be a distribution. Then*

$$D_{\mathrm{struct}}(P^* \| G) = \sum_i I_{P^*}(X_i; \{X_1, \ldots X_{i-1}\} - \mathbf{Pa}_i \mid \mathbf{Pa}_i) \ .$$

This proposition shows that $D_{\mathrm{struct}}(P^* \| G) = 0$ if and only if G is an *I-map* of P^*; that is, all the independence statements encoded in G are also true of P^*. Small values of $D_{\mathrm{struct}}(P^* \| G)$ indicate that while G is not an I-map of P^*, the dependencies not captured by G are "weak." We note that $D_{\mathrm{struct}}(P^* \| G)$ is a one-sided error measure, in the sense that it penalizes structures for representing wrong independence statements, but does not penalize structures for representing redundant dependence statements. In particular, *complete* network structures (i.e., ones to which we cannot add edges without introducing cycles) have no inherent error, since they do not represent any conditional independencies.

We can postulate now that the difference between the overall error (as measured by the entropy distance) and the inherent error is due to errors introduced in the estimation of the CPDs. Note that when we learn a local structure, some of this additional error may be due to the induction of an inappropriate local structure, such as a local structure that makes assumptions of context-specific independencies that do not hold in the target distribution. As with global structure, we can measure the inherent error in the local structure learned. Let G be a network structure, and let $S_{L_1}, \ldots, S_{L_n}$ be structures for the CPDs of G. The *inherent local error* of

G and $S_{L_1}, \ldots, S_{L_n}$ is

$$D_{\text{local}}(P^* \| G, \{S_{L_1}, \ldots, S_{L_n}\}) = \min_{\Theta_{L_1}, \ldots, \Theta_{L_n}} D(P \| (G, \{(S_{L_1}, \Theta_{L_1}), \ldots, (S_{L_n}, \Theta_{L_n})\})).$$

From the above, we get the following expected generalization of Proposition 5.1.

Proposition 5.3: *Let G be a network structure, let $S_{L_1}, \ldots, S_{L_n}$ be local structure for the CPDs of G, and let P^* be a distribution. Then*

$$D_{\text{local}}(P^* \| G, \{S_{L_1}, \ldots, S_{L_n}\}) = D(P^* \| (G, \mathcal{L}^*)),$$

where $\mathcal{L}^*$ is such that $P(X_i \mid \Upsilon_{L_i}) = P^*(X_i \mid \Upsilon_{L_i})$ for all i.

From the definitions of inherent error above it follows that for any network $B = (G, \mathcal{L})$,

$$D(P^* \| P_B) \geq D_{\text{local}}(P^* \| G, \{S_{L_1}, \ldots, S_{L_n}\}) \geq D_{\text{struct}}(P^* \| G).$$

Using these measures in the evaluation of our experiments, we can measure the "quality" of the global independence assumptions made by a network structure (D_{struct}), the quality of the local and global independence assumptions made by a network structure and a local structure (D_{local}), and the total error, which also includes the quality of the parameters.

5.3. RESULTS

We want to characterize the error in the induced models as a function of the number of samples used by the different learning algorithms for the induction. Thus, we plot *learning curves* where the x-axis displays the number of training instances N, and the y-axis displays the error of the learned model. In general, these curves exhibit exponential decrease in the error. This makes visual comparisons between different learning procedures hard, since the differences in the large-sample range ($N \geq 8000$) are obscured, and, when a logarithmic scale is used for the x-axis, the differences at the small-sample range are hard to visualize. See for example Figure 3(a) and (b).

To address this problem, we propose a normalization of these curves, motivated by the theoretical results of Friedman and Yakhini (1996). They show that learning curves for Bayesian networks generally behave as a linear function of $\frac{\log N}{N}$. Thus, we plot the error scaled by $\frac{N}{\log N}$. Figure 5(a) shows the result of the application of this normalization to the curves in Figure 3. Observe that the resulting curves are roughly constant. The thin dotted diagonal lines in Figure 5(a) correspond to the lines of constant error in Figure 3. We plot these lines for entropy distances of $1/2^i$ for $i = 0, \ldots, 6$.

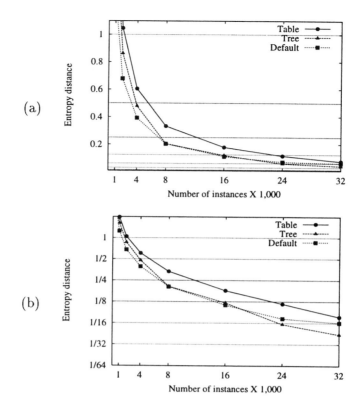

Figure 3. (a) Error curves showing the entropy distance achieved by procedures using the MDL score in the **Alarm** domain. The x-axis displays the number of training instances N, and the y-axis displays the entropy distances of the induced network. (b) The same curves with logarithmic y-axis. Each point is the average of learning from 10 independent data sets.

Figures 4 and 5 display the entropy distance of networks learned via the BDe and MDL scores (Table 2 summarizes these values.) In all the experiments, the learning curves appear to converge to the target distribution: eventually they would intersect the dotted line of ϵ entropy distance for all $\epsilon > 0$. Moreover, all of them appear to (roughly) conform to the behavior specified by the results of Friedman and Yakhini.

With respect to the entropy distance, tree-based procedures performed better in all our experiments than table-based procedures. With few exceptions, the default-based procedures also performed better than the table-based procedures in the **Alarm** and **Insurance** domains. The default-based methods performed poorly in the **Hailfinder** domain.

As a general rule, we see a constant gap in the the curves corresponding

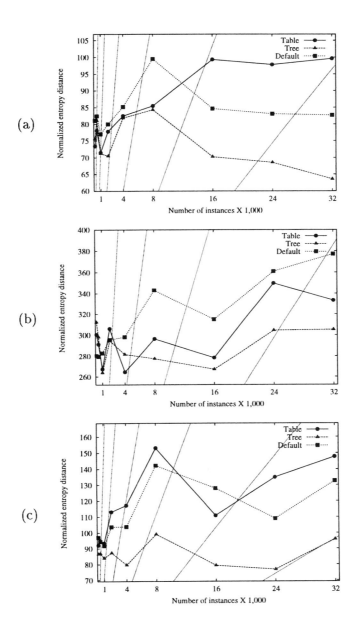

Figure 4. Normalized error curves showing the entropy distance achieved by procedures using the BDe (with $N' = 1$) score in the (a) Alarm domain, (b) Hailfinder domain, and (c) Insurance domain. The x-axis displays the number of training instances N, and the y-axis displays the normalized entropy distances of the induced network (see Section 5.2).

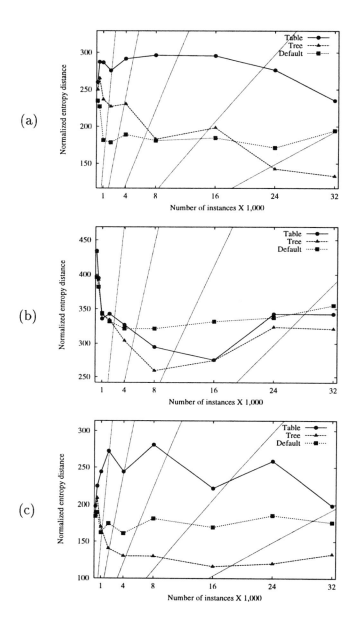

Figure 5. Normalized error curves showing the entropy distance achieved by procedures using the MDL score in the (a) Alarm domain, (b) Hailfinder domain, and (c) Insurance domain.

to different representations. Thus, for a fixed N, the error of the procedure representing local structure is a constant fraction of the error of the corresponding procedure that does not represent local structure (i.e., learns tabular CPDs). For example, in Figure 4(a) we see that in the large-sample region (e.g., $N \geq 8000$), the errors of procedures that use trees and default tables are approximately 70% and 85% (respectively) of the error of the table-based procedures. In Figure 5(c) the corresponding ratios are 50% and 70%.

Another way of interpreting these results is obtained by looking at the number of instances needed to reach a particular error rate. For example, In Figure 4(a), the tree-based procedure reaches the error level of $\frac{1}{32}$ with approximately 23,000 instances. On the other hand, the table-based procedure barely reaches that error level with 32,000 instances. Thus, if we want to ensure this level of performance, we would need to supply the table-based procedure with 9,000 additional instances. This number of instances might be unavailable in practice.

We continued our investigation by examining the network structures learned by the different procedures. We evaluated the inherent error, D_{struct}, of the structures learned by the different procedures. In all of our experiments, the inherent error of the network structures learned via tree-based and default-based procedures is smaller than the inherent error of the networks learned by the corresponding table-based procedure. For example, examine the D_{struct} column in Tables 3 and 4. From these results, we conclude that the network structures learned by procedures using local representations make fewer mistaken assumptions of global independence, as predicted by our main hypothesis.

Our hypothesis also predicts that procedures that learn local representation are able to assess fewer parameters by making local assumptions of independence in the CPDs. To illustrate this, we measured the inherent local error, D_{local}, and the number of parameters needed to quantify these networks. As we can see in Tables 3 and 4, the networks learned by these procedures exhibit smaller inherent error, D_{struct}; but they require fewer parameters, and their inherent local error, D_{local}, is roughly the same as that of networks learned by the table-based procedures. Hence, instead of making global assumptions of independence, the local representation procedures make the local assumptions of independence that better capture the regularities in the target distribution and require fewer parameters. As a consequence, the parameter estimation for these procedures is more accurate.

Finally, we investigated how our conclusions depend on the particular choices we made in the experiments. As we will see, the use of local structure leads to improvements regardless of these choices. We examined two aspects of the learning process: the choice of the parameters for the priors and in the search procedure.

We start by looking at the effect of changing the equivalent sample size N'. Heckerman et al. (1995a) show that the choice of N' can have drastic effects on the quality of the learned networks. On the basis of on their experiments in the Alarm domain, Heckerman et al. report that $N' = 5$ achieves the best results. Table 5 shows the effect of changing N' from 1 to 5 in our experiments. We see that the choice of N' influences the magnitude of the errors in the learned networks, and the sizes of the error gaps between the different methods. Yet these influences do not suggest any changes on the benefits of local structures.

Unlike the BDe score, the MDL score does not involve an explicit choice of priors. Nonetheless, we can use Bayesian averaging to select the parameters for the structures that have been learned by the MDL score, as opposed to using maximum likelihood estimates. In Table 6 we compare the error between the maximum likelihood estimates and Bayesian averaging with $N' = 1$. As expected, averaging leads to smaller errors in the parameter estimation, especially for small sample sizes. However, with the exception of the Alarm domain, Bayesian averaging does not improve the score for large samples (e.g., $N = 32,000$). We conclude that even though changing the parameter estimation technique may improve the score in some instances, it does not change our basic conclusions.

Finally, another aspect of the learning process that needs further investigation is the heuristic search procedure. A better search technique can lead to better induced models as illustrated in the experiments of Heckerman et al. (1995a). In our experiments we modified the search by initializing the greedy search procedure with a more informed starting point. Following Heckerman et al. (1995a) we used the *maximal branching* as a starting state for the search. A maximal branching network is one of the highest-scoring network among these where $|\mathbf{Pa}_i| \leq 1$ for all i. A maximal branching can be found in an efficient manner (e.g., in low-order polynomial time) (Heckerman et al., 1995a). Table 7 reports the results of this experiment. In the Alarm domain, the use of maximal branching as an initial point led to improvements in all the learning procedures. On the other hand, in the Insurance domain, this choice of for a starting point led to a worse error. Still, we observe that the conclusions described above regarding the use of local structure held for these runs as well.

6. Conclusion

The main contribution of this article is the introduction of structured representations of the CPDs in the learning process, the identification of the benefits of using these representations, and the empirical validation of our hypothesis. As we mentioned in the introduction (Section 1), we are not the first to consider efficient representations for the CPDs in the context of learning. However, to the best of our knowledge, we are the first to consider and demonstrate the effects that these representations may have on the learning of the global structure of the network.

In this paper we have focused on the investigation of two fairly simple, structured representations of CPDs: trees and default tables. There are certainly many other possible representation of CPDs, based, for example, on decision graphs, rules, and CNF formulas: see Boutilier et al. (1996). Our choice was mainly due to the availability of efficient computational tools for learning the representations we use. The refinement of the methods studied in this paper to incorporate these representations deserves further attention. In the machine learning literature, there are various approaches to learning trees, all of which can easily be incorporated in the learning procedures for Bayesian networks. In addition, certain interactions among the search procedures for global and local structures can be exploited, to reduce the computational cost of the learning process. We leave these issues for future research.

It is important to distinguish between the local representations we examine in this paper and the noisy-or and logistic regression models that have been examined in the literature. Both noisy-or and logistic regression (as applied in the Bayesian network literature) attempt to estimate the CPD with a *fixed* number of parameters. This number is usually linear in the number of parents in the CPD. In cases where the target distribution does not satisfy the assumptions embodied by these models, the estimates of CPDs produced by these methods can arbitrarily diverge from the target distribution. On the other hand, our local representations involve learning the structure of the CPD, which can range from a lean structure with few parameters to a complex structure with an exponential number of parameters. Thus, our representations can scale up to accommodate the complexity of the training data. This ensures that, in theory, they are asymptotically correct: given enough samples, they will construct a close approximation of the target distribution.

In conclusion, we have shown that the induction of local structured representation for CPDs significantly improves the performance of procedures for learning Bayesian networks. In essence, this improvement is due to the fact that we have changed the *bias* of the learning procedure to reflect the nature of the distribution in the data more accurately.

TABLE 2. Summary of entropy distance for networks learned by the procedure using the MDL score and BDe score with $N' = 1$.

Domain	Size (× 1,000)	MDL Score			BDe Score		
		Table	Tree	Defualt	Table	Tree	Default
Alarm	0.25	5.7347	5.5148	5.1832	1.6215	1.6692	1.7898
	0.50	3.5690	3.2925	2.8215	0.9701	1.0077	1.0244
	1.00	1.9787	1.6333	1.2542	0.4941	0.4922	0.5320
	2.00	1.0466	0.8621	0.6782	0.2957	0.2679	0.3040
	4.00	0.6044	0.4777	0.3921	0.1710	0.1697	0.1766
	8.00	0.3328	0.2054	0.2034	0.0960	0.0947	0.1118
	16.00	0.1787	0.1199	0.1117	0.0601	0.0425	0.0512
	24.00	0.1160	0.0599	0.0720	0.0411	0.0288	0.0349
	32.00	0.0762	0.0430	0.0630	0.0323	0.0206	0.0268
Hailfinder	0.25	9.5852	9.5513	8.7451	6.6357	6.8950	6.1947
	0.50	4.9078	4.8749	4.7475	3.6197	3.7072	3.4746
	1.00	2.3200	2.3599	2.3754	1.8462	1.8222	1.9538
	2.00	1.3032	1.2702	1.2617	1.1631	1.1198	1.1230
	4.00	0.6784	0.6306	0.6671	0.5483	0.5841	0.6181
	8.00	0.3312	0.2912	0.3614	0.3329	0.3117	0.3855
	16.00	0.1666	0.1662	0.2009	0.1684	0.1615	0.1904
	24.00	0.1441	0.1362	0.1419	0.1470	0.1279	0.1517
	32.00	0.1111	0.1042	0.1152	0.1081	0.0989	0.1223
Insurance	0.25	4.3750	4.1940	4.0745	2.0324	1.9117	2.1436
	0.50	2.7909	2.5933	2.3581	1.1798	1.0784	1.1734
	1.00	1.6841	1.1725	1.1196	0.6453	0.5799	0.6335
	2.00	1.0343	0.5344	0.6635	0.4300	0.3316	0.3942
	4.00	0.5058	0.2706	0.3339	0.2432	0.1652	0.2153
	8.00	0.3156	0.1463	0.2037	0.1720	0.1113	0.1598
	16.00	0.1341	0.0704	0.1025	0.0671	0.0480	0.0774
	24.00	0.1087	0.0506	0.0780	0.0567	0.0323	0.0458
	32.00	0.0644	0.0431	0.0570	0.0479	0.0311	0.0430

TABLE 3. Summary of inherent error, inherent local error, and number of parameters for the networks learned by the table-based and the tree-based procedures using the BDe score with $N' = 1$.

Domain	Size (× 1,000)	Table D	D_{struct}/D_{local}	Param	Tree D	D_{local}	D_{struct}	Param
Alarm	1	0.4941	0.1319	570	0.4922	0.1736	0.0862	383
	4	0.1710	0.0404	653	0.1697	0.0570	0.0282	453
	16	0.0601	0.0237	702	0.0425	0.0154	0.0049	496
	32	0.0323	0.0095	1026	0.0206	0.0070	0.0024	497
Hailfinder	1	1.8462	1.2166	2066	1.8222	1.1851	1.0429	1032
	4	0.5483	0.3434	2350	0.5841	0.3937	0.2632	1309
	16	0.1684	0.1121	2785	0.1615	0.1081	0.0758	1599
	32	0.1081	0.0770	2904	0.0989	0.0701	0.0404	1715
Insurance	1	0.6453	0.3977	487	0.5799	0.3501	0.2752	375
	4	0.2432	0.1498	724	0.1652	0.0961	0.0654	461
	16	0.0671	0.0377	938	0.0480	0.0287	0.0146	525
	32	0.0479	0.0323	968	0.0311	0.0200	0.0085	576

TABLE 4. Summary of inherent error, inherent local error, and number of parameters for the networks learned by the table-based and tree-based procedures using the MDL score.

Domain	Size (× 1,000)	Table D	D_{struct}/D_{local}	Param	Tree D	D_{local}	D_{struct}	Param
Alarm	1	1.9787	0.5923	361	1.6333	0.4766	0.3260	289
	4	0.6044	0.2188	457	0.4777	0.1436	0.0574	382
	16	0.1787	0.0767	639	0.1199	0.0471	0.0189	457
	32	0.0762	0.0248	722	0.0430	0.0135	0.0053	461
Hailfinder	1	2.3200	1.0647	1092	2.3599	1.1343	0.9356	1045
	4	0.6784	0.4026	1363	0.6306	0.3663	0.2165	1322
	16	0.1666	0.1043	1718	0.1662	0.1107	0.0621	1583
	32	0.1111	0.0743	1864	0.1042	0.0722	0.0446	1739
Insurance	1	1.6841	1.0798	335	1.1725	0.5642	0.4219	329
	4	0.5058	0.3360	518	0.2706	0.1169	0.0740	425
	16	0.1341	0.0794	723	0.0704	0.0353	0.0187	497
	32	0.0644	0.0355	833	0.0431	0.0266	0.0140	544

TABLE 5. Summary of entropy distance for procedures that use the BDe score with $N' = 1$ and $N' = 5$.

Domain	Size (× 1,000)	$N' = 1$ Table	Tree	Default	$N' = 5$ Table	Tree	Default
Alarm	1	0.4941	0.4922	0.5320	0.3721	0.3501	0.3463
	4	0.1710	0.1697	0.1766	0.1433	0.1187	0.1308
	16	0.0601	0.0425	0.0512	0.0414	0.0352	0.0435
	32	0.0323	0.0206	0.0268	0.0254	0.0175	0.0238
Hailfinder	1	1.8462	1.8222	1.9538	1.4981	1.5518	1.6004
	4	0.5483	0.5841	0.6181	0.4574	0.4859	0.5255
	16	0.1684	0.1615	0.1904	0.1536	0.1530	0.1601
	32	0.1081	0.0989	0.1223	0.0996	0.0891	0.0999
Insurance	1	0.6453	0.5799	0.6335	0.5568	0.5187	0.5447
	4	0.2432	0.1652	0.2153	0.1793	0.1323	0.1921
	16	0.0671	0.0480	0.0774	0.0734	0.0515	0.0629
	32	0.0479	0.0311	0.0430	0.0365	0.0284	0.0398

TABLE 6. Summary of entropy distance for procedures that use the MDL score for learning the structure and local structure combined with two methods for parameter estimation.

Domain	Size (× 1,000)	Maximum Likelihood Table	Tree	Default	Bayesian, $N' = 1$ Table	Tree	Default
Alarm	1	1.9787	1.6333	1.2542	0.8848	0.7495	0.6015
	4	0.6044	0.4777	0.3921	0.3251	0.2319	0.2229
	16	0.1787	0.1199	0.1117	0.1027	0.0730	0.0779
	32	0.0762	0.0430	0.0630	0.0458	0.0267	0.0475
Hailfinder	1	2.3200	2.3599	2.3754	1.7261	1.7683	1.8047
	4	0.6784	0.6306	0.6671	0.5982	0.5528	0.6091
	16	0.1666	0.1662	0.2009	0.1668	0.1586	0.1861
	32	0.1111	0.1042	0.1152	0.1133	0.0964	0.1120
Insurance	1	1.6841	1.1725	1.1196	1.1862	0.7539	0.8082
	4	0.5058	0.2706	0.3339	0.3757	0.1910	0.2560
	16	0.1341	0.0704	0.1025	0.1116	0.0539	0.0814
	32	0.0644	0.0431	0.0570	0.0548	0.0368	0.0572

TABLE 7. Summary of entropy distance for two methods for initializing the search, using the the BDe score with $N' = 1$.

Domain	Size ($\times$ 1,000)	Empty Network			Maximal Branching Network		
		Table	Tree	Default	Table	Tree	Default
Alarm	1	0.4941	0.4922	0.5320	0.4804	0.5170	0.4674
	4	0.1710	0.1697	0.1766	0.1453	0.1546	0.1454
	16	0.0601	0.0425	0.0512	0.0341	0.0350	0.0307
	32	0.0323	0.0206	0.0268	0.0235	0.0191	0.0183
Hailfinder	1	1.8462	1.8222	1.9538	1.7995	1.7914	1.9972
	4	0.5483	0.5841	0.6181	0.6220	0.6173	0.6633
	16	0.1684	0.1615	0.1904	0.1782	0.1883	0.1953
	32	0.1081	0.0989	0.1223	0.1102	0.1047	0.1162
Insurance	1	0.6453	0.5799	0.6335	0.6428	0.6350	0.6502
	4	0.2432	0.1652	0.2153	0.2586	0.2379	0.2242
	16	0.0671	0.0480	0.0774	0.1305	0.0914	0.1112
	32	0.0479	0.0311	0.0430	0.0979	0.0538	0.0856

Acknowledgments

The authors are grateful to an anonymous reviewer and to Wray Buntine and David Heckerman for their comments on previous versions of this paper and for useful discussions relating to this work.

Part of this research was done while both authors were at the Fockwell Science Center, [4] Palo Alto Laboratory. Nir Friedman was also at Stanford University at the time. The support provided by Fockwell and Stanford University is gratefully acknowledged. In addition, Nir Friedman was supported in part by an IBM graduate fellowship and NSF Grant IFI-95-03109.

A preliminary version of this article appeared in the *Proceedings, 12*[th] *Conference on Uncertainty in Artificial Intelligence*, 1996.

References

I. Beinlich, G. Suermondt, R. Chavez, and G. Cooper. The ALARM monitoring system: A case study with two probabilistic inference techniques for belief networks. In *Proc. 2'nd European Conf. on AI and Medicine.* Springer-Verlag, Berlin, 1989.

R. R. Bouckaert. Properties of Bayesian network learning algorithms. In R. López de Mantarás and D. Poole, editors, *Proc. Tenth Conference on Uncertainty in Artificial Intelligence (UAI '94)*, pages 102–109. Morgan Kaufmann, San Francisco, CA, 1994.

C. Boutilier, N. Friedman, M. Goldszmidt, and D. Koller. Context-specific independence in Bayesian networks. In E. Horvitz and F. Jensen, editors, *Proc. Twelfth Conference on Uncertainty in Artificial Intelligence (UAI '96)*, pages 115–123. Morgan Kaufmann, San Francisco, CA, 1996.

W. Buntine. *A theory of learning classification rules.* PhD thesis, University of Technology, Sydney, Australia, 1991.

W. Buntine. Theory refinement on Bayesian networks. In B. D. D'Ambrosio, P. Smets, and P. P. Bonissone, editors, *Proc. Seventh Annual Conference on Uncertainty Artificial Intelligence (UAI '92)*, pages 52–60. Morgan Kaufmann, San Francisco, CA, 1991.

W. Buntine. Learning classification trees. In D. J. Hand, editor, *Artificial Intelligence Frontiers in Statistics*, number III in AI and Statistics. Chapman & Hall, London, 1993.

D. M. Chickering. Learning Bayesian networks is NP-complete. In D. Fisher and H.-J. Lenz, editors, *Learning from Data: Artificial Intelligence and Statistics V*. Springer Verlag, 1996.

G. F. Cooper and E. Herskovits. A Bayesian method for the induction of probabilistic networks from data. *Machine Learning*, 9:309–347, 1992.

T. M. Cover and J. A. Thomas. *Elements of Information Theory.* John Wiley & Sons, New York, 1991.

M. H. DeGroot. *Optimal Statistical Decisions.* McGraw-Hill, New York, 1970.

F. J. Diez. Parameter adjustment in Bayes networks: The generalized noisy or-gate. In D. Heckerman and A. Mamdani, editors, *Proc. Ninth Conference on Uncertainty in Artificial Intelligence (UAI '93)*, pages 99–105. Morgan Kaufmann, San Francisco, CA, 1993.

N. Friedman and Z. Yakhini. On the sample complexity of learning Bayesian networks. In E. Horvitz and F. Jensen, editors, *Proc. Twelfth Conference on Uncertainty in*

---

[4]All products and company names mentioned in this article are the trademarks of their respective holders.

Artificial Intelligence (UAI '96). Morgan Kaufmann, San Francisco, CA, 1996.

D. Heckerman and J. S. Breese. A new look at causal independence. In R. López de Mantarás and D. Poole, editors, *Proc. Tenth Conference on Uncertainty in Artificial Intelligence (UAI '94)*, pages 286–292. Morgan Kaufmann, San Francisco, CA, 1994.

D. Heckerman, D. Geiger, and D. M. Chickering. Learning Bayesian networks: The combination of knowledge and statistical data. *Machine Learning*, 20:197–243, 1995.

D. Heckerman. A tutorial on learning Bayesian networks. Technical Report MSR-TR-95-06, Microsoft Research, 1995.

W. Lam and F. Bacchus. Learning Bayesian belief networks: An approach based on the MDL principle. *Computational Intelligence*, 10:269–293, 1994.

R. Musick. *Belief Network Induction*. PhD thesis, University of California, Berkeley, CA, 1994.

R. M. Neal. Connectionist learning of belief networks. *Artificial Intelligence*, 56:71–113, 1992.

J. Pearl. *Probabilistic Reasoning in Intelligent Systems*. Morgan Kaufmann, San Francisco, CA, 1988.

J. R. Quinlan and R. Rivest. Inferring decision trees using the minimum description length principle. *Information and Computation*, 80:227–248, 1989.

J. R. Quinlan. *C4.5: Programs for Machine Learning*. Morgan Kaufmann, San Francisco, CA, 1993.

J. Rissanen. *Stochastic Complexity in Statistical Inquiry*. World Scientific, River Edge, NJ, 1989.

S. Russell, J. Binder, D. Koller, and K. Kanazawa. Local learning in probabilistic networks with hidden variables. In *Proc. Fourteenth International Joint Conference on Artificial Intelligence (IJCAI '95)*, pages 1146–1152. Morgan Kaufmann, San Francisco, CA, 1995.

G. Schwarz. Estimating the dimension of a model. *Annals of Statistics*, 6:461–464, 1978.

J. E. Shore and R. W. Johnson. Axiomatic derivation of the principle of maximum entropy and the principle of minimum cross-entropy. *IEEE Transactions on Information Theory*, IT-26(1):26–37, 1980.

D. J. Spiegelhalter and S. L. Lauritzen. Sequential updating of conditional probabilities on directed graphical structures. *Networks*, 20:579–605, 1990.

S. Srinivas. A generalization of the noisy-or model. In D. Heckerman and A. Mamdani, editors, *Proc. Ninth Conference on Uncertainty in Artificial Intelligence (UAI '93)*, pages 208–215. Morgan Kaufmann, San Francisco, CA, 1993.

C. Wallace and J. Patrick. Coding decision trees. *Machine Learning*, 11:7–22, 1993.

ASYMPTOTIC MODEL SELECTION FOR DIRECTED NETWORKS WITH HIDDEN VARIABLES

DAN GEIGER

Computer Science Department
Technion, Haifa 32000, Israel
dang@cs.technion.ac.il

DAVID HECKERMAN

Microsoft Research, Bldg 9S
Redmond WA, 98052-6399
heckerma@microsoft.com

AND

CHRISTOPHER MEEK

Carnegie-Mellon University
Department of Philosophy
meek@cmu.edu

Abstract. We extend the Bayesian Information Criterion (BIC), an asymptotic approximation for the marginal likelihood, to Bayesian networks with hidden variables. This approximation can be used to select models given large samples of data. The standard BIC as well as our extension punishes the complexity of a model according to the dimension of its parameters. We argue that the dimension of a Bayesian network with hidden variables is the rank of the Jacobian matrix of the transformation between the parameters of the network and the parameters of the observable variables. We compute the dimensions of several networks including the naive Bayes model with a hidden root node.

This manuscript was previously published in *The Proceedings of the Twelfth Conference on Uncertainty in Artificial Intelligence*, 1996, Morgan Kaufmann.

1. Introduction

Learning Bayesian networks from data extends their applicability to situations where data is easily obtained and expert knowledge is expensive. Consequently, it has been the subject of much research in recent years (e.g., Heckerman, 1995a; Buntine, 1996). Researchers have pursued two types of approaches for learning Bayesian networks: one that uses independence tests to direct a search among valid models and another that uses a score to search for the best scored network—a procedure known as *model selection*. Scores based on exact Bayesian computations have been developed by (e.g.) Cooper and Herskovits (1992), Spiegelhalter et al. (1993), Buntine (1994), and Heckerman et al. (1995), and scores based on minimum description length (MDL) have been developed in Lam and Bacchus (1993) and Suzuki (1993).

We consider a Bayesian approach to model selection. Suppose we have a set $\{X_1, \ldots, X_n\} = \mathbf{X}$ of discrete variables, and a set $\{\mathbf{x}_1, \ldots, \mathbf{x}_N\} = D$ of cases, where each case is an instance of some or of all the variables in $\mathbf{X}$. Let $(S, \boldsymbol{\theta}_s)$ be a Bayesian network, where S is the network structure of the Bayesian network, a directed acyclic graph such that each node X_i of S is associated with a random variable X_i, and $\boldsymbol{\theta}_s$ is a set of parameters associated with the network structure. Let S^h be the hypothesis that precisely the independence assertions implied by S hold in the true or objective joint distribution of $\mathbf{X}$. Then, a Bayesian measure of the goodness-of-fit of network structure S to D is $p(S^h|D) \propto p(S^h)p(D|S^h)$, where $p(D|S^h)$ is known as the *marginal likelihood of D given S^h*.

The problem of model selection among Bayesian networks with hidden variables, that is, networks with variables whose values are not observed is more difficult than model selection among networks without hidden variables. First, the space of possible networks becomes infinite, and second, scoring each network is computationally harder because one must account for all possible values of the missing variables (Cooper and Herskovits, 1992). Our goal is to develop a Bayesian scoring approach for networks that include hidden variables. Obtaining such a score that is computationally effective and conceptually simple will allow us to select a model from among a set of competing models.

Our approach is to use an asymptotic approximation of the marginal likelihood. This asymptotic approximation is known as the Bayesian Information Criteria (BIC) (Schwarz, 1978; Haughton, 1988), and is equivalent to Rissanen's (1987) minimum description length (MDL). Such an asymptotic approximation has been carried out for Bayesian networks by Herskovits (1991) and Bouckaert (1995) when no hidden variables are present. Bouckaert (1995) shows that the marginal likelihood of data D given a network structure S is given by

$$p(D|S^h) = H(S,D)N - 1/2 \dim(S) \log(N) + O(1) \tag{1}$$

where N is the sample size of the data, $H(S,D)$ is the entropy of the probability distribution obtained by projecting the frequencies of observed cases into the conditional probability tables of the Bayesian network S, and $\dim(S)$ is the number of parameters in S. Eq. 1 reveals the qualitative preferences made by the Bayesian approach. First, with sufficient data, a network structure that is an I-map of the true distribution is more likely than a network structure that is not an I-map of the true distribution. Second, among all network structures that are I-maps of the true distribution, the one with the minimum number of parameters is more likely.

Eq. 1 was derived from an explicit formula for the probability of a network given data by letting the sample size N run to infinity and using a Dirichlet prior for its parameters. Nonetheless, Eq. 1 does not depend on the selected prior. In Section 3, we use Laplace's method to rederive Eq. 1 without assuming a Dirichlet prior. Our derivation is a standard application of asymptotic Bayesian analysis. This derivation is useful for gaining intuition for the hidden-variable case.

In section 4, we provide an approximation to the marginal likelihood for Bayesian networks with hidden variables, and give a heuristic argument for this approximation using Laplace's method. We obtain the following equation:

$$\begin{aligned} \log p(S|D) \approx \\ \log p(S|D, \hat{\boldsymbol{\theta}}_s) - 1/2 \dim(S, \hat{\boldsymbol{\theta}}_s) \log(N) \end{aligned} \tag{2}$$

where $\hat{\boldsymbol{\theta}}_s$ is the *maximum likelihood* (ML) value for the parameters of the network and $\dim(S, \hat{\boldsymbol{\theta}}_s)$ is the dimension of S at the ML value for $\boldsymbol{\theta}_s$. The dimension of a model can be interpreted in two equivalent ways. First, it is the number of free parameters needed to represent the parameter space near the maximum likelihood value. Second, it is the rank of the Jacobian matrix of the transformation between the parameters of the network and the parameters of the observable (non-hidden) variables. In any case, the dimension depends on the value of $\hat{\boldsymbol{\theta}}_s$, in contrast to Eq. 1, where the dimension is fixed throughout the parameter space.

In Section 5, we compute the dimensions of several network structures, including the naive Bayes model with a hidden class node. In Section 6, we demonstrate that the scoring function used in AutoClass sometimes diverges from $p(S|D)$ asymptotically. In Sections 7 and 8, we describe how our heuristic approach can be extended to Gaussian and sigmoid networks.

2. Background

We introduce the following notation for a Bayesian network. Let r_i be the number of states of variable X_i, $\mathbf{Pa}_i$ be the set of variables corresponding to the parents of node X_i, and $q_i = \prod_{X_l \in \mathbf{Pa}_i} r_l$ be the number of states of $\mathbf{Pa}_i$. We use the integer j to index the states of $\mathbf{Pa}_i$. That is, we write $\mathbf{Pa}_i = \mathbf{pa}_i^j$ to denote that the parents of X_i are assigned its jth state. We use θ_{ijk} to denote the true probability or *parameter* that $X_i = x_i^k$ given that $\mathbf{Pa}_i = \mathbf{pa}_i^j$. Note that $\sum_{k=1}^{r_i} \theta_{ijk} = 1$. Also, we assume $\theta_{ijk} > 0$. In addition, we use $\boldsymbol{\theta}_{ij} = \{\theta_{ijk} | 2 \leq k \leq r_i\}$ to denote non-redundant parameters associated with node i for a given instance of the parents $\mathbf{Pa}_i$, and $\boldsymbol{\theta}_i = \{\boldsymbol{\theta}_{ij} | 1 \leq j \leq q_i\}$ to denote the parameters associated with node i. Thus, $\boldsymbol{\theta}_s = \{\boldsymbol{\theta}_i | 1 \leq i \leq n\}$. When S is unambiguous, we use $\boldsymbol{\theta}$ instead of $\boldsymbol{\theta}_s$.

To compute $p(D|S^h)$ in closed form for many network structures, several assumptions are usually made. First, the data D is assumed to be a random sample from some Bayesian network $(S, \boldsymbol{\theta}_s)$. Second, for each network structure, the parameter sets $\boldsymbol{\theta}_1, \ldots, \boldsymbol{\theta}_n$ are mutually independent (global independence, Spiegelhalter and Lauritzen, 1990), and the parameter sets $\boldsymbol{\theta}_{i1}, \ldots, \boldsymbol{\theta}_{iq_i}$ for each i are assumed to be mutually independent (local independence, Spiegelhalter and Lauritzen, 1990). Third, if a node has the same parents in two distinct networks, then the distribution of the parameters associated with this node are identical in both networks (parameter modularity, Heckerman et al., 1995). Fourth, each case is complete. Fifth, the prior distribution of the parameters associated with each node is Dirichlet—that is, $p(\boldsymbol{\theta}_{ij}|S^h) \propto \prod_k \theta_{ijk}^{\alpha_{ijk}}$ where α_{ijk} can be interpreted as the equivalent number of cases seen in which $X_i = x_i^k$ and $\mathbf{Pa}_i = \mathbf{pa}_i^j$.

Using these assumptions, Cooper and Herskovits (1992) obtained the following exact formula for the marginal likelihood:

$$p(D|S^h) = \prod_{i=1}^{n} \prod_{j=1}^{q_i} \frac{\Gamma(\alpha_{ij})}{\Gamma(\alpha_{ij} + N_{ij})} \prod_{k=1}^{r_i} \frac{\Gamma(\alpha_{ijk} + N_{ijk})}{\Gamma(\alpha_{ijk})}$$

where N_{ijk} is the number of cases in D in which $X_i = x_i^k$ and $\mathbf{Pa}_i = \mathbf{pa}_i^j$. We call this expression the *Cooper–Herskovits scoring function*.

The last assumption is made for the sake of convenience. Namely, the parameter distributions before and after complete data are seen are in the same family: the Dirichlet family. Geiger and Heckerman (1995) provide a characterization of the Dirichlet distribution, which shows that the fifth assumption is implied from the first three assumptions and from one additional assumption that if S_1 and S_2 are equivalent Bayesian networks (i.e., they represent the same sets of independence assumptions), then the events S_1^h and S_2^h are equivalent as well (hypothesis equivalence, Heckerman et al., 1995). This assumption was made explicit, because it does not hold for causal networks where two arcs with opposing directions correspond to distinct hypotheses (Heckerman, 1995b). To satisfy these assumptions, Heckerman et al. (1995) show that one must use

$$\alpha_{ijk} = \alpha \; q(X_i = x_i^k, \mathbf{Pa}_i = \mathbf{pa}_i^j)$$

in the Cooper–Herskovits scoring function, where $q(X_1, \ldots, X_n)$ is the joint probability distribution of $\mathbf{X}$ obtained from an initial or prior Bayesian network specified by the user, and α is the user's effective sample size or confidence in the prior network.

The Cooper–Herskovits scoring function does not lend itself to a qualitative analysis. Nonetheless, by letting N grow to infinity yet keeping N_{ij}/N and N_{ijk}/N finite, Eq. 1 can be derived by expanding $\Gamma(\cdot)$ using Sterling's approximation. This derivation hinges on the assumptions of global and local independence and on a Dirichlet prior, although, as we show, the result still holds without these assumptions. Intuitively, with a large sample size N, the data washes away any contribution of the prior.

3. Assymptotics Without Hidden Variables

We shall now rederive Herskovits' (1991) and Bouckaert's (1995) asymptotic result. The technique we use is Laplace's method, which is to expand the log likelihood of the data around the maximum likelihood value, and then approximate the peak using a multivariate-normal distribution.

Our derivation bypasses the need to compute $p(D_N|S^h)$ for data D_N of a sample size N, which requires the assumptions discussed in the previous section. Instead, we compute $\lim_{N\to\infty} p(D_N|S^h)$. Furthermore, our derivation only assumes that the prior for $\boldsymbol{\theta}$ around the maximum likelihood value is positive. Finally, we argue in the next section that our derivation can be extended to Bayesian networks with hidden variables.

We begin by defining $f(\boldsymbol{\theta}) \equiv \log p(D_N|\boldsymbol{\theta}, S^h)$. Thus,

$$p(D_N|S^h) = \int p(D_N|\boldsymbol{\theta}, S^h) \; p(\boldsymbol{\theta}|S^h) \; d\boldsymbol{\theta} =$$
$$\int \exp\{f(\boldsymbol{\theta})\} \; p(\boldsymbol{\theta}|S^h) \; d\boldsymbol{\theta} \qquad (3)$$

Assuming $f(\boldsymbol{\theta})$ has a maximum—the ML value $\hat{\boldsymbol{\theta}}$—we have $f'(\hat{\boldsymbol{\theta}}) = 0$. Using a Taylor-series expansion of $f(\boldsymbol{\theta})$ around the ML value, we get

$$f(\boldsymbol{\theta}) \approx f(\hat{\boldsymbol{\theta}}) + 1/2(\boldsymbol{\theta} - \hat{\boldsymbol{\theta}})f''(\boldsymbol{\theta})(\boldsymbol{\theta} - \hat{\boldsymbol{\theta}}) \qquad (4)$$

where $f''(\boldsymbol{\theta})$ is the Hessian of f—the square matrix of second derivatives with respect to every pair of variables $\{\theta_{ijk}, \theta_{i'j'k'}\}$. Consequently, from Eqs. 3 and 4,

$$\log p(D|S^h) \approx f(\hat{\boldsymbol{\theta}})+ \tag{5}$$
$$\log \int \exp\{1/2(\boldsymbol{\theta} - \hat{\boldsymbol{\theta}})f''(\boldsymbol{\theta})(\boldsymbol{\theta} - \hat{\boldsymbol{\theta}})\}p(\boldsymbol{\theta}|S^h)d\boldsymbol{\theta}$$

We assume that $-f''(\boldsymbol{\theta})$ is positive-definite, and that, as N grows to infinity, the peak in a neighborhood around the maximum becomes sharper. Consequently, if we ignore the prior, we get a normal distribution around the peak. Furthermore, if we assume that the prior $p(\boldsymbol{\theta}|S^h)$ is not zero around $\hat{\boldsymbol{\theta}}$, then as N grows it can be assumed constant and so removed from the integral in Eq. 5. The remaining integral is approximated by the formula for multivariate-normal distributions:

$$\int \exp\{1/2(\boldsymbol{\theta} - \hat{\boldsymbol{\theta}})f''(\boldsymbol{\theta})(\boldsymbol{\theta} - \hat{\boldsymbol{\theta}})\}d\boldsymbol{\theta} \approx$$
$$\sqrt{2\pi} \det \left[-f''(\hat{\boldsymbol{\theta}})\right]^{d/2} \tag{6}$$

where d is the number of parameters in $\boldsymbol{\theta}$, $d = \prod_{i=1}^{n}(r_i - 1)q_i$. As N grows to infinity, the above approximation becomes more precise because the entire mass becomes concentrated around the peak. Plugging Eq. 6 into Eq. 5 and noting that $\det \left[-f''(\hat{\boldsymbol{\theta}})\right]$ is proportional to N yields the BIC:

$$p(D_N|S^h) \approx p(D_N|\hat{\boldsymbol{\theta}}, S^h) - \frac{d}{2}\log(N) \tag{7}$$

A careful derivation in this spirit shows that, under certain conditions, the relative error in this approximation is $O_p(1)$ (Schwarz, 1978; Haughton, 1988).

For Bayesian networks, the function $f(\boldsymbol{\theta})$ is known. Thus, all the assumptions about this function can be verified. First, we note that $f''(\boldsymbol{\theta})$ is a block diagonal matrix where each block A_{ij} corresponds to variable X_i and a particular instance j of $\mathbf{Pa}_i$, and is of size $(r_i - 1)^2$. Let us examine one such A_{ij}. To simplify notation, assume that X_i has three states. Let w_1, w_2 and w_3 denote θ_{ijk} for $k = 1, 2, 3$, where i and j are fixed. We consider only those cases in D_N where $\mathbf{Pa}_i = j$, and examine only the observations of X_i. Let D'_N denote the set of N values of X_i obtained in this process. With each observation, we associate two indicator functions x_i and y_i. The function x_i is one if X_i gets its first value in case i and is zero otherwise. Similarly, y_i is one if X_i gets its second value in case i and is zero otherwise.

The log likelihood function of D'_N is given by

$$\lambda(w_1, w_2) = \log \prod_{i=1}^{N} w_1^{x_i} w_2^{y_i} (1 - w_1 - w_2)^{1-x_i-y_i} \qquad (8)$$

To find the maximum, we set the first derivative of this function to zero. The resulting equations are called the maximum likelihood equations:

$$\lambda_{w_1}(w_1, w_2) = \sum_{i=1}^{N} \left[\frac{x_i}{w_1} - \frac{1 - x_i - y_i}{1 - w_1 - w_2} \right] = 0$$

$$\lambda_{w_2}(w_1, w_2) = \sum_{i=1}^{N} \left[\frac{y_i}{w_2} - \frac{1 - x_i - y_i}{1 - w_1 - w_2} \right] = 0$$

The only solution to these equations is given by $w_1 = \overline{x} = \sum_i x_i/N$, $w_2 = \overline{y} = \sum_i y_i/N$, which is the maximum likelihood value. The Hessian of $\lambda(w_1, w_2)$ at the ML value is given by

$$\lambda''(w_1, w_2) = \begin{pmatrix} \lambda''_{w_1 w_1} & \lambda''_{w_1 w_2} \\ \lambda''_{w_1 w_1} & \lambda''_{w_2 w_2} \end{pmatrix} =$$

$$-N \begin{pmatrix} \frac{1}{\overline{x}} + \frac{1}{1-\overline{x}-\overline{y}} & \frac{1}{1-\overline{x}-\overline{y}} \\ \frac{1}{1-\overline{x}-\overline{y}} & \frac{1}{\overline{y}} + \frac{1}{1-\overline{x}-\overline{y}} \end{pmatrix} \qquad (9)$$

This Hessian matrix decomposes into the sum of two matrices. One matrix is a diagonal matrix with positive numbers $1/\overline{x}$ and $1/\overline{y}$ on the diagonal. The second matrix is a constant matrix in which all elements equal the positive number $1/(1 - \overline{x} - \overline{y})$. Because these two matrices are positive and non-negative definite, respectively, the Hessian is positive definite. This argument also holds when X_i has more than three values.

Because the maximum likelihood equation has a single solution, and the Hessian is positive definite, and because as N increases the peak becomes sharper (Eq.9), all the conditions for the general derivation of the BIC are met. Plugging the maximum likelihood value into Eq. 7, which is correct to $O(1)$, yields Eq. 1.

4. Assymptotics With Hidden Variables

Let us now consider the situation where S contains hidden variables. In this case, we can not use the derivation in the previous section, because the log-likelihood function $\log p(D_N|S^h, \boldsymbol{\theta})$ does not necessarily tend toward a *peak* as the sample size increases. Instead, the log-likelihood function can tend toward a *ridge*. Consider, for example, a network with one arc

$H \to X$ where H has two values h and $\bar{h}$ and X has two values x and $\bar{x}$. Assume that only values of X are observed—that is, H is hidden. Then, the likelihood function is given by $\prod_i w^{x_i}(1-w)^{1-x_i}$ where $w = \theta_h \theta_{x|h} + (1-\theta_h)\theta_{x|\bar{h}}$, and x_i is the indicator function that equals one if X gets value x in case i and zero otherwise. The parameter w is the true probability that $X = x$ unconditionally. The ML value is unique in terms of w: it attains its maximum when $w = \sum_i x_i/N$. Nonetheless, any solution for $\boldsymbol{\theta}$ to the equation

$$\sum_i x_i/N = \theta_h \theta_{x|h} + (1-\theta_h)\theta_{x|\bar{h}}$$

will maximize the likelihood of the data. In this sense, the network structure $H \to X$ has only one non-redundant parameter. In this section, we provide an informal argument describing how to identify a set of non-redundant parameters for any Bayesian network with hidden variables.

Given a Bayesian network for domain $\mathbf{X}$ with observable variables $\mathbf{O} \subset \mathbf{X}$, let $W = \{w_\mathbf{o}|\mathbf{o} \in \mathbf{O}\}$ denote the parameters of the true joint probability distribution of $\mathbf{O}$. Corresponding to every value of $\boldsymbol{\theta}$ is a value of W. That is, S defines a (smooth) map g from $\boldsymbol{\theta}$ to W. The range of g (with the exception of a measure-zero set of points) is a curved manifold M in the space defined by W.[1] Now, consider $g(\hat{\boldsymbol{\theta}})$, the image of all ML values of $\boldsymbol{\theta}$. In a small region around $g(\hat{\boldsymbol{\theta}})$, the manifold M will resemble Euclidean space with some dimension d. That is, in a small region around $g(\hat{\boldsymbol{\theta}})$, M will look like R^d with orthogonal coordinates $\Phi = \{\phi_1, \ldots, \phi_d\}$. Thus, the log-likelihood function written as a function of Φ—$\log p(D_N|\Phi)$—will become peaked as the sample size increases, and we can apply the BIC approximation:

$$\log p(D_N|S^h) \approx \log p(D_N|\hat{\Phi}, S^h) - \frac{d}{2}\log N \qquad (10)$$

Note that $\log p(D_N|\hat{\Phi}, S^h) = \log p(D_N|\hat{\boldsymbol{\theta}}, S^h)$.

It remains to understand what d is and how it can be found. When considering a linear transformation $j : R^n \to R^m$, the transformation is a matrix of size $n \times m$. The dimension d of the image of j equals the rank of the matrix. When $k : R^n \to R^m$ is a smooth mapping, it can be approximated locally as a linear transformation, where the Jacobian matrix $J(\mathbf{x})$ serves as the linear transformation matrix for the neighborhood of $\mathbf{x} \in R^n$. The dimension of the image of k in a small region around $k(\mathbf{x})$ is the rank of $J(\mathbf{x})$ (Spivak, 1979). This observation holds when the rank of the Jacobian matrix does not change in a small ball around $\mathbf{x}$, in which case $\mathbf{x}$ is called a *regular point*.

---

[1] For terminology and basic facts in differential geometry, see Spivak (1979).

Returning to our problem, the mapping from $\boldsymbol{\theta}$ to W is a polynomial function of $\boldsymbol{\theta}$. Thus, as the next theorem shows, the rank of the Jacobian matrix $\left[\frac{\partial \boldsymbol{\theta}}{\partial W}\right]$ is almost everywhere some fixed constant d, which we call the *regular rank* of the Jacobian matrix. This rank is the number of non-redundant parameters of S—that is, the dimension of S.

Theorem 1 *Let $\boldsymbol{\theta}$ be the parameters of a network S for variables $\mathbf{X}$ with observable variables $\mathbf{O} \subset \mathbf{X}$. Let W be the parameters of the true joint distribution of the observable variables. If each parameter in W is a polynomial function of $\boldsymbol{\theta}$, then* $\operatorname{rank}\left[\frac{\partial \boldsymbol{\theta}}{\partial W}(\boldsymbol{\theta})\right] = d$ *almost everywhere, where d is a constant.*

Proof: Because the mapping from $\boldsymbol{\theta}$ to W is polynomial, each entry in the matrix $J(\boldsymbol{\theta}) = \left[\frac{\partial \boldsymbol{\theta}}{\partial W}(\boldsymbol{\theta})\right]$ is a polynomial in $\boldsymbol{\theta}$. When diagonalizing J, the leading elements of the first d lines remain polynomials in $\boldsymbol{\theta}$, whereas all other lines, which are dependent given every value of $\boldsymbol{\theta}$, become identically zero. The rank of $J(\boldsymbol{\theta})$ falls below d only for values of $\boldsymbol{\theta}$ that are roots of some of the polynomials in the diagonalized matrix. The set of all such roots has measure zero. $\square$

Our heuristic argument for Eq. 10 does not provide us with the error term. Researchers have shown that $O_p(1)$ relative errors are attainable for a variety of statistical models (e.g., Schwarz, 1978, and Haughton, 1988). Although the arguments of these researchers do not directly apply to our case, it may be possible to extend their methods to prove our conjecture.

5. Computations of the Rank

We have argued that the second term of the BIC for Bayesian networks with hidden variables is the rank of the Jacobian matrix of the transformation between the parameters of the network and the parameters of the observable variables. In this section, we explain how to compute this rank, and demonstrate the approach with several examples.

Theorem 1 suggests a random algorithm for calculating the rank. Compute the Jacobian matrix $J(\boldsymbol{\theta})$ symbolically from the equation $W = g(\boldsymbol{\theta})$. This computation is possible since g is a vector of polynomials in $\boldsymbol{\theta}$. Then, assign a random value to $\boldsymbol{\theta}$ and diagonalize the numeric matrix $J(\boldsymbol{\theta})$. Theorem 1 guarantees that, with probability 1, the resulting rank is the regular rank of J. For every network, select—say—ten values for $\boldsymbol{\theta}$, and determine r to be the maximum of the resulting ranks. In all our experiments, *none* of the randomly chosen values for $\boldsymbol{\theta}$ accidentally reduced the rank.

We now demonstrate the computation of the needed rank for a naive Bayes model with one hidden variable H and two feature variables X_1 and X_2. Assume all three variables are binary. The set of parameters $W = g(\boldsymbol{\theta})$

$$
\begin{pmatrix}
\theta_h\theta_{x_2|h} & \theta_h\theta_{x_1|h} & (1-\theta_h)\theta_{x_2|\bar{h}} & (1-\theta_h)\theta_{x_1|\bar{h}} & \theta_{x_1|h}\theta_{x_2|h} - \theta_{x_1|\bar{h}}\theta_{x_2|\bar{h}} \\
-\theta_h\theta_{x_2|h} & \theta_h\theta_{\bar{x}_1|h} & -(1-\theta_h)\theta_{x_2|\bar{h}} & (1-\theta_h)\theta_{\bar{x}_1|\bar{h}} & \theta_{\bar{x}_1|h}\theta_{x_2|h} - \theta_{\bar{x}_1|\bar{h}})\theta_{x_2|\bar{h}} \\
(1-\theta_h\theta_{x_2|h}) & -\theta_h\theta_{x_1|h} & (1-\theta_h)\theta_{\bar{x}_2|\bar{h}} & -(1-\theta_h)\theta_{x_1|\bar{h}} & \theta_{x_1|h}\theta_{\bar{x}_2|h} - \theta_{x_1|\bar{h}}\theta_{\bar{x}_2|\bar{h}})
\end{pmatrix}
$$

Figure 1.   The Jacobian matrix for a naive Bayesian network with two binary feature nodes

is given by

$$
w_{x_1x_2} = \theta_h\theta_{x_1|h}\theta_{x_2|h} + (1-\theta_h)\theta_{x_1|\bar{h}}\theta_{x_2|\bar{h}}
$$

$$
w_{\bar{x}_1x_2} = \theta_h(1-\theta_{x_1|h})\theta_{x_2|h} + (1-\theta_h)(1-\theta_{x_1|\bar{h}})\theta_{x_2|\bar{h}}
$$

$$
w_{x_1\bar{x}_2} = \theta_h\theta_{x_1|h}(1-\theta_{x_2|h}) + (1-\theta_h)\theta_{x_1|\bar{h}}(1-\theta_{x_2|\bar{h}})
$$

The 3×5 Jacobian matrix for this transformation is given in Figure 5 where $\theta_{\bar{x}_i|h} = 1 - \theta_{x_i|h}$ $(i = 1,2)$. The columns correspond to differentiation with respect to $\theta_{x_1|h}, \theta_{x_2|h}, \theta_{x_1|\bar{h}}, \theta_{x_2|\bar{h}}$ and θ_h, respectively. A symbolic computation of the rank of this matrix can be carried out; and it shows that the regular rank is equal to the dimension of the matrix—namely, 3. Nonetheless, as we have argued, in order to compute the regular rank, one can simply choose random values for $\boldsymbol{\theta}$ and diagonalize the resulting numerical matrix. We have done so for naive Bayes models with one binary hidden root node and $n \le 7$ binary observable non-root nodes. The size of the associated matrices is $(1+2n) \times (2^n - 1)$. The regular rank for $n = 3,\ldots,7$ was found to be $1+2n$. We conjecture that $1+2n$ is the regular rank for all $n > 2$. For $n = 1,2$, the rank is 1 and 3, respectively, which is the size of the full parameter space over one and two binary variables. The rank can not be greater than $1 + 2n$ because this is the maximum possible dimension of the Jacobian matrix. In fact, we have proven a lower bound of $2n$ as well.

Theorem 2 *Let S be a naive Bayes model with one binary hidden root node and $n > 2$ binary observable non-root nodes. Then*

$$
2n \le r \le 2n + 1
$$

where r is the regular rank of the Jacobian matrix between the parameters of the network and the parameters of the feature variables.

The proof is obtained by diagonalizing the Jacobian matrix symbolically, and showing that there are at least $2n$ independent lines.

The computation for $3 \le n \le 7$ shows that, for naive Bayes models with a binary hidden root node, there are no redundant parameters. Therefore, the best way to represent a probability distribution that is representable by such a model is to use the network representation explicitly.

Nonetheless, this result does not hold for all models. For example, consider the following *W structure*:

$$A \rightarrow C \leftarrow H \rightarrow D \leftarrow B$$

where H is hidden. Assuming all five variables are binary, the space over the observables is representable by 15 parameters, and the number of parameters of the network is 11. In this example, we could not compute the rank symbolically. Instead, we used the following Mathematica code.

There are 16 functions (only 15 are independent) defined by $W = g(\boldsymbol{\theta})$. In the Mathematica code, we use $fijkl$ for the true joint probability $w_{a=i,b=j,c=k,d=l}$, cij for the true conditional probability $\theta_{c=0|a=i,h=j}$, dij for $\theta_{d=0|b=i,h=j}$, a for $\theta_{a=0}$, b for $\theta_{b=0}$, and $h0$ for $\theta_{h=0}$.

The first function is given by

$$f0000\,[a\_, b\_, h0\_, c00\_, \ldots, c11\_, d00\_, \ldots, d11\_] :=$$
$$a * b * (h0 * c00 * d00 + (1 - h0) * c01 * d01)$$

and the other functions are similarly written. The Jacobian matrix is computed by the command *Outer*, which has three arguments. The first is D which stands for the differentiation operator, the second is a set of functions, and the third is a set of variables.

$$J\,[a\_, b\_, h0\_, c00\_, \ldots, c11\_, d00\_, \ldots, d11\_] :=$$
$$Outer[D, \{f0000\,[a, b, h0, c00, c01, \ldots, d11],$$
$$f0001\,[a, b, h0, c00, \ldots, c11, d00, \ldots, d11],$$
$$\ldots,$$
$$f1111\,[a, b, h0, c00, \ldots, c11, d00, \ldots, d11]\},$$
$$\{a, b, h0, c00, c01, c10, c11, d00, d01, d10, d11\}]$$

The next command produces a diagonalized matrix at a random point with a precision of 30 decimal digits. This precision was selected so that matrix elements equal to zero would be correctly identified as such.

$$N[RowReduce[J[a, b, h0, c00, \ldots, c11, d00, \ldots, d11]/.\{$$
$$a \rightarrow \text{Random[Integer}, \{1, 999\}]/1000,$$
$$b \rightarrow \text{Random[Integer}, \{1, 999\}]/1000,$$
$$\ldots,$$
$$d11 \rightarrow \text{Random[Integer}, \{1, 999\}]/1000\}], 30]$$

The result of this Mathematica program was a diagonalized matrix with 9 non-zero rows and 7 rows containing all zeros. The same counts were obtained in ten runs of the program. Hence, the regular rank of this Jacobian matrix is 9 with probability 1.

The interpretation of this result is that, around almost every value of $\boldsymbol{\theta}$, one can locally represent the hidden W structure with only 9 parameters. In contrast, if we encode the distribution using the network parameters ($\boldsymbol{\theta}$) of the W structure, then we must use 11 parameters. Thus, two of the network parameters are locally redundant. The BIC approximation punishes this W structure according to its most efficient representation, which uses 9 parameters, and not according to the representation given by the W structure, which requires 11 parameters.

It is interesting to note that the dimension of the W structure is 10 if H has three *or* four states, and 11 if H has 5 states. We do not know how to predict when the dimension changes as a result of increasing the number of hidden states without computing the dimension explicitly. Nonetheless, the dimension can not increase beyond 12, because we can average out the hidden variable in the W structure (e.g., using arc reversals) to obtain another network structure that has only 12 parameters.

6. AutoClass

The AutoClass clustering algorithm developed by Cheeseman and Stutz (1995) uses a naive Bayes model.[2] Each state of the hidden root node H represents a cluster or class; and each observable node represents a measurable feature. The number of classes k is unknown a priori. AutoClass computes an approximation of the marginal likelihood of a naive Bayes model given the data using increasing values of k. When this probability reaches a peak for a specific k, that k is selected as the number of classes.

Cheeseman and Stutz (1995) use the following formula to approximate the marginal likelihood:

$$\log p(D|S) \approx$$
$$\log p(D_c|S) + \log p(D|S, \hat{\boldsymbol{\theta}}_s) - \log p(D_c|S, \hat{\boldsymbol{\theta}}_s)$$

where D_c is a database consistent with the expected sufficient statistics as computed by the EM algorithm. Although Cheeseman and Stutz suggested this approximation in the context of simple AutoClass models, it can be used to score any Bayesian network with discrete variables as well as other models (Chickering and Heckerman, 1996). We call this approximation the *CS scoring function*.

Using the BIC approximation for $p(D_c|S)$, we obtain

$$\log p(D|S) \approx \log p(D|S, \hat{\boldsymbol{\theta}}_s) - d'/2 \log N$$

---

[2]The algorithm can handle conditional dependencies among continuous variables.

where d' is the number of parameters of the network. (Given a naive Bayes model with k classes and n observable variables each with b states, $d' = nk(b-1) + k - 1$.) Therefore, the CS scoring function will converge asymptotically to the BIC and hence to $p(D|S)$ whenever d' is equal to the regular rank of S (d). Given our conjecture in the previous section, we believe that the CS scoring function will converge to $p(D|S)$ when the number of classes is two. Nonetheless, d' is not always equal to d. For example, when $b = 2, k = 3$ and $n = 4$, the number of parameters is 14, but the regular rank of the Jacobian matrix is 13. We computed this rank using Mathematica as described in the previous section. Consequently, the CS scoring function will not always converge to $p(D|S)$.

This example is the only one that we have found so far; and we believe that incorrect results are obtained only for rare combinations of b, k and n. Nonetheless, a simple modification to the CS scoring function yields an approximation that will asymptotically converge to $p(D|S)$:

$$\log p(D|S) \approx \log p(D_c|S) + \log p(D|S, \hat{\boldsymbol{\theta}}_s) - \\ \log p(D_c|S, \hat{\boldsymbol{\theta}}_s) - d/2 \log N + d'/2 \log N$$

Chickering and Heckerman (1996) show that this scoring function is often a better approximation for $p(D|S)$ than is the BIC.

7. Gaussian Networks

In this section, we consider the case where each of the variables $\{X_1, \ldots, X_n\} = \mathbf{X}$ are continuous. As before, let $(S, \boldsymbol{\theta}_s)$ be a Bayesian network, where S is the network structure of the Bayesian network, and $\boldsymbol{\theta}_s$ is a set of parameters associated with the network structure. A Gaussian network is one in which the joint likelihood is that of a multivariate Gaussian distribution that is a product of local likelihoods. Each local likelihood is the linear regression model

$$p(x_i|\mathbf{pa}_i, \boldsymbol{\theta}_i, S) = N(m_i + \Sigma_{X_j \in \mathbf{Pa}_i} b_{ji} x_j, v_i)$$

where $N(\mu, v)$ is a normal (Gaussian) distribution with mean μ and variance $v > 0$, m_i is a conditional mean of X_i, b_{ji} is a coefficient that represents the strength of the relationship between variable X_j and X_i, v_i is a variance,[3] and $\boldsymbol{\theta}_i$ is the set of parameters consisting of m_i, v_i, and the b_{ji}. The parameters $\boldsymbol{\theta}_s$ of a Gaussian network with structure S is the set of all $\boldsymbol{\theta}_i$.

---

[3] m_i is the mean of X_i conditional on all parents being zero, b_{ji} corresponds to the partial regression coefficient of X_i on X_j given the other parents of X_i, and v_i corresponds to the residual variance of X_i given the parents of X_i.

To apply the techniques developed in this paper, we also need to specify the parameters of the observable variables. Given that the joint distribution is multivariate-normal and that multivariate-normal distributions are closed under marginalization, we only need to specify a vector of means for the observed variables and a covariance matrix over the observed variables. In addition, we need to specify how to transform the parameters of the network to the observable parameters. The transformation of the means and the transformation to obtain the observable covariance matrix can be accomplished via the *trek-sum rule* (for a discussion, see Glymour et al. 1987).

Using the trek-sum rule, it is easy to show that the observable parameters are all sums of products of the network parameters. Given that the mapping from $\boldsymbol{\theta}_s$ to the observable parameters is W is a polynomial function of $\boldsymbol{\theta}$, it follows from Thm. 1 that the rank of the Jacobian matrix $\left[\frac{\partial \boldsymbol{\theta}_s}{\partial W}\right]$ is almost everywhere some fixed constant d, which we again call the *regular rank* of the Jacobian matrix. This rank is the number of non-redundant parameters of S—that is, the dimension of S.

Let us consider two Gaussian models. We use Mathematica code similar to the code in Section 5 to compute their dimensions, because we can not perform the computation symbolically. As in the previous experiments, none of the randomly chosen values of $\boldsymbol{\theta}_s$ accidentally reduces the rank.

Our first example is the naive-Bayes model

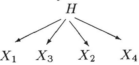

in which H is the hidden variable and the X_i are observed. There are 14 network parameters: 5 conditional variances, 5 conditional means, and 4 linear parameters. The marginal distribution for the observed variables also has 14 parameters: 4 means, 4 variances, and 6 covariances. Nonetheless, the analysis of the rank of the Jacobian matrix tells us that the dimension of this model is 12. This follows from the fact that this model imposes *tetrad* constraints (see Glymour et al. 1987). In this model the three tetrad constraints that hold in the distribution over the observed variables are

$$cov(X_1, X_2)cov(X_3, X_4) - cov(X_1, X_3)cov(X_2, X_4) = 0$$
$$cov(X_1, X_4)cov(X_2, X_3) - cov(X_1, X_3)cov(X_2, X_4) = 0$$
$$cov(X_1, X_4)cov(X_2, X_3) - cov(X_1, X_2)cov(X_3, X_4) = 0$$

two of which are independent. These two independent tetrad constraints lead to the reduction of dimensionality.

Our second example is the W structure described in Section 5 where each of the variables is continuous. There are 14 network parameters: 5 conditional means, 5 conditional variances, and 4 linear parameters. The marginal distribution for the observed variables has 14 parameters, whereas the analysis of the rank of the Jacobian matrix tells us that the dimension of this model is 12. This coincides with the intuition that many values for the variance of H and the linear parameters for $C \leftarrow H$ and $H \rightarrow D$ produce the same model for the observable variables, but once any two of these parameters are appropriately set, then the third parameter is uniquely determined by the marginal distribution for the observable variables.

8. Sigmoid Networks

Finally, let us consider the case where each of the variables $\{X_1, \ldots, X_n\} = \mathbf{X}$ is binary (discrete), and each local likelihood is the generalized linear model

$$p(x_i|\mathbf{pa}_i, \boldsymbol{\theta}_i, S) = \mathrm{Sig}(a_i + \Sigma_{X_j \in \mathbf{Pa}_i} b_{ji} x_j)$$

where $\mathrm{Sig}(x)$ is the *sigmoid function* $\mathrm{Sig}(x) = \frac{1}{1+e^{-x}}$. These models, which we call *sigmoid networks*, are useful for learning relationships among discrete variables, because these models capture non-linear relationships among variables yet employ only a small number of parameters (Neal, 1992; Saul et al., 1996).

Using techniques similar to those in Section 5, we can compute the rank of the Jacobian matrix $\left[\frac{\partial \boldsymbol{\theta}_s}{\partial W}\right]$. We can not apply Thm. 1 to conclude that this rank is almost everywhere some fixed constant, because the local likelihoods are non-polynomial sigmoid functions. Nonetheless, the claim of Thm. 1 holds also for analytic transformations, hence a regular rank exists for sigmoid networks as well (as confirmed by our experiments).

Our experiments show expected reductions in rank for several sigmoid networks. For example, consider the two-level network

H_1 H_2

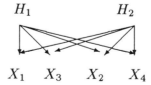

X_1 X_3 X_2 X_4

This network has 14 parameters. In each of 10 trials, we found the rank of the Jacobian matrix to be 14, indicating that this model has dimension 14. In contrast, consider the three-level network.

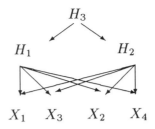

This network has 17 parameters, whereas the dimension we compute is 15. This reduction is expected, because we could encode the dependency between the two variables in the middle level by removing the variable in the top layer and adding an arc between these two variables, producing a network with 15 parameters.

References

Bouckaert, R. (1995). *Bayesian belief networks: From construction to inference.* PhD thesis, University Utrecht.

Buntine, W. (1994). Operations for learning with graphical models. *Journal of Artificial Intelligence Research,* 2:159–225.

Buntine, W. (1996). A guide to the literature on learning graphical models. *IEEE Transactions on Knowledge and Data Engineering,* 8:195–210.

Cheeseman, P. and Stutz, J. (1995). Bayesian classification (AutoClass): Theory and results. In Fayyad, U., Piatesky-Shapiro, G., Smyth, P., and Uthurusamy, R., editors, *Advances in Knowledge Discovery and Data Mining,* pages 153–180. AAAI Press, Menlo Park, CA.

Chickering, D. and Heckerman, D. (1996). Efficient approximations for the marginal likelihood of incomplete data given a Bayesian network. In *Proceedings of Twelfth Conference on Uncertainty in Artificial Intelligence,* Portland, OR, pages 158–168. Morgan Kaufmann.

Cooper, G. and Herskovits, E. (1992). A Bayesian method for the induction of probabilistic networks from data. *Machine Learning,* 9:309–347.

Geiger, D. and Heckerman, D. (1995). A characterization of the Dirichlet distribution with application to learning Bayesian networks. In *Proceedings of Eleventh Conference on Uncertainty in Artificial Intelligence,* Montreal, QU, pages 196–207. Morgan Kaufmann. See also Technical Report TR-95-16, Microsoft Research, Redmond, WA, February 1995.

Glymour, C., Scheines, R., Spirtes, P., and Kelly, K. (1987). *Discovering Causal Structure.* Acedemic Press.

Haughton, D. (1988). On the choice of a model to fit data from an exponential family. *Annals of Statistics,* 16:342–355.

Heckerman, D. (1995a). A tutorial on learning Bayesian networks. Technical Report MSR-TR-95-06, Microsoft Research, Redmond, WA. Revised November, 1996.

Heckerman, D. (1995b). A Bayesian approach for learning causal networks. In *Proceedings of Eleventh Conference on Uncertainty in Artificial Intelligence,* Montreal, QU, pages 285–295. Morgan Kaufmann.

Heckerman, D., Geiger, D., and Chickering, D. (1995). Learning Bayesian networks: The combination of knowledge and statistical data. *Machine Learning,* 20:197–243.

Herskovits, E. (1991). *Computer-based probabilistic network construction.* PhD thesis, Medical Information Sciences, Stanford University, Stanford, CA.

Lam, W. and Bacchus, F. (1993). Using causal information and local measures to learn

Bayesian networks. In *Proceedings of Ninth Conference on Uncertainty in Artificial Intelligence,* Washington, DC, pages 243–250. Morgan Kaufmann.

Neal, R. (1992). Connectionist learning of belief networks. *Artificial Intelligence,* 56:71–113.

Rissanen, J. (1987). Stochastic complexity (with discussion). *Journal of the Royal Statistical Society, Series B,* 49:223–239 and 253–265.

Saul, L., Jaakkola, T., and Jordan, M. (1996). Mean field theory for sigmoid belief networks. *Journal of Artificial Intelligence Research,* 4:61–76.

Schwarz, G. (1978). Estimating the dimension of a model. *Annals of Statistics,* 6:461–464.

Spiegelhalter, D., Dawid, A., Lauritzen, S., and Cowell, R. (1993). Bayesian analysis in expert systems. *Statistical Science,* 8:219–282.

Spiegelhalter, D. and Lauritzen, S. (1990). Sequential updating of conditional probabilities on directed graphical structures. *Networks,* 20:579–605.

Spivak, M. (1979). *A Comprehensive Introduction to Differential Geometry 1, 2nd edition.* Publish or Perish, Berkeley, CA.

Suzuki, J. (1993). A construction of Bayesian networks from databases based on an MDL scheme. In *Proceedings of Ninth Conference on Uncertainty in Artificial Intelligence,* Washington, DC, pages 266–273. Morgan Kaufmann.

A HIERARCHICAL COMMUNITY OF EXPERTS

GEOFFREY E. HINTON

BRIAN SALLANS

AND

ZOUBIN GHAHRAMANI
Department of Computer Science
University of Toronto
Toronto, Ontario, Canada M5S 3H5
{hinton,sallans,zoubin}@cs.toronto.edu

Abstract. We describe a directed acyclic graphical model that contains a hierarchy of linear units and a mechanism for dynamically selecting an appropriate subset of these units to model each observation. The non-linear selection mechanism is a hierarchy of binary units each of which gates the output of one of the linear units. There are no connections from linear units to binary units, so the generative model can be viewed as a logistic belief net (Neal 1992) which selects a skeleton linear model from among the available linear units. We show that Gibbs sampling can be used to learn the parameters of the linear and binary units even when the sampling is so brief that the Markov chain is far from equilibrium.

1. Multilayer networks of linear-Gaussian units

We consider hierarchical generative models that consist of multiple layers of simple, stochastic processing units connected to form a directed acyclic graph. Each unit receives incoming, weighted connections from units in the layer above and it also has a bias (see figure 1). The weights on the connections and the biases are adjusted to maximize the likelihood that the layers of "hidden" units would produce some observed data vectors in the bottom layer of "visible" units.

The simplest kind of unit we consider is a linear-Gaussian unit. Following the usual Bayesian network formalism, the joint probability of the

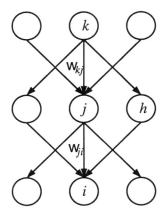

Figure 1.   Units in a belief network.

states of all the units in the network is the product of the local probability of each unit given the states of its parents, which for layered networks are the units in the layer above. The state of each unit in the top layer has a Gaussian distribution with a learned mean and variance. Given the states, y_k of units in the top layer, we can compute the top-down input, $\hat{y}_j$ to each unit, j, in the next layer down:

$$\hat{y}_j = b_j + \sum_k w_{kj} y_k \qquad (1)$$

where b_j is the bias of unit j, k is an index over all units in the layer above and w_{kj} is the weight on the top-down connection from k to j. The state of unit j is then Gaussian distributed with mean $\hat{y}_j$ and a variance σ_j^2 that is learned from data.

The generative model underlying factor analysis (Everitt, 1984) consists of one hidden layer of linear-Gaussian units (the factors) that send weighted connections (the factor loadings) to a visible layer of linear-Gaussian units.

Linear models with Gaussian noise have two important advantages: They often provide good models of continuous data and they are easy to fit even when many of the linear variables are unobserved. Given the states of any subset of the linear units it is tractable to compute the posterior distribution across the unobserved units and once this distribution is known, it is straightforward to use the EM algorithm to update all the parameters of the model. Unfortunately, linear models ignore all the higher order statistical structure in the data so they are inappropriate for tasks like vision in which higher-order structure is crucial.

One sensible way to extend linear models is to use a mixture of M of them (Ghahramani and Hinton, 1996; Hinton et al., 1997). This retains tractability because the full posterior distribution can be found by computing the posterior across each of the M models and then normalizing. However, a mixture of linear models is not flexible enough to represent the kind of data that is typically found in images. If an image can have several different objects in it, the pixel intensities cannot be accurately modelled by a mixture unless there is a separate linear model for each possible *combination* of objects. Clearly, the efficient way to represent an image that contains n objects is to use a "distributed" representation that contains n separate parts, but this cannot be achieved using a mixture because the non-linear selection process in a mixture consists of picking *one* of the linear models. What we need is a non-linear selection process that can pick arbitrary subsets of the available linear-Gaussian units so that some units can be used for modelling one part of an image, other units can be used for modelling other parts, and higher level units can be used for modelling the redundancies between the different parts.

2. Multilayer networks of binary-logistic units

Multilayer networks of binary-logistic units in which the connections form a directed acyclic graph were investigated by Neal (1992). We call them logistic belief nets or LBN's. In the generative model, each unit computes its top-down input, $\hat{s}_j$, in the same way as a linear-Gaussian unit, but instead of using this top-down input as the mean of a Gaussian distribution it uses it to determine the probability of adopting each if the two states 1 and 0:

$$\hat{s}_j = b_j + \sum_k w_{kj} s_k \tag{2}$$

$$p(s_j = 1 | \{s_k : k \in \mathrm{pa}_j\}) = \sigma(\hat{s}_j) = \frac{1}{1 + e^{-\hat{s}_j}} \tag{3}$$

where pa_j is the set of units that send generative connections to unit j (the "parents" of j), and $\sigma(\cdot)$ is the logistic function. A binary-logistic unit does not need a separate variance parameter because the single statistic $\hat{s}_j$ is sufficient to define a Bernouilli distribution.

Unfortunately, it is exponentially expensive to compute the exact posterior distribution over the hidden units of an LBN when given a data point, so Neal used Gibbs sampling: With a particular data point clamped on the visible units, the hidden units are visited one at a time. Each time hidden unit u is visited, its state is stochastically selected to be 1 or 0 in proportion to two probabilities. The first, $P^{\alpha \setminus s_u = 1} = p(s_u = 1, \{s_k^\alpha : k \neq u\})$ is the joint probability of generating the states of all the units in the network (including u) if u has state 1 and all the others have the state defined by the current configuration of states, α. The second, $P^{\alpha \setminus s_u = 0}$, is the same quantity if u has state 0. When calculating these probabilities, the states of all the other units are held constant. It can be shown that repeated application of this stochastic decision rule eventually leads to hidden state configurations being selected according to their posterior probabilities.

Because the LBN is acyclic it is easy to compute the joint probability P^α of a configuration, α, of states of all the units.

$$P^\alpha = \prod_i p(s_i^\alpha | \{s_k^\alpha : k \in \mathrm{pa}_i\} \tag{4}$$

where s_i^α is the binary state of unit i in configuration α.

It is convenient to work in the domain of negative log probabilities which are called energies by analogy with statistical physics. We define E^α to be $-\ln P^\alpha$.

$$E^\alpha = - \sum_u \left(s_u^\alpha \ln \hat{s}_u^\alpha + (1 - s_u^\alpha) \ln(1 - \hat{s}_u^\alpha) \right) \tag{5}$$

where s_u^α is the binary state of unit u in configuration α, $\hat{s}_u^\alpha$ is the top-down expectation generated by the layer above, and u is an index over all the units in the net.

The rule for stochastically picking a new state for u requires the ratio of two probabilities and hence the difference of two energies

$$\Delta E_u^\alpha = E^{\alpha \backslash s_u=0} - E^{\alpha \backslash s_u=1} \tag{6}$$

$$p(s_u = 1 | \{s_k^\alpha : k \neq u\}) = \sigma(\Delta E_u^\alpha) \tag{7}$$

All the contributions to the energy of configuration α that do not depend on s_j can be ignored when computing ΔE_j^α. This leaves a contribution that depends on the top-down expectation $\hat{s}_j$ generated by the units in the layer above (see Eq. 3) and a contribution that depends on both the states, s_i, and the top-down expectations, $\hat{s}_i$, of units in the layer below (see figure 1)

$$\Delta E_j^\alpha = \ln \hat{s}_j^\alpha - \ln(1 - \hat{s}_j^\alpha) + \sum_i \left[s_i^\alpha \ln \hat{s}_i^{\alpha \backslash s_j=1} + (1 - s_i^\alpha) \ln \left(1 - \hat{s}_i^{\alpha \backslash s_j=1} \right) \right.$$
$$\left. - s_i^\alpha \ln \hat{s}_i^{\alpha \backslash s_j=0} - (1 - s_i^\alpha) \ln \left(1 - \hat{s}_i^{\alpha \backslash s_j=0} \right) \right] \tag{8}$$

Given samples from the posterior distribution, the generative weights of a LBN can be learned by using the online delta rule which performs gradient ascent in the log likelihood of the data:

$$\Delta w_{ji} = \epsilon s_j (s_i - \hat{s}_i) \tag{9}$$

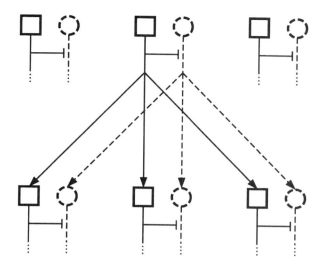

Figure 2. Units in a community of experts, a network of paired binary and linear units. Binary units (solid squares) gate the outputs of corresponding linear units (dashed circles) and also send generative connections to the binary units in the layer below. Linear units send generative connections to linear units in the layer below (dashed arrows).

3. Using binary units to gate linear units

It is very wasteful to use highly non-linear binary units to model data that is generated from continuous physical processes that behave linearly over small ranges. So rather than using a multilayer binary network to generate data directly, we use it to synthesize an appropriate linear model by selecting from a large set of available linear units. We pair a binary unit with each hidden linear unit (figure 2) and we use the same subscript for both units within a pair. We use y for the real-valued state of the linear unit and s for the state of the binary unit. The binary unit gates the output of the linear unit so Eq. 1 becomes:

$$\hat{y}_j = b_j + \sum_k w_{kj} y_k s_k \qquad (10)$$

It is straightforward to include weighted connections from binary units to linear units in the layer below, but this was not implemented in the examples we describe later. To make Gibbs sampling feasible (see below) we prohibit connections from linear units to binary units, so in the generative model the states of the binary units are unaffected by the linear units and are chosen using Eq. 2 and Eq. 3. Of course, during the inference process the states of the linear units do affect the states of the binary units.

Given a data vector on the visible units, it is intractable to compute the posterior distribution over the hidden linear and binary units, so an approximate inference method must be used. This raises the question of whether the learning will be adversely affected by the approximation errors that occur during inference. For example, if we use Gibbs sampling for inference and the sampling is too brief for the samples to come from the equilibrium distribution, will the learning fail to converge? We show in section 6 that it is not necessary for the brief Gibbs sampling to approach equilibrium. The only property we really require of the sampling is that it get us closer to equilibrium. Given this property we can expect the learning to improve a bound on the log probability of the data.

3.1. PERFORMING GIBBS SAMPLING

The obvious way to perform Gibbs sampling is to visit units one at a time and to stochastically pick a new state for each unit from its posterior distribution given the current states of all the other units. For a binary unit we need to compute the energy of the network with the unit on or off. For a linear unit we need to compute the quadratic function that determines how the energy of the net depends on the state of the unit.

This obvious method has a significant disadvantage. If a linear unit, j, is gated out by its binary unit (*i.e.*, $s_j = 0$) it cannot influence the units below it in the net, but it still affects the Gibbs sampling of linear units like k that send inputs to it because these units attempt to minimize $(y_j - \hat{y}_j)^2/2\sigma_j^2$. So long as $s_j = 0$ there should be no net effect of y_j on the units in the layer above. These units completely determine the distribution of y_j, so sampling from y_j would provide no information about their distributions. The effect of y_j on the units in the layer above during inference is unfortunate because we hope that most of the linear units will be gated out most of the time and we do not want the teeming masses of unemployed linear units to disturb the delicate deliberations in the layer above. We can avoid this noise by integrating out the states of linear units that are gated out. Fortunately, the correct way to integrate out y_j is to simply ignore the energy contribution $(y_j - \hat{y}_j)^2/2\sigma_j^2$.

A second disadvantage of the obvious sampling method is that the decision about whether or not to turn on a binary unit depends on the particular value of its linear unit. Sampling converges to equilibrium faster if we integrate over all possible values of y_j when deciding how to set s_j. This integration is feasible because, given all other units, y_j has one Gaussian posterior distribution when $s_j = 1$ and another Gaussian distribution when $s_j = 0$. During Gibbs sampling, we therefore visit the binary unit in a pair first and integrate out the linear unit in deciding the state of the binary unit. If the binary unit gets turned on, we then pick a state for the linear unit from the relevant Gaussian posterior. If the binary unit is turned off it is unnecessary to pick a value for the linear unit.

For any given configuration of the binary units, it is tractable to compute the full posterior distribution over all the selected linear units. So one interesting possibility is to use Gibbs sampling to stochastically pick states for the binary units, but to integrate out *all* of the linear units when making these discrete decisions. To integrate out the states of the selected linear units we need to compute the exact log probability of the observed data using the selected linear units. The change in this log probability when one of the linear units is included or excluded is then used in computing the energy gap for deciding whether or not to select that linear unit. We have not implemented this method because it is not clear that it is worth the computational effort of integrating out all of the selected linear units at the beginning of the inference process when the states of some of the binary units are obviously inappropriate and can be improved easily by only integrating out one of the linear units.

Given samples from the posterior distribution, the incoming connection weights of both the binary and the linear units can be learned by using the online delta rule which performs gradient ascent in the log likelihood of the data. For the binary units the learning rule is Eq. 9. For linear units the rule is:

$$\Delta w_{ji} = \epsilon \, y_j s_j (y_i - \hat{y}_i) s_i / \sigma_i^2 \qquad (11)$$

The learning rule for the biases is obtained by treating a bias as a weight coming from a unit with a state of 1.[1]

The variance of the local noise in each linear unit, σ_j^2, can be learned by the online rule:

$$\Delta \sigma_j^2 = \epsilon \, s_j \left[(y_j - \hat{y}_j)^2 - \sigma_j^2 \right] \qquad (12)$$

Alternatively, σ_j^2 can be fixed at 1 for all hidden units and the effective local noise level can be controlled by scaling the incoming and outgoing weights.

4. Results on the bars task

The noisy bars task is a toy problem that demonstrates the need for sparse distributed representations (Hinton et al., 1995; Hinton and Ghahramani, 1997). There are four stages in generating each $K \times K$ image. First a global orientation is chosen, either horizontal or vertical, with both cases being equally probable. Given this choice, each of the K bars of the appropriate orientation is turned on independently with probability 0.4. Next, each active bar is given an intensity, chosen from a uniform distribution. Finally,

---

[1] We have used w_{ji} to denote both the weights from binary units to binary units and from linear units to linear units; the intended meaning should be inferred from the context.

independent Gaussian noise is added to each pixel. A sample of images generated in this way is shown in figure 3(a).

a   b

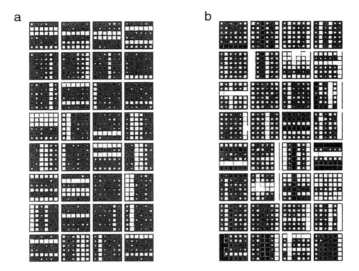

Figure 3.   a) Training data for the noisy bars problem. b) Images generated by the trained network. The area of each square represents the value of the corresponding pixel in the 6 × 6 images. White represents positive values and black represents negative values.

We trained a 3-layer network on the 6 × 6 noisy bars problem. The network consisted of one pair of units in the top hidden layer, where each pair consists of a linear-Gaussian unit gated by its corresponding binary logistic unit; 24 pairs of units in the first hidden layer; and 36 linear-Gaussian units in the visible layer. The network was trained for 12 passes through a data set of of 1000 images, with a learning rate of 0.04 and a weight decay parameter of 0.04. The images were presented in a different, random order for each pass.

For each image presented, 16 Gibbs sampling iterations were performed. Gibbs sampling was performed by visiting each pair of units in a layer in random order, where for each pair the binary unit was visited first, followed by the linear unit. Of the 16 network states visited, the first four were discarded, and the next 12 were used for learning. The weights from the linear units in the first hidden layer to the units in the visible layer were constrained to be positive. Without this constraint, the trained model still generates images from the correct distribution, but the solution is not so easily interpreted. The result of training is shown in figure 4.

The trained network is using 12 of the linear-Gaussian units in the first hidden layer to represent each of the 12 possible horizontal and vertical

a

b

c

d

e

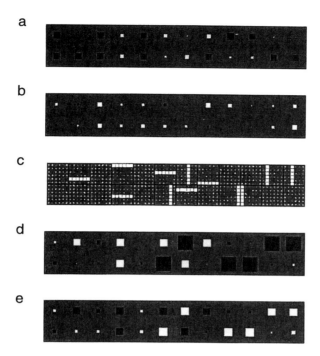

Figure 4. Generative weights and biases of a three-layered network after being trained on the noisy bars problem. a) Weights from the top layer linear-Gaussian unit to the 24 middle layer linear-Gaussian units. b) Biases of the middle layer linear units. c) Weights from the 24 middle layer linear units to the 36 visible units. d) Weights from the top layer binary logistic unit to the 24 middle layer binary logistic units. e) Biases of the middle layer binary logistic units.

bars. The top level binary unit is selecting the linear units in the first hidden layer that represent horizontal bars by exciting the corresponding binary units; these binary units are biased to be off otherwise. Similarly, the binary units that correspond to vertical bars, which are often active due to positive biases, are being inhibited by the top binary unit. The top linear unit is simply acting as an additional bias on the linear units in the first hidden layer. Examples of data generated by the trained network are shown in figure 3(b).

The network was shown novel images, and 10 iterations of Gibbs sampling were performed. After the final iteration, the top level binary unit was found to be off for 90% of vertical images, and on for 84% of horizontal images.

5. Results on handwritten digits

We trained a similar three-layer network on handwritten twos and threes from the CEDAR CDROM 1 database (Hull, 1994). The digits were scaled to an 8×8 grid, and the 256-gray-scale pixel values were rescaled to lie within $[0, 1]$. The 2000 digits were divided into a training set of 1400 digits, and a test set of 600 digits, with twos and threes being equally represented in both sets. A small subset of the training data is shown in figure 5(a).

a   b

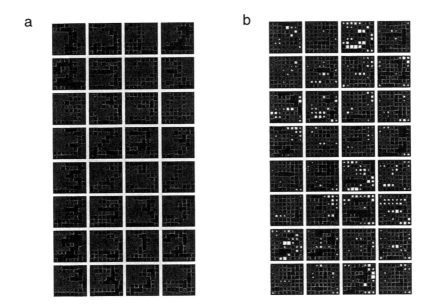

Figure 5. a) A subset of the training data. b) Images generated by the trained network. For clarity, black represents positive values in this figure.

The network consisted of a single pair of units in the top hidden layer, 24 pairs of units in the first hidden layer, and 64 linear-Gaussian units in the visible layer. During training, the network made 43 passes through the data set, with a learning rate of 0.01 and a weight decay parameter of 0.02. Gibbs sampling was performed as in the bars problem, with 4 discarded Gibbs sampling iterations, followed by 12 iterations used for learning. For this task, there were no constraints placed on the sign of the weights from the linear-Gaussian units in the first hidden layer to the units in the visible layer. The result of training is shown in figure 6.

In this case, the network uses all 24 linear units in the first hidden layer to represent digit features. Some of the features are global, while others are

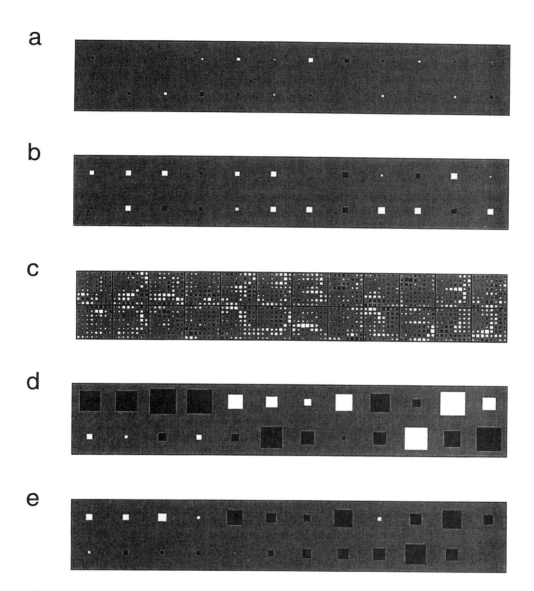

Figure 6. Generative weights and biases of a three-layered network after being trained on handwritten twos and threes. a) Weights from the top layer linear-Gaussian unit to the 24 middle layer linear-Gaussian units. b) Biases of the middle layer linear-Gaussian units. c) Weights from the 24 middle layer linear-Gaussian units to the 36 visible units. d) Weights from the top layer binary logistic unit to the 24 middle layer binary logistic units. e) Biases of the middle layer binary logistic units.

highly localized. The top binary unit is selecting the linear units in the first hidden layer that correspond to features found predominantly in threes, by exciting the corresponding binary units. Features that are exclusively used in twos are being gated out by the top binary unit, while features that can be shared between digits are being only slightly excited or inhibited. When the top binary unit is off, the features found in threes are are inhibited by strong negative biases, while features used in twos are gated in by positive biases on the corresponding binary units. Examples of data generated by the trained network are shown in figure 5(b).

The trained network was shown 600 test images, and 10 Gibbs sampling iterations were performed for each image. The top level binary unit was found to be off for 94% of twos, and on for 84% of threes. We then tried to improve classification by using prolonged Gibbs sampling. In this case, the first 300 Gibbs sampling iterations were discarded, and the activity of the top binary unit was averaged over the next 300 iterations. If the average activity of the top binary unit was above a threshold of 0.32, the digit was classified as a three; otherwise, it was classified as a two. The threshold was found by calculating the optimal threshold needed to classify 10 of the training samples under the same prolonged Gibbs sampling scheme. With prolonged Gibbs sampling, the average activity of the top binary unit was found to be below threshold for 96.7% of twos, and above threshold for 95.3% of threes, yielding an overall successful classification rate of 96% (with no rejections allowed). Histograms of the average activity of the top level binary unit are shown in figure 7.

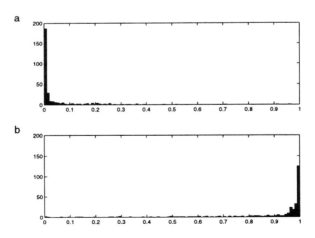

Figure 7. Histograms of the average activity of the top level binary unit, after prolonged Gibbs sampling, when shown novel handwritten twos and threes. a) Average activity for twos in the test set. b) Average activity for threes in the test set.

6. Why brief Gibbs sampling works

There are two major difficulties in using Gibbs sampling for maximum likelihood learning in a neural network:

1. The learning algorithm is usually derived by assuming that Gibbs sampling produces samples from the equilibrium distribution. But when the weights are large, there can be high energy barriers that make convergence to the equilibrium distribution very slow. Moreover, it is generally very hard to measure whether convergence has been achieved.

2. Even if the samples do come from the equilibrium distribution, non-uniform sampling noise can have unfortunate effects. The weights can be strongly repelled from regions where the sampling noise is high, even if the estimated gradient of the log likelihood with respect to the weights is unbiased. A familiar example of this phenomenon is that gravel accumulates at the sides of a road, even if the road is flat, because there is higher variance in the movement of the gravel where the traffic is. In networks with binary logistic units this effect causes the weights to be repelled from values that cause hidden units to be on about half the time, since they then have much higher variance than when they are firmly on or firmly off. This prevents uncommitted hidden units from sitting around in their middle range and following small gradients of the log likelihood. The variance repulsion causes them to wander into useless regions where they are always on or always off.

The sampling noise can easily be estimated by repeating exactly the same sampling procedure several times. It should then be possible for simple gradient methods to cancel out the effects of non-uniform variance by using a smaller learning rate when the variance in the estimated gradient is high.

The failure to approach equilibrium seems like a far less tractable problem than the sampling noise and makes Gibbs sampling seem an unpromising candidate as a model of real neural computation. Fortunately, the EM algorithm can be generalized so that each iteration improves a lower bound on the log likelihood (Neal and Hinton, 1993). In this form, the only property required of Gibbs sampling is that it get closer to equilibrium on each iteration. There is a sensible objective function for the learning that can be improved even if the sampling is far from equilibrium.

Suppose that Gibbs sampling produces a distribution Q over the hidden state configurations. We define the *free energy* of the network as the the expected energy under Q minus the entropy of Q:

$$F = \sum_\alpha Q_\alpha E_\alpha - \left(-\sum_\alpha Q_\alpha \ln Q_\alpha\right) \qquad (13)$$

If Q is the posterior distribution over hidden configurations given E, then F is equal to the negative log probability of the configuration of the visible units under the model defined by E. Otherwise, F exceeds the negative log probability of visible configuration by the Kullback-Leibler divergence between Q and P:

$$F = -\ln p(\text{visible}) + \sum_\alpha Q_\alpha \ln \frac{Q_\alpha}{P_\alpha} \qquad (14)$$

The EM algorithm consists of coordinate descent in F (Neal and Hinton, 1993): a full M step minimizes F with respect to the parameters that determine E, and a full E step minimizes F with respect to Q, which is achieved by setting Q equal to the posterior distribution over the hidden configurations given E.

A major advantage of viewing EM as coordinate descent in F is that it justifies partial E-steps which improve F without fully minimizing it with respect to the distribution Q. We define Q^t to be the distribution reached at the end of partial E-step t and E^t to be the energy function used during partial E-step t. Partial M-step t occurs after partial E-step t and updates the energy function to E^{t+1}.

To eliminate sampling noise, imagine that we have an infinite ensemble of identical networks so that we can compute the exact Q distribution produced by a few sweeps of Gibbs sampling. Provided we start the Gibbs sampling in each network from the hidden configuration at the end of the previous partial E-step we are guaranteed that $F^{t+1} \leq F^t$ because the gradient M-step ensures that:

$$\sum_\alpha Q_\alpha^t E_\alpha^{t+1} \leq \sum_\alpha Q_\alpha^t E_\alpha^t \qquad (15)$$

while Gibbs sampling, however brief, ensures that:

$$\sum_\alpha Q_\alpha^{t+1} E_\alpha^{t+1} + Q_\alpha^{t+1} \ln Q_\alpha^{t+1} \leq \sum_\alpha Q_\alpha^t E_\alpha^{t+1} + Q_\alpha^t \ln Q_\alpha^t. \qquad (16)$$

In practice, we try to approximate an infinite ensemble by using a very small learning rate in a single network so that many successive partial E-steps are performed using very similar energy functions. But it is still nice to know that with a sufficiently large ensemble it is possible for a simple learning algorithm to improve a bound on the log probability of the visible configurations even when the Gibbs sampling is far from equilibrium.

Changing the parameters can move the equilibrium distribution further from the current distribution of the Gibbs sampler. The E step ensures that the Gibbs sampler will chase this shifting equilibrium distribution. One worrisome consequence of this is that the equilibrium distribution may end up very far from the initial distribution of the Gibbs sampler. Therefore, when presented a new data point for which we don't have a previous remembered Gibbs sample, inference can take a very long time since the Gibbs sampler will have to reach equilibrium from its initial distribution.

There are at least three ways in which this problem can be finessed:

1. Explicitly learn a bottom-up initialization model. At each iteration t, the initialization model is used for a fast bottom-up recognition pass. The Gibbs sampler is initialized with the activities produced by this pass and proceeds from there. The bottom-up model is trained using the difference between the next sample produced by the Gibbs sampler and the activities it produced bottom-up.

2. Force inference to recapitulate learning. Assume that we store the sequence of weights during learning, from which we can obtain the sequence of corresponding energy functions. During inference, the Gibbs sampler is run using this sequence of energy functions. Since energy functions tend to get peakier during learning, this procedure should have an effect similar to annealing the temperature during sampling. Storing the entire sequence of weights may be impractical, but this procedure suggests a potentially interesting relationship between inference and learning.

3. Always start from the same distribution and sample briefly. The Gibbs sampler is initialized with the same distribution of hidden activities at each time step of learning and run for only a few iterations. This has the effect of penalizing models with an equilibrium distribution that is far from the distributions that the Gibbs sampler can reach in a few samples starting from its initial distribution.[2] We used this procedure in our simulations.

7. Conclusion

We have described a probabilistic generative model consisting of a hierarchical network of binary units that select a corresponding network of linear units. Like the mixture of experts (Jacobs et al., 1991; Jordan and Jacobs, 1994), the binary units gate the linear units, thereby choosing an appropriate set of linear units to model nonlinear data. However, unlike the mixture of experts, each linear unit is its own expert, and any subset of experts can

---

[2]The free energy, F, can be interpreted as a penalized negative log likelihood, where the penalty term is the Kullback-Leibler divergence between the approximating distribution Q_α and the equilibrium distribution (Eq. 14). During learning, the free energy can be decreased either by increasing the log likelihood of the model, or by decreasing this KL divergence. The latter regularizes the model towards the approximation.

be selected at once, so we call this network a hierarchical community of experts.

Acknowledgements

We thank Peter Dayan, Michael Jordan, Radford Neal and Michael Revow for many helpful discussions. This research was funded by NSERC and the Ontario Information Technology Research Centre. GEH is the Nesbitt-Burns Fellow of the Canadian Institute for Advanced Research.

References

Everitt, B. S. (1984). *An Introduction to Latent Variable Models*. Chapman and Hall, London.

Ghahramani, Z. and Hinton, G. E. (1996). The EM algorithm for mixtures of factor analyzers. Technical Report CRG-TR-96-1 [ftp://ftp.cs.toronto.edu/pub/zoubin/tr-96-1.ps.gz], Department of Computer Science, University of Toronto.

Hinton, G. E., Dayan, P., Frey, B. J., and Neal, R. M. (1995). The wake-sleep algorithm for unsupervised neural networks. *Science*, 268:1158–1161.

Hinton, G. E., Dayan, P., and Revow, M. (1997). Modeling the manifolds of Images of handwritten digits. *IEEE Trans. Neural Networks*, 8(1):65–74.

Hinton, G. E. and Ghahramani, Z. (1997). Generative models for discovering sparse distributed representations. *Phil. Trans. Roy. Soc. London B*, 352:1177–1190.

Hull, J. J. (1994). A database for handwritten text recognition research. *IEEE Transactions on Pattern Analysis and Machine Intelligence*, 16(5):550–554.

Jacobs, R. A., Jordan, M. I., Nowlan, S. J., and Hinton, G. E. (1991). Adaptive mixture of local experts. *Neural Computation*, 3:79–87.

Jordan, M. I. and Jacobs, R. (1994). Hierarchical mixtures of experts and the EM algorithm. *Neural Computation*, 6:181–214.

Neal, R. M. (1992). Connectionist learning of belief networks. *Artificial Intelligence*, 56:71–113.

Neal, R. M. and Hinton, G. E. (1993). A new view of the EM algorithm that justifies incremental and other variants. Unpublished manuscript [ftp://ftp.cs.utoronto.ca/pub/radford/em.ps.z], Department of Computer Science, University of Toronto.

AN INFORMATION-THEORETIC ANALYSIS OF HARD AND SOFT ASSIGNMENT METHODS FOR CLUSTERING

MICHAEL KEARNS
AT&T Labs – Research
Florham Park, New Jersey

YISHAY MANSOUR
Tel Aviv University
Tel Aviv, Israel

AND

ANDREW Y. NG
Massachusetts Institute of Technology
Cambridge, Massachusetts

Abstract. Assignment methods are at the heart of many algorithms for unsupervised learning and clustering — in particular, the well-known *K-means* and *Expectation-Maximization* (EM) algorithms. In this work, we study several different methods of assignment, including the "hard" assignments used by *K*-means and the "soft" assignments used by EM. While it is known that *K*-means minimizes the distortion on the data and EM maximizes the likelihood, little is known about the systematic differences of behavior between the two algorithms. Here we shed light on these differences via an information-theoretic analysis. The cornerstone of our results is a simple decomposition of the expected distortion, showing that *K*-means (and its extension for inferring general parametric densities from unlabeled sample data) must implicitly manage a trade-off between how similar the data assigned to each cluster are, and how the data are *balanced* among the clusters. How well the data are balanced is measured by the entropy of the partition defined by the hard assignments. In addition to letting us predict and verify systematic differences between *K*-means and EM on specific examples, the decomposition allows us to give a rather general argument showing that *K*-means will consistently find densities with less "overlap" than EM. We also study a third natural assignment method that we call *posterior* assignment, that is close in spirit to the soft assignments of EM, but leads to a surprisingly different algorithm.

1. Introduction

Algorithms for density estimation, clustering and unsupervised learning are an important tool in machine learning. Two classical algorithms are the K-*means* algorithm (MacQueen, 1967; Cover and Thomas, 1991; Duda and Hart, 1973) and the *Expectation-Maximization* (EM) algorithm (Dempster *et al.*, 1977). These algorithms have been applied in a wide variety of settings, including parameter estimation in hidden Markov models for speech recognition (Rabiner and Juang, 1993), estimation of conditional probability tables in belief networks for probabilistic inference (Lauritzen, 1995), and various clustering problems (Duda and Hart, 1973).

At a high level, K-means and EM appear rather similar: both perform a two-step iterative optimization, performed repeatedly until convergence. The first step is an *assignment* of data points to "clusters" or density models, and the second step is a *reestimation* of the clusters or density models based on the current assignments. The K-means and EM algorithms differ only in the manner in which they assign data points (the first step). Loosely speaking, in the case of two clusters [1], if P_0 and P_1 are density models for the two clusters, then K-means assigns x to P_0 if and only if $P_0(x) \geq P_1(x)$; otherwise x is assigned to P_1. We call this *hard* or *Winner-Take-All* (WTA) assignment. In contrast, EM assigns x fractionally, assigning x to P_0 with weight $P_0(x)/(P_0(x) + P_1(x))$, and assigning the "rest" of x to P_1. We call this *soft* or *fractional* assignment. A third natural alternative would be to again assign x to only one of P_0 and P_1 (as in K-means), but to *randomly* assign it, assigning to P_0 with *probability* $P_0(x)/(P_0(x) + P_1(x))$. We call this *posterior* assignment.

Each of these three assignment methods can be interpreted as classifying points as belonging to one (or more) of two distinct populations, solely on the basis of probabilistic models (densities) for these two populations. An alternative interpretation is that we have three different ways of inferring the value of a "hidden" (unobserved) variable, whose value would indicate which of two sources had generated an observed data point. How these assignment methods differ in the context of unsupervised learning is the subject of this paper.

In the context of unsupervised learning, EM is typically viewed as an algorithm for mixture density estimation. In classical density estimation, a finite training set of unlabeled data is used to derive a hypothesis density. The goal is for the hypothesis density to model the "true" sampling density as accurately as possible, typically as measured by the Kullback-Leibler

---

[1] Throughout the paper, we concentrate on the case of just two clusters or densities for simplicity of development. All of our results hold for the general case of K clusters or densities.

(KL) divergence. The EM algorithm can be used to find a *mixture* density model of the form $\alpha_0 P_0 + (1 - \alpha_0) P_1$. It is known that the mixture model found by EM will be a local minimum of the log-loss (Dempster *et al.*, 1977) (which is equivalent to a local maximum of the likelihood), the empirical analogue of the KL divergence.

The K-means algorithm is often viewed as a *vector quantization* algorithm (and is sometimes referred to as the *Lloyd-Max* algorithm in the vector quantization literature). It is known that K-means will find a local minimum of the *distortion* or *quantization error* on the data (MacQueen, 1967), which we will discuss at some length.

Thus, for both the fractional and WTA assignment methods, there is a natural and widely used iterative optimization heuristic (EM and K-means, respectively), and it is known what *loss function* is (locally) minimized by each algorithm (log-loss and distortion, respectively). However, relatively little seems to be known about the precise relationship between the two loss functions and their attendant heuristics. The structural similarity of EM and K-means often leads to their being considered closely related or even roughly equivalent. Indeed, Duda and Hart (Duda and Hart, 1973) go as far as saying that K-means can be viewed as "an approximate way to obtain maximum likelihood estimates for the means", which is the goal of density estimation in general and EM in particular. Furthermore, K-means is formally equivalent to EM using a mixture of Gaussians with covariance matrices ϵI (where I is the identity matrix) in the limit $\epsilon \to 0$. In practice, there is often some conflation of the two algorithms: K-means is sometimes used in density estimation applications due to its more rapid convergence, or at least used to obtain "good" initial parameter values for a subsequent execution of EM.

But there are also simple examples in which K-means and EM converge to rather different solutions, so the preceding remarks cannot tell the entire story. What quantitative statements can be made about the systematic differences between these algorithms and loss functions?

In this work, we answer this question by giving a new interpretation of the classical distortion that is locally minimized by the K-means algorithm. We give a simple information-theoretic decomposition of the expected distortion that shows that K-means (and any other algorithm seeking to minimize the distortion) must manage a trade-off between how well the data are *balanced* or distributed among the clusters by the hard assignments, and the *accuracy* of the density models found for the two sides of this assignment. The degree to which the data are balanced among the clusters is measured by the *entropy* of the partition defined by the assignments. We refer to this trade-off as the *information-modeling* trade-off.

The information-modeling trade-off identifies two significant ways in which K-means and EM differ. First, where EM seeks to model the *entire* sampling density Q with a *mixture* model $\alpha_0 P_0 + (1 - \alpha_0)P_1$, K-means is concerned with explicitly identifying *distinct* subpopulations Q_0 and Q_1 of the sampling density, and finding good models P_0 and P_1 for each *separately*. Second, the choice of subpopulations identified by K-means may be strongly influenced by the entropy of the partition they define; in EM this influence is entirely absent. The first of these differences is the intuitive result of the differing assignment methods, and we formalize it here; the second is less obvious, but actually can determine the behavior of K-means even in simple examples, as we shall see.

In addition to letting us predict and explain the behavior of K-means on specific examples, the new decomposition allows us to derive a general prediction about how K-means and EM differ: namely, that K-means will tend to find density models P_0 and P_1 that have less "overlap" with each other compared to those found by EM. In certain simple examples, this bias of K-means is apparent; here we argue that it is a rather general bias that depends little on the sampling density or the form of the density models P_0 and P_1 used by the algorithms.

The mathematical framework we use also allows us to analyze the variant of K-means that maintains unequal weightings of the density models P_0 and P_1; we show that the use of this weighting has an interesting effect on the loss function, essentially "erasing" the incentive for finding a partition with high entropy. We also study the posterior assignment method mentioned above, and show that despite the resulting loss function's algebraic similarity to the iterative optimization performed by EM, it differs rather dramatically.

Our results should be of some interest to anyone applying EM, K-means and their variants to problems of unsupervised learning.

2. A Loss Decomposition for Hard Assignments

Suppose that we have densities P_0 and P_1 over X, and a (possibly randomized) mapping F that maps $x \in X$ to either 0 or 1; we will refer to F as a *partition* of X. We think of F as "assigning" points to exactly one of P_0 and P_1, and we think of P_b ($b \in \{0, 1\}$) as a density model for the points assigned to it. F may flip coins to determine the assignment of x, but must always output a value in $\{0, 1\}$; in other words, F must make "hard" assignments. We will call such a triple $(F, \{P_0, P_1\})$ a *partitioned density*. In this section, we propose a measure of goodness for partitioned densities and explore its interpretation and consequences.

In all of the settings we consider in this paper, the partition F will actually be *determined* by P_0 and P_1 (and perhaps some additional parameters), but we will suppress the dependency of F on these quantities for notational brevity. As simple examples of such hard assignment methods, we have the two methods discussed in the introduction: *WTA* assignment (used by K-means), in which x is assigned to P_0 if and only if $P_0(x) \geq P_1(x)$, and what we call *posterior* assignment, in which x is assigned to P_b with probability $P_b(x)/(P_0(x) + P_1(x))$. The soft or fractional assignment method used by EM does not fall into this framework, since x is fractionally assigned to *both* P_0 and P_1.

Throughout the development, we will assume that unclassified data is drawn according to some fixed, unknown density or distribution Q over X that we will call the *sampling* density. Now given a partitioned density $(F, \{P_0, P_1\})$, what is a reasonable way to measure how well the partitioned density "models" the sampling density Q? As far as the P_b are concerned, as we have mentioned, we might ask that the density P_b be a good model of the sampling density Q *conditioned* on the event $F(x) = b$. In other words, we imagine that F partitions Q into two distinct subpopulations, and demand that P_0 and P_1 *separately* model these subpopulations. It is not immediately clear what criteria (if any) we should ask F to meet; let us defer this question for a moment.

Fix any partitioned density $(F, \{P_0, P_1\})$, and define for any $x \in X$ the *partition loss*

$$\chi(x) = \mathbf{E}\left[-\log(P_{F(x)}(x))\right] \qquad (1)$$

where the expectation is only over the (possible) randomization in F. We have suppressed the dependence of χ on the partitioned density under consideration for notational brevity, and the logarithm is base 2. If we ask that the partition loss be minimized, we capture the informal measure of goodness proposed above: we first use the assignment method F to assign x to either P_0 or P_1; and we then "penalize" only the *assigned* density P_b by the log loss $-\log(P_b(x))$. We can define the *training* partition loss on a finite set of points S, and the *expected* partition loss with respect to Q, in the natural ways.

Let us digress briefly here to show that in the special case that P_0 and P_1 are multivariate Gaussian (normal) densities with means μ_0 and μ_1, and identity covariance matrices, and the partition F is the WTA assignment method, then the partition loss on a set of points is equivalent to the well-known *distortion* or *quantization error* of μ_0 and μ_1 on that set of points (modulo some additive and multiplicative constants). The distortion of x with respect to μ_0 and μ_1 is simply $(1/2) \min(\|x - \mu_0\|^2, \|x - \mu_1\|^2) = (1/2)\|x - \mu_{F(x)}\|^2$, where $F(x)$ assigns x to the nearer of μ_0 and μ_1 according to Euclidean distance (WTA assignment). Now for any x, if P_b is the d-dimensional Gaussian $(1/(2\pi)^{(d/2)})e^{-(1/2)\|x - \mu_b\|^2}$ and F is WTA assignment with respect to the P_b, then the partition loss on x is

$$-\log(P_{F(x)}(x)) \;=\; \log\left((2\pi)^{d/2}e^{(1/2)||x-\mu_{F(x)}||^2}\right) \tag{2}$$

$$=\; (1/2)||x - \mu_{F(x)}||^2 \log(e) + (d/2)\log 2\pi. \tag{3}$$

The first term in Equation (3) is the distortion times a constant, and the second term is an additive constant that does not depend on x, P_0 or P_1. Thus, minimization of the partition loss is equivalent to minimization of the distortion. More generally, if x and μ are equal dimensioned real vectors, and if we measure distortion using any distance metric $d(x,\mu)$ that can be expressed as a function of $x - \mu$, (that is, the distortion on x is the smaller of the two distances $d(x,\mu_0)$ and $d(x,\mu_1)$,) then again this distortion is the special case of the partition loss in which the density P_b is $P_b(x) = (1/Z)e^{-d(x,\mu_b)}$, and F is WTA assignment. The property that $d(x,\mu)$ is a function of $x - \mu$ is a sufficient condition to ensure that the normalization factor Z is independent of μ; if Z depends on μ, then the partition loss will include an additional μ-dependent term besides the distortion, and we cannot guarantee in general that the two minimizations are equivalent.

Returning to the development, it turns out that the expectation of the partition loss with respect to the sampling density Q has an interesting decomposition and interpretation. For this step we shall require some basic but important definitions. For any fixed mapping F and any value $b \in \{0,1\}$, let us define $w_b = \mathbf{Pr}_{x \in Q}[F(x) = b]$, so $w_0 + w_1 = 1$. Then we define Q_b by

$$Q_b(x) = Q(x) \cdot \mathbf{Pr}[F(x) = b]/w_b \tag{4}$$

where here the probability is taken only over any randomization of the mapping F. Thus, Q_b is simply the distribution Q conditioned on the event $F(x) = b$, so F "splits" Q into Q_0 and Q_1: that is, $Q(x) = w_0 Q_0(x) + w_1 Q_1(x)$ for all x. Note that *the definitions of w_b and Q_b depend on the partition F* (and therefore on the P_b, when F is determined by the P_b).

Now we can write the expectation of the partition loss with respect to Q:

$$\mathbf{E}_{x \in Q}[\chi(x)]$$

$$= w_0 \mathbf{E}_{x_0 \in Q_0}\left[-\log(P_0(x_0))\right] + w_1 \mathbf{E}_{x_1 \in Q_1}\left[-\log(P_1(x_1))\right] \tag{5}$$

$$= w_0 \mathbf{E}_{x_0 \in Q_0}\left[\log\frac{Q_0(x_0)}{P_0(x_0)} - \log(Q_0(x_0))\right]$$

$$+ w_1 \mathbf{E}_{x_1 \in Q_1}\left[\log\frac{Q_1(x_1)}{P_1(x_1)} - \log(Q_1(x_1))\right] \tag{6}$$

$$= w_0 KL(Q_0||P_0) + w_1 KL(Q_1||P_1) + w_0 \mathcal{H}(Q_0) + w_1 \mathcal{H}(Q_1) \tag{7}$$

$$= w_0 KL(Q_0||P_0) + w_1 KL(Q_1||P_1) + \mathcal{H}(Q|F). \tag{8}$$

Here $KL(Q_b||P_b)$ denotes the Kullback-Leibler divergence from Q_b to P_b, and $\mathcal{H}(Q|F)$ denotes $\mathcal{H}(x|F(x))$, the entropy of the random variable x, distributed according to Q, when we are given its (possibly randomized) assignment $F(x)$.

This decomposition will form the cornerstone of all of our subsequent arguments, so let us take a moment to examine and interpret it in some detail. First, let us remember that every term in Equation (8) depends on all of F, P_0 and P_1, since F and the P_b are themselves coupled in a way that depends on the assignment method. With that caveat, note that the quantity $KL(Q_b||P_b)$ is the natural measure of how well P_b models its respective side of the partition defined by F, as discussed informally above. Furthermore, the weighting of these terms in Equation (8) is the natural one. For instance, as w_0 approaches 0 (and thus, w_1 approaches 1), it becomes less important to make $KL(Q_0||P_0)$ small: if the partition F assigns only a negligible fraction of the population to category 0, it is not important to model that category especially well, but very important to accurately model the dominant category 1. In isolation, the terms $w_0 KL(Q_0||P_0) + w_1 KL(Q_1||P_1)$ encourage us to choose P_b such that the two sides of the split of Q defined by P_0 and P_1 (that is, by F) are in fact modeled well by P_0 and P_1. But these terms are not in isolation.

The term $\mathcal{H}(Q|F)$ in Equation (8) measures the *informativeness* of the partition F defined by P_0 and P_1, that is, how much it reduces the entropy of Q. More precisely, by appealing to the symmetry of the mutual information $\mathcal{I}(x, F(x))$, we may write (where x is distributed according to Q):

$$\mathcal{H}(Q|F) = \mathcal{H}(x|F(x)) \tag{9}$$
$$= \mathcal{H}(x) - \mathcal{I}(x, F(x)) \tag{10}$$
$$= \mathcal{H}(x) - (\mathcal{H}(F(x)) - \mathcal{H}(F(x)|x)) \tag{11}$$
$$= \mathcal{H}(x) - (\mathcal{H}_2(w_0) - \mathcal{H}(F(x)|x)) \tag{12}$$

where $\mathcal{H}_2(p) = -p\log(p) - (1-p)\log(1-p)$ is the binary entropy function. The term $\mathcal{H}(x) = \mathcal{H}(Q)$ is independent of the partition F. Thus, we see from Equation (12) that F *reduces* the uncertainty about x by the amount $\mathcal{H}_2(w_0) - \mathcal{H}(F(x)|x)$. Note that if F is a deterministic mapping (as in WTA assignment), then $\mathcal{H}(F(x)|x) = 0$, and a good F is simply one that maximizes $\mathcal{H}(w_0)$. In particular, *any* deterministic F such that $w_0 = 1/2$ is optimal in this respect, regardless of the resulting Q_0 and Q_1. In the general case, $\mathcal{H}(F(x)|x)$ is a measure of the randomness in F, and a good F must trade off between the competing quantities $\mathcal{H}_2(w_0)$ (which, for example, is *maximized* by the F that flips a coin on every x) and $-\mathcal{H}(F(x)|x)$ (which is always *minimized* by this same F).

Perhaps most important, we expect that there may be competition between the *modeling* terms $w_0 KL(Q_0||P_0) + w_1 KL(Q_1||P_1)$ and the *partition information* term $\mathcal{H}(Q|F)$. If P_0 and P_1 are chosen from some parametric class $\mathcal{P}$ of densities of limited complexity (for instance, multivariate Gaussian distributions), then the demand that the $KL(Q_b||P_b)$ be small can be interpreted as a demand that the partition F yield Q_b that are "simple" (by virtue of their being well-approximated, in the KL divergence sense, by densities lying in $\mathcal{P}$). This demand may be in tension with the demand that F be informative, and Equation (8) is a prescription for how to manage this competition, which we refer to in the sequel as the *information-modeling trade-off*.

Thus, if we view P_0 and P_1 as implicitly defining a hard partition (as in the case of WTA assignment), then the partition loss provides us with one particular way of evaluating the goodness of P_0 and P_1 as models of the sampling density Q. Of course, there are other ways of evaluating the P_b, one of them being to evaluate the *mixture* $(1/2)P_0 + (1/2)P_1$ via the KL divergence $KL(Q||(1/2)P_0+(1/2)P_1)$ (we will discuss the more general case of nonequal mixture coefficients shortly). This is the expression that is (locally) minimized by standard density estimation approaches such as EM, and we would particularly like to call attention to the ways in which Equation (8) differs from this expression. Not only does Equation (8) differ by incorporating the penalty $\mathcal{H}(Q|F)$ for the partition F, but instead of asking that the mixture $(1/2)P_0 + (1/2)P_1$ model the entire population Q, each P_b is only asked to — and only given credit for — modeling its respective Q_b. We will return to these differences in considerably more detail in Section 4.

We close this section by observing that if P_0 and P_1 are chosen from a class $\mathcal{P}$ of densities, and we constrain F to be the WTA assignment method for the P_b, there is a simple and perhaps familiar iterative optimization algorithm for locally minimizing the partition loss on a set of points S over all choices of the P_b from $\mathcal{P}$ — we simply repeat the following two steps until convergence:

- (WTA Assignment) Set S_0 to be the set of points $x \in S$ such that $P_0(x) \geq P_1(x)$, and set S_1 to be $S - S_0$.
- (Reestimation) Replace each P_b with $argmin_{P \in \mathcal{P}}\{-\sum_{x \in S_b} \log(P(x))\}$.

As we have already noted, in the case that the P_b are restricted to be Gaussian densities with identity covariance matrices (and thus, only the means are parameters), this algorithm reduces to the classical K-means algorithm. Here we have given a natural extension for estimating P_0 and P_1 from a general parametric class, so we may have more parameters than just the means. With some abuse of terminology, we will simply refer to our generalized version as K-means. The reader familiar with the EM algorithm for choosing P_0 and P_1 from $\mathcal{P}$ will also recognize this algorithm as simply a "hard" or WTA assignment variant of *unweighted* EM (that is, where the mixture coefficients must be equal).

It is easy to verify that K-means will result in a local minimum of the partition loss over P_b chosen from $\mathcal{P}$ using the WTA assignment method. Let us rename this special case of the partition loss the K-*means loss* for convenience.

The fact that K-means locally minimizes the K-means loss, combined with Equation (8), implies K-means must implicitly manage the information-modeling trade-off. Note that although K-means will not increase the K-means loss at any iteration, this does *not* mean that each of the terms in Equation (8) will not increase; indeed, we will see examples where this is not the case. It has been often observed in the vector quantization litera-ture (Gersho, 1982) that at each iteration, the means estimated by K-means must in fact be the true means of the points assigned to them — but this does not imply, for instance, that the terms $KL(Q_b||P_b)$ are nonincreasing (because, for example, Q_b can also change with each iteration).

Finally, note that we can easily generalize Equation (8) to the K-cluster case:

$$\mathbf{E}_Q[\chi(x)] = \sum_{i=1}^{K} w_i KL(Q_i||P_i) + \mathcal{H}(Q|F). \tag{13}$$

Note that, as in Equation (11), $\mathcal{H}(Q|F) = \mathcal{H}(x) - (\mathcal{H}(F(x)) - \mathcal{H}(F(x)|x))$, where x is distributed according to Q, and that for general K, $\mathcal{H}(F(x))$ is now an $O(\log(K))$ quantity.

3. Weighted K-Means

As we have noted, K-means is a hard-assignment variant of the *unweighted* EM algorithm (that is, where the mixture coefficients are forced to be $1/2$, or $1/K$ in the general case of K densities). There is also a natural gener-alization of K-means that can be thought of as a hard-assignment variant of *weighted* EM. For any class $\mathcal{P}$ of densities over a space X, *weighted K-means* over $\mathcal{P}$ takes as input a set S of data points and outputs a pair of densities $P_0, P_1 \in \mathcal{P}$, as well as a weight $\alpha_0 \in [0,1]$. (Again, the general-ization to the case of K densities and K weights is straightforward.) The algorithm begins with random choices for the $P_b \in \mathcal{P}$ and α_0, and then repeatedly executes the following three steps:

- (WTA Assignment) Set S_0 to be the set of points $x \in S$ such that $\alpha_0 P_0(x) \geq (1 - \alpha_0)P_1(x)$, and set S_1 to be $S - S_0$.
- (Reestimation) Replace each P_b with $argmin_{P \in \mathcal{P}}\{-\sum_{x \in S_b} \log(P(x))\}$.
- (Reweighting) Replace α_0 with $|S_0|/|S|$.

Now we can again ask the question: what loss function is this algorithm (locally) minimizing? Let us fix F to be the *weighted WTA partition*, given by $F(x) = 0$ if and only if $\alpha_0 P_0(x) \geq (1 - \alpha_0)P_1(x)$. Note that F is deterministic, and also that in general, α_0 (which is an adjustable parameter of the weighted K-means algorithm) is *not* necessarily the same as w_0 (which is defined by the current weighted WTA partition, and depends on Q).

It turns out that weighted K-means will *not* find P_0 and P_1 that give a local minimum of the unweighted K-means loss, but of a slightly different loss function whose expectation differs from that of the unweighted K-means loss in an interesting way. Let us define the *weighted K-means* loss of P_0 and P_1 on x by

$$- \log \left(\alpha_0^{1-F(x)}(1 - \alpha_0)^{F(x)} P_{F(x)}(x) \right) \tag{14}$$

where again, F is the weighted WTA partition determined by P_0, P_1 and α_0. For any data set S, define $S_b = \{x \in S : F(x) = b\}$. We now show that weighted K-means will in fact not increase the weighted K-means loss on S with each iteration. Thus[2]

$$-\sum_{x \in S} \log \left(\alpha_0^{1-F(x)}(1 - \alpha_0)^{F(x)} P_{F(x)}(x) \right)$$

$$= -\sum_{x \in S_0} \log(\alpha_0 P_0(x)) - \sum_{x \in S_1} \log((1 - \alpha_0)P_1(x)) \tag{15}$$

$$= -\sum_{x \in S_0} \log(P_0(x)) - \sum_{x \in S_1} \log(P_1(x))$$
$$\quad -|S_0| \log(\alpha_0) - |S_1| \log(1 - \alpha_0). \tag{16}$$

Now

$$-|S_0| \log(\alpha_0) - |S_1| \log(1 - \alpha_0)$$

$$= -|S| \left(\frac{|S_0|}{|S|} \log(\alpha_0) + \frac{|S_1|}{|S|} \log(1 - \alpha_0) \right) \tag{17}$$

which is an entropic expression minimized by the choice $\alpha_0 = |S_0|/|S|$. But this is exactly the new value of α_0 computed by weighted K-means from the current assignments S_0, S_1. Furthermore, the two summations in Equation (16) are clearly reduced by reestimating P_0 from S_0 and P_1 from S_1 to obtain the densities P_0' and P_1' that minimize the log-loss over S_0 and S_1 respectively, and these are again exactly the new densities computed

---

[2] We are grateful to Nir Friedman for pointing out this derivation to us.

by weighted K-means. Thus, weighted K-means decreases the weighted K-means loss (given by Equation (14) of $(F, \{P_0, P_1\})$ on S at each iteration, justifying our naming of this loss.

Now for a fixed P_0 and P_1, what is the expected weighted K-means loss with respect to the sampling density Q? We have

$$\mathbf{E}_{x \in Q} \left[-\log \left(\alpha_0^{1-F(x)} (1 - \alpha_0)^{F(x)} P_{F(x)}(x) \right) \right]$$
$$= \mathbf{E}_{x \in Q} \left[-\log(P_{F(x)}(x)) \right] - w_0 \log(\alpha_0) - w_1 \log(1 - \alpha_0) \quad (18)$$

where $w_b = \mathbf{Pr}_{x \in X}[F(x) = b]$ as before. The first term on the right-hand side is just the expected partition loss of $(F, \{P_0, P_1\})$. The last two terms give the cross-entropy between the binary distributions $(w_0, w_1) = (w_0, 1 - w_0)$ and $(\alpha_0, 1 - \alpha_0)$. For a fixed $(F, \{P_0, P_1\})$, there is not much we can say about this cross-entropy; but for weighted K-means, we know that at convergence we must have $\alpha_0 = |S_0|/|S|$ (for this is how weighted K-means reassigns α_0 at each iteration), and $|S_0|/|S| = \hat{w}_0$ is simply the empirical estimate of w_0. Thus, in the limit of large samples we expect $\hat{w}_0 \to w_0$, and thus

$$- w_0 \log(\hat{w}_0) - w_1 \log(\hat{w}_1) \to \mathcal{H}_2(w_0). \quad (19)$$

Combining Equation (19) with Equation (18) and our general decomposition for partition loss in Equation (8) gives that *for the P_0, P_1 and α_0 found by weighted K-means,*

$$\mathbf{E}_{x \in Q} \left[-\log \left(\alpha_0^{1-F(x)} (1 - \alpha_0)^{F(x)} P_{F(x)}(x) \right) \right]$$
$$= w_0 KL(Q_0 || P_0) + w_1 KL(Q_1 || P_1) + \mathcal{H}(Q|F)$$
$$\quad - w_0 \log(\hat{w}_0) - w_1 \log(\hat{w}_1) \quad (20)$$
$$= w_0 KL(Q_0 || P_0) + w_1 KL(Q_1 || P_1) + \mathcal{H}(Q) - \mathcal{H}_2(w_0)$$
$$\quad - w_0 \log(\hat{w}_0) - w_1 \log(\hat{w}_1) \quad (21)$$
$$\approx w_0 KL(Q_0 || P_0) + w_1 KL(Q_1 || P_1) + \mathcal{H}(Q). \quad (22)$$

Thus, since $\mathcal{H}(Q)$ does not depend on the P_b or α_0, we may think of the (generalization) goal of weighted K-means as finding $(F, \{P_0, P_1\})$ that minimizes the sum $w_0 KL(Q_0 || P_0) + w_1 KL(Q_1 || P_1)$. This differs from the goal of unweighted K-means in two ways. First of all, the introduction of the weight α_0 has changed our definition of the partition F, and thus has changed the definition of Q_0 and Q_1, even for fixed P_0, P_1 (unweighted K-means corresponds to fixing $\alpha_0 = 1/2$). But beyond this, the introduction of the weight α_0 has also removed the bias towards finding an "informative" partition F. Thus, *there is no information-modeling trade-off for weighted K-means*; the algorithm will try to minimize the modeling terms

$w_0 KL(Q_0 \| P_0) + w_1 KL(Q_1 \| P_1)$ only. Note, however, that this is still quite different from the *mixture* KL divergence minimized by EM.

4. K-Means vs. EM: Examples

In this section, we consider several different sampling densities Q, and compare the solutions found by K-means (both unweighted and weighted) and EM. In each example, there will be significant differences between the error surfaces defined over the parameter space by the K-means losses and the KL divergence. Our main tool for understanding these differences will be the loss decompositions given for the unweighted K-means loss by Equation (8) and for the weighted K-means loss by Equation (22). It is important to remember that the solutions found by one of the algorithms should not be considered "better" than those found by the other algorithms: we simply have different loss functions, each justifiable on its own terms, and the choice of which loss function to minimize (that is, which algorithm to use) determines which solution we will find.

Throughout the following examples, the instance space X is simply $\Re$. We compare the solutions found by (unweighted and weighted) EM and (unweighted and weighted) K-means when the output is a pair $\{P_0, P_1\}$ of Gaussians over $\Re$ — thus $P_0 = \mathcal{N}(\mu_0, \sigma_0)$ and $P_1 = \mathcal{N}(\mu_1, \sigma_1)$, where $\mu_0, \sigma_0, \mu_1, \sigma_1 \in \Re$ are the parameters to be adjusted by the algorithms. (The weighted versions of both algorithms also output the weight parameter $\alpha_0 \in [0, 1]$.) In the case of EM, the output is interpreted as representing a *mixture* distribution, which is evaluated by its KL divergence from the sampling density. In the case of (unweighted or weighted) K-means, the output is interpreted as a partitioned density, which is evaluated by the expected (unweighted or weighted) K-means loss with respect to the sampling density. Note that the generalization here over the classical vector quantization case is simply in allowing the Gaussians to have non-unit variance.

In each example, the various algorithms were run on 10 thousand examples from the sampling density; for these 1-dimensional problems, this sample size is sufficient to ensure that the observed behavior is close to what it would be running directly on the sampling density.

Example (A). Let the sampling density Q be the symmetric Gaussian mixture

$$Q = 0.5\mathcal{N}(-2, 1.5) + 0.5\mathcal{N}(2, 1.5). \tag{23}$$

See Figure 1. Suppose we initialized the parameters for the algorithms as $\mu_0 = -2$, $\mu_1 = 2$, and $\sigma_0 = \sigma_1 = 1.5$. Thus, each algorithm begins its search from the "true" parameter values of the sampling density. The behavior of unweighted EM is clear: we are starting EM at the global minimum of its expected loss function, the KL divergence; by staying where it begins, EM can enjoy a solution that perfectly models the sampling density Q (that is, KL divergence 0). The same is also true of weighted EM: the presence or absence of the weighting parameter α_0 is essentially irrelevant here, since the optimal value for this parameter is $\alpha_0 = 0.5$ for this choice of Q.

What about unweighted K-means? Let us examine each of the terms in the decomposition of the expected partition loss given in Equation (8). The term $\mathcal{H}(Q|F)$ is already minimized by the initial choice of parameters: the WTA partition F is simply $F(x) = 0$ if and only if $x \leq 0$, which yields $w_0 = 1/2$ and $\mathcal{H}_2(w_0) = 1$. The terms $w_0 KL(Q_0 \| P_0)$ and $w_1 KL(Q_1 \| P_1)$, however, are a different story. Notice that Q_0 — which is Q conditioned on the event $F(x) = 0$, or $x \leq 0$ — is *not* $\mathcal{N}(-2, 1.5)$. Rather, it is $\mathcal{N}(-2, 1.5)$ "chopped off" above $x = 0$, but with the tail of $\mathcal{N}(2, 1.5)$ below $x = 0$ added on. Equivalently, it is $\mathcal{N}(-2, 1.5)$ with its tail above $x = 0$ reflected back below $x = 0$. Clearly, the tail reflection operation on $\mathcal{N}(-2, 1.5)$ that results in Q_0 moves the mean of Q_0 *left* of -2 (since the tail reflection moved mass left), and *reduces* the variance below 1.5 (since the tail has moved towards the final mean). Thus, with respect to only the term $w_0 KL(Q_0 \| P_0)$, the best choice of μ_0 should be smaller than the initial value of -2, and the best choice of σ_0 should be smaller than the initial value of 1.5. Symmetric remarks apply to the term $w_1 KL(Q_1 \| P_1)$. Furthermore, as long as the movements of μ_0 and μ_1, and σ_0 and σ_1, are *symmetric*, then the WTA partition F will remain *unchanged* by these movements — thus, it is possible to improve the terms $w_b KL(Q_b \| P_b)$ from the initial conditions *without* degrading the initially optimal value for the term $\mathcal{H}(Q|F)$. We make essentially the same prediction for weighted K-means, as the optimal performance is achieved for $\alpha_0 = 0.5$.

Performing the experiment on the finite sample, we find that after 8 iterations, K-means has converged to the solution

$$\mu_0 = -2.130, \sigma_0 = 1.338, \mu_1 = 2.131, \sigma_1 = 1.301 \qquad (24)$$

which yields $w_0 = 0.500$. As predicted, the means have been pushed out from the origin, and the variances reduced. Naturally, the KL divergence from the sampling density Q to the *mixture model* is inferior to that of the starting parameters, while its expected K-means loss is superior.

Let us remark that in this simple example, it would have been easy to predict the behavior of K-means directly. The point is that the decomposition of Equation (8) provides a *justification* of this behavior that cannot be provided by regarding K-means as a coarse approximation to EM. We now move on to some examples where the behavior of the various algorithms is more subtle.

Example (B). We now examine an example in which the term $\mathcal{H}(Q|F)$ directly *competes* with the KL divergences. Let the sampling density Q be the single unit-variance Gaussian $Q(x) = \mathcal{N}(0, 1)$; see Figure 2. Consider the initial choice of parameters $\mu_0 = 0$, $\sigma_0 = 1$, and P_1 at some very distant location, say $\mu_0 = 100$, $\sigma_0 = 1$. We first examine the behavior of unweighted K-means. The WTA partition F defined by these settings is $F(x) = 0$ if and only if $x < 50$. Since Q has so little mass above $x = 50$, we have $w_0 \approx 1$, and thus $\mathcal{H}(Q|F) \approx \mathcal{H}(Q)$: the partition is not informative. The term $w_1 KL(Q_1 || P_1)$ in Equation (8) is negligible, since $w_1 \approx 0$. Furthermore, $Q_0 \approx \mathcal{N}(0, 1)$ because even though the tail reflection described in Example (A) occurs again here, the tail of $\mathcal{N}(0, 1)$ above $x = 50$ is a negligible part of the density. Thus $w_0 KL(Q_0 || P_0) \approx 0$, so $w_0 KL(Q_0 || P_0) + w_1 KL(Q_1 || P_1) \approx 0$. In other words, if all we cared about were the KL divergence terms, these settings would be near-optimal.

But the information-modeling trade-off is at work here: by moving P_1 closer to the origin, our KL divergences may degrade, but we obtain a more informative partition. Indeed, after 32 iterations unweighted K-means converges to

$$\mu_0 = -0.768, \sigma_0 = 0.602, \mu_1 = 0.821, \sigma_1 = 0.601 \tag{25}$$

which yields $w_0 = 0.509$.

The information-modeling tradeoff is illustrated nicely by Figure 3, where we simultaneously plot the unweighted K-means loss and the terms $w_0 KL(Q_0 || P_0) + w_1 KL(Q_1 || P_1)$ and $\mathcal{H}_2(w_0)$ as a function of the number of iterations during the run. The plot clearly shows the increase in $\mathcal{H}_2(w_0)$ (meaning a decrease in $\mathcal{H}(Q|F)$), with the number of iterations, and an increase in $w_0 KL(Q_0 || P_0) + w_1 KL(Q_1 || P_1)$. The fact that the gain in partition information is worth the increase in KL divergences is shown by the resulting decrease in the unweighted K-means loss. Note that it would be especially difficult to justify the solution found by unweighted K-means from the viewpoint of density estimation.

As might be predicted from Equation (22), the behavior of *weighted* K-means is dramatically different for this Q, since this algorithm has no incentive to find an informative partition, and is only concerned with the KL divergence terms. We find that after 8 iterations it has converged to

$$\mu_0 = 0.011, \sigma_0 = 0.994, \mu_1 = 3.273, \sigma_1 = 0.033 \tag{26}$$

with $\alpha_0 = w_0 = 1.000$. Thus, as expected, weighted K-means has chosen a completely uninformative partition, in exchange for making $w_b KL(Q_b || P_b) \approx 0$. The values of μ_1 and σ_1 simply reflect the fact that at convergence, P_1 is assigned only the few rightmost points of the 10 thousand examples.

Note that the behavior of both K-means algorithms is rather different from that of EM, which will prefer $P_0 = P_1 = \mathcal{N}(0, 1)$ resulting in the mixture $(1/2)P_0 + (1/2)P_1 = \mathcal{N}(0, 1)$. However, the solution found by weighted

K-means is "closer" to that of EM, in the sense that weighted K-means effectively eliminates one of its densities and fits the sampling density with a single Gaussian.

Example (C). A slight modification to the sampling distribution of Example (B) results in some interesting and subtle difference of behavior for our algorithms. Let Q be given by

$$Q = 0.95\mathcal{N}(0, 1) + 0.05\mathcal{N}(5, 0.1). \tag{27}$$

Thus, Q is essentially as in Example (B), but with addition of a small distant "spike" of density; see Figure 4.

Starting unweighted K-means from the initial conditions $\mu_0 = 0, \sigma_0 = 1, \mu_1 = 0, \sigma_1 = 5$ (which has $w_0 = 0.886, \mathcal{H}(w_0) = 0.513$ and $w_0 KL(Q_0\|P_0) + w_1 KL(Q_1\|P_1) = 2.601$), we obtain convergence to the solution

$$\mu_0 = -0.219, \sigma_0 = 0.470, \mu_1 = 0.906, \sigma_1 = 1.979 \tag{28}$$

which is shown in Figure 5 (and has $w_0 = 0.564, \mathcal{H}(w_0) = 0.988$, and $w_0 KL(Q_0\|P_0) + w_1 KL(Q_1\|P_1) = 2.850$). Thus, as in Example (B), unweighted K-means starts with a solution that is better for the KL divergences, and worse for the partition information, and elects to degrade the former in exchange for improvement in the latter. However, it is interesting to note that $\mathcal{H}(w_0) = \mathcal{H}(0.564) = 0.988$ is still bounded significantly away from 1; presumably this is because any *further* improvement to the partition information would *not* be worth the degradation of the KL divergences. In other words, this solution found is a minimum of the K-means loss where there is truly a *balance* of the two terms: movement of the parameters in one direction causes the loss to increase due to a decrease in the partition information, while movement of the parameters in another direction causes the loss to increase due to an increase in the modeling error.

Unlike Example (B), there is also another (local) minimum of the unweighted K-means loss for this sampling density, at

$$\mu_0 = 0.018, \sigma_0 = 0.997, \mu_1 = 4.992, \sigma_1 = 0.097 \tag{29}$$

with the suboptimal unweighted K-means loss of 1.872. This is clearly a local minimum where the KL divergence terms are being minimized, at the expense of an uninformative partition ($w_0 = 0.949$). It is also essentially the same as the solution chosen by weighted K-means (regardless of the initial conditions), which is easily predicted from Equation (22).

Not surprisingly, in this example weighted K-means converges to a solution close to that of Equation (29).

Example (D). Let us examine a case in which the sampling density is a mixture of *three* Gaussians:

$$Q = 0.25\mathcal{N}(-10, 1) + 0.5\mathcal{N}(0, 1) + 0.25\mathcal{N}(10, 1). \tag{30}$$

See Figure 6. Thus, there are three rather distinct subpopulations of the sampling density. If we run unweighted K-means on 10 thousand examples from Q from the initial conditions $\mu_0 = -5$, $\mu_1 = 5$, $\sigma_0 = \sigma_1 = 1$, (which has $w_0 = 0.5$) we obtain convergence to

$$\mu_0 = -3.262, \sigma_0 = 4.789, \mu_1 = 10.006, \sigma_1 = 0.977 \qquad (31)$$

which has $w_0 = 0.751$. Thus, unweighted K-means sacrifices the initial optimally informative partition in exchange for better KL divergences. (Weighted K-means converges to approximately the same solution, as we might have predicted from the fact that even the unweighted algorithm did not choose to maximize the partition information.) Furthermore, note that it has modeled two of the subpopulations of Q ($\mathcal{N}(-10,1)$ and $\mathcal{N}(0,1)$) using P_0 and modeled the other ($\mathcal{N}(10,1)$) using P_1. This is natural "clustering" behavior — the algorithm prefers to group the middle subpopulation $\mathcal{N}(0,1)$ with either the left or right subpopulation, rather than "splitting" it. In contrast, unweighted EM from the same initial conditions converges to the approximately symmetric solution

$$\mu_0 = -4.599, \sigma_0 = 5.361, \mu_1 = 4.689, \sigma_1 = 5.376. \qquad (32)$$

Thus, unweighted EM chooses to *split* the middle population between P_0 and P_1. The difference between K-means and unweighted EM in this example is a simple illustration of the difference between the two quantities $w_0 KL(Q_0\|P_0) + w_1 KL(Q_1\|P_1)$ and $KL(Q\|\alpha_0 P_0 + (1-\alpha_0)P_1)$, and shows a natural case in which the behavior of K-means is perhaps preferable from the clustering point of view. Interestingly, in this example the solution found by *weighted* EM is again quite close to that of K-means.

5. K-Means Forces Different Populations

The partition loss decomposition given by Equation (8) has given us a better understanding of the loss function being minimized by K-means, and allowed us to explain some of the differences between K-means and EM on specific, simple examples. Are there any *general* differences we can identify? In this section we give a derivation that strongly suggests a bias inherent in the K-means algorithm: namely, a bias towards finding component densities that are as "different" as possible, in a sense to be made precise.

Let $V(P_0, P_1)$ denote the *variation distance* [3] between the densities P_0 and P_1:

$$V(P_0, P_1) = \int_x |P_0(x) - P_1(x)| dx. \qquad (33)$$

---

[3] The ensuing argument actually holds for any distance metric on densities.

Note that $V(P_0, P_1) \leq 2$ always. Notice that due to the triangle inequality, for any partitioned density $(F, \{P_0, P_1\})$,

$$V(Q_0, Q_1) \leq V(Q_0, P_0) + V(P_0, P_1) + V(Q_1, P_1). \tag{34}$$

Let us assume without loss of generality that $w_0 = \mathbf{Pr}_{x \in Q}[F(x) = 0] \leq 1/2$. Now in the case of unweighted or weighted K-means (or indeed, any other case where a deterministic partition F is chosen), $V(Q_0, Q_1) = 2$, so from Equation (34) we may write

$$
\begin{aligned}
V(P_0, &P_1) \\
\geq\ & 2 - V(Q_0, P_0) - V(Q_1, P_1) & (35) \\
=\ & 2 - 2(w_0 V(Q_0, P_0) + w_1 V(Q_1, P_1) \\
& + ((1/2) - w_0) V(Q_0, P_0) + ((1/2) - w_1) V(Q_1, P_1)) & (36) \\
\geq\ & 2 - 2(w_0 V(Q_0, P_0) + w_1 V(Q_1, P_1)) - 2((1/2) - w_0) V(Q_0, P_0) & (37) \\
\geq\ & 2 - 2(w_0 V(Q_0, P_0) + w_1 V(Q_1, P_1)) - 2(1 - 2w_0). & (38)
\end{aligned}
$$

Let us examine Equation (38) in some detail. First, let us assume $w_0 = 1/2$, in which case $2(1 - 2w_0) = 0$. Then Equation (38) lower bounds $V(P_0, P_1)$ by a quantity that approaches the maximum value of 2 as $V(Q_0, P_0) + V(Q_1, P_1)$ approaches 0. Thus, to the extent that P_0 and P_1 succeed in approximating Q_0 and Q_1, P_0 and P_1 must differ from each other. But the partition loss decomposition of Equation (8) includes the terms $KL(Q_b||P_b)$, which are directly encouraging P_0 and P_1 to approximate Q_0 and Q_1. It is true that we are conflating two different technical senses of approximation (variation distance KL divergence). But more rigorously, since $V(P, Q) \leq 2 \ln 2 \sqrt{KL(P||Q)}$ holds for any P and Q, and for all x we have $\sqrt{x} \leq x + 1/4$, we may write

$$
\begin{aligned}
V(P_0, &P_1) \\
\geq\ & 2 - 4 \ln 2 \left(w_0 KL(Q_0||P_0) + w_1 KL(Q_1||P_1) + 1/4 \right) - 2(1 - 2w_0) & (39) \\
=\ & 2 - \ln 2 - 4 \ln 2 \left(w_0 KL(Q_0||P_0) + w_1 KL(Q_1||P_1) \right) - 2(1 - 2w_0) & (40)
\end{aligned}
$$

Since the expression $w_0 KL(Q_0||P_0) + w_1 KL(Q_1||P_1)$ directly appears in Equation (8), we see that K-means is attempting to minimize a loss function that encourages $V(P_0, P_1)$ to be large, at least in the case that the algorithm finds roughly equal weight clusters ($w_0 \approx 1/2$) — which one might expect to be the case, at least for unweighted K-means, since there is the entropic term $-\mathcal{H}_2(w_0)$ in Equation (12). For weighted K-means, this entropic term is eliminated.

In Figure 7, we show the results of a simple experiment supporting the suggestion that K-means tends to find densities with less overlap than EM does. In the experiment, the sampling density Q was a mixture of two one-dimensional, unit-variance Gaussians with varying distance between the means (the horizontal axis). The vertical axis shows the variation distance between the two target Gaussians (dark line) as a reference, and the variation distance between P_0 and P_1 for the solutions found by EM (grey line near solid line), and for unweighted K-means (lowest of the top three grey lines), posterior loss gradient descent, which is discussed in the next section (middle of the top three grey lines), and weighted K-means (top grey line).

6. A New Algorithm: The Posterior Partition

The WTA assignment method is one way of making hard assignments on the basis of P_0 and P_1. But there is another natural hard assignment method — perhaps even more natural. Suppose that we *randomly* assign any fixed x to P_b with probability $P_b(x)/(P_0(x) + P_1(x))$. Thus, we assign x to P_b with the posterior probability that x was generated by P_b under the prior assumption that the sampling density is $(1/2)P_0+(1/2)P_1$ (which, of course, may not be true). We call this F the *posterior* partition.

One nice property of the posterior partition compared to WTA assignment is that it avoids the potential "truncation" resulting from WTA assignment mentioned in Example (A) — namely, that even when P_0 and P_1 have the same form as the true sampling mixture components, we cannot make the terms $KL(Q_b||P_b)$ zero. (Recall that this occurred when the sampling density was a Gaussian mixture, the P_b were Gaussian, but WTA assignment resulted in Q_b that were each Gaussian with one tail "reflected back.") But if F is the posterior partition, and $Q = (1/2)\tilde{Q}_0 + (1/2)\tilde{Q}_1$, and $P_0 = \tilde{Q}_0$, $P_1 = \tilde{Q}_1$ then

$$Q_b(x) \quad = \quad Q(x) \cdot \mathbf{Pr}[F(x) = b]/w_b \tag{41}$$

$$= \quad (\tilde{Q}_0(x) + \tilde{Q}_1(x)) \left(\frac{\tilde{Q}_b(x)}{\tilde{Q}_0(x) + \tilde{Q}_1(x)} \right) \tag{42}$$

$$= \quad \tilde{Q}_b(x) \tag{43}$$

$$= \quad P_b(x). \tag{44}$$

So, if P_0 and P_1 are such that $Q = (1/2)P_0 + (1/2)P_1$, then by the above derivation $w_b KL(Q_b||P_b) = 0$. Thus, the KL divergence terms in the expected partition loss given by Equation (8) encourage us to model the sampling density under this definition of F. For this reason, it is tempting to think that the use of the posterior partition will lead us closer to density estimation than will WTA assignments. However, the situation is more subtle than this, again because of the competing constraint for an informative partition. We will see an example in a moment.

Now, under the posterior partition F, the partition loss of $(F, \{P_0, P_1\})$ on a fixed point x is

$$
\begin{aligned}
\mathbf{E}[\chi(x)] &= \mathbf{E}\left[-\log P_{F(x)}(x)\right] \\
&= -\frac{P_0(x)}{P_0(x) + P_1(x)}\log P_0(x) - \frac{P_1(x)}{P_0(x) + P_1(x)}\log P_1(x) \quad (45)
\end{aligned}
$$

where here the expectation is taken over only the randomization of F; we will call this special case of the partition loss the *posterior loss*. The posterior loss on a sample S is then simply the summation of the right-hand-side of Equation (45) over all $x \in S$.

Example (A) Revisited. Recall that the sampling density in Example (A) is

$$
Q = 0.5\mathcal{N}(-2, 1.5) + 0.5\mathcal{N}(2, 1.5) \quad (46)
$$

and that if we start at $P_0 = \tilde{Q}_0 = \mathcal{N}(-2, 1.5)$, $P_1 = \tilde{Q}_1 = \mathcal{N}(2, 1.5)$, then K-means (both weighted and unweighted) will move the means away from the origin symmetrically, since a maximally informative partition F is preserved by doing so, and the KL divergences are improved. Under the posterior partition definition of F, the KL divergences *cannot* be improved from these initial conditions — but the informativeness of the partition can! This is because our general expression for $\mathcal{H}(x|F(x))$ is $\mathcal{H}(x) - (\mathcal{H}_2(w_0) - \mathcal{H}(F(x)|x))$ (here x is distributed according to Q). In the K-means choice of F, the term $\mathcal{H}(F(x)|x)$ was 0, as F was deterministic. Under the posterior partition, at the stated initial conditions $\mathcal{H}_2(w_0) = \mathcal{H}_2(1/2) = 1$ still holds, but now $\mathcal{H}(F(x)|x)) \neq 0$, because F is probabilistic. Thus, it is at least possible that there is a better solution — for instance, by reducing the variances of P_0 and P_1, or by moving their means symmetrically away from the origin, we may be able to preserve $\mathcal{H}_2(w_0) = \mathcal{H}_2(1/2) = 1$ while reducing $\mathcal{H}(F(x)|x))$. This is indeed the case: starting from the stated initial parameter values, 53 steps of gradient descent on the training posterior loss (see below for a discussion of the algorithmic issues arising in finding a local minimum of the posterior loss) results in the solution

$$
\mu_0 = -2.140, \sigma_0 = 1.256, \mu_1 = 2.129, \sigma_1 = 1.233 \quad (47)
$$

at which point the gradients with respect to all four parameters are smaller than 0.03 in absolute value. This solution has an expected posterior loss of 2.55, as opposed to 2.64 for the initial conditions. Of course, the KL divergence of $(1/2)P_0 + (1/2)P_1$ to the sampling density has increased from the initial conditions.

What algorithm should one use in order to minimize the expected posterior loss on a sample? Here it seems worth commenting on the algebraic similarity between Equation (45) and the iterative minimization performed by EM. In (unweighted) EM, if we have a current solution $(1/2)P_0+(1/2)P_1$, and sample data S, then our next solution is $(1/2)P_0' + (1/2)P_1'$, where P_0' and P_1' minimize

$$-\sum_{x \in S} \left(\frac{P_0(x)}{P_0(x) + P_1(x)} \log(P_0'(x)) \right.$$
$$\left. + \frac{P_1(x)}{P_0(x) + P_1(x)} \log(P_1'(x)) \right). \qquad (48)$$

While the summand in Equation (48) and the right-hand-side of Equation (45) appear quite similar, there is a crucial difference. In Equation (48) there is a *decoupling* between the posterior prefactors $P_b(x)/(P_0(x)+P_1(x))$ and the log-losses $-\log(P_b'(x))$: our current guesses P_b *fix* the posterior prefactors for each x, and then we minimize the resulting weighted log-losses $-\log(P_b'(x))$ with respect to the P_b', giving our next guess. In Equation (45), no such decoupling is present: in order to evaluate a potential solution P_b', we must use the log-losses *and* posteriors determined by the P_b'. An informal way of explaining the difference is that in EM, we can use our current guess (P_0, P_1) to generate random labels for each x (using the posteriors $P_b(x)/(P_0(x) + P_1(x))$), and then minimize the log-losses of the x together with their labels to get P_0', P_1'. For the posterior loss, to evaluate (P_0', P_1') we must generate the labels according to (P_0', P_1') as well. Thus, there is no obvious iterative algorithm to minimize the expected posterior loss. An alternative is to let $\mathcal{P}$ be a smoothly parameterized class of densities, and resort to gradient descent on the parameters of P_0 and P_1 to minimize the posterior loss.

An even more intriguing difference between the posterior loss and the standard mixture log-loss can be revealed by examining their derivatives. Let us fix two densities P_0 and P_1 over X, and a point $x \in X$. If we think of P_0 and P_1 as representing the mixture $(1/2)P_0 + (1/2)P_1$, and we define $L_{log} = -\log((1/2)P_0(x)+(1/2)P_1(x))$ to be the mixture log-loss on x, then

$$\frac{\partial L_{log}}{\partial P_0(x)} = \frac{1}{\ln(2)} \frac{-1}{P_0(x) + P_1(x)}. \qquad (49)$$

This derivative has the expected behavior. First, it is always negative, meaning that the mixture log-loss on x is always decreased by increasing $P_0(x)$, as this will give more weight to x under the mixture as well. Second, as $P_0(x) + P_1(x) \to 0$, the derivative goes to $-\infty$.

In contrast, if we define the posterior loss on x

$$L_{post} = -\frac{P_0(x)}{P_0(x) + P_1(x)} \log P_0(x) - \frac{P_1(x)}{P_0(x) + P_1(x)} \log P_1(x) \quad (50)$$

then we obtain

$$\frac{\partial L_{post}}{\partial P_0(x)}$$

$$= \frac{1}{P_0(x) + P_1(x)} \left[-\log P_0(x) + \frac{P_0(x)}{P_0(x) + P_1(x)} \log P_0(x) \right.$$

$$\left. + \frac{P_1(x)}{P_0(x) + P_1(x)} \log P_1(x) - \frac{1}{\ln(2)} \right]. \qquad (51)$$

This derivative shows further curious differences between the mixture log-loss and the posterior loss. Notice that since $1/(P_0(x) + P_1(x)) \geq 0$, the sign of the derivative is determined by the bracketed expression in Equation (51). If we define $R_0(x) = P_0(x)/(P_0(x) + P_1(x))$, then this bracketed expression can be rewritten as

$$(1 - R_0(x)) \log \frac{1 - R_0(x)}{R_0(x)} - \frac{1}{\ln(2)} \qquad (52)$$

which is a function of $R_0(x)$ only. Figure 8 shows a plot of the expression in Equation (52), with the value of $R_0(x)$ as the horizontal axis. From the plot we see that $\partial L_{post}/\partial P_0(x)$ can actually be *positive* — namely, the point x can exhibit a *repulsive* force on P_0. This occurs when the ratio $R_0(x) = P_0(x)/(P_0(x) + P_1(x))$ falls below a certain critical value (approximately 0.218). The explanation for this phenomenon is straightforward once we have Equation (8): as long as P_0 models x somewhat poorly (that is, gives it small probability), it is preferable that x be modeled as poorly as possibly by P_0, so as to make the assignment of x to P_1 as deterministic as possible. It is interesting to note that clustering algorithms in which data points have explicit repulsive effects on distant centroids have been proposed in the literature on K-means and self-organizing maps (Hertz *et al.*, 1991).

From the preceding discussion, it might be natural to expect that, as for K-means, minimizing the posterior loss over a density class $\mathcal{P}$ would be more likely to lead to P_0 and P_1 that are "different" from one another than, say, classical density estimation over $\mathcal{P}$. This intuition derives from the fact that P_0 and P_1 repel each other in the sense given above. As for K-means, this can be shown in a fairly general manner (details omitted).

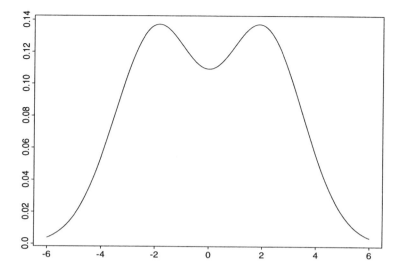

Figure 1: The sampling density for Example (A).

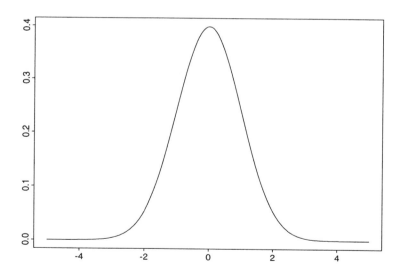

Figure 2: The sampling density for Example (B).

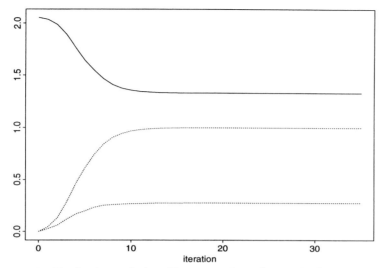

Figure 3: Evolution of the K-means loss (top plot) and its decomposition for Example (B): KL divergences $w_0 KL(Q_0 \| P_0) + w_1 KL(Q_1 \| P_1)$ (bottom plot) and partition information gain $\mathcal{H}_2(w_0)$ (middle plot), as a function of the iteration of unweighted K-means running on 10 thousand examples from $Q = \mathcal{N}(0, 1)$.

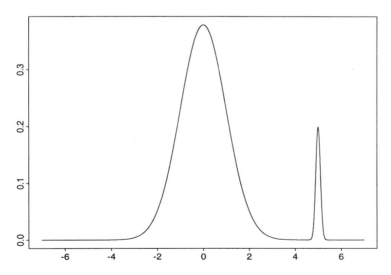

Figure 4: Plot of the sampling mixture density $Q = 0.95\mathcal{N}(0, 1) + 0.05\mathcal{N}(5, 0.1)$ for Example (C).

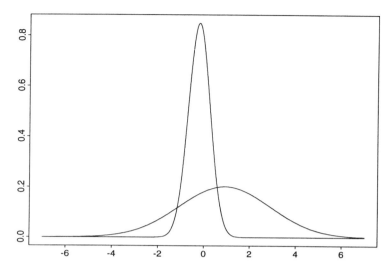

Figure 5: P_0 and P_1 found by unweighted K-means for the sampling density of Example (C).

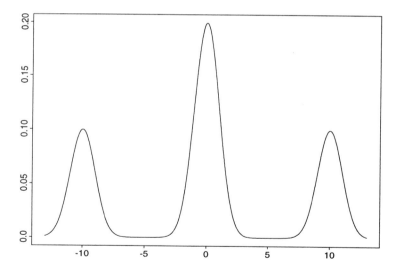

Figure 6: The sampling density for Example (D).

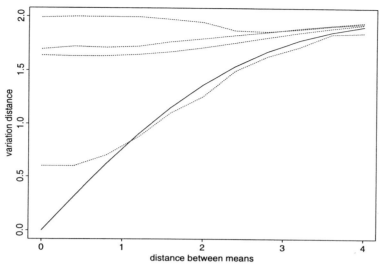

Figure 7: Variation distance $V(P_0, P_1)$ as a function of the distance between the sampling means for EM (bottom grey line), unweighted K-means (lowest of top three grey lines), posterior loss gradient descent (middle to top three grey lines), and weighted K-means (top grey line). The dark line plots $V(Q_0, Q_1)$.

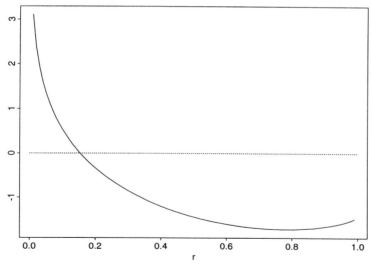

Figure 8: Plot of Equation (52) (vertical axis) as a function of $R_0 = R_0(x)$ (horizontal axis). The line $y = 0$ is also plotted as a reference.

References

T.M. Cover and J.A. Thomas. *Elements of Information Theory.* Wiley-Interscience, 1991.

A.P. Dempster, N.M. Laird, and D.B. Rubin. Maximum-likelihood from incomplete data via the em algorithm. *Journal of the Royal Statistical Society B*, 39:1–39, 1977.

R.O. Duda and P.E. Hart. *Pattern Classification and Scene Analysis.* John Wiley and Sons, 1973.

A. Gersho. On the structure of vector quantizers. *IEEE Transactions on Information Theory*, 28(2):157–166, 1982.

J. Hertz, A. Krogh, and R.G. Palmer. *Introduction to the Theory of Neural Computation.* Addison-Wesley, 1991.

S. L. Lauritzen. The EM algorithm for graphical association models with missing data. *Computational Statistics and Data Analysis*, 19:191–201, 1995.

J. MacQueen. Some methods for classification and analysis of multivariate observations. In *Proceedings of the Fifth Berkeley Symposium on Mathematics, Statistics and Probability*, volume 1, pages 281–296, 1967.

L. Rabiner and B. Juang. *Fundamentals of Speech Recognition.* Prentice Hall, 1993.

LEARNING HYBRID BAYESIAN NETWORKS FROM DATA

STEFANO MONTI
Intelligent Systems Program
University of Pittsburgh
901M CL, Pittsburgh, PA – 15260

AND

GREGORY F. COOPER
Center for Biomedical Informatics
University of Pittsburgh
8084 Forbes Tower, Pittsburgh, PA – 15261

Abstract. We illustrate two different methodologies for learning *Hybrid Bayesian networks*, that is, Bayesian networks containing both continuous and discrete variables, from data. The two methodologies differ in the way of handling continuous data when learning the Bayesian network structure. The first methodology uses discretized data to learn the Bayesian network structure, and the original non-discretized data for the parameterization of the learned structure. The second methodology uses non-discretized data both to learn the Bayesian network structure and its parameterization. For the direct handling of continuous data, we propose the use of artificial neural networks as probability estimators, to be used as an integral part of the scoring metric defined to search the space of Bayesian network structures. With both methodologies, we assume the availability of a complete dataset, with no missing values or hidden variables.

We report experimental results aimed at comparing the two methodologies. These results provide evidence that learning with discretized data presents advantages both in terms of efficiency and in terms of accuracy of the learned models over the alternative approach of using non-discretized data.

1. Introduction

Bayesian belief networks (BNs), sometimes referred to as probabilistic networks, provide a powerful formalism for representing and reasoning under uncertainty. The construction of BNs with domain experts often is a difficult and time consuming task [16]. Knowledge acquisition from experts is difficult because the experts have problems in making their knowledge explicit. Furthermore, it is time consuming because the information needs to be collected manually. On the other hand, databases are becoming increasingly abundant in many areas. By exploiting databases, the construction time of BNs may be considerably decreased.

In most approaches to learning BN structures from data, simplifying assumptions are made to circumvent practical problems in the implementation of the theory. One common assumption is that all variables are discrete [7, 12, 13, 23], or that all variables are continuous and normally distributed [20]. We are interested in the task of learning BNs containing both continuous and discrete variables, drawn from a wide variety of probability distributions. We refer to these BNs as *Hybrid Bayesian networks*. The learning task consists of learning the BN structure, as well as its parameterization.

A straightforward solution to this task is to discretize the continuous variables, so as to be able to apply one of the well established techniques available for learning BNs containing discrete variables only. This approach has the appeal of being simple. However, discretization can in general generate spurious dependencies among the variables, especially if "local" discretization strategies (i.e., discretization strategies that do not consider the interaction between variables) are used[1]. The alternative to discretization is the direct modeling of the continuous data as such. The experiments described in this paper use several real and synthetic databases to investigate whether the discretization of the data degrades structure learning and parameter estimation when using a Bayesian network representation.

The use of artificial neural networks (ANNs) as estimators of probability distributions presents a solution to the problem of modeling probabilistic relationships involving mixtures of continuous and discrete data. It is particularly attractive because it allows us to avoid making strong parametric assumptions about the nature of the probability distribution governing the relationships among the participating variables. They offer a very general *semi-parametric* technique for modeling both the probability mass of dis-

---

[1]Most discretization techniques have been devised with the classification task in mind, and at best they take into consideration the interaction between the class variable and the feature variables individually. "Global" discretization for Bayesian networks learning, that is, discretization taking into consideration the interaction between all dependent variables, is a promising and largely unexplored topic of research, recently addressed in the work described in [19].

crete variables and the probability density of continuous variables. On the other hand, as it was shown in the experimental evaluation in [28] (where only discrete data was used), and as it is confirmed by the evaluation reported in this paper, the main drawback of the use of ANN estimators is the computational cost associated with their training when used to learn the BN structure.

In this paper we continue the work initiated in [28], and further explore the use of ANNs as probability distribution estimators, to be used as an integral part of the scoring metric defined to search the space of BN structures. We perform an experimental evaluation aimed at comparing the new learning method with the simpler alternative of learning the BN structure based on discretized data. The results show that discretization is an efficient and accurate method of model selection when dealing with mixtures of continuous and discrete data.

The rest of the paper is organized as follows. In Section 2 we briefly introduce the Bayesian belief network formalism and some basics of how to learn BNs from data. In Section 3, we describe our learning method, and define the ANN-based scoring metric used to search the space of BN structures. In Section 4, we describe the use of artificial neural networks as probability distribution estimators. Finally, in Section 5 we present experimental results aimed at evaluating the efficacy of the proposed learning procedure, and at comparing it with a simple alternative based on the discretization of the continuous variables. We conclude the paper with a discussion of the results and with some suggestions for further research.

2. Background

A Bayesian belief network is defined by a triple (G, Ω, P), where $G = (\mathcal{X}, E)$ is a directed acyclic graph with a set of nodes $\mathcal{X} = \{x_1, \ldots, x_n\}$ representing domain variables, and with a set of arcs $E = \{(x_i, x_j) \mid x_i, x_j \in \mathcal{X}, x_i \neq x_j\}$ representing probabilistic dependencies among domain variables; Ω is the space of possible instantiations of the domain variables[2]; and P is a probability distribution over the instantiations in Ω. Given a node $x \in \mathcal{X}$, we use π_x to denote the set of parents of x in $\mathcal{X}$. In Figure 1, we give an example of a simple Bayesian network structure, derived in part from [11]. By looking at the network structure, and by giving a causal interpretation to the links displayed, we see that *metastatic cancer* (x_1) is a cause of *brain tumor* (x_3), and that it can also cause an increase in *total serum calcium* (x_2). Furthermore, *brain tumor* can cause *papilledema* (x_5), and both *brain*

---

[2]An instantiation ω of all n variables in $\mathcal{X}$ is an n-uple of values $\{x'_1, \ldots, x'_n\}$ such that $x_i = x'_i$ for $i = 1 \ldots n$.

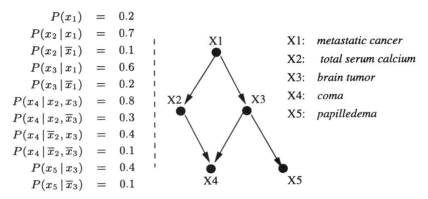

$$
\begin{aligned}
P(x_1) &= 0.2 \\
P(x_2 \mid x_1) &= 0.7 \\
P(x_2 \mid \overline{x}_1) &= 0.1 \\
P(x_3 \mid x_1) &= 0.6 \\
P(x_3 \mid \overline{x}_1) &= 0.2 \\
P(x_4 \mid x_2, x_3) &= 0.8 \\
P(x_4 \mid x_2, \overline{x}_3) &= 0.3 \\
P(x_4 \mid \overline{x}_2, x_3) &= 0.4 \\
P(x_4 \mid \overline{x}_2, \overline{x}_3) &= 0.1 \\
P(x_5 \mid x_3) &= 0.4 \\
P(x_5 \mid \overline{x}_3) &= 0.1
\end{aligned}
$$

X1: *metastatic cancer*

X2: *total serum calcium*

X3: *brain tumor*

X4: *coma*

X5: *papilledema*

Figure 1. A simple belief network, with set of nodes $x = \{x_1, x_2, x_3, x_4, x_5\}$, and parent sets $\pi_{x_1} = \emptyset$, $\pi_{x_2} = \pi_{x_3} = \{x_1\}$, $\pi_{x_4} = \{x_2, x_3\}$, $\pi_{x_5} = \{x_3\}$. All the nodes represent binary variables, taking values from the domain $\{True, False\}$. We use the notation $\overline{x}_i$ to denote $(x_i = False)$. The probability tables give the values of $p(x_i \mid \pi_{x_i})$ only, since $p(\overline{x}_i \mid \pi_{x_i}) = 1 - p(x_i \mid \pi_{x_i})$.

tumor and an increase in *total serum calcium* can cause a patient to lapse into a *coma* (x_4).

The key feature of Bayesian networks is their explicit representation of conditional independence among events (domain variables). In particular, each variable is independent of its non-descendants given its parents. This property is usually referred to as the *Markov property*, and it allows for the parsimonious representation of the multivariate joint probability distribution over $\mathcal{X}$ in terms of the univariate conditional distributions $P(x_i \mid \pi_i, \boldsymbol{\theta}_i)$ of each variable x_i given its parents π_i, with $\boldsymbol{\theta}_i$ the set of parameters needed to fully characterize the conditional probability. For example, with reference to the Bayesian network of Figure 1, where all the variables are discrete, each set of parameters $\boldsymbol{\theta}_i$ is represented by means of a lookup table, with each entry in the table corresponding to the conditional probability $P(x_i' \mid \pi_i', \boldsymbol{\theta}_i)$ for a given instantiation of the variable x_i and its parents π_i.

The probability of any complete instantiation of $\mathcal{X}$ can then be computed from the probabilities in the belief network. In fact, it has been shown [29, 35] that the joint probability of any particular instantiation of all n variables in a belief network can be calculated as follows:

$$
P(x_1', \ldots, x_n') = \prod_{i=1}^{n} P(x_i' \mid \pi_{x_i}', \boldsymbol{\theta}_i) \, . \tag{1}
$$

[3]For a comprehensive guide to the literature on learning probabilistic networks, see [6].

2.1. LEARNING BAYESIAN BELIEF NETWORKS[3]

In a Bayesian framework, ideally classification and prediction would be performed by taking a weighted average over the inferences of every possible BN containing the domain variables[4]. Since this approach is usually computationally infeasible, due to the large number of possible Bayesian networks, often an attempt has been made to select a high scoring Bayesian network for classification. We will assume this approach in the remainder of this paper.

The basic idea of the Bayesian approach is to maximize the probability $P(B_S \,|\, \mathcal{D}) = P(B_S, \mathcal{D})/P(\mathcal{D})$ of a network structure B_S given a database of cases $\mathcal{D}$. Because for all network structures the term $P(\mathcal{D})$ is the same, for the purpose of model selection it suffices to calculate $P(B_S, \mathcal{D})$ for all B_S.

So far, the Bayesian metrics studied in detail typically rely on the following assumptions: 1) given a BN structure, all cases in $\mathcal{D}$ are drawn independently from the same distribution (*random sample* assumption); 2) there are no cases with missing values (*complete database* assumption; some more recent studies have relaxed this assumption [1, 8, 10, 21, 37]); 3) the parameters of the conditional probability distribution of each variable are independent (*global parameter independence* assumption); and 4) for discrete variables the parameters associated with each instantiation of the parents of a variable are independent (*local parameter independence* assumption). The last two assumptions can be restated more formally as follows. Let $\Theta_{B_S} = \{\boldsymbol{\theta}_1, \dots, \boldsymbol{\theta}_n\}$ be the complete set of parameters for the BN structure B_S, with each of the $\boldsymbol{\theta}_i$'s being the set of parameters that fully characterize the conditional probability $P(x_i \,|\, \pi_i)$. Also, when all the variables in π_i are discrete, let $\boldsymbol{\theta}_i = \{\theta_{i1}, \dots, \theta_{iq_i}\}$, where θ_{ij} is the set of parameters defining a distribution that corresponds to the j-th of the q_i possible instantiations of the parents π_i. From Assumption 3 it follows that $P(\Theta_{B_S} \,|\, B_S) = \prod_i P(\boldsymbol{\theta}_i \,|\, B_S)$, and from assumption 4 it follows that $P(\boldsymbol{\theta}_i \,|\, B_S) = \prod_j P(\theta_{ij} \,|\, B_S)$ [36].

The application of these assumptions allows for the following factorization of the probability $P(B_S, \mathcal{D})$:

$$P(B_S, \mathcal{D}) = P(B_S)P(\mathcal{D} \,|\, B_S) = P(B_S) \prod_{i=1}^{n} s(x_i, \pi_i, \mathcal{D}) \,, \qquad (2)$$

where each $s(x_i, \pi_i, \mathcal{D})$ is a term measuring the contribution of x_i and its parents π_i to the overall score of the network structure B_S. The exact form of the terms $s(x_i \pi_i, \mathcal{D})$ slightly differs in the Bayesian scoring metrics de-

---

[4]See the work described in [24, 25] for interesting applications of the *Bayesian model averaging* approach.

fined so far, and for the details we refer the interested reader to the relevant literature [7, 13, 23]. To date, closed-form expressions for $s(x_i \, \pi_i, \mathcal{D})$ have been worked out for the cases when both x_i and π_i are discrete variables, or when both x_i and π_i are continuous (sets of) variables normally distributed; little work been done in applying BN learning methods to domains not satisfying these constraints. Here, we only describe the metric for the discrete case defined by Cooper and Herskovits in [13], since it is the one we use in the experiments.

Given a Bayesian network B_S for a domain $\mathcal{X}$, let r_i be the number of states of variable x_i, and let $q_i = \prod_{x_s \in \pi_i} r_s$ be the number of possible instantiations of π_i. Let θ_{ijk} denote the multinomial parameter corresponding to the conditional probability $P(x_i = k \,|\, \pi_i = j)$, where j is used to index the instantiations of π_i, with $\theta_{ijk} > 0$, and $\sum_k \theta_{ijk} = 1$. Also, given the database $\mathcal{D}$, let N_{ijk} be the number of cases in the database where $x_i = k$ and $\pi_i = j$, and let $N_{ij} = \sum_k N_{ijk}$ be the number of cases in the database where $\pi_i = j$, irrespective of the state of x_i. Given the assumptions described above, and provided all the variables in $\mathcal{X}$ are discrete, the probability $P(\mathcal{D}, B_S)$ for a given Bayesian network structure B_S is given by

$$P(\mathcal{D}, B_S) = P(B_S) \prod_{i=1}^{n} \prod_{j=1}^{q_i} \frac{\Gamma(r_i)}{\Gamma(N_{ij} + r_i)} \prod_{k=1}^{r_i} \Gamma(N_{ijk}), \tag{3}$$

where Γ is the gamma function[5].

Once a scoring metric is defined, a search for a high-scoring network structure can be carried out. This search task (in several forms) has been shown to be NP-hard [4, 9]. Various heuristics have been proposed to find network structures with a high score. One such heuristic is known as K2 [13], and it implements a greedy forward stepping search over the space of network structures. The algorithm assumes a given ordering on the variables. For simplicity, it also assumes a non-informative prior over parameters and structure. In particular, the prior probability distribution over the network structures is assumed to be uniform, and thus, it can be ignored in comparing network structures.

As previously stated, the Bayesian scoring metrics developed so far either assume discrete variables [7, 13, 23], or continuous variables normally distributed [20]. In the next section, we propose one generalization which allows for the inclusion of both discrete and continuous variables with arbitrary probability distributions.

---

[5]Cooper and Herskovits [13] defined Equation (3) using factorials, although the generalization to gamma functions is straightforward.

3. An ANN-based scoring metric

In this section, we describe in detail the use of artificial neural networks as probability distribution estimators, to be used in the definition of a decomposable scoring metric for which no restrictive assumptions on the functional form of the class, or classes, of the probability distributions of the participating variables need to be made. The first three of the four assumptions described in the previous section are still needed. However, the use of ANN estimators allows for the elimination of the assumption of local parameter independence. In fact, the conditional probabilities corresponding to the different instantiations of the parents of a variable are represented by the same ANN, and they share the same network weights and the same training data. Furthermore, the use of ANNs allows for the seamless representation of probability functions containing both continuous and discrete variables.

Let us denote with $\mathcal{D}_l \equiv \{C_1, \ldots, C_{l-1}\}$ the set of the first $l-1$ cases in the database, and with $x_i^{(l)}$ and $\pi_i^{(l)}$ the instantiations of x_i and π_i in the l-th case respectively. The joint probability $P(B_S, \mathcal{D})$ can be written as

$$
P(B_S, \mathcal{D}) = P(B_S)P(\mathcal{D} \mid B_S) = P(B_S) \prod_{l=1}^{m} P(C_l \mid \mathcal{D}_l, B_S) =
$$

$$
= P(B_S) \prod_{l=1}^{m} \prod_{i=1}^{n} P(x_i^{(l)} \mid \pi_i^{(l)}, \mathcal{D}_l, B_S). \tag{4}
$$

If we assume uninformative priors, or decomposable priors on network structures, of the form $P(B_S) = \prod_i P(\pi_i)$, where $P(\pi_i)$ is the probability that π_i are the parents of x_i, the probability $P(B_S, \mathcal{D})$ is decomposable. In fact, we can interchange the two products in Equation 4, so as to obtain

$$
P(B_S, \mathcal{D}) = \prod_{i=1}^{n} [\, P(\pi_i) \prod_{l=1}^{m} P(x_i^{(l)} \mid \pi_i^{(l)}, \mathcal{D}_l, B_S) \,] = \prod_{i=1}^{n} s(x_i, \pi_i, \mathcal{D}), \tag{5}
$$

where $s(x_i, \pi_i, \mathcal{D})$ is the term between square brackets, and it is only a function of x_i and its parents in the network structure B_S (the prior $P(\pi_i)$ can be neglected if we assume a uniform prior over the network structures). The derivation illustrated in Equations 4 and 5 corresponds to the application of the prequential analysis discussed by Dawid in [14, 15]. Usually, the above decomposition is carried out in log terms, and it is interpreted as a predictive score, i.e., as a measure of the success of the model S in predicting the data $\mathcal{D}$. In fact, as it is shown more clearly in Equation 4, we form a predictive distribution of each case $C^{(l)}$ given the cases $\mathcal{D}_l = \{x^{(1)}, \ldots, x^{(l-1)}\}$ already seen. Hence, the name of prequential analysis, which suggests sequential prediction. It corresponds to a theoretically sound form of cross-validation.

From a Bayesian perspective, each of the $P(x_i \mid \pi_i, \mathcal{D}_l, B_S)$ terms should be computed as follows:

$$P(x_i \mid \pi_i, \mathcal{D}_l, B_S) = \int_{\boldsymbol{\theta}_i} P(x_i \mid \pi_i, \boldsymbol{\theta}_i, B_S) P(\boldsymbol{\theta}_i \mid \mathcal{D}_l, B_S) d\boldsymbol{\theta}_i \, .$$

In most cases this integral does not have a closed-form solution; the following MAP approximation can be used instead:

$$P(x_i \mid \pi_i, \mathcal{D}_l, B_S) = P(x_i \mid \pi_i, \tilde{\boldsymbol{\theta}}_i, B_S) \, , \tag{6}$$

with $\tilde{\boldsymbol{\theta}}_i$ the posterior mode of $\boldsymbol{\theta}_i$, i.e., $\tilde{\boldsymbol{\theta}}_i = \mathrm{argmax}_{\boldsymbol{\theta}_i} \{ P(\boldsymbol{\theta}_i \mid \mathcal{D}_l, B_S) \}$. As a further approximation, we use the maximum likelihood (ML) estimator $\hat{\boldsymbol{\theta}}_i$ instead of the posterior mode $\tilde{\boldsymbol{\theta}}_i$. The two quantities are actually equivalent if we assume a uniform prior probability for $\boldsymbol{\theta}_i$, and are asymptotically equivalent for any choice of positive prior. The approximation of Equation (6) corresponds to the application of the *plug-in* prequential approach discussed by Dawid [14].

Artificial neural networks can be designed to estimate $\hat{\boldsymbol{\theta}}_i$ in both the discrete and the continuous case. Several schemes are available for training a neural network to approximate a given probability distribution, or density. In the next section, we describe the *softmax* model for discrete variables [5], and the *mixture density network* model introduced by Bishop in [2], for modeling conditional probability densities.

Notice that even if we adopt the ML approximation, the number of terms to be evaluated to calculate $P(\mathcal{D} \mid B_S)$ is still very large (mn terms, where m is the number of cases, or records, in the database, and n is the number of variables in $\mathcal{X}$), in most cases prohibitively so. The computation cost can be reduced by introducing a further approximation. Let $\hat{\boldsymbol{\theta}}_i(l)$ be the ML estimator of $\boldsymbol{\theta}_i$ with respect to the dataset $\mathcal{D}_l$. Instead of estimating a distinct $\hat{\boldsymbol{\theta}}_i(l)$ for each $l = 1, \ldots, m$, we can group consecutive cases in batches of cardinality t, and estimate a new $\hat{\boldsymbol{\theta}}_i(l)$ for each addition of a new batch to the dataset $\mathcal{D}_l$ rather than for each addition of a new case. Therefore, the same $\hat{\boldsymbol{\theta}}_i(l)$, estimated with respect to the dataset $\mathcal{D}_l$, is used to compute each of the t terms $P(x_i^{(l)} \mid \pi_i^{(l)}, \hat{\boldsymbol{\theta}}_i(l), B_S), \ldots, P(x_i^{(l+t-1)} \mid \pi_i^{(l+t-1)}, \hat{\boldsymbol{\theta}}_i(l), B_S)$.

With this approximation we implicitly make the assumption that, given our present belief about the value of each $\hat{\boldsymbol{\theta}}_i$, at least t new cases are needed to revise this belief. We thus achieve a t-fold reduction in the computation needed, since we now need to estimate only m/t $\hat{\boldsymbol{\theta}}_i$'s for each x_i, instead of the original m. In fact, application of this approximation to the computation of a given $s(x_i, \pi_i, \mathcal{D})$ yields:

$$s(x_i, \pi_i, \mathcal{D}) \quad = \quad \prod_{l=1}^{m} P(x_i^{(l)} \mid \pi_i^{(l)}, \hat{\boldsymbol{\theta}}_i(l), B_S)$$

$$= \prod_{k=0}^{m/t-1} \prod_{l=tk+1}^{t(k+1)} P(x_i^{(l)} \mid \pi_i^{(l)}, \hat{\boldsymbol{\theta}}_i(tk), B_S). \tag{7}$$

With regard to the choice of an appropriate value for t, we can – for example – select a constant value for t, or we can choose to increment t as a function of $|\mathcal{D}_l|$. The second approach seems preferable. When estimating $\hat{\boldsymbol{\theta}}_i(l)$, this estimate will be very sensitive to the addition of new cases when l is small, but it will become increasingly insensitive to the addition of new cases as l grows. For example, when $l = 1$, adding a new case to the training data set means doubling it, while if $l = 10,000$ an additional case in the data set is very unlikely to make a significant difference.

A scheme for the incremental updating of t can be summarized in the equation $t = \lceil \lambda l \rceil$, where l is the number of cases already seen (i.e., the cardinality of $\mathcal{D}_l$), and $0 < \lambda \leq 1$. For example, assuming we set $\lambda = 0.5$, given a data set of 50 cases, the updating scheme $t = \lceil 0.5l \rceil$ would require the training of the ANN estimators of $\hat{\boldsymbol{\theta}}_i(l)$ for $l = 1, 2, 3, 5, 8, 12, 18, 27, 41$.

4. ANN probability estimators

In this section, we describe two models for the representation of conditional probability distributions with neural networks. These are the *softmax* model for discrete variables [5], and the *mixture density network* model introduced by Bishop in [2], for modeling conditional probability densities.

4.1. SOFTMAX MODEL FOR DISCRETE VARIABLES

Let x_i be a discrete variable with r_i values and with a set of parents $\pi_i = \pi_i^c \cup \pi_i^d$, where π_i^c is the set of continuous parents, and π_i^d is the set of discrete parents. The conditional probability distribution $P(x_i \mid \pi_i)$ is approximated by a neural network with r_i output units, and r_{π_i} input units, where $r_{\pi_i} = |\pi_i^c| + \sum_{x_j \in \pi_i^d}(r_j - 1)$. The representation of a discrete input variable taking r_j values by means of $r_j - 1$ indicator variables is common practice in statistical regression. The r_i output units define the conditional probabilities $P(x_i = v_k \mid \pi_i)$, $k = 1, \ldots, r_i$, as follows:

$$P(x_i = v_k \mid \pi_i) = \frac{e^{f_k(\pi_i)}}{\sum_{j=1}^{n_i} e^{f_j(\pi_i)}}, \tag{8}$$

where $f_k(\pi_i)$ is the linear output of the k-th output unit corresponding to the network input π_i. Notice that the probability $P(x_i = v_k \mid \pi_i)$ can be interpreted as the probability of class membership of π_i, i.e., as the probability that π_i belongs to the k-th of r_i classes. It has been proved that a neural network thus configured, with a sum-of-squares or cross-entropy error function, leads to network outputs that estimate Bayesian a posteriori probabilities of class membership [3, 32].

4.2. *MIXTURE DENSITY NETWORKS FOR CONTINUOUS VARIABLES*

The approximation of probability distributions by means of finite mixture models is a well established technique, widely studied in the statistics literature [17, 38]. Bishop [2] describes a class of network models that combine a conventional neural network with a finite mixture model, so as to obtain a general tool for the representation of conditional probability distributions.

The probability $P(x_i \mid \pi_i, \mathcal{D}_l, B_S)$ can be approximated by a finite mixture of normals as is illustrated in the following equation (where we dropped the conditioning on $\mathcal{D}_l$ and B_S for brevity):

$$P(x_i \mid \pi_i) = \sum_{k=1}^{K} \alpha_k(\pi_i)\phi_k(x_i \mid \pi_i) \,, \tag{9}$$

where K is the number of mixture components, $0 \leq \alpha_k \leq 1$, $k = 1, \ldots, K$, and $\sum_k \alpha_k = 1$, and where each of the kernel functions $\phi_k(x_i \mid \pi_i)$ is a normal density of the form:

$$\phi_k(x_i \mid \pi_i) = c \exp \left\{ -\frac{(x_i - \mu_k(\pi_i))^2}{2\sigma_k(\pi_i)^2} \right\} \tag{10}$$

with c the normalizing constant, and $\mu_k(\pi_i)$ and $\sigma_k(\pi_i)^2$ the conditional mean and variance respectively. The parameters $\alpha_k(\pi_i)$, $\mu_k(\pi_i)$, and $\sigma_k(\pi_i)^2$ can be considered as continuous functions of π_i. They can therefore be estimated by a properly configured neural network. Such a neural network will have three outputs for each of the K kernel functions in the mixture model, for a total of $3K$ outputs. The set of input units corresponds to the variables in π_i. It can be shown that a Gaussian mixture model such as the one given in Equation (9) can – with an adequate choice for K – approximate to an arbitrary level of accuracy any probability distribution. Therefore, the representation given by Equations (9) and (10) is completely general, and allows us to model arbitrary conditional distributions. More details on the mixture density network model can be found in [2].

Notice that the mixture density network model assumes a given number K of kernel components. In our case, this number is not given, and needs to be determined. The determination of the number of components of a mixture model is probably the most difficult step, and a completely general solution strategy is not available. Several strategies are proposed in [31, 33, 38]. However, most of the techniques are computationally expensive, and given our use of mixture models, minimizing the computational cost of the selection process becomes of paramount importance. Given a set of alternative model orders $\mathcal{K} = \{1, \ldots, K^{\max}\}$, we consider two alternative strategies for the selection of the best order $K \in \mathcal{K}$: model selection based on a test set held out during training ("hold-out"), and model selection based on the *Bayesian Information Criterion* (BIC) [30, 34].

Model selection by hold-out is performed by splitting the dataset $\mathcal{D}_l$ into a training set $\mathcal{D}_l^{\text{train}}$ and a test set $\mathcal{D}_l^{\text{test}}$. A mixture density network $\mathcal{M}_K$ is then trained on the training set $\mathcal{D}_l^{\text{train}}$ for each $K \in \mathcal{K}$, and the model order K that maximizes the probability $P(\mathcal{D}_l^{\text{test}} \mid \hat{\theta}, \mathcal{M}_K)$ is selected, where $\hat{\theta}$ is the ML estimator with respect to $\mathcal{D}_l^{\text{train}}$.

Model selection based on BIC aims at finding the model order K that maximizes $P(\mathcal{D}_l \mid \mathcal{M}_K)$. BIC provides the following asymptotic approximation:

$$P(\mathcal{D}_l \mid \mathcal{M}_K) = P(\mathcal{D}_l \mid \hat{\theta}, \mathcal{M}_K) - \frac{d}{2} \log l + O(1) \qquad (11)$$

where d is the number of parameters in the model $\mathcal{M}_K$ (in our case, the number of weights of the neural network), l is the size of the dataset, and $\hat{\theta}$ is the ML estimator of the parameters of $\mathcal{M}_K$ (in our case, $\hat{\theta}$ is given by the outputs $\{\alpha_k(\pi_i), \mu_k(\pi_i), \sigma_k(\pi_i)^2 \mid k = 1, \ldots, K\}$ of the trained neural network). Given certain regularity conditions, the error bound for Equation 11 is $O(1)$.

Since repeating the model order selection for each prequential term (i.e., for the estimation of each $\hat{\theta}_i(l)$) would be computationally too costly, we select the model order based on the whole dataset $\mathcal{D}$, and we then use the same selected order in each prequential term.

4.3. ANN TRAINING

For the training of the ANNs, we use the conjugate-gradient optimization algorithm described in [27]. This algorithm shows much faster convergence to the (possibly local) maximum than backpropagation. Currently, we do not use any regularization technique to control for over-fitting.

The number of hidden units is selected as a function of the number of inputs. More specifically, we set the number of hidden units to be half the number of input units, with a minimum of three hidden units. The ANN's weights are randomly initialized with real values in the interval $(-.5, .5)$. This, however, is only true for the ANN corresponding to the first prequential term of the scoring metric. The ANNs corresponding to subsequent prequential terms have their weights initialized to the weights of the ANN for the previous prequential term. More specifically, for a given $s(x_i, \pi_i, \mathcal{D}_l)$ term, we need to train several ANNs, one for each of the prequential terms $P(x_i \mid \pi_i, \mathcal{D}_l, B_S)$, $l = 1, \ldots, m$. Given the ANN trained on the database $\mathcal{D}_l$, we can use the weights of that network as the initialization of the weights for the ANN to be trained on the database $\mathcal{D}_{l+1}$ (or $\mathcal{D}_{l+t}$ if we use the updating scheme described at the end of Section 3). This strategy will be particularly beneficial for large sized $\mathcal{D}_l$, where the addition of a new case (or a few new cases) will not change significantly the estimated probability.

5. Experimental evaluation

In this section we describe the experimental evaluation we conducted to test the viability of use of the ANN-based scoring metric. We first describe the experimental design. We then present the results and discuss them.

5.1. EXPERIMENTAL DESIGN

The experimental evaluation is primarily aimed at determining whether the new scoring metric, given by Equations (7), (8), and (9), which is applicable to continuous variables as well as to discrete variables, offers any advantage over the use of the scoring metric of Equation (3), which is applied to discretized data. To this end, we considered two learning algorithms:

- Algorithm A1 first performs a discretization of the data; then it searches for the highest scoring network structure based on the scoring metric of Equation (3); finally it estimates the parameters of the discovered structure by using ANN estimators applied to the original continuous data.
- Algorithm A2 searches for the highest scoring BN structure using the ANN-based scoring metric of Equation (7) applied to the original continuous data, and it also estimates the parameters of the discovered structure by means of ANN estimators.

We would expect the structure search by A1 to be faster than the structure search by A2, but possibly less accurate, due to the information loss resulting from discretization.

The discretization technique used with the algorithm A1 is a simple "constant density" discretization, whereby the value range of the continuous variable is partitioned into a given number of *bins* so that an approximately equal number of contiguous data points is assigned to each bin.

To make the comparison of the two algorithms simpler, the experiments were designed so as to compare the performance of the two algorithms in discovering the set of parents of a given response, or *class* variable. The evaluation is aimed at testing both the predictive accuracy of the two algorithms, and their capability of discovering relevant structural patterns in the data. With regard to the first goal, real data is fully appropriate, and it allows for a better testing of the robustness of the assumptions made. With regard to the second goal, simulated data generated from Bayesian networks whose structure and parameterization are known is more appropriate, since the generating BN represents the gold standard with which we can compare the model(s) selected by the learning procedure.

To assess the predictive accuracy of the two algorithms, we measured mean square error (MSE) and log score (LS) with respect to the class variable y on a test set distinct from the training set. The mean square error is computed with the formula:

$$\text{MSE} = \frac{1}{L} \sum_{\mathcal{D}^{\text{test}}} [\, y^{(l)} - \hat{y}(\pi_y^{(l)}) \,]^2 \,, \tag{12}$$

where $\mathcal{D}^{\text{test}}$ is a test set of cardinality L, $y^{(l)}$ is the value of y in the l-th case of $\mathcal{D}^{\text{test}}$, and $\hat{y}(\pi_y^{(l)})$ is the value of y predicted by the learned BN for the given instantiation $\pi_y^{(l)}$ of y's parents. More specifically, $\hat{y}(\pi_y^{(l)})$ is the expectation of y with respect to the conditional probability $P(y \mid \pi_y^{(l)})$.

Similarly, the log-score LS is computed with the formula:

$$\text{LS} = -\log P(\mathcal{D}^{\text{test}}) = -\sum_{\mathcal{D}^{\text{test}}} \log P(y^{(l)} \mid \pi_y^{(l)}) \,, \tag{13}$$

where $P(y^{(l)} \mid \pi_y^{(l)})$ is the conditional probability for y in the learned BN. With both MSE and LS the lower the score the better the model.

For the evaluation with real databases, we used databases from the data repository at UC Irvine [26]. In particular, we used the databases AUTO-MPG and ABALONE. These databases were selected because their class variable can be treated as a continuous variable. In the database AUTO-MPG the class variable is `miles-per-gallon`. In the database ABALONE the class variable is an integer proportional to the age of the mollusk, and can thus be treated as a continuous variable. The database AUTO-MPG has a total of 392 cases over eight variables, of which two variables are discrete, and six are continuous. The database ABALONE has a total of 4177 cases over nine variables, of which only one variable is discrete. All continuous variables were normalized.

Since we are only interested in selecting the set of parents of the response variable, the only relevant ordering of the variables needed for the search algorithm is the partial ordering that has the response variable as the successor of all the other variables.

All the statistics reported are computed over ten simulations. In each simulation, 10% of the cases is randomly selected as the test set, and the learning algorithms use the remaining 90% of the cases for training. Notice that in each simulation the test set is the same for the two algorithms.

For the evaluation with simulated databases, we designed the experiments with the goal of assessing the capability of the scoring metrics to correctly identify the set of parents of a given variable. To this purpose,

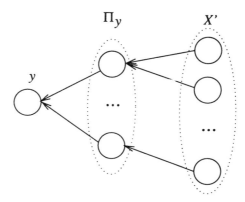

Figure 2.   General structure of the synthetic BNs used in the experiments, with π_y denoting the parents of y, and with $\mathcal{X}'$ the indirect ancestors of y.

synthetic BNs were generated as follows. We considered a domain $\mathcal{X}$ containing 8 continuous variables. One of the variables in $\mathcal{X}$ is randomly selected to be the response variable y. A given number n_π of variables is then randomly select from $\mathcal{X} - \{y\}$ to be y's parents. Let us denote this set of variables with π_y. All the remaining variables are randomly assigned as parents of the variables in π_y. Let us denote this set of variables with $\mathcal{X}' = \mathcal{X} - (\{y\} \cup \pi_y)$. The designation of the variables in $\mathcal{X}'$ as parents of π_y is aimed at testing the effectiveness of the scoring metrics at identifying conditional independencies (i.e., at determining the conditional independence $y \perp \mathcal{X}' \mid \pi_y$). In Figure 2, we show a prototypical structure for the BNs used in the experiments.

For a given BN structure, the parameterization is in terms of finite mixtures of linear models. That is, each conditional probability $P(x_i \mid \pi_i)$ is modeled as a finite mixture of linear models as follows:

$$P(x_i \mid \pi_i) = \sum_{k=1}^{K} \alpha_k N(\mu_k(\pi_i), \sigma_k) \tag{14}$$

$$\mu_k(\pi_i) = \beta_{0k} + \sum_{x_j \in \pi_i} \beta_{jk} x_j \,,$$

where $N(\mu, \sigma)$ denotes a Normal distribution with mean μ and standard deviation σ. All σ_k are real numbers randomly drawn from a uniform distribution over the interval $[1, 10]$. All the regression parameters β_{jk}'s are real numbers randomly drawn from a uniform distribution over the interval $|\beta_{jk}| \in [1, K + 1]$, where K is the number of mixture components. This choice of interval is justified by the fact that we would like the resulting conditional distributions to depart significantly from a singly peaked curve, as the number of mixture components increases. Therefore, we choose to increase the magnitude of the regression parameters with the number of mixture components, in an attempt to obtain a multimodal shape for the corresponding conditional probability function. The α_k are real numbers randomly drawn from a uniform distribution over the interval $(0, 1]$, then normalized to sum to 1.

Several simulations were run for different combinations of parameter settings. In particular: i) the number n_π of parents of y in the generating synthetic network, was varied from 1 to 4; ii) the number K of mixture components used in Equation (14) was varied from 3 to 7 (Note: this is the number of linear models included in the mixtures used to *generate* the database); and iii) the number of bins used in the discretization was either 2 or 3. Furthermore, in the algorithm A2, the strategy of order selection for the mixture density network (MDN) model was either hold-out or BIC (see Section 4). Finally, we chose the maximum admissible MDN model order (referred to as $K^{\max}$ in Section 4) to be 5. That is, the best model order was selected from the range $1, \ldots, 5$. Finally, we ran simulations with datasets of different cardinality. In particular, we used datasets of cardinality 300, 600, and 900.

For each parameter setting, both algorithms were run five times, and in each run 20% of the database cases were randomly selected as test set, and the remaining 80% of the database cases were used for training.

We ran several simulations, whereby a simulation consists of the following steps:

- a synthetic Bayesian network B_S is generated as described above;
- a database $\mathcal{D}$ of cases is generated from B_S by Markov simulation;
- the two algorithms A1 and A2 are applied to the database $\mathcal{D}$ and relevant statistics on the algorithms' performance are collected.

The collected statistics for the two algorithms were then compared by means of standard statistical tests. In particular, for the continuous statistics, namely, the MSE, and the LS, we used a simple t-test, and the Welch-modified two-sample t-test for samples with unequal variance. For the discrete statistics, namely, number of arcs added and omitted, we used a median test (the Wilcoxon test).

5.2. RESULTS

Figure 3 and Figure 4 summarize the results of the simulations with real and synthetic databases, respectively. As a general guideline, for each discrete measure (such as the number of arcs added or omitted) we report the 3-tuple *(min, median, max)*. For each continuous measure (such as the log-score) we report mean and standard deviation.

DB	P1			P2			+			−		
auto-mpg	2	2	2	2	2.5	4	0	1	2	0	0	1
abalone	3	4	4	0	3	4	0	1	2	1	2	4

DB	MSE1		MSE2		LS1		LS2		time-ratio	
auto-mpg	0.13	0.01	0.14	0.02	0.25	0.04	0.28	0.07	40	5
abalone	0.92	0.06	1.09	0.3	1.31	0.06	1.41	0.14	42	12

Figure 3. Comparison of algorithms A1 and A2 on real databases. The first table reports statistics about the structural differences of the models learned by the two algorithms. In particular, P1 and P2 are the number of parents of the response variable discovered by the two algorithms A1 and A2 respectively. The number of arcs added (+) and omitted (−) by A2 with respect to A1 are also shown. For each measure, the 3-tuple *(min, median, max)* is shown. The second table reports mean and standard deviation of the mean square error (MSE), of the log-score (LS), and of the ratio of the computational time of A2 to the computational time of A1 (time-ratio).

With regard to the performance of the two algorithms when coupled with the two alternative MDN model selection criteria (namely, the BIC-based model selection, and the "hold-out" model selection), neither of the two criteria is significantly superior. Therefore, we report the results corresponding to the use of the BIC-based model selection only.

In Figure 3 we present the results of the comparison of the two learning algorithms based on the real databases. In particular we report: the number of parents P1 and P2 discovered by the two algorithms A1 and A2; the corresponding mean square error MSE and the log-score LS; and the ratio of the computational time for A2 to the computational time for A1, denoted with *time-ratio*.

In Figure 4 we present the results of the comparison of the two learning algorithms based on the simulated databases. In particular, the first table of Figure 4 reports the number of arcs added (+) and the number of arcs omitted (−) by each algorithm with respect to the gold standard Bayesian network GS (i.e., the synthetic BN used to generate the database). It also reports the number of arcs added (+) and omitted (−) by algorithm A2 with respect to algorithm A1. The second table of Figure 4 reports the measures MSE and LS for the two algorithms A1 and A2, and the time-ratio.

Notice that the statistics shown in Figure 4 are computed over different

# of cases	GS *vs* A1						GS *vs* A2						A1 *vs* A2					
	+			−			+			−			+			−		
300	0	0	2	0	1	4	0	0	2	0	1	3	0	0	2	0	0	2
600	0	0	1	0	0.5	3	0	0	3	0	1	3	0	0	3	0	0	2
900	0	0	1	0	0	3	0	1	3	0	0	3	0	1	3	0	0	2

# of cases	MSE1		MSE2		LS1		LS2		time-ratio
300	0.72	0.33	0.73	0.33	0.93	0.35	0.96	0.33	29	7
600	0.73	0.32	0.74	0.33	0.77	0.34	0.80	0.37	36	10
900	0.78	0.30	0.78	0.32	0.91	0.27	0.92	0.28	35	8

Figure 4. Comparison of algorithms A1 and A2 on simulated databases. In the first table, the comparison is in term of the structural differences of the discovered networks; each entry reports the 3-tuple *(min, median, max)*. In the second table, the comparison is in terms of predictive accuracy; each entry reports mean and standard deviation of the quantities MSE and LS. It also reports the time ratio, given by the ratio of the computational time for A2 to the computational time for A1.

settings as stated in the previous section on experimental design.

The statistical analysis of the results reported in Figure 3 and Figure 4 shows that the difference in the prediction accuracy of the two algorithms is not statistically significant, either in terms of the mean square error, or in terms of the log-score. On the other hand, the two algorithms differ significantly when we compare the structure of the BNs they discover. In particular, with regard to the real databases, algorithm A2 tends to select a significantly larger number of parents for the response variable than algorithm A1 ($p \ll .01$). With regard to the simulated databases, algorithm A2 tends to add more extra arcs than algorithm A1 ($p \ll .01$), while the difference in the number of arcs omitted by the two algorithms is not statistically significant (remember that the number of arcs added and omitted is computed with respect to the gold standard BNs used to generate the databases). An unexpected result is the decreased prediction accuracy of both algorithms when using the dataset of 900 cases with respect to the prediction accuracy of the two algorithms when using the dataset of 600 cases. The fact that both algorithms' performance decreases suggests that this is due to an anomaly from sampling. However the point grants further verification by testing the algorithms on larger datasets.

5.3. DISCUSSION

The results shown in Figures 3 and 4 support the hypothesis that discretization of continuous variables does not decrease the accuracy of recovering the structure of BNs from data. They also show that using discretized continuous variables to construct a BN structure (algorithm A1) is significantly faster (by a factor ranging from about 30 to 40) than using untransformed continuous variables (algorithm A2). Also, the predictions based on A1 are at least as accurate as (and often more accurate than) the predictions based on A2.

Another important aspect differentiating the two learning methods is the relative variability of the results for algorithm A2 compared with the results for algorithm A1, especially with regard to the structure of the learned models. In Figures 3 and 4 the number of parents of the class variable discovered by algorithm A1 over multiple simulations remains basically constant (e.g., 2 parents in the database AUTO-MPG, 4 parents in the database ABALONE). This is not true for algorithm A2, where the difference between the minimum and maximum number of arcs discovered is quite high (e.g., when applied to the database ABALONE, A2 discovers a minimum of 0 parents and a maximum of 4 parents). These results suggest that the estimations based on the ANN-based scoring metric are not very stable, probably due to the tendency of ANN-based search to get stuck in local maxima in the search space.

6. Conclusions

In this paper, we presented a method for learning hybrid BNs, defined as BNs containing both continuous and discrete variables. The method is based on the definition of a scoring metric that makes use of artificial neural networks as probability estimators. The use of the ANN-based scoring metric allows us to search the space of BN structures without the need for discretizing the continuous variables. We compared this method to the alternative of learning the BN structure based on discretized data.

The main purpose of this work was to test whether discretization would or would not degrade the accuracy of the discovered BN structure and parameter estimation accuracy. The experimental results presented in this paper suggest that discretization of variables permits the rapid construction of relatively high fidelity Bayesian networks when compared to a much slower method that uses continuous variables. These results do not of course rule out the possibility that we can develop faster and more accurate continuous variable learning methods than the one investigated here. However, the results do lend support to discretization as a viable method for addressing the problem of learning hybrid BNs.

Acknowledgments

We thank Chris Bishop and Moises Goldszmidt for their useful comments on a preliminary version of this manuscript. This work was funded by grant IRI-9509792 from the National Science Foundation.

References

1. J. Binder, D. Koller, S. Russel, and K. Kanazawa. Adaptive probabilistic networks with hidden variables. *Machine Learning*, 1997. To appear.
2. C. Bishop. Mixture density networks. Technical Report NCRG/4288, Neural Computing Research Group, Department of Computer Science, Aston University, Birmingham B4 7ET, U.K., February 1994.
3. C. Bishop. *Neural Networks for Pattern Recognition*. Oxford University Press, Oxford, 1995.
4. R. Bouckært. Properties of learning algorithms for Bayesian belief networks. In *Proceedings of the 10th Conference of Uncertainty in Artificial Intelligence*, pages 102–109, San Francisco, California, 1994. Morgan Kaufmann Publishers.
5. J. Bridle. Probabilistic interpretation of feedforward classification network outputs, with relationships to statistical pattern recognition. In *Neuro-computing: Algorithms, Architectures and Applications*. Springer Verlag, New York, 1989.
6. W. Buntine. A guide to the literature on learning probabilistic networks from data. *IEEE Transactions on Knowledge and Data Engineering*, 8(3), 1996.
7. W. L. Buntine. Theory refinement on Bayesian networks. In *Proceedings of the 7th Conference of Uncertainty in AI*, pages 52–60, 1991.
8. P. Cheeseman and J. Stutz. Bayesian classification (AutoClass): Theory and results. In U. M. Fayyad, G. Piatetsky-Shapiro, P. Smyth, and R. Uthurasamy, editors, *Advances in Knowledge Discovery and Data Mining*. MIT Press, 1996.
9. D. M. Chickering, D. Geiger, and D. Heckerman. Learning Bayesian networks: search methods and experimental results. In *Proceedings of 5th Workshop on Artificial Intelligence and Statistics*, pages 112–128, January 1995.
10. D. M. Chickering and D. Heckerman. Efficient approximation for the marginal likelihood of incomplete data given a Bayesian network. In *Proceedings of the 12-th Conference of Uncertainty in AI*, 1996.
11. G. F. Cooper. NESTOR: A computer-based medical diagnostic that integrates causal and probabilistic knowledge. Technical Report HPP-84-48, Dept. of Computer Science, Stanford University, Palo Alto, California, 1984.
12. G. F. Cooper and E. Herskovits. A Bayesian method for constructing Bayesian belief networks from databases. In *Proceedings of the 7th Conference of Uncertainty in Artificial Intelligence*, pages 86–94, Los Angeles, CA, 1991.
13. G. F. Cooper and E. Herskovits. A Bayesian Method for the Induction of Probabilistic Networks from Data. *Machine Learning*, 9:309–347, 1992.
14. A. Dawid. Present position and potential developments: Some personal views. Statistical theory. The prequential approach (with discussion). *Journal of Royal Statistical Society A*, 147:278–292, 1984.
15. A. Dawid. Prequential analysis, stochastic complexity and Bayesian inference. In J.M. Bernardo *et al*, editor, *Bayesian Statistics 4*, pages 109–125. Oxford University Press, 1992.

16. M. Druzdzel, L. C. van der Gaag, M. Henrion, and F. Jensen, editors. *Building probabilistic networks: where do the numbers come from?*, IJCAI-95 Workshop, Montreal, Québec, 1995.

17. B. Everitt and D. Hand. *Finite mixture distributions.* Chapman and Hall, 1981.

18. U. Fayyad and R. Uthurusamy, editors. *Proceedings of the First International Conference on Knowledge Discovery and Data Mining (KDD-95)*, Montreal, Québec, 1995. AAAI Press.

19. N. Friedman and M. Goldszmidt. Discretization of continuous attributes while learning Bayesian networks. In L. Saitta, editor, *Proceedings of 13-th International Conference on Machine Learning*, pages 157–165, 1996.

20. D. Geiger and D. Heckerman. Learning Gaussian networks. In R. L. de Mantras and D. Poole, editors, *Prooceedings of the 10th Conference of Uncertainty in AI*, San Francisco, California, 1994. Morgan Kaufmann.

21. D. Geiger, D. Heckerman, and C. Meek. Asymptotic model selection for directed networks with hidden variables. Technical Report MSR-TR-96-07, Microsoft Research, May 1996.

22. W. Gilks, S. Richardson, and D. Spiegelhalter. *Markov Chain Monte Carlo in Practice.* Chapman & Hall, 1996.

23. D. Heckerman, D. Geiger, and D. M. Chickering. Learning Bayesian networks: The combination of knowledge and statistical data. *Machine Learning*, 20:197–243, 1995.

24. D. Madigan, S. A. Andersson, M. D. Perlman, and C. T. Volinsky. Bayesian model averaging and model selection for Markov equivalence classes of acyclic digraphs. *Communications in Statistics – Theory and Methods*, 25, 1996.

25. D. Madigan, A. E. Raftery, C. T. Volinsky, and J. A. Hoeting. Bayesian model averaging. In *AAAI Workshop on Integrating Multiple Learned Models*, 1996.

26. C. Merz and P. Murphy. Machine learning repository. University of California, Irvine, Department of Information and Computer Science, 1996. http://www.ics.uci.edu/ mlearn/MLRepository.html.

27. M. Moller. A scaled conjugate gradient algorithm for fast supervised learning. *Neural Networks*, 6:525–533, 1993.

28. S. Monti and G. F. Cooper. Learning Bayesian belief networks with neural network estimators. In M. Mozer, M. Jordan, and T. Petsche, editors, *Advances in Neural Information Processing Systems 9: Proceedings of the 1996 Conference*, 1997.

29. J. Pearl. *Probabilistic Reasoning in Intelligent Systems: Networks of Plausible Inference.* Morgan Kaufman Publishers, Inc., 1988.

30. A. E. Raftery. Bayesian model selection in social research (with discussion). *Sociological Methodology*, pages 111–196, 1995.

31. A. E. Raftery. Hypothesis testing and model selection. In Gilks *et al* [22], chapter 10, pages 163–188.

32. M. Richard and R. Lippman. Neural network classifiers estimate Bayesian a-posteriori probabilities. *Neural Computation*, 3:461–483, 1991.

33. C. Robert. Mixtures of distributions: Inference and estimation. In Gilks *et al* [22], chapter 24, pages 441–464.

34. G. Schwarz. Estimating the dimension of a model. *Annals of Statistics*, 6:461–464, 1996.

35. R. Shachter. Intelligent probabilistic inference. In L. K. . J. Lemmer, editor, *Uncertainty in Artificial Intelligence 1*, pages 371–382, Amsterdam, North-Holland, 1986.

36. D. Spiegelhalter, A. Dawid, S. Lauritzen, and R. Cowell. Bayesian analysis in expert systems. *Statistical Science*, 8(3):219–283, 1993.

37. B. Thiesson. Accelerated quantification of Bayesian networks with incomplete data. In Fayyad and Uthurusamy [18], pages 306–311.

38. D. Titterington, A. Smith, and U. Makov. *Statistical Analysis of Finite Mixture Distributions.* Wiley, New York, 1985.

A MEAN FIELD LEARNING ALGORITHM FOR UNSUPERVISED NEURAL NETWORKS

LAWRENCE SAUL

AT&T Labs – Research
180 Park Ave D-130
Florham Park, NJ 07932

AND

MICHAEL JORDAN

Massachusetts Institute of Technology
Center for Biological and Computational Learning
79 Amherst Street, E10-034D
Cambridge, MA 02139

Abstract. We introduce a learning algorithm for unsupervised neural networks based on ideas from statistical mechanics. The algorithm is derived from a mean field approximation for *large, layered* sigmoid belief networks. We show how to (approximately) infer the statistics of these networks without resort to sampling. This is done by solving the mean field equations, which relate the statistics of each unit to those of its Markov blanket. Using these statistics as target values, the weights in the network are adapted by a local delta rule. We evaluate the strengths and weaknesses of these networks for problems in statistical pattern recognition.

1. Introduction

Multilayer neural networks trained by backpropagation provide a versatile framework for statistical pattern recognition. They are popular for many reasons, including the simplicity of the learning rule and the potential for discovering hidden, distributed representations of the problem space. Nevertheless, there are many issues that are difficult to address in this framework. These include the handling of missing data, the statistical interpretation of hidden units, and the problem of unsupervised learning, where there are no explicit error signals.

One way to handle these problems is to view these networks as probabilistic models. This leads one to consider the units in the network as random variables, whose statistics are encoded in a joint probability distribution. The learning problem, originally one of function approximation, now becomes one of density estimation under a latent variable model; the objective function is the log-likelihood of the training data. The probabilistic semantics in these networks allow one to infer target values for hidden units, even in an unsupervised setting.

The Boltzmann machine[1] was the first neural network to be endowed with probabilistic semantics. It has a simple Hebb-like learning rule and a fully probabilistic interpretation as a Markov random field. A serious problem for Boltzmann machines, however, is computing the statistics that appear in the learning rule. In general, one has to rely on approximate methods, such as Gibbs sampling or mean field theory[2], to estimate these statistics; exact calculations are not tractable for layered networks. Experience has shown, however, that sampling methods are too slow, and mean field approximations too impoverished[3], to be used in this way.

A different approach has been to recast neural networks as layered belief networks[4]. These networks have a fully probabilistic interpretation as directed graphical models[5, 6]. They can also be viewed as *top-down* generative models for the data that is encoded by the units in the bottom layer[7, 8, 9]. Though it remains difficult to compute the statistics of the hidden units, the directionality of belief networks confers an important advantage. In these networks one can derive a simple lower bound on the likelihood and develop learning rules based on maximizing this lower bound.

The Helmholtz machine[7, 8] was the first neural network to put this idea into practice. It uses a fast, bottom-up recognition model to compute the statistics of the hidden units and a simple stochastic learning rule, known as wake-sleep, to adapt the weights. The tradeoff for this simplicity is that the recognition model cannot handle missing data or support certain types of reasoning, such as *explaining away*[5], that rely on top-down and bottom-up processing.

In this paper we consider an algorithm based on ideas from statistical mechanics. Our lower bound is derived from a mean field approximation for sigmoid belief networks[4]. The original derivation[10] of this approximation made no restrictions on the network architecture or the location of visible units. The purpose of the current paper is to tailor the approximation to networks that represent hierarchical generative models. These are multilayer networks whose visible units occur in the bottom layer and whose topmost layers contain large numbers of hidden units.

The mean field approximation that emerges from this specialization is interesting in its own right. The *mean field equations*, derived by maximizing the lower bound on the log-likelihood, relate the statistics of each unit to those of its Markov blanket. Once estimated, these statistics are used to fill in target values for hidden units. The learning algorithm adapts the weights in the network by a local delta rule. Compact and intelligible, the approximation provides an attractive computational framework for probabilistic modeling in layered belief networks. It also represents a viable alternative to sampling, which has been the dominant paradigm for inference and learning in large belief networks.

While this paper builds on previous work, we have tried to keep it self-contained. The organization of the paper is as follows. In section 2, we examine the modeling problem for unsupervised networks and give a succinct statement of the learning algorithm. (A full derivation of the mean field approximation is given in the appendix.) In section 3, we assess the strengths and weaknesses of these networks based on experiments with handwritten digits. Finally, in section 4, we present our conclusions, as well as some directions for future research.

2. Generative models

Suppose we are given a large sample of binary (0/1) vectors, then asked to model the process by which these vectors were generated. A multilayer network (see Figure 1) can be used to parameterize a generative model of the data in the following way. Let S_i^ℓ denote the ith unit in the ℓth layer of the network, h_i^ℓ its bias, and $J_{ij}^{\ell-1}$ the weights that feed into this unit from the layer above. We imagine that each unit represents a binary random variable whose probability of activation, in the data-generating process, is conditioned on the units in the layer above. Thus we have:

$$P(S_i^\ell = 1|S^{\ell-1}) = \sigma\left(\sum_j J_{ij}^{\ell-1}S_j^{\ell-1} + h_i^\ell\right),\tag{1}$$

where $\sigma(z) = [1 + e^{-z}]^{-1}$ is the sigmoid function. We denote by σ_i^ℓ the squashed sum of inputs that appears on the right hand side of eq. (1). The joint distribution over all the units in the network is given by:

$$P(S) = \prod_{\ell i}(\sigma_i^\ell)^{S_i^\ell}(1 - \sigma_i^\ell)^{1-S_i^\ell}\tag{2}$$

A neural network, endowed with probabilistic semantics in this way, is known as a sigmoid belief network[4]. Layered belief networks were proposed as hierarchical generative models by Hinton et al[7].

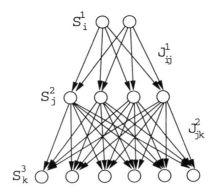

Figure 1. A multilayer sigmoid belief network that parameterizes a generative model for the units in the bottom layer.

The goal of unsupervised learning is to model the data by the units in the bottom layer. We shall refer to these units as visible (V) units, since the data vectors provide them with explicit target values. For the other units in the network—the hidden (H) units—appropriate target values must be inferred from the probabilistic semantics encoded in eq. (2).

2.1. MAXIMUM LIKELIHOOD ESTIMATION

The problem of unsupervised learning, in this framework, is essentially one of density estimation. A network with many hidden units can parameterize a large family of distributions over the visible units. The learning problem is to find the weights J_{ij}^{ℓ} and biases h_i^{ℓ} that make the statistics of the visible units match those of the data.

One simple approach to learning is to maximize the log-likelihood[1] of the training sample. The likelihood of each data vector is obtained from its marginal distribution,

$$P(V) = \sum_H P(H, V), \tag{3}$$

where by definition $P(H, V) = P(S)$ is the joint distribution over all units (hidden and visible). We can derive local learning rules by computing the gradients of the log-likelihood, $\ln P(V)$, with respect to the weights and biases of the network. For each data vector, this gives the on-line updates:

$$\Delta J_{ij}^{\ell} \quad \propto \quad \mathrm{E}\left[(S_i^{\ell+1} - \sigma_i^{\ell+1})S_j^{\ell}\right], \tag{4}$$

$$\Delta h_i^{\ell} \quad \propto \quad \mathrm{E}\left[S_i^{\ell} - \sigma_i^{\ell}\right], \tag{5}$$

---

[1] For simplicity of exposition, we do not consider forms of regularization (e.g., penalized likelihoods, cross-validation) that may be necessary to prevent overfitting.

where $E[\cdots]$ denotes an expectation with respect to the conditional distribution, $P(H|V)$. Note that the updates take the form of a delta rule, with unit activations σ_i^ℓ being matched to target values S_i^ℓ. Many authors[4, 18] have noted the associative, error-correcting nature of gradient-based learning rules in belief networks.

2.2. MEAN FIELD LEARNING

In general, it is intractable[11, 12] to calculate the likelihood in eq. (3) or the statistics in eqs. (4–5). It is also time-consuming to estimate them by sampling from $P(H|V)$. One way to proceed is based on the following idea[7]. Suppose we have an approximate distribution, $Q(H|V) \approx P(H|V)$. Using Jensen's inequality, we can form a lower bound on the log-likelihood from:

$$\ln P(V) \geq \sum_H Q(H|V) \ln \left[\frac{P(H,V)}{Q(H|V)} \right]. \tag{6}$$

If this bound is easy to compute, then we can derive learning rules based on maximizing the bound. Though one cannot guarantee that such learning rules always increase the actual likelihood, they provide an efficient alternative to implementing the learning rules in eqs. (4–5).

Our choice of $Q(H|V)$ is motivated by ideas from statistical mechanics. The mean field approximation[13] is a general method for estimating the statistics of large numbers of correlated variables. The starting point of the mean field approximation is to consider factorized distributions of the form:

$$Q(H|V) = \prod_\ell \prod_{i \in H} (\mu_i^\ell)^{S_i^\ell} (1 - \mu_i^\ell)^{1-S_i^\ell} \tag{7}$$

The parameters μ_i^ℓ are the mean values of S_i^ℓ under the distribution $Q(H|V)$, and they are chosen to maximize the lower bound in eq. (6). A full derivation of the mean field theory for these networks, starting from eqs. (6) and (7), is given in the appendix. Our goal in this section, however, is to give a succinct statement of the learning algorithm. In what follows, we therefore present only the main results, along with a number of useful intuitions.

For these networks, the mean field approximation works by keeping track of two parameters, $\{\mu_i^\ell, \xi_i^\ell\}$ for each unit in the network. Roughly speaking, these parameters are stored as approximations to the true statistics of the hidden units: $\mu_i^\ell \approx E[S_i^\ell]$ approximates the mean of S_i^ℓ, while $\xi_i^\ell \approx E[\sigma_i^\ell]$ approximates the average value of the squashed sum of inputs. Though only the first of these appears explicitly in eq. (7), it turns out that both are needed to compute a lower bound on the log-likelihood. The values of $\{\mu_i^\ell, \xi_i^\ell\}$ depend on the states of the visible units, as well as the weights and biases of the network. They are computed by solving the *mean field equations:*

$$\mu_i^\ell = \sigma\left[\sum_j J_{ij}^{\ell-1}\mu_j^{\ell-1} + h_i^\ell + \sum_j J_{ji}^\ell(\mu_j^{\ell+1} - \xi_j^{\ell+1}) - \frac{1}{2}(1 - 2\mu_i^\ell)\sum_j(J_{ji}^\ell)^2\xi_j^{\ell+1}(1 - \xi_j^{\ell+1})\right] \quad (8)$$

$$\xi_i^\ell = \sigma\left[\sum_j J_{ij}^{\ell-1}\mu_j^{\ell-1} + h_i^\ell + \frac{1}{2}(1 - 2\xi_i^\ell)\sum_j(J_{ij}^{\ell-1})^2\mu_j^{\ell-1}(1 - \mu_j^{\ell-1})\right]. \quad (9)$$

These equations couple the parameters of each unit to those in adjacent layers. The terms inside the brackets can be viewed as effective influences (or "mean fields") on each unit in the network. The reader will note that sigmoid belief networks have twice as many mean field parameters as their undirected counterparts[2]. For this we can offer the following intuition. Whereas the parameters μ_i^ℓ are determined by top-down and bottom-up influences, the parameters ξ_i^ℓ are determined only by top-down influences. The distinction—essentially, one between parents and children—is only meaningful for directed graphical models.

The procedure for solving these equations is fairly straightforward. Initial guesses for $\{\mu_i^\ell, \xi_i^\ell\}$ are refined by alternating passes through the network, in which units are updated one layer at a time. We alternate these passes in the bottom-up and top-down directions so that information is propagated from the visible units to the hidden units, and vice versa. The visible units remain clamped to their target values throughout this process. Further details are given in the appendix.

The learning rules for these networks are designed to maximize the bound in eq. (6). An expression for this bound, in terms of the weights and biases of the network, is derived in the appendix; see eq. (24). Gradient ascent in J_{ij}^ℓ and h_i^ℓ leads to the learning rules:

$$\Delta J_{ij}^\ell \propto \left[\left(\mu_i^{\ell+1} - \xi_i^{\ell+1}\right)\mu_j^\ell - J_{ij}^\ell\xi_i^{\ell+1}(1 - \xi_i^{\ell+1})\mu_j^\ell(1 - \mu_j^\ell)\right], \quad (10)$$

$$\Delta h_i^\ell \propto (\mu_i^\ell - \xi_i^\ell). \quad (11)$$

Comparing these learning rules to eqs. (4–5), we see that the mean field parameters fill in for the statistics of S_i^ℓ and σ_i^ℓ. This is, of course, what makes the learning algorithm tractable. Whereas the statistics of $P(H|V)$ cannot be efficiently computed, the parameters $\{\mu_i^\ell, \xi_i^\ell\}$ can be found by solving the mean field equations. We obtain a simple on-line learning algorithm by solving the mean field equations for each data vector in the training set, then adjusting the weights by the learning rules, eqs. (10) and (11).

The reader may notice that the rightmost term of eq. (10) has no counterpart in eq. (4). This term, a regularizer induced by the mean field approximation, causes J_{ij}^ℓ to be decayed according to the mean-field statistics of $\sigma_i^{\ell+1}$ and S_j^{ℓ}. In particular, the weight decay is suppressed if either $\xi_i^{\ell+1}$ or μ_j^{ℓ} is saturated near zero or one; in effect, weights between highly correlated units are *burned in* to their current values.

3. Experiments

We used a large database of handwritten digits to evaluate the strengths and weaknesses of these networks. The database[16] was constructed from NIST Special Databases 1 and 3. The examples in this database were deslanted, downsampled, and thresholded to create 10×10 binary images. There were a total of 60000 examples for training and 10000 for testing; these were divided roughly equally among the ten digits ZERO to NINE. Our experiments had several goals: (i) to evaluate the speed and performance of the mean field learning algorithm; (ii) to assess the quality of multilayer networks as generative models; (iii) to see whether classifiers based on generative models work in high dimensions; and (iv) to test the robustness of these classifiers with respect to missing data.

We used the mean field algorithm from the previous section to learn generative models for each digit. The generative models were parameterized by four-layer networks with $4 \times 12 \times 36 \times 100$ architectures. Each network was trained by nine passes[2] through the training examples. Figure 2 shows a typical plot of how the score computed from eq. (6) increased during training. To evaluate the discriminative capabilities of these models, we trained ten networks, one for each digit, then used these networks to classify the images in the test set. The test images were labeled by whichever network assigned them the highest likelihood score, computed from eq. (6). Each of these experiments required about nineteen CPU hours on an SGI R10000, or roughly 0.12 seconds of processing time per image per network. We conducted five such experiments; the error rates were $4.9\% (\times 2)$, $5.1\% (\times 2)$, and 5.2%. By comparison, the error rates[3] of several k-nearest neighbor algoriths were: 6.3% $(k = 1)$, 5.8% $(k = 3)$, 5.5% $(k = 5)$, 5.4% $(k = 7)$, and 5.5% $(k = 9)$. These results show that the networks have learned noisy but essentially accurate models of each digit class. This is confirmed by looking at images sampled from the generative model of each network; some of these are shown in figure 3.

One advantage of generative models for classification is the seamless handling of missing data. Inference in this case is simply performed on the

---

[2]The first pass through the training examples was used to initialize the biases of the bottom layer; the rest were used for learning. The learning rate followed a fixed schedule: 0.02 for four epochs and 0.005 for four epochs.

[3]All the error rates in this paper apply to experiments with 10×10 binary images. The best backpropagation networks[16], which exploit prior knowledge and operate on 20×20 greyscale images, can obtain error rates less than one percent.

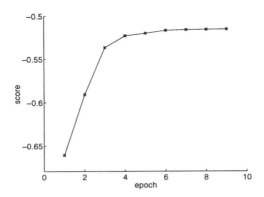

Figure 2. Plot of the lower bound on the log-likelihood, averaged over training patterns, versus the number of epochs, for a $4 \times 12 \times 36 \times 100$ network trained on the digit TWO. The score has been normalized by $100 \times \ln 2$.

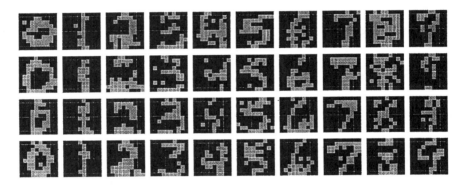

Figure 3. Synthetic images sampled from each digit's generative model.

pruned network in which units corresponding to missing pixels have been removed (i.e., marginalized). We experimented by randomly labeling a certain fraction, f, of pixels in the test set as missing, then measuring the number of classification errors versus f. The solid line in figure 4 shows a plot of this curve for one of the mean field classifiers. The overall performance degrades gradually from 5% error at $f = 0$ to 12% error at $f = 0.5$.

One can also compare the mean field networks to other types of generative models. The simplest of these is a mixture model in which the pixel values (within each mixture component) are conditionally distributed as independent binary random variables. Models of this type can be trained by an Expectation-Maximization (EM) algorithm[19] for maximum likelihood estimation. Classification via mixture models was investigated in a separate set of experiments. Each experiment consisted of training ten mixture models, one for each digit, then using the mixture models to classify the

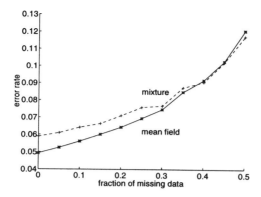

Figure 4. Plot of classification error rate versus fraction of missing pixels in the test set. The solid curve gives the results for the mean field classifier; the dashed curve, for the mixture model classifier.

digits in the test set. The mixture models had forty mixture components and were trained by ten iterations of EM. The classification error rates in five experiments were 5.9%(×3) and 6.2%(×2); the robustness of the best classifier to missing data is shown by the dashed line in figure 4. Note that while the mixture models had roughly the same number of free parameters as the layered networks, the error rates were generally higher. These results suggest that hierarchical generative models, though more difficult to train, may have representational advantages over mixture models.

4. Discussion

The trademarks of neural computation are simple learning rules, local message-passing, and hierarchical distributed representations of the problem space. The backpropagation algorithm for multilayer networks showed that many supervised learning problems were amenable to this style of computation. It remains a challenge to find an unsupervised learning algorithm with the same widespread potential.

In this paper we have developed a mean field algorithm for unsupervised neural networks. The algorithm captures many of the elements of neural computation in a sound, probabilistic framework. Information is propagated by local message-passing, and the learning rule—derived from a lower bound on the log-likelihood—combines delta-rule adaptation with weight decay and burn-in. All these features demonstrate the advantages of tailoring a mean field approximation to the properties of layered networks.

It is worth comparing our approach to methods based on Gibbs sampling[4]. One advantage of the mean field approximation is that it enables one to compute a lower bound on the marginal likelihood, $P(V)$. Estimating these likelihoods by sampling is not so straightforward; indeed, it is considerably harder than estimating the statistics of individual units. In a recent study, Frey et al[15] reported that learning by Gibbs sampling was an extremely slow process for sigmoid belief networks.

Mean field algorithms are evolving. The algorithm in this paper is considerably faster and easier to implement than our previous one[10, 15]. There are several important areas for future research. Currently, the overall computation time is dominated by the iterative solution of the mean field equations. It may be possible to reduce processing times by fine tuning the number of mean field updates or by training a feed-forward network (i.e., a bottom-up recognition model[7, 8]) to initialize the mean field parameters close to solutions of eqs. (8–9). In the current implementation, we found the processing times (per image) to scale linearly with the number of weights in the network. An interesting question is whether mean field algorithms can support massively parallel implementations.

With better algorithms come better architectures. There are many possible elaborations on the use of layered belief networks as hierarchical generative models. Continuous-valued units, as opposed to binary-valued ones, would help to smooth the output of the generative model. We have not exploited any sort of local connectivity between layers, although this structure is known to be helpful in supervised learning[16]. An important consideration is how to incorporate prior knowledge about the data (e.g., translation/rotation invariance[20]) into the network. Finally, the synthetic images in figure 3 reveal an inherent weakness of top-down generative models; while these models require an element of stochasticity to model the variability in the data, they lack a feedback mechanism (i.e., relaxation[21]) to clean up noisy pixels. These extensions and others will be necessary to realize the full potential of unsupervised neural networks.

ACKNOWLEDGEMENTS

The authors acknowledge useful discussions with T. Jaakkola, H. Seung, P. Dayan, G. Hinton, and Y. LeCun and thank the anonymous reviewers for many helpful suggestions.

A. Mean field approximation

In this appendix we derive the mean field approximation for large, layered sigmoid belief networks. Starting from the factorized distribution for $Q(H|V)$, eq. (7), our goal is to maximize the lower bound on the log-likelihood, eq. (6). This bound consists of the difference between two terms:

$$\ln P(V) \geq \left[-\sum_H Q(H|V)\ln Q(H|V)\right] - \left[-\sum_H Q(H|V)\ln P(H,V)\right].$$
(12)

The first term is simply the entropy of the mean field distribution. Because $Q(H|V)$ is fully factorized, the entropy is given by:

$$-\sum_H Q(H|V)\ln Q(H|V) = -\sum_{i\ell\in H}\left[\mu_i^\ell \ln \mu_i^\ell + (1-\mu_i^\ell)\ln(1-\mu_i^\ell)\right]$$
(13)

We identify the second term in eq. (12) as (minus) the mean field energy; the name arises from interpreting $P(H,V) = e^{\ln P(H,V)}$ as a Boltzmann distribution. Unlike the entropy, the energy term in eq. (12) is not so straightforward.

The difficulty in evaluating the energy stems from the form of the joint distribution, eq. (2). To see this, let

$$z_i^\ell = \sum_j J_{ij}^{\ell-1} S_j^{\ell-1} + h_i^\ell$$
(14)

denote the weighted sum of inputs into unit S_i^ℓ. From eqs. (1) and (2), we can write the joint distribution in sigmoid belief networks as:

$$\ln P(S) = -\sum_{\ell i}\left\{S_i^\ell \ln\left[1+e^{-z_i^\ell}\right] + (1-S_i^\ell)\ln\left[1+e^{z_i^\ell}\right]\right\}$$
(15)

$$= \sum_{\ell i}\left\{S_i^\ell z_i^\ell - \ln\left[1+e^{z_i^\ell}\right]\right\}.$$
(16)

The difficulty in evaluating the mean field energy is the logarithm on the right hand side of eq. (16). This term makes it impossible to perform the averaging of $\ln P(S)$ in closed form, even for the simple distribution, eq. (7).

Clearly, another approximation is needed to evaluate $\langle \ln[1+e^{z_i^\ell}]\rangle$, averaged over the distribution, $Q(H|V)$. We can make progress by studying the sum of inputs, z_i^ℓ, as a random variable in its own right. Under the distribution $Q(H|V)$, the right hand side of eq. (14) is a weighted sum of independent random variables with means $\mu_j^{\ell-1}$ and variances $\mu_j^{\ell-1}(1-\mu_j^{\ell-1})$. The number of terms in this sum is equal to the number of hidden units in the $(\ell-1)$th layer of the network. In large networks, we expect the statistics of this sum—or more precisely, the mean field distribution $Q(z_i^\ell|V)$—to be governed by a central limit theorem. In other words, to a very good approximation, $Q(z_i^\ell|V)$ assumes a normal distribution with mean and variance:

$$\langle z_i^\ell \rangle = \sum_j J_{ij}^{\ell-1}\mu_j^{\ell-1} + h_i^\ell,$$
(17)

$$\left\langle (\delta z_i^\ell)^2 \right\rangle = \sum_j (J_{ij}^{\ell-1})^2 \mu_j^{\ell-1} (1 - \mu_j^{\ell-1}). \tag{18}$$

In what follows, we will use the approximation that $Q(z_i^\ell|V)$ is Gaussian to simplify the mean field theory for sigmoid belief networks. The approximation is well suited to layered networks where each unit receives a large number of inputs from the (hidden) units in the preceding layer.

The asymptotic form of $Q(z_i^\ell|V)$ and the logarithm term in eq. (16) motivate us to consider the following lemma. Let z denote a Gaussian random variable with mean $\langle z \rangle$ and variance $\langle \delta z^2 \rangle$, and consider the expected value, $\langle \ln[1 + e^z] \rangle$. For any real number ξ, we can form the upper bound[22]:

$$\langle \ln[1 + e^z] \rangle = \langle \ln[e^{\xi z} e^{-\xi z} (1 + e^z)] \rangle, \tag{19}$$

$$= \xi \langle z \rangle + \langle \ln[e^{-\xi z} + e^{(1-\xi)z}] \rangle, \tag{20}$$

$$\leq \xi \langle z \rangle + \ln \langle e^{-\xi z} + e^{(1-\xi)z} \rangle, \tag{21}$$

where the last line follows from Jensen's inequality. Since z is Gaussian, it is straightforward to perform the averages on the right hand side. This gives us an upper bound on $\langle \ln[1 + e^z] \rangle$ expressed in terms of the mean and variance:

$$\langle \ln[1 + e^z] \rangle \leq \frac{1}{2} \xi^2 \langle \delta z^2 \rangle + \ln \left[1 + e^{\langle z \rangle + (1-2\xi)\langle \delta z^2 \rangle / 2} \right]. \tag{22}$$

In what follows, we will use this bound to approximate the exact value of $\langle \ln[1 + e^{z_i^\ell}] \rangle$. Recall from eq. (16) that these are the intractable averages that appear in the mean field energy; we are therefore motivated to find the value of ξ that makes the bound as tight as possible. The right hand side of eq. (22) is minimized when:

$$\xi = \sigma \left[\langle z \rangle + \frac{1}{2}(1 - 2\xi)\langle \delta z^2 \rangle \right]. \tag{23}$$

Eq. (23) has a unique solution in the interval $\xi \in [0, 1]$. Given values for $\langle z \rangle$ and $\langle \delta z^2 \rangle$, it is easily solved by iteration; in fact, the iteration $\xi \leftarrow \sigma \left[\langle z \rangle + \frac{1}{2}(1 - 2\xi)\langle \delta z^2 \rangle \right]$ is guaranteed to tighten the upper bound in eq. (22). We can understand eq. (23) as a self-consistent approximation for computing $\xi \approx \langle \sigma(z) \rangle$ where z is a Gaussian random variable. To see this, consider the limiting behaviors: $\langle \sigma(z) \rangle \to \sigma(\langle z \rangle)$ as $\langle \delta z^2 \rangle \to 0$ and $\langle \sigma(z) \rangle \to \frac{1}{2}$ as $\langle \delta z^2 \rangle \to \infty$. Eq. (23) captures both these limits and interpolates smoothly between them for finite $\langle \delta z^2 \rangle$.

Equipped with the lemma, eq. (22), we can proceed to deal with the intractable terms in the mean field energy. Unable to compute the average over $Q(H|V)$ exactly, we instead settle for the tightest possible bound. This is done by introducing a new mean field parameter, ξ_i^ℓ, for each unit in the network, then substituting ξ_i^ℓ and the statistics of z_i^ℓ into eq. (22). Note that these terms appear in eq. (6) with an overall minus sign; thus, to the extent that $Q(z_i^l|V)$ is well approximated by a Gaussian distribution, the upper bound in eq. (22) translates[4] into a lower bound on the log likelihood.

Assembling all the terms in eq. (12), we obtain an objective function for the mean field approximation:

$$
\begin{aligned}
\ln P(V) \;\geq\; & -\sum_{i\ell\in H}\left[\mu_i^\ell\ln\mu_i^\ell + (1-\mu_i^\ell)\ln(1-\mu_i^\ell)\right] + \sum_{ij\ell}J_{ij}^{\ell-1}\mu_i^\ell\mu_j^{\ell-1} \quad (24)\\
& +\sum_{i\ell}h_i^\ell\mu_i^\ell - \frac{1}{2}\sum_{ij\ell}(\xi_i^\ell)^2(J_{ij}^{\ell-1})^2\mu_j^{\ell-1}(1-\mu_j^{\ell-1})\\
& -\sum_{i\ell}\ln\left\{1+e^{h_i^\ell+\sum_j[J_{ij}^{\ell-1}\mu_j^{\ell-1}+\frac{1}{2}(1-2\xi_i^\ell)(J_{ij}^{\ell-1})^2\mu_j^{\ell-1}(1-\mu_j^{\ell-1})]}\right\}
\end{aligned}
$$

The mean field parameters are chosen to maximize eq. (24) for different settings of the visible units. Equating their gradients to zero gives the mean field equations, eqs. (8–9). Likewise, computing the gradients for J_{ij}^ℓ and h_i^ℓ gives the learning rules in eqs. (10–11).

The mean field equations are solved by finding a local maximum of eq. (24). This can be done in many ways. The strategy we chose was cyclic stepwise ascent—fixing all the parameters except one, then locating the value of that parameter that maximizes eq. (24). This procedure for solving the mean field equations can be viewed as a sequence of local message-passing operations that "match" the statistics of each hidden unit to those of its Markov blanket[5]. For the parameters ξ_i^ℓ, new values can be found by iterating eq. (9); it is straightforward to show that this iteration always leads to an increase in the objective function. On the other hand, iterating eq. (8) for μ_i^ℓ does *not* always lead to an increase in eq. (24); hence, the optimal values for μ_i^ℓ cannot be found in this way. Instead, for each update, one must search the interval $\mu_i^\ell\in[0,1]$ using some sort of bracketing procedure[17] to find a local maximum in eq. (24). This is necessary to ensure that the mean field parameters converge to a solution of eqs. (8–9).

---

[4]Our earlier work[10] showed how to obtain a strict lower bound on the log likelihood; i.e., the earlier work made no appeal to a Gaussian approximation for $Q(z_i^\ell|V)$. For the networks considered here, however, we find the difference between the approximate bound and the strict bound to be insignificant in practice. Moreover, the current algorithm has advantages in simplicity and interpretability.

References

1. D. Ackley, G. Hinton, and T. Sejnowski. A learning algorithm for Boltzmann machines. *Cognitive Science* **9**:147–169 (1985).
2. C. Peterson and J. R. Anderson. A mean field theory learning algorithm for neural networks. *Complex Systems* **1**:995–1019 (1987).
3. C. Galland. The limitations of deterministic Boltzmann machine learning. *Network* **4**:355–379.
4. R. Neal. Connectionist learning of belief networks. *Artificial Intelligence* **56**:71–113 (1992).
5. J. Pearl. *Probabilistic Reasoning in Intelligent Systems*. Morgan Kaufmann: San Mateo, CA (1988).
6. S. Lauritzen. *Graphical Models*. Oxford University Press: Oxford (1996).
7. G. Hinton, P. Dayan, B. Frey, and R. Neal. The wake-sleep algorithm for unsupervised neural networks. *Science* **268**:1158–1161 (1995).
8. P. Dayan, G. Hinton, R. Neal, and R. Zemel. The Helmholtz machine. *Neural Computation* **7**:889–904 (1995).
9. M. Lewicki and T. Sejnowski. Bayesian unsupervised learning of higher order structure. In M. Mozer, M. Jordan, and T. Petsche, eds. *Advances in Neural Information Processing Systems* **9**: . MIT Press: Cambridge (1996).
10. L. Saul, T. Jaakkola, and M. Jordan. Mean field theory for sigmoid belief networks. *Journal of Artificial Intelligence Research* **4**:61–76 (1996).
11. G. Cooper. Computational complexity of probabilistic inference using Bayesian belief networks. *Artificial Intelligence* **42**:393-405 (1990).
12. P. Dagum and M. Luby. Approximately probabilistic reasoning in Bayesian belief networks is NP-hard. *Artificial Intelligence* **60**:141-153 (1993).
13. G. Parisi. *Statistical Field Theory*. Addison-Wesley: Redwood City (1988).
14. J. Hertz, A. Krogh, and R.G. Palmer. *Introduction to the Theory of Neural Computation*. Addison-Wesley: Redwood City (1991).
15. B. Frey, G. Hinton, and P. Dayan. Does the wake-sleep algorithm produce good density estimators? In D. Touretzky, M. Mozer, and M. Hasselmo, eds. *Advances in Neural Information Processing Systems* **8**:661-667. MIT Press: Cambridge, MA (1996).
16. Y. LeCun, L. Jackel, L. Bottou, A. Brunot, C. Cortes, J. Denker, H. Drucker, I. Guyon, U. Muller, E. Sackinger, P. Simard, and V. Vapnik. Comparison of learning algorithms for handwritten digit recognition. In *Proceedings of ICANN'95*.
17. W. Press, B. Flannery, S. Teukolsky, and W. Vetterling. *Numerical Recipes*. Cambridge University Press: Cambridge (1986).
18. S. Russell, J. Binder, D. Koller, and K. Kanazawa. Local learning in probabilistic networks with hidden variables. In *Proceedings of IJCAI-95*.
19. A. Dempster, N. Laird, and D. Rubin. 1977. Maximum likelihood from incomplete data via the EM algorithm. *Journal of the Royal Statistical Society* B39:1–38.
20. P. Simard, Y. LeCun, and J. Denker. Efficient pattern recognition using a new transformation distance. In S. Hanson, J. Cowan, and C. Giles, eds. *Advances in Neural Information Processing Systems* **5**:50–58. Morgan Kaufmann: San Mateo, CA (1993).
21. S. Geman and D. Geman. Stochastic relaxation, Gibbs distributions, and the Bayesian restoration of images. *IEEE Transactions on Pattern Analysis and Machine Intelligence* **6**:721–741 (1984).
22. H. Seung. Annealed theories of learning. In J.-H. Oh, C. Kwon, and S. Cho, eds. *Neural Networks: The Statistical Mechanics Perspective, Proceedings of the CTP-PRSRI Joint Workshop on Theoretical Physics*. World Scientific: Singapore (1995).

EDGE EXCLUSION TESTS FOR GRAPHICAL GAUSSIAN MODELS

PETER W. F. SMITH

Department of Social Statistics,
The University, Southampton, SO9 5NH UK.

AND

JOE WHITTAKER

Department of Mathematics and Statistics,
University of Lancaster, LA1 4YF, UK.
email: joe.whittaker@lancaster.ac.uk

Summary

Testing that an edge can be excluded from a graphical Gaussian model is an important step in model fitting and the form of the generalised likelihood ratio test statistic for this hypothesis is well known. Herein the modified profile likelihood test statistic for this hypothesis is obtained in closed form and is shown to be a function of the sample partial correlation. Related expressions are given for the Wald and the efficient score statistics. Asymptotic expansions of the exact distribution of this correlation coefficient under the hypothesis of conditional independence are used to compare the adequacy of the chi-squared approximation of these and Fisher's Z statistics. While no statistic is uniformly best approximated, it is found that the coefficient of the $O(n^{-1})$ term is invariant to the dimension of the multivariate Normal distribution in the case of the modified profile likelihood and Fisher's Z but not for the other statistics. This underlines the importance of adjusting test statistics when there are large numbers of variables, and so nuisance parameters in the model.

Similar comparisons are effected for the Normal approximation to the signed square-rooted versions of these statistics.

Keywords: Asymptotic expansions; Conditional independence; Edge exclusion; Efficient score; Fisher's Z; Graphical Gaussian models; Modified profile likelihood; Signed square-root tests; Wald statistic.

1. Introduction

Dempster (1972) introduced graphical Gaussian models where the structure of the inverse variance matrix, rather than the variance matrix itself, is modelled. The idea is to simplify the joint Normal distribution of p continuous random variables by testing if a particular element ω_{ij} of the p by p inverse variance matrix Ω can be set to zero. The remaining elements are nuisance parameters and the hypothesis is composite. Wermuth (1976) showed that fitting these models is equivalent to testing for conditional independence between the corresponding elements of the random vector X. Speed and Kiiveri (1986) showed that the test corresponds to testing if the edge connecting the vertices corresponding to X_i and X_j in the conditional independence graph can be eliminated. Hence such tests are known as edge exclusion tests. For an introduction to this material see Lauritzen (1989) or Whittaker (1990).

Many graphical model selection procedures start by making the $\binom{p}{2}$ single edge exclusion tests, evaluating the (generalised) likelihood ratio statistic and comparing it to a chi-squared distribution. However, this is only asymptotically correct, and may be poor, as is the case for models with discrete observations (Kreiner, 1987; Frydenburg and Jensen, 1989). One approach taken by Davison, Smith and Whittaker (1991) is to use the exact conditional distribution of a test statistic, where available. However, the exact conditional test for edge exclusion for the graphical Gaussian case is equivalent to the unconditional test, and is based on the square of the sample partial correlation coefficient whose null distribution is a beta (Davison, Smith and Whittaker, 1991). Thus in practice the exact test should be used. This statistic is the same as would be derived from a t-test for testing for a zero coefficient in multiple regression. Fisher's Z transformation is also based on the sample partial correlation coefficient and allows Normal tables to be used to a reasonable degree of approximation. It is of interest to assess which of several competing statistics has an exact distribution best approximated by the chi-squared over a varying number of nuisance parameters.

To achieve this aim, explicit expressions for the modified profile likelihood ratio, Wald and efficient score statistics are obtained. This involves inverting the information matrix and calculating the determinant of a relevant submatrix. These test statistics turn out to be functions of the sample partial correlation coefficient and it is natural to compare them with Fisher's Z transformation.

In Section 2, after inverting the information matrix, the Wald and efficient score test statistics for excluding a single edge from a graphical Gaussian model are constructed. In Section 3 a test based on the modified profile likelihood is presented which requires the evaluation of the information determinant. Section 4 contains an assessment, using Taylor series expansions, of the chi-squared approximation to the null distributions. The derivation for the modified profile test statistic requires an extra layer of asymptotic argument. The likelihood ratio test and a test based on Fisher's Z statistic are considered for comparison. The final section contains a discussion of possible generalisations. The related set of signed square-rooted statistics with asymptotic standard Normal distribution are considered in an appendix.

2. Graphical Gaussian Models

The random p-dimensional vector X has a multivariate Normal distribution with density

$$f(x; \Omega) = (2\pi)^{-p/2} |\Omega|^{1/2} \exp\{-\frac{1}{2} x^T \Omega x\},$$

where $\Omega = \Sigma^{-1}$ is the inverse of the variance matrix. Since only the correlation structure of the data is of interest, the mean is taken to be zero. The log-likelihood function for $\omega = \text{vec}(\Omega)$, the vector of the $p(p+1)/2$ distinct elements of Ω, for a single observation, x, is

$$
\begin{aligned}
l(\omega; x) &= c + \frac{1}{2} \log |\Omega| - \frac{1}{2} \text{tr}(\Omega x x^T) \\
&= c + \frac{1}{2} \log |\Omega| - \frac{1}{2} \omega^T J s, \quad (1)
\end{aligned}
$$

where $s = \text{vec}(xx^T)$ and J is a diagonal matrix containing 1s corresponding to elements of ω of the form ω_{ii} and 2s corresponding to elements of ω of the form $\omega_{ij}, i \neq j$. For example, if $p = 3$ and

$$
\omega = \begin{pmatrix} \omega_{12} \\ \omega_{13} \\ \omega_{23} \\ \omega_{11} \\ \omega_{22} \\ \omega_{33} \end{pmatrix}, \quad \text{then} \quad J = \begin{pmatrix} 2 & & & & & \\ & 2 & & & O & \\ & & 2 & & & \\ & & & 1 & & \\ & O & & & 1 & \\ & & & & & 1 \end{pmatrix},
$$

where the Os indicate that all the remaining elements of the matrix are zeros. The interest parameters are held in the leading part of the vector ω.

Graphical Gaussian models form a linear exponential family with canonical parameter ω and canonical statistic a linear function of s. The score function is

$$U(\omega) = \frac{1}{2} \frac{\partial}{\partial \omega} \log |\Omega| - \frac{1}{2} J s = \frac{1}{2} J (\sigma - s), \quad (2)$$

where $\sigma = \text{vec}(\Sigma)$ is (a linear function of) the mean value parameter. The observed (and expected) information matrix is

$$\mathcal{I} = -\frac{\partial}{\partial \omega^T} U(\omega) = -\frac{1}{2} J \frac{\partial}{\partial \omega^T} \sigma. \tag{3}$$

The inverse, $\mathcal{K}$, of this information matrix is required to compute the test statistics.

Consider more generally a linear exponential family model with p-dimensional canonical parameter θ, canonical statistics t and log-likelihood $\theta^T t(x) - \kappa(\theta) - h(x)$ (Barndorff-Nielsen, 1988, p87). The information matrix for the canonical parameter, $\mathcal{I}_\theta$, can be expressed as

$$\mathcal{I}_\theta = \frac{\partial}{\partial \theta^T} \tau(\theta), \tag{4}$$

where $\tau = \frac{\partial}{\partial \theta} \kappa(\theta)$ is the mean-value mapping. As the mean-value mapping is bijective (Barndorff-Nielsen, 1978, p121),

$$\frac{\partial}{\partial \theta^T} \tau \cdot \frac{\partial}{\partial \tau^T} \theta = I,$$

the identity matrix. Hence the inverse of the information matrix can be computed from

$$\mathcal{I}_\theta^{-1} = \frac{\partial}{\partial \tau} \theta^T. \tag{5}$$

This result (5) does not appear well-known, though a form appears in Efron (1978) and, in a different expression, in Amari (1982, 1985, p106). One corollary is that

$$\mathcal{I}_\tau = (\mathcal{I}_\theta)^{-1}. \tag{6}$$

To find the inverse $\mathcal{K} = \mathcal{I}^{-1}$ for the graphical Gaussian model apply (5) to (3) to give

$$\mathcal{K} = -2 \frac{\partial}{\partial \sigma} \omega^T J^{-1}.$$

The partial derivatives of the elements of a p-dimensional symmetric matrix $A = \{a_{ij}\}$ with respect to the elements of its inverse $B = \{b_{rs}\}$ are known (see Graybill, 1983, Corollary 10.8.10 or McCullagh, 1987) and are as follows:

$$\frac{\partial a_{ij}}{\partial b_{rs}} = \begin{cases} -a_{ir} a_{js} & \text{if } r = s \\ -(a_{ir} a_{js} + a_{is} a_{jr}) & \text{if } r \neq s \end{cases} \qquad i, j, r, s = 1, \dots, p.$$

Hence the inverse information matrix of ω can be obtained explicitly. So, in a sample of size n, the covariance between the maximum likelihood estimates (mles) of any two elements of the inverse variance matrix, asymptotically, is

$$\text{cov}(\widehat{\omega}_{ij} \widehat{\omega}_{rs}) = \frac{1}{n} (\omega_{ir} \omega_{js} + \omega_{is} \omega_{jr}). \tag{7}$$

Cox and Wermuth (1990) obtained the inverse of the information matrix for graphical Gaussian models by another method using a result of Isserlis (1918).

Excluding the edge connecting vertices 1 and 2 in a graphical Gaussian model corresponds to accepting the null hypothesis $H_0 : \omega_{12} = 0$. The alternative is $H_A : \omega_{12}$ unspecified. The remaining distinct elements of Ω are nuisance parameters. The likelihood ratio test statistic for excluding a single edge from a graphical Gaussian model is

$$T_l = -n \log (1 - r^2_{12|rest}), \tag{8}$$

where $r_{12|rest}$ is the sample partial correlation of X_1 and X_2 adjusted for the remainder $X_3, \ldots, X_p$. The latter can be expressed in terms of the mles of elements of the inverse variance matrix as

$$r_{12|rest} = -\widehat{\omega}_{12}(\widehat{\omega}_{11}\widehat{\omega}_{22})^{-1/2}, \tag{9}$$

see for example, Whittaker (1990, p189). Below are derived the Wald and efficient score test statistics for the null hypothesis.

2.1. THE WALD TEST

The Wald statistic T_w (Cox and Hinkley, 1974, p314, 323) based on a quadratic approximation of the likelihood function at its maximum, for excluding a single edge from a graphical Gaussian model, is $\widehat{\omega}^2_{12}/\widehat{\mathrm{var}}(\widehat{\omega}_{12})$. The asymptotic variance of $\widehat{\omega}_{12}$ from equation (7) is

$$\mathrm{var}\,\widehat{\omega}_{12} = \frac{1}{n}(\omega_{11}\omega_{22} + \omega^2_{12}), \tag{10}$$

and so leads to the closed form

$$
\begin{aligned}
T_w &= \frac{n\,\widehat{\omega}^2_{12}}{\widehat{\omega}_{11}\widehat{\omega}_{22} + \widehat{\omega}^2_{12}} \\
&= \frac{n\,r^2_{12|rest}}{1 + r^2_{12|rest}}
\end{aligned}
\tag{11}
$$

using (9) above.

2.2. THE EFFICIENT SCORE TEST

The efficient score test T_s (Cox and Hinkley, 1974, p315, 324) is based on the conditional distribution of the score statistic for the interest parameter given the score statistic for the nuisance parameter, evaluated under the null hypothesis. From (2) the score is

$$U(\tilde{\omega}_{12}) = \tilde{\sigma}_{12} - s_{12},$$

where tilde denotes evaluation under the null hypothesis, with conditional variance

$$\frac{1}{n}(\omega_{11}\omega_{22} + \omega_{12}^2)^{-1}. \tag{12}$$

Evaluation of these requires estimates of ω_{12}, ω_{11}, ω_{22} and σ_{12} under the null hypothesis. Under $H_0 : \omega_{12} = 0$ the mles of Ω and Σ are

$$\tilde{\omega}_{12} = 0, \tag{13}$$

$$\tilde{\omega}_{ii} = \hat{\omega}_{ii}(1 - r_{12|rest}^2) \qquad\qquad i = 1, 2 \tag{14}$$

$$\tilde{\sigma}_{ij} = s_{ij} \qquad\qquad i, j \neq 1, 2 \tag{15}$$

$$\tilde{\sigma}_{12} = \cdot \frac{-r_{12|rest}}{(\hat{\omega}_{11}\hat{\omega}_{22})^{1/2}(1 - r_{12|rest}^2)} + s_{12}. \tag{16}$$

Equation (13) restates the null hypothesis. Speed and Kiiveri (1986) showed that for all unconstrained ω_{ij} the mles of the corresponding σ_{ij} are equal to s_{ij}, hence (15). The other two equations are new and their proofs are given in Appendix C.

The corollary of interest is the closed form expression for the score

$$\begin{aligned} T_s &= n\,(\tilde{\sigma}_{12} - s_{12})^2\,\hat{\omega}_{11}\hat{\omega}_{22}(1 - r_{12|rest}^2)^2 \\ &= n\,r_{12|rest}^2, \end{aligned} \tag{17}$$

using (16).

3. The Modified Profile Likelihood Ratio Test

The modified profile likelihood function (Barndorff-Nielsen, 1983, 1988), explicitly designed to take account of nuisance parameters, can be analytically expressed in the Gaussian context, and is an obvious candidate on which to base a test statistic. A number of authors have developed this work and for linear exponential families have calculated the modified profile log-likelihood function: equations (10) of Cox and Reid (1987), (5.2) of Davison (1988) and (6) of Pierce and Peters (1992). Taking this as the starting point, the corresponding test statistic, in the canonical parameterisation, is

$$T_m = T_l + \log\frac{|\hat{\mathcal{I}}_{bb}|}{|\tilde{\mathcal{I}}_{bb}|}. \tag{18}$$

The term T_l is the ordinary log-likelihood ratio test at (8) and $\mathcal{I}_{bb}$ is the information submatrix corresponding to the nuisance parameter ω_b. Here the parameter ω is partitioned into the interest parameter indexed by a (={12}) and the nuisance parameter indexed by b, so $\omega = (\omega_a, \omega_b)$.

Note that in this version of the test statistic the ordinary mles have been used, rather than those obtained from maximising the modified profile likelihood directly; the latter is analytically difficult, see the comments of Cox and Reid (1987) and Pierce and Peters (1992).

The following lemma gives an explicit form for the determinant of the information matrix required to evaluate (18): if $\mathcal{I}$ is the information matrix for a graphical Gaussian model with the canonical parameterisation, then

$$|\mathcal{I}| = 2^{-p}|\Sigma|^{p+1}. \tag{19}$$

To prove this note that taking determinants of (3) gives

$$|\mathcal{I}| = (-2)^{-p(p+1)/2}|J|\left|\frac{\partial}{\partial \omega^T}\,\sigma\right|.$$

The last term on the right is the Jacobian of the transformation $\Sigma = \Sigma\Omega\Sigma$ from Ω to Σ and (Deemer and Olkin, 1951, Theorem 3.7; Muirhead, 1982, p59) equals in absolute value $|\Sigma|^{p+1}$. This establishes the result.

The main result of this section is that the modified profile likelihood ratio test statistic for $H_0 : \omega_{12} = 0$, where the underlying distribution is the p-dimensional Normal, is

$$T_m = -(n - p + 1)\log\left(1 - r^2_{12|rest}\right) + \log\left(1 + r^2_{12|rest}\right). \tag{20}$$

To prove this, the following identities (Whittaker 1990, p149, 169) are used

$$|\mathcal{I}_{bb}| = |\mathcal{I}||\mathcal{K}_{aa}| \quad \text{and} \quad \frac{|\widehat{\Sigma}|}{|\widetilde{\Sigma}|} = 1 - r^2_{12|rest},$$

where $\mathcal{K}_{aa}$ is the submatrix of the inverse of the information matrix corresponding to the interest parameter ω_a.

Equation (18) is evaluated by, firstly using the first identity, followed by applying lemma (19) to give

$$\log\frac{|\widehat{\mathcal{I}}_{bb}|}{|\widetilde{\mathcal{I}}_{bb}|} = (p+1)\log\frac{|\widehat{\Sigma}|}{|\widetilde{\Sigma}|} + \log\frac{|\widehat{\mathcal{K}}_{aa}|}{|\widetilde{\mathcal{K}}_{aa}|}$$

$$= (p+1)\log\left(1 - r^2_{12|rest}\right) + \log\frac{|\widehat{\mathcal{K}}_{aa}|}{|\widetilde{\mathcal{K}}_{aa}|} \tag{21}$$

using the second identity and noting that the $\log 2^p$ terms cancel. The last term on the right is simplified by $\mathcal{K}_{aa} = \omega_{11}\omega_{22} + \omega_{12}^2$ as already utilised in the expressions (10) and (12). So

$$
\begin{aligned}
\frac{\widehat{\mathcal{K}}_{aa}}{\widetilde{\mathcal{K}}_{aa}} &= \frac{\widehat{\omega}_{11}\widehat{\omega}_{22} + \widehat{\omega}_{12}^2}{\widehat{\omega}_{11}\widehat{\omega}_{22}(1 - r_{12|rest}^2)^2} \\
&= \frac{1 + r_{12|rest}^2}{(1 - r_{12|rest}^2)^2}.
\end{aligned}
\tag{22}
$$

Finally, combining (21) and (22) and substituting into (18) gives

$$
\begin{aligned}
T_m &= -n \log{(1 - r_{12|rest}^2)} + (p+1) \log{(1 - r_{12|rest}^2)} \\
&\quad + \log \left\{ \frac{1 + r_{12|rest}^2}{(1 - r_{12|rest}^2)^2} \right\} \\
&= -(n - p - 1) \log{(1 - r_{12|rest}^2)} + \log \left\{ \frac{1 + r_{12|rest}^2}{(1 - r_{12|rest}^2)^2} \right\} \tag{23} \\
&= -(n - p + 1) \log{(1 - r_{12|rest}^2)} + \log{(1 + r_{12|rest}^2)}.
\end{aligned}
$$

Note that (23) shows that the modified test statistic is the ordinary likelihood ratio test statistic where n has been replaced by $n - p - 1$, a multiplicative correction, plus another term which is the log of the ratio of the asymptotic variances of the interest parameter evaluated under H_0 and H_A. The adjustment to the multiplicative term is not directly related to dimension of the nuisance parameters, although this might be expected if adjusting for the number of degrees of freedom used up by estimating these parameters. Instead this term is reduced by one more than the number of variables for which the sample partial correction coefficient is adjusted. This is similar to the case of linear regression where the degrees of freedom are reduced: one for the mean and one for each variable included in the model. This modified test is a function of the sample partial correlation coefficient alone, which is a maximal invariant for the problem (see Davison, Smith and Whittaker, 1991); as are the tests derived in the previous section.

4. The Null Distributions

Moran (1970) (see also Hayakawa, 1975 and Harris and Peers, 1980) showed that in general the likelihood ratio, Wald and efficient score statistics have the same asymptotic power. It has been shown here that for excluding a single edge from a graphical Gaussian model the four statistics: the generalised likelihood ratio, the Wald, the efficient score and the modified profile likelihood, are functions of the sample partial correlation coefficient, as is the test based on Fisher's Z transformation. Consequently the tests have exactly the same power provided the null distributions are correct.

Under the null hypothesis, the square of the sample partial correlation coefficient from a sample of size n from a p-dimensional Normal distribution has a Beta$(\frac{1}{2}, \frac{n-p}{2})$ distribution. For example, see Muirhead (1982, p188). That is

$$f_U(u) = \frac{1}{B(\frac{1}{2}, \frac{n-p}{2})} u^{-1/2}(1-u)^{(n-p-2)/2}, \quad 0 < u < 1,$$

where $u = r_{12|rest}^2$ and $B(\cdot, \cdot)$ is the beta function. By using the relevant transformation, the exact null distribution of the statistics above can be obtained. Following Barndorff-Nielsen and Cox (1989, Chapter 3) and expanding the log of the density functions in powers of n^{-1}, the adequacy of the asymptotic chi-squared approximation can be assessed.

Consider first the likelihood ratio test. With $t = -n \log(1-u)$ the density of T_l under the null hypothesis is

$$
\begin{aligned}
f_l(t) &= \frac{1}{B(\frac{1}{2}, \frac{n-p}{2})} u^{-1/2}(1-u)^{(n-p-2)/2} \cdot \frac{1-u}{n}, \quad 0 < u < 1, \\
&= \frac{1}{nB(\frac{1}{2}, \frac{n-p}{2})} \{1 - \exp(-t/n)\}^{-1/2} \exp\{-t(n-p)/2n\}, \quad t > 0,
\end{aligned}
$$

since $u = 1 - \exp(-t/n)$. Using Stirling's approximation, taking logs and expanding gives

$$\log f_l(t) = -\frac{1}{2}\{t + \log(2\pi t)\} + \frac{1}{4}(t-1)(2p+1)n^{-1} + O(n^{-2}).$$

The leading term of this expansion corresponds to the χ_1^2 distribution and so

$$f_l(t) = g_\chi(t)[1 + \frac{1}{4}(t-1)(2p+1)\,n^{-1}] + O(n^{-2}), \quad t > 0,$$

where $g_\chi(t)$ is the density function of a χ_1^2 random variable. Finally integrating, from 0 to x, term by term, gives the expansion for the cumulative distribution function as

$$
\begin{aligned}
F_l(x) &= G_\chi(x) + \frac{1}{4}(2p+1)\,n^{-1}\int_0^x (t-1)g_\chi(t)dt + O(n^{-2}) \\
&= G_\chi(x) - \frac{1}{2}(2p+1)\,n^{-1}\left(\frac{x}{2\pi}\right)^{1/2}\exp(-x/2) + O(n^{-2}) \\
&= G_\chi(x) - \frac{1}{2}(2p+1)\,x\,g_\chi(x)\,n^{-1} + O(n^{-2}), \quad x > 0,
\end{aligned}
$$

TABLE 1. Coefficients of the $O(n^{-1})$ term in the asymptotic expansions of the density and distribution functions of the five test statistics.

	$a(t)$	$b(x)$
likelihood	$\frac{1}{4}(t-1)(2p+1)$	$-\frac{1}{2}(2p+1)\,x$
modified	$\frac{5}{4}(t-1)$	$-\frac{5}{2}\,x$
Wald	$\frac{1}{4}(t-1)(2p+1)+3t(3-t)$	$-\frac{1}{2}(2p+1-3x)\,x$
score	$\frac{1}{4}(t-1)(2p+1)+t(3-t)$	$-\frac{1}{2}(2p+1-x)\,x$
Fisher	$\frac{1}{12}(3-6t+t^2)$	$-\frac{1}{6}(x-3)\,x$

where $G_\chi(x)$ is the distribution function of a χ_1^2 random variable.

These expressions are of the form

$$
\begin{aligned}
f_l(t) &= g_\chi(t) + a_l(t)\,g_\chi(t)n^{-1} + O(n^{-2}) \\
F_l(x) &= G_\chi(x) + b_l(x)\,g_\chi(x)\,n^{-1} + O(n^{-2}),
\end{aligned}
\tag{24}
$$

with a and b appropriately defined.

The approximations for the five test statistics considered are of a similar form and are displayed in Table 1. The expansions for the Wald and efficient score tests are similarly derived and details are included in Appendix A.

In the case of the modified profile likelihood test, where

$$
f_m(t) = \frac{1}{B(\frac{1}{2},\frac{n-p}{2})} u^{-1/2}(1-u)^{(n-p-2)/2}\cdot\frac{1-u^2}{n-p+2+(n-p)u},\quad 0<u<1,
\tag{25}
$$

it is not possible to obtain a transformation u in terms of t explicitly. However, a function $u^*(t)$, can be found such that

$$
u = u^*(t) + O(n^{-3})
$$

and leads to the evaluation of the coefficients a_m and b_m displayed in the table above; see Appendix B for details.

Fisher's statistic,

$$
Z_f = \frac{1}{2}\log\left(\frac{1+r_{12|rest}}{1-r_{12|rest}}\right),
$$

can be used to test for a zero partial correlation coefficient. Under the null hypothesis, it has expectation zero and variance $1/[(n-p+2)-3] = 1/(n-p-1)$. See Fisher (1970, Ex. 30, p204) or Muirhead (1982, p160 and Theorem 5.3.1). Usually Z_f is standardised and compared with a standard

Normal distribution. However here, for comparison, the null distribution of $T_f = (n-p-1)Z_f^2$ is considered and the terms in the asymptotic expansion are given. Details are included in Appendix A as the derivation is similar to that of the likelihood ratio above.

The second term $b.(x) g_\chi(x) n^{-1}$ in the distribution function expansion gives $F.(x) - G_\chi(x)$. If this coefficient is negative then the test will reject too few hypotheses (a conservative test) whereas if the coefficient is positive too many will be rejected (a liberal test).

The striking feature of Table 1 is that to order n^{-1} the distribution of the modified profile likelihood ratio test and Fisher's Z_f statistics do not depend on p; hence to this accuracy their distributions do not depend on the number of nuisance parameters. The expansions of the modified profile likelihood and the likelihood ratio density functions are the same when $p = 2$. In general the actual sizes of the other three tests are increasing with p and hence when the coefficient of n^{-1} becomes negative the adequacy of the chi-squared approximation decreases with p. When the number of nuisance parameters is large, that is large p, all the tests are on the conservative side.

Inspection of Table 2 reveals that to order n^{-1}, for a 5% test, the likelihood ratio and efficient score tests are always conservative, whereas the Wald test rejects too few hypotheses for p less than 6 and too many for larger p. For a 1% test the likelihood ratio test is again always conservative and so is the efficient score test apart from when $p = 2$. The Wald test is liberal until p equals 10. As expected the modified profile statistic does well, but surprisingly so does Fisher's statistic.

5. Discussion

The asymptotic expansions of the null distribution functions given in Table 1 above (i) allow a comparison of test accuracy among the five statistics considered here, (ii) make explicit how nuisance parameters affect the tests to varying degrees, and (iii) indicate the effect of sample size. The closed form expressions, of interest in their own right, enable the detailed calculation of these expansions. The main conclusion is that the modified profile likelihood test (and Fisher's Z_f test) do not depend on the dimension p of the vector X. From Table 2 these two tests are in general more accurate than the others. For large p this superiority is uniform, since the accuracy of the others deteriorates. The implication is that it is important to modify the statistic when p is large and n is small. Interestingly the adjusting factor depends linearly on p rather than the number of nuisance parameters in the model which is $O(p^2)$.

The signed square root version of the test statistics discussed in Ap-

TABLE 2. Achieved significance levels for the Wald, efficient Score, Likelihood, Modified profile likelihood and Fisher's test statistics, with varying sample size n and dimension p.

Nominal level 5%

n	p	W	S	L	M	F
10	2	0.0126	0.0566	0.0786	0.0786	0.0516
	6	0.0585	0.1025	0.1245		
	10	0.1043	0.1483	0.1703		
20	2	0.0313	0.0533	0.0643	0.0643	0.0508
	6	0.0542	0.0762	0.0872		
	10	0.0771	0.0991	0.1101		
30	2	0.0375	0.0522	0.0595	0.0595	0.0505
	6	0.0528	0.0675	0.0748		
	10	0.0681	0.0828	0.0901		
50	2	0.0425	0.0513	0.0557	0.0557	0.0503
	6	0.0517	0.0605	0.0649		
	10	0.0609	0.0697	0.0741		
200	2	0.0481	0.0503	0.0514	0.0514	0.0501
	6	0.0504	0.0526	0.0537		
	10	0.0527	0.0549	0.0560		

Nominal level 1%

n	p	W	S	L	M	F
10	2	0.0178	0.0070	0.0193	0.0193	0.0123
	6	0.0029	0.0219	0.0342		
	10	0.0120	0.0368	0.0491		
20	2	0.0039	0.0085	0.0147	0.0147	0.0111
	6	0.0036	0.0159	0.0221		
	10	0.0110	0.0234	0.0296		
30	2	0.0007	0.0090	0.0131	0.0131	0.0108
	6	0.0057	0.0140	0.0181		
	10	0.0107	0.0189	0.0230		
50	2	0.0044	0.0094	0.0119	0.0119	0.0105
	6	0.0074	0.0124	0.0148		
	10	0.0104	0.0154	0.0178		
200	2	0.0086	0.0098	0.0105	0.0105	0.0101
	6	0.0094	0.0106	0.0112		
	10	0.0101	0.0113	0.0120		

pendix D lead to much the same conclusions.

These conclusions will generalise to situations in the wider context of graphical model selection: in particular the cases of excluding several edges simultaneously, single edge exclusion from a non-saturated model, and of models involving discrete and mixed variables. All but Fisher's test generalise conceptually, but it is hard to find closed form expressions. The results of the paper suggest that modifying the profile likelihood is most rewarding, and this can always be done numerically. A small simulation study for excluding two edges indicated this to be the case, Smith (1990). In particular these show that the modified profile give the most accurate p-values and its accuracy is least affected by an increase in the number of nuisance parameters.

Acknowledgements: We should like to thank Antony Davison for some extremely valuable comments on an earlier version of this paper. The work of the first author was supported by a SERC studentship.

6. References

Amari, S-I. (1982). Geometrical theory of asymptotic ancillarity and conditional inference. *Biometrika*, **69**, 1–17.

Amari, S-I. (1985). *Differential-Geometric Methods in Statistics*. Lecture Notes in Statistics 28, Springer-Verlag: Heidelberg.

Barndorff-Nielsen, O.E. (1978). *Information and Exponential Families in Statistical Theory*. Wiley: New York.

Barndorff-Nielsen, O.E. (1983). On a formula for the distribution of the maximum likelihood estimator. *Biometrika*, **70**, 343–365.

Barndorff-Nielsen, O.E. (1986). Inference on full or partial parameters based on the standardized signed log likelihood ratio. *Biometrika*, **73**, 307–322.

Barndorff-Nielsen, O.E. (1988). *Parametric Statistical Models and Likelihood*. Lecture Notes in Statistics 50, Springer-Verlag: Heidelberg.

Barndorff-Nielsen, O.E. (1990a). A note on the standardised signed log likelihood ratio. *Scand. J. Statist.*, **17** 157–160.

Barndorff-Nielsen, O.E. (1990b). Approximate probabilities. *J. R. Statist. Soc.B*, **52**, 485–496.

Barndorff-Nielsen, O.E. and Cox, D.R. (1989). *Asymptotic Techniques for Use in Statistics*. Chapman and Hall: London.

Cox, D.R. and Hinkley, D. V. (1974). *Theoretical Statistics*. Chapman and Hall: London.

Cox, D.R. and Reid, N. (1987). Parameter orthogonality and approximate conditional inference, (with discussion). *J. R. Statist. Soc. B*, **49**, 1–39.

Cox, D.R. and Wermuth, N. (1990). An approximation to maximum likelihood estimates in reduced models. *Biometrika*, **77**, 747–761.

Davison, A. C. (1988). Approximate conditional inference in generalised linear models. *J. R. Statist. Soc. B*, **50**, 445–462.

Davison, A. C., Smith, P.W.F. and Whittaker, J. (1991). An exact conditional test for covariance selection. *Austral. J. Statist.*, **33**, 313–318.

Deemer, W.L. and Olkin, O. (1951). The jacobians of certain matrix transformations useful in multivariate analysis. *Biometrika*, **38**, 345–367.

Dempster, A.P. (1972). Covariance selection. *Biometrics*, **28**, 157–175.

Efron, B. (1978). The geometry of exponential families. *Ann. Statist.*, **6**, 362–376.

Fisher, R.A. (1970). *Statistical Methods for Research Workers*, 14th Edition. Hafner Press: New York.

Fraser, D.A.S. (1991). Statistical inference: likelihood to significance. *J. Amer. Statist. Soc.*, **86**, 258–265.

Frydenburg, M. and Jensen, J.L. (1989). Is the 'improved likelihood ratio statistic' really improved for the discrete case? *Biometrika*, **76**, 655–661.

Graybill, F.A. (1983). *Matrices with Applications in Statistics*. 2nd Edition. Wadsworth: California.

Harris, P. and Peers, H.W. (1980). The local power of the efficient score test statistic. *Biometrika*, **67**, 525–529.

Hayakawa, T. (1975). The likelihood ratio criterion for a composite hypothesis under a local alternative. *Biometrika*, **62**, 451–460.

Isserlis, L. (1918). On a formula for the product-moment coefficient of any order of a normal frequency distribution in any number of variables. *Biometrika*, **12**, 134–139.

Kreiner, S. (1987). Analysis of multi-dimensional contingency tables by exact conditional tests: techniques and strategies. *Scand. J. Stat.*, **14**.

Lauritzen, S.L. (1989). Mixed graphical association models. *Scand. J. Statist.*, **16**, 273–306.

McCullagh, P. (1987). *Tensor Methods in Statistics*. Chapman and Hall: London.

Moran, P. A. P. (1970). On asymptotically optimal tests of composite hypotheses. *Biometrika*, **57**, 45–55.

Muirhead, R.J. (1982). *Aspects of Multivariate Statistical Theory*. Wiley: New York.

Pierce, D.A. and Peters, D. (1992). Practical use of higher order asymptotics for multiparameter exponential families (with discussion). *J. R. Statist. Soc. B*, **54**, 701–737.

Smith, P.W.F. (1990). *Edge Exclusion Tests for Graphical Models*. Unpublished Ph.D. thesis. Lancaster University.

Speed, T.P. and Kiiveri, H. (1986). Gaussian Markov distributions over finite graphs. *Ann. Statist.*, **14**, 138–150.

Wermuth, N. (1976). Analogies between multiplicative models in contingency tables and covariance selection. *Biometrics*, **32**, 95–108.

Whittaker, J. (1990). *Graphical Models in Applied Multivariate Statistics.* Wiley: Chichester.

Appendix A: Expansions of the Density Functions for the Wald and Efficient Score Test Statistics in Section 4

The Wald test statistic for excluding a single edge from a graphical Gaussian models is

$$T_w = \frac{n\,u}{1+u},$$

where $u = r^2_{12|rest}$. Under the null hypothesis $H_0 : \omega_{12} = 0$

$$f_r(u) = \frac{1}{B(\frac{1}{2}, \frac{n-p}{2})} u^{-1/2}(1-u)^{(n-p-2)/2}, \quad 0 < u < 1.$$

Putting $t = n\,u/(1+u)$ gives the density function of T_w as

$$
\begin{aligned}
f_w(t) &= \frac{1}{B(\frac{1}{2}, \frac{n-p}{2})} u^{-1/2}(1-u)^{(n-p-2)/2} \cdot \frac{(1+u)^2}{n}, \quad 0 < u < 1 \\
&= \frac{1}{B(\frac{1}{2}, \frac{n-p}{2})} \left(\frac{t}{n-t}\right)^{-1/2} \left(1 - \frac{t}{n-t}\right)^{(n-p-2)/2} \cdot \frac{n}{(n-t)^2},
\end{aligned}
$$

$0 < t < \frac{n}{2}$, since $u = t/(n-t)$. Using Stirling's approximation, taking logs and expanding gives

$$\log f_l(t) = -\frac{1}{2}\{t + \log(2\pi t)\} + \frac{1}{4}\{(t-1)(2p-1) + 3\,t(3-t)\}\,n^{-1} + O(n^{-2}).$$

The leading term of this expansion corresponds to the χ_1^2 distribution and so

$$f_w(t) = g_\chi(t)[1 + \frac{1}{4}\{(t-1)(2p+1) + 3\,t(3-t)\}\,n^{-1}] + O(n^{-2}), \quad 0 < t < \frac{n}{2},$$

where $g_\chi(t)$ is the density function of a χ_1^2 random variable. Finally integrating from 0 to x, term by term, gives the expansion for the cumulative distribution function as

$$
\begin{aligned}
F_w(x) &= G_\chi(x) + \frac{1}{4}n^{-1}\int_0^x \{(t-1)(2p+1) + 3\,t(3-t)\}g_\chi(t)dt + O(n^{-2}) \\
&= G_\chi(x) - \frac{1}{2}n^{-1}(2p+1-3x)\left(\frac{x}{2\pi}\right)^{1/2}\exp(-x/2) + O(n^{-2}) \\
&= G_\chi(x) - \frac{1}{2}(2p+1-3x)\,x\,g_\chi(x)\,n^{-1} + O(n^{-2}), \quad x > 0,
\end{aligned}
$$

where $G_\chi(x)$ is the distribution function of a χ_1^2 random variable.

The efficient score test statistic for excluding a single edge from a graphical Gaussian model is

$$
T_s = n\,u.
$$

Putting $t = n\,u$ gives the density function of T_s under the null hypothesis as

$$
\begin{aligned}
f_s(t) &= \frac{1}{B(\frac{1}{2}, \frac{n-p}{2})}u^{-1/2}(1-u)^{(n-p-2)/2}\cdot\frac{1}{n}, \quad 0 < u < 1, \\
&= \frac{1}{n\,B(\frac{1}{2}, \frac{n-p}{2})}\left(\frac{t}{n}\right)^{-1/2}\left(1-\frac{t}{n}\right)^{(n-p-2)/2}, \quad 0 < t < n,
\end{aligned}
$$

since $u = t/n$. Using Stirling's approximation, taking logs and expanding gives

$$
\log f_s(t) = -\frac{1}{2}\{t + \log(2\pi t)\} + \frac{1}{4}\{(t-1)(2p+1) + t(3-t)\}\,n^{-1} + O(n^{-2}).
$$

Now this expansion is identical to that for the Wald statistic, apart from $3\,t(3-t)$ is replaced by $t(3-t)$. Hence

$$
\begin{aligned}
f_s(t) &= g_\chi(t)[1 + \frac{1}{4}\{(t-1)(2p+1) + t(3-t)\}\,n^{-1}] + O(n^{-2}), 0 < t < n, \\
F_s(x) &= G_\chi(x) - \frac{1}{2}(2p+1-x)\,x\,g_\chi(x)\,n^{-1} + O(n^{-2}), \quad x > 0.
\end{aligned}
$$

Under the null hypothesis the density function of $R = R_{12|rest}$ is

$$
f_R(r) = \frac{1}{B(\frac{1}{2}, \frac{n-p}{2})}(1-r^2)^{(n-p-2)/2}, \quad -1 < r < 1,
$$

Muirhead (1982, p188). So the density function of T_f is

$$
\begin{aligned}
f_f(t) &= \frac{1}{B(\frac{1}{2}, \frac{n-p}{2})}(1 - r^2)^{(n-p-2)/2} \cdot \frac{2(1-r^2)}{(n-p-1)\,\log\left(\frac{1+r}{1-r}\right)} \\
&= \frac{1}{B(\frac{1}{2}, \frac{n-p}{2})}\frac{2(1-r^2)^{(n-p)/2}}{(n-p-1)\,\log\left(\frac{1+r}{1-r}\right)},
\end{aligned}
$$

where

$$
r = \frac{\exp[2\{t/(n-p-1)\}^{1/2}] - 1}{\exp[2\{t/(n-p-1)\}^{1/2}] + 1}.
$$

Expanding the log of $f_f(t)$ as before gives

$$
\log f_f(t) = g_\chi(t) + \frac{1}{12}(3 - 6t + t^2)n^{-1} + O(n^{-2}).
$$

Hence

$$
\begin{aligned}
f_f(t) &= g_\chi(t)[1 + \frac{1}{12}(3 - 6t + t^2)n^{-1}] + O(n^{-2}), \quad t > 0, \\
F_f(x) &= G_\chi(x) - \frac{1}{6}(x - 3)\,x\,g_\chi(x)\,n^{-1} + O(n^{-2}), \quad x > 0.
\end{aligned}
$$

Appendix B: The Derivation of $u^*(t)$ in Section 4

Recall $t = -(n - p + 1)\,\log(1 - u) + \log(1 + u)$, where $u = r^2_{12|rest}$. Put

$$
\begin{aligned}
u_1 &= 1 - \exp\{-t/(n - p + 1)\} \\
&= u + (1 - u)\,\log(1 + u)n^{-1} + O(n^{-2}).
\end{aligned}
$$

So $u = u_1 + O(n^{-1})$. Then put

$$
\begin{aligned}
u_2 &= u_1 - (1 - u_1)\,\log(1 + u_1)n^{-1} \\
&= u + \frac{1}{2}n^{-2}(1 - u)\,\log(1 + u)\left(2p + \log(1 + u) - \frac{4}{1+u}\right) + O(n^{-3}).
\end{aligned}
$$

So $u = u_2 + O(n^{-2})$. Finally put

$$
\begin{aligned}
u_3 &= u_2 - \frac{1}{2}n^{-2}(1 - u_2)\,\log(1 + u_2)\left(2p + \log(1 + u_2) - \frac{4}{1+u_2}\right) \\
&= u + O(n^{-3}).
\end{aligned}
$$

Recursively substituting for u_2 and then u_1 gives u_3 as a function of t which is a equal to u to order n^{-2} and hence is the required $u^*(t)$. Then a_m and b_m are obtained by substituting $u^*(t)$ in (25) and expanding as for the other test statistics.

Appendix C: Proofs of (14) and (16)

Since $\Omega = \Sigma^{-1}$ (and mles are invariant under continuous transformations)

$$\tilde{\omega}_{ii} = \frac{|\tilde{\Sigma}_{ii}|}{|\tilde{\Sigma}|},$$

where $|\Sigma_{ii}|$ is the co-factor of σ_{ii} and so does not contain σ_{12} when $i = 1$ or 2. By (15), $|\tilde{\Sigma}_{ii}| = |\hat{\Sigma}_{ii}|$, for $i = 1, 2$, and hence

$$
\begin{aligned}
\tilde{\omega}_{ii} &= \frac{|\hat{\Sigma}_{ii}|\,|\hat{\Sigma}|}{|\tilde{\Sigma}|\,|\hat{\Sigma}|} \\
&= \hat{\omega}_{ii}(1 - r^2_{12|rest}),
\end{aligned}
$$

which proves (14).

For (16) note that

$$0 = \tilde{\omega}_{12}(= \tilde{\omega}_{21}) = \frac{|\tilde{\Sigma}_{21}|}{|\tilde{\Sigma}|} \quad \Longrightarrow \quad |\tilde{\Sigma}_{21}| = 0, \tag{26}$$

where $|\tilde{\Sigma}_{21}|$ is the cofactor of σ_{21}. Expanding $|\tilde{\Sigma}_{21}|$ about the first row of $\tilde{\Sigma}_{21}$ gives

$$|\tilde{\Sigma}_{21}| = -\sum_{k=2}^{p} \tilde{\sigma}_{1k}|[\tilde{\Sigma}_{21}]_{1k}|, \tag{27}$$

where $|[\Sigma_{21}]_{1k}|$ is the cofactor of σ_{1k} from the submatrix of Σ without the first column and second row. So $|[\tilde{\Sigma}_{21}]_{1k}|$ does not contain $\tilde{\sigma}_{12}$ $(= \tilde{\sigma}_{21})$ and hence, by (15), is equal to $|[\hat{\Sigma}_{21}]_{1k}|$ for all k. Combining (26) and (27) gives

$$
\begin{aligned}
0 = -|\tilde{\Sigma}_{21}| &= \sum_{k=2}^{p} \tilde{\sigma}_{1k}|[\hat{\Sigma}_{21}]_{1k}| \\
&= \tilde{\sigma}_{12}|[\hat{\Sigma}_{21}]_{12}| + \sum_{k=3}^{p} \hat{\sigma}_{1k}|[\hat{\Sigma}_{21}]_{1k}|, \quad \text{since } \tilde{\sigma}_{1k} = \hat{\sigma}_{1k},\, k \neq 2 \\
&= (\tilde{\sigma}_{21} - \hat{\sigma}_{12})|[\hat{\Sigma}_{21}]_{12}| + \sum_{k=2}^{p} \hat{\sigma}_{1k}|[\hat{\Sigma}_{21}]_{1k}| \\
&= (\tilde{\sigma}_{12} - \hat{\sigma}_{12})|[\hat{\Sigma}_{21}]_{12}| - |\hat{\Sigma}_{21}|.
\end{aligned}
$$

By rearranging,

$$\tilde{\sigma}_{12} = \frac{|\hat{\Sigma}_{21}|}{|[\hat{\Sigma}_{21}]_{12}|} + \hat{\sigma}_{12}$$

$$= \frac{|\widehat{\Sigma}_{21}|}{|\widehat{\Sigma}|} \frac{|\widehat{\Sigma}|}{|[\widehat{\Sigma}_{21}]_{12}|} + \widehat{\sigma}_{12}$$

$$= \frac{\widehat{\omega}_{12}}{\widehat{\omega}_{11}\widehat{\omega}_{22} - \widehat{\omega}_{12}^2} + \widehat{\sigma}_{12}.$$

Substituting $r_{12|rest}$ for $-\widehat{\omega}_{12}(\widehat{\omega}_{11}\widehat{\omega}_{22})^{-1/2}$ and s_{12} for $\widehat{\sigma}_{12}$ gives the result (16).

Appendix D: Signed Square-root Tests

There is recent interest in deriving modifications of signed square-root tests with null distributions better approximated by the Normal distribution (Barndorff-Nielsen, 1986, 1990a, 1990b; Fraser, 1991; Pierce and Peters, 1992); in part, this is because one-side hypotheses have especial relevance in applied studies.

The signed square-root versions of the Wald, efficient score and likelihood ratio test statistics are given by $Z = \text{sgn}\,(r_{12|rest})T^{1/2}$ together with (8), (11) and (17). The statistic proposed by Barndorff-Nielsen (1986) is calculated by directly modifying the square-root test statistic, Z_l. (Note that modification and square-rooting do not commute.) From equation (8) of Pierce and Peters (1992)

$$Z_m = Z_l + \frac{1}{2Z_l} \log \frac{|\widehat{\mathcal{I}}_{bb}|}{|\widetilde{\mathcal{I}}_{bb}|} - \frac{1}{Z_l} \log \frac{Z_l}{Z_w}. \tag{28}$$

The relevant values for substitution are obtained from (8), (11), (21) and (22); giving a closed form expression which again is a function of the sample partial correlation, but is too complicated to write here.

Asymptotic expansions can be calculated to compare the Wald, efficient score and likelihood ratio tests along with Fisher's Z_f test. The resulting expansion for the densities are similar to those in Section 4 with the arguments replaced by their squares, and correspondingly the chi-square density function replaced by that for the Normal. The cumulative distribution functions can then be obtained by integration bearing in mind that the Wald and efficient score have lower bounds. It is not possible to invert Z_m, not even to the required order, so a comparison for the modified statistic cannot be given.

Numerical results are given in Table 3, but comparison with Table 2 reveals nothing new.

TABLE 3. Achieved significance levels for the signed square root versions of the Wald, efficient Score, Likelihood, and Fisher's test statistics, with varying sample size n and dimension p.

Nominal level 5%

n	p	W	S	L	M	F
10	2	0.0368	0.0597	0.0712	na	0.0496
	6	0.0707	0.0936	0.1051		
	10	0.1046	0.1276	0.1390		
20	2	0.0434	0.0549	0.0606	na	0.0498
	6	0.0604	0.0718	0.0776		
	10	0.0773	0.0888	0.0945		
30	2	0.0456	0.0532	0.0571	na	0.0499
	6	0.0569	0.0645	0.0684		
	10	0.0682	0.0759	0.0797		
50	2	0.0474	0.0519	0.0542	na	0.0499
	6	0.0541	0.0587	0.0610		
	10	0.0609	0.0655	0.0678		
200	2	0.0493	0.0505	0.0511	na	0.0500
	6	0.0510	0.0522	0.0528		
	10	0.0527	0.0539	0.0545		

Nominal level 1%

n	p	W	S	L	M	F
10	2	0.0074	0.0094	0.0178	na	0.0112
	6	0.0050	0.0218	0.0302		
	10	0.0174	0.0342	0.0426		
20	2	0.0013	0.0097	0.0139	na	0.0106
	6	0.0075	0.0159	0.0201		
	10	0.0137	0.0221	0.0263		
30	2	0.0042	0.0098	0.0126	na	0.0104
	6	0.0083	0.0139	0.0167		
	10	0.0125	0.0181	0.0209		
50	2	0.0065	0.0099	0.0116	na	0.0102
	6	0.0090	0.0124	0.0140		
	10	0.0115	0.0148	0.0165		
200	2	0.0091	0.0100	0.0104	na	0.0101
	6	0.0097	0.0106	0.0110		
	10	0.0104	0.0112	0.0116		

HEPATITIS B: A CASE STUDY IN MCMC

D. J. SPIEGELHALTER
MRC Biostatistics Unit
Institute of Public Health
Cambridge CB2 2SR
UK

N. G. BEST
Dept Epidemiology and Public Health
Imperial College School of Medicine at St Mary's
London W2 1PG
UK

W. R. GILKS
MRC Biostatistics Unit
Institute of Public Health
Cambridge CB2 2SR
UK

AND

H. INSKIP
MRC Environmental Epidemiology Unit
Southampton General Hospital
Southampton SO16 6YD

1. Introduction

This chapter features a worked example using Bayesian graphical modelling and the most basic of MCMC techniques, the Gibbs sampler, and serves to introduce ideas that are developed more fully in other chapters. This case study first appeared in Gilks, Richardson and Spiegelhalter (1996), and frequent reference is made to other chapters in that book.

Our data for this exercise are serial antibody-titre measurements, obtained from Gambian infants after hepatitis B immunization. We begin our analysis with an initial statistical model, and describe the use of the Gibbs sampler to obtain inferences from it, briefly touching upon issues of convergence, presentation of results, model checking and model criticism. We then step through some elaborations of the initial model, emphasizing the comparative ease of adding realistic complexity to the traditional, rather simplistic, statistical assumptions; in particular, we illustrate the accommodation of covariate measurement error. The Appendix contains some details of a freely available software package (BUGS, Spiegelhalter *et al.*, 1994), within which all the analyses in this chapter were carried out.

We emphasize that the analyses presented here cannot be considered the definitive approach to this or any other dataset, but merely illustrate some of the possibilities afforded by computer-intensive MCMC methods. Further details are provided in other chapters in this volume.

2. Hepatitis B immunization

2.1. BACKGROUND

Hepatitis B (HB) is endemic in many parts of the world. In highly endemic areas such as West Africa, almost everyone is infected with the HB virus during childhood. About 20% of those infected, and particularly those who acquire the infection very early in life, do not completely clear the infection and go on to become chronic carriers of the virus. Such carriers are at increased risk of chronic liver disease in adult life and liver cancer is a major cause of death in this region.

The Gambian Hepatitis Intervention Study (GHIS) is a national programme of vaccination against HB, designed to reduce the incidence of HB carriage (Whittle *et al.*, 1991). The effectiveness of this programme will depend on the duration of immunity that HB vaccination affords. To study this, a cohort of vaccinated GHIS infants was followed up. Blood samples were periodically collected from each infant, and the amount of surface-antibody was measured. This measurement is called the *anti-HBs titre*, and is measured in milli-International Units (mIU). A similar study in neighbouring Senegal concluded that for all infants

$$\text{anti-HBs titre} \propto \frac{1}{t}, \tag{1}$$

where t denotes time since the infant's final vaccination, and the constant of proportionality may vary between infants (Coursaget *et al.*, 1991). This is equivalent to a linear relationship between log titre and log time:

$$y = \alpha_i - 1 \times \log t, \tag{2}$$

where y denotes log anti-HBs titre and α_i is constant after the final dose of vaccine for each infant i.

Here we analyse the GHIS data to validate the findings of Coursaget *et al.* (1991). In particular, we investigate the plausibility of individuals having a common gradient of minus 1, as in (2). This relationship, if true, would provide a simple tool for predicting individual protection against HB, via (1).

2.2. PRELIMINARY ANALYSIS

Figure 1 shows the raw data, plotted on a log-log scale, for a subset of 106 infants from the GHIS follow-up study. These infants each had a *baseline* anti-HBs titre measurement taken at the time of the final vaccination, and at least two titre measurements taken subsequently. For these infants, a total of 288 post-baseline measurements were made (30 infants with two measurements, 76 with three) at approximately six-monthly intervals after final vaccination.

Initial examination of the data in Figure 1 suggests that it might be reasonable to fit straight lines to the data for each infant, but that these lines should be allowed to have different intercepts and possibly different gradients. Of particular note is the infant labelled with a '*' in Figure 1, whose titre apparently rose from 1 mIU at 826 days to 1329 mIU at day 1077. This somewhat atypical behaviour could be thought of as an outlier with respect to the change of titre over time, i.e. an outlying gradient; or due to one or both of the measurements being subject to extraneous error, i.e. outlying observations.

As a preliminary exploratory analysis, for each infant in Figure 1 we fitted a straight line:

$$E[y_{ij}] = \alpha_i + \beta_i \left(\log t_{ij} - \log 730 \right), \tag{3}$$

where E denotes expectation and subscripts ij index the jth post-baseline observation for infant i. We standardized $\log t$ around $\log 730$ for numerical

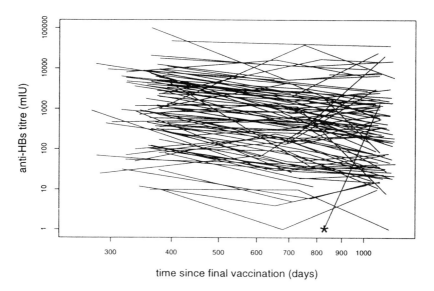

Figure 1. Raw data for a subset of 106 GHIS infants: straight lines connect anti-HBS measurements for each infant.

stability; thus the intercept α_i represents estimated log titre at two years post-baseline. The regressions were performed independently for each infant using ordinary least squares, and the results are shown in Figure 2.

The distribution of the 106 estimated intercepts $\{\hat{\alpha}_i\}$ in Figure 2 appears reasonably Gaussian apart from the single negative value associated with infant '*' mentioned above. The distribution of the estimated gradients $\{\hat{\beta}_i\}$ also appears Gaussian apart from a few high estimates, particularly that for infant '*'. Thirteen (12%) of the infants have a positive estimated gradient, while four (4%) have a 'high' estimated gradient greater than 2.0. Plotting estimated intercepts against gradients suggests independence of α_i and β_i, apart from the clear outlier for infant '*'. This analysis did not explicitly take account of baseline log titre, y_{i0}: the final plot in Figure 2 suggests a positive relationship between y_{i0} and α_i, indicating that a high baseline titre predisposes towards high subsequent titres.

Our primary interest is in the population from which these 106 infants were drawn, rather than in the 106 infants themselves. Independently applying the linear regression model (3) to each infant does not provide a basis for inference about the population; for this, we must build into our model assumptions about the underlying population distribution of α_i and β_i. Thus we are concerned with 'random-effects growth-curve' models. If

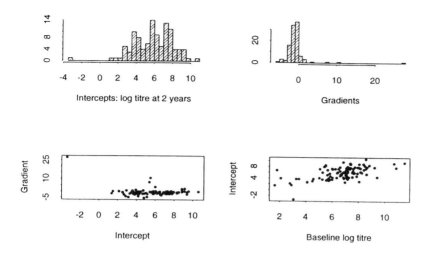

Figure 2. Results of independently fitting straight lines to the data for each of the infants in Figure 1.

we are willing to make certain simplifying assumptions and asymptotic approximations, then a variety of techniques are available for fitting such models, such as restricted maximum likelihood or penalized quasi-likelihood (Breslow and Clayton, 1993). Alternatively, we can take the more general approach of simulating 'exact' solutions, where the accuracy of the solution depends only the computational care taken.

3. Modelling

This section identifies three distinct components in the construction of a full probability model, and applies them in the analysis of the GHIS data:

- Specification of model quantities and their qualitative conditional independence structure: we and other authors in this volume find it convenient to use a *graphical* representation at this stage.
- Specification of the parametric form of the direct relationships between these quantities: this provides the likelihood terms in the model. Each of these terms may have a standard form but, by connecting them together according to the specified conditional-independence structure, models of arbitrary complexity may be constructed.
- Specification of prior distributions for parameters: see Gilks *et al.* (1996) for a brief introduction to Bayesian inference.

3.1. STRUCTURAL MODELLING

We make the following minimal structural assumptions based on the exploratory analysis above. The y_{ij} are independent conditional on their mean μ_{ij} and on a parameter σ that governs the sampling error. For an individual i, each mean lies on a 'growth curve' such that μ_{ij} is a deterministic function of time t_{ij} and of intercept and gradient parameters α_i and β_i. The α_i are independently drawn from a distribution parameterized by α_0 and σ_α, while the β_i are independently drawn from a distribution parameterized by β_0 and σ_β.

Figure 3 shows a *directed acyclic graph* (DAG) representing these assumptions (*directed* because each link between nodes is an arrow; *acyclic* because, by following the directions of the arrows, it is impossible to return to a node after leaving it). Each quantity in the model appears as a node in the graph, and directed links correspond to direct dependencies as specified above: solid arrows are probabilistic dependencies, while dashed arrows show functional (deterministic) relationships. The latter are included to simplify the graph but are collapsed over when identifying probabilistic relationships. Repetitive structures, of blood-samples within infants for example, are shown as stacked 'sheets'. There is no essential difference between any node in the graph in that each is considered a random quantity, but it is convenient to use some graphical notation: here we use a double rectangle to denote quantities assumed fixed by the design (i.e. sampling times t_{ij}), single rectangles to indicate observed data, and circles to represent all unknown quantities.

To interpret the graph, it will help to introduce some fairly self-explanatory definitions. Let v be a node in the graph, and V be the set of all nodes. We define a 'parent' of v to be any node with an arrow emanating from it pointing to v, and a 'descendant' of v to be any node on a directed path starting from v. In identifying parents and descendants, deterministic links are collapsed so that, for example, the parents of y_{ij} are α_i, β_i and σ. The graph represents the following formal assumption: for any node v, if we know the value of its parents, then no other nodes would be informative concerning v except descendants of v. The genetic analogy is clear: if we know your parents' genetic structure, then no other individual will give any additional information concerning your genes except one of your descendants. Thomas and Gauderman (1996) illustrate the use of graphical models in genetics.

Although no probabilistic model has yet been specified, the conditional independencies expressed by the above assumptions permit many properties of the model to be derived; see for example Lauritzen *et al.* (1990), Whittaker (1990) or Spiegelhalter *et al.* (1993) for discussion of how to read

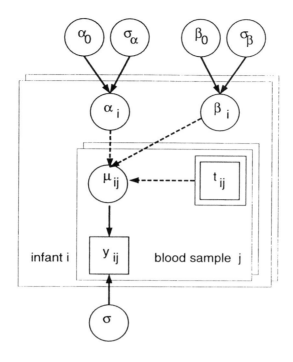

Figure 3.   Graphical model for hepatitis B data.

off independence properties from DAGs. It is important to understand that the graph represents properties of the full model before any data is observed, and the independence properties will change when conditioning on data. For example, although nodes that have no common 'ancestor' will be initially marginally independent, such as α_i and β_i, this independence will not necessarily be retained when conditioning upon other quantities. For example, when y_{i1}, y_{i2}, y_{i3} are observed, dependence between α_i and β_i may be induced.

Our use of a graph in this example is primarily to facilitate communication of the essentials of the model without needing algebra. However, as we now show, it forms a convenient basis for the specification of the full joint distribution of all model quantities.

3.2. PROBABILITY MODELLING

The preceding discussion of graphical models has been in terms of conditional independence properties without necessarily a probabilistic interpretation. If we wish to construct a full probability model, it can be shown (Lauritzen *et al.*, 1990) that a DAG model is equivalent to assuming that the joint distribution of all the random quantities is fully specified in terms of the conditional distribution of each node given its parents:

$$P(V) = \prod_{v \in V} P(v \mid \text{parents}[v]), \tag{4}$$

where $P(.)$ denotes a probability distribution. This factorization not only allows extremely complex models to be built up from local components, but also provides an efficient basis for the implementation of some forms of MCMC methods.

For our example, we therefore need to specify exact forms of 'parent–child' relationships on the graph shown in Figure 3. We shall make the initial assumption of normality both for within- and between-infant variability, although this will be relaxed in later sections. We shall also assume a simple linear relationship between expected log titre and log time, as in (3). The likelihood terms in the model are therefore

$$y_{ij} \sim N(\mu_{ij}, \sigma^2), \tag{5}$$

$$\mu_{ij} = \alpha_i + \beta_i(\log t_{ij} - \log 730), \tag{6}$$

$$\alpha_i \sim N(\alpha_0, \sigma_\alpha^2), \tag{7}$$

$$\beta_i \sim N(\beta_0, \sigma_\beta^2), \tag{8}$$

where '$\sim$' means 'distributed as', and $N(a, b)$ generically denotes a normal distribution with mean a and variance b. Scaling $\log t$ around $\log 730$ makes the assumed prior independence of gradient and intercept more plausible, as suggested in Figure 2.

3.3. PRIOR DISTRIBUTIONS

To complete the specification of a full probability model, we require prior distributions on the nodes without parents: σ^2, α_0, σ_α^2, β_0 and σ_β^2. These nodes are known as 'founders' in genetics. In a scientific context, we would often like these priors to be not too influential in the final conclusions, although if there is only weak evidence from the data concerning some secondary aspects of a model, such as the degree of smoothness to be expected in a set of adjacent observations, it may be very useful to be able to include external information in the form of fairly informative prior distributions. In hierarchical models such as ours, it is particularly important to avoid casual use of standard improper priors since these may result in improper posterior distributions (DuMouchel and Waternaux, 1992); see also Clayton (1996) and Carlin (1996).

The priors chosen for our analysis are

$$\alpha_0, \beta_0 \sim N(0, 10\,000), \tag{9}$$

$$\sigma^{-2}, \sigma_\alpha^{-2}, \sigma_\beta^{-2} \sim Ga(0.01, 0.01), \tag{10}$$

where $Ga(a, b)$ generically denotes a gamma distribution with mean a/b and variance a/b^2. Although these are proper probability distributions, we might expect them to have minimal effect on the analysis since α_0 and β_0 have standard deviation 100, and the inverse of the variance components (the precisions) all have prior standard deviation 10. Examination of the final results shows these prior standard deviations are at least an order of magnitude greater than the corresponding posterior standard deviations.

4. Fitting a model using Gibbs sampling

We estimate our model by Gibbs sampling using the BUGS software (Gilks *et al.*, 1994; Spiegelhalter *et al.*, 1996). See Gilks *et al.* (1996) for a description of Gibbs sampling.

In general, four steps are required to implement Gibbs sampling:

- starting values must be provided for all unobserved nodes (parameters and any missing data);
- full conditional distributions for each unobserved node must be constructed and methods for sampling from them decided upon;
- the output must be monitored to decide on the length of the 'burn-in' and the total run length, or perhaps to identify whether a more computationally efficient parameterization or MCMC algorithm is required;
- summary statistics for quantities of interest must be calculated from the output, for inference about the true values of the unobserved nodes.

For a satisfactory implementation of Gibbs sampling, a fifth step should also be added: to examine summary statistics for evidence of lack of fit of the model.

We now discuss each of these steps briefly; further details are provided elsewhere in this volume.

4.1. INITIALIZATION

In principle, the choice of starting values is unimportant since the Gibbs sampler (or any other MCMC sampler) should be run long enough for it to 'forget' its initial states. It is useful to perform a number of runs with widely dispersed starting values, to check that the conclusions are not sensitive to the choice of starting values (Gelman, 1996). However, very extreme starting values could lead to a very long burn-in (Raftery, 1996). In severe cases, the sampler may fail to converge towards the main support of the posterior distribution, this possibility being aggravated by numerical instability in the extreme tails of the posterior. On the other hand, starting the simulation at the mode of the posterior is no guarantee of success if the sampler is not mixing well, i.e. if it is not moving fluidly around the support of the posterior.

We performed three runs with starting values shown in Table 1. The first run starts at values considered plausible in the light of Figure 2, while the second and third represent substantial deviations in initial values. In particular, run 2 is intended to represent a situation in which there is low measurement error but large between-individual variability, while run 3 represents very similar individuals with very high measurement error.

From these parameters, initial values for for α_i and β_i were independently generated from (7) and (8). Such 'forwards sampling' is the default strategy in the BUGS software.

Parameter	Run 1	Run 2	Run 3
α_0	5.0	20.0	-10.00
β_0	-1.0	-5.0	5.00
σ_α	2.0	20.0	0.20
σ_β	0.5	5.0	0.05
σ	1.0	0.1	10.00

TABLE 1. Starting values for parameters in three runs of the Gibbs sampler

4.2. SAMPLING FROM FULL CONDITIONAL DISTRIBUTIONS

Gibbs sampling works by iteratively drawing samples from the full conditional distributions of unobserved nodes in the graph. The full conditional distribution for a node is the distribution of that node given current or known values for all the other nodes in the graph. For a directed graphical model, we can exploit the structure of the joint distribution given in (4). For any node v, we may denote the remaining nodes by V_{-v}, and from (4) it follows that the full conditional distribution $P(v|V_{-v})$ has the form

$$
\begin{aligned}
P(v \mid V_{-v}) \quad &\propto \quad P(v, V_{-v}) \\
&\propto \quad \text{terms in } P(V) \text{ containing } v \\
&= \quad P(v \mid \text{parents}[v]) \times \\
&\qquad \prod_{w \in children[v]} P(w \mid \text{parents}[w]), \qquad (11)
\end{aligned}
$$

where $\propto$ means 'proportional to'. (The proportionality constant, which ensures that the distribution integrates to 1, will in general be a function of the remaining nodes V_{-v}.) We see from (11) that the full conditional distribution for v contains a *prior* component $P(v \mid \text{parents}[v])$ and *likelihood* components arising from each child of v. Thus the full conditional for any node depends only on the values of its parents, children, and co-parents, where 'co-parents' are other parents of the children of v.

For example, consider the intercept term α_i. The general prescription of (11) tells us that the full conditional distribution for α_i is proportional to the product of the prior for α_i, given by (7), and n_i likelihood terms, given by (5, 6), where n_i is the number of observations on the ith infant. Thus

$$
P(\alpha_i \mid \cdot) \quad \propto \quad \exp\left\{ -\frac{(\alpha_i - \alpha_0)^2}{2\sigma_\alpha^2} \right\} \times
$$
$$
\prod_{j=1}^{n_i} \exp\left\{ -\frac{[y_{ij} - \alpha_i - \beta_i(\log t_{ij} - \log 730)]^2}{2\sigma^2} \right\}, \quad (12)
$$

where the '$\cdot$' in $P(\alpha_i \mid \cdot)$ denotes all data nodes and all parameter nodes except α_i, (i.e. $V_{-\alpha_i}$). By completing the square for α_i in the exponent of (12), it can be shown that $P(\alpha_i \mid \cdot)$ is a normal distribution with mean

$$
\frac{\frac{\alpha_0}{\sigma_\alpha^2} + \frac{1}{\sigma^2} \sum_{j=1}^{n_i} y_{ij} - \beta_i(\log t_{ij} - \log 730)}{\frac{1}{\sigma_\alpha^2} + \frac{n_i}{\sigma^2}}
$$

and variance

$$
\frac{1}{\frac{1}{\sigma_\alpha^2} + \frac{n_i}{\sigma^2}}.
$$

The full conditionals for β_i, α_0 and β_0 can similarly be shown to be normal distributions.

The full conditional distribution for the precision parameter σ_α^{-2} can also be easily worked out. Let τ_α denote σ_α^{-2}. The general prescription (11) tells us that the full conditional for τ_α is proportional to the product of the prior for τ_α, given by (10), and the 'likelihood' terms for τ_α, given by (7) for each i. These are the likelihood terms for τ_α because the α_i parameters are the only children of τ_α. Thus we have

$$
P(\tau_\alpha \mid \cdot) \quad \propto \quad \tau_\alpha^{0.01-1} e^{-0.01\tau_\alpha} \prod_{i=1}^{106} \tau_\alpha^{\frac{1}{2}} \exp\left\{ -\frac{1}{2}\tau_\alpha (\alpha_i - \alpha_0)^2 \right\}
$$
$$
= \quad \tau_\alpha^{0.01+\frac{106}{2}-1} \exp\left\{ -\tau_\alpha \left(0.01 + \frac{1}{2}\sum_{i=1}^{106} (\alpha_i - \alpha_0)^2 \right) \right\}
$$
$$
\propto \quad \text{Ga}\left(0.01 + \frac{106}{2}, \; 0.01 + \frac{1}{2}\sum_{i=1}^{106} (\alpha_i - \alpha_0)^2 \right).
$$

Thus the full conditional distribution for τ_α is another gamma distribution. The full conditional distributions for σ_β^{-2} and σ^{-2} can similarly be shown to be gamma distributions.

In this example, all full conditionals reduce to normal or gamma distributions, from which sampling is straightforward (see for example Ripley, 1987). In many applications, full conditional distributions do not simplify so conveniently. However, several techniques are available for efficiently sampling from such distributions; see Gilks (1996).

4.3. MONITORING THE OUTPUT

The values for the unknown quantities generated by the Gibbs sampler must be graphically and statistically summarized to check mixing and convergence. Here we illustrate the use of Gelman and Rubin (1992) statistics on three runs of length 5 000 iterations, started as in Table 1. Details of the method of Gelman and Rubin are given by Gelman (1996). Each run took around two minutes on a SPARCstation 10 using BUGS, and the runs were monitored using the suite of S-functions called CODA (Best *et al.*, 1995). Figure 4 shows the trace of the sampled values of β_0 for the three runs: while runs 1 and 2 quickly settled down, run 3 took around 700 iterations to stabilize.

Table 2 shows Gelman–Rubin statistics for four parameters being monitored (b_4 is defined below). For each parameter, the statistic estimates the reduction in the pooled estimate of its variance if the runs were continued indefinitely. The estimates and their 97.5% points are near 1, indicating that reasonable convergence has occurred for these parameters.

Parameter	Estimate	97.5% quantile
β_0	1.03	1.11
σ_β	1.01	1.02
σ	1.00	1.00
b_4	1.00	1.00

TABLE 2.   Gelman–Rubin statistics for four parameters

The Gelman–Rubin statistics can be calculated sequentially as the runs proceed, and plotted as in Figure 5: such a display would be a valuable tool in parallel implementation of a Gibbs sampler. These plots suggest discarding the first 1 000 iterations of each run and then pooling the remaining $3 \times 4\,000$ samples.

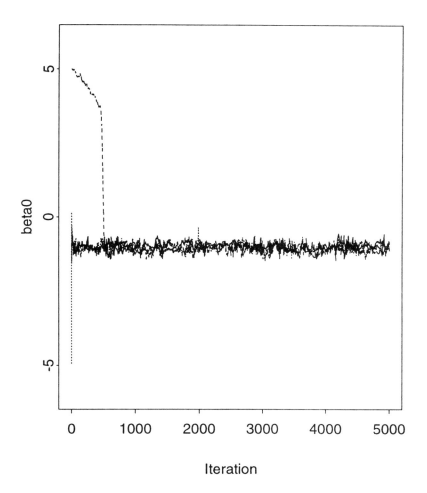

Figure 4. Sampled values for β_0 from three runs of the Gibbs sampler applied to the model of Section 3; starting values are given in Table 1: run 1, solid line; run 2, dotted line; run 3, broken line.

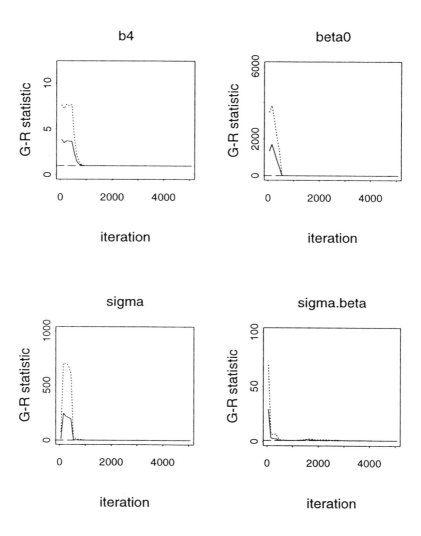

Figure 5. Gelman–Rubin statistics for four parameters from three parallel runs. At each iteration the median and 97.5 centile of the statistic are calculated and plotted, based on the sampled values of the parameter up to that iteration. Solid lines: medians; broken lines: 97.5 centiles. Convergence is suggested when the plotted values closely approach 1.

4.4. INFERENCE FROM THE OUTPUT

Figure 6 shows kernel density plots of the sampled values. There is clear evidence of variability between the gradients, although the absolute size of the variability is not great, with σ_β estimated to be around 0.3. The underlying gradient β_0 is concentrated around minus 1: this value is of particular interest, as noted in Section 2.1. Summary statistics for this model are provided in Table 3 (see page 18), in the column headed 'GG'.

4.5. ASSESSING GOODNESS-OF-FIT

Standard maximum likelihood methods provide a natural basis for goodness-of-fit and model comparison, since the parameter estimates are specifically designed to minimize measures of deviance that may be compared between alternative nested models. Cox and Solomon (1986) also consider classical tests for detecting departures from standard within-subject assumptions in such data, assuming independence between subjects. In contrast, MCMC methods allow the fitting of multi-level models with large numbers of parameters for which standard asymptotic likelihood theory does not hold. Model criticism and comparison therefore require particular care. Gelfand (1996), Raftery (1996), Gelman and Meng (1996), George and McCulloch (1996) and Phillips and Smith (1996) describe a variety of techniques for assessing and improving model adequacy.

Here, we simply illustrate the manner in which standard statistics for measuring departures from an assumed model may be calculated, although we again emphasize that our example is by no means a definitive analysis. We define a standardized residual

$$r_{ij} = \frac{y_{ij} - \mu_{ij}}{\sigma}$$

with mean zero and variance 1 under the assumed error model. These residuals can be calculated at each iteration (using current values of μ_{ij} and σ), and can be used to construct summary statistics. For example, we can calculate a statistic that is intended to detect deviations from the assumed normal error model. Various functions of standardized residuals could be considered, and here we calculate

$$b_4 = \frac{1}{288} \sum_{ij} r_{ij}^4,$$

the mean fourth moment of the standardized residual. If the error distribution is truly normal then this statistic should be close to 3; see Gelman and Meng (1996) for more formal assessment of such summary statistics.

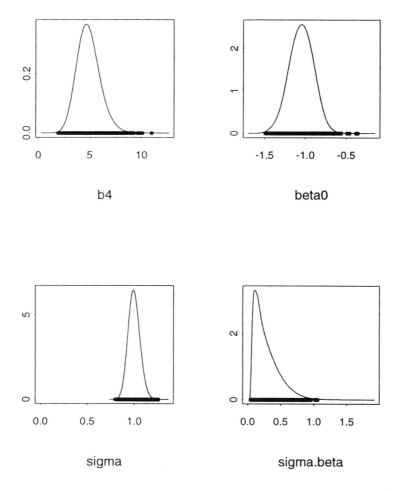

Figure 6. Kernel density plots of sampled values for parameters of the model of Section 3 based on three pooled runs, each of 4 000 iterations after 1 000 iterations burn-in. Results are shown for β_0, the mean gradient in the population; σ_β, the standard deviation of gradients in the population; σ, the sampling error; and b_4, the standardized fourth moment of the residuals.

Figure 6 clearly shows that sampled values of b_4 are substantially greater than 3 (mean = 4.9; 95% interval from 3.2 to 7.2). This strongly indicates that the residuals are not normally distributed.

5. Model elaboration

5.1. HEAVY-TAILED DISTRIBUTIONS

The data and discussion in Section 2 suggest we should take account of apparent outlying observations. One approach is to use heavy-tailed distributions, for example t distributions, instead of Gaussian distributions for the intercepts α_i, gradients β_i and sampling errors $y_{ij} - \mu_{ij}$.

Many researchers have shown how t distributions can be easily introduced within a Gibbs sampling framework by representing the precision (the inverse of the variance) of each Gaussian observation as itself being a random quantity with a suitable gamma distribution; see for example Gelfand *et al.* (1992). However, in the BUGS program, a t distribution on ν degrees of freedom can be specified directly as a sampling distribution, with priors being specified for its scale and location, as for the Gaussian distributions in Section 3. Which value of ν should we use? In BUGS, a prior distribution can be placed over ν so that the data can indicate the degree of support for a heavy- or Gaussian-tailed distribution. In the results shown below, we have assumed a discrete uniform prior distribution for ν in the set

$$\{ \ 1, 1.5, 2, 2.5, \ldots, 20, 21, 22, \ldots, 30, 35, 40, 45, 50, 75,$$
$$100, 200, \ldots, 500, 750, 1000 \ \}.$$

We fitted the following models:

GG   Gaussian sampling errors $y_{ij} - \mu_{ij}$; Gaussian intercepts α_i and gradients β_i, as in Section 3;

GT   Gaussian sampling errors; t-distributed intercepts and gradients;

TG t-distributed samping errors; Gaussian intercepts and gradients;

TT t-distributed samping errors; t-distributed intercepts and gradients.

Results for these models are given in Table 3, each based on 5 000 iterations after a 1 000-iteration burn-in. Strong auto-correlations and cross-correlations in the parameters of the t distributions were observed, but the β_0 sequence was quite stable in each model (results not shown).

We note that the point estimate of β_0 is robust to secondary assumptions about distributional shape, although the width of the interval estimate is

Parameter		GG	GT	TG	TT
β_0	mean	−1.05	−1.13	−1.06	−1.11
	95% c.i.	−1.33, −0.80	−1.35, −0.93	−1.24, −0.88	−1.26, −0.93
σ_β	mean	0.274	0.028	0.033	0.065
	95% c.i.	0.070, 0.698	0.007, 0.084	0.004, 0.111	0.007, 0.176
ν	mean	∞	∞	3.5	2.5
	95% c.i.			2.5, 3.5	2, 3.5
ν_α	mean	∞	12	∞	19
	95% c.i.		4, 20		5, 30
ν_β	mean	∞	1	∞	16
	95% c.i.		1, 1		8.5, 26

TABLE 3. Results of fitting models GG, GT, TG and TT to the GHIS data: posterior means and 95% credible intervals (c.i). Parameters ν, ν_α and ν_β are the degrees of freedom in t distributions for sampling errors, intercepts and gradients, respectively. Degrees of freedom $= \infty$ corresponds to a Gaussian distribution.

reduced by 35% when allowing t distributions of unknown degrees of freedom for both population and sampling distributions. Gaussian sampling errors and t distributions for regression coefficients (model GT) leads to overwhelming belief in very heavy (Cauchy) tails for the distribution of gradients, due to the outlying individuals ($\hat{\nu}_\beta \approx 1$). Allowing the sampling error alone to have heavy tails (model TG) leads to a confident judgement of a heavy-tailed sampling distribution ($\hat{\nu} \approx 3.5$), while allowing t distributions at all levels (model TT) supports the assumption of a heavy-tailed sampling distribution ($\hat{\nu} \approx 2.5$) and a fairly Gaussian shape for intercepts and gradients ($\hat{\nu}_\alpha \approx 19$, $\hat{\nu}_\beta \approx 16$).

5.2. INTRODUCING A COVARIATE

As noted in Section 2.2, the observed baseline log titre measurement, y_{i0}, is correlated with subsequent titres. The obvious way to adjust for this is to replace the regression equation (6) with

$$\mu_{ij} = \alpha_i + \gamma(y_{i0} - y_{.0}) + \beta_i(\log t_{ij} - \log 730), \qquad (13)$$

where $y_{.0}$ is the mean of the observations $\{y_{i0}\}$. In (13), the covariate y_{i0} is 'centred' by subtracting $y_{.0}$: this will help to reduce posterior correlations between γ and other parameters, and consequently to improve mixing in the Gibbs sampler. See Gilks and Roberts (1996) for further elaboration of this point.

As for all anti-HBS titre measurements, y_{i0} is subject to measurement error. We are scientifically interested in the relationship between the 'true' underlying log titres μ_{i0} and μ_{ij}, where μ_{i0} is the unobserved 'true' log titre on the ith infant at baseline. Therefore, instead of the obvious regression model (13), we should use the 'errors-in-variables' regression model

$$\mu_{ij} = \alpha_i + \gamma(\mu_{i0} - y_{.0}) + \beta_i(\log t_{ij} - \log 730). \qquad (14)$$

Information about the unknown μ_{i0} in (14) is provided by the measurement y_{i0}. We model this with

$$y_{i0} \sim \mathrm{N}(\mu_{i0},\ \sigma^2). \qquad (15)$$

Note that we have assigned the same variance σ^2 to both y_{ij} in (5) and y_{i0} in (15), because we believe that y_{ij} and y_{i0} are subject to the same sources of measurement (sampling) error.

We must also specify a prior for μ_{i0}. We choose

$$\mu_{i0} \sim \mathrm{N}(\theta,\ \phi^2), \qquad (16)$$

where the hyperparameters θ and ϕ^{-2} are assigned vague but proper Gaussian and gamma prior distributions.

Equations (14–16) constitute a measurement-error model, as discussed further by Richardson (1996). The measurement-error model (14–16) forms one component of our complete model, which includes equations (5) and (7–10). The graph for the complete model is shown in Figure 7, and the results from fitting both this model and the simpler model with a fixed baseline (13) instead of (14–16), are shown in Table 4.

Parameter		Fixed baseline (13)	Errors in baseline (14–16)
β_0	mean	−1.06	−1.08
	95% c.i.	−1.32, −0.80	−1.35, −0.81
σ_β	mean	0.31	0.24
	95% c.i.	0.07, 0.76	0.07, 0.62
γ	mean	0.68	1.04
	95% c.i.	0.51, 0.85	0.76, 1.42

TABLE 4. Results of fitting alternative regression models to the GHIS data: posterior means and 95% credible intervals

We note the expected result: the coefficient γ attached to the covariate measured with error increases dramatically when that error is properly taken into account. Indeed, the 95% credible interval for γ under the

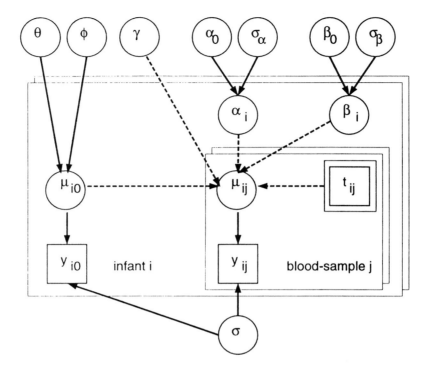

Figure 7. Graphical model for the GHIS data, showing dependence on baseline titre, measured with error.

errors-in-baseline model does not contain the estimate for γ under the fixed-baseline model. The estimate for σ_β from the errors-in-baseline model suggests that population variation in gradients probably does not have a major impact on the rate of loss of antibody, and results (not shown) from an analysis of a much larger subsample of the GHIS data confirm this. Setting $\sigma_\beta = 0$, with the plausible values of $\gamma = 1$, $\beta_0 = -1$, gives the satisfyingly simple model:

$$\frac{\text{titre at time } t}{\text{titre at time } 0} \propto \frac{1}{t},$$

which is a useful elaboration of the simpler model given by (1).

6. Conclusion

We have provided a brief overview of the issues involved in applying MCMC to full probability modelling. In particular, we emphasize the possibility for constructing increasingly elaborate statistical models using 'local' associations which can be expressed graphically and which allow straightforward implementation using Gibbs sampling. However, this possibility for complex modelling brings associated dangers and difficulties; we refer the reader to other chapters in Gilks, Richardson and Spiegelhalter (1996) for deeper discussion of issues such as convergence monitoring and improvement, model checking and model choice.

Acknowledgements

The BUGS project is supported by a grant from the UK Economic and Social Science Research Council's initiative for the Analysis of Large and Complex Datasets. The GHIS was generously funded by a grant from the Direzione Generale per la Cooperazione allo Sviluppo of the Ministry of Foreign Affairs of Italy. The GHIS was conducted at the Medical Research Council Laboratories, The Gambia, under the auspices of the International Agency for Research on Cancer.

References

Best, N. G., Cowles, M. K. and Vines, S. K. (1995) *CODA: Convergence Diagnosis and Output Analysis software for Gibbs Sampler output: Version 0.3.* Cambridge: Medical Research Council Biostatistics Unit.

Breslow, N. E. and Clayton, D. G. (1993) Approximate inference in generalized linear mixed models. *J. Am. Statist. Ass.*, **88**, 9–25.

Carlin, B. P. (1996) Hierarchical longitudinal modelling. In *Markov Chain Monte Carlo in Practice* (eds W. R. Gilks, S. Richardson and D. J. Spiegelhalter), pp. 303–320. London: Chapman & Hall.

Clayton, D. G. (1996) Generalized linear mixed models. In *Markov Chain Monte Carlo in Practice* (eds W. R. Gilks, S. Richardson and D. J. Spiegelhalter), pp. 275–302. London: Chapman & Hall.

Coursaget, P., Yvonnet, B., Gilks, W. R., Wang, C. C., Day, N. E., Chiron, J. P. and Diop-Mar, I. (1991) Scheduling of revaccinations against Hepatitis B virus. *Lancet*, **337**, 1180–3.

Cox, D. R. and Solomon, P. J. (1986) Analysis of variability with large numbers of small samples. *Biometrika*, **73**, 543–54.

DuMouchel, W. and Waternaux, C. (1992) Discussion on hierarchical models for combining information and for meta-analyses (by C. N. Morris and S. L. Normand). In *Bayesian Statistics 4* (eds J. M. Bernardo, J. O. Berger, A. P. Dawid and A. F. M. Smith), pp. 338–341. Oxford: Oxford University Press.

Gelfand, A. E. (1996) Model determination using sampling-based methods. In *Markov Chain Monte Carlo in Practice* (eds W. R. Gilks, S. Richardson and D. J. Spiegelhalter), pp. 145–162. London: Chapman & Hall.

Gelfand, A. E., Smith, A. F. M. and Lee, T.-M. (1992) Bayesian analysis of constrained parameter and truncated data problems using Gibbs sampling. *J. Am. Statist. Ass.*, **87**, 523–32.

Gelman, A. (1996) Inference and monitoring convergence. In *Markov Chain Monte Carlo in Practice* (eds W. R. Gilks, S. Richardson and D. J. Spiegelhalter), pp. 131–144. London: Chapman & Hall.

Gelman, A. and Meng, X.-L. (1996) Model checking and model improvement. In *Markov Chain Monte Carlo in Practice* (eds W. R. Gilks, S. Richardson and D. J. Spiegelhalter), pp. 189–202. London: Chapman & Hall.

Gelman, A. and Rubin, D. B. (1992) Inference from iterative simulation using multiple sequences (with discussion). *Statist. Sci.*, **7**, 457–511.

George, E. I. and McCulloch, R. E. (1996) Stochastic search variable selection. In *Markov Chain Monte Carlo in Practice* (eds W. R. Gilks, S. Richardson and D. J. Spiegelhalter), pp. 203–214. London: Chapman & Hall.

Gilks, W. R. (1996) Full conditional distributions. In *Markov Chain Monte Carlo in Practice* (eds W. R. Gilks, S. Richardson and D. J. Spiegelhalter), pp. 75–88. London: Chapman & Hall.

Gilks, W. R. S. Richardson and D. J. Spiegelhalter). (1996) Strategies for improving MCMC. In *Markov Chain Monte Carlo in Practice* (eds W. R. Gilks, S. Richardson and D. J. Spiegelhalter), pp. 89–114. London: Chapman & Hall.

Gilks, W. R. and Roberts, G. O. (1996) Strategies for improving MCMC. In *Markov Chain Monte Carlo in Practice* (eds W. R. Gilks, S. Richardson and D. J. Spiegelhalter), pp. 89–114. London: Chapman & Hall.

Gilks, W. R., Richardson, S. and Spiegelhalter, D. J. (1996) Introducing Markov chain Monte Carlo. In *Markov Chain Monte Carlo in Practice* (eds W. R. Gilks, S. Richardson and D. J. Spiegelhalter), pp. 1–20. London: Chapman & Hall.

Gilks, W. R., Thomas, A. and Spiegelhalter, D. J. (1994) A language and program for complex Bayesian modelling. *The Statistician*, **43**, 169–78.

Lauritzen, S. L., Dawid, A. P., Larsen, B. N. and Leimer, H.-G. (1990) Independence properties of directed Markov fields. *Networks*, **20**, 491–505.

Phillips, D. B. and Smith, A. F. M. (1996) Bayesian model comparison via jump diffusions. In *Markov Chain Monte Carlo in Practice* (eds W. R. Gilks, S. Richardson and D. J. Spiegelhalter), pp. 215–240. London: Chapman & Hall.

Raftery, A. E. (1996) Hypothesis testing and model selection. In *Markov Chain Monte Carlo in Practice* (eds W. R. Gilks, S. Richardson and D. J. Spiegelhalter), pp. 163–188. London: Chapman & Hall.

Richardson, S. (1996) Measurement error. In *Markov Chain Monte Carlo in Practice* (eds W. R. Gilks, S. Richardson and D. J. Spiegelhalter), pp. 401–418. London: Chapman & Hall.

Ripley, B. D. (1987) *Stochastic Simulation*. New York: Wiley.

Spiegelhalter, D. J., Dawid, A. P., Lauritzen, S. L. and Cowell, R. G. (1993) Bayesian analysis in expert systems (with discussion) *Statist. Sci.*, **8**, 219–83.

Spiegelhalter, D. J., Thomas, A. and Best, N. G. (1996) Computation on Bayesian graphical models. In *Bayesian Statistics 5*, (eds J. M. Bernardo, J. O. Berger, A. P. Dawid and A. F. M. Smith), pp 407–425. Oxford: Oxford University Press.

Spiegelhalter, D. J., Thomas, A., Best, N. G. and Gilks, W. R. (1994) *BUGS: Bayesian inference Using Gibbs Sampling, Version 0.30.* Cambridge: Medical Research Council Biostatistics Unit.

Thomas, D. C. and Gauderman, W. J. (1996) Gibbs sampling methods in genetics. In *Markov Chain Monte Carlo in Practice* (eds W. R. Gilks, S. Richardson and D. J. Spiegelhalter), pp. 419–440. London: Chapman & Hall.

Whittaker, J. (1990) *Graphical Models in Applied Multivariate Analysis.* Chichester: Wiley.

Whittle, H. C., Inskip, H., Hall, A. J., Mendy, M., Downes, R. and Hoare, S. (1991) Vaccination against Hepatitis B and protection against viral carriage in The Gambia. *Lancet*, **337**, 747–750.

Appendix: BUGS

BUGS is a program which provides a syntax for specifying graphical models and a command language for running Gibbs sampling sessions. An idea of the syntax can be obtained from the model description shown below, corresponding to the errors-in-variables model described in equations (5, 7–10, 14–16) and shown in Figure 7.

```
{
    for(i in 1:I){

        for(j in 1:n[i]){
            y[i,j]    ~ dnorm(mu[i,j],tau);
            mu[i,j] <- alpha[i] + gamma * (mu0[i] - mean(y0[]))
                            + beta[i] * (log.time[j] - log(730));
        }

#   covariate with measurement error
        y0[i]     ~ dnorm(mu0[i],tau);
        mu0[i]    ~ dnorm(theta, phi);

# random lines
        beta[i]  ~ dnorm(beta0, tau.beta);
        alpha[i] ~ dnorm(alpha0, tau.alpha);

    }


# prior distributions
    tau         ~ dgamma(0.01,0.01);
    gamma       ~ dnorm(0,0.0001);
    alpha0      ~ dnorm(0,0.0001);
```

```
beta0       ~ dnorm(0,0.0001);
tau.beta    ~ dgamma(0.01,0.01);
tau.alpha   ~ dgamma(0.01,0.01);
theta       ~ dnorm(0.0, 0.0001);
phi         ~ dgamma(0.01, 0.01);


sigma       <- 1/sqrt(tau);
sigma.beta  <- 1/sqrt(tau.beta);
sigma.alpha <- 1/sqrt(tau.alpha);
}
```

The essential correspondence between the syntax and the graphical representation should be clear: the relational operator ~ corresponds to 'is distributed as' and <- to 'is logically defined by'. Note that BUGS parameterizes the Gaussian distribution in terms of mean and precision (= 1/variance). The program then interprets this declarative model description and constructs an internal representation of the graph, identifying relevant prior and likelihood terms and selecting a sampling method. Further details of the program are given in Gilks *et al.* (1994) and Spiegelhalter *et al.* (1996).

The software will run under UNIX and DOS, is available for a number of computer platforms, and can be freely obtained, together with a manual and extensive examples from http://www.mrc-bsu.cam.ac.uk/bugs/, or contact the authors at bugs@mrc-bsu.cam.ac.uk.

PREDICTION WITH GAUSSIAN PROCESSES:

FROM LINEAR REGRESSION TO LINEAR PREDICTION AND BEYOND

C. K. I. WILLIAMS

Neural Computing Research Group, Aston University
Birmingham B4 7ET, UK

Abstract. The main aim of this paper is to provide a tutorial on regression with Gaussian processes. We start from Bayesian linear regression, and show how by a change of viewpoint one can see this method as a Gaussian process predictor based on priors over functions, rather than on priors over parameters. This leads in to a more general discussion of Gaussian processes in section 4. Section 5 deals with further issues, including hierarchical modelling and the setting of the parameters that control the Gaussian process, the covariance functions for neural network models and the use of Gaussian processes in classification problems.

1. Introduction

In the last decade neural networks have been used to tackle regression and classification problems, with some notable successes. It has also been widely recognized that they form a part of a wide variety of non-linear statistical techniques that can be used for these tasks; other methods include, for example, decision trees and kernel methods. The books by Bishop (1995) and Ripley (1996) provide excellent overviews.

One of the attractions of neural network models is their flexibility, i.e. their ability to model a wide variety of functions. However, this flexibility comes at a cost, in that a large number of parameters may need to be determined from the data, and consequently that there is a danger of "overfitting". Overfitting can be reduced by using weight regularization, but this leads to the awkward problem of specifying how to set the regularization parameters (e.g. the parameter α in the weight regularization term $\alpha \mathbf{w}^T \mathbf{w}$ for a weight vector $\mathbf{w}$.)

The Bayesian approach is to specify an hierarchical model with a prior distribution over hyperparameters such as α, then to specify the prior distribution of the weights relative to the hyperparameters. This is connected to data via an "observations" model; for example, in a regression context, the value of the dependent variable may be corrupted by Gaussian noise. Given an observed dataset, a posterior distribution over the weights and hyperparameters (rather than just a point estimate) will be induced. However, for neural network models this posterior cannot usually be obtained analytically; computational methods used include approximations (MacKay, 1992) or the evaluation of integrals using Monte Carlo methods (Neal, 1996).

In the Bayesian approach to neural networks, a prior on the weights of a network induces a prior over functions. An alternative method of putting a prior over functions is to use a *Gaussian process* (GP) prior over functions. This idea has been used for a long time in the spatial statistics community under the name of "kriging", although it seems to have been largely ignored as a general-purpose regression method. Gaussian process priors have the advantage over neural networks that at least the lowest level of a Bayesian hierarchical model can be treated analytically. Recent work (Williams and Rasmussen, 1996, inspired by observations in Neal, 1996) has extended the use of these priors to higher dimensional problems that have been traditionally tackled with other techniques such as neural networks, decision trees *etc* and has shown that good results can be obtained.

The main aim of this paper is to provide a tutorial on regression with Gaussian processes. The approach taken is to start with Bayesian linear regression, and to show how by a change of viewpoint one can see this method as a Gaussian process predictor based on priors over functions, rather than performing the computations in parameter-space. This leads in to a more general discussion of Gaussian processes in section 4. Section 5 deals with further issues, including hierarchical modelling and the setting of the parameters that control the Gaussian process, the covariance functions for neural network models and the use of Gaussian processes in classification problems.

2. Bayesian regression

To apply the Bayesian method to a data analysis problem, we first specify a set of probabilistic models of the data. This set may be finite, countably infinite or uncountably infinite in size. An example of the latter case is when the set of models is indexed by a vector in $\mathbb{R}^m$. Let a member of this set be denoted by $\mathcal{H}_\alpha$, which will have a *prior* probability $P(\mathcal{H}_\alpha)$. On observing some data $\mathcal{D}$, the *likelihood* of hypothesis $\mathcal{H}_\alpha$ is $P(\mathcal{D}|\mathcal{H}_\alpha)$. The *posterior* probability of $\mathcal{H}_\alpha$ is then given by

$$\text{posterior} \quad \propto \quad \text{prior} \times \text{likelihood} \tag{1}$$

$$P(\mathcal{H}_\alpha|\mathcal{D}) \quad \propto \quad P(\mathcal{H}_\alpha)P(\mathcal{D}|\mathcal{H}_\alpha). \tag{2}$$

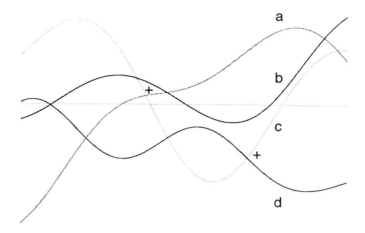

Figure 1. The four possible curves (labelled a, b, c and d) and the two data points (shown with + signs).

The proportionality can be turned into an equality be dividing through by $P(\mathcal{D}) = \sum_\alpha P(\mathcal{D}|\mathcal{H}_\alpha)P(\mathcal{H}_\alpha)$ (where the summation may be interpreted as an integration where appropriate).

Suppose we are now asked to make a prediction using this set of probabilistic models; say we are to predict some quantity y. Under each of the individual models the prediction for y is given by $P(y|\mathcal{H}_\alpha)$. The combined prediction is

$$P(y) = \sum_\alpha P(y|\mathcal{H}_\alpha)P(\mathcal{H}_\alpha|\mathcal{D}). \tag{3}$$

In this paper we will discuss the Bayesian approach to the regression problem, i.e. the discovery of the relationship between input (or independent) variables $\mathbf{x}$ and the output (or dependent) variable y. In the rest of this section we illustrate the Bayesian method with only a finite number of hypotheses; the case of an uncountably infinite set is treated in section 3.

We are given four different curves denoted $f_a(x), f_b(x), f_c(x)$ and $f_d(x)$ which correspond to the hypotheses labelled by $\mathcal{H}_a, \mathcal{H}_b, \mathcal{H}_c$ and $\mathcal{H}_d$; see the illustration in Figure 1. Each curve $\mathcal{H}_\alpha$ has a prior probability $P(\mathcal{H}_\alpha)$; if there is no reason *a priori* to prefer one curve over another, then each prior probability is $1/4$.

The data $\mathcal{D}$ is given as input-output pairs $(\mathbf{x}_1, t_1), (\mathbf{x}_2, t_2), \ldots, (\mathbf{x}_n, t_n)$. Assuming that the targets t_i are generated by adding independent Gaussian noise of variance σ_ν^2 to the underlying function evaluated at $\mathbf{x}_i$, the likelihood of model $\mathcal{H}_\alpha$ (for $\alpha \in \{a, b, c, d\}$) when the data point $(\mathbf{x}_i, t_i)$ is observed is

$$P(t_i|\mathbf{x}_i, \mathcal{H}_\alpha) = \frac{1}{(2\pi\sigma_\nu^2)^{1/2}} \exp -\frac{(t_i - f_\alpha(x_i))^2}{2\sigma_\nu^2}. \tag{4}$$

The likelihood of each hypothesis given all n data points is simply $\prod_i P(t_i|\mathbf{x}_i, \mathcal{H}_\alpha)$.

Let us assume that the standard deviation of the noise is much smaller (say less than $1/10$) than the overall y-scale of Figure 1. On observing one data point (the left-most $+$ in Figure 1), the likelihood (or data fit) term given by equation 4 is much higher for curves a, b and c than for curve d. Thus the posterior distribution after the first data point will now have less weight on $\mathcal{H}_d$ and correspondingly more on hypotheses $\mathcal{H}_a, \mathcal{H}_b$ and $\mathcal{H}_c$. A second data point is now observed (the right-most $+$ in Figure 1). Only curve c fits both of of these data points well, and thus the posterior will have most of its mass concentrated on this hypothesis. If we were to make predictions at a new x point, it would be curve c that had the largest contribution to this prediction.

From this example it can be seen that Bayesian inference is really quite straightforward, at least in principle; we simply evaluate the posterior probability of each alternative, and combine these to make predictions. These calculations are easily understood when there are a finite number of hypotheses, and they can also be carried out analytically in some cases when the number of hypotheses is infinite, as we shall see in the next section.

3. From linear regression ...

Let us consider what may be called "generalized linear regression", which we take to mean linear regression using a fixed set of m basis functions $\{\phi_i(\mathbf{x})\}$. Thus the regression function will have the form $y(x) = \sum_{i=1}^{m} w_i\phi_i(x) = \mathbf{w}^T\phi(\mathbf{x})$, for some vector of "weights" $\mathbf{w}$. If there is a Gaussian prior distribution on the weights and we assume Gaussian noise then there are two equivalent ways of obtaining the regression function, (i) by performing the computations in weight-space, and (ii) by taking a Gaussian process view. In the rest of this section we will develop these two methods and demonstrate their equivalence.

3.1. THE WEIGHT-SPACE VIEW

Let the weights have a prior distribution which is Gaussian and centered on the origin, $\mathbf{w} \sim N(\mathbf{0}, \Sigma_w)$, i.e.

$$P(\mathbf{w}) = \frac{1}{(2\pi)^{m/2}|\Sigma_w|^{1/2}} \exp\{-\frac{1}{2}\mathbf{w}^T\Sigma_w^{-1}\mathbf{w}\}. \tag{5}$$

Although a common choice for the prior (e.g. in ridge regression) is to set $\Sigma_w \propto I_m$, it may be more sensible to choose Σ_w so as to approximate a Gaussian process (see section 5.3).

Again, assuming that the targets t_i are generated by Gaussian noise of variance σ_ν^2 from the underlying function, the likelihood of $\mathbf{w}$ is

$$P(t_1, t_2, \ldots, t_n | \mathbf{w}) = \frac{1}{(2\pi\sigma_\nu^2)^{n/2}} \prod_{i=1}^{n} \exp\{-\frac{(t_i - y(x_i; \mathbf{w}))^2}{2\sigma_\nu^2}\}. \tag{6}$$

The posterior distribution for the weights is given by

$$P(\mathbf{w}|D) = \frac{P(D|\mathbf{w})P(\mathbf{w})}{P(D)} \tag{7}$$

where $P(D) = \int P(D|\mathbf{w})P(\mathbf{w})d\mathbf{w}$. As the prior and likelihood are Gaussian, the posterior is also Gaussian. The posterior mean value of the weights $\mathbf{w}_{MP}$ is the choice of $\mathbf{w}$ that minimizes the quadratic form

$$E = \frac{1}{2\sigma_\nu^2} \sum_{i}^{n} (t_i - \mathbf{w}^T \phi(\mathbf{x}_i))^2 + \frac{1}{2}\mathbf{w}^T \Sigma_w^{-1} \mathbf{w}. \tag{8}$$

Let $\beta = 1/\sigma_\nu^2$, let Φ be the $n \times m$ design matrix

$$\Phi = \begin{pmatrix} \phi_1(\mathbf{x}_1) & \phi_2(\mathbf{x}_1) & \cdots & \phi_m(\mathbf{x}_1) \\ \phi_1(\mathbf{x}_2) & \phi_2(\mathbf{x}_2) & \cdots & \phi_m(\mathbf{x}_2) \\ \vdots & \vdots & \vdots & \vdots \\ \phi_1(\mathbf{x}_n) & \phi_2(\mathbf{x}_n) & \cdots & \phi_m(\mathbf{x}_n) \end{pmatrix} \tag{9}$$

and let $\mathbf{t}$ denote the vector of targets. Then we can rewrite equation 8 as

$$E = \frac{\beta}{2}(\mathbf{t} - \Phi\mathbf{w})^T(\mathbf{t} - \Phi\mathbf{w}) + \frac{1}{2}\mathbf{w}^T\Sigma_w^{-1}\mathbf{w} \tag{10}$$

$$= \frac{1}{2}\mathbf{w}^T(\Sigma_w^{-1} + \beta\Phi^T\Phi)\mathbf{w} - \beta\mathbf{w}^T\Phi^T\mathbf{t} + \frac{\beta}{2}\mathbf{t}^T\mathbf{t}, \tag{11}$$

and $\mathbf{w}_{MP}$ is the minimizer of this quadratic form, i.e. it is the solution of

$$(\Sigma_w^{-1} + \beta\Phi^T\Phi)\mathbf{w}_{MP} = \beta\Phi^T\mathbf{t}. \tag{12}$$

Let $A = \Sigma_w^{-1} + \beta\Phi^T\Phi$. Then $\mathbf{w}_{MP} = \beta A^{-1}\Phi^T\mathbf{t}$ and the posterior covariance matrix for the weights is A^{-1}.

The mean prediction for a new input $\mathbf{x}_*$ (under the weight-space view) is

$$\mu_{ws}(\mathbf{x}_*) = \phi^T(\mathbf{x}_*)\mathbf{w}_{MP} = \beta\phi^T(\mathbf{x}_*)A^{-1}\Phi^T\mathbf{t}. \tag{13}$$

We can also obtain "error bars" for this prediction; the variance about the mean is given by

$$\sigma_y^2(\mathbf{x}_*) = E_{w|\mathcal{D}}[(y(\mathbf{x}_*) - \mu_{ws}(\mathbf{x}_*))^2] \tag{14}$$

$$= \phi^T(\mathbf{x}_*)E_{w|\mathcal{D}}[(\mathbf{w} - \mathbf{w}_{MP})(\mathbf{w} - \mathbf{w}_{MP})^T]\phi(\mathbf{x}_*) \tag{15}$$

$$= \phi^T(\mathbf{x}_*)A^{-1}\phi(\mathbf{x}_*). \tag{16}$$

To obtain the predictive variance var $t(\mathbf{x}_*)$ it is necessary to add σ_ν^2 to $\sigma_y^2(\mathbf{x}_*)$ to account for the additional variance due to the noise, since the two sources of variation are uncorrelated.

The Bayesian approach to linear regression is discussed in most texts on Bayesian statistics, for example Box and Tiao (1973).

3.2. THE FUNCTION-SPACE VIEW

In the previous section the uncertainty in the problem was described through a probability distribution over the weights. It is also possible to deal directly with uncertainty with respect to the function values at the points we are interested in. This is the stochastic process or function-space view of the problem. A stochastic process $Y(\mathbf{x})$ is a collection of random variables indexed by $\mathbf{x}$. In the cases considered below, $\mathbf{x}$ will usually be a vector in $\mathbb{R}^p$ where p is the dimensionality of $\mathbf{x}$-space. A general stochastic process is specified by giving the probability distributions of any finite subset $(Y(\mathbf{x}_1), Y(\mathbf{x}_2), \ldots, Y(\mathbf{x}_k))$ in a consistent way. Gaussian processes are a subset of stochastic processes that can be specified by giving only the mean vector and covariance matrix for any finite subset of points. In fact we shall further specialize and consider only Gaussian processes which have zero mean.

In the function-space view of linear regression we consider the kinds of function that can be generated from a fixed set of basis functions with random weights. The Y value at a particular point $\mathbf{x}$ in the input space is a random variable $Y(\mathbf{x}) = \sum_j W_j \phi_j(\mathbf{x})$, which is simply a linear combination of the Gaussian random variables $\mathbf{W}$, where $\mathbf{W} \sim N(\mathbf{0}, \Sigma_w)$ as in equation 5. (The notation $\mathbf{W}$ indicates that the weights are viewed as random variables.) We can calculate the mean and covariance functions for the stochastic process,

$$E_w[Y(\mathbf{x})] = 0 \tag{17}$$

$$E_w[Y(\mathbf{x})Y(\mathbf{x}')] = \phi^T(\mathbf{x})\Sigma_w\phi(\mathbf{x}'). \tag{18}$$

In fact since it is derived as a linear combination of Gaussian random variables it is clear that Y is a Gaussian process. Some examples of sample functions are shown in Figure 2(b), using the basis functions shown in

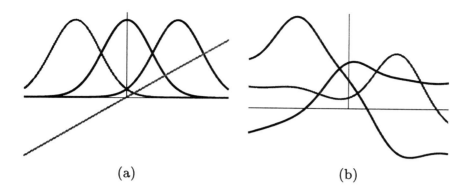

Figure 2. (a) shows four basis functions, and (b) shows three sample functions generated by taking different linear combinations of these basis functions.

Figure 2(a). The sample functions are obtained by drawing samples of $\mathbf{W}$ from $N(\mathbf{0}, \Sigma_w)$.

3.3. PREDICTION USING GAUSSIAN PROCESSES

We will first consider the general problem of prediction using a Gaussian process, and then focus on the particular Gaussian process derived from linear regression. The key observation is that rather than deal with complicated entities such as priors on function spaces, we can consider just the function values at the $\mathbf{x}$ points that concern us, namely the training points $\mathbf{x}_1, \ldots, \mathbf{x}_n$ and the test point $\mathbf{x}_*$ whose y-value we wish to predict. Thus we need only consider finite-dimensional objects, namely covariance matrices.

Consider $n + 1$ random variables $(Z_1, Z_2, \ldots, Z_n, Z_*)$ which have a joint Gaussian distribution with mean $\mathbf{0}$ and covariance matrix K_+. Let the $(n + 1) \times (n + 1)$ matrix K_+ be partitioned into a $n \times n$ matrix K, a $n \times 1$ vector $\mathbf{k}$ and a scalar k_*

$$K_+ = \begin{pmatrix} K & \mathbf{k} \\ \mathbf{k}^T & k_* \end{pmatrix} \tag{19}$$

If particular values are observed for the first n variables, i.e. $Z_1 = z_1, Z_2 = z_2, \ldots, Z_n = z_n$, then the conditional distribution for Z_* is Gaussian (see, e.g. von Mises, 1964, section 9.3) with

$$E[Z_*] = \mathbf{k}^T K^{-1} \mathbf{z} \tag{20}$$
$$\text{var}[Z_*] = k_* - \mathbf{k}^T K^{-1} \mathbf{k} \tag{21}$$

where $\mathbf{z}^T = (z_1, z_2, \ldots, z_n)$. Notice that the predicted mean (equation 20) is a linear combination of the z's.

3.4. LINEAR REGRESSION USING THE FUNCTION-SPACE VIEW

Returning to the linear regression case, we are interested in calculating the distribution of $Y(\mathbf{x}_*) = Y_*$, given the noisy observations $(t_1, \ldots, t_n)$. To do this we calculate the joint distribution of $(T_1, T_2, \ldots, T_n, Y_*)$ and then condition on the specific values $T_1 = t_1, T_2 = t_2, \ldots, T_n = t_n$ to obtain the desired distribution $P(Y_*|\mathbf{t})$. Of course this distribution will be a Gaussian so we need only compute its mean and variance.

The distribution for $(T_1, T_2, \ldots, T_n, Y_*)$ is most easily derived by first considering the joint distribution of $\mathbf{Y}_+ = (Y_1, Y_2, \ldots, Y_n, Y_*)$. Under the linear regression model this is given by $\mathbf{Y}_+ \sim N(\mathbf{0}, \Phi_+ \Sigma_w \Phi_+^T)$, where Φ_+ is an extended Φ matrix with an additional bottom row $\phi_* = \phi(\mathbf{x}_*) = (\phi_1(\mathbf{x}_*), \phi_2(\mathbf{x}_*), \ldots, \phi_m(\mathbf{x}_*))$. Under the partitioning used in equation 19, the structure of $\Phi_+ \Sigma_w \Phi_+^T$ can be written

$$\Phi_+ \Sigma_w \Phi_+^T = \begin{pmatrix} \Phi \Sigma_w \Phi^T & \Phi \Sigma_w \phi_* \\ \phi_*^T \Sigma_w \Phi^T & \phi_*^T \Sigma_w \phi_* \end{pmatrix}. \tag{22}$$

The joint distribution for $T_1, \ldots T_n, Y_*$ can be found by realizing that the T's are obtained by corrupting the corresponding Y's with Gaussian noise, and hence that $(T_1, \ldots T_n, Y_*) \sim N(\mathbf{0}, \Phi_+ \Sigma_w \Phi_+^T + E_+)$, where E_+ is the $n \times n$ matrix $\sigma_\nu^2 I_n$ bordered on the right and bottom by bands of zeros. (The reason that E_+ is not $\sigma_\nu^2 I_{n+1}$ is that we are predicting Y_*, not T_*.) Conditioning on $T_1 = t_1, T_2 = t_2, \ldots, T_n = t_n$ and using equations 20 and 21, we obtain

$$E[Y_*] = \mu_{fs}(\mathbf{x}_*) = \phi_*^T \Sigma_w \Phi^T P^{-1} \mathbf{t} \tag{23}$$

$$\text{var}[Y_*] = \phi_*^T \Sigma_w \phi_* - \phi_*^T \Sigma_w \Phi^T P^{-1} \Phi \Sigma_w \phi_* \tag{24}$$

where we have defined $P = (\Phi \Sigma_w \Phi^T + \sigma_\nu^2 I_n)$. Note that if the number of basis functions (m) is less than the number of data points (n), as will often be the case, then the covariance matrix $\Phi \Sigma_w \Phi^T$ will be rank-deficient, i.e. it will have some zero eigenvalues, so that the probability of points lying outside a linear subspace will be zero. However, the addition of $\sigma_\nu^2 I_n$ ensures that P will be strictly positive definite.

The challenge is now to show that these results for the mean and variance are consistent with the expressions obtained in section 3.1. To obtain the formula for the mean as in equation 13 we note that

$$A \Sigma_w \Phi^T = \Phi^T + \beta \Phi^T \Phi \Sigma_w \Phi^T = \beta \Phi^T (\sigma_\nu^2 I + \Phi \Sigma_w \Phi^T) = \beta \Phi^T P. \tag{25}$$

By multiplying through by A^{-1} and P^{-1} we obtain $\Sigma_w \Phi^T P^{-1} = \beta A^{-1} \Phi^T$, which can be substituted into equation 23 to yield the desired result.

The equivalence of the two expressions for the variance can be proved by using the following matrix identity (the Woodbury formula, Press *et al*, 1992, section 2.7)

$$(X + YZ)^{-1} = X^{-1} - X^{-1}Y(I + ZX^{-1}Y)^{-1}ZX^{-1} \qquad (26)$$

on $A^{-1} = (\Sigma_w^{-1} + \beta\Phi^T\Phi)^{-1}$ to obtain

$$A^{-1} = \Sigma_w - \Sigma_w\Phi^T(\sigma_\nu^2 I + \Phi\Sigma_w\Phi^T)^{-1}\Phi\Sigma_w, \qquad (27)$$

which may be substituted into equation 16 to give equation 24.

Given that the weight-space and function-space views are equivalent, it is interesting to ask which of the two methods is computationally more efficient. In the weight-space approach it is necessary to form and invert the matrix A which is of dimension $m \times m$. Similarly for the function-space view one has to form and invert the $n \times n$ matrix P. As the inversion of a $l \times l$ matrix takes time $O(l^3)$, it is natural to choose the method which takes less time. Usually for simple linear regression problems $m \ll n$ and so the weight-space view will be preferred. But for other kinds of linear prediction (see section 4) m can be infinite and thus the function-space view is the only tenable one.

4. ... to linear prediction ...

As we have already seen in section 3.3, if the prior is a general Gaussian process and we assume a Gaussian noise model, then the predicted y-value is just some linear combination of the t-values; the method is said to be a *linear smoother* (Hastie and Tibshirani, 1990) or a *linear predictor*. In section 3 we have seen how linear regression can be seen from a function-space viewpoint. This opens up further possibilities, as linear regression with a prior on the weights is just one way of specifying the covariance between points $\mathbf{x}$ and $\mathbf{x}'$. In general the covariance function $C(\mathbf{x}, \mathbf{x}')$ of a zero-mean Gaussian process $Y(\mathbf{x})$ is defined as $E[Y(\mathbf{x})Y(\mathbf{x}')]$. Formally, the covariance function can be any function that will generate a non-negative definite covariance matrix for any set of points $(\mathbf{x}_1, \mathbf{x}_2, \ldots, \mathbf{x}_k)$. It is non-trivial to come up with functions that obey this condition, although several families are known in the literature.

One well-known class is the stationary and isotropic covariance functions where $C(\mathbf{x}, \mathbf{x}') = C(|\mathbf{x} - \mathbf{x}'|) = C(h)$, where $|\cdot|$ denotes the Euclidean norm. These can be derived as the characteristic function (or Fourier transform) of an isotropic probability density[1]. For example $C(h) = \exp(-(h/\sigma)^\nu)$

---

[1]In fact Bochner's theorem (see, e.g. Wong, 1971) states that the positive definite functions $C(h)$ which are continuous at 0 and satisfy $C(0) = 1$ are exactly the characteristic functions.

is a valid covariance function for all dimensions p and for $0 < \nu \leq 2$, corresponding to the multivariate Cauchy and Gaussian distributions when $\nu = 1$ and $\nu = 2$ respectively. Note that in this case σ sets the correlation length-scale of the random field, although other covariance functions (e.g. those corresponding to power-law spectral densities[2]) may have no preferred length scale.

Samples from Gaussian processes can have very different properties depending on the choice of the covariance function. For example in 1-d, the Ornstein-Uhlenbeck process (with covariance function $e^{-|h|}$) has very rough sample paths which are not mean-square differentiable. On the other hand, choosing $C(x, x') = \sigma_0^2 + \sigma_1^2 xx'$ (which arises from $y = \mathbf{w}^T \phi(\mathbf{x})$ with $\phi(\mathbf{x}) = (1, x)^T$ and $\mathbf{w} \sim N(\mathbf{0}, \text{diag}(\sigma_0^2, \sigma_1^2))$) leads to straight-line sample paths of the form $y = w_0 + w_1 x$. It should also be noted that the covariance function $C(h) = e^{-h^2}$ gives rise to sample paths that are infinitely mean-square differentiable.

Given a covariance function which is assumed to characterize the data $\mathcal{D}$, it is easy to make predictions for new test points; we simply use equations 20 and 21; as in section 3.4 the overall covariance function will be made up of the prior covariance function and a noise term. If the covariance function is unknown (as will always be the case in practice) but is assumed to come from some parametric class, then maximum likelihood estimation or a Bayesian approach can be taken; this is discussed in section 5.2 below.

Prediction with Gaussian processes is certainly not a very recent topic; the basic theory goes back to Wiener and Kolmogorov in the 1940's and applications to multivariate regression are discussed in Whittle (1963). ARMA models for time series are Gaussian process models. Gaussian process prediction is also well known in the geostatistics field (Journel and Huijbregts, 1978; Cressie, 1993) where it is known as "kriging", although this literature naturally has focussed mostly on two- and three-dimensional input spaces. Wahba has been influential in promoting the use of spline techniques for regression problems; her work dates back to Kimeldorf and Wahba (1970), although Wahba (1990) provides a useful overview. Essentially splines correspond to Gaussian processes with a particular choice of covariance function[3].

Gaussian process prediction was also suggested by O'Hagan (1978), and is widely used in the analysis of computer experiments (e.g Sacks *et al*, 1989), although in this application it is assumed that the observations are noise-free. A connection to neural networks was made by Poggio

---

[2]For stationary covariance functions the spectral density is the Fourier transform of the covariance function.

[3]Technically splines require generalized covariance functions (see Cressie §5.4), and they have a power-law spectral density $S(\omega) \propto \omega^{-\beta}$ with $\beta > 0$.

and Girosi (1990) and Girosi, Jones and Poggio (1995) with their work on Regularization Networks. When the covariance function $C(\mathbf{x}, \mathbf{x}')$ depends only on $h = |\mathbf{x} - \mathbf{x}'|$, the predictor derived in equation 20 has the form $\sum_i c_i C(|\mathbf{x} - \mathbf{x}_i|)$ and may be called a *radial basis function* (or RBF) network.

4.1. COVARIANCE FUNCTIONS AND EIGENFUNCTIONS

It turns out that general Gaussian processes can be viewed as Bayesian linear regression with an infinite number of basis functions. One possible basis set is the *eigenfunctions* of the covariance function. A function $\phi(\cdot)$ that obeys the integral equation over the domain $\mathcal{R}$

$$\int_{\mathcal{R}} C(\mathbf{x}, \mathbf{x}')\phi(\mathbf{x})d\mathbf{x} = \lambda\phi(\mathbf{x}') \qquad (28)$$

is called an eigenfunction of C with eigenvalue λ. In general there are an infinite number of eigenfunctions, which we label $\phi_1(\mathbf{x}), \phi_2(\mathbf{x}), \ldots$. The eigenfunctions are orthogonal and can be chosen to be normalized so that $\int_{\mathcal{R}} \phi_i(\mathbf{x})\phi_j(\mathbf{x})\, d\mathbf{x} = \delta_{ij}$ where δ_{ij} is the Kronecker delta.

Mercer's theorem (see, e.g. Wong, 1971) states that the covariance function can be expressed as

$$C(\mathbf{x}, \mathbf{x}') = \sum_{i=1}^{\infty} \lambda_i \phi_i(\mathbf{x})\phi_i(\mathbf{x}'). \qquad (29)$$

This decomposition is just the infinite-dimensional analogue of the diagonalization of a real symmetric matrix. Note that if $\mathcal{R}$ is $\mathbb{R}^p$, then the summation in equation 29 can become an integral. This occurs, for example, in the spectral representation of stationary covariance functions. However, it can happen that the spectrum is discrete even if $\mathcal{R}$ is $\mathbb{R}^p$ as long as $C(\mathbf{x}, \mathbf{x}')$ decays fast enough.

The equivalence with Bayesian linear regression can now be seen by taking the prior weight matrix Σ_w to be the diagonal matrix $\Lambda = \mathrm{diag}(\lambda_1, \lambda_2, \ldots)$ and choosing the eigenfunctions as the basis functions; equation 29 and the equivalence of the weight-space and function-space views demonstrated in section 3 completes the proof.

The fact that an input vector can be expanded into an infinite-dimensional space $(\phi_1(\mathbf{x}), \phi_2(\mathbf{x}), \ldots)$ but that the necessary computations can be carried out efficiently due to Mercer's theorem has been used in some other contexts, for example in the method of potential functions (due to Aizerman, Braverman and Rozoner, 1964) and in support vector machines (Vapnik, 1995). In support vector regression the prior over functions is as described above, but instead of using a squared error loss function (which corresponds to Gaussian noise), a modified version of the l_1 error metric $|t_i - y_i|$ is used, called the ϵ-insensitive loss function. Finding the *maximum a posteriori* (or MAP) y-values for the training points and test point can now be achieved using quadratic programming (see Vapnik, 1995 for details).

5. ... and beyond ...

In this section some further details are given on the topics of modelling issues, adaptation of the covariance function, computational issues, the covariance function for neural networks and classification with Gaussian processes.

5.1. MODELLING ISSUES

As we have seen above, there is a wide variety of covariance functions that can be used. The use of stationary covariance functions is appealing as usually one would like the predictions to be invariant under shifts of the origin in input space. From a modelling point of view we wish to specify a covariance function so that nearby inputs will give rise to similar predictions. Experiments in Williams and Rasmussen (1996) and Rasmussen (1996) have demonstrated that the following covariance function seems to work well in practice:

$$C(\mathbf{x}^{(i)}, \mathbf{x}^{(j)}) = v_0 \exp\{-\frac{1}{2}\sum_{l=1}^{p}\alpha_l(x_l^{(i)} - x_l^{(j)})^2\}$$
$$+a_0 + a_1\sum_{l=1}^{p}x_l^{(i)}x_l^{(j)} + v_1\delta(i,j), \qquad (30)$$

where $\theta \overset{def}{=} (\log v_0, \log v_1, \log \alpha_1, \ldots, \log \alpha_p, \log a_0, \log a_1)$ is the vector of adjustable parameters. The parameters are defined to be the log of the variables in equation (30) since they are positive scale-parameters.

The covariance function is made up of three parts; the first term, a linear regression term (involving a_0 and a_1) and a noise term $v_1\delta(i,j)$. The first term expresses the idea that cases with nearby inputs will have highly correlated outputs; the α_l parameters allow a different distance measure for each input dimension. For irrelevant inputs, the corresponding α_l will become small, and the model will ignore that input. This is closely related to the Automatic Relevance Determination (ARD) idea of MacKay and Neal (MacKay, 1993; Neal 1996). The v_0 variable gives the overall scale of the local correlations, a_0 and a_1 are variables controlling the scale of the bias and linear contributions to the covariance. A simple extension of the linear regression part of the covariance function would allow a different

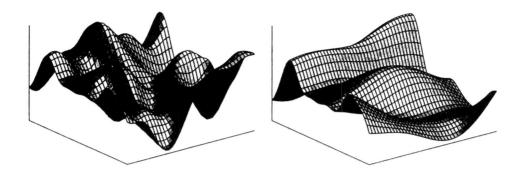

Figure 3. Functions drawn at random from the ARD prior. In the left hand plot $\alpha_1 = \alpha_2$ while on the right $\alpha_1 = 10\alpha_2$.

hyperparameter a_{1i} for each of the input dimensions. The last term accounts for the noise on the data; v_1 is the variance of the noise.

The ARD idea was demonstrated for Gaussian processes in an experiment described in Williams and Rasmussen (1996), where irrelevant inputs were added to a regression task. By adapting the α parameters as described in section 5.2 below, their values for the irrelevant inputs became very small, successfully indicating the irrelevance of these inputs.

A graphical example of ARD is given in Figure 3. The left hand panel shows a sample from the prior when $\alpha_1 = \alpha_2$. Notice that the length-scale of variation is the same on both axes. In the right hand panel $\alpha_1 = 10\alpha_2$, indicating much slower variation along the x_2 axis. In the limit as $\alpha_2 \to 0$, the x_2 coordinate is irrelevant.

5.2. ADAPTING THE COVARIANCE FUNCTION

Given a covariance function it is straightforward to make predictions for new test points. However, in practical situations we are unlikely to know which covariance function to use. One option is to choose a parametric family of covariance functions (with a parameter vector $\boldsymbol{\theta}$) and then either to estimate the parameters (for example, using the method of maximum likelihood) or to use a Bayesian approach where a posterior distribution over the parameters is obtained.

These calculations are facilitated by the fact that the log likelihood $l = \log P(\mathcal{D}|\boldsymbol{\theta})$ can be calculated analytically as

$$l = -\frac{1}{2}\log \det K - \frac{1}{2}\mathbf{t}^T K^{-1}\mathbf{t} - \frac{n}{2}\log 2\pi. \tag{31}$$

It is also possible to express analytically the partial derivatives of the log likelihood with respect to the hyperparameters, using the equation

$$\frac{\partial l}{\partial \theta_i} = -\frac{1}{2}\text{tr}\left(K^{-1}\frac{\partial K}{\partial \theta_i}\right) + \frac{1}{2}\mathbf{t}^T K^{-1}\frac{\partial K}{\partial \theta_i}K^{-1}\mathbf{t}, \tag{32}$$

as derived, for example, in Mardia and Marshall (1984). The evaluation of the likelihood and the partial derivatives takes time $O(n^3)$. Given l and its derivatives with respect to $\boldsymbol{\theta}$ it is straightforward to feed this information to an optimization package in order to obtain a local maximum of the likelihood. An alternative to maximum likelihood estimation of the parameters is to use a cross-validation (CV) or generalized cross-validation (GCV) method, as discussed in Wahba (1990). However, it would appear that it is difficult to use these methods when a large number of parameters are involved.

In general one may be concerned about making point estimates when the number of parameters is large relative to the number of data points, or if some of the parameters may be poorly determined, or if there may be local maxima in the likelihood surface. For these reasons the Bayesian approach of defining a prior distribution over the parameters and then obtaining a posterior distribution once the data $\mathcal{D}$ has been seen is attractive. To make a prediction for a new test point $\mathbf{x}_*$ one simply averages over the posterior distribution $P(\boldsymbol{\theta}|\mathcal{D})$, i.e.

$$P(y_*|\mathcal{D}) = \int P(y_*|\boldsymbol{\theta}, \mathcal{D})P(\boldsymbol{\theta}|\mathcal{D})d\boldsymbol{\theta}. \tag{33}$$

It is not possible to do this integration analytically in general, but numerical methods may be used. If $\boldsymbol{\theta}$ is of sufficiently low dimension, then techniques involving grids in $\boldsymbol{\theta}$-space can be used. See, for example the paper by Handcock and Stein, (1993).

If $\boldsymbol{\theta}$ is high-dimensional it is very difficult to locate the regions of parameter-space which have high posterior density by gridding techniques or importance sampling. In this case Markov chain Monte Carlo (MCMC) methods may be used. These work by constructing a Markov chain whose equilibrium distribution is the desired distribution $P(\boldsymbol{\theta}|\mathcal{D})$; the integral in equation 33 is then approximated using samples from the Markov chain.

Two standard methods for constructing MCMC methods are the Gibbs sampler and Metropolis-Hastings algorithms (see, e.g., Gelman *et al*, 1995). However, the conditional parameter distributions are not amenable to Gibbs sampling if the covariance function has the form given by equation 30, and the Metropolis-Hastings algorithm does not utilize the derivative information that is available, which means that it tends to have an inefficient random-walk behaviour in parameter-space. Following the work of Neal

(1996) on Bayesian treatment of neural networks, Williams and Rasmussen (1996) and Rasmussen (1996) have used the Hybrid Monte Carlo method of Duane *et al* (1987) to obtain samples from $P(\boldsymbol{\theta}|\mathcal{D})$. Rasmussen (1996) carried out a careful comparison of the Bayesian treatment of Gaussian process regression with several other state-of-the-art methods on a number of problems and found that its performance is comparable to that of Bayesian neural networks as developed by Neal (1996), and consistently better than the other methods.

5.3. COMPUTATIONAL ISSUES

Equations 20 and 21 require the inversion of a $n \times n$ matrix. When n is of the order of a few hundred then this is quite feasible with modern computers. However, once $n \sim O(1000)$ these computations can be quite time consuming, especially if this calculation must be carried out many times in an iterative scheme as discussed above in section 5.2. It is therefore of interest to consider approximate methods.

One possible approach is to approximate the matrix inversion step needed for prediction, i.e. the computation of $K^{-1}\mathbf{z}$ in equation 20. Gibbs and MacKay (1997a) have used the conjugate gradients (CG) algorithm for this task, based on the work of Skilling (1993). The algorithm iteratively computes an approximation to $K^{-1}\mathbf{z}$; if it is allowed to run for n iterations it takes time $O(n^3)$ and computes the exact solution to the linear system, but by stopping the algorithm after $k < n$ iterations an approximate solution is obtained. Note also that when adjusting the parameters of the covariance matrix, the solution of the linear system that was obtained with the old parameter values will often be a good starting point for the new CG iteration.

When adjusting the parameters one also needs to be able to calculate quantities such as $\text{tr}(K^{-1}\partial K/\partial\theta_i)$. For large matrices this computation can be approximated by using the "randomized trace method". Observe that if $\mathbf{d} \sim N(0, I_n)$, then $E[\mathbf{d}^T M \mathbf{d}] = \text{tr}M$, and thus the trace of a matrix M may be estimated by averaging $\mathbf{d}^T M \mathbf{d}$ over several $\mathbf{d}$'s. This method has been used in the splines literature by Hutchinson (1989) and Girard (1989) and also by Gibbs and MacKay (1997a) following the independent work of Skilling (1993). Similar methods can be brought to bear on the calculation of $\log \det K$.

An alternative approximation scheme for Gaussian processes is to project the covariance kernel onto a finite number of basis functions, i.e. to find the Σ_w in equation 5 which leads to the best approximation of the covariance function. This method has been discussed by Silverman (1985), Wahba (1990) Zhu and Rohwer (1996) and Hastie (1996). However, if we also can

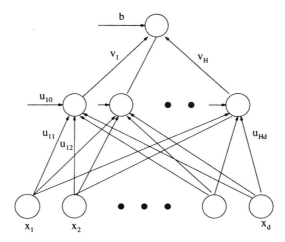

Figure 4. The architecture of a network with a single hidden layer.

choose which basis functions we wish to use then the m eigenfunctions which have the largest eigenvalues should be used. This truncated expansion makes sense when the eigenvalues in equation 29 decay to zero fast enough so that the sum $\sum_{i=1}^{\infty} \lambda_i$ converges. The technique is an infinite-dimensional analogue of principal components analysis, and is discussed, for example, in Zhu *et al* (1997).

There may well be other methods of speeding up the computations; one possible example is to ignore data points which are far away from the test point when making predictions, thereby producing a smaller matrix to be inverted.

5.4. THE COVARIANCE FUNCTION OF NEURAL NETWORKS

My own interest in using Gaussian processes for regression was sparked by Radford Neal's observation (Neal, 1996), that under a Bayesian treatment, the functions produced by a neural network with certain kinds of prior distribution over its weights will tend to a Gaussian process prior over functions as the number of hidden units in the network tends to infinity. In the remainder of this section the covariance function for a neural network with a single hidden layer is derived.

Consider a network which takes an input $\mathbf{x}$, has one hidden layer with H units and then linearly combines the outputs of the hidden units with a bias b to obtain $f(\mathbf{x})$. The mapping can be written

$$f(\mathbf{x}) = b + \sum_{j=1}^{H} v_j h(\mathbf{x}; \mathbf{u}_j) \tag{34}$$

where $h(\mathbf{x}; \mathbf{u})$ is the hidden unit transfer function (which we shall assume is bounded) which depends on the input-to-hidden weights $\mathbf{u}$. This architecture is important because it has been shown by Hornik (1993) that networks with one hidden layer are universal approximators as the number of hidden units tends to infinity, for a wide class of transfer functions (but excluding polynomials). Let b and the v's have independent zero-mean distributions of variance σ_b^2 and σ_v^2 respectively, and let the weights $\mathbf{u}_j$ for each hidden unit be independently and identically distributed. Denoting all weights by $\mathbf{w}$, we obtain (following Neal, 1996)

$$E_{\mathbf{w}}[f(\mathbf{x})] = 0 \tag{35}$$

$$E_{\mathbf{w}}[f(\mathbf{x})f(\mathbf{x}')] = \sigma_b^2 + \sum_j \sigma_v^2 E_{\mathbf{u}}[h_j(\mathbf{x}; \mathbf{u})h_j(\mathbf{x}'; \mathbf{u})] \tag{36}$$

$$= \sigma_b^2 + H\sigma_v^2 E_{\mathbf{u}}[h(\mathbf{x}; \mathbf{u})h(\mathbf{x}'; \mathbf{u})] \tag{37}$$

where equation 37 follows because all of the hidden units are identically distributed. The final term in equation 37 becomes $\omega^2 E_{\mathbf{u}}[h(\mathbf{x}; \mathbf{u})h(\mathbf{x}'; \mathbf{u})]$ by letting σ_v^2 scale as ω^2/H.

The sum in equation 36 is over H identically and independently distributed random variables. As the transfer function is bounded, all moments of the distribution will be bounded and hence the Central Limit Theorem can be applied, showing that the stochastic process will converge to a Gaussian process in the limit as $H \to \infty$.

By evaluating $E_{\mathbf{u}}[h(\mathbf{x})h(\mathbf{x}')]$ for all $\mathbf{x}$ and $\mathbf{x}'$ in the training and testing sets we can obtain the covariance function needed to describe the neural network as a Gaussian process. These expectations are, of course, integrals over the relevant probability distributions of the biases and input weights. For some choices of transfer function and weight priors these integrals can be calculated analytically. For Gaussian weight priors and a transfer function that is either (i) the error function $\Phi(z) = 2/\sqrt{\pi} \int_0^z e^{-t^2} dt$ or (ii) a Gaussian, explicit expressions for the covariance functions are given in Williams (1997a) and Williams (1997b).

One attraction of using infinite neural networks (represented as GPs) is that the full Bayesian computation should be much easier than with finite networks in some circumstances. Finite networks require integration over the joint posterior in weight-space and (hyper)parameter space, and currently this high-dimensional integration can only be tackled with MCMC methods. With GPs, in effect the integration over the weights can be done exactly (using equations 20 and 21) so that only the integration over the parameters remains. This should lead to improved computational efficiency for GP predictions over neural networks, particularly for problems where n is not too large.

5.5. CLASSIFICATION PROBLEMS

Given an input $\mathbf{x}$, the aim of a classifier is to produce an estimate of the posterior probabilities for each class $P(k|\mathbf{x})$, where $k = 1, \ldots C$ indexes the C classes. Naturally we require that $0 \leq P(k|\mathbf{x}) \leq 1$ for all k and that $\sum_k P(k|\mathbf{x}) = 1$. A naïve application of the regression method for Gaussian processes using, say, targets of 1 when an example of class k is observed and 0 otherwise will not obey these constraints.

For the two-class classification problem it is only necessary to represent $P(1|\mathbf{x})$, since $P(2|\mathbf{x}) = 1 - P(1|\mathbf{x})$. An easy way to ensure that the estimate $\pi(\mathbf{x})$ of $P(1|\mathbf{x})$ lies in $[0,1]$ is to obtain it by passing an unbounded value $y(\mathbf{x})$ through a the logistic transfer function $\sigma(z) = 1/(1 + e^{-z})$ so that $\pi(\mathbf{x}) = \sigma(y(\mathbf{x}))$. The input $y(\mathbf{x})$ to the logistic function will be called the *activation*. In the simplest method of this kind, logistic regression, the activation is simply computed as a linear combination of the inputs, plus a bias, i.e. $y(\mathbf{x}) = \mathbf{w}^T\mathbf{x} + b$. Using a Gaussian process or other flexible methods allow $y(\mathbf{x})$ to be a non-linear function of the inputs. An early reference to this approach is the work of Silverman (1978).

For the classification problem with more than two classes, a simple extension of this idea using the "softmax" function (Bridle, 1990) gives the predicted probability for class k as

$$\pi(k|\mathbf{x}) = \frac{\exp y_k(\mathbf{x})}{\sum_m \exp y_m(\mathbf{x})}. \tag{38}$$

For the rest of this section we shall concentrate on the two-class problem; extension of the methods to the multi-class case is relatively straightforward.

By defining a Gaussian process prior over the activation $y(\mathbf{x})$ automatically induces a prior over $\pi(\mathbf{x})$, as illustrated in Figure 5.5. To make predictions for a test input $\mathbf{x}_*$ when using fixed parameters in the GP we would like to compute $\hat{\pi}_* = \int \pi_* P(\pi_*|\mathbf{t}, \boldsymbol{\theta}) \, d\pi_*$, which requires us to find $P(\pi_*|\mathbf{t}, \boldsymbol{\theta}) = P(\pi(\mathbf{x}_*)|\mathbf{t}, \boldsymbol{\theta})$ for a new input $\mathbf{x}_*$. This can be done by finding the distribution $P(y_*|\mathbf{t}, \boldsymbol{\theta})$ (y_* is the activation of π_*) as given by

$$P(y_*|\mathbf{t}, \boldsymbol{\theta}) = \int P(y_*, \mathbf{y}|\mathbf{t}, \boldsymbol{\theta}) d\mathbf{y} = \frac{1}{P(\mathbf{t}|\boldsymbol{\theta})} \int P(y_*, \mathbf{y}|\boldsymbol{\theta}) P(\mathbf{t}|\mathbf{y}) d\mathbf{y} \tag{39}$$

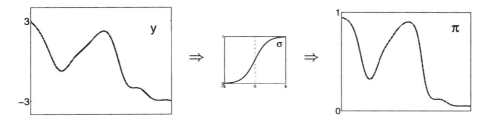

Figure 5. $\pi(\mathbf{x})$ is obtained from $y(\mathbf{x})$ by "squashing" it through the sigmoid function σ.

and then using the appropriate Jacobian to transform the distribution. When $P(\mathbf{t}|\mathbf{y})$ is Gaussian then the integral in equation 39 can be computed exactly to give equations 20 and 21. However, the usual expression for $P(\mathbf{t}|\mathbf{y}) = \prod_i \pi_i^{t_i}(1 - \pi_i)^{1-t_i}$ for classification data (where the t's take on values of 0 or 1), means that the marginalization to obtain $P(y_*|\mathbf{t}, \boldsymbol{\theta})$ is no longer analytically tractable.

Faced with this problem there are two routes that we can follow: (i) to use an analytic approximation to the integral in equation 39 or (ii) to use Monte Carlo methods, specifically MCMC methods, to approximate it. These two methods will be considered in turn.

The first analytic method we shall consider is Laplace's approximation, where the integrand $P(y_*, \mathbf{y}|\mathbf{t}, \boldsymbol{\theta})$ is approximated by a Gaussian distribution centered at a maximum of this function with respect to $y_*, \mathbf{y}$ with an inverse covariance matrix given by $-\nabla\nabla \log P(y_*, \mathbf{y}|\mathbf{t}, \boldsymbol{\theta})$. Finding a maximum can be carried out using the Newton-Raphson (or Fisher scoring) iterative method on $\mathbf{y}$, which then allows the approximate distribution of y_* to be calculated. This is also the method used to calculate the *maximum a posteriori* estimate of y_*. For more details see Green and Silverman (1994) §5.3 and Barber and Williams (1997).

An alternative analytic approximation is due to Gibbs and MacKay (1997b). Instead of using the Laplace approximation they use variational methods to find approximating Gaussian distributions that bound the marginal likelihood $P(\mathbf{t}|\boldsymbol{\theta})$ above and below, and then use these approximate distributions to predict $P(y_*|\mathbf{t}, \boldsymbol{\theta})$ and thus $\hat{\pi}(\mathbf{x}_*)$.

For the analytic approximation methods, there is also the question of what to do about the parameters $\boldsymbol{\theta}$. Maximum likelihood and GCV approaches can again be used as in the regression case (e.g. O'Sullivan *et al*, 1986). Barber and Williams (1997) used an approximate Bayesian scheme based on the Hybrid Monte Carlo method whereby the marginal likelihood $P(\mathbf{t}|\boldsymbol{\theta})$ (which is not available analytically) is replaced by the Laplace approximation of this quantity. Gibbs and MacKay (1997b) estimated $\boldsymbol{\theta}$ by maximizing their lower bound on $P(\mathbf{t}|\boldsymbol{\theta})$.

Recently Neal (1997) has developed a MCMC method for the Gaussian process classification model. This works by generating samples from $P(\mathbf{y}, \boldsymbol{\theta}|\mathcal{D})$ in a two stage process. Firstly, for fixed $\boldsymbol{\theta}$, each of the n individual y_i's are updated sequentially using Gibbs sampling. This "sweep" takes time $O(n^2)$ once the matrix K^{-1} has been computed (in time $O(n^3)$), so it actually makes sense to perform quite a few Gibbs sampling scans between each update of the parameters, as this probably makes the Markov chain mix faster. Secondly, the parameters are updated using the Hybrid Monte Carlo method.

It should also be noted that MCMC method for Gaussian processes can be applied to other situations. For example Neal (1997) describes how to use it for a regression problem where the noise model is assumed to be t-distributed rather than the standard Gaussian distribution. This is important as the t-distribution is widely used when it is desired that the noise model be "robust", i.e. less sensitive to outliers than the Gaussian model. The MCMC approach can also be used in a hierarchical regression model where it is assumed that the noise process has a variance that depends on $\mathbf{x}$, and that this noise-field $N(\mathbf{x})$ is drawn from a prior generated from an independent Gaussian process $Z(\mathbf{x})$ by $N(\mathbf{x}) = \exp Z(\mathbf{x})$ (see Goldberg et al, 1997).

6. Discussion

In this paper I have shown how to move from simple Bayesian linear regression to regression with Gaussian processes, and have discussed some of the issues in using Gaussian process prediction for the kinds of problem that neural networks have also been used on.

There are still further elaborations that can be made. One weakness of the method described above is that the covariance functions used are stationary, which means that the length-scales over which interactions occur are the same everywhere in the input space. This is a very strong assumption, and can be relaxed in a number of ways. One appealing method is to warp the original input space $\mathbf{x}$ into another space, say $\boldsymbol{\xi}$, which may be taken to be of the same dimension as $\mathbf{x}$, and then to use a stationary covariance function in $\boldsymbol{\xi}$-space. This is, roughly speaking, the approach proposed by Sampson and Guttorp (1992). Of course this warping is defined by co-ordinate functions $\xi_i(\mathbf{x}), i = 1, \ldots p$, which may again be modelled with Gaussian processes[4], so one can derive a hierarchical Gaussian process model.

---

[4]It may be desirable to impose the condition that the $\mathbf{x}$ to $\boldsymbol{\xi}$ mapping should be bijective.

It is also interesting to consider the differences between finite neural network and Gaussian process priors. One difference is that in functions generated from finite neural networks, the effects of individual basis functions can be seen. For example, with sigmoidal units a steep step may be observed where one basis function (with large weights) comes into play. A judgement about whether this type of behaviour is appropriate or not should depend on prior beliefs about the problem at hand. Of course it is also possible to compare finite neural networks and Gaussian process predictions empirically. This has been done by Rasmussen (1996), where GP predictions (using MCMC for the parameters) were compared to those from Neal's MCMC Bayesian neural networks. These results show that for a number of problems, the predictions of GPs and Bayesian neural networks are similar, and that both methods outperform several other widely-used regression techniques.

ACKNOWLEDGEMENTS

I thank David Barber, Chris Bishop, David MacKay, Radford Neal, Manfred Opper, Carl Rasmussen, Richard Rohwer, Francesco Vivarelli and Huaiyu Zhu for helpful discussions about Gaussian processes over the last few years, and David Barber, Chris Bishop and David MacKay for comments on the manuscript.

References

Aizerman, M. A., E. M. Braverman, and L. I. Rozoner (1964). Theoretical foundations of the potential function method in pattern recognition learning. *Automation and Remote Control* **25**, 821–837.

Barber, D. and C. K. I. Williams (1997). Gaussian Processes for Bayesian Classification via Hybrid Monte Carlo. In M. C. Mozer, M. I. Jordan, and T. Petsche (Eds.), *Advances in Neural Information Processing Systems 9*. MIT Press.

Bishop, C. M. (1995). *Neural Networks for Pattern Recognition*. Oxford: Clarendon Press.

Box, G. E. P. and G. C. Tiao (1973). *Bayesian Inference in Statistical Analysis*. Reading, Mass.: Addison-Wesley.

Bridle, J. (1990). Probabilistic interpretation of feedforward classification network outputs, with relationships to statistical pattern recognition. In F. Fougelman-Soulie and J. Herault (Eds.), *NATO ASI series on systems and computer science*. Springer-Verlag.

Cressie, N. A. C. (1993). *Statistics for Spatial Data*. New York: Wiley.

Duane, S., A. D. Kennedy, B. J. Pendleton, and D. Roweth (1987). Hybrid Monte Carlo. *Physics Letters B* **195**, 216–222.

Gelman, A., J. B. Carlin, H. S. Stern, and D. B. Rubin (1995). *Bayesian Data Analysis*. London: Chapman and Hall.

Gibbs, M. and D. J. C. MacKay (1997a). Efficient Implementation of Gaussian Processes. Draft manuscript, available from
`http://wol.ra.phy.cam.ac.uk/mackay/homepage.html`.

Gibbs, M. and D. J. C. MacKay (1997b). Variational Gaussian Process Classifiers. Draft manuscript, available via http://wol.ra.phy.cam.ac.uk/mackay/homepage.html.

Girard, D. (1989). A fast "Monte Carlo cross-validation" procedure for large least squares problems with noisy data. *Numer. Math.* **56**, 1–23.

Girosi, F., M. Jones, and T. Poggio (1995). Regularization Theory and Neural Networks Architectures. *Neural Computation* **7(2)**, 219–269.

Goldberg, P. W., C. K. I. Williams, and C. M. Bishop (1997). Regression with Input-dependent Noise: A Gaussian Process Treatment. Accepted to NIPS*97.

Green, P. J. and B. W. Silverman (1994). *Nonparametric regression and generalized linear models*. London: Chapman and Hall.

Handcock, M. S. and M. L. Stein (1993). A Bayesian Analysis of Kriging. *Technometrics* **35(4)**, 403–410.

Hastie, T. (1996). Pseudosplines. *Journal of the Royal Statistical Society B* **58**, 379–396.

Hastie, T. J. and R. J. Tibshirani (1990). *Generalized Additive Models*. London: Chapman and Hall.

Hornik, K. (1993). Some new results on neural network approximation. *Neural Networks* **6** (8), 1069–1072.

Hutchinson, M. (1989). A stochastic estimator for the trace of the influence matrix for Laplacian smoothing splines. *Communications in statistics:Simulation and computation* **18**, 1059–1076.

Journel, A. G. and C. J. Huijbregts (1978). *Mining Geostatistics*. Academic Press.

Kimeldorf, G. and G. Wahba (1970). A correspondence between Bayesian estimation of stochastic processes and smoothing by splines. *Annals of Mathematical Statistics* **41**, 495–502.

MacKay, D. J. C. (1992). A Practical Bayesian Framework for Backpropagation Networks. *Neural Computation* **4(3)**, 448–472.

MacKay, D. J. C. (1993). Bayesian Methods for Backpropagation Networks. In J. L. van Hemmen, E. Domany, and K. Schulten (Eds.), *Models of Neural Networks II*. Springer.

Mardia, K. V. and R. J. Marshall (1984). Maximum likelihood estimation for models of residual covariance in spatial regression. *Biometrika* **71(1)**, 135–146.

Neal, R. M. (1997). Monte Carlo Implementation of Gaussian Process Models for Bayesian Regression and Classification. Draft manuscript, available from http://www.cs.toronto.edu/~radford/.

Neal, R. M. (1996). *Bayesian Learning for Neural Networks*. New York: Springer. Lecture Notes in Statistics 118.

O'Hagan, A. (1978). Curve Fitting and Optimal Design for Prediction (with discussion). *Journal of the Royal Statistical Society B* **40(1)**, 1–42.

O'Sullivan, F., B. S. Yandell, and W. J. Raynor (1986). Automatic Smoothing of Regression Functions in Generalized Linear Models. *Journal of the American Statistical Association* **81**, 96–103.

Poggio, T. and F. Girosi (1990). Networks for approximation and learning. *Proceedings of IEEE* **78**, 1481–1497.

Press, W. H., S. A. Teukolsky, W. T. Vetterling, and B. P. Flannery (1992). *Numerical Recipes in C* (second ed.). Cambridge University Press.

Rasmussen, C. E. (1996). *Evaluation of Gaussian Processes and Other Methods for Nonlinear Regression*. Ph.D. thesis, Dept. of Computer Science, University of Toronto. Available from http://www.cs.utoronto.ca/~carl/.

Ripley, B. (1996). *Pattern Recognition and Neural Networks*. Cambridge, UK: Cambridge University Press.

Sacks, J., W. J. Welch, T. J. Mitchell, and H. P. Wynn (1989). Design and Analysis of Computer Experiments. *Statistical Science* **4(4)**, 409–435.

Sampson, P. D. and P. Guttorp (1992). Nonparametric estimation of nonstationary covariance structure. *Journal of the American Statistical Association* **87**, 108–119.

Silverman, B. W. (1978). Density Ratios, Empirical Likelihood and Cot Death. *Applied Statistics* **27(1)**, 26–33.

Silverman, B. W. (1985). Some aspects of the spline smoothing approach to non-parametric regression curve fitting (with discussion). *J. Roy. Stat. Soc. B* **47(1)**, 1–52.

Skilling, J. (1993). Bayesian numerical analysis. In W. T. Grandy, Jr. and P. Milonni (Eds.), *Physics and Probability.* Cambridge University Press.

Vapnik, V. N. (1995). *The Nature of Statistical Learning Theory.* New York: Springer Verlag.

von Mises, R. (1964). *Mathematical Theory of Probability and Statistics.* Academic Press.

Wahba, G. (1990). *Spline Models for Observational Data.* Society for Industrial and Applied Mathematics. CBMS-NSF Regional Conference series in applied mathematics.

Whittle, P. (1963). *Prediction and regulation by linear least-square methods.* English Universities Press.

Williams, C. K. I. (1997a). Computation with infinite neural networks. Submitted to *Neural Computation.*

Williams, C. K. I. (1997b). Computing with infinite networks. In M. C. Mozer, M. I. Jordan, and T. Petsche (Eds.), *Advances in Neural Information Processing Systems 9.* MIT Press.

Williams, C. K. I. and C. E. Rasmussen (1996). Gaussian processes for regression. In D. S. Touretzky, M. C. Mozer, and M. E. Hasselmo (Eds.), *Advances in Neural Information Processing Systems 8,* pp. 514–520. MIT Press.

Wong, E. (1971). *Stochastic Processes in Information and Dynamical Systems.* New York: McGraw-Hill.

Zhu, H. and R. Rohwer (1996). Bayesian Regression Filters and the Issue of Priors. *Neural Computing and Applications* **4**, 130–142.

Zhu, H., C. K. I. Williams, R. J. Rohwer, and M. Morciniec (1997). Gaussian Regression and Optimal Finite Dimensional Linear Models. Technical Report NCRG/97/011, Aston University, UK. Available from `http://www.ncrg.aston.ac.uk/Papers/` .

Contributors

Nicky G. Best
Department of Epidemiology
and Public Health
Imperial College School of Medicine
London W2 1PG
UK

Christopher M. Bishop
Microsoft Research
St. George House
1 Guildhall Street
Cambridge CB2 3NH
UK

Joachim M. Buhmann
Institut für Informatik III
Universität Bonn
Römerstr. 164
D-53117 Bonn
GERMANY

Gregory F. Cooper
Forbes Tower, Suite 8084
University of Pittsburgh
Pittsburgh, PA 15213-2582
USA

Robert G. Cowell
School of Mathematics, Actuarial
Science and Statistics
City University
Northampton Square
London EC1V 0HB
UK

Rina Dechter
Information and Computer Science
University of California
Irvine, CA 92697
USA

Nir Friedman
Computer Science Division
387 Soda Hall
University of California
Berkeley, CA 94720
USA

Dan Geiger
Computer Science Department
Technion
Haifa, 32000
ISRAEL

Zoubin Ghahramani
Department of Computer Science
University of Toronto
Toronto, Ontario M5S 3H5
CANADA

Wally R. Gilks
MRC Biostatistics Unit
Institute of Public Health
University Forvie Site
Robinson Way
Cambridge CB2 2SR
UK

Moises Goldszmidt
SRI International
333 Ravenswood Ave., EK329
Menlo Park, CA 94025
USA

David Heckerman
Microsoft Research
One Microsoft Way
Redmond, WA 98052
USA

Geoffrey E. Hinton
Department of Computer Science
University of Toronto
Toronto, Ontario M5S 3H5
CANADA

Hazel Inskip
MRC Environmental Epidemiology
Unit
Southampton General Hospital
Southampton SO16 6YD
UK

Tommi S. Jaakkola
Department of Computer Science
University of California
Santa Cruz, CA 95064
USA

Michael I. Jordan
Massachusetts Institute of Technology
E25-229
Cambridge, MA 02139
USA

Michael J. Kearns
AT&T Labs – Research
Room A201
180 Park Avenue
Florham Park, NJ 07932
USA

Uffe Kjærulff
Department of Computer Science
Aalborg University
Fredrik Bajers Vej 7E
DK-9220 Aalborg O
DENMARK

David J. C. MacKay
Cavendish Laboratory
Madingley Road
Cambridge CB3 0HE
UK

Yishay Mansour
Department of Computer Science
School of Mathematical Sciences
Tel-Aviv University
Tel-Aviv 69978
ISRAEL

Christopher Meek
Microsoft Research
One Microsoft Way
Redmond, WA 98052
USA

Stefano Monti
Intelligent Systems Program
University of Pittsburgh
901M CL
Pittsburgh, PA 15260
USA

Radford M. Neal
Department of Statistics and
Department of Computer Science
University of Toronto
100 St. George Street
Toronto, Ontario M5S 3G3
CANADA

Andrew Y. Ng
Artificial Intelligence Laboratory
MIT
Cambridge, MA 02139
USA

Thomas S. Richardson
Department of Statistics
Box 354322
University of Washington
Seattle, WA 98195-4322
USA

Brian Sallans
Department of Computer Science
University of Toronto
Toronto, Ontario M5S 3H5
CANADA

Lawrence K. Saul
AT&T Labs – Research
180 Park Avenue
Florham Park, NJ 07932
USA

Peter W. F. Smith
Department of Social Statistics
The University
Southampton, SO9 5NH
UK

David J. Spiegelhalter
MRC Biostatistics Unit
Institute of Public Health
University Forvie Site
Robinson Way
Cambridge CB2 2SR
UK

Milan Studený
Institute of Information Theory
and Automation
Academy of Sciences of Czech
Republic
Pod vodárenskou věží 4
182 08 Prague
CZECH REPUBLIC

Jirina Vejnarová
Laboratory of Intelligent Systems
University of Economics
Ekonomická 957
148 00 Prague
CZECH REPUBLIC

Joe Whittaker
Department of Mathematics and Statistics
Lancaster University
Lancaster LA1 4YF
UK

Christopher K. I. Williams
Neural Computing Research Group
Aston University
Birmingham B4 7ET
UK

INDEX

A

acceptance rate 190

adaptive rejection sampling method 222

Adler's overrelaxation method 209

ancestral sets 20, 21

approximation methods
    see Gaussian approximation
    see Laplace approximation
    see sampling methods
    see variational methods
    chi-squared 563

artificial neural networks (ANNs)
    see neural networks

asymptotic expansion 462, 563, 569, 571

augmented graph 95

AutoClass 342, 472

autocorrelation time 211

automatic relevance determination (ARD) 610

B

basis function 393, 602, 606

Baum-Welch algorithm 400
    see also EM algorithm

Bayes' factor 328

Bayes' theorem 10

Bayesian information criterion (BIC) 332, 466, 472, 531

Bayesian networks 52, 76, 313, 373, 422, 462, 464, 522

BDe score 337, 430

belief networks
    see Bayesian networks

belief updating

    see inference

beta prior 308

between-separated models 244

binomial sampling 307

Boltzmann
    distribution 117, 170, 358, 408
    machine 116, 134, 178, 542

bucket elimination 75

BUGS 193, 583, 597

burn-in period 201, 583

C

canonical parameter 557

causality
    causal graph 248, 344, 465
    causal knowledge 344
    causal Markov condition 344

causal relationships 234, 303, 343

CG-potentials 17

chain graphs 231, 235, 238

chain graph Markov properties
    Andersson-Madigan-Perlman property 239
    Lauritzen-Wermuth-Frydenberg Markov property 238

characteristic random variable 434, 435, 439, 441, 444

Cheeseman-Stutz scoring function 472

classification 340, 383, 616

clique 19, 53

clique-marginal representation 23, 41

clustering
    central 367, 383, 386, 391, 406, 496